Women's Encyclopedia of Natural Medicine

WOMEN'S ENCYCLOPEDIA OF NATURAL MEDICINE

Alternative Therapies and Integrative Medicine

by

Tori Hudson, N.D.

Foreword by Christiane Northrup, M.D.

KEATS PUBLISHING

LOS ANGELES

NTC/Contemporary Publishing Group

Women's Encyclopedia of Natural Medicine is not intended as medical advice. Its intent is solely informational and educational. Please consult a health professional should the need for one be indicated.

Library of Congress Cataloging-in-Publication Data

Hudson, Tori.
    Women's encyclopedia of natural medicine: alternative therapies and integrative medicine / by Tori Hudson ; foreword by Christiane Northrup.
      p.   cm.
    Includes bibliographical references and index.
    ISBN 0-87983-788-8
    1. Gynecology—Popular works.   2. Naturopathy—Popular works.
3. Generative organs, Female—Diseases—Alternative treatment.
I. Northrup, Christiane.   II. Title.
RG121.H927 1998
618.1'06—dc21   99-17382
                                                                  CIP

Published by Keats, a division of NTC/Contemporary Publishing Group, Inc.
4255 West Touhy Avenue, Lincolnwood, Illinois 60646-1975 U.S.A.

Design by Andrea Reider

Printed and bound in the United States of America
International Standard Book Number: 0-87983-788-8
10 9 8 7 6 5 4 3

To

The women who have sought my advice as a naturopathic physician
and lent me their trust and confidence

The women in medicine

The women who have made a difference in my life

CONTRIBUTORS

The following people contributed to writing or reviewing material in the following sections:

Susanna Reid, Ph.D., N.D.   Cancer Prevention

Sandoval Melin, N.D., Ph.D.   Exercise Therapeutics, Cancer Prevention

Elizabeth Newhall, M.D.   Contraception; selected entries in PMS, Pregnancy,
                                   Cervical Dysplasia, Fibrocystic Breasts

Judy Fulop, N.D. candidate, 1999   Endometriosis

Vicki Noble   Pregnancy

Patricia Burford, M.D.   Osteoporosis

Contents

FOREWORD

I've long been a fan of the work of Dr. Tori Hudson, the foremost national leader in naturopathic and botanical medicine specifically for women. And unbeknownst to her, Dr. Hudson has been a guiding light for me in using botanical and naturopathic approaches to women's health problems for many years. Long before herbal medicine enjoyed its current mainstream acceptance, my patients who were interested in natural approaches to their gynecologic problems brought me copies of Dr. Hudson's articles and even the text that she wrote for her students to fill in the information gap about gynecology and natural medicines that existed in the naturopathic training program where she teaches. In this text entitled *Gynecology and Naturopathic Medicine: A Treatment Manual*, Dr. Hudson set down natural treatment protocols that she had used effectively for years to treat the kind of women's health problems that I was seeing every day, ranging from irregular periods and menstrual cramps to hot flashes. As a conventionally trained allopathic gynecologist, I was gratified to learn about and help my patients apply some of Dr. Hudson's gentle, natural and plant-based approaches. They were an excellent complement to the standard gynecologic care I was already practicing.

So when Dr. Hudson called and told me about her new book, I was delighted. Here in one volume is everything a woman needs to know to begin applying gentle, natural, naturopathic solutions to her health problems on her own, along with guidance about when she needs to seek professional help. Many of these solutions are available at your local natural food store. Some are even available in your own kitchen. Many naturopathic approaches stand alone as a viable, safe, and effective treatment option. Others can be used in an integrative approach along with conventional medicine. Some women and situations will require the most conventional of medical treatments. Dr. Hudson's book helps to sort through these options. In general, the naturopathic treatments outlined in this book offer safer and gentler solutions to many women's health problems that can be applied to help rebalance the body and restore it to health long before more serious conditions develop.

Women have used the healing power of plants since the beginning of time. Now Dr. Hudson brings her years of scientific and clinical expertise to the field of natural, plant-based healing, and helps make it safer and more effective for women than ever before. This is a book that should be in every woman's health library and every alternative practitioner's library, and is a resource for the new breed of conventional practitioners open to a more integrative health care system.

Christiane Northrup, M.D., author of *Women's Bodies, Women's Wisdom*

ACKNOWLEDGMENTS

Throughout the course of writing this book, I have had overwhelming moments of gratitude for all the people that have helped. I resisted this project for some time and actually said no to the publisher on more than one occasion. Norman Goldfind, of Keats Publishing at the time, persisted in finding ways to influence and encourage me, accommodate his production schedule, and assist me in taking on the project and getting the job done. Although it has challenged my already insistent workaholic personality, at some point in the last few months I finally had that feeling of excitement, and I am grateful for having said yes.

Over the course of this book, I have learned the value of a well-informed, talented, thorough, supportive, yet full of constructive feedback, editor. Phyllis Herman has embodied all of these skills, and I thank her for her diligence, patience, and vital role in this book.

Now that I am nearing the completion date, I can reflect on the magnitude of the work involved and the people who made significant contributions to the final product. Dr. Susanna Reid worked with me from almost the very beginning when she was still a student at the National College of Naturopathic Medicine. If it were not for her, I would not have learned to use a computer. Thanks to her weekly tutoring, I have finally achieved at least a functional level of competence. Susanna has been critically involved in the research of information for this book and in planning its organization and format. Special thanks to Susanna for her skill, hard work, and commitment. I also want to thank Dr. Sandoval Melin for his expertise in the area of exercise. Sandoval has elevated the role of exercise therapeutics in the book and is literally responsible for its inclusion from start to finish. Many thanks to his other talent, that of reviewer for errors large and small, prior to the official editing. His meticulous reading, corrections, and suggestions have greatly contributed to the quality of the book. Both Susanna and Sandoval made a special contribution to the chapter on cancer prevention. These two people deserve an extraordinary amount of credit, and I am forever grateful for their assistance in seeing me through this project. Both Dr. Reid and Dr. Melin are now in practice in Stamford, Connecticut, as naturopathic physicians.

Dr. Elizabeth Newhall has generously given of her time and expertise as an obstetrician and gynecologist. I thank her for her review of several chapters for their conventional medicine content, her direct contributions to a few of the chapters, and the excellent information she provided on contraception. If it were not for her generous sharing of her conventional medical knowledge over the last seven years, my expertise in women's health would not have been complete.

I am fortunate to have a very talented and supportive sister, Karen Hudson, and her partner, Terry Hulse. Thanks to them, my former life as a techno-peasant is now behind me. They have held my hand during my virgin voyage into computerland, and made it possible for me to leave the land of the technologically impaired. In addition, not many women have the good fortune to have a sister that knows everything you do not know. Being in business together at our clinic, A Woman's Time, is the perfect blend of what we each do best. Our joint commitment of delivering health care options to women is our work and our play.

My family has been very supportive throughout my career and throughout this project. My mother, Pat Lawrence, has provided me with lifelong love, support, and trust, and has always made it clear that I am worthy and special. She's also the one that keeps me in touch with what the media are communicating about alternative medicine. Not everyone has their own clipping service from all the popular magazines and regular updates on what's happening on the Oprah show, 20/20, and the rest. Her husband, Dick, is my special project man. All the things I haven't had time for—hanging the Christmas lights, cleaning the gutters, staining the deck—what a guy! My father, Ken Guenther, made it possible for me to go back to school and receive an education in naturopathic medicine, and I thank him for providing the support and resources for allowing me to pursue a career as a naturopathic physician. My dad, Jack Hudson, who passed away at too young an age, gave me the gift of learning and doing all the things normally reserved for boys. My niece, Jana, delights me with her spirit. May you find what you seek.

Sheila Frodermann and Judy Fulop are two students at the National College of Naturopathic Medicine who have put many hours into this project: Sheila, as the library assistant who fetched articles, spent many a day at the copy machine, and helped read, sift, and sort—it is she who is responsible for my having filing cabinets as roommates; Judy, for her contribution on the research and compilation of the endometriosis information and her relentless pursuit of knowledge. They will both be fine naturopathic physicians.

Sometimes I cannot believe my good fortune to have Doug Stapf in my life—trusted business partner at Vitanica, easygoing Texan friend, fellow basketball fan, the most excellent of men one could hope to know and work with.

Having become a naturopathic physician in 1984, I am honored to be an alumna and faculty member of the National College of Naturopathic Medicine (NCNM) these last fourteen-plus years. The National College of Naturopathic Medicine is the oldest college of naturopathic medicine in the United States, and the expertise and experience of its faculty in the field of natural medicine are exceeded by no other college in the country. I honor the faculty, administration, and employees of NCNM for their commitment and vision.

Several other people have lent their professional, business, academic, and personal support and extended themselves in various ways: Dr. Guru Sandesh Khalsa, academic dean at the National College of Naturopathic Medicine (NCNM); Dr. Chris Meletis, medical director, NCNM; Clyde Jensen, Ph.D., president of NCNM; Sharon McFarland of Transitions for Health; Dr. Marcus Laux, Dr. Eileen Stretch, Dr. Cindy Phillips, Dr. Kimberly Windstar, Dr. Steve Austin, Dr. Michael Murray, Dr. Tom Kruzel, Dr. Don Brown, Dr. David Shefrin, naturopathic physicians; the associates in my office, Dr. Barbara McDonald, Dr. Deah Baird, naturopathic physicians; Dr. Paul Kucera, Dr. Joanne Nelson, Dr. Bruce Dana, Dr. Angela Kalisik, Dr. Mike McClung, Dr. Trish Burford, Dr. Phillipa Ribbink, Dr. Lydia Collins, Dr. Marcy Barnhart, Dr. Brenda Kehoe, Dr. Sue Johnson, medical doctors in the Portland community; Dr. Agatha Thrash, Rick Volchok, Theresa Baisley, Vicki Noble, Dee Packard, Kate Krider, and Patti Kochler.

I also want to thank the students at the National College of Naturopathic Medicine, my colleagues, and all the women I have treated over these last fourteen-plus years. I am a better teacher, better physician, and better person because of you.

For those who have played with, worked with, nourished, and loved me, you have brought about my evolution as a human being.

Finally, we all owe our gratitude to the women who seek safe, effective, respectful medicine and choices in their health care. You have changed history on more than one occasion and protected our humanness.

Introduction

I've spent the last twenty years studying, practicing, teaching, and evolving as a naturopathic physician. Two themes have been consistent: natural medicine and the health care of women.

Alternative medicine has come to be the popular term used to distinguish natural, noninvasive therapies from conventional medicine. Whether the terms *alternative medicine, complementary medicine, natural medicine,* or *holistic medicine* are used, they all reflect the transformation that is occurring in health care: a focus on disease prevention, the promotion of healthy lifestyle habits, and the treatment of disease with natural, nontoxic, and less invasive therapies. At the center of this transformation is a distinct system called naturopathic medicine.

The roots of naturopathic medicine are seen in the healing traditions of Egypt, India, China, Greece, Germany, South and Central America, Africa, and native North America. The European hydrotherapy tradition had a strong influence on the development of naturopathy, and by the end of the nineteenth century, Benedict Lust, a physician trained in the water-cure methods of Europe, came to America and began using the term *naturopathy* to describe an eclectic combination of natural healing principles and methods.

The first college of naturopathic medicine in the United States opened in New York City in 1902. It taught a system of medicine that included nutritional therapy, natural dietetics, herbal medicine, homeopathy, manipulation, exercise therapy, hydrotherapy, electrotherapy, and stress reduction techniques.

Naturopathic medicine grew and flourished from the early 1900s until the mid-1930s. At that point in history, the conventional medical profession began to influence the health care system in several ways. By abandoning some of its barbaric bloodletting therapies and toxic mercury dosing, naturopathy was able to replace them with more effective and less toxic treatments. With therapies more acceptable to the public, subsidies from wealthy foundations, the support of the developing pharmaceutical industry, and political savvy and legislation in its favor, conventional medicine was able to restrict the use of unorthodox doctors, midwives, herbalists, and others and gain a virtual monopoly on the health care system.

Fortunately, alternative medicine and naturopathic medicine have seen a rebirth in the last fifteen to twenty years, and especially in the last five. A public hungry for choices in their health care, an increased awareness about the role of diet and lifestyle in cancer and chronic disease, the aging of the baby boomer generation, and the failures of certain aspects of modern conventional medicine and the health insurance industry to deal with people and their health problems respectfully, carefully, fairly, and effectively have been responsible for this resurgence. Conventional medicine has brought great insights, successes, and miracles of what human intelligence can accomplish. Natural medicine has matured, particularly in the areas of scientific research, educational institutions, virtual numbers of licensed practitioners, and professionalism, and is now poised to serve those who seek its gentle ways.

Naturopathic medicine is its own distinct healing art and is best defined by its principles and its therapies. Simply put in modern terms, naturopathic physicians are primary health care providers, family physicians who specialize in natural medicine. The following seven principles are the foundation for naturopathic medicine:

1. **The Healing Power of Nature** (*vis medicatrix naturae*). The body has the inherent ability to establish, maintain, and restore health. The physician's role is to facilitate and augment this process with the aid of natural, nontoxic therapies; to act to identify and remove obstacles to health and recovery; and to support the creation of a healthy internal and external environment.
2. **First, Do No Harm** (*primum no nocere*). Naturopathic physicians seek to do no harm with medical treatment by employing safe, effective, less invasive, and natural therapies.
3. **Identify and Treat the Cause** (*tolle causam*). Naturopathic physicians are not only trained to investigate and diagnose diseases, they are also trained to view things more holistically and look for an underlying cause, be it physical, mental, or emotional. Symptoms are viewed as expressions of the body's attempt to heal but are not the cause of disease. The physician must evaluate fundamental underlying causes on all levels, using treatment that includes addressing the root cause rather than just suppressing symptoms.
4. **Treat the Whole Person.** Health and disease are conditions of the whole organism, involving a complex interaction of physical, spiritual, mental, emotional, genetic, environmental, and social/cultural/economic factors. The physician must treat the whole person by taking all of these factors into account. Homeostasis and harmony of functions of all aspects of the individual are essential to recovery from disease, prevention of future health problems, and maintenance of wellness.

5. **Physician as Teacher** (*docere*). The naturopathic physician's major role is to educate, empower, and motivate the patient to take responsibility for health. The physician educates about risk factors, hereditary susceptibility, lifestyle habits, and preventive measures, and makes recommendations on how to avoid or minimize future chronic health problems. A healthy attitude, diet, exercise, and other lifestyle habits serve as the cornerstone of our recommendations.
6. **Prevention Is the Best Cure.** The ultimate goal of naturopathic medicine is prevention. This is accomplished through education and promotion of lifestyle habits and through natural therapeutic recommendations. The emphasis is on building health rather than on fighting disease.
7. **Establish Health and Wellness.** The primary goals of naturopathic physicians are to establish and maintain optimum health and to promote wellness. They strive to increase the patient's level of wellness, characterized by a positive emotional state, regardless of the level of health or disease.

In addition to these seven principles, there are two principles that I believe are fundamental not only to natural medicine, but fundamental to good medicine: the principle of resonance and the principle of choice. Let me explain. Resonance is basically an issue of compatibility. What approach, what therapy, what herb, or what of any substance is compatible with this particular patient in this particular moment and set of life circumstances? The selection of the therapeutic approach that is resonant with the individual is the therapy that will create the most healing momentum. Picture a child on a swing. You stand behind the child pushing her forward so she can achieve the most momentum, and swinging then becomes effortless. If you push her at the right moment, your force is perfectly timed with her body motion and the rhythm of the swing. The perfect timing sends her smoothly and easily higher, and with the slightest effort she can keep swinging forever. If you push her at the wrong moment, the swinging becomes jerky, she loses speed and height, and the rhythm is disrupted. It then takes a great deal of effort to regain momentum, speed, and height. The perfect effortless swing comes from the perfectly timed and perfect forcefulness of the "push." This is resonance. The person with the health problem is the child on the swing. The person who pushes the swing is the physician and the therapy she uses. Any medicine, natural or pharmaceutical, can be resonant. The art of medicine is to know when to use what, for whom, and for how long. I believe the most profound healing principle in the practice of medicine is the principle of resonance, not whether the medicine is natural or synthetic, alternative or conventional, or a "naturopathic" philosophy versus conventional "allopathic" philosophy. The healing method is the medicine that is right for that person. The true goal of a physician is to perceive what is resonant with that individual.

Dr. John Bastyr was considered by most naturopathic physicians to be the modern patriarch of naturopathic medicine. A whole new generation of naturopaths looked to him for their wisdom as the holder of true naturopathic medicine. The story goes, a young naturopathic medical student asked Dr. Bastyr, "How are we supposed to know what therapy to choose when there are so many different medicines and systems to choose from?" Dr. Bastyr calmly and quickly responded, "Choose what works." Another question was posed to Dr. Bastyr: "How can you tell an excellent physician from a good physician?" Dr. Bastyr's answer: "The results."

My second guiding principle is that of choice. Each patient chooses what is right for her. The doctor's role is to educate about the health problem, about the options, including their pros and cons, and to share resources. The goal is to provide the context in which the patient can make an informed decision. The physician must be perceptive and must listen, investigate, evaluate, educate, offer recommendations, and then create an environment where the individual can make a decision for herself. The individual seeking my help gets to choose. It may be black cohosh, or it may be estrogen. It may be a rigorous naturopathic health regimen, or it may be surgery. It may be an integrated combination, a "complementary" approach using the best of two worlds. Choice is a powerful force. The force of individual responsibility, empowerment, and self-direction. Choice fosters will, desire,

discipline, and motivation. Freedom of choice occurs in an environment of equality and respect between physician and patient.

These two principles, resonance and choice, are what motivate me toward the vision of an integrative health care model. I no longer believe in a fractionated approach to health and healing where alternative medicine is on one side and conventional medicine is on the other. There is a spectrum of options that go from simple to complex, from the least intervention to the most aggressive intervention, and from the most natural therapy to the most synthetic or technological. We need all of it. Human intelligence has created incredible tools and techniques. The physician who is educated and aware of all the options, and learns to understand how and when best to use all these choices on behalf of someone who is ill and suffering, is the true physician in my book. An integrative model incorporates the natural/naturopathic perspective and the conventional perspective and knows the strengths and weaknesses of each in different circumstances. When we can do something effectively and safely with nontoxic, natural medicines with far fewer side effects, then what would stop us? If we can't, or it's too risky to wait and find out, then let's move up the ladder to more invasive, riskier medicines with more side effects but which may work better or be a more appropriate choice because the risk of the disease is greater than the risks of the treatment.

Naturopathic and other alternative medicine disciplines have their strengths and their weaknesses. Conventional medicine has its strengths and its weaknesses. I encourage consumer and practitioner alike to advocate for practitioners of all disciplines to integrate their intelligence, experience, and energies to build cooperative working relationships with each other so that they can truly help people to choose what works best for them.

In addition to recommendations on lifestyle, diet, and exercise, naturopathic physicians utilize a vast array of therapeutic tools to promote health and treat illnesses. Naturopathic physicians are trained in what is called the "eclectic" tradition. They have a broad range of therapies and tend to use a selected mixture of these therapies when treating their patients. Naturopathic therapies include dietary and lifestyle changes, clinical nutrition (nutritional supplementation), botanical medicine (herbs), homeopathy, Chinese medicine and acupuncture, hydrotherapy, manipulation, physical therapies, psychotherapy, and minor surgery. Some naturopathic physicians receive extra training and licensure to practice obstetrics and natural childbirth.

And now for the second consistent theme in my life: the delivery of health care to women. Modern women are the first women in history to enjoy the luxury of anticipating that their lives will be healthy, long, and self-directed. This awareness of opportunities and choices is leading them today to seek the benefits of natural medicine in ever-increasing numbers. More dominant and discriminating consumers of health care than men or children, and quicker to grasp the advantages of a vitalistic, holistic healing art, their innate wisdom has already led to many significant changes in conventional medicine in recent years. Women insisted on "natural childbirth," and now it is the goal of most pregnant women and available everywhere. They have too long felt the restrictions of paternalistic conventional medicine with its uniformity and lack of individualization of healing approaches and are therefore more than ready to embrace the natural principle of "treating the individual." Moreover, the success of natural treatments in relieving disease and suffering has done much to effect its popularity. The now well-recognized neglect of women in allopathic conventional research and the failure to prioritize women's health in general have left a profound gap in health care that alternative medicine is well poised to fill.

Women want safe, effective, affordable medicine. Women want to be educated about their bodies and their health. Women want to make choices in their health care that they have determined are right for them. By philosophy, by design, and by commitment, alternative healing systems have the package to offer women what they want.

Beginning with the AMA's exclusion of women in the late 1800s, orthodox medicine's lack of respect for women both as healers and patients has been all too obvious. Today, significantly more empowered women have come to reject the dictums of orthodox medicine in greater numbers. Women intuit the limitations of the biomechanical model to completely explain physiological processes. Despite the orthodox physician's uniform advocacy for menopausal hormone replacement therapy for all, only a fraction, less than 20 percent of women comply; 90 percent of the women who begin HRT stop within the first year of use. Partially a failure of access, it is a profound testimonial to their lack of trust in conventional medicine's safety, efficacy, and commitment to their well-being.

The creation of synthetic hormones in the 1950s and 1960s was unquestionably revolutionary for women in that it suddenly allowed personal life autonomy through successful fertility control and the elimination of the hot flashes and mood swings of menopause. Women's lives were changed forever. However, with hormones coming as they did on the heels of the "miracle medicine era" in which antibiotics and vaccines led the general public to believe medicine could do no wrong, the consequences of hormone excess and side effects were not anticipated or quickly recognized and dealt with. And still today, most conventional practitioners will recommend a postmenopausal lifetime on HRT even though the data have begun to clearly show that the risk of breast cancer increases after five years of use. Consequently, many women distrust and fear hormonal medicine and their conventional physicians. Unfortunately, this fear and mistrust then lead to the denial of a medicine (HRT) that in some cases may achieve more benefit than risk. Here's where the integrated wisdom and approach come in. While clearly not a panacea, hormones are not all bad and have important uses for selected individuals. We can also use a combination of a reduced dose of hormones along with soy and herbal medicines to bring about the most benefit with the least risk.

Women today are insisting on participating in their health care decisions in a way conventional medicine is just beginning to recognize. I believe that the baby boomer menopausal woman is having and will continue to have a more significant impact on our health care model than any other previous group of health care consumers. Menopausal women today reject the notion of a single therapeutic modality being essential for all women undergoing a natural process. They reject the notion of taking a drug for the rest of their lives, especially if they have other options, especially if they can do other things to help prevent osteoporosis and heart disease, and especially if that drug increases their risk of a life-threatening disease.

Women are the biggest consumers of health care in America. A recent menopause supplement to *OB-GYN,* the journal of the American College of Ob-Gyn, states, "Focus groups, involving women age forty to sixty, reveal that women know more about herbal medicines than about estrogen. . . ." That seems an impressive testimonial to the power of alternative medicine in its alliance with the natural wisdom of women to define their own health care standards. It is an invitation to alternative medicine to continue to provide women with the wider, healthier options they seek. Fifty percent of American women will be menopausal by the year 2015, and they will provide alternative medicine the greatest opportunity yet to serve our communities.

In addition to practitioner-delivered natural health care, natural medicine offers safe and effective self-care options for many common conditions such as vaginitis, PMS, fibrocystic breasts, menopause, bladder infections, and more, further expanding women's health care autonomy. I support the self-care approach to healing. Much of the practice of medicine is not particularly difficult or complex. Education and resources can provide a lot of very practical information. One of the things I've tried to do in this book is not only to provide some self-care treatments for common female disorders but also to provide guidelines about when self-care is not appropriate. Health care is a team approach: the patient, the practitioner, the therapies. The team can include both the alternative and the conventional practitioner—and, better still, those that talk to each other on behalf of the patient.

Choice in doctors and medical approaches, involvement in the health care process, healthy lifestyles, and safer, nontoxic natural therapies are recognized by today's women as essential to health and well-being. Women highly value the longer time spent in discussion with their alternative provider as well as the careful, complete, and respectful collection of their histories. They value processing their options thoroughly and individually. This unique quality of alternative health care systems is rare in conventional medicine and is one of the chief reasons women seek alternative care.

Naturopathic physicians and other providers of alternative medicine must seek to verify the "scientific" truth of their medicines whenever possible— by research and by modifying the mechanistic model when necessary to suit their vitalistic philosophy. They must continue to stand by their tradition of resonance between patient and therapy, ever seeking the resonance for a particular woman with a particular problem at a particular time in her life.

Last, alternative medicine must recognize that conventional medicine, while inadequate alone, is here to stay and offers important options and lifesaving measures. Likewise, conventional medicine must recognize that natural therapies are a fundamental healing tradition of all cultures, and that modern alternative medicine is also here to stay. The more practitioners make themselves aware of these options, the better they can guide women in selecting from all options, both naturopathic and conventional. A combined, well-thought-out cooperative and integrative approach is often the best that medicine has to offer. Our open-mindedness will be rewarded manifold by the improved health of women and their increased satisfaction and trust in their health care providers.

CHAPTER ONE

ABNORMAL UTERINE BLEEDING

⤳ Overview

Changes in the amount of menstrual blood flow, duration, and pattern are among the most common health concerns that women face. Although these changes cause a lot of anxiety for women and do warrant a medical evaluation, most cases of abnormal bleeding are due to benign and easily addressed conditions. Whether alternative or conventional treatments are used for intervention, prompt evaluation is highly recommended.

There are many causes of abnormal bleeding, but our main purpose in this chapter is to discuss a benign hormonal cause of bleeding called dysfunctional uterine bleeding (DUB), abnormal uterine bleeding without any demonstrable organic cause. First, we need a little background and overview on abnormal bleeding in general.

A wide variety of clinical disorders can manifest as abnormal bleeding from the vagina. What is considered abnormal bleeding depends on the age of the patient. The bleeding can take many forms, including heavy and/or prolonged menses (*menorrhagia*), intermenstrual bleeding (*metrorrhagia*), frequent menses (*polymenorrhea*), infrequent menses (*oligomenorrhea*), heavy and irregular intermenstrual bleeding (*menometrorrhagia*), or postmenopausal bleeding. Normal menses are defined as vaginal bleeding that occurs approximately every 28 days (with a range of 21 to 35 days) and lasts for 4 to 7 days. Abnormal bleeding is bleeding that occurs more frequently than every 21 days, less frequently than every 35 days, lasts more than 7 days, is unusually heavy or light, or occurs after menopause. In addition, vaginal bleeding is considered heavy if a woman loses more than 80 ml of blood per cycle (normal is 30 to 35 ml).

Benign Abnormal Bleeding

The causes of abnormal bleeding can be benign, premalignant, or malignant. Benign causes can be further subdivided as either organic or hormonal. Organic disorders are all benign causes of bleeding that are not hormonal. This may include systemic health problems, abnormal pregnancy, foreign bodies, trauma, infections, and growths.

Systemic diseases that are associated with problems in how the blood clots are called coagulopathies and can cause heavy vaginal bleeding. Heavy bleeding in a teenage girl may be caused by a coagulopathy called von Willebrand's disease. In fact, 20 percent of teenage girls with severe menorrhagia have a significant coagulation problem. A decrease in the number of blood platelets (thrombocytopenia) can also cause abnormal bleeding. Other systemic diseases, such as hypothyroidism and severe liver diseases, can also cause prolonged menses, heavy menses, or intermenstrual bleeding.

An abnormal pregnancy is the most common cause of abnormal vaginal bleeding in women who are of reproductive age. Any type of miscarriage can present with abnormal bleeding that is also often associated with cramping pains. Women with an ectopic pregnancy can present with abnormal bleeding as can those with a molar pregnancy.

Abnormal bleeding in children can be caused by foreign bodies that they may have placed in their vaginas while playing. The most common foreign body in women of reproductive age is an IUD. Women with IUDs will tend to have heavier menses and sometimes intermenstrual bleeding.

Trauma during intercourse can cause vaginal bleeding, for example in postmenopausal women who may have a dry vagina with thinning vaginal tissue. Just the friction of normal vaginal penetration during sex may be traumatic to this sensitive tissue. There are other situations where trauma may be experienced in a violent situation such as sexual abuse and rape. In children or adolescents, sexual abuse must be considered in cases of traumatic vaginal bleeding. Traumatic bleeding may also occur after gynecological procedures such as biopsies and instrumentation.

Occasionally, a uterine infection called chronic endometritis can present with abnormal vaginal bleeding or spotting. Other symptoms are often associated with this infection. These may include a vaginal discharge, fever, abdominal/pelvic pain, or lower back pain.

Perhaps one of the most common causes of abnormal bleeding is growths known as myomas, more commonly referred to as uterine fibroids. These tend to be more common in women over the age of 30, particularly when women are in their forties. There are different kinds of fibroids that are discussed in Chapter 17, but the submucous fibroids tend to be the most troublesome in terms of bleeding, most typically heavy bleeding. Fortunately, they represent only about 5–10 percent of all fibroids.

Endometrial polyps can also cause abnormal bleeding, but the bleeding is usually not heavy. Adenomyosis, or a variant of endometriosis, may result in very heavy bleeding that is associated with menstrual cramping. Endometriosis itself can also cause irregular changes in the menstrual cycle but not typically heavy menses. Finally, bleeding may result from cervical polyps or a simple inflammation of the cervix called cervicitis. Cervical polyps and cervicitis tend to present with intermenstrual bleeding or spotting after intercourse.

Malignant Abnormal Bleeding

Now let us look at the premalignant and malignant causes of bleeding. Vaginal cancer accounts for only 2 percent of malignancies of the female genital tract. Eighty-five percent of the primary vaginal cancers are squamous cell carcinoma. The most common symptoms of invasive squamous cell cancer include vaginal bleeding or foul-smelling discharge. Pain is usually a late symptom.

The tragedy of another cancer, cervical cancer, is that it is a preventable disease. It is preceded by a prolonged precancerous state in almost all cases and can be detected at its early precancerous states by annual pap smears. These earlier states of abnormal cells and cervical dysplasias are easily treatable conditions. Cervical cancer accounts for approximately 18 percent of female genital cancer in the United States. The peak incidence of cervical cancer is from 35 to 39 and 60 to 64 years of age. Vaginal bleeding after vaginal sexual activity is the most common symptom occurring in cancer of the cervix. In women with advanced disease, a foul-smelling discharge may be present.

Endometrial hyperplasia is an increased growth of the lining of the uterus (endometrium) and a subsequent thickening. Most cases of endometrial hyperplasia revert to normal, either spontaneously or with hormonal treatment. Some may persist, and others can progress to endometrial cancer. Endometrial hyperplasia may occur in any age group but is most commonly seen in older women. Chronic lack of ovulation, as seen in the teenage years, after menopause, and in polycystic ovary disease, is a condition where we may see endometrial hyperplasia. Endometrial hyperplasia can be simple or complex, and atypical or without atypia. These distinctions are very important when it comes to treatment and management and can best be made with a procedure called an endometrial biopsy. Pelvic ultrasound has improved to the point where it can detect thickening of the endometrium. Once thickening is observed, a biopsy will probably be recommended to further evaluate the situation.

Some endometrial hyperplasias will progress to cancer of the endometrium, i.e., uterine cancer. As in cervical dysplasia and cervical cancer, endometrial hyperplasia is the precancerous state; its adequate treatment will prevent the development of endometrial cancer. This is the most common malignancy of the female genital tract and accounts for approximately 7 percent of all cancers in women. The average age of patients with endometrial cancer is 59 years; the highest range for the incidence is age 50 to 59 years in postmenopausal women. The most common symptom associated with endometrial cancer is abnormal uterine bleeding. Typically, the bleeding is in the form of spotting, especially in postmenopausal women.

Dysfunctional Uterine Bleeding (DUB)

DUB can occur at any age but is most common at either end of the reproductive age span. Adolescents account for about 20 percent of DUB cases due to hypothalamic immaturity after the first menstrual cycle. Perimenopausal women account for approximately 50 percent of DUB cases due to waning ovarian function. As the ovary ages, it becomes less efficient in completing the ovulatory process. Initially there is a decrease in progesterone production, which causes shorter cycles. As the aging process progresses, ovulation becomes less frequent, resulting in a variable length of the menstrual cycle and a variation in the duration of the flow. Eventually, the lack of ovulation puts women in an estrogen-dominant state in the presence of too little progesterone. Ovulation must occur in order to produce progesterone. Women who are in a state of chronic anovulation tend to have an excess of estrogen in the body. This excess estrogen is what disrupts the normal pattern of menstruation.

The remaining 30 percent of cases of DUB occur among women age 20 to 40, generally as a result of polycystic ovarian syndrome, elevated prolactin levels, emotional stress, obesity, weight loss due to anorexia, or athletic training.

The actual cause of DUB is not completely clear. One theory is that the fluctuating estrogen levels seen in chronic lack of ovulation can cause intermittent estrogen withdrawal bleeding. Another theory is that the continuous estrogen stimulation leads to a thickening of the endometrium, which actually needs more estrogen in order to maintain itself. Eventually, the need for estrogen surpasses the production and breakthrough bleeding results. Another theory is that some areas of the endometrium outgrow their blood supply, and subsequent bleeding occurs due to the lack of progesterone.

There are also cases of DUB that are not due to anovulation but rather occur even though there is regular monthly ovulation. Ovulatory DUB is defined as heavy menses in women who ovulate and who do not have a coagulopathy or any uterine abnormality. The cause of this form of DUB is not clear, although several theories exist.

❧ Diagnosis

The key to accurate diagnosis of DUB is the medical history. Several pertinent pieces of information will facilitate diagnosis:

- Previous menstrual patterns for the last three months
- The presence or absence of pain along with the bleeding
- Heaviness of the flow (number of pads or tampons per day and how often they are changed when saturated)
- Contraceptive methods, if any
- Symptoms of pregnancy
- Dates and histories of past pregnancies
- Premenstrual symptoms
- Recent abdominal, pelvic, or vaginal trauma
- Clotting problems
- Easy bruising or bleeding
- Symptoms of systemic diseases
- History of taking estrogens without adequate progesterone/progestins
- History of sexually transmitted diseases
- Past gynecologic history

A physical exam will involve visualizing the cervix, feeling the contour and size of the uterus, and general palpation of the pelvic area. Laboratory testing may include:

- Pap smear
- Thyroid function tests
- Pregnancy test
- Complete blood count to rule out anemia
- Follicle stimulating hormone (FSH)/luteinizing hormone (LH)
- Liver function tests
- Prolactin levels
- Adrenal function studies
- Pelvic ultrasound to identify uterine fibroids or measure endometrial thickness
- Testing for sexually transmitted diseases

An endometrial biopsy may be recommended to actually test the tissue itself. This is a simple procedure done in the practitioner's office in which the clinician inserts a small narrow plastic instrument called a pipelle into the uterine cavity, creating a slight vacuum and extracting tissue by rotating the pipelle while it is being moved in and out within the cavity. It only takes about 30 to 60 seconds, but women can experience mild to significant cramping during that time. A local anesthetic is usually not required, and the cramping generally subsides very quickly once the procedure is over. Endometrial pipelle biopsies can determine the presence of endometrial hyperplasia, uterine cancer, infection (endometritis), a disrupted hormonal effect, a lack of estrogen as is seen in postmenopausal women, or a uterine polyp.

If the procedure is done at the right time, it can also be used to verify ovulation. If the endometrium has proliferated (as reported on the biopsy report), when the woman's next bleeding episode occurs within 10 to 12 days, it is generally an indication of a lack of ovulation. Tests such as saline infusion sonohysterography (SIS—an ultrasound procedure that gives a three-dimensional view so as not to miss any portion of the uterine cavity), hysteroscopy (a procedure that involves dilating the cervix so that a small lighted scope can be inserted to visualize the intrauterine cavity), or a dilation and curettage (D&C) may be recommended in addition to or instead of the pelvic ultrasound and the pipelle biopsy in selected cases to improve accuracy of the results.

KEY CONCEPTS

- Seek and utilize a health care practitioner who will distinguish DUB from benign, premalignant, and malignant causes. If benign, is the cause organic or hormonal?
- Workup will include a medical history and may include a physical exam and further laboratory tests.
- Do not self-treat unless assured that the cause is DUB.
- Practitioners may presume a diagnosis of DUB temporarily and recommend a further workup depending on response to the treatment.

PREVENTION

- Reduce stress.
- Avoid taking any form of estrogen without adequate progesterone or progestins in order to prevent endometrial hyperplasia and endometrial cancer.
- Engage in healthy lifestyle habits.
- Protect yourself against sexually transmitted diseases.
- Use well-tolerated forms of contraception.
- Have regular medical visits, including an annual physical exam.

❧ Overview of Alternative Treatments

The goals of alternative treatment for DUB are the same as the goals of conventional treatment: control the bleeding, prevent and treat anemia, restore an acceptable menstrual pattern, and prevent endometrial hyperplasia/endometrial cancer.

Repeated episodes of heavier and prolonged bleeding should be distinguished from acute hemorrhage. My general guidelines are: If a woman is saturating a super tampon or heavy pad more often than every hour for 6 to 8 hours or more she needs some form of prescription hormone intervention. Even heavier bleeding (i.e., saturating pads every half hour or less) will most likely require surgical intervention. Monitoring physical symptoms, blood pressure, pulse, and hemoglobin and hematocrit levels will help to determine management of these more semi-urgent and urgent cases. Use of high dose natural estrogens and natural progesterone may be substituted in some cases of heavier semi-acute bleeding, although the net effect is the same as when using conventional hormones. Licensed naturopathic physicians can prescribe natural hormones and conventional hormones in many of the states in which they are licensed and would approach these dramatic situations with an equally high degree of concern and astuteness. They may integrate acute antihemorrhagic botanicals or nutrients in combination with the hormonal therapies.

Less dramatic cases, but still heavy menstrual flow, will be best managed with both an immediate plan for the semi-acute bleeding episode, which should slow down within one to four days, and a comprehensive plan that should bring results in one to four months.

A comprehensive plan may include the use of soy and flax products to regulate the menstrual cycle, herbal extracts to address immediate bleeding episodes, nutrients such as bioflavonoids and bromelain for their natural anti-inflammatory effect, herbal extracts for their ability to bring about ovulation and orderly stimulation of ovarian function, and herbs for their tonifying and astringent effects.

The concept of tissue tonification is a key feature of the philosophy of herbal medicine. It is thought that gynecological conditions associated with bleeding may occur as a result of poor tissue tone of the mucus membranes, poor uterine tone, and a constitutional weakness of the tissues that presents as generalized lack of tissue integrity, in this case, the uterus. The astringents (herbs that slow the loss of body fluids, i.e., menstrual bleeding) are the herbs most likely to affect tissue tone, while the uterine tonics and the emmenagogues (herbs to promote menses) are most likely to affect uterine tone. Traditionally, the ability of an astringent herb to stop bleeding has been attributed to the tannin content of the plants. Uterine tone is related to the ability of the uterus to function as a smooth muscle. When the uterine tone is normal, there is a normalization of menstrual flow. A hypertonic uterus can be associated with a delayed menses and cramping uterine pains. A hypotonic uterus is frequently accompanied by heavy bleeding and a feeling of pelvic congestion.

Stress reduction has an underappreciated but significant influence on irregular menses and DUB. A disruption in the messages between the hypothalamus (which produces gonadotropin-releasing hormones) and the anterior pituitary (which releases FSH and LH, follicle-stimulating and luteinizing hormones) brings about a mistiming of the release of these hormones and a subsequent lack of ovulation and/or estrogen and progesterone production by the ovary. The timing of the release of these pituitary hormones, as well as of estrogen and progesterone, is what determines a normal, regular menstrual cycle. This timing can be adversely affected by stress, and, by the same token, the timing can be improved by stress reduction. A third hormone produced by the pituitary, prolactin, also plays an important role in the menstrual cycle. Increased production of prolactin can inhibit the maturation of ovarian follicles and induce menstrual abnormalities and sterility. Prolactin release is often stress-related.

Nutrition

Consume a whole foods diet rich in whole grains, fruits, vegetables, legumes, quality cooking oils (canola and olive), nuts, and seeds. Emphasize fish high in omega-3 oils (salmon, tuna, sardines, halibut, mackerel, herring) and reduce saturated animal fats (beef, chicken, butter, cheese) to promote the preferred prostaglandin pathways that are discussed in Chapters 9 and 11 (Heart Disease and Menstrual Cramps). These preferred prostaglandins will reduce inflammation and thereby may help to reduce heavy and profuse menstrual flows.

Foods high in iron in particular should be incorporated into the general diet when heavy blood loss persists on a monthly basis. The single greatest nutritional contributor to iron-deficiency anemia is the refining of breads and cereals. Although we do have iron "enriched" flour, it is still about one-third the content of the iron contained in whole-wheat flour. Brewer's yeast and wheat germ are both excellent sources supplying about 18 and 8 mg respectively per ½ cup. Blackstrap molasses is not only one of the richest sources of iron but also of many other minerals. It supplies about 9 mg of iron per tablespoon; dark unrefined molasses, 1.5 mg, and sugar, none. Single foods high in iron probably cannot surpass the amount found in liver and then kidneys. However, I do not recommend these because it is very difficult to get organic products, and these organs accumulate many metabolic wastes. Apricots and eggs are also rather high in iron. We often think of dark green leafy vegetables as high in iron, although it may be difficult to absorb in this form. Foods such as yogurt, sour fruits, and citrus juices can aid the absorption of iron.

Two foods stand out in their ability to regulate the menstrual cycle: flaxseeds and soy protein. Flaxseeds contain a group of phytoestrogens called lignans that have been shown to have weakly estrogenic and antiestrogenic properties. Two specific lignans, enterodiol and enterolactone, are absorbed after formation in the intestinal tract from plant precursors particularly abundant in flaxseeds.

The ingestion of flaxseed powder and its effect on the menstrual cycle was studied in 18 normally cycling women.[1] Each woman consumed her usual omnivorous, low fiber diet for three cycles and her usual diet supplemented with 10 grams per day of flaxseed for another three cycles. All women were instructed to avoid soy foods. The second and third flax cycles were compared to the second and third control diet cycles. Three nonovulatory cycles occurred among the 18 women during the control diet (36 total cycles) compared to none during the 36 flaxseed cycles. The ovulatory flax cycles were consistently associated with about one more day in the luteal phase (second half of the cycle) when compared to the ovulatory non-flax cycles. Only one day longer before you bleed and a slight increase in the number of ovulations may not seem like much. However, over a period of months and years, the cumulative effect not only has implications for regulating the menstrual cycle but may also play a positive role in reducing the risk of breast and other hormonally dependent cancers.

The influence of a diet containing soy protein on the length of the menstrual cycle in premenopausal women has also been studied.[2] Sixty grams of soy protein containing 45 mg of isoflavones (a phytoestrogen compound found in high amounts in soy) was given daily for one month in a study lasting nine months (Table 1.1). A significant increase in the length of the follicular phase (first half of the menstrual cycle) by an average of 2.5 days and/or delayed menstruation was observed in the six women who consumed the soy protein. Again, as with flaxseeds, soy protein has a role not only in contributing to the regularity and lengthening of the menstrual cycle, but adding 2.5 days per month and lengthening the number of days from one menses to another may in part contribute to a lower incidence of breast cancer.[3]

Nutritional Supplements

Vitamin A

A deficiency of vitamin A may be a contributing factor in the menorrhagia of adult women. A deficiency of vitamin A impairs enzyme activity and hormone production in the ovaries of animals,[4] and serum levels of vitamin A have been found to be lower in women with menorrhagia than in healthy women.[5] In this study, vitamin A was used as a treatment in 40 women who had diagnosed menorrhagia as a result of a diverse array of causes. In the group who received 60,000 IU of vitamin A for 35 days, menstruation returned to normal in 23 women (57.5 percent) for a period of at least three months. A significant decrease in the amount of blood or a reduction in the duration of the menses or both was obtained in 14 women (35 percent). The vitamin A was ineffective in 3 of the 40 women (7.5 percent). The overall result with vitamin A therapy showed that 92.5 percent of the 40 cases of menorrhagia were cured or alleviated.

It is important to understand that 60,000 IU of vitamin A given for long periods of time could lead to vitamin A toxicity, but generally this would only occur if doses in excess of 50,000 IU were used for several years. Smaller doses may produce toxicity

TABLE 1.1   **Isoflavone Content of Soybeans**

Food	Serving Size	Isoflavones
Textured soy protein granules	¼ cup	62 mg
Nutlettes breakfast cereal	¼ cup	61 mg
Roasted soynuts	¼ cup	60 mg
Tempeh	½ cup	35 mg
Tofu; low fat and regular	½ cup	35 mg
Soy beverage powders (variable with brands)	1–2 scoops	20–50 mg
Regular soy milk	1 cup	30 mg
Low fat soy milk	1 cup	20 mg
Roasted soy butter	2 tbsp	17 mg

symptoms if there are problems in storage and transport of vitamin A. These problems are generally only found in people with cirrhosis of the liver, hepatitis, or malnutrition, and in children and adolescents. However, for a period of only one month, as in the above study, vitamin A toxicity is of virtually no concern, and I would not hesitate to use it for this amount of time, or up to three months. Using lower doses of 25,000 IU for longer periods of time should be considered in those cases where ongoing treatment is necessary to control menorrhagia.

Vitamin A

60,000 IU per day for 1–3 months
10,000–25,000 IU ongoing, if necessary

Note: Vitamin E improves vitamin A storage and utilization, and zinc is required to mobilize vitamin A. A deficiency of zinc, vitamin C, protein, or thyroid hormone may impair the conversion of carotenes to vitamin A. Provitamin A carotenes such as beta carotene require these nutrients for their conversion to vitamin A.

B Complex

There may be a correlation between a nutritional deficiency of vitamin B complex and menorrhagia and metrorrhagia. It has been shown that the liver loses its ability to inactivate estrogen in vitamin B-complex deficiency. We know that some cases of heavy menses and intermenstrual bleeding are due to an excess of estrogen. Therefore, supplementing with a complex of B vitamins may restore the proper

metabolism of estrogen and thus have a role in treating DUB. A study done over 50 years ago was undertaken to determine if the B-complex vitamin was effective in the treatment of these menstrual conditions. Although the study done in the 1940s was not up to today's scientific standards, a series of consecutive cases showed that a B-complex preparation was effective in "prompt" improvement in both menorrhagia and metrorrhagia.[6] The B-complex preparations used orally in the study were usually given in daily doses providing 3–9 mg of thiamin, 4.5–9 mg of riboflavin, and up to 60 mg of niacin.

Vitamin B-100 Complex

1–2 daily

Vitamin K

Vitamin K deficiency is pretty rare, but its role in the manufacture of clotting factors like prothrombin and clotting factors VII, IX, and X has obvious implications for women with heavy or prolonged menses. Even when the cause of the excessive bleeding is not a clotting disorder, it may be prudent to use vitamin K as part of a comprehensive treatment plan. Fat-soluble chlorophyll is a good source of vitamin K and is found in fresh green juices. Consider increasing the intake of green leafy vegetables and/or supplementing with 150–500 mcg per day of vitamin K.

Vitamin K

150–500 mcg per day

Vitamin C

Vitamin C helps to reduce heavy bleeding by strengthening the capillaries and preventing their fragility. In at least one study, vitamin C was able to reduce heavy bleeding in 87 percent of the women.[7] Vitamin C also is an important supplement for women who have acquired iron deficient anemia from menstrual blood loss. It helps to increase iron absorption and can be used to prevent anemia as well as to treat it.

Vitamin C
2,000–4,000 mg per day

Bioflavonoids

Like vitamin C, bioflavonoids have demonstrated a significant ability to reduce heavy menstrual bleeding by strengthening the vessel walls of the capillaries in women with menorrhagia.[7] Bioflavonoids also can have an antiestrogen effect on the uterus by occupying the estrogen receptor sites and thus limiting the estrogen-stimulating effect on the endometrium. This effect can then help to reduce bleeding. Just as conventional medicine prescribes nonsteroidal anti-inflammatories to reduce heavy bleeding, alternative medicine has natural anti-inflammatories like bioflavonoids to be used for the same purpose. Foods high in bioflavonoids (and vitamin C) include grape skins, cherries, blackberries, blueberries, and the pulp and white rind of citrus fruits.

Bioflavonoids
1,000–2,000 mg per day

Botanicals

Chaste Tree (*Vitex agnus castus*)

Chaste tree is probably the best-known herb in all of Europe for hormonal imbalances in women. Since at least the time of the Greeks, chaste tree has been used for the full scope of menstrual disorders: heavy menses, lack of ovulation, frequent and infrequent menses, irregular menses, and a complete lack of menses. Chaste tree has been repeatedly studied in Germany, and, although the fruit was used traditionally, it is the seeds that are mainly used for medicine in Europe and in this country. Consequently, most of the testing has been done on the seeds. Chaste tree acts on the hypothalamus and pituitary glands. It increases LH production and mildly inhibits the release of FSH. The result is a shift in the ratio of estrogen to progesterone and consequently produces a "progesterone-like" effect.[8] The ability of chaste tree to raise progesterone levels is then an indirect effect and not a direct hormonal action.[9] Chaste tree has also been shown to inhibit prolactin release by the pituitary gland, particularly under stress.[10]

The first major study on chaste tree was published in 1954.[11] Although some of the women studied had amenorrhea (lack of menses), which we will discuss in Chapter 2, nine women had scant or infrequent menstrual flows, and six of them experienced more frequent menses and an improvement by an increase in bleeding. A dramatic improvement was seen in 40 patients with cystic hyperplasia (excessive proliferation of the endometrium). Although this condition is not technically DUB, but rather endometrial hyperplasia, it is impressive that chaste tree was able to bring about enough of a progesterone effect to reduce the hyperplasia.

A study observing 126 women with menstrual disorders involved taking 15 drops of a chaste tree liquid extract three times daily over several menstrual cycles.[12] In 33 women who had frequent menses (polymenorrhea), the duration between periods lengthened from an average of 20.1 days to 26.3 days. In 58 patients with excessive bleeding (menorrhagia), the number of heavy bleeding days was shortened.

As mentioned earlier, chaste tree has an ability to inhibit prolactin production. A double-blind placebo-controlled study was able to examine the effect of a chaste tree preparation on 52 women with luteal phase defects due to elevated prolactin levels.[13] The dose given was 20 mg chaste tree daily for three months. After three months of treatment, prolactin release was significantly reduced in those taking chaste tree. The shortened luteal phase was normalized as was the decrease in progesterone production.

Chaste tree is the most important herb to normalize and regulate the menstrual cycle. Chaste tree is not a fast-acting herb; do not hesitate to use it over a long period of time. In fact, results may not be achieved until after four to six months. It is not an herb to be relied on for immediate relief, and it will not be effective in reducing semi-acute bleeding episodes.

Chaste tree
*liquid extract 30–60 drops per day or
.6–.75% standardized extract, 175–215 mg per day*

Human and animal studies have determined chaste tree to be safe for most menstruating women. It is not recommended during pregnancy, although this is not an absolute contraindication, and women should not worry if they become pregnant while taking chaste tree for the first trimester. Chaste tree is completely safe during lactation, and there are no known interactions with other drugs. Minimal side effects have included itching, occasional rash, and possibly a lowered libido.

Ginger (*Zingiber officinale*)

Ginger has been shown to inhibit prostaglandin synthetase,[14] the enzyme believed to be related to the altered prostaglandin-2 ratio associated with excessive menstrual loss.[15] The most potent constituent appears to be gingerol, the pungent ingredient in the ginger. Inhibition of prostaglandin and leukotriene formation could explain ginger's traditional use as an anti-inflammatory agent, and anti-inflammatories are effective in reducing the flow from heavy and protracted menses.

Ginger
*1–4 grams dry powder per day
for semi-acute blood loss*

Traditional Astringent Herbs

Astringent herbs form a large category of tannin containing plants that are used to reduce blood loss from the reproductive tract as well as from the bowel, stomach, respiratory tract, and skin. In the reproductive tract, the astringent herbs are used to correct uterine or cervical bleeding. The astringents most effective in uterine blood loss are often high in tannins, but other constituents also explain their mechanism of action. The following herbs are the major astringent and hemostatic herbs used in gynecological problems:

With tannins
- Yarrow (*Achillea millefolium*)
- Ladies' mantle (*Alchemilla vulgaris*)
- Cranesbill (*Geranium maculatum*)
- Beth root* (*Trillium erectum*)
- Greater periwinkle (*Vinca major*)

Cranesbill

This astringent herb, high in tannic acid, was relied on by early American Indians to treat diarrhea, dysentery, leukorrhea, and chronic menorrhagia, especially cases of prolonged bleeding. Cranesbill was used by early practitioners of natural medicine (the eclectic physicians) to achieve prompt and predictable results in cases of menorrhagia without any unpleasant side effects.

Without tannins
- Horsetail (*Equisetum arvense*)
- Goldenseal (*Hydrastis canadensis*)
- Shepherd's purse (*Capsella bursa pastoris*)

Shepherd's Purse

Shepherd's purse is a mild astringent that contains saponins, choline, acetylcholine, and tyramine, all likely to be helpful in female reproductive health.[16] Chemical analysis shows that it can coagulate blood.[17] Its best use is in combination with other astringent and hemostatic herbs for uterine bleeding, particularly when there is extremely heavy flow. Shepherd's purse is a good choice for both semi-acute situations and chronic recurring episodes of DUB.

---

*See "Dosage" on page 10.

Uterine Tonics

In traditional herbal medicine, uterine tone determines the ease of menstrual flow. If the uterus is "hypertonic," then it may be difficult to initiate menses in a timely manner. If the uterus is hypotonic, there may be heavy bleeding. In either case, improving uterine tone will tend to normalize and regulate menstrual bleeding. Two categories of herbs are said to have the most effect on uterine tone and therefore bleeding:

1. The uterine tonics or amphoterics that regulate tone (both reduce excess tone and increase tone in states of laxity):
   - Dong quai (*Angelica sinensis*)
   - Blue cohosh (*Caulophyllum thalictroides*)
   - Helonias (*Chamaelirium luteum*)
   - Squaw vine (*Mitchella repens*)
   - Raspberry leaves (*Rubus idaeus*)
   - Life root (*Senecio aureus*)

Life Root

Life root, also known as ragwort, is a time honored "female regulator" that has been used consistently in traditional herbal medicine for menstrual cramps, menorrhagia, suppressed menstruation, and other disturbances of the reproductive tract. It is a classic uterine tonic that has been used to tonify a soft, boggy uterus, including laxity of the uterine ligaments. It adds tone and structure to the nervous and muscular structures of the reproductive female organs and regulates the quantity of the monthly flow.

2. The uterine stimulants or emmenagogues that increase tone or muscular activity and serve to initiate the onset of menses:
   - Squaw vine (*Mitchella repens*)
   - Yarrow (*Achillea millefolium*)
   - Chaste tree (*Vitex agnus castus*)
   - Pennyroyal* (*Mentha pulegium*)
   - Mugwort (*Artemisia vulgaris*)
   - Blue cohosh (*Caulophyllum thalictroides*)

Blue Cohosh

This perennial herb grows all over the United States, and it is the root or rhizome that is used medicinally. The chemical constituents include al-

kaloids, saponins, phytosterols, and many minerals. As an emmenagogue that promotes the onset of menstrual flow, it would seem odd to use it as a treatment for menorrhagia. Yet, traditionally, blue cohosh, when used with other astringent herbs, acts as a uterine tonic and in fact helps to regulate the menses and the amount of flow.

Astringent and uterine tonic herbs can be used in combination formulations and used for weeks to several months. Use as a tea, liquid extract, or powdered capsule.

Traditional Herbs for Semi-acute and Acute Blood Loss

- Cinnamon* (*Cinnamomum verum*)
- Life root (*Senecio aureus*)
- Canadian fleabane* (*Eregeron canadensis*)
- Greater periwinkle (*Vinca major*)
- Shepherd's purse (*Capsella bursa pastorus*)
- Yarrow (*Achillea millefolium*)
- Savin (*Sabina officinalis*)

DOSAGE

*The herbs that are starred may be toxic if given in inappropriate doses, so correct dosing is very important. Use a botanical reference text.

Essential oil of cinnamon: 1–5 drops every 3–4 hours.

Other herbs: Do not exceed 20 drops every 2 hours or 1 cap every 4 hours if using a single herb. Several herbs may be used in combination, and in these cases it is important to consult a reference book or an herbal practitioner to know the dose limitations.

Natural Hormones

Natural Progesterone

Cyclic natural progesterone can be used to correct infrequent menses, heavy menses, and sometimes intermenstrual bleeding. This therapy substitutes for what the body is not producing due to the lack of ovulation. A woman must ovulate in order to produce adequate levels of progesterone. Natural

SAMPLE TREATMENT PLAN FOR ABNORMAL UTERINE BLEEDING

Chronic recurring menorrhagia

- Bioflavonoids, 1,000 mg twice per day
- Vitamin A, 60,000 IU per day up to 3 months
- Chaste tree (standardized extract) 175 mg per day; or ½–1 tsp daily
- Combination herbal product using astringents and uterine tonics
- Consider natural progesterone cream, ¼–½ tsp 12–21 days/month

Semi-acute menorrhagia

- Bioflavonoids, 1,000 mg 2–3 times daily
- Combination herbal products using astringents and uterine tonics; use equal parts of a liquid extract of:

  Yarrow

  Greater periwinkle

  Shepherd's purse

  Life root

  20–30 drops every 2–3 hours

  If you choose to use one of the more toxic herbs, such as cinnamon or beth root, be sure not to exceed recommended doses.

- Oral micronized progesterone: 200–400 mg per day for 7–12 days followed by a cyclic hormone product for 21 days on and 7 days off

If no change in 24 to 48 hours, high dose estrogens may be needed to stop the immediate bleeding, followed by a progesterone regimen.

Oligomenorrhea (infrequent menses)

- Chaste tree berry

  .6–.75% standardized extract: one 175–215 mg capsule daily, or liquid extract: ½–1 tsp daily
- Combination herbal emmenagogue:

Squawvine	1½ oz
Yarrow	1 oz
Blue cohosh	1 oz
Pennyroyal	½ oz 20 drops every 2–3 hours.

- Natural progesterone cream

  Apply ¼ tsp 1–2 times daily, day 7 to day 14 of cycle

  Apply ½ tsp 1–2 times daily, day 15 to day 26

Polymenorrhea (frequent menses)

- Chaste tree

  Standardized extract: 175 mg daily, or liquid extract: 30–60 drops daily
- Natural progesterone cream: ¼–½ tsp twice daily, 21 days on, 7 days off (during menstrual flow)
- Some cases may require higher doses of oral micronized progesterone
- Some cases may require a natural estrogen/natural progesterone formulation that requires more individualized dosing

progesterone, which is made from extracts of Mexican wild yam or soybeans, is an exact chemical duplicate of progesterone produced by the human body. Because natural progesterone is biochemically identical to human progesterone, it is generally very well tolerated by women. The disadvantages to the natural hormone include a short half-life (three to six hours) that requires giving it two to three times a day. Natural progesterone can be delivered by injection, sublingual tablets, rectal or vaginal suppositories, oral capsules or tablets, and topical creams. Dosing is dependent on the delivery system and the characteristic bleeding problems. When treating women with DUB, the amount of progesterone given must be adequate to convert the endometrium for complete sloughing to avoid endometrial hyperplasia. Continuous progesterone can be effective in controlling menorrhagia.

NATURAL PROGESTERONE

200 mg is thought to be equivalent to 10 mg of synthetic progestin (medroxyprogesterone acetate) when used to regulate abnormal bleeding.

Oral Dosage: 100 mg twice daily given 7 to 12 days per month for infrequent menses, menorrhagia, and, occasionally, intermenstrual bleeding

Cream Dosage (product that contains at least 400 mg progesterone per ounce): ¼–½ tsp 2 to 3 times daily for 12 to 21 days per month for cases of mild menorrhagia, infrequent menses, and, occasionally, intermenstrual bleeding

Sublingual tablets: 50–75 mg twice daily for 12 to 21 days per month for cases of mild menorrhagia

---

Natural Estradiol

To control an acute bleeding episode, the use of natural estradiol should be just as effective as one of the dosing regimens of conjugated estrogens. These hormones are prescription items and should be administered by a practitioner qualified to use them. One high-dose regimen would be 2 mg of estradiol every 4 hours for 24 hours, a single daily dose for 7 to 10 days, followed by oral micronized progesterone, 200 mg for 7 to 12 days.

❧ Conventional Medicine Approach

When the diagnosis is definitely DUB, it is preferable to use medical, not surgical, treatments. There are several effective medical methods for the treatment of DUB, but a definitive diagnosis will ultimately be necessary.

The goals of conventional treatment for DUB are to control bleeding, prevent endometrial hyperplasia/cancer, prevent/treat anemia, and restore quality of life. Concurrent treatment of the hormone dysfunction is also necessary. To control an acute bleeding episode, 10 mg of oral conjugated estrogens (or the equivalent) administered daily in four divided doses (2.5 mg 4 times daily) is usually effective. If bleeding is not controlled within the first 24 hours, higher doses (20 mg) may be effective. It must be determined whether the cause of the bleeding may be organic, such as miscarriage.

Once the bleeding has stopped, oral estrogen therapy is continued at the same dosage for a total of 21 days; the addition of a progestin, such as medroxyprogesterone acetate (MPA), 10 mg daily, should be added for the last 7 to 10 days of those 21 days. At the end of the 21 days, both hormones are stopped.

Oral contraceptives containing estrogen and progestin are also used to stop acute bleeding, although they are often not as effective as the high doses of estrogen alone. Three tablets of an oral contraceptive containing progestin plus 50 mcg of estrogen taken every 24 hours in divided doses usually will provide sufficient estrogen to stop acute bleeding while at the same time providing the progestin. Treatment is continued for at least one week after the bleeding stops.

The treatment of choice for the majority of women with anovulatory DUB is a progestin medication. It is used for the long-term management of DUB only after the acute episode has been controlled. Either MPA or norethindrone (NE) in doses of 5–10 mg daily for 10 to 14 days significantly reduces heavy menstrual blood loss in most women with DUB due to anovulation.

Nonsteroidal anti-inflammatory drugs (NSAIDs) are also used to reduce blood loss, especially in women who have DUB but still have normal ovulation. When NSAIDs are taken during the episode of menorrhagia and ovulatory DUB, the effect is a

20–50 percent reduction in blood loss. The following anti-inflammatories are usually given for the first three days of menses or throughout the heavy menstrual flow and seem to have similar effects:

- Mefenamic acid (500 mg, 3 times daily)
- Ibuprofen (400 mg, 3 times daily)
- Meclofenamate sodium (100 mg, 3 times daily)
- Naproxen sodium (275 mg every 6 hours after a loading dose of 550 mg)

NSAIDs may be used alone in some cases or combined with an oral contraceptive or progestin in other cases.

Other more sophisticated medical regimens may be used to intervene that involve antifibrinolytic agents, progesterone-releasing IUDs, androgenic steroids (danazol), and GnRH agonists (which essentially induce a medical menopause). Therapies such as GnRH agonists are expensive and have significant side effects, and their use is limited to women who fail to respond to other methods of drug management and who don't want surgery.

There are basically three surgical options that may be considered in individual cases. Dilation and curettage (D&C) can be both diagnostic and therapeutic. A D&C is the quickest way to stop bleeding; therefore, it is the treatment of choice in women with DUB who suffer from low blood volume due to heavy menstrual blood loss. The problem with a D&C is that it is only temporary in most cases and cures the problem a minority of the time. Endometrial ablation is a more recent procedure and is being used with increasing frequency for the treatment of women without uterine lesions who have not responded to medical therapy for menorrhagia. The desirable aspect of endometrial ablation is that it will avoid a hysterectomy, making it a viable option for many women. Endometrial ablation should not be used in women who wish to maintain their ability to carry a pregnancy, or when there are growths in the uterus or a pathology.

Hysterectomy, surgical removal of the uterus, should be reserved for the woman with other indications for hysterectomy, such as a uterine fibroid or uterine prolapse or other pathology. Some women may choose a hysterectomy, but given the effectiveness of drug treatments, D&Cs, and now endometrial ablation, a hysterectomy for DUB should only be used to treat persistent ovulatory DUB after other treatments have failed and the menstrual blood loss is persistently excessive.

〜 Seeing a Licensed Primary Health Care Practitioner*

.Changes in the pattern or amount of menstrual blood flow is one of the most common health concerns of women. Even though many of these cases are of no serious concern, a woman with abnormal bleeding distinctly different from her familiar history should do the cautious thing and be seen by a licensed health care practitioner. After a thorough medical history is taken, a physical exam and further laboratory testing may be requested not only to adequately diagnose the cause of the problem but also to determine if excessive blood loss has caused an anemic state.

The most worrisome situation is an acute bleeding episode. As stated earlier, bleeding that meets or exceeds saturation of a super tampon or heavy pad every hour for six to eight hours or more requires prescription hormone intervention. Bleeding that is even more severe will require immediate medical attention to assess the need for a surgical intervention and management of the dangers of acute blood loss.

A licensed naturopathic physician may work in tandem with conventional medical colleagues to cooperate on an integrated approach to optimize the patient outcome.

---

*N.D. = Naturopathic Doctor; M.D. = Medical Doctor; D.O. = Osteopathic Doctor; N.P. = Nurse Practitioner; P.A. = Physician's Assistant

CHAPTER TWO

AMENORRHEA

 Overview

Traditionally, amenorrhea (absence of menstrual bleeding) has been classified as either primary or secondary. In the United States, females normally experience the onset of their first menstrual period between the ages of 9 and 18. It has been estimated that the prevalence of amenorrhea in the general U.S. female population during the reproductive years is 1.8–3 percent, the prevalence in college-aged women is 2.6–5 percent, and amenorrhea may be seen in 20 percent of women reporting infertility. Primary amenorrhea means that no vaginal bleeding has ever occurred by the time of expected initial onset (usually age 16). Secondary amenorrhea means that vaginal bleeding has previously occurred but has now ceased—for three months in a woman with a history of regular cyclic bleeding or for six months in a woman with a history of irregular periods. The causes of primary amenorrhea are often very complex, and approximately 40 percent turn out to have a chromosomal defect. Absence of a vagina is next in frequency, followed by testicular feminization syndrome. Other causes of primary and secondary amenorrhea are often overlapping. Causes of amenorrhea can be organized into four classifications: disorders of the vagina or uterus, disorders of the ovary, disorders of the anterior pituitary gland, and disorders of the central nervous system. Determining the cause of amenorrhea is one of the most challenging tasks in gynecology.

The majority of amenorrheic young women have very low levels of estrogen, and a minority will have subnormal noncyclic estrogen levels unopposed by progesterone due to a lack of ovulation. This distinction is important in considering the long-term implications of amenorrhea. Hypoestrogenic amenorrhea is associated with loss of bone mineral density that is associated with an increased risk later in life of osteoporosis and fractures. Lipid levels in the bloodstream are also negatively affected by prolonged hypoestrogenic states, and this is associated with an increased risk of cardiovascular disease. Amenorrhea without ovulation is associated with an increased risk of endometrial hyperplasia and uterine cancer because of the lack of progesterone and the presence of what is called an "unopposed" estrogen state.

This requires the medical knowledge of a qualified primary care practitioner, often a specialist in endocrinology who can rule out or consider an array of potential diseases and disorders of the hypothalamus, pituitary gland, ovaries, thyroid, and/or uterus.

The Normal Menstrual Cycle

Normal menstruation results from a complex chain of events initiated in the central nervous system:

1. The hypothalamus secretes gonadotropin-releasing hormone (GnRH) that regulates pituitary function.
2. The anterior pituitary produces luteinizing hormone (LH) and follicle-stimulating hormone (FSH) that govern ovarian function.
3. The ovaries respond to these gonadotropins by synthesizing the steroid hormones estradiol and progesterone that affect uterine function.
4. The uterus has a cavity capable of endometrial thickening and shedding according to the levels of ovarian hormones in the blood, and an outflow tract (vagina) to allow the emptying of menstrual flow.

The menstrual cycle can best be broken into three phases.

1. *Menstrual phase* (menstruation): Days 1–5
   - Estrogen and progesterone withdrawn before onset of menstrual flow
   - Shedding of endometrial lining
2. *Proliferative phase* (follicular): Days 6–14
   - Regrowth of endometrial tissue
   - Secretion of FSH by the pituitary gland
   - Development in ovary of a mature graafian follicle containing a mature egg
   - Secretion of increasing amounts of estrogen by graafian follicle
   - Suppression of FSH when estrogen level becomes high, leading to secretion of LH by pituitary gland
3. *Secretory phase* (luteal): Days 15–28
   - Rupture of graafian follicle releasing egg (ovulation) starts the secretory phase
   - Movement of egg through fallopian tube to uterus
   - Formation of corpus luteum at site of ruptured follicle
   - Production of progesterone by corpus luteum
   - Stimulation by progesterone of endometrial cell growth
   - Significant decrease in progesterone level if implantation does not occur; menstrual phase then begins again

A good history is the most important part of the medical evaluation. The history will include evaluating for pregnancy, menstrual history, emotional stress, weight gain or weight loss, alcohol use or abuse, dietary habits, exercise habits, medications, narcotics, drug abuse, acute or chronic illnesses, accidents or injuries, infertility, metabolic disease, immune system abnormalities, tuberculosis, hot flashes, breast discharge, headaches, and family history.

A physical and pelvic exam will confirm the most likely causes as suggested by the history. During the pelvic exam, the practitioner will attempt to determine if there is an adequate estrogen effect on the cervix and vagina, check for the size of the ovaries, assure the normalcy of the uterus and vagina, and observe for the presence or absence of secondary sex characteristics (e.g., breasts and pubic hair). The thyroid gland will also be checked, and laboratory tests will be chosen selectively to document the suspected diagnosis.

Due to the complexity of amenorrhea and the diverse array of causes, it is impossible to address each potential cause in this chapter. The guiding rule in the management of amenorrhea is to diagnose before treating. The appropriate management depends not only on the diagnosis but also on the presenting problem. Each woman must then be treated according to the specific causative factors involved. Consequently, in the alternative treatment discussion, we will largely focus on four states:

1. *Hypergonadotropic hypogonadism.* The pituitary secretes elevated amounts of its hormones, but the ovary does not respond. Example: premature ovarian failure
2. *Hyperprolactinemia.* The pituitary secretes too much prolactin. Examples: certain drugs, pituitary tumors, hypothyroid disease
3. *Hypogonadotropic hypogonadism.* Reduced secretion of FSH and LH that results in failure of the ovarian follicle to develop and hence, a lack of secretion of estradiol by the ovaries. Examples: psychological stress, weight loss, genetic diseases
4. *Normogonadotropic anovulation.* Normal FSH and LH, but the cyclic nature of the pulsed secretions is disrupted. The ovarian follicles develop and estrogen is produced, but at some stage the follicles do not fully mature. Thus, there is no ovulation but there is no sign of estrogen defi-

FIGURE 2.1 Normal Menstrual Cycle

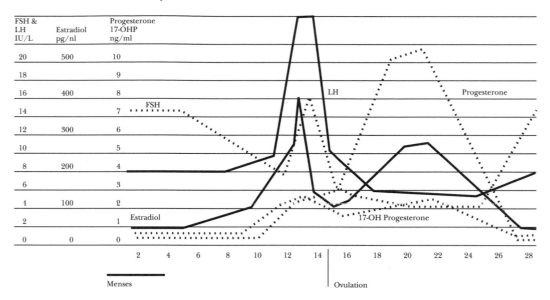

<table>
<tr><td colspan="3">

KEY CONCEPTS

</td></tr>
</table>

<table>
<tr>
<td valign="top">

KEY CONCEPTS

- Successful management of amenorrhea depends on an accurate diagnosis.
- Amenorrhea is a symptom, not a diagnosis.
- The absence of menses in itself has no deleterious effect on health, but it may be a presenting symptom of an underlying disorder that requires treatment.
- A licensed primary health care practitioner is needed to conduct a careful history, examination, and possible tests.
- The most common cause of secondary amenorrhea is pregnancy.
- Prolonged amenorrhea prior to menopause is a risk factor for osteoporosis.

</td>
<td valign="top">

PREVENTION

- Adequate calories in the diet.
- Adequate levels of dietary fat.
- Regular daily eating habits.
- Avoid being underweight.
- Avoid obesity.
- Avoid excessive exercise.
- Stress reduction and stress management.
- Women with hypoestrogenic amenorrhea must be vigilant about prevention of osteoporosis and coronary artery disease.
- Women with anovulatory amenorrhea must be monitored for endometrial thickening and the development of endometrial hyperplasia, a precancerous state, and endometrial cancer.

</td>
</tr>
</table>

ciency; rather, there is a progesterone deficiency. Example: polycystic ovary syndrome

❧ Overview of Alternative Treatments

A licensed alternative primary care practitioner such as a naturopathic physician must first make an accurate diagnosis as to the cause of the amenorrhea, utilizing a medical history, physical exam, and possibly laboratory testing. Naturopathic physicians

often see patients who are on extreme diets initiated due to some other health concern; sometimes these diets are inappropriate for that individual and are now the cause of the amenorrhea. Insufficient calories, insufficient dietary fat, and cholesterol may be the culprit in some of these cases. Other health-conscious individuals may have become too thin with a combination of diet and exercise, and they may have acquired amenorrhea because of too little body fat. Exercise-induced amenorrhea is very common.

A holistic approach to the patient with amenorrhea will require exploring not only the mental/spiritual, emotional, and physical aspects of a woman's current health in looking for an underlying cause but also a meticulous and logical medical workup will be integrated with some of the more mind/body-oriented perspectives.

Specific dietary counseling may be warranted and, as I mentioned, the practitioner may find herself in the unusual position of advocating an increase in cholesterol and other fats in the diet. She may also counsel some patients to gain weight or to exercise less. Guidance about stress reduction must also be offered due to the disrupting effect of stress on the menstrual cycle.

The goal of a natural therapeutic treatment plan for amenorrhea is to address the specific underlying cause as would conventional medicine, but, unique to natural medicine, the goal is also to take a more constitutional approach and address the whole person. Even in cases where something specific like an elevated prolactin level may be the cause, the practitioner would want to address the mental/emotional component, support the digestion, provide tonifying and nutritive support to the reproductive system in general, and more. This organ-specific as well as constitutional approach is a common theme in many alternative medicine disciplines, and especially naturopathic medicine.

The natural therapies presented in this chapter are limited to dealing with these four general states:

1. Ovarian failure
2. Hyperprolactinemia
3. Inadequate estrogen production
4. Chronic lack of ovulation

Keep in mind that causes such as thyroid disorders, tumors, systemic diseases, genetic disorders, and others will require therapies to specifically address those underlying problems, which are beyond the scope of this book.

Nutrition

Both weight loss and obesity can be associated with amenorrhea. A range of weight-loss problems are associated with amenorrhea including crash diets, mal-nutrition, and life-threatening anorexia nervosa. Anorexia nervosa occurs almost exclusively in young white middle- to upper-class women under age 25. The family situation of a young woman with anorexia is very often success-achievement-appearance oriented. The pattern usually starts with a diet to control weight and a fear of excess weight when in fact the weight being gained is due to normal maturing. Besides amenorrhea, constipation is a common symptom and often accompanied by abdominal pain. There is often a preoccupation with food that may manifest itself by large intakes of lettuce, raw vegetables, and low calorie foods. Other manifestations may be chaotic eating habits and eating times, radical diets, missed meals, and bingeing episodes.

Bulimia is a syndrome of episodic and secretive binge eating followed by self-induced vomiting, fasting, or the use of laxatives and diuretics. Bulimic behavior is frequently seen in about half of women with anorexia nervosa. Girls and women with bulimia often have a high incidence of depressive symptoms and a problem with shoplifting, usually food. Body weight in "pure" bulimics fluctuates but does not fall to the low levels seen in anorectics. Teenagers with low body weight, amenorrhea, and hyperactivity (excellent grades and many extracurricular activities) need astute evaluation for an eating disorder. A careful and sensitive approach and education of the relationship between the amenorrhea and the low body weight is often the only impetus needed to return to more normal habits. Others will need psychological counseling, consistent support, and monitoring for calorie intake in order to break the established patterns. The earlier the recognition of the problem, the more successful the intervention. Family members, friends, and health care practitioners should pay particular attention to weight and diet in young women with amenorrhea.

Obese women exhibit several abnormalities in their hormone profile. Elevated serum concentrations of androstenedione, testosterone, and DHEA-sulfate are associated more closely with the pattern of fat distribution than to the body fat mass.[1] High levels of these hormones, called androgens, are known to be a cause of menstrual irregularities including amenorrhea, hirsutism (abnormal body hair growth), as well as other metabolic disturbances. Usually, chronic anovulation caused by the hormonal abnormalities is the cause of the menstrual irregularity in women with significant amounts of excess body fat. A reduction of the excess body weight by reducing calories in the diet, increasing physical exercise, and possibly other weight-management interventions will result in beneficial changes in the hormonal profile, including a marked reduction of androgenic hormones and their effects. [1]

Some women may have low body weight but do not have an eating disorder or exercise-induced amenorrhea. This may be a metabolism issue, a hereditary factor, or a diet that is extremely low in fat although not low in calories. Women who take in insufficient calories, such as strict vegetarians who eat no animal products or others with extreme diets, may have insufficient dietary fat and low cholesterol. Adequate cholesterol is needed to manufacture hormones. If no cholesterol is found in the diet and the liver is not manufacturing adequate cholesterol, then these women may have amenorrhea due to insufficient hormone levels. Strict vegetarian diets are admirable, but they are not right for everyone's metabolism. Measuring the cholesterol level can be telling in such cases. If cholesterol is low (below 120), a change in vegetarian philosophy will probably be necessary so that some animal products can be included in the diet in order to bring up the cholesterol levels.

Sometimes it is difficult to find the best nutritional program for one's body type and lifestyle. Nutritional counseling and nutritional analyses with a qualified practitioner can be very helpful for people who don't have the time or interest to read and experiment on their own. No one diet plan is right for everyone. Not everyone needs to eat from all the food groups, not everyone can be a vegetarian, and not everyone responds well to a high protein or high complex carbohydrate diet.

In addition to proper food choices, another basic general principle for good nutrition is regularity. Just as going to bed and rising at regular times with a certain amount of sleep assures adequate energy and vitality, regular mealtimes and consistency in eating habits lead to good digestion and absorption of nutrients necessary for normal physiology.

Not all nutritional habits for women with amenorrhea are related to dietary fat, calories, body weight, or eating disorders. Some nutritional guidance is relevant to the prevention of osteoporosis, a potential consequence of amenorrhea. In Chapter 12, I discuss the importance of dark green leafy vegetables, whole grains, soy foods, and other mineral-rich foods. This would be an important chapter for amenorrheic women to read and follow.

Supplements

Vitamin A and the Carotenes

In looking back through old studies on amenorrhea, I came across references to hypercarotenemia and amenorrhea. Carotenemia, an abnormal elevation of plasma carotene levels, may result from an excessive ingestion of carotene-rich vegetables, anorexia, and impaired ability of the body to metabolize carotenes.[2–4] Carotenemia has been linked with menstrual dysfunction and amenorrhea in some women, generally in association with weight loss. In 1968, elevated carotene levels were observed in nine of twelve women with anorexia nervosa,[5] and it was suggested that carotenemia was caused by an abnormality in fat metabolism. A small study conducted later reported that six patients with amenorrhea and weight loss had carotenemia.[6] Surprisingly though, these women did not ingest increased amounts of carotenes in their diet, again it was thought that mobilization of fat stores secondary to the loss in weight might be responsible for their hypercarotenemia. Another group of researchers found elevated serum carotene levels in women with anorexia nervosa, but not in women with normal or abnormal menstrual function.[4]

In 1971, a small study examined six women with elevated serum carotene levels who had excessive intake of carrots or pumpkins.[7] The researcher described what he called "golden ovaries" and noted that amenorrhea developed in the two younger patients and irregular menstrual bleeding in the four older patients. For some time it was thought that exercise-induced amenorrhea in long-distance runners was associated with hypercarotenemia, but that association was disproven, and no difference in carotene levels was observed.[8]

I found no reference to amenorrhea or menstrual irregularities associated with taking carotene supplements, and, as of this writing, I don't believe amenorrhea has been reported as a side effect of beta carotene ingestion. However, I found the information interesting, and I will probably encourage women who are experiencing significant weight loss and amenorrhea to eat lesser amounts of carotene foods for the time being. I would also be inclined to reduce their vitamin A and carotene supplementation if they were on high doses for some other medical reason.

Calcium

One of the serious long-term consequences of amenorrhea is a lower bone density and a potential for osteoporosis and an increased risk for fractures later in life. Even when calcium intake is the same between amenorrheic women and women who menstruate normally, there is a decrease in calcium absorption and an increase in calcium excretion in estrogen-deficient women. Even though there is still much to be learned about the effect of estrogen on bone, there is ample evidence that a lack of estrogen increases the daily calcium requirement.[9] As a result, I recommend a daily intake of either calcium carbonate, (1,200–1,500 mg per day), or calcium citrate (600–750 mg per day), to maintain calcium balance in low-estrogen states in women of reproductive age.

Calcium carbonate
1,200–1,500 mg per day
or
Calcium citrate
600–750 mg per day

Additional Vitamins and Minerals

Many other minerals and nutrients have an effect on bone density and are relevant to the prevention of osteoporosis in amenorrheic women. Magnesium, manganese, zinc, copper, boron, vitamin K, vitamin D,

and other nutrients determine bone health, each in their own way. In Chapter 12, I discuss this in detail. For women with amenorrhea, osteoporosis prevention measures, including nutritional supplementation, are vital in assuring future bone health.

Botanicals

Chaste Tree (*Vitex agnus castus*)

Chaste tree is probably the best-known herb in all of Europe for hormonal imbalances in women. Since at least the time of the Greeks, chaste tree has been used for the full scope of menstrual disorders, including amenorrhea.

Chaste tree acts on the hypothalamus and pituitary glands by increasing LH production and mildly inhibits the release of FSH. The result is a shift in the ratio of estrogen to progesterone, in favor of progesterone. This is, in fact, a corpus luteum-like hormone effect.[10] The ability of chaste tree to raise progesterone levels in the body is therefore an indirect effect and not a direct hormonal action.[11] This progesterone-like effect can then become a tool in treating some women with amenorrhea. Amenorrhea that is caused by lack of ovulation and therefore lack of progesterone production should result in a progesterone-induced menses when progesterone is given. Progesterone-induced menses indicates an intact reproductive system that lacks cyclicity. It suggests that the body is producing enough FSH to stimulate the ovaries, and that the ovaries can develop follicles. Furthermore, it indicates that follicular production of estrogen is sufficient to cause the lining of the uterus (endometrium) to grow and that the sloughed endometrium is able to pass through the cervical opening and the vagina. This then most likely tells us that the problem is a dysfunction in the hypothalamus or pituitary. The ability of chaste tree to modulate the hypothalamus or pituitary then makes this herb an obvious choice.

The first major study on chaste tree was published in 1954.[12] Fifty-seven women suffering from a variety of menstrual disorders were given chaste tree on a daily basis. Fifty patients developed a cycle in phase with menses while seven women did not respond. Of the fifty women, six with secondary amenorrhea demonstrated one or more cyclic menstruations. Of the nine women who had scant or infrequent menstrual flow, six experienced a shortening of the menstrual interval and an increase in bleeding.

Twenty women with secondary amenorrhea were admitted to a six-month study using chaste tree liquid extract at 40 drops daily.[13] Laboratory testing was done to measure progesterone, FSH, and LH, and pap smears were done at the beginning of the study, at three months, and at six months. At the end of the six-month study, the researchers were able to evaluate fifteen of the women. Ten out of the fifteen women had a return of their menstrual cycles. Testing showed that values for progesterone and LH increased, and FSH values either did not change or decreased slightly.

When using chaste tree, don't expect immediate results. It's not the same as giving progesterone, even natural progesterone. You don't give it, stop it, and then expect a withdrawal bleed a few days later like you would if giving progesterone or progestins. Chaste tree is more of a medium-range plan; usually it begins to take effect after three or four months.

Chaste tree also inhibits prolactin release by the pituitary gland, particularly under stress. The mechanism of action appears to involve the ability of chaste tree to bind dopamine receptors and then inhibit prolactin release in the pituitary.[14, 15] A double-blind, placebo-controlled study examined the effect of a chaste tree (*Vitex*) preparation on 52 women with luteal phase defects due to hyperprolactinemia.[16] The daily dose of the *Vitex* extract was 20 mg, and the study lasted for three months. Laboratory tests were done at two different times of the month—at the beginning of the study and again at the end of the three months. Prolactin release was significantly reduced in the *Vitex* group. The short luteal phase (second half of the cycle) was normalized, and the decreased progesterone production was normalized. No side effects were noted, and two women became pregnant. Since elevated prolactin levels cause some cases of amenorrhea, chaste tree is also indicated for these cases.

> **Chaste tree**
> *40 drops tincture, or*
> *175 mg of standardized extract per day*

Black Cohosh (*Cimicifuga racemosa*)

Black cohosh has become one of the most significant women's herbs in all of botanical medicine. Also known as snakeroot or rattleroot, this plant belongs to the buttercup family and is indigenous to the eastern part of North America. The native peoples of Canada and America used black cohosh for many different indications, such as uterine pains during menses and childbirth, rheumatism, rattlesnake bites, and general malaise. Black cohosh was introduced to Western gynecology in the middle of the eighteenth century and was used in the treatment of menopausal symptoms.[17]

The exact mechanism of how black cohosh works has yet to be elucidated. We attribute most of its gynecological effects to its "estrogen-like" action. The primary constituents in black cohosh extract are glycosides with particular importance attached to the triterpene glycosides, mainly cimicifugoside and actein. Other characteristic constituents are the flavonoids, resins, volatile oils, fatty acids, tannins, phytosterols, alkaloids, cimicifugin, and salicylic acid. Due to their steroid, hormone-like chemical structure, triterpene glycosides are assumed to interfere with receptors in the pituitary gland and the hypothalamus. Although the constituents in black cohosh may be able to bind to receptors in the pituitary or hypothalamus, these constituents do not seem to be able to bind to receptors in target organs. The effects of a black cohosh preparation on LH and FSH secretion were investigated in a study on menopausal women. After a treatment of two months, LH (but not FSH) levels were significantly reduced in the black cohosh–treated group.[18]

Many studies have been done using black cohosh preparations in menopausal women. These studies and the further use of this valuable plant in menopausal women will be discussed in much detail in Chapter 10. For women who have amenorrhea due to hypoestrogen states, black cohosh will have an important role not only in relieving some of the symptoms related to this state that is similar to menopause but also in helping to support the regularity of the menstrual cycle. It should be noted, however, that the benefits of black cohosh on risk factors associated with menopause such as osteoporosis and cardiovascular disease have not been established.

Black cohosh
40–80 mg standardized extract twice daily

Traditional Herbs—Uterine Stimulants

Uterine stimulants or emmenagogues increase tone or muscular activity and serve to initiate the onset of menses and stimulate reproductive function. Most important are the herbs that cause shedding of the endometrium and stimulate normal menstrual cycles in the absence of pregnancy.

- Partridgeberry/squaw vine (*Mitchella repens*)
- Yarrow flower (*Achillea millefolium*)
- Chaste tree (*Vitex agnus castus*)
- Pennyroyal* (*Mentha pulegium*)
- Mugwort (*Artemisia vulgaris*)
- Blue cohosh (*Caulophyllum thalictroides*)
- Water pepper (*Polygonum hydropiper*)

* **Important Caution:** Do not use essential oil of pennyroyal internally in any situation.

Water Pepper[19]

In a medical journal of 1846, Dr. Thomas Ogier, a surgeon and obstetrician, published an herbal approach for amenorrhea.[20] He maintained that administering a tincture of water pepper successfully treated a case of obstinate amenorrhea. The woman was given one teaspoon of tincture of water pepper three times a day in a glass of water. On the second day she complained of a slight burning at the pit of the stomach, which continued for three or four days; on the sixth day she had a yellowish discharge which continued until the tenth day. On the tenth day, her menses appeared. On the second day after the discharge appeared, she was directed to take the dose only once a day and discontinue it

on the fifth day. The menses lasted six days. Exactly how the water pepper works is not known.

Traditional Herbs—Phytoestrogens

Phytoestrogens are by and large nonsteroidal hormone-like constituents found in over 300 medicinal and edible plants. With the currently available evidence, soybeans are probably the richest edible source of phytoestrogens. Some plant compounds, such as lignans, found in flaxseeds, are not phytoestrogens but when ingested are converted to estrogens in the intestines. Many herbs contain phytoestrogen compounds, and this topic is discussed further in Chapter 10.

There are many herbs in addition to black cohosh that contain phytoestrogen compounds and have a role in amenorrhea. We cannot say that we fully understand how they work, but we know that they support the reproductive cycle and relieve menopausal symptoms in women who are appropriately menopausal as well as women who are prematurely amenorrheic and essentially prematurely menopausal. These herbs include:

- Alfalfa (*Medicago sativa*)
- Black cohosh (*Cimicifuga racemosa*)
- Dong quai (*Angelica sinensis*)
- Flaxseed (*Linum usitatissimum*)
- Ginseng (*Panax ginseng*)
- Hops (*Humulus lupulus*)
- Licorice (*Glycyrrhiza glabra*)
- Red clover (*Trifollium pratense*)

Traditional Herbs—Progesterone Precursors

A number of herbs contain diosgenin or sarsasapogenin and related compounds:

- Bloodroot (*Sanguinaria canadensis*)
- Blue cohosh (*Caulophyllum thalictroides*)
- Fenugreek (*Trigonella foenumgraecum*)
- Sarsaparilla (*Smilax officinalis*)
- Wild yam (*Dioscorea spp*)
- Yucca (*Yucca spp*)

These compounds can be converted in the laboratory to various hormones including progesterone, which in turn can be converted to adrenal steroids and then to testosterone or estrogens. Even though diosgenin from plants is used by pharmaceutical companies to synthesize various hormones, there is very little scientific information on diosgenin-containing plants and their relationship to human metabolism. Until someone is able to do a proper study, we have to assume that no plant directly increases progesterone levels.

Natural Hormones

Progesterone can be used for both diagnosis and treatment. Progesterone-induced menses indicates that there are adequate estrogen levels and that anatomical problems causing obstruction of the outflow of blood are not present.

Onset of menstruation after intramuscular injection of 150 mg of progesterone in oil suggests that anovulation is the most likely explanation of the amenorrhea. The progesterone challenge test is considered positive if uterine bleeding (even a few days of "spotting") occurs and correlates with a serum estradiol level of 40 g/mL or higher. Oral micronized progesterone administered for 10 days at 400 mg per day will induce complete secretary changes in the endometrium and induce a menses in a woman whose uterus has been adequately stimulated by estrogen. Lack of vaginal bleeding after progesterone challenge suggests either inadequate priming of the endometrial lining or absence of an endometrial cavity or some kind of obstruction.

A natural estrogen formulation, estriol 2 mg/estrone 0.250/estradiol 0.250, one pill twice daily, (equivalent to 1.25 mg/day of conjugated equine estrogens) is then given for 21 days, with 200 mg of oral micronized progesterone/day added for the last week of the estrogen therapy. Withdrawal bleeding should occur within 14 days; even spotting is sufficient to count as withdrawal bleeding. Absence of uterine bleeding under these circumstances indicates uterine end-organ failure that may result from congenital malformation of the uterus and vagina or from distortion of the endometrial cavity by intrauterine adhesions (due to tuberculous endometritis, also called Asherman's syndrome). Conventional practitioners will have a protocol using conjugated equine estrogens and progestins.

The woman who is hypoestrogenic and is not a candidate for induction of ovulation requires hormone replacement therapy. This can be accomplished with natural hormone replacement therapy, as well as conventional hormone replacement therapy, if the doses are adequate and monitoring is done to assure adequate hormone levels in the blood. The long-term impact of the hypoestrogenic state in terms of cardiovascular disease and osteoporosis is dependent on normal reproductive age levels of hormones. Younger women who insist on using alternative medicine need to fully understand their risks of premature states of insufficient hormone production. If the herbal, nutritional, and lifestyle interventions are not sufficient to stimulate the menstrual cycle, they must understand that bone loss in amenorrheic women shows the same pattern over time as that seen in postmenopausal women.[21] The loss is most rapid in the first few years, emphasizing the need for early treatment.

Natural hormones in a prescription that is considered to be equivalent to conventional hormones should be used. A good schedule is the following: on days 1 through 25 each month, take estriol 1 mg/estrone 0.125/estradiol 0.125 (tri-estrogen) one pill twice daily; on days 16 through 25, add oral natural progesterone 100 mg twice daily. Beginning medication on the first of every month establishes an easily remembered routine. Some practitioners use a bi-estrogen formulation instead of the tri-estrogen formulation. In this case, the formula would be estriol 1 mg/estradiol 0.250 mg (bi-estrogen), one pill twice daily.

Menstruation generally occurs within three days after the last pills, the 28th day of each month. Bleeding that occurs at any other time may indicate that the body's own function has returned. The natural hormone replacement program should then be discontinued and the patient monitored for the return of ovulation.

Natural progesterone creams may be used in selected cases to help maintain a monthly cycle in women with anovulatory amenorrhea once this diagnosis has been established. Some women only need this monthly lower-dose hormone support during the second half of a monthly cycle. The typical dosing recommendations are from ¼–½ tsp applied to the palms, inner forearms, and chest twice daily from day 15 to day 25. This cycle can be repeated. In the event that menstruation does not occur, it may be necessary to return to the estrogen/progesterone plan and/or herbal/nutritional therapies that induce ovulation such as chaste tree extract.

Exercise

Most cross-sectional studies analyzed suggest that female competitive athletes, whether runners[22–27] or body builders[28, 29] have increased incidence of menstrual cycle disturbance, shorter luteal phases, and amenorrhea than do sedentary controls. Because of subject self-selection and consequent oversampling, results of these studies must be interpreted with caution.[30] Prospective studies have found no hormonal changes in women following one year of endurance training[31] and, up to 1994, had not detected induction of secondary amenorrhea by exercise.[30]

In her excellent review, Bonen,[30] states that secondary amenorrhea "is difficult to induce by exercise alone." She concludes that some of the factors thought to be associated with exercise-induced amenorrhea—type, duration, intensity of exercise, age of menarche, training before menarche, and training history—remain speculative and that, in fact, little is known about the true incidence of secondary amenorrhea in athletic populations.

The higher incidence rates of secondary amenorrhea detected in competitive athletes appear related to metabolic factors. In weightlifters and bodybuilders, the appearance of luteal-phase disturbances and oligo- or amenorrhea is directly related to drastic reduction in caloric intake prior to competition combined with increases in strenuous exercise. For example, Sandoval[32] found that female bodybuilders, examined for a period of 48 hours before competition, achieved a degree of leanness similar to their male counterparts. Kleiner[33] found in female bodybuilders, competing at the 1988 National Physique Committee's Junior USA Bodybuilding Championships, a 9.8 percent body fat (males, 6.0 percent).

That bodybuilding competitive athletes reduce caloric intake to drastic levels in pre-competition is made clear by the amount of calories ingested post-competition. In a group of female bodybuilders she studied for one month pre- and post-competition, Walberg-Rankin[29] detected a twofold increase in caloric intake and a tenfold increase in fat intake post-event as compared to pre-event. Furthermore, these unhealthy practices are followed by college-age women who compete in bodybuilding events[34] and competing women bodybuilders train harder and longer in all body areas than their male counterparts.[32]

In this context, it is not surprising that in Walberg's study, 86 percent of female competitive bodybuilders (not on birth control pills) reported menstrual dysfunction, and, in Kleiner's, 81 percent of female elite bodybuilders had contest-related amenorrhea for one or two months pre-contest.

The picture is similar for competitive female runners whose caloric intake is inadequate or falls below the constant draining of energy demanded by their sports. Time and again, menstrual cycle disturbances in these populations have been shown to be related to inadequate caloric intake combined with strenuous, abrupt increases in running distances.[22, 30, 35–37] Amenorrhea usually is not seen in athletes with high percent body fat.[37]

In addition, amenorrheic athletes show dangerous reductions in mean trabecular bone density as compared to eumenorrheic counterparts (–42 percent).[38] Exercise may intensify these effects.[36]

Finally, as shown by Bonen, menstrual disturbances are quite common in the general population of sedentary women. Different factors—weight change, starvation, crowding, travel, communal living, exercise, and severe stress of any kind—have been implicated in altered menstrual cyclicity.[39] Ronkainen and colleagues[40] found increased abnormalities in the menstrual cycles of women during the short sunlight days of fall.

Thus, amenorrhea appears to have multiple etiologic relationships. Inappropriate exercise is only one of them.

Exercise Recommendations

If a woman has documented secondary amenorrhea not due to pregnancy, a careful history of eating and exercising habits is critical. In addition, her body

SAMPLE TREATMENT PLAN FOR AMENORRHEA

Ovarian failure

Diet: A whole foods diet using plenty of grains, beans (especially soy beans), fruits, vegetables (especially dark leafy greens), nuts and seeds (especially flaxseeds), fish (salmon, tuna, halibut, sardines)

Exercise: Regular aerobic and weight-bearing exercise 30–60 minutes, 4–7 days per week

Black cohosh extract: Standardized extract, 40–80 mg twice daily

Natural hormone replacement: Estriol 1 mg/estradiol 0.125 mg/estrone 0.125; 1 capsule two times daily, days 1–25 or continuous. Add oral micronized progesterone, 100 mg twice daily, days 16–25 each month.

Note: Conventional hormone replacement therapy may be more appropriate for some patients. Check blood level of estradiol after three months to see if the formula is adequately raising the hormone level. Some patients do better on one hormone product and formulation versus another. Each woman is different and unique and requires an individualized approach.

Mineral supplementation: Calcium/magnesium/boron/vitamin D/other trace minerals and nutrients (see Chapter 12)

Hyperprolactinemia

Chaste tree extract: 40 drops or 175 mg capsule of standardized extract per day

Hypoestrogen states (often associated with weight loss, psychological states, anorexia nervosa)

Diet: Increase calories, dietary protein, fat, and carbohydrates
Regular meals using whole foods
Avoid extreme dieting
Increase soy foods and flaxseeds

Lifestyle: Counseling (for eating disorders)
Stress management counseling and practices
Reduce exercise from excessive to moderate

Mineral supplementation: Calcium/magnesium/boron/vitamin D, other trace minerals and nutrients (see Chapter 12)

Black cohosh: Standardized extract, 40–80 mg twice daily

Natural hormone replacement: Estriol 1 mg/estrone 0.125/estradiol 0.125; 1 capsule twice daily, days 1–25; add oral micronized progesterone 100 mg twice daily, days 16–25.

Chronic anovulation

Diet: Reduce carbohydrates and increase protein in the diet (chronic anovulation can lead to hyperinsulinemia and overweight/obesity). Diets such as the Zone Diet can be very helpful in this situation to reduce the hyperinsulinemia and provide better weight management. Increase soy foods and flaxseeds. Emphasize whole grains, fruits, vegetables, nuts, seeds, fish (salmon, tuna, sardines, halibut), organic chicken/turkey, low-fat dairy products, eggs, and beans

Chaste tree extract: 40 drops or 175 mg capsule of standardized extract once daily

Oral natural progesterone: 400 mg per day for 10 days

Natural progesterone cream: ¼–½ tsp twice daily, days 16–25. Or ¼ tsp 1–2 times daily, days 7–14; ¼–½ tsp twice daily, days 15–25.

weight and percent body fat should be ascertained and compared to the normal ranges for her body build and age. A bone densitometry test, particularly of the lumbar spine and proximal femur, also is highly desirable.

In case the history and tests recommended indicate that the calories consumed are inadequate to maintain ideal body weight, the bone mass density is below normal range, and the body fat is <15 percent, the recommended course is:

- Adapt diet to individual needs; particularly emphasize protein, calcium, magnesium, vitamin D, zinc, copper, and chromium.[40]
- Reduce or stop intensive training, particularly running, until cycling resumes.
- Modify type of exercise. Instead of running, do moderate walking (30 minutes/day) and add a regular program of moderate weight lifting for 30 minutes, 3 times per week.
- Avoid competition in sports, in the job, and elsewhere.

❧ Conventional Medicine Approach

Successful management of women with amenorrhea depends on an accurate diagnosis.[41] A careful history and examination and often simple laboratory investigations will most likely yield an accurate diagnosis in order to offer appropriate treatment in the majority of cases. A physical exam should assess the signs of secondary sexual characteristics (e.g., breast development) and the presence or absence of abnormal body hair. Pelvic ultrasound may be helpful in determining whether or not the ovaries are enlarged with many small cysts. Blood tests to measure FSH, LH, prolactin, estradiol, testosterone, and thyroid function may be used to help determine the diagnosis. On the basis of this information, women with amenorrhea can be classified into the four groups mentioned earlier in this chapter.

Treatments for each group:

1. *Hypergonadotropic hypogonadism.* Hormone replacement therapy with estrogen will induce secondary sexual characteristics in girls with primary amenorrhea and in combination with cyclic progestins will prevent the consequences of osteo-porosis and cardiovascular disease. The standard program for hormone replacement therapy is the following: on days 1 to 25 of each month, 0.625 mg conjugated estrogens (Premarin); on days 16 to 25, 10 mg of medroxyprogesterone acetate is added (Provera). Beginning the medication on the first of every month establishes a routine that is easy to remember. An alternate method would be to give 0.625 mg of Premarin daily and Provera 2.5 mg three weeks of the month and none for one week.

2. *Hyperprolactinemia.* Treatment with dopamine agonists (e.g., bromocriptine, cabergoline, quinagolide) leads to reduction in prolactin secretion and inhibition of tumor growth in most women with tumor-related hyperprolactinemia.[42] Surgical resection of the tumor is required in some cases when the tumor does not shrink. Women with prolactinomas are usually advised to avoid pregnancy for several months.

3. *Hypogonadotropic hypogonadism.* In the majority of women with this classification, no organic disease can be identified in the hypothalamus or anterior pituitary. Management of hypothalamic amenorrhea associated with weight loss must focus primarily on trying to correct the underlying cause of the weight loss. Amenorrhea from anorexia nervosa, bulimia, and exercise-induced weight loss all require prompt diagnosis and treatment. Some women will require hospitalization in a controlled environment. Dietary counseling, psychological counseling, and advice about exercise may all prove to be sufficient to correct the problem and restore ovarian function. If amenorrhea persists for more than 12 months, then some form of hormone replacement therapy should be considered to prevent the long-term consequences of a low estrogen state, such as osteoporosis and cardiovascular disease. Some women with hypothalamic amenorrhea are administered GnRH. This is given by injection with a portable programmable pump that releases the GnRH every 1 to 2 hours to simulate the body's pulsatile secretions. Women with rare disorders such as Sheehan's syndrome, a pituitary disease, are given hormones of FSH and LH.

4. *Chronic anovulation.* About 30 percent of women with secondary amenorrhea have concentrations of FSH and LH within the normal range. They may have subtle abnormalities in the pattern of the secretions,

such as is the case with polycystic ovary syndrome. Many women with these disorders present with irregular menstrual patterns more often than secondary amenorrhea. Women who do not ovulate show no signs of estrogen deficiency but rather experience problems related to continued exposure to estrogen that is not opposed by progesterone. Under these conditions, the endometrium may become hyperplastic. Polycystic ovaries are associated in the majority of women with normal FSH/LH and anovulation. Polycystic ovary syndrome describes the association of polycystic ovaries with obesity, hirsutism, anovulation, and irregular bleeding.

Treatment for polycystic ovary syndrome often is concerned with stimulating a regular sloughing of the endometrium, and various progestin regimens may be used to accomplish this. Antiestrogens such as clomiphene and tamoxifen are sometimes given to induce ovulation and will restore fertility in most women in this group.

✎ Seeing a Licensed Primary Health Care Practitioner*

All women with amenorrhea should be evaluated by a licensed primary care practitioner because of the diverse array of potential diseases and disorders.

*N.D. = Naturopathic Doctor; M.D. = Medical Doctor; D.O. = Osteopathic Doctor; N.P. = Nurse Practitioner; P.A. = Physician's Assistant

Some of these conditions are very unfamiliar, such as Asherman's syndrome, Cushing's disease, Sheehan's syndrome, and pituitary-secreting tumors. Other causes are not so rare but can be complex, such as malnutrition, anorexia nervosa, hyperthyroidism, polycystic ovary syndrome, and pituitary disorders. Other causes are rather straightforward; for example, hypothyroidism, strenuous exercise, pregnancy, and stress-related amenorrhea. Fortunately, most women/girls with amenorrhea have relatively simple problems that can be managed easily by primary care physicians, whether they are alternative medicine practitioners, conventional practitioners, or a team approach using the best choices of each.

After an evaluation has been done and a diagnosed cause has been determined, then natural therapies can be considered as the primary therapy, and in other cases they will serve as an addition and be integrated with the conventional treatment. Conventional treatments may be necessary in many cases of amenorrhea, but dosing regimens may be lower when natural therapies are used as part of an integrated plan.

CHAPTER THREE

CANCER PREVENTION

⤳ *Overview*

The good news about cancer is that it is largely preventable. Recent conservative estimates attribute 30 percent of cancer deaths in the U.S. population (women and men) to cigarette smoking and 30 percent to diet. The responsibility of diet in cancer reduction has been estimated at 35 percent by other researchers, who, after more than a decade since the estimate was done, still consider it a "reasonable estimate." A 1995 review of the available evidence concluded that changes in lifestyle likely reduced cancer risk.[1] These lifestyle parameters, all of them modifiable, include smoking cigarettes, excessive sun exposure, alcohol consumption, low consumption of fruits and vegetables, and little or no physical activity.

In women, the reduction of cancer incidence and mortality by dietary manipulation may be much higher than in men. Based on international and intranational comparisons, researchers have concluded that almost 60 percent of cancers in American women were attributable to dietary factors. The figure for men was just above 40 percent.

However, the risk of female cancer is a real threat to women in industrialized societies. In the United States, the estimates of the American Cancer Society for 1998 indicate that more than 250,000 women will develop some type of breast or genital cancer and that more than 70,000 will die from female cancer during that year. (See Table 3.1 for a breakdown of these totals.) The majority (69 percent) of all new female cancer cases arise in the breast; this has become the second most damaging female cancer in this country. It is responsible for the deaths of 44,000 women a year.

Cancer statistics may be made to look much more encouraging. For example, if you are 30 years old, your risk of developing breast cancer in the next 12 months would be 1 in 5,900. If you are 80 years old, your risk would be 1 in 290. The statistics for other types of female cancers are even more encouraging.

In addition, early detection techniques and more and more sophisticated forms of chemical treatment apparently have significantly reduced mortality among women with female cancer. The five-year average survival rate for four types of female cancer (breast, cervix, endometrium, ovary) in white women was 56.5 percent in 1960 and 72.5 percent in 1986. The figures for breast cancer were 63 percent and 86 percent, respectively. Unfortunately, for reasons outside the scope of this discussion, the survival rates for African-American women are much smaller than those for Caucasian-American women. Only 39 percent of African-American women were alive five years after diagnosis of female cancer in 1960. The figure for 1986 was 56 percent.

TABLE 3.1   **Estimated New Cases of Cancer and Cancer Deaths in U.S. Women During 1998**

Type of Cancer	New Cases	Deaths
Breast	178,700	43,500
Cervix	13,700	4,900
Ovary	25,400	14,500
Uterus and corpus	36,100	6,300
Vulva	3,200	800
Vagina	2,000	600

As you can see, you are not condemned to develop a female cancer in your lifetime. Far from it. The risks, however, are real enough to justify the mustering of your energy to minimize them as much as is possible and reasonable. In case you have not yet assumed a pro-active stance toward female cancers, I would encourage you to do so. There are behaviors that you can adopt to protect your life from the intrusion of disease. Many of these behaviors are outlined in the course of this chapter.

The discussion that follows is, of necessity, selective and reflects the bias of its author. It includes a distilling of information from hundreds of different studies selected from among the thousands that research has produced in the last three decades on the subject of female cancers. One of the important criteria for their selection was date of publication. In most cases, the more recent studies were chosen. All along, an effort has been made to account for studies that contradicted our biases.

This chapter has two major sections. The first discusses behaviors that, in most instances, you can change if you so choose. Those factors such as age or close relatives with the disease that remain outside the realm of choice have been purposefully left out.

In a basic sense, the prevention of female cancers hinges on reversing the risk factors for these diseases outlined in the first section. For example, little or no ingestion of fruit is shown to increase a woman's risk for female cancers, whereas the daily intake of three to five servings of raw fruits is protective.

The main objective of the second section is to scientifically validate that the reversal of some of the major risk factors for female cancer represents behaviors clearly associated with the prevention of these same cancers. In addition, this section elucidates, whenever possible, the mechanisms explaining why the behaviors, whose adoption is recommended, work to prevent or reduce the risk of developing female cancers.

Factors Shown to Increase the Risk of Female Cancers

The discussion of risk factors may be somewhat confusing—some factors appear to increase the risk for one type of cancer while reducing it for another. When this is the case, perhaps it is best to err on the side of caution. A case in point is hormone replacement therapy (HRT). A recent review of all studies published in the English language concerning hormone replacement and breast cancer was done by the Harvard Center for Cancer Prevention. The Hill criteria for demonstrating a causal relationship (consistency, dose-response pattern, biologic plausibility, temporality, strength of association, and coherence) were used to determine what association might exist between breast cancer and hormones. The report of this work, published in June 1998 in the *Journal of the National Cancer Institute*, concluded that "it is evident that postmenopausal hormones cause breast cancer."[2] While no causal relationship has yet been demonstrated between HRT and the incidence of ovarian and endometrial cancers, a positive association also exists between these parameters. In contrast, HRT appears to reduce the risk for cervical cancer, but if the hormones are taken in the form of oral contraceptives, cervical cancer risk may be increased, although other studies show a protective effect.

Moreover, known risk factors can explain only a small percentage of cancers, as for example, 25–30 percent of breast cancers. In other words, 70–75 percent of breast cancer cases cannot be explained by presently known factors. However, despite the fact that much more is unknown than known about why cancer arises in humans, I am convinced that minimization or, when possible, elimination of risk factors presently is the best and most reasonable available means to prevent development of cancer or to live with it if present.

Clearly, cancer impacts women's lives. Although, as we have seen, the numbers of women who develop cancer are relatively small, even one cancer is one too many. However, the vast majority of cancers can be prevented by the consistent practice of a few simple behaviors. Appropriate changes in habits of living—diet, nutrition, exercise—may cut female cancer risk by at least 70 percent.

Nonmodifiable Risk Factors

Nonmodifiable risk factors for female cancers include age and a history of close female relatives with the disease. Since these factors are not "preventable," they remain outside the scope of this discussion. However, gene mutations, such as BRCA1, BRCA2, and p53, merit appraisal. These mutations have been linked to increased risk of breast and ovarian cancers. Mutations of the recently identified genes BRCA1 and BRCA2 are thought responsible for 5–10 percent of new breast cancer cases.

One of the most frequently mutated genes in cancer, p53, a tumor suppressor gene, also is implicated in breast cancer risk. Normally, it blocks the growth and division of genetically damaged cells. When mutated, however, p53 allows the cell to transmit potentially carcinogenic material to the cell's progeny.

The past two decades in cancer research have provided much insight into the beginnings of cancer. It is clear that mutations that lead to the transformation of proto-oncogenes into oncogenes (genes that promote cancer), inhibition of suppressor genes, and deregulation of genes governing cell differentiation and division play central roles in the initiation and promotion of cancer. The recent discovery of telomerase, the enzyme that builds the telomeres (the caps at the ends of chromosomes)

and is shortened after each cell division, has shed light into mechanisms of cancer cell immortality that may lead to early detection of cancer.

Despite the central role played by genes in cancer genesis, one must be cognizant of the fact that the environment plays the major role in the appearance of the disease. If the genetic load will account for a maximum of 10 percent of new cases of breast cancer (about 18,000 cases), the environment will be responsible for more than 160,000 in 1998. Perera[3] put in sharp perspective genes and environment when she wrote:

> The likelihood of tumor development is increased by impairment of the immune system and by such disorders as hormonal imbalances, hepatitis, and chronic lung disease. Convincing evidence also indicates that a diet low in fruits and vegetables containing antioxidants and other nutrients (such as vitamins A, C, and E) increases the probability of acquiring diverse cancers. . . . I would emphasize . . . that in most cases, calculations of risk based on single genetic characteristics will be incomplete and could even be misleading. *The effect of any one, single-acting gene can be modulated by environmental influences, by other genes, by health and nutritional status, and by an array of other host characteristics* (italics mine).

Modifiable Risk Factors

Hormonal Factors

Though still arguable, hormone replacement therapy has been shown to cause breast cancer. Additionally, it is associated with increased risk for endometrial and ovarian cancers. While a woman who takes both estrogen and progesterone has a lesser risk for endometrial cancer than a woman who is taking estrogen only, she nevertheless has a higher risk than a woman not on HRT, even if she is taking progesterone for more than 10 days a month.

Long-term use of hormones given as birth control pills (BCP) increases a woman's risk for breast cancer. Moreover, for each year she uses BCP, her risk increases 3.3 percent. Thus, if she takes BCP for 10 years, her relative risk would be 1.38 or a 38 percent increase in breast cancer risk. Increased risk has been found in women less than 36 years old

TABLE 3.2 **BRCA1 and BRCA2 Mutations and Effects on Breast and Ovarian Cancer Risks**

Type of Cancer	Proposed Gene	Estimated Risk
Breast cancer, women	BRCA1	50–80% by age 70 years
	BRCA2	Similar to BRCA1
Ovarian cancer	BRCA1	26–85% by age 70 years
	BRCA2	<10% by age 70 years

who used BCP for more than four years (especially if begun before age 20) and for 46- to 54-year-olds who had used them recently. The BCP may also increase a woman's risk of cervical cancer, although there is conflicting data. Women who had used BCP, as compared with those who had never used it, had double the risk of developing cervical cancer; moreover, if a woman used the BCP for more than 12 years, her risk quadrupled.

Fortunately, the use of BCP may have some redeeming features. Besides giving a woman the ability to prevent unwanted pregnancy, BCP usage has been shown to decrease the risk for ovarian cancer, a very difficult one to treat, and endometrial cancers.

Diethylstilbestrol (DES), administered to women unable to carry their pregnancy to term, likely increases their breast cancer risk, as well as the risk for cervical and vaginal cancers in their daughters. Having a first-degree relative (sister or mother) with breast or ovarian cancer increases a woman's risk of developing identical cancers. Similarly, the presence of the BRCA1 mutation increases a woman's risk for breast and ovarian cancers (see Table 3.2). Breast cancer incidence is also associated with BRCA2 and p53 mutations.

Tamoxifen, a selective estrogen receptor modulator (SERM), attaches to estrogen receptors in breast tissue, thus displacing estrogen from the sites and inhibiting its action. It is being used as a chemopreventive agent for breast cancer recurrence. It has reduced breast cancer incidence in high-risk women and the rate of same-side and opposite-side breast tumor recurrences in women with breast cancer. It is important to realize, however, that its use is not completely without danger. Tamoxifen has been linked with increases in gastrointestinal, endometrial, and ovarian cancers, as well as thromboembolic episodes. A recent study

found, however, that if the administration of this drug is accompanied by annual screening of patients for gynecologic cancer, this increase of endometrial cancer could be prevented.

Reproductive Factors

Reproductive factors associated with female cancer incidence include:

1. Nulliparity (never having given birth)
2. Being more than 20 years old at birth of first child
3. Having begun menstruating before age 14
4. Having short menstrual cycles
5. Having anovulatory cycles
6. Beginning menopause past age 55

With the exception of anovulatory cycles, which are related to decreased risk of breast cancer, most of the other factors correlate positively with increased risk of breast, ovarian, and endometrial cancers. The first two risk factors correlate negatively with cervical cancer, and the latter is also associated with decreased risk of ovarian and vulvar cancers.

Lifestyle and Environmental Factors

A sedentary lifestyle increases the risk of all female cancers: breast, cervical, ovarian, endometrial, vaginal, and vulvar. So does smoking. Recently, a tobacco-specific and potent carcinogen was found in significantly higher concentrations in the cervical mucus of female smokers than non-smokers. Smokers also had more exfoliated cervical cells and smoking-related DNA damage, which could represent early signs of cancer initiation. Current cigarette smoking increased by more than six times the odds for vulvar cancer *in situ* and three times for invasive vulvar cancers. Except for one study, all others found a strong link between smoking and the risk for cervical cancer. Moreover, smoking was linked to endometrial cancer in postmenopausal but not in premenopausal women.

The link between smoking and breast cancer risk is confusing. For example, a recent study suggested that smoking may reduce breast cancer risk in BRCA1 and BRCA2 gene mutation carriers.[4] Additionally, a 1998 review of certain environmental factors and breast cancer risk indicated that the effects of smoking on breast cancer development may depend on host susceptibility, subtypes of the disease, and lifetime exposure.[5] Moreover, the Nurses' Health Study revealed that smoking early in life is a "modifiable cause of breast cancer in a subpopulation of genetically susceptible women."[6] To round out the confusion, a population-based case-control study of 242 breast cancer patients in Switzerland concluded that smoking was related to estrogen receptor positive (ER+) and estrogen receptor negative (ER−) breast cancer in both pre- and postmenopausal women.[7]

An association between female cancers and other environmental factors, such as pesticides, has long been suspected. Repeatedly, however, the evidence for the association is scanty and inconsistent and, therefore, not fully convincing. Elevated risk of breast cancer has been linked to exposure to electromagnetic fields, pesticides, ionizing radiation, chlorinated solvents, and polychlorinated biphenyls, as well as working as a beautician or in the pharmaceutical industry or living in the San Francisco Bay area. Vulvar cancer incidence is associated with working in garment laundering or cleaning, or as a household maid or servant. The list implicates some kind of persistent chemical exposure in the increased risks detected, which is not an unreasonable deduction.

Cervical cancer risk increases with multiple sexual partners, age at first sexual intercourse experience (the younger the woman, the greater the risk), and frequent douching. Frequent douching also seems to increase the risk for vaginal cancer. Vulvar cancer risk increased as the number of sexual partners increased—more than five partners increased a woman's risk two to three times, particularly if the woman was young.

Diet, Nutrition, and Related Factors

Calories, Fat, Meat, and Alcohol Generally, the relationship between dietary factors and female cancers offers no surprises. Regular use of animal fats (saturated fats) leads to elevated risk of all female cancers studied thus far—breast, ovarian, and endometrial cancers. One study,[8] however, found no relationship between ovarian cancer risk and saturated fat intake. Nevertheless, the general trend is that increased total dietary fat, meat, alcohol, and elevated calorie consumption increases the risk for female cancers. The association between calorie consumption and female cancer risk is strongest in postmenopausal women. One study found no association between alcohol or meat intake and vulvar cancer. Another failed to relate increased total dietary fat consumption with ovarian cancer risk.

Fruits, Vegetables, and Fiber The relationship is also as expected between low consumption of fruits, vegetables, or fiber and female cancer risk. Elevated female cancer risk was consistently found to be related to low intake of these dietary items.

Dairy Products The relationship of milk and cheese consumption with female cancer is less straightforward. While one study[9] found a positive correlation for milk intake and breast cancer risk, two others[10, 11] found that milk decreased breast cancer incidence. Milk intake also decreased the risk of cervical, but not of ovarian, cancer. In fact, one study[12] found that galactose (a simple sugar part of the molecule of the milk sugar, lactose) increased ovarian cancer risk. Conflicting evidence was found for endometrial cancer: skim milk and yogurt intake decreased its risk, while milk increased it.

These conflicting data may result from a number of different factors: (1) another parameter, not yet identified, may be the reason for the apparent conflict; (2) researcher bias—one's beliefs may color one's interpretation of the facts; (3) participant bias—subjects' self-selection; (4) answers given to questions in interviews or questionnaires by participants often unintentionally reflect what participants thought the interviewer wanted to hear, rather than what the facts really were.

One study,[12] the first to uncover the possible relationship between galactose and ovarian cancer, raises caution in relation to the indiscriminate use of some popular foods. The authors found a "highly significant trend" for ovarian cancer in women consuming yogurt at least once a month—nearly twice as large as for women who reported less frequent yogurt consumption. Eating cottage cheese at least once a month also elevated the risk for the same cancer. Hormone and/or pesticide residues in the milk may be responsible for these disturbing results.

Body Mass and Weight Body mass index (BMI), the ratio of weight to height, correlates inversely with cancer incidence in premenopausal women. In postmenopausal women, the correlation is positive but weak. In other words, within certain limits, the premenopausal woman might benefit from moderately elevated body mass! For the postmenopausal woman, the benefit appears to result from moderately decreased body mass.

A high current BMI was associated with lower breast cancer incidence in premenopausal women. However, this was reversed in postmenopausal women. A high BMI at age 18 appeared protective for both pre- and postmenopausal women. Conversely, weight gain after age 18 was associated with increased cancer incidence in postmenopausal, but not in premenopausal, women. Both high birth weight and leanness at age 7 increased the incidence of breast cancer in both pre- and postmenopausal women.

Increased BMI also related to increased risk of ovarian, endometrial, and vulvar cancers but was inversely related to cervical cancer risk.

Fish and Omega-3 Oils Conflicting results also have been observed with fish and omega-3 oil consumption. While some studies found that an increased intake of these foods was associated with decreased breast and cervical cancers, others found that they were associated with increased ovarian and endometrial cancer risk.

Legumes and Refined Carbohydrates While consumption of legumes (including soy) decreased breast, ovarian, and endometrial cancer incidence, the use of sugar, refined carbohydrates (e.g., desserts), and/or soft drinks increased the risk of breast and en-

dometrial cancers. (A lengthy discussion on soy will appear below under prevention of female cancers.)

In summary, research results on the association between foods, weight, BMI, and alcohol and the risk of female cancers are conflicting and, therefore, difficult to interpret. Dogmatic extrapolation of these results to any individual woman is inadvisable.

Some trends, however, are clearly discernible and can provide the basis for guidance. For example, all studies consulted agree that fruits and vegetables are protective against all female cancers. Additionally, we were unable to find conflicting results regarding the regular use of meat or alcohol: accumulating and consistent evidence suggests that the more often a woman eats meat or drinks alcoholic beverages, the greater her risk of developing female cancer. Legumes (e.g., soy and other beans, peas, and lentils), on the contrary, exhibit a protective effect that is consistent across the research.

Mental/Emotional Factors

The feeling that certain personality types are more prone to cancer than others has been around for centuries.* Lock and Colligan write: "The second-century physician Galen noted that 'melancholic' women were more prone to breast cancer than their more 'sanguine' counterparts." More recently, in the 1950s, researchers in a veterans' hospital in Long Beach, California, were impressed by a cluster of features that seemed to characterize patients with rapidly growing tumors. These people were "polite, apologetic, consistently serious, over-cooperative, over-nice, over-anxious, painfully sensitive, passive. . . ." Other researchers confirmed this suspicion and found, in addition, other characteristics in the prone-to-cancer personality. For example, investigators in New York and Philadelphia described their cancer patients as incapable of dealing with stress and caught in a kind of emotional rigidity, "choosing to affect a permanent pleasant attitude and personality regardless of the bleakness of their inner lives."

Still other investigators, this time at Kings College Hospital in London in the 1970s, described their

---

*This discussion is based on *The Healer Within: The New Medicine of Mind and Body* by Lock and Colligan. New York: New American Library (1986: 158–76).

breast cancer patients as appearing to be "holding their emotions, especially anger, in check."

Finally, doctors at the Malignant Melanoma Clinic in San Francisco, with the help of psychologists, dubbed this pattern of behavior the Type C personality, as contrasted to A (angry, tense, hard-driving) or B (relaxed, confident) type. According to these researchers, the C-type patients had one dominant characteristic, "the nonexpression of emotion," especially "negative" emotions. They were model patients, "compliant in the extreme."

In contrast, cancer survivors appeared to be those individuals who had learned to express their emotions and were in touch with their feelings and physical needs—they had developed "a way to deal with the stresses of life."

More recent studies have confirmed the relationship between this "anti-emotion" personality and cancer. A Dutch study, involving 9,705 women, 131 of whom developed breast cancer during 1989 through 1994, found significant increased risk of the disease in women having a first-degree relative with breast cancer, nulliparity, or anti-emotionality.[13]

The study of the relationship between stress and female cancer incidence has elicited conflicting results. Three studies[14–16] showed that stressful life events increased breast cancer risk. Another study, in contrast, found no "important associations" between these two parameters. One reason for this disparity could be that the latter study looked at the number of stressful events, rather than their severity. When researchers have distinguished between severe life events and ongoing long-term difficulties, they find no association between ongoing long-term difficulties and development of breast cancer but find that the more severe the event is, the greater the danger of coming down with the disease. Experiencing a single, major life event was potentially more damaging, particularly with deficient or nonexistent coping skills, than regular exposure to stress.

❧ Prevention of Female Cancers

Having identified modifiable factors commonly associated with female cancer risk, our task now is to help motivated readers develop strategies shown to alter these factors, giving their bodies the best chance to remain free of cancer.

Four strategies show the greatest promise in the prevention of female cancers. These are: never smoking cigarettes, limiting alcohol, practicing regular exercise, and using appropriate nutrition. The risks of smoking cigarettes and excessive alcohol use are well known. I will, therefore, discuss in some depth the practice of exercise and the use of appropriate nutrition and will add other behaviors in the discussion that follows.

The judicious, persistent, joyful, and lifelong adherence to diets that emphasize the consumption of foods in as close-to-nature a condition as possible, to a life of movement, physical and intellectual, from which tobacco, in all its forms, and probably alcohol, have been eliminated, offers the average U.S. woman the bargain of her life: a minimum of 70 percent reduction in her risk of developing female cancers.

Diet and Diet-Related Behaviors

Recently, the American Cancer Society suggested the following nutritional guidelines to prevent cancer.

1. Choose most of the foods you eat from plant sources.
   - Eat five or more servings of fruits and vegetables each day.
   - Eat other foods from plant sources, such as breads, cereals, grain products, rice, pasta, or beans several times each day.
2. Limit your intake of fatty foods, particularly from animal sources.
   - Choose foods low in fat.
   - Limit consumption of meats, especially high fat meats.
3. Limit consumption of alcoholic beverages, if you drink at all.

Vegetables

Increased consumption of vegetables may reduce female cancer risk in several ways. Vegetables appear to:

1. Increase the cytotoxic (cell-killing) activity of important cancer-detecting natural killer (NK) cells

2. Inhibit the formation of neoplastic cells by changing the fatty acid content of cell membranes.

3. Restrict cancer development, especially breast cancer, through one of their components, glucarate, which is found in cruciferous vegetables. The effects of glucarate may be explained in at least two ways: It regulates hormone levels, thereby regulating cell growth, and inhibits the effect of known carcinogens on cancer initiation.

4. Protect against cancer-causing chemicals. Cruciferous vegetables, such as broccoli, broccoli sprouts, cauliflower, cabbage, Brussels sprouts, and kohlrabi also contain large amounts of glucoraphanin, a precursor to sulforaphane and other isothiocyanates. In animal studies, these substances have been shown to increase the enzymes that protect the cell from damage by cancer-causing chemicals.

5. Reduce breast cancer risk. Cruciferous vegetables also contain indoles, chemicals that appear to stimulate enzymes that render estrogen less effective, thus decreasing the risk of breast cancer.

6. Inhibit the action of cancer-causing chemicals. Vegetables like garlic, onions, leeks, and chives contain phytochemical allyl sulfides that have been shown to inhibit chemically induced carcinogenesis.

7. Decrease oxidative damage to DNA. Carotene-containing vegetables (carrots, sweet potatoes, squash) have been shown to decrease oxidative and other damage to DNA in humans.

Research on vegetarian women has demonstrated that they excrete two to three times more estrogens in their feces than do their omnivorous counterparts. They also have 50 percent lower mean plasma levels of unconjugated estrone and estradiol than omnivores. Additionally, they have lower urinary estriol levels, an indication that less free estriol is absorbed in the intestines. They also have reduced levels of prolactin. Increased levels of prolactin have been associated with enhanced breast cancer growth in postmenopausal women. In terms of female cancer risk, the results of the studies consulted suggest, without exception, reduced risk of female cancers in vegetarian women.

In summary, pre- and postmenopausal women can only benefit from a larger-than-average intake of fresh organic vegetables daily. A diet rich in vegetables will protect their cells from carcinogens, decrease their blood levels of damaging high levels of estrogens, and render their cells immune to injury from oxidative processes.

Fruits

The following discussion elucidates how certain components of fresh fruit may work to reduce female cancer risk. In all probability other components of fruits (and other foods) will be discovered and studied and their effects ascertained. Although this type of research has the benefit of explaining how certain substances may or may not prevent cancer risk, it tends to separate substances that, in a natural context, work together. It is our feeling that eating a cup of fresh organic strawberries will offer any woman much greater benefit than a few milligrams of ellagic acid.

Recent research consistently has found that consumption of whole fruits is associated with decreased occurrence of female cancers and has identified several anticarcinogenic substances in fruits.

1. Ellagic acid and other naturally occurring plant phenolics, such as caffeic and ferulic acids, also found in nuts and trees, appear to inhibit the action of aflatoxins and nitrosamines, two known powerful carcinogens. Ellagic acid is found primarily in strawberries, raspberries, cranberries, loganberries, cherries, oranges, and grapes. Cooking does not appear to destroy it.

2. Carotenoids, another component of many fruits, especially apricots, cantaloupe, peaches, and nectarines, decrease oxidative damage to DNA in humans, thereby reducing DNA mutations, one of the first steps in cancer initiation.

3. Limonene, a dietary monoterpene found in lemons and oranges, prevents cancer initiation in animals by inducing the production of carcinogen-metabolizing enzymes. It also inhibits the cancer promotion/progression phase by inducing tumor cell death, tumor cell redifferentiation, and/or post-translational isoprenylation of cell growth-regulating proteins.

4. Citrus flavonoids, such as tangeretin and nobiletin, found in citrus fruits, induce apoptosis

of cancer cells, thereby inhibiting tumor growth without negatively affecting immune cells.

5. Vitamin C is found in large amounts in many fruits and vegetables. Examination of epidemiological data from 33 of 46 studies revealed that vitamin C has significant protective effects both on cancer mortality and incidence.

Soy

Population studies have demonstrated reduced breast cancer deaths among women whose diets include large amounts of soy products. This is true of women in Asia, China, and Japan. For example, data published by the American Cancer Society in 1998 show that 21.1 U.S., 22 Canadian, 22.1 German, 26.5 English, and 19.7 French women per 100,000 women died from breast cancer each year between 1992 and 1995, whereas only 5 Chinese and 6.8 Japanese women died during the same time period from the same disease.[17] Additionally, the observation that female Asian immigrants, who decrease intake of soy-based foods and adopt a "Western" diet, over time die of breast cancer at rates similar to those of their adopted country strongly implicates environmental factors in breast cancer risk, e.g., diets poor in soy and rich in animal products.

Soy, available as soybeans, tofu, soy milk, tempeh, miso, soy nuts (roasted), and powders, is being studied intensively because it appears to help optimize health in numerous ways. Its role in the prevention and treatment of cancer is well documented. Consistently encouraging results have been obtained in this area whether researchers used the whole soybean or some of its bioactive components. Soybeans contain several anticarcinogenic compounds: isoflavones, protease inhibitors, phytic acid, saponins, phytosterols, and phenolic acids. Two of the isoflavones, daidzein and genistein, have been researched most often.

Ingestion of whole soybeans, miso, or genistein conferred protection from breast cancer in animals. When young animals were fed genistein they were less susceptible to chemically induced breast cancer as adults than their counterparts who ate no isoflavones. A note of caution emerges from animal studies—the offspring of genistein-fed pregnant animals showed an increased risk of developing breast cancer later in life. Genistein appeared to have similar effects to those of estradiol (E2) on the mammary glands and reproductive systems of the offspring. Unfortunately, I was unable to locate any studies in which the whole soy foods were used and, therefore, could not ascertain whether or not whole soy induces these untoward effects. However, studies do show that women who consumed higher amounts of soy products had reduced incidence of hormone-related cancers, including breast cancer.

Laboratory testing of the effects of soy products on breast cells has elucidated some of the mechanisms for the anticarcinogenic activity of soy. Soy products:

- inhibit proteases and decrease carcinogenic activity
- reduce serum estradiol levels: when measured on days 11 and 22 of the menstrual cycle, estradiol levels were inversely associated with a woman's intake of soy products; soy protein isolate elevates plasma estradiol levels in premenopausal, but not in postmenopausal women
- increase plasma levels of sex-hormone-binding globulin (SHBG)
- inhibit angiogenesis (blood vessel formation)
- have antioxidating activity
- induce differentiation of cancer cells
- have antiestrogenic activity
- limit cancer growth; soy contains low levels of methionine, thereby limiting the polyamines required for cancer growth
- increase cancer cell apoptosis (cell death) by inducing p53
- may reduce insulin resistance, thereby decreasing levels of bioavailable estrogen

In addition, many studies have shown the anticancer activity of two compounds of soy, genistein and daidzein.

Since soy isoflavones function as weak estrogens, concern about their consumption by postmenopausal women has been voiced. As a response to this concern, a recent study of postmenopausal women[18] used a daily intake of 165 mg of isoflavones (estimated to correspond to 0.3 mg of Premarin) either in the form of soybeans or dried defatted soybean flour. After four weeks, no estrogenic effects were detected except for a small effect in the vaginal lining. The reason for this apparently protective effect of soy isoflavones even in postmenopausal women is that these substances bind weakly to estrogen receptors. Thus they block the biological estrogens (estrone, estradiol, and estriol) from binding to the same receptors and inhibit their effects. The net result of this action is to reduce prolonged exposure to high levels of estrogen and, in turn, prevent the incidence of estrogen-dependent female cancers.

It is also of interest to understand that for daidzein and genistein to function as anticarcinogens in the body, they first must be transformed into bioavailable forms (e.g., equol) by intestinal-friendly bacteria (microflora). Moreover, the microflora's ability to produce the bioavailable soy isoflavones appears dependent on a woman's diet: women who consume more carbohydrates, plant protein, and dietary fiber have a more balanced microfloral environment than their counterparts who consume a meat-based diet.

Table 3.3 indicates the content of isoflavonoids and lignans per 100 grams of different plant foods. Lignans are a different type of phytoestrogen, poorly represented in soy but found in large amounts in flax and pumpkin seeds. There are approximately 21.3 mg of genistein and 7.6 mg of daidzein in 3.5 ounces of firm tofu, nearly 370 mg of the lignan secoisolariciresinol in 100 mg of flaxseed, and more than 21 mg of the same lignan in pumpkin seeds. Dr. B. A. Stoll recommended a daily intake of at least 100 mg of isoflavones "to beat breast cancer."[19]

For women who may have difficulty eating enough tofu daily to provide these amounts of isoflavones, powdered preparations of these substances are available and may easily be supplemented to the diet. It is important to note here that a powder containing a mixture of isoflavones and lignans, rather than isolated substances like genistein, is the better choice.

Flaxseeds

Flaxseeds are the most abundant source of dietary lignans. Secoisolariciresinol, the major precursor of lignans found in flaxseeds, must be transformed into bioavailable forms by the gut microflora before it can be absorbed into the blood circulation and be of benefit in preventing female cancer. Again, it is important to realize how important a balanced microflora is to health. Antibiotics destroy or greatly imbalance gut microflora. After a dose of antibiotics was given to young women, researchers found that their intestinal flora was deranged and had not returned to normal 40 days later.

Lignans can also be found in some whole grains, fruits, berries, some vegetables, and other seeds. The lignans are located in the outer layers of the seeds or grains and are concentrated in the aleurone layer. Modern milling techniques that remove the aleurone layer and produce "polished" rice and "white" breads eliminate from many Western tables most of the lignans found in grains.

In animal studies, flaxseed ingestion has been found to reduce cell proliferation and nuclear aberrations in breast cells. Both of these parameters are early signs of carcinogenesis in tissue.

Fiber

A low fat diet, rich in insoluble fiber, has been shown to decrease the circulation of estrogens between the intestines and the liver and decrease plasma estrogen levels, thereby potentially reducing the risk of hormone-related cancers. However, studies on dietary fiber have yielded conflicting results. A 1992 study found no relationship between these parameters,[21] while four others found an inverse relationship between them.[22-25] The discrepancy may stem from differing fiber composition depending on whether the participants used whole (lignan-rich) or refined (lignan-depleted) grains.

Two other studies also showed the importance of fiber-rich foods in the prevention of breast cancer. One of these compared the diets of postmenopausal omnivorous and vegetarian American women in Boston[26] and the other, premenopausal omnivorous and vegetarian Finnish women in Helsinki.[27] These groups were further subdivided into women with breast cancer and women without the disease. The results of these studies clearly indicated that the only significant difference between women with and

TABLE 3.3   **Average Isoflavonoid and Lignan Content in Selected Plant Foods**[20]

Food	Isoflavones mcg/100 grams		Lignans mcg/100 grams
	Genistein	*Daidzein*	
Soybean flour	96,900	67,400	130
Firm tofu	21,300	7,600	0
Soft tofu	18,700	7,300	0
Hatcho Miso	14,500	13,700	0
Soy drink	2,100	700	0
Soy-milk formula	310	30	0
Flaxseed	0	0	369,900
Flaxseed, crushed and defatted	0	0	546,000
Clover seed	323	178	13.2
Sunflower seed	13.9	8.00	610
Poppy seed	6.7	17.9	14.0
Caraway seed	8.0	0.14	221
Wheat (whole grain)	0	0	32.9
White wheat meal	Trace	Trace	8.1
Wheat bran	6.9	3.5	110
Oat meal	0	0	13.4
Oat bran	0	0	23.8
Barley (whole grain)	7.7	14.0	58.0
Barley bran	16.3	6.4	62.6
Rye meal (whole grain)	0	0	47.1
Rye bran	0	0	132
Triticale (whole grain)	1.7	1.6	38.8
Triticale meal	1.1	1.9	21.4
Chick-peas	76.3	11.4	8.4
Mung bean	365	9.7	172
Mung bean sprouts	1902	745	468
Dahl	60.3	30.3	240
Pumpkin seeds	1.53	0.56	21,370
Soy oil	0.40	0.02	1.20
Chinese soy sauce	Trace	20.5	26.9
Carrots	1.7	1.6	192
Garlic	1.45	2.08	379
Broccoli	6.6	4.7	414
Cranberry	0	0	1,510
Peanuts	82.6	49.7	333
Earl Grey black tea	0	29.0	1,590
Japanese green tea	Not determined	Trace	2,460

See also the soy/isoflavone table on page 148 of Chapter 10.

women without breast cancer was the intake of grains: women with breast cancer ate less grain and grain fibers than their counterparts. These results were independent of the women's menopausal status.

Whole grains contain high amounts of lignans, and these have been shown to reduce the circulation of estrogens, increase plasma sex-hormone-binding-globulin values, and reduce free estradiol and testosterone, all of which may translate into diminished cancer risk. An added mechanism for the effect of whole grains on cancer risk reduction was proposed in a recent review: fiber decreases insulin resistance, which reduces bioavailable estrogen, which in turn diminishes the risk of breast cancer.

In June 1998, the *International Journal of Cancer* published the results of a study of 10,000 women with cancer, who were compared to 8,000 controls without the disease. All participants were questioned about their diet. The investigators concluded: "High intake of whole grain foods consistently reduced risk of (cancer) at all sites, except thyroid." Breast and ovarian cancers were included in this group of cancers.[28]

Dairy Products

Most epidemiological studies found a positive relationship between eating dairy products (milk, cheese, etc.) and increasing one's risk of female cancers. Even low-fat milk consumption appeared to increase this risk. In contrast, however, a few studies found a protective role for dairy, or no relationship between female cancers and dairy products.

Normal, untreated cow's milk contains insulin-growth factor I (IGF-I), which has been shown to be a powerful stimulator of breast cancer cell proliferation in vitro. Pasteurization does not destroy IGF-I. Whether IGF-I, a peptide, is of harm to humans remains in doubt. Proteins and peptides in general are not absorbed into the circulation until broken down into their constituent amino acids. However, there is evidence suggesting that epidermal growth factor (EGF), a peptide with similar molecular structure and weight to those of IGF-I, was absorbed intact from infants' guts and that the enzyme bovine milk xanthine oxidase (BMXO) was also absorbed intact, even in adults who consumed large amounts of milk. Moreover, bovine growth hormone (bGH), commonly added to cow's feed today, increases by two to four times the bovine plasma and milk levels of IGF-I.

These results suggest that IGF-I may be absorbed intact into the blood circulation, making the consumption of these treated milk and milk products an increased female cancer risk.

Fish

Fish consumption does not appear to be protective for all female cancers. While it was linked to decreased risk of breast and cervical cancers in several studies, it was related to the increased risk of ovarian and endometrial cancers.

Two studies in particular merit extended discussion. The first one examined data from 533,276 Norwegian women relating to their intake of fish and subsequent incidence of and mortality from breast cancer. The results showed lowest incidence and mortality rates among women married to fishermen in northern Norway. In general, northern Norwegians consume twice as much fish as the national average, and, among these, the women studied consumed twice as much fish (80 g/day) as did other women in their community.[29]

The second study offers a possible explanation for the apparent discrepancy in the results of studies examining relationship of fish intake to female cancer incidence and mortality. Swedish researchers studied breast cancer rates among two groups of women married to fishermen. One group lived on the eastern shores of the Baltic Sea, notable for its organochlorine-polluted waters; the other, on the shores of the North Sea, a much less polluted body of water. Breast cancer rates in these two groups were compared to expected levels in the general population. The results were as follows: Baltic Sea women had higher-than-expected breast cancer incidence, while North Sea women had lower-than-expected rates.[30] The difference between these two groups of women is that one ate fish from polluted waters and the other ate fish from less polluted waters.

The degree of water contamination and consequent levels of pollutants in fish from different locations is a possible confounding variable in fish studies that may account for the outcome discrepancies noted.

In brief, despite popular emphasis on the benefits of eating fish (reduced breast cancer risk and possibly of other female cancers), the fact remains that not all fish are alike. Fish from polluted waters—sea, river, or lake—may also be polluted and, probably, harmful to women if eaten regularly and in large amounts. Although this is increasingly difficult, before eating fish or, for that matter any food you buy, try to check its origin.

Garlic

Garlic provides an inexpensive and easily obtainable dietary protection against female cancers. Its benefits have been demonstrated in numerous studies. For example, garlic-treated animal breast cells exposed to a carcinogen (DMBA) showed reduced binding of DMBA with their DNA and, hence, less carcinogenic damage.[31] Growth of cultured animal breast cancer cells was significantly inhibited when oil-based garlic preparations were added to the cultures.[32] Additionally, garlic-fed animals with artificially induced breast cancer showed delayed onset of tumors and decreased tumor incidence.[33] Moreover, continuous garlic treatment, "which started before the DMBA and persisted for the entire duration of the study, was most effective in tumor suppression."[34]

The chemopreventive effect of garlic was also demonstrated in a cervical carcinoma animal model study. The oral dosage of garlic, 400 mg/kg of body weight for two weeks before and four weeks following continuous carcinogen exposure, significantly reduced the incidence of cancer. In the controls, the incidence of cervical carcinomas was 73 percent. It was only 23 percent in the garlic-treated animals.[35]

An Iowa study of 34,388 postmenopausal women found that garlic intake reduced breast cancer risk. A Chinese study also found that ingestion of allium vegetables (garlic and onions) was protective. In contrast, a study from the Netherlands of women and men found no association between onion or leek consumption or garlic supplementation and breast cancer incidence.[36]

The reasons for the unexpected results obtained by the Netherlands study are not known. However, possible confounding factors that might have not been accounted for and skewed the results are dietary fat, soy and soy product ingestion, fish consumption, mineral content of the soil, water, and soil contaminants, and the quality of garlic supplements (e.g., absence of allicin).

Moreover, John Pinto of the Memorial Sloan-Kettering Cancer Center in New York is quoted as saying, "There is growing evidence that garlic or its derivatives may be able to prevent the development of at least six different cancers," including breast cancer. The mechanism suggested by this researcher for the effects of this vegetable on cancer risk is that garlic may stimulate glutathione-S-transferase, an enzyme known to inhibit carcinogenesis.[37]

Fats

The results of studies examining the relationship between dietary fat intake and female cancers are, at best, confusing. The confusion engendered by conflicting outcomes has been attributed to the failure of some studies to distinguish between different types of fats. However, discrepancies exist even in studies looking at the same type of fat.

A door out of this impasse is to look for trends despite the confusion, and trends do exist. Generally, the following trends are clear. Diets which are positively related to increased risk of female cancers are:

- rich in total fat
- rich in saturated (animal) fat
- low in monounsaturated fat
- rich in linoleic acid (the major omega-6 polyunsaturated fat)
- low in linolenic acid (the major omega-3 polyunsaturated fat)

Total Dietary Fat

Numerous studies point to high dietary fat intake as a factor in the increased incidence of breast, ovarian, and endometrial cancers, while others find either a decrease in risk of breast cancer or no relationship with breast, ovarian, or endometrial cancers. Dr. O. J. Hunter, from the Harvard School of Public Health, believes that "results from prospective studies do not support the hypothesis that fat intake in middle life is associated with breast cancer risk during up to ten years of follow-up. It is possible that the type of fat, rather than total fat intake, is important."[38]

It seems that the type of study, not only the type of fat, also elicits different results. For example, ecological studies, which look at trends, clearly demonstrate a positive association between breast cancer risk and dietary fat intake; case-control and cohort studies, on the other hand, generally do not support this conclusion.

Saturated Fats

The large majority of studies on dietary saturated (animal) fats and female cancer risk support a positive association of saturated fat with breast, ovarian, and endometrial cancers. One study, however, found no relationship between these parameters.[39]

Polyunsaturated Fats

The major polyunsaturated fats (PUFAs) in foods are of two types: omega-6 (linoleic acid) and omega-3 (linolenic acid). The chief sources of omega-6 fatty acids are safflower, sunflower and corn oils, and the chief source of omega-3 fatty acids is fish. Since fish is not a major item in U.S. diets, the ratio of omega-6 to omega-3 fats is 10 to 1. The U.S. government has not established dietary guidelines for the consumption of these fats. The Canadian recommendation for this ratio is 4 to 1, which many researchers feel is protective against cancer. Perhaps, the 10 to 1 ratio is partly responsible for the increased incidence of female cancers in North America.

Monounsaturated Fats

Monounsaturated fats remind us of Mediterranean diets that generally have been related to decreased risk of heart disease and also cancer. In fact, many studies have found an inverse relationship between risk of breast and endometrial cancers and the intake of monounsaturated fats.

The major monounsaturated fatty acid in foods is the omega-9 oleic acid. It is found in large amounts in olives and avocados. It is the chief component of olive oil.

Dietary fat intake, although confusing in its relationship to female cancer risk and prevention, is a topic of major importance in this regard. Its ramifications may reach farther than the individual woman's risk. In fact, a recent study in female animals demonstrated that the mother's high fat intake during pregnancy increased breast cancer risk among the female offspring.[40]

Nutritional Supplements

Most of the studies referenced below examined participants' intake of foods and calculated the amount of particular nutrients, such as vitamin C and others found in them. It is, therefore, a somewhat dubious extrapolation to infer that the results obtained by these studies were specifically due to the nutrient discussed. The term "nutritional supplements" is generally understood to mean a capsule or a tablet containing a specified amount of a nutrient extracted from foods or prepared in a laboratory from synthetic chemicals. These extractions, used as self-medication or as a prescription by alternative medicine practitioners, probably are not as important in the protection of a woman from female cancer as her choice of foods containing high levels of these nutrients.

Vitamin C

Numerous studies have looked at the effect of vitamin C on female cancer risk. Most of them have found that it reduces breast, cervical, ovarian, and endometrial cancer risk. However, a few studies, including the Nurses' Health Study, have found no beneficial effect of this vitamin in breast cancer.

When vitamin C was combined with breast cancer cells in a laboratory experiment, it stopped tumor growth. The larger the dose of the vitamin, the greater were its effects. Moreover, vitamin C reduced cervical tumor incidence by 33 percent in animals exposed to cervical carcinogens. The reduction was higher during the initiation phase of the cancer than later in its course.

I quote below the summary of the opinion on vitamin C and cancer prevention from the 1990 National Cancer Institute Symposium:

> Of 46 reports on epidemiologic studies, 33 described significant protective effects on cancer mortality or incidence. Strong epidemiologic evidence indicates that vitamin C, or other components in fruit, is protective against cancers of the esophagus, larynx, oral cavity, and pancreas. Evidence also exists for a protective effect against cancers of the stomach, rectum, lung, breast, and endometrial cervix.[41]

Additionally, the National Cancer Institute (NCI) has the following statement on its Web site:

> Preliminary evidence from experiments with laboratory animals and from population studies suggests that foods rich in vitamin C inhibit the initial development of some forms of cancer. However, the mechanism of protection is unclear. It is also uncertain whether the protection seen in population studies is the result of vitamin C or some other component in the diet, such as beta carotene. Further study is necessary to determine whether dietary or supplemental vitamin C has a role in cancer prevention and, if so, to determine the maximum safe dose. The NCI currently is sponsoring such studies.[42]

Rich sources of vitamin C are citrus fruits, rose hips, black currants, cranberries, broccoli, Brussels sprouts, kale, collard greens, turnips, beets, cabbage, beet greens, strawberries, and watercress.

CoQ-10

No research support exists for the use of coenzyme Q-10 (CoQ-10) as a preventive agent against female cancers. American and Danish physicians have used CoQ-10 to reduce metastatic disease in breast cancer. It has also been used to protect the hearts of women and men treated with adriamycin (a chemotherapeutic agent).

Dehydroepiandrosterone (DHEA)

Women with low blood levels of DHEA have been shown to have increased risk for breast and ovarian cancers.

DHEA was studied in animals with artificially induced mammary cancer. It reduced the number of animals that acquired the disease, as well as the number of tumors that formed per animal. It was not as effective as the antiestrogen EM-800. Neither of these agents was as effective separately as they were when combined.[43]

Selenium

The Nurses' Health Study reported no association between selenium, as measured in the participants' toenails, and breast cancer risk; however, a more recent study, using the same method of measuring selenium levels, found that lower levels of this mineral tended to be associated with high risk. No such contradictions were reported in studies in which selenium was measured in the blood of the participants. In these studies, low blood levels of selenium were associated with increased incidence of breast cancer.

Vitamin E

The literature consulted on vitamin E reported either a significant inverse association or no association of this vitamin with female cancer risk. In a recent study of 36,265 women and men, women who had low levels of serum vitamin E, as well as low levels of serum selenium, had three times the risk of hormone-related cancers.

Vitamin E emerges from numerous animal, in vitro, and epidemiological investigations as a strong antioxidant, protecting cells' DNA from free radical damage. Free radicals appear to play a major role in the initiation of cancer.

Carotenoids

Carotenoids, the orange pigments in many fruits and vegetables, are precursors for certain forms of vitamin A. Our liver possesses the enzymatic ability to perform the transformation of half of beta carotene, for example, into retinol, a form of vitamin A. Numerous studies have found that dietary carotenoids found in cantaloupe and carrots were protective against breast, cervical, ovarian, and endometrial cancers. Beta carotene, the most often studied carotenoid, showed a diminished protective role when the diet was high in fat.

Several possible mechanisms have been proposed to explain the anticarcinogenic activity of carotenoids: (1) they increase cell differentiation, a property lost by tumor cells; (2) they have antioxidative activity—at low oxygen tensions (the normal condition in tissues) they are effective oxygen radical scavengers; (3) they enhance the immune response—perhaps increasing production of tumor necrosis factor (TNF); (4) they are associated with decreased breast density as observed on mammograms (this association does not exist for vitamin A).

The following foods contain significant amounts of carotenoids (the foods are listed in order of carotenoid content from the high to low): collards, spinach, butternut squash, cantaloupe, watermelon, carrots, beet greens, whole apples, broccoli, acorn squash, apricots, papaya, peaches, oranges (pulp), yellow squash, green peppers, zucchini, blackberries, and avocados.

Folate

Folate, also called folic acid, is one of the B vitamins. It appears to be protective against breast, cervical, and endometrial cancers. Also, a European team recently found a possible role for folate in decreasing ovarian cancer.

Folate appears to be exceptionally beneficial in the treatment of preneoplastic cervical lesions (see Chapter 4), but not in more advanced disease. In fact, one study found that while folate was ineffective in reversing low- to moderate-grade cervical intraepithelial neoplasia (CIN), beta-trans retinoic acid was effective in reversing moderate neoplasia, but not severe CIN.

Curiously, one study found that when low levels of antioxidants coexisted with low levels of folic acid there were significant increases in cervical cancer. This result suggests that the effects of folate on cervical cancer may be improved by the simultaneous administration of antioxidants.

Botanical Medicine

Immune Enhancers

Immune competence, the ability of the immune system to protect from disease, has been advanced as one of the most important factors in preventing and treating female cancers. Studies suggest that an incompetent immune system greatly increases a woman's risk of developing female cancers, whereas, a fully competent immune system appears to significantly reduce her risk. Although tentative, this hypothesis is extremely attractive because there are numerous noninvasive ways of improving immune system function. Among these, plants occupy an honorable position.

Botanicals commonly used as immune enhancers are echinacea, Oregon grape, goldenseal, European mistletoe, angelica, licorice, and ginseng.

Green Tea

A recent review of numerous laboratory studies shows green tea to inhibit effects of carcinogens both in vitro and in vivo. The authors ascribe these results to the polyphenols and other antioxidants found in the green tea.[44] Other plausible mechanisms for the inhibitory effects of green tea on carcinogenesis have been described elsewhere and include increased serum sex-hormone-binding globulin and decreased serum estradiol levels.[45]

Similar results were seen in women with breast cancer. For example, increased consumption of green tea before diagnosis of breast cancer significantly improved the odds of survival and decreased axillary node metastasis and cancer recurrence. In addition, green tea drinking appears to modulate cancer chemotherapy in a positive fashion. The oral administration of green tea to animals enhanced 2.5 times the inhibitory effects of doxorubicin (a chemotherapeutic agent) on tumor growth. These effects were limited to the cancer cells and didn't seem to affect normal tissue, and they extended to ovarian cancer, normally resistant to doxorubicin. The results suggest that drinking green tea may enhance the effects of chemotherapy in women with breast and ovarian cancers.

Exercise

The ability of much-publicized tamoxifen (45 percent reduction in breast cancer recurrences, in a recent study)[46] pales when compared with the effects of concerted regular physical effort. Recent studies of the effects of physical exertion (in job or recreation) on breast cancer risk demonstrate an inverse dose-response relationship between these two parameters that forecast benefits for the prevention of female cancers that exceed those of tamoxifen.

The phrase "inverse dose-response relationship" needs explanation. Inverse simply means that *more* physical exertion translated into *less* cancer incidence. Dose-response, a very important marker for establishing causality between parameters under study, establishes that incremental changes in one parameter produce related one-directional incremental changes in the other.

For example, a study published in the *New England Journal of Medicine* in 1997 showed certain relationships between levels of physical activity and breast cancer risk in pre- and postmenopausal women (see Table 3.4).

As physical exertion behavior increases from sedentary to walking to heavy manual labor, the risk of breast cancer decreases proportionately (inverse dose-response relationship) from 1.00 to 0.82 to 0.48 and from 1.00 to 0.87 to 0.78 in pre- and postmenopausal women, respectively.

Thus, in this study, women who used their muscles the most had the least risk of breast cancer—a reduction of 52 percent for premenopausal and of 22 percent for postmenopausal women.

Consistently physically active women with BMI <22.8 showed a 72 percent reduction in breast cancer risk as compared to sedentary counterparts!

When one adds to these figures the equally remarkable effects of a diet rich in fruits, vegetables, whole grains, and legumes and of a life free from tobacco and alcohol, the risk of female cancer is reduced to levels far below those attained by even the most renowned of drugs.

One of the explanations for this ability of simple changes to achieve superior results is that cancer, recent research suggests, is a core disease, pretty much at the center of life itself. Subtle changes in DNA structure, caused by at present undetectable variations in the chemical soup that bathes our cells and with which they constantly interact, lead to the production of modified chemical messengers that elicit abnormal signals. Derangement gradually sets in. Other undetectable mutations occur. One cell begins to divide clonally in the depths of some tissue. When the tumor is finally detected, the initial cell has divided a billion times and measures about one centimeter (a little more than a quarter of an inch). The process to this state took an average of 30 years. Cancer arises from imbalance that persists, that the body fails to correct, a dysbiosis, a derangement of life processes. In this regard, it is obvious that the undetectable imbalance that produced the cancer (probably a series of genetic mutations in genes that control cell growth and differentiation) cannot be corrected by killing the cancer, since it precedes the tumor. The killing of the cancer (the present conventional approach: "We have to keep our eye on the prize, which is to kill the tumor"[48]) undoubtedly saves and prolongs the life of many individuals with cancer. It does so, however, at the cost of more biological imbalance and, often, increased risk for other cancers.

That cancer treatment and prevention must be approached much more comprehensively than hitherto is a direction now clearly validated by scientific research. As clearly validated is also the fact that nothing can correct biological imbalance and restore chemical equilibrium better than quality nutrition and muscular exertion when they assume central focus in a woman's life.

Miscellaneous

Aspirin

A 1998 study in the *Lancet* reported that women who used one dose of aspirin per week over a period of six months had a decreased risk of ovarian cancer. Although interesting, the results of this study need to be interpreted in the light of negative side effects of regular aspirin intake, such as stomach bleeding. The authors of the study appear to adhere to this cautionary stance as they conclude that the result of their study "cannot yet be regarded as one which would prompt a public health recommendation."[49] We think that there is plenty of evidence suggesting that the use of foods and other means as preventive measures against cancer risk offers greater advantages and does not have untoward side effects.

TABLE 3.4 **Adjusted Relative Risk of Breast Cancer According to Menopausal Status and the Level of Physical Activity**[47]

Level of Physical Activity	Premenopausal Relative Risk	Postmenopausal Relative Risk
Recreational		
Sedentary	1.00	1.00
Moderate	.77	1.00
Regular (>4hr/wk)	.53	.67
Occupational		
Sedentary	1.00	1.00
Walking	.82	.87
Lifting or heavy manual labor	.48	.78

SUGGESTED PLAN FOR THE PREVENTION OF FEMALE CANCERS

Nutrition

General Guidelines

- Vary diet from meal to meal, but do not eat too many varieties at one meal.
- Eat a substantial breakfast.
- Eat slowly and chew your food thoroughly.
- Eliminate eating between meals.
- Separate your meals by at least 5 hours.
- Avoid drinking water with the meal.
- Eat at the same times, or nearly so, every day.
- Use organic foods as much as possible.

Limit intake of

- Meat (replace as much as possible with cold-water fish from unpolluted waters)
- Alcohol (even in small amounts)
- Saturated (animal) fat
- Polyunsaturated fat (corn, safflower, sunflower oils)
- Total dietary fat
- Calories (to maintain ideal body weight)

Daily Specific Suggestions

Vary the kind of following food items from day to day:

- 3–5 servings of fresh fruits
- 3–5 servings of fresh vegetables
- 2–4 servings of whole grains
- 1–2 servings of legumes (with enough soy foods to provide 50–100 mg isoflavones)
- Increase the regular use of nuts, seeds, and olives.

Other specific suggestions

- 1–2 Tbs. of freshly-ground flaxseeds daily
- Limit daily intake of sugars to 1 Tbs.
- 8–10 glasses of pure water (between meals)

Miscellaneous

- Green tea: 1–2 cups daily
- Multi-vitamin/mineral daily (produced from natural sources)
- Consult your health care practitioner about additional supplementation.

Exercise

- Exercise daily in the open air, as much as possible away from pollution.
- Walk/run/bike/row/ski/swim daily for more than 30 minutes at 60–80% capacity. (consult your health care practitioner about your desirable level of exertion).
- Strength train 3 times a week on alternate days.
- Warm up joints before beginning any exercise session.
- Stretch muscles used after each exercise session.

General Suggestions

- Eliminate smoking.
- Avoid pesticides, herbicides, fungicides, and other pollutants.
- If using meat or any other animal products, use hormone and pesticide-free sources.
- Make a practice of expressing your feelings.
- Take a day off each week. Get away from your normal environment. Go to the woods. Do some leisurely walking. Drink pure water throughout the day. Breathe the fresh air. When tired, sit down, read a book, or simply let the silence embrace you. At the regular times, eat simple, natural, unprepared foods like fruits, vegetables, nuts, seeds, olives, bread. Make this day your day, your weekly spiritual, physical, mental, and emotional recreation. Let nothing interfere with it.

〜 *A Word of Caution to the Reader*

In attempting to change habits, perseverance is important. However, perhaps even more important is to avoid rigidity. The implementation of the suggested plan for prevention of female cancers is a task that requires monumental changes in daily habits of life for some of us. Discouragement is a strong possibility as you face this task. It is, therefore, essential that one adopt the program gradually and with moderation. Do not feel guilty for occasional departures from the plan. Just try again. Life is a series of detours and returns. In brief, accept and express yourself, avoid guilt, and cultivate awareness, love, and joy.

CERVICAL DYSPLASIA

 Overview

Over the past four decades, cervical cancer rates have dropped dramatically in most developed countries. It presently ranks third in cancer deaths of American women but remains the leading cause of death from cancer among women in developing countries who do not enjoy the same access to diagnosis and early treatment.[1] This improvement in our health is attributable to the commonly available and annually recommended Pap smear whereby early premalignant lesions can be found and treated, most often with fairly simple office techniques. The incidence varies among ethnic groups—from 4.5 per 100,000 Japanese Americans to 7.2 per 100,000 white women to 12.2 per 100,000 black women, to a high of 18.4 per 100,000 Hispanics. Compare these numbers to a Peruvian incidence of 55 per 100,000 or India's 47 per 100,000.[1] The differences among ethnic groups are due to variance in risk factors, as well as access to preventive care.

Before there is cervical cancer, there is virtually always its precursor, cervical dysplasia, which is 100 percent treatable. The terminology can be off-putting, but if you take the time to wade through the next couple of sentences, you'll see how straightforward and redundant it all is! Another name that dysplasia goes by is cervical intraepithelial neoplasia (CIN for short), which is further subdivided by severity into mild, moderate, or severe, or CIN I, CIN II, and CIN III.[2]

Cervical cancer and dysplasia have long been recognized as sexually transmitted diseases, and over the past decade the causal role of the human papillomavirus (HPV, warts, condyloma) became irrefutable. This association is reflected in yet another, simpler rating system in use since 1988, of simply low- and high-grade lesions or, more specifically, low-grade squamous intraepithelial lesions (low-grade SIL) and high-grade SIL.

About 90 percent of dysplasias have been attributed to concomitant or prior HPV infection.[3] Low-grade SIL now replaces mild dysplasia and CIN I, and includes changes of simple infection with the human papillomavirus. Moderate and severe dysplasia, or CIN II and CIN III, are now combined into high-grade SIL. All these terms are still being used, however.

Progression to cervical cancer increases with severity. Mostly, though, it is a slow-growing process, occurring over about 10 to 15 years in most women who are untreated. The progression varies according to which of the 60 or so subtypes of virus one is infected with. The most aggressive types, HPV 16 and 18, can transform susceptible tissue into cancer in about 18 months, but this is the exception, not the norm. Most women with the human papillomavirus never get dysplasia at all. Some estimate that as many as 70 percent of us are or have been infected in our lifetime. On the other hand, only about 10 women per 100,000 get cervical cancer.

In addition to eliminating dysplasia through treatment, there can be a significant amount of spontaneous regression of even the most severe forms, thanks to our well-functioning immune systems. Spontaneous regression of HPV-CIN I and HPV-CIN II has been documented to be as high as 50 percent to 40 percent respectively, with numbers improving the longer women are followed (usually one to three years). Almost 70 percent resolution of HPV alone was observed.[3] The same study shows about 30 percent regression of even severe dysplasia, but only about 14 percent if there is also HPV found. However, 12 percent of the severe dysplasias progressed to invasive cervical cancer over the same time, which is why mere observation can be dangerous. Women with HPV detected on Pap smear tests progress to dysplasia about 30 percent of the time over three years, compared to about 3 percent of women with normal Paps.[3]

Mild dysplasia is picked up in about 1 percent of women visiting their private gynecologist, and about 14 percent of women who visit designated sexually transmitted disease clinics,[3] so you can see how incidence varies with population. Besides HPV, other risks include early age at first intercourse, giving birth before age 22, cigarette smoking, low socioeconomic status, and possibly, although not conclusively, oral contraceptive use. It is difficult to separate out the effects of sexual activity without barrier protection (condoms or diaphragms) from that conferred by ingesting the hormones. For whatever reason, women who use these barrier methods have less dysplasia.

What exactly is dysplasia? The mucous membrane that covers the cervix changes in adolescence from more bumpy columnar cells, like those that also line the uterus, to squamous cells, like those that line the mouth, through a normal process called metaplasia. Where these two types of cells meet is called the squamocolumnar junction—and it is here that our cells are most susceptible to premalignant transformation. The Pap smear is a sampling of the cells taken from this area and looked at microscopically. Squamous cells make up all of our external body surfaces that are characteristically smooth, like our skin, for example.

The very bottom layer of cells are called basal cells. They are the largest and roundest with the biggest nuclei. As the cells progress toward the surface, they become smaller, flatter, and ultimately lose their nuclei before they get to the top. In mild dysplasia, the basal cell layer is thicker, up to one-third the total thickness of the tissue; in moderate dysplasia, they occupy the bottom and into the middle third; severe dysplasia extends to the top third. Carcinoma "in situ" is not an invasive malignancy, but rather the extension of the immature basal cells to the very top of the thickness. While it does carry a higher risk of conversion to true cancer, it too is completely treatable.

Another Pap smear result you may receive is "atypia"—which is really a kind of fence-sitting call. The cells are not changed enough to warrant the abnormal label, but they are not quite normal either. Usually atypia is either an early abnormal change or evidence of tissue repairing itself, as following a birth or vaginal infection. These Pap tests are usually just repeated, but if atypia persists, the woman should be evaluated.

Evaluation of an abnormal test result is done by a method called colposcopy, which is a lot like using binoculars to view the cervix. The colposcope magnifies the cervix, and white vinegar is applied to make the abnormal areas show up. Tiny biopsies are taken of these areas, a few millimeters at most. These then are examined by the pathologist and graded into mild, moderate, or severe as described above.

I tell women the only way they are going to get cervical cancer is to chain smoke cigarettes, have a dozen boyfriends, and never go to the doctor. While clearly a glib exaggeration, it makes the point that cervical cancer is a sexually transmitted disease, greatly promoted by smoking, but one which usually grows slowly over years from its precursor, dysplasia, and one completely treatable in all of its earliest forms.

❧ Overview of Alternative Treatments

Cervical dysplasia is an excellent example of what preventive medicine can accomplish because, in almost all cases, it is a preventable disease. Through lifestyle habits, dietary factors, nutritional supplementation, and regular Pap smears, most all cases

KEY CONCEPTS

- Cervical dysplasia is a sexually transmitted disease.
- The human papillomavirus (HPV) causes virtually all cases of cervical dysplasia, although most women with HPV never get dysplasia.
- Cervical dysplasia is either low-grade or high-grade and, if left untreated, or if the body is not able to reverse it on its own, will progress to cervical cancer.
- Cervical cancer is a preventable disease.
- Pap smears are screening tests, not diagnostic tests.

PREVENTION CONCEPTS

- Annual Pap smears are the single most important factor in preventing cervical cancer and on detecting earlier grades of cervical dysplasia.
- The use of condoms during intercourse is a significant tool in preventing exposure to HPV and reducing the risk of cervical dysplasia.
- Reduce sexual risk factors: multiple partners, sexual exposure to men who have genital warts, sexual exposure to men sexually exposed to women with genital warts or cervical dysplasia, intercourse prior to age eighteen.
- Avoid smoking.
- Eat a healthy whole foods diet rich in green, yellow, and orange vegetables.
- Use folic acid supplementation if using oral contraceptives.
- HIV-positive women and women who are immune suppressed because of kidney dialysis or immune-suppressive medications are at higher risk for cervical dysplasia and cervical cancer and need more frequent screening.

of cervical dysplasia and its consequence, cervical cancer, could have been avoided.

Natural medicine perspectives on cervical dysplasia are consistent with conventional medicine's understanding that the human papillomavirus causes virtually all cases and that this virus is sexually transmitted. Many cofactors serve as co-carcinogens in the development such as smoking, nutrient deficiencies, possibly oral contraceptives, and immune deficiency. Where natural medicine diverges in its approach is in the attention to advising patients about what they can do about these cofactors. In addition, there are nutrients that can be used in supplement form both to prevent the progression of cervical dysplasia to cervical cancer and reverse dysplasia to normal.

Cervical dysplasia is both a local problem involving the local immunity and health of the cervical tissue and a systemic problem involving general immune health and resistance to viral exposure.

The overriding goals of natural treatments are to reduce exposure to the human papillomavirus, reduce cofactors (smoking), correct nutrient deficiencies specific to the incidence of dysplasias, improve local immune response, strengthen general immune health, and prevent the progression to cervical cancer.

Nutrition

Cervical cancer has been studied in relationship to many dietary factors. In general, diets high in vitamin C, carotenoids, vitamin E, selenium, and other substances found in fruits and vegetables have been found to be protective in at least some studies.[4-8] In the treatment sections of this chapter, I emphasize a vegetarian diet, one that is high in fruits and vegetables, especially yellow-orange ones like carrots, yellow squash, cantaloupe, peaches, corn, etc. In China, where cervical cancer is one of the most common female cancers, consumption of both animal foods (including meat, eggs, and fish) and green vegetables was significantly correlated with a lower death rate from cervical cancer.[9] Even though these studies have shown this dietary correlation, at least one study in the United States among white women showed that risk of cervical dysplasia and cervical cancer was not affected by increased consumption of vegetables, yellow-orange vegetables, fruits, or legumes.[10] Nonetheless, there is enough evidence to support a change in diet to include more of the beneficial vegetables.

Nutritional Supplements

Carotenes

Most people have heard of beta carotene, but maybe they have not heard of all the other carotenes. These include alpha carotene, cryptoxanthin, lutein, xanthein, and lycopene. The studies done to investigate the relationship between beta carotene levels and cervical dysplasia have largely involved either dietary analyses or measurements of plasma levels or levels in the cells of the cervix. Beta carotene deficiency in the cervical cells was concluded to have an etiologic role in the development of cervical dysplasia.[11] It has also been suspected that other carotenes like lycopene, found in tomatoes, are more responsible for an improvement in dysplasia than is beta or the other carotenes.[12] We can also find documentation that a significant decrease in plasma beta carotene levels is found in women with either cervical dysplasia or cancer of the cervix.[13]

My own research study used beta carotene supplementation as one part of a multifactorial supplementation and local treatment protocol. In this study of dysplasias, including cervical atypia, mild, moderate, and severe dysplasia, and carcinoma in situ, I found a high success rate using this combination protocol. Most of the women were given supplements of 150,000 units of mixed natural carotenes daily for a minimum of three months. Of 43 women studied, 38 patients returned to normal, three patients had partial improvements, 2 stayed the same, and none of the patients progressed to a worse state of dysplasia during the course of the natural treatment protocol.[14, 15] The full treatment protocols for each degree of dysplasia are described in the treatment plan section of this chapter.

Overall, my approach has been to recommend increased sources of carotenes in the diet as well as supplementation. More information has come to light recently regarding some of the potential concerns about using beta carotene by itself, especially in women who are at higher risk for lung cancer. Currently, I am avoiding beta carotene supplementation in those women, even though there is enough evidence now to suspect that the problem, if there truly is one, is due to the use of synthetic beta carotene. That is why I only recommend products that have mixed carotenes and natural carotenes (see Resources). Careful label-reading is essential. If it doesn't say "natural," then the product has synthetic beta carotene. The preferred products will state the kind of carotenes used, because manufacturers know it is something that sets their product apart from others and also explains why the cost might be greater.

Do not be alarmed if your skin turns an orange tint when supplementing with high amounts of carotenes. It is merely a pigment and is not a sign of liver toxicity. Carotenes are not toxic. Vitamin A is toxic in high doses, but not carotenes. True jaundice spares the palms and turns the whites of the eye yellow.

Carotenes
Use mixed, natural carotenes,
150,000 IU per day
(See treatment plans; lower doses of 25,000–
50,000 IU may be used for prevention.)

Vitamin A

Dietary vitamin A has been found in some studies to be one of several nutrients that may protect against cervical cancer. It is not always easy to sort out the difference between one nutrient and the other. However, it has been reported that women with lower dietary intakes of total vitamin A are significantly more likely to have severe dysplasia or carcinoma in situ than women with a higher intake of these nutrients.[16]

The use of topical vitamin A was successful in a study of 301 women who received either four consecutive 24-hour applications of retinoid or placebo, followed by two more applications at three and six months applied with a collagen sponge in a cervical cap. Retinoic acid increased the complete regression rate of moderate dysplasia from 27 percent in the placebo group to 43 percent in the treatment group. Women with severe dysplasia failed to respond.[17]

One of the earlier and more well-known studies on topical vitamin A and dysplasia was done at the University of Arizona. As in the above study, all patients were evaluated with Pap smears, colposcopy, and biopsies. In the Arizona study, the vitamin A was delivered to 20 women via a cervical cap that was lined with a collagen sponge. In 50 percent (10/20) of the patients, disease completely disappeared. Of the 10 patients with a complete response, 5 had mild and 5 moderate dysplasia.[18] No difference in response rate was seen in patients with mild and moderate dysplasia; too few patients had severe dysplasia to evaluate. All patients had dysplasia on the ectocervix (external surface of the cervix); no one in the study had dysplasia in the endocervix.

In my own research, vitamin A suppositories were applied topically as part of a multifactorial systemic and local treatment plan. The protocol is described at the end of this chapter.

Vitamin C

The possible role of vitamin C in preventing cervical dysplasia is of special interest because vitamin C is involved in collagen synthesis, detoxifies chemical carcinogens, interferes with the formation of chemical carcinogens, and modulates the immune system. It has been demonstrated in more than one study that there is a significant decrease in vitamin C intake as well as plasma levels of vitamin C in patients with cervical dysplasia.[19, 20]

Vitamin C supplementation has not been studied by itself as a treatment for cervical dysplasia. It was a part of the comprehensive treatment protocol in my research study.

Vitamin C
2,000–6,000 mg per day (See treatment plans; lower doses of 1,000 to 2,000 mg per day may be used for prevention.)

Folic Acid

There have been several studies using folic acid supplementation in women with mild and moderate cervical dysplasia. As is often the case, the conclusion as to its benefit is not crystal clear or consistent in all studies. In one positive study, women with mild or moderate dysplasia received 10 mg daily of folic acid supplementation or placebo for three months. All of these women had used oral contraceptives for at least six months and continued to do so. The results showed significant improvement or normalization of Pap smears and biopsies at the end of the treatment period.[21] In patients with folic acid deficiency, changes can occur in the cells of the cervix called megaloblastic abnormalities. This has been observed more often in women who are taking oral contraceptives. In another study, women taking 10 mg of folic acid daily for three weeks (while continuing oral contraceptives) showed a striking reversion of the megaloblastic changes toward the normal.[22] The regression-to-normal rate was observed to be 20 percent in this study and 100 percent in another.[23] Folic acid supplementation should be considered effective in preventing dysplasia from progressing as well. [19]

When doses as high as 10 mg per day are given, two points must be kept in mind. The first is that most retail natural foods stores have folic acid available only in capsules up to 800 mcg (less that 1 mg). Higher doses of folic acid are available only by prescription from your medical doctor or licensed alternative practitioner. There is a prescription liquid form available where one drop is equal to 5 mg, which proves to be a very cost-effective and efficient way to supplement. The second issue is that with high doses of folic acid, you can mask a vitamin B_{12} anemia. To avoid this, take either a multiple vitamin-mineral, B-complex, or B_{12} supplement along with the daily folic acid.

Folic acid
*2.5–10 mg per day
(See treatment plans; lower doses of 800–2,400 mcg per day may be used for prevention.)*

Botanicals

Traditional herbal medicine includes the use of many plants for systemic immune support. No plants have been studied by themselves in relationship to the human papilloma virus and cervical dysplasia that I am aware of, although many plants are known to act both as immune modulators and to be antiviral in their activity.

This concept of immune support is an important part of preventive medicine as well as in reversing and preventing the progression of cervical dysplasia. Since up to 80 percent of the U.S. sexually active adult population carries the human papillomavirus and less than 5 percent actually have a visible lesion or abnormal Pap smears, it is common sense that most people's bodies have the ability to prevent the virus from causing an actual diseased state. Specifically, their immune systems are doing a better job at keeping them healthy. This is true for women both systemically and in the vagina. There is local immune tissue in the cervical epithelium, and the immune status of this tissue is in part responsible for resistance to the virus.

This is the background logic for both systemic immune support and local immune support. As part of the research protocol, you will see the use of a systemic botanical formula including thuja, echinacea, ligusticum, and goldenseal. You will also notice herbal suppositories containing many traditional herbs for immune support, antiviral activity, and squamous cell repair. These include myrrh, echinacea, usnea, goldenseal, marshmallow root, geranium, and yarrow.

Lifestyle Habits

Sexuality

Early age at first intercourse (before age 18) with unprotected sex and/or multiple heterosexual partners with unprotected sex are associated with an increased risk of cervical dysplasia and cervical cancer. Due to the current belief that most all cases of cervical dysplasia involve HPV and that HPV is transmitted with sexual contact, women can best protect themselves from exposure to the virus by requiring condoms with intercourse. Even if a male partner does not have visible genital warts, he can have nonvisible genital warts and can also carry the virus in the semen. HPV can be transmitted in all of these conditions.

If the partner is female, it is more difficult to contract the virus and cervical dysplasia, but not impossible. Avoiding genital-to-genital contact if the partner has known genital warts, or practicing safer sex may be advisable. It is considered very low risk for the virus alone to be transmitted between women, although it is theoretically possible. Both heterosexual and homosexual women ask about the risk of transmitting or contracting the virus through oral sex. Again, this is theoretically possible, and there are conditions when the wart virus may lodge in the larynx and oral cavity. However, these cases are *extremely* rare and so it is left to each person to make that judgment on her own. If one of the partners is immuno-compromised (HIV-positive, transplant patient, chronic hepatitis), then she is more vulnerable to contracting HPV, and precautions are definitely warranted.

Smoking

Probably the single most important cofactor in the development of cervical dysplasia and cervical cancer is smoking. Smokers have a two- to threefold increase in the incidence of cervical dysplasia.[24] Some studies indicate that the incidence compared to nonsmokers is even greater than that. Nicotine is actually concentrated in the glands of the cervix where it then acts as a carcinogenic compound. Other mechanisms may also contribute. Smoking may alter immune function such that the cervical tissue is more susceptible to the virus, causing abnormal development. Smoking also affects the levels and distribution of ascorbic acid. Ascorbic acid in the cells of the cervix and the vagina and plasma levels of ascorbic acid are reduced in smokers.[25] Cervical dysplasia is yet one more reason to stop smoking.

Oral Contraceptives

Many women and practitioners believe that hormonal contraception is associated with cervical cancer. That is probably because earlier studies suggested that oral contraceptive (OC) use increased the risk of cervical neoplasia, both invasive and precancerous cervical dysplasias.[26] Recently, however, studies that are controlled for sexual history have been reassuring. Three large, well-controlled studies looked at invasive cervical cancer and OC use and did not find statistically significant associations compared with women who never used OCs.[27–29] There was no overall change in risk of invasive cervical cancer; however, one of the three studies (Parazzini) did find a modestly increased risk in long-term OC users. The other two studies failed to find a significantly increased risk of invasive cervical cancer even with long-term OC use. The definition of long-term use is not always consistent, but some define it as more than five years of use. Two other recent studies assessed OC use and risk of cervical dysplasia, and neither of these found any statistically significant associations.[30, 31]

One disturbing finding with OC use is an association with an increase in the incidence of a rare cancer of the cervix called adenocarcinoma. This is

CRITERIA AND GUIDELINES FOR TREATMENT SELECTION

Note: Not all of these treatments are appropriate for self-care. Some of the treatments such as the escharotic treatment need to be administered by a licensed health care practitioner trained in women's health. In addition, not all cases of cervical dysplasia are appropriate for the natural treatment protocols. Licensed practitioners familiar with diagnosing and treating cervical dysplasias should be consulted to assist in making appropriate and safe decisions. For practitioners who will be reading this book, the following criteria may be helpful in determining the appropriate treatment:

I. Criteria for Naturopathic Protocol

1. Cervical atypia.
2. Cervical atypia with condyloma.
3. Low-grade squamous intraepithelial neoplasia: endocervical curettage is negative with a satisfactory colposcopy.
4. High-grade squamous intraepithelial neoplasia: endocervical curettage is negative with a satisfactory colposcopy.
5. Low-grade squamous intraepithelial neoplasia: endocervical curettage is positive with a satisfactory colposcopy, but either the patient is at low risk for more serious disease or at the discretion of the practitioner.
6. High-grade squamous intraepithelial neoplasia: endocervical curettage is positive, with a satisfactory colposcopy, but the patient is at low risk or at the discretion of the practitioner.

(These cases would most likely include only the moderate dysplasia cases. It is possible to treat severe dysplasia and carcinoma in situ in selected cases, but this is definitely a judgment call and should be considered very carefully.)

II. Referrals for Colposcopy with Biopsies

1. Persistent atypical squamous cells on Pap test (two consecutive atypical Pap smears or two in 18 months).
2. Atypical squamous cells of undetermined significance with visible condyloma or a history of condyloma.
3. Low-grade squamous intraepithelial lesions: high-risk patient.
4. Persistent low-grade squamous intraepithelial lesions.
5. High-grade squamous intraepithelial lesions.
6. Atypical glandular cells of undetermined significance; consider endometrial biopsy as well.
7. Adenocarcinoma in situ.
8. Pap smear diagnosis of microinvasion or frank invasion.
9. Endometrial cells present in a postmenopausal woman even if the cells are benign; also needs an endometrial biopsy.
10. A patient that may not follow through with the recommended follow-up Pap smear after an abnormal Pap result.
11. Visible unknown cervical lesion, regardless of the Pap smear test result.
12. Initial exam of a DES daughter.
13. Unexplained or persistent cervical bleeding.
14. Vulvar condyloma with abnormal Pap smear test result.
15. To be used for follow-up after treatment plan is completed, especially in high-grade squamous intraepithelial lesions.

III. Referrals for Conization or LEEP

1. Pap smear results show more than one grade of dysplasia different than that seen on colposcopy or reported on in the biopsy.
2. Biopsy squamous intraepithelial lesions with three to four quadrants involved.
3. Unsatisfactory colposcopy with any degree of squamous intraepithelial lesions on biopsy.
4. The patient may not be a good candidate for more ongoing treatments and the closer follow-up required by alternative treatments.
5. No improvement in pathology with using the initial naturopathic plan or repeated alternate plan.

Practitioner discretions

6. Positive endocervical curettage with any degree of squamous intraepithelial lesions.
7. High-risk patients: Their last Pap test was more than one year previous, a history of genital warts, a history of cervical dysplasia, smokers, multiple sexual partners with lack of safe sex practices.

IV. Referrals for Consideration of Hysterectomy

1. Microinvasive cervical cancer.
2. Frank invasive cervical cancer.
3. Adenocarcinoma.

BOTANICAL FORMULA I		BOTANICAL FORMULA II	
	Ounces		*Ounces*
Red clover	1	Thuja	1
Dandelion root	1½	Echinacea	1½
Licorice root	1	Goldenseal root	½
Goldenseal root	½	Ligusticum	1

SAMPLE TREATMENT FOR ATYPIA

Initial Naturopathic Plan

Topical

Week 1   Vitamin A suppository nightly for
               6 nights*

Week 2   Herbal vaginal suppository nightly for
               6 nights*

Week 3   Vitamin A suppository nightly for
               6 nights

Week 4   Herbal vaginal suppository nightly for
               6 nights

Systemic

Treatment	*Daily dosage*
Folic acid	10 mg
Vitamin C	6 grams
Beta carotene	150,000 IU
Multiple vitamin/mineral	follow label directions
Botanical Formula I	½ tsp, twice daily

Use systemic treatment for 3 months until
follow-up.

Constitutional

Vegetarian diet for 3 months until follow-up.

Alternative Naturopathic Plan

Topical

Week 1   Vitamin A suppository nightly for
               6 nights
               One Vaginal Depletion Pack with
               vitamin A *or* two Vag Pack suppositories

Week 2   Herbal vaginal suppository nightly for
               6 nights
               One Vaginal Depletion Pack with
               vitamin A *or* two Vag Pack suppositories

Week 3   Vitamin A suppository nightly for
               6 nights
               One Vaginal Depletion Pack with
               vitamin A *or* two Vag Pack suppositories

Week 4   Herbal vaginal suppository nightly for
               6 nights
               One Vaginal Depletion Pack with
               vitamin A *or* two Vag Pack suppositories

Systemic

	Daily dosage
Vitamin C	6 grams
Beta carotene	150,000 IU
Folic acid	10 mg for 3 months, then 2.5 mg
Multiple vitamin/mineral	follow label directions
Botanical Formula I	½ tsp, twice daily

Systemic treatment for 3 months until follow-up.

Constitutional

Vegetarian diet for 3 months until follow-up.

* For contents of and resources for vitamin A suppositories,
herbal vaginal suppositories, vag pack suppositories, and
condyloma suppositories see Resources.

ATYPIA

Maintenance Plan for 3 Months (after normal Pap smear)

	Daily dosage
Vitamin C	2 grams
Beta carotene	150,000 IU
Folic acid	2.5 mg
Multiple vitamin/ mineral	follow label directions
Vegetarian diet	

Comments: Findings of atypia on two separate Pap smears within 18 months warrant a colposcopy.

Additional Therapies to Consider

	Daily dosage
Zinc	30 mg
Vitamin E	400 IU
Selenium	400 mcg

Alternating sitz baths* twice per week for 4 weeks

* See Appendix C for directions.

---

a less common variant of squamous cervical cancer. It does appear that the incidence of this disease has increased over the past several decades, while the incidence of invasive squamous cervical cancer has decreased since the pill was introduced. Two recent studies[28, 32] that were relatively large and well-controlled in design found a modest but statistically significant increased risk of invasive cervical adenocarcinoma in OC users with over 12 years of use. However, it is still important to remember that the cause of cervical cancer is the human papillomavirus, a sexually transmitted disease.

Psychological Factors

The association between psychosocial factors and cervical dysplasia has been the subject of several investigations. Significant life stressors were found to be correlated including low coping style, pessimism, a high degree of social alienation, high anxiety states, and feeling threatened.[33, 34] Some of the patients studied were experiencing stress at the time of the assessment, and others had their stressors largely zero to six months prior to assessment. In general, life stressors with negative impact over the previous six months showed a direct, positive association with level of dysplasia, while coping style showed a less prominent effect.

SAMPLE TREATMENT FOR MILD DYSPLASIA (CIN I, LOW-GRADE SIL)

Initial Naturopathic Plan

Topical

Week 1   Vitamin A suppository nightly for 6 nights*

2 Vag Pack suppositories for 1 night

Week 2   Herbal vaginal suppository nightly for 6 nights*

2 Vag Pack suppositories for 1 night

Week 3   Vitamin A suppository (Vital-A) nightly for 6 nights

2 Vag Pack suppositories for 1 night

Week 4   Herbal vaginal suppository (Herbal-C) nightly for 6 nights.

2 "Vag Pack" suppositories for 1 night

Systemic

	Daily dosage
Vitamin C	6 grams
Beta carotene	150,000 IU
Folic acid	10 mg
Multiple vitamin/ mineral	follow label directions
Botanical Formula I	½ tsp, twice daily

Use systemic treatment for 3 months until follow-up Pap smear.

Constitutional

Vegetarian diet for 3 months until follow-up

* See Resources

Alternate Naturopathic Plan

Topical

Escharotic treatment* twice per week for 3 weeks

After the last escharotic treatment:

Week 1   Vitamin A suppository nightly for 6 nights

Week 2   Herbal vaginal suppository nightly for 6 nights

Week 3   Vitamin A suppository nightly for 6 nights

Week 4   Herbal vaginal suppository nightly for 6 nights

Systemic

	Daily dosage
Vitamin C	6 grams
Beta carotene	200,000 IU
Folic acid	10 mg
Multiple vitamin/ mineral	follow label directions
Selenium	400 mcg

Use systemic treatment for 3 months until follow-up.

Constitutional

Vegetarian diet for 3 months until follow-up

* Instructions at end of this chapter

Additional Therapies to Consider

	Daily dosage
Zinc	30 mg
Vitamin E	800 IU
Selenium	400 mcg

Alternating hot and cold sitz baths twice weekly for 4 weeks during suppository routine.

Maintenance Plan for 6–12 Months

	Daily dosage
Vitamin C	2 grams
Beta carotene	150,000 IU
Folic acid	2.5 mg
Multiple vitamin/ mineral	follow label directions
Vegetarian diet	

Sample Treatment for Mild Dysplasia and Condyloma (CIN I, low-grade SIL)

Initial Naturopathic Plan

Local

Escharotic treatment* twice per week for 4 weeks
    After the last escharotic treatment:

Week 1   Vitamin A suppository nightly for
        6 nights[†]

Week 2   Herbal vaginal suppository nightly
        for 6 nights[†]

Week 3   Vitamin A suppository nightly for
        6 nights

Week 4   Herbal vaginal suppository nightly
        for 6 nights

Systemic

	Daily dosage
Vitamin C	6 grams
Beta carotene	150,000 IU
Folic acid	10 mg
Multiple vitamin/ mineral	follow label directions
Lomatium Isolate	5 drops, twice daily
Botanical Formula II	½ tsp, twice daily

Use systemic treatment for 3 months until
follow-up.

Constitutional

Vegetarian diet for 3 months until follow-up

* Instructions at end of this chapter

† See Resources

Alternate Naturopathic Plan

Local

Escharotic treatment twice per week for 5 weeks

After the last escharotic treatment, follow with 4
weeks of suppositories:

Week 1   Vitamin A suppository nightly for
        6 nights

Week 2   Herbal vaginal suppository nightly
        for 6 nights

Week 3   Vitamin A suppository nightly for
        6 nights

Week 4   Herbal vaginal suppository nightly
        for 6 nights

Systemic

	Daily dosage
Vitamin C	6 grams
Beta carotene	200,000 IU
Folic acid	10 mg for 3 months
Multiple vitamin/ mineral	follow label directions
Lomatium Isolate	5 drops, twice daily
Botanical Formula I	½ tsp, twice daily

Use systemic treatment for 3 months until
follow-up.

Constitutional

Vegetarian diet for additional 3 months

Additional Therapies to Consider

Condyloma suppository instead of herbal suppository: Vitamin A, thuja, and lomatium*

Alternating sitz baths twice weekly for 4 weeks
during suppository routine.

	Daily dosage
Zinc	30 mg
Vitamin E	800 IU
Selenium	400 mcg

* See Resources

Maintenance Plan for One Year

	Daily dosage
Vitamin C	3 grams
Beta carotene	150,000 IU
Folic acid	2.5 mg
Multiple vitamin/ mineral	follow label directions
Vegetarian diet	
Lomatium Isolate	5 drops, twice daily
Botanical Formula II	alternating one month on, one month off

Vitamin A and Condyloma suppositories every
other week every third month:

Week 1   Vitamin A suppository nightly for
        6 nights

Week 3   Condyloma suppository nightly for
        6 nights

SAMPLE TREATMENT FOR MODERATE DYSPLASIA (CIN II, HIGH-GRADE SIL)

Initial Naturopathic Plan

Local

Week 1   Vitamin A suppository nightly for
         6 nights*
         2 Vag Pack suppositories for
         1 night*

Week 2   Herbal vaginal suppository nightly
         for 6 nights*
         2 Vag Pack suppositories for 1 night

Week 3   Vitamin A suppository nightly for
         6 nights
         2 Vag Pack suppositories for 1 night

Week 4   Herbal vaginal suppository nightly
         for 6 nights
         2 Vag Pack suppositories for 1 night

Week 5   Vitamin A suppository nightly for
         6 nights
         2 Vag Pack suppositories for 1 night

Week 6   Herbal vaginal suppository nightly
         for 6 nights
         2 Vag Pack suppositories for 1 night

Systemic

	Daily dosage
Folic acid	10 mg
Vitamin C	6 grams
Multiple vitamin/ mineral	follow label directions
Beta carotene	150,000 IU
Botanical Formula I	½ tsp, twice daily

Use systemic treatment for 3 months until
follow-up.

Constitutional

Vegetarian diet for 3 months until follow-up

* See Resources

Alternate Naturopathic Plan

Topical

Escharotic treatment* twice per week for 4 weeks
After the last escharotic treatment:

Week 1   Vitamin A suppository nightly for
         6 nights

Week 2   Herbal vaginal suppository nightly
         for 6 nights

Week 3   Vitamin A suppository nightly for
         6 nights

Week 4   Herbal vaginal suppository nightly
         for 6 nights

Systemic

	Daily dosage
Vitamin C	6 grams
Beta carotene	200,000 IU
Folic acid	10 mg for 3 months
Selenium	400 mcg
Multiple vitamin/ mineral	follow label directions

Use systemic treatment for 3 months until
follow-up.

Constitutional

Vegetarian diet for 3 months until follow-up

* Instructions at end of this chapter

Additional Therapies to Consider

	Daily dosage
Zinc	30 mg
Vitamin E	800 IU
Selenium	400 mcg

Alternating sitz baths twice weekly for 4 weeks
during suppository routine.

Maintenance Plan for One Year

	Daily dosage
Vitamin C	3 grams
Beta carotene	150,000 IU
Folic acid	2.5 mg
Multiple vitamin/ mineral	follow label directions
Vegetarian diet	

SAMPLE TREATMENT FOR MODERATE DYSPLASIA AND CONDYLOMA (CIN II, HIGH-GRADE SIL)

Initial Naturopathic Plan

Local

Escharotic treatment* twice per week for 4 weeks
After the last escharotic treatment:

Week 1	Vitamin A suppository nightly for 6 nights†
Week 2	Herbal vaginal suppository nightly for 6 nights†
Week 3	Vitamin A suppository nightly for 6 nights
Week 4	Herbal vaginal suppository nightly for 6 nights

Systemic

	Daily dosage
Folic acid	10 mg
Vitamin C	6 grams
Beta carotene	150,000 IU
Lomatium Isolate	5 drops, twice daily
Botanical Formula II	½ tsp, twice daily
Multiple vitamin/ mineral	follow label directions

Use systemic treatment for 3 months until follow-up.

Constitutional

Vegetarian diet for 3 months until follow-up

* Instructions at end of this chapter
† See Resources

Alternate Naturopathic Plan

Local

Escharotic treatment twice per week for 5 weeks
After the last escharotic treatment, follow with 4 weeks of suppositories:

Week 1	Vitamin A suppository nightly for 6 nights
Week 2	Condyloma vaginal suppository nightly for 6 nights
Week 3	Vitamin A suppository nightly for 6 nights
Week 4	Condyloma vaginal suppository nightly for 6 nights*

Systemic

	Daily dosage
Vitamin C	6 grams
Beta carotene	200,000 IU
Folic acid	10 mg
Selenium	400 mcg
Multiple vitamin/ mineral	follow label directions
Botanical Formula II	½ tsp, twice daily

Use systemic treatment for 3 months until follow-up.

Constitutional

Vegetarian diet for additional 3 months

* See Resources

Additional Therapies to Consider

	Daily dosage
Zinc	30 mg
Vitamin E	800 IU
Selenium	400 mcg

Alternating sitz baths twice weekly for 4 weeks during suppository routine.

Maintenance Plan for One Year

	Daily dosage
Vitamin C	3 grams
Beta carotene	150,000 IU
Multiple vitamin/ mineral	follow label directions
Folic acid	2.5 mg
Lomatium Isolate	5 drops, twice daily
Botanical Formula II	alternating one month on, one month off

Vitamin A and condyloma suppositories every other week every third month:

Week 1	Vitamin A suppository nightly for 6 nights
Week 3	Condyloma suppository nightly for 6 nights

Vegetarian diet

SAMPLE TREATMENT FOR SEVERE DYSPLASIA (CIN III, HIGH-GRADE SIL)

Initial Naturopathic Plan

Local

Escharotic treatment* twice per week for 5 weeks
After the last escharotic treatment:

Week 1   Vitamin A suppository nightly for
        6 nights†

Week 2   Herbal vaginal suppository nightly
        for 6 nights†

Week 3   Vitamin A suppository nightly for
        6 nights

Week 4   Herbal vaginal suppository nightly
        for 6 nights

Systemic

	Daily dosage
Folic acid	10 mg
Vitamin C	6 grams
Beta carotene	150,000 IU
Multiple vitamin/ mineral	follow label directions
Botanical Formula I	½ tsp, twice daily

Use systemic treatment for 3 months until follow-up.

Constitutional

Vegetarian diet for 3 months until follow-up

* Instructions at end of this chapter
† See Resources

Alternate Naturopathic Plan

Local

Escharotic treatment twice per week for 8 weeks
After the last escharotic treatment, follow with 4 weeks of suppositories:

Week 1   Vitamin A suppository nightly for
        6 nights

Week 2   Herbal vaginal suppository nightly
        for 6 nights

Week 3   Vitamin A suppository nightly for
        6 night

Week 4   Herbal vaginal suppository nightly for
        6 nights

Systemic

	Daily dosage
Vitamin C	6 grams
Beta carotene	200,000 IU
Folic acid	10 mg
Selenium	400 mcg
Multiple vitamin/ mineral	follow label directions
Botanical Formula I	½ tsp, twice daily

Use systemic treatment for 3 months until follow-up.

Constitutional

Vegetarian diet for 3 months until follow-up

Additional Therapies to Consider

	Daily dosage
Zinc	30 mg
Vitamin E	800 IU
Selenium	400 mcg
Pyridoxine	50 mg, 3 times daily

Alternating sitz baths twice weekly for 4 weeks during suppository routine.

Maintenance Plan for One Year

	Daily dosage
Vitamin C	3 grams
Beta carotene	150,000 IU
Folic acid	2.5 mg
Vitamin E	400 IU
Multiple vitamin/ mineral	follow label directions
Botanical Formula I	Alternating one month on, one month off

Vegetarian diet

SAMPLE TREATMENT FOR SEVERE DYSPLASIA AND CONDYLOMA (CIN III, HIGH-GRADE SIL)

Initial Naturopathic Plan

Local

Escharotic treatment* twice per week for 5 weeks
After the last escharotic treatment:

Week 1   Vitamin A suppository nightly for
       6 nights†

Week 2   Herbal vaginal suppository nightly for
       6 nights†

Week 3   Vitamin A suppository nightly for
       6 nights

Week 4   Herbal vaginal suppository nightly for
       6 nights

Systemic

	Daily dosage
Folic acid	10 mg
Vitamin C	6 grams
Beta carotene	180,000 IU
Selenium	400 mcg
Multiple vitamin/ mineral	follow label directions
Lomatium Isolate	5 drops, twice daily
Botanical Formula II	½ tsp, twice daily

Use systemic treatment for 3 months until follow-up.

Constitutional

Vegetarian diet for 3 months until follow-up

* Instructions at end of this chapter

† See Resources

Alternate Naturopathic Plan

Local

Escharotic treatment twice per week for 5 weeks
   After the last escharotic treatment, follow with
   4 weeks of suppositories:

Week 1   Vitamin A suppository nightly for
       6 nights

Week 2   Condyloma vaginal suppository nightly
       for 6 nights

Week 3   Vitamin A suppository nightly for
       6 nights

Week 4   Condyloma vaginal suppository nightly
       for 6 nights*

Systemic

	Daily dosage
Vitamin C	10 grams
Beta carotene	200,000 IU
Folic acid	10 mg
Selenium	400 mcg
Lomatium Isolate	5 drops, twice daily
Botanical Formula II	½ tsp, 4 times daily

Use systemic treatment for 3 months until follow-up.

Constitutional

Vegetarian diet for 3 months until follow-up

* See Resources

Additional Therapies to Consider

	Daily dosage
Zinc	30 mg
Vitamin E	800 IU
Pyridoxine	50 mg

Alternating sitz baths twice weekly for 4 weeks during suppository routine.

Maintenance Plan for One Year

	Daily dosage
Vitamin C	3 grams
Folic acid	10 mg
Beta carotene	150,000 IU
Multiple vitamin/ mineral	follow label directions
Lomatium Isolate	5 drops, twice daily
Botanical Formula II	alternating one month on, one month off.

Vitamin A and condyloma suppository every other week every third month:

Week 1   Vitamin A suppository nightly for
       6 nights

Week 3   Condyloma suppository nightly for
       6 nights

Vegetarian diet

SAMPLE TREATMENT FOR CARCINOMA IN SITU (CIN III, HIGH-GRADE SIL)

Initial Naturopathic Plan

Local

Escharotic treatment* twice per week for 5 weeks
After the last escharotic treatment:

Week 1   Vitamin A suppository nightly for
            6 nights†
Week 2   Herbal vaginal suppository nightly for
            6 nights†
Week 3   Vitamin A suppository nightly for
            6 nights
Week 4   Herbal vaginal suppository nightly for
            6 nights

Systemic

	Daily dosage
Folic acid	10 mg
Vitamin C	6 grams
Beta carotene	180,000 IU
Selenium	400 mcg
Multiple vitamin/ mineral	follow label directions
Botanical Formula I	½ tsp, twice daily

Use systemic treatment for 3 months until follow-up.

Constitutional

Vegetarian diet for 3 months until follow-up

* Instructions at end of this chapter
† See Resources

Alternate Naturopathic Plan

Local

Escharotic treatment twice per week for 8 weeks
After the last escharotic treatment, follow with
4 weeks of suppositories:

Week 1   Vitamin A suppository nightly for
            6 nights
Week 2   Condyloma vaginal suppository nightly
            for 6 nights

Week 3   Vitamin A suppository nightly for
            6 nights
Week 4   Condyloma vaginal suppository nightly
            for 6 nights*

Systemic

	Daily dosage
Vitamin C	10 grams
Beta carotene	200,000 IU
Folic acid	10 mg
Selenium	400 mcg
Multiple vitamin/ mineral	follow label directions
Botanical Formula I	½ tsp, 3–4 times a day

Use systemic treatment for 3 months until follow-up.

Constitutional

Vegetarian diet for 3 months until follow-up
* See Resources

Additional Therapies to Consider

	Daily dosage
Zinc	30 mg
Vitamin E	800 IU
Selenium	400 mcg
Pyridoxine	50 mg, 3 times a day
Lomatium Isolate	5 drops, twice daily

Alternating sitz baths twice weekly for 4 weeks during suppository routine.

Maintenance Plan for One Year

	Daily dosage
Vitamin C	3 grams
Beta carotene	150,000 IU
Folic acid	2.5 mg
Multiple vitamin/ mineral	follow label directions
Vitamin E	400 IU
Botanical Formula I	Alternating one month on, one month off.

Vegetarian diet

CERVICAL ESCHAROTIC TREATMENT INSTRUCTIONS
(For the Practitioner)

1. Before beginning the treatment, prepare the following items:
   a. $ZnCl_2$/Sanguinaria mixture. Take ¼ tsp $ZnCl_2$ solution and place in empty cup. Add ¾ tsp sanguinaria tincture to this same bottle. This will now be the mixture used for one treatment.
   b. One cup distilled water.
   c. ⅛ cup calendula succus.
   d. A cup containing two powdered bromelain capsules or tablets ("Cervical Buft").

2. Insert speculum and visualize the cervix.

3. Blot the cervix dry with large cotton swab or cotton ball on the end of a ring forceps.

4. Dip a large cotton swab into the distilled water and then squeeze out the water with your fingers. Place the damp swab into the bromelain and attempt to thickly cover the face of the cervix with the powder. This will have to be repeated two to four times in order to cover properly. The same step must be done in the endocervical canal with a small cotton tip applicator; i.e., dampen it, place in the bromelain, and apply to endocervix one to three times. Use a new cotton tip applicator each time.

5. Leave the bromelain on the cervix and in the endocervical canal for 15 minutes. A GYN lamp should be placed facing the vagina so that gentle heat is provided during this portion of the treatment.

6. Now remove the bromelain by placing a large cotton swab in the calendula succus and then applying it to the cervix, thus washing off the bromelain. This must also be done with a small cotton tip applicator to the endocervical canal. Be liberal; repeat two to four times. Take a dry large swab and absorb the washings that have pooled in the vagina.

7. Now soak a large swab in the $ZnCl_2$/Sanguinaria mixture that you prepared earlier. Apply this to the cervix once. Repeat this procedure with a small cotton tip applicator and insert in the endocervical canal. Leave on for one minute. If this causes pain, wash the cervix with a small amount of distilled water. Avoid contact of the $ZnCl_2$/Sanguinaria mixture with the vaginal wall.

8. Wash off the $ZnCl_2$/Sanguinaria mixture with swabs of calendula solution. Wash the endocervical canal as well with a cotton tip applicator. Absorb the liquid that has pooled in the vagina with a dry cotton swab.

9. Insert two "Vag Pack" suppositories. Using forceps or other appropriate instruments, attempt to have the suppositories lie lengthwise across the cervix. Instruct the patient to leave the suppositories in place for 24 hours (using small sanitary napkin due to leakage).

10. After the last escharotic treatment:

    Week 1   Vitamin A suppository nightly for 6 nights

    Week 2   Herbal vaginal suppository nightly for 6 nights, or in cases with HPV, use condyloma suppository

    Week 3   Vitamin A suppository nightly for 6 nights

    Week 4   Herbal vaginal or condyloma suppository nightly for 6 nights

Note: The Escharotic Treatment is best done twice a week with two full days between treatments. There is a kit available called the "Cervical Escharotic Treatment Kit" that supplies all materials necessary for 10 treatments. See Resources.

❧ *Conventional Medicine Approach*

The degree of aggression used to combat simple human papillomavirus waxes and wanes through the years, and from provider to provider. Many of us thought for years we could eradicate it, if we only persisted compulsively for long enough, but even this fails in some. While HPV can be dormant for decades, recurrence is always possible. Only close observation through the acute viral stage of cervical infection in low-risk patients is now recommended by some, hoping the patient's immune system will ultimately clear, or make dormant, the infection without transforming the cervical cells to dysplasia. We have seen this work at least as often as not. Others feel HPV should be treated at least on the cervix, like mild dysplasia, and be ablated (removed in some way). Many doctors give patients the option, considering their lifestyle, other risk factors, prior history, and immune system status. Everyone agrees that partners might also be infected, but not all practitioners recommend that they be evaluated to detect tiny, flat, otherwise invisible warts that can be present but not seen with the naked eye. Estimates are that as many as 50–80 percent of male partners are infected when examined with vinegar and magnification to reveal otherwise unseen "subclinical" condyloma.[35]

Most everyone agrees on how to manage any degree of dysplasia, with or without HPV: remove it. The procedures generally used are cryotherapy, a conization with a scalpel, laser ablation, or loop electrosurgical excision procedure, referred to as LEEP. All of them remove the entire transformation zone and allow new cells to replace the old. They all work upward of 90 percent of the time when used correctly.

Cryotherapy is the oldest and cheapest. The cervical tissue is literally frozen solid, to a depth probably about half a centimeter, using concentrated nitrous oxide gas in the office. It cramps but not badly for the three or so minutes it takes,

and then slowly over the next ten days to two weeks the devitalized tissue comes out as a heavy watery discharge. The cervix looks quite new again in about a month. This method works best for small, mild lesions on the surface of the cervix, which are fortunately the most common. The probe is too small to really cover big lesions, and the penetration of the freeze is too uncertain for severe ones.

Conization with laser has been used for many years and is the perfect tool for very large lesions. Unlike cryotherapy, the depth of destruction can be precisely controlled, so much less of the underlying normal tissue need be interrupted. Dysplasia is a very superficial disease, only about 2–4 millimeters at most, so laser really would be the perfect tool if cost were no object. The disadvantage is the huge cost for the machine, and the fact that most hospitals have them only in the operating room. Although only local anesthesia is necessary, the cost of being in that room is high. Consequently, this option is reserved for those with wide areas that can really be treated in no other way. Conization with a surgical scalpel is also done in the operating room.

LEEP is the most commonly used, and one of the great inventions of the past 10 years. LEEP uses an electrocautery tool in the office with local anesthesia. The squamocolumnar junction with the dysplasia is excised in a tiny plug of tissue. Any other areas of abnormality can simply be excised. The beauty of this procedure is that not only can it be done in the office instead of the operating room but it also removes much less of the good tissue under the dysplasia than the old cone biopsy that it has largely replaced. Importantly, LEEP provides a specimen (unlike the laser and cryo), which can be examined pathologically to confirm complete eradication of disease. The tissue regenerates quite rapidly and healthily. There is no effect on fertility or sexuality. All patients are followed with frequent Pap smears for the next two years.

❧ Seeing a Licensed Primary Health Care Practitioner*

Accurate and adequate diagnosis and evaluation is the key to knowing which is the most appropriate treatment for your case. Colposcopy (magnification) and cervical biopsies are the specific diagnostic methods for evaluation. Pap smears are not diagnostic; they are screening tests. When your physician recommends that you need a colposcopy and biopsy, this is good advice. They are not recommending treatment; they are recommending accurate diagnosis.

Decisions regarding treatments such as a LEEP, cone biopsy, or hysterectomy versus one of the natural treatment protocols require a medical history, Pap smear report, colposcopy report, biopsy/pathology report, and a working knowledge of the advantages and disadvantages of each of the treatments. If your conventional practitioner is not aware of the research on the natural treatment protocols or is biased without knowledge, then she is not the most appropriate person to help you make the right decision. Likewise, if your alternative practitioner is not aware of the clinical indications for the conventional treatments as distinguished from the clinical indications for the safety and efficacy of the alternative treatment plan or is biased without knowledge, then she too is not the most appropriate person to help you make the right decision.

---

*N.D. = Naturopathic Doctor; M.D. = Medical Doctor; D.O. = Osteopathic Doctor; N.P. = Nurse Practitioner; P.A. = Physician's Assistant

CHAPTER FIVE

CONTRACEPTION

Overview

Around the same time suffragettes were securing the right to vote, other women, most notably Margaret Sanger, desperately sought to provide women a means of "family limitation,"[1] later called birth control. The political struggle to legitimize contraception and bring it into the medical arena was long and fierce. Sanger was jailed on obscenity charges more than once, and finally fled the country rather than face a trial she ultimately won years later. Any public discussion of reproduction was judged obscene under the prevailing Comstock Law. Although women frequently died in childbirth or struggled to feed families of six to ten or more, they were forbidden information concerning fertility regulation that was literally life-saving. Although diaphragms and condoms gradually became more readily available (the first diaphragms in use in America were smuggled from Europe through Canada by Sanger and her husband), it was not until the Supreme Court decision *Griswald v. Connecticut* in 1966 that married women's rights to access birth control became assured.

While we modern women lament the absence of a perfect fertility control option, the mere fact that the birthrate has fallen so drastically these past 50 years illustrates both women's desire to have fewer children and the efficacy of the combined methods in achieving that goal. Nevertheless, even with the current availability of contraception, fully 57 percent of American pregnancies today are unintended.[2] Perhaps our difficulty with the issue relates to our prudish roots. Safe, effective birth control does exist, although failures, whether human or methodological, occur with each. The best we can do is choose wisely and minimize human error. In addition to natural family planning or fertility awareness methods, there are three general categories—hormonal contraception, barrier contraception, and the intrauterine device. After-the-fact (emergency) "contraception," like the next-day pill and abortion, complete the list of fertility control methods. Sterilization, the most common method of fertility control, is a safe surgical procedure for either men or women. This method is used by about 20 percent[3] of couples; yet it, too, has a failure rate of about 1 in 400.

Fertility Awareness

Many couples successfully rely on this drug-free and device-free method that depends on identifying a woman's fertile periods and abstaining from intercourse during those times. However, to achieve the lowest failure rates of 1–10 percent requires relatively long periods of abstinence each month—at least 10 and up to 20 days—depending on cycle length and predictability. The average pregnancy rate with most who use this method is 20 percent, clearly less than the 85 percent rate experienced with no method at all. More pregnancies result from taking chances during fertile times than from difficulty deciphering the methods.[4] These methods work best when women have a cycle length that is predictable. Ovulation is then predicted most accurately, and intercourse is restricted for the least amount of time. Barrier methods can be combined with the calendar method pretty effectively during the restricted time, but spermicide can obscure the cervical mucus method. All variations of this method assume that an ovulated egg can be fertilized for up to 24 hours, and that sperm can survive in the female reproductive tract for about three but possibly up to seven days.[4] Amazingly, one might become pregnant up to a week after the last intercourse! So much for romantically planning conception location, or dating a pregnancy simply from the timing of sex.

Combining all the methods somewhat probably works the best; for example, many women are quite good at predicting when they ovulate from a variety of symptoms (such as pelvic pain or *mittelschmerz*), but this is an after-the-fact awareness. To successfully avoid pregnancy, you have to be able to predict ovulation about five to seven days in advance or else avoid exposure completely during the first half of the cycle. Obviously noncoital activities are permissible at all times; this method does not require actual abstinence, just avoidance of procreational sex.

Calendar Methods

Rhythm, the oldest of birth control schemes, relies on a 28-day cycle, with ovulation occurring on day 14—exactly midcyle. Intercourse must be avoided for at least three days before and after ovulation—days 11 through 17 at least, and optimally seven days before and for at least four days after. If menses are not this clockwork, another calendar method is useful that takes into account cycle variance. First gather information about cycle length over enough time to figure out how wide is the range. You must know the longest and the shortest cycle length you

experience—day 1 being the first day of menses and the last day being the one just before menses resume. Subtract 20 from the shortest cycle to get the first fertile day (day 4 in a 24-day cycle). Subtract 10 from the longest cycle (day 22 in a 32-day cycle) to get the last fertile day. Thus, a woman with cycles ranging from 25–30 days avoids intercourse days 5 through 20 (25 − 20 = 5, and 30 − 10 = 20). Read through this paragraph two or three times to make sure you understand it.

Cervical Mucus

This method uses the recognition of "fertile mucus" to predict ovulation. It depends on the physiological fact of the presence of slippery thin mucus at the cervical orifice around ovulation. You can easily learn to discern fertile mucus by experimenting with egg white, which resembles fertile mucus. Use your index finger to gather mucus from as close to the uterine opening as possible. Fertile mucus stretches between thumb and index fingers as they are separated, just like raw egg white, without breaking in the middle. Nonfertile mucus is more tacky and breaks apart easily at short distances between the fingers. Experiment with an egg white, then try room temperature butter—you will see the difference. Imagine the sperm swimming easily between long slippery parallel strands of mucus around ovulation, which is thought to ease transport into the uterus and may also modify the sperm so that it is capable of fertilizing the egg. Ovulation usually occurs in the middle or toward the end of the fertile mucus time; thus it is best to determine your length of fertility in advance a few cycles before relying on this method. Obviously semen, spermicides, vaginal creams, or lubricants can adulterate the mucus and make this assessment unreliable. Experiment.

Basal Body Temperature

Basal body temperature is measured by taking one's temperature the very first thing in the morning before getting out of bed and before any activity at all. Wake up, reach over, take the temperature, record.

Plotting these numbers daily over a few months will show a nice pattern of ovulation. The temperature may drop a bit (usually around half a degree) just before ovulation, and then goes up about a degree from there (now half a degree over baseline) just after ovulation. Ovum release probably occurs the day *before* the elevation[3] and persists until the menses. Elevation longer than the expected 12–14 days is presumptive evidence of pregnancy. You can find thermometers that stretch out the couple of degrees around 98 to demonstrate this rise more obviously, but you can use any thermometer if you are willing to precisely plot the points.

❧ *Barrier Methods*

Barrier methods include anything that imposes a barrier between egg and sperm, and include condoms, diaphragm, cervical cap, and any of the spermicides. Only the condom physically prevents contact. The diaphragm and cap are both methods of holding spermicide against the cervix; they don't really keep egg from meeting sperm. Without spermicide, these methods are not greatly effective. Most condoms are impregnated with spermicide as well these days, because of the presumed protection nonoxynol-9 provides against sexually transmitted diseases. Nonoxynol-9 kills gonorrhea, herpes, trichomonas, syphilis, and HIV in vitro,[4] which may or may not translate into reduced transmission of these diseases between humans. Because some organisms, like HIV, are intracellular, they may not get exposed to the spermicide in vivo (i.e., during sexual intercourse) in the same way, and therefore protection may be compromised. In fact, nonoxynol-9 is rather irritating to some, and the irritation may result in vaginal mucosa (the lining of the vagina) that is *more* susceptible to the AIDS virus. It is safe to use nonoxynol-9 unless it irritates you; in that case, don't.

Condoms should obviously be used with any new sexual partner to protect against sexually transmitted diseases. Alone as a method of birth control, they can be highly effective. If used consistently and properly, failure rates are reputed to be as low as 3 percent, although actual use failure rates are closer

to 10 percent. Using condoms with an intravaginal spermicide provides essentially 100 percent safety from pregnancy. This combination is the best over-the-counter method.

Healthy noninfected couples who choose condoms may prefer the comfort of lambskin condoms; the pores of these condoms are too big to protect well against viral-size organisms, but they do just fine in keeping out sperm. Condoms, a very old tried-and-true method, are enjoying a surge in popularity.

Caps and diaphragms work similarly; both hold spermicide against the cervix. Both lessen the likelihood a woman's cervix will be exposed to the wart virus, protecting her against cervical cancer and its precursor, dysplasia. Condoms also bar this virus and are even more protective of the vagina. Caps come in fewer sizes, so not all women can be appropriately fitted, and they are a bit harder to put in correctly. Effectiveness rates with perfect use are as high as 95 percent, although, for some reason, this number is consistently lower in women who have given birth. Caps have the advantage of being able to be left in with ongoing efficacy for as long as 48 hours without the addition of extra spermicide. Diaphragms, on the other hand, are easier to fit and easier to put in. They must be left in for at least six hours after intercourse, and any additional intercourse during that six hours must be preceded by the addition of an applicator of additional spermicide. For those who are sexually active frequently, the cap is much less messy.

❧ *Intrauterine Devices*

Intrauterine devices are in a contraceptive class all by themselves, and may arguably be the most "natural"—or the least invasive—high-efficacy form of birth control. Rumors persist that Cleopatra had a gold ring in her uterus that prevented pregnancy and allowed a healthy, active love life. And, of course, the camel drivers are said to have put small rocks in their camels uteruses to prevent pregnancy on the long roads they traveled. These may just be good stories, but for those women who are good candidates, IUDs are simple, cheap, highly efficacious, reversible, and have a minimal impact on underlying physiological processes. IUDs are used much more commonly in Europe than in the United States, largely because of the persistent fear American women and providers both still harbor from the Dalkon Shield debacle during the 1970s.

Modern IUDs became popular with the introduction of the Lippes Loop (not presently on the market) in the early 1960s, when as many as 10 percent of contracepting women used this method. The failure rate was about 2 percent, although the expulsion rate (coming out with the menstrual flow) was reported as high as 12–20 percent.[3]

While this method can make heavy crampy periods worse, for those women with moderate or light menses it is a method that requires no mess or loss of spontaneity, and can be used effectively for years on end without loss of efficacy. Even at a cost of $200–$300, this is a minimal expense if used over a 10-year period. Women loved the Lippes Loop.

Then came the 1960s, free love, and the Dalkon Shield. Unprotected sex was common. Unfortunately, this device traumatized the cervix on insertion, and the string was made of a material that was a perfect conduit for bacteria to ascend into the uterus. Pelvic inflammatory disease increased dramatically, essentially due to the prevalence of sexually transmitted diseases, and infertility resulted. Yet, the company did not recall the device for 10 years—at least 5 years after the problems were known. The reputation of the IUD was tarnished forever, and a good contraceptive method is all but lost to women who might well benefit from it today.

There are presently very few IUDs in the United States because manufacturers just don't want to take a chance on a device that has become so unpopular. Lippes Loops are still available and in use around the world (although not available in the United States). Copper was added to increase efficacy in the 1980s, which allowed smaller and better-tolerated devices to be used. The Paragard copper T fails less than 1 percent of the time[4] and lasts for at least 10 years. Fertility is unchanged over baseline in women who do not contract sexually transmitted diseases. The device comes in only one size, and so is better tolerated in a uterus that has carried a pregnancy. It can be put in during nursing for ex-

cellent carefree contraception that will not interfere with lactation. The mechanism of action is now fairly well documented as a sterile inflammatory spermicidal response in the endometrial cavity. It is not felt to be an abortifacient. Women (especially mothers) in monogamous relationships who are not at risk for STDs are perfect candidates, if their menses are normal. Unfortunately, many doctors are still unfairly prejudiced about this method, so consulting a family planning clinic may be your best bet if you would like to try an IUD.

Insertion is an office procedure that is a little crampy, but not bad. You should be offered an antibiotic to prevent infection. If you do become pregnant, the IUD should be removed. Pregnancies will be interrupted about half the time. If desired, ultrasound can be used to minimize disruption of a wanted pregnancy.

⊗ Birth Control Pills (BCPs)

Never has there been a more perfect love/hate relationship than that between women and hormonal contraception or birth control pills. In 1951, Margaret Sanger is credited with convincing Gregory Pincus (who ultimately synthesized the first oral contraceptive) that his research in fertilization could be used to create an oral contraceptive. Available for the first time in the 1960s, oral contraceptives were truly a revolutionary medical option for women. Women readily embraced the option of having fewer children, and the dramatically lower birthrate that resulted has persisted, undoubtedly due to the pill's continued widespread use. Women's maternal burden was lifted for the first time in history. It is fascinating to speculate how the newfound sexual freedom for women affected the course of female/male politics. That's the good news.

Unfortunately, the hormonal content—estrogen and progesterone—was much higher than today's pills, and smoking was more common. Both factors affected what is always the course of any new medicine—the downside became obvious only with mass use. It soon became apparent that cardiovascular disease, including heart attacks, strokes, and pulmonary emboli were more frequent in women who used birth control pills. But even though "more frequent," these diseases are still exceedingly rare in the healthy population of young women who are the usual pill takers. It is also true that these risks are dose related, and have fallen measurably as the estrogen and progesterone content of pills has fallen 4 and 10 times respectively since their initial use. The FDA-approved package insert states:

> The information contained in this package insert is principally based on studies carried out in patients who used oral contraceptives with formulations containing 0.05 mg or *higher* of estrogen. The effects of long-term use with lower-dose formulations of both estrogens and progestogens remain to be determined.

The only pills in common use today have 20–40 mcg of estrogen, and only one or two formulations containing 50 mcg are even available. Moreover, the studies documenting these higher risks in the earlier days did not control for other risk factors like smoking, high blood pressure, obesity, and so forth—all known to independently increase a woman's risk. I like the way Felicia Stuart describes pill risk.[4]

> If you were to draw a line 215 meters high (the height of a 70-story building) to represent 100,000 young nonsmoking pill users, and then draw a line beside it to represent the number of pill users in the United States who die each year from complications related to higher-dose pills, that second line would be about 0.5 centimeters high [about one-fifth of an inch]. In comparison, the line representing the number of U.S. women who would die of pregnancy-related problems would be just under 2.5 centimeters high [about an inch]. A line representing maternal mortality in developing countries would be 25 centimeters to 1.5 meters tall [10 inches to just under five feet].

Risks attendant to birth control use must be measured against the risk of the pregnancies they prevent. We are fortunate to live in the time of the lowest maternal mortality ever—and still the risk of oral contraception we all worry about is one-fifth that of pregnancy. If we can manage to avoid pregnancy in other ways, presumably they are safer than the pills.

There are also some other significant health benefits attributable to the pill—for example, an 80 percent reduction in ovarian cancer and a 50 percent reduction in uterine cancer with about a decade of use.[3] Assessing an individual's risk/benefit ratio requires individualization based on health status, family history, and so forth. If one's risk of all cardiovascular disease doubles with use (it does), that sounds worrisome. But if doubling one's risk means going from a risk of 1 in 10,000 to 2 in 10,000, that doesn't sound so bad. This is just another way of looking at the same fact. Incidentally, this risk is not even close to the risk we take driving our car to work or school.

Smokers older than thirty-five, however, should not use the birth control pill. Most other women at higher risk of heart disease, like those with diabetes, hypertension, or elevated cholesterol, should consider other options as well—but even in these conditions, pills are usually safer than an undesired pregnancy. Blood pressure needs to be followed in all pill-takers, and, if elevated significantly by use, another birth control method must be chosen.

Breast Cancer and the Pill

Much attention has been given to the relationship between the pill and breast cancer, and slowly some answers emerge. The Centers for Disease Control (CDC) conducted a study in the 1980s called the "Cancer and Steroid Hormone Study" which looked at nearly 5,000 cases of breast cancer and 5,000 healthy control women and concluded that there was no increased risk of breast cancer in women who had used the pill.[3] Another recently published study[5] concluded that there is a slight, but measurable increase in the incidence of breast cancer for current BCP users and for the first 10 years after stopping the pill. At that point, women revert to their baseline risk, with the risk falling in the interim. A relative risk of 1.24 translates differently in a twenty-year-old woman versus a 40-year-old woman. If the risk of breast cancer at 20 is 1 in 5,000 (or less), then a relative risk of 1.24 increases it to 1 in 4,000. However, if a woman is 40 and the risk of breast cancer is about 1 in 250, a relative risk of 1.24 increases her risk to 1 in 200. Thus, the increase is clearly more significant in an older woman. In this age group, of 1,000 40-year-old women who take the pill, one will contract breast cancer as a consequence. For comparison, in the postmenopausal age group, it is estimated that 1 in 100 women on estrogen replacement will get breast cancer as a consequence. Only about 15 percent of breast cancers occur in women less than age 45,[6] which is when most of us take oral contraceptives. The cancers in former users are generally of a less advanced stage than the cancers of nonusers, and benign breast disease (cysts, fibrosis, breast pain, swelling) is generally improved by BCP use.

Before deciding for or against BCPs, consider your risk for breast cancer (although most women who get breast cancer are not at risk, and most at risk don't get it),[6] whether pregnancy poses a risk, and any other health risks and benefits related to BCP use.

Other Health Benefits of the BCP

Several years ago, the FDA began to require that, in addition to risks, pill manufacturers list benefits, because they are so significant. Some women actually take birth control pills for the health benefits they offer. They protect from uterine and ovarian cancers in the general population, but we aren't sure yet about those in families with a higher incidence. They protect from pregnancy nearly 100 percent of the time, although even with perfect use, there is still about 1 pregnancy in 1,000 women per year, and with common human error, a 2 percent failure rate is more accurate. As a bonus, they reduce heavy, painful menses in everyone.

About 80–90 percent of "functional" ovarian cysts (those related to ovulation, the most common type) are eliminated.[4] Women who suffer from endometriosis can frequently reduce their ongoing pain by suppressing the disease with oral contraceptives. Women with polycystic ovaries and abnormal male pattern hair growth can decrease hair growth with BCPs because they measurably reduce the androgens in these women. Interestingly, because of the thickening in cervical mucus that BCPs induce, it is less likely that women who take them will get pelvic inflammatory disease if they are un-

lucky enough to get gonorrhea or chlamydia in the cervix. Fertility is spared in this way.

Nutritional Supplements for Pill Users

Women on oral contraceptives may want to take nutritional supplementation to adjust for some of the biochemical alterations caused by the pill. Women on BCPs have a higher requirement for folate,[7] and this may be especially true for women who have had cervical dysplasia. The frequent ingestion of the steroids found in the pill depresses levels of riboflavin, pyridoxine, vitamin B_{12}, ascorbic acid, and zinc.[8] Supplement dosages vary, but the following recommendations would be appropriate as a preventive measure.

	Daily Dosage
Folic acid	800 mcg–2.5 mg
Vitamin B_{12}	100–1,000 mcg
Vitamin B_6 (pyridoxine)	50–100 mg
Vitamin B_2 (riboflavin)	5–10 mg
Vitamin C	500–3,000 mg
Zinc	15–45 mg

Additional considerations may include liver support to aid in the metabolism of the steroids. There are many options here, including a lipotropic supplement and herbs such as root or dandelion root, burdock root, and mild thistle.

Side Effects

Many women prefer not to take birth control pills because they see them as an unnatural form of birth control. Others are concerned, rightly so, about some of the issues that have been raised here, but some women just plain don't feel good on them. Some women have bloating, breast tenderness/pain, headaches, mood swings, depression, weight gain, nausea, and breakthrough bleeding. Other women may experience significant, more serious side effects such as complete hair loss, blood clots, high blood pressure, heart attack, and elevated liver enzymes.

There are many kinds of birth control pills today, and fortunately they are significantly lower in dose than they used to be; they caused far greater side effects in the past. The pills vary in their estrogen and progestin dosages, and others have different kinds of estrogens and progestins. A woman may tolerate one pill extremely poorly and another pill very well. The pill is clearly not a natural form of birth control, but for some women the benefits do outweigh the downside. If you do choose to use birth control pills, remember that one of the advantages to barrier methods of contraception (diaphragms, cervical caps, condoms) is the reduced incidence of STDs, especially pelvic inflammatory disease. Condoms are the best method of contraception that also offers a "safer sex" method. Diaphragms and cervical caps do not provide for safer sex, but they will stop sexually transmitted diseases from ascending into the uterus and pelvic region. These are important considerations when choosing your method of contraception.

Other Forms of Hormonal Contraception

All the newer forms of hormonal contraception in the past few years, such as Norplant implants and Depoprovera (Depot medroxyprogesterone acetate or DMPA) injections contain progesterone only. They can have many of the same nuisance side effects of combination pills—weight gain, irritability, depression. They have a lower failure rate, because compliance is not required on a daily basis—only once every three months for the DMPA shot and every five years for the Norplant. Both work by suppressing ovulation to an extent, neither as completely as the combination BCP, but this mechanism is augmented by even thicker cervical mucus that impedes the sperm at the cervix. They aren't as good for cyst suppression because of this. Norplant boasts the lowest systemic hormone dose of any hormonal method, because it is released at such a steady low dose by the implants. As a consequence, menses are irregular in up to 40 percent of women. This tends to improve over time and is tolerated better by some than others.

DMPA, on the other hand, suppresses menses entirely by one year of use, and it can take up to a year for fertility to return. There is concern that inadequate estrogen for bone density protection will be available as a consequence of the obvious estrogen suppression it causes. There is reversible bone loss over time on Depoprovera, and the FDA has required the company to do a prospective study of bone density in users. Because both of these methods are impossible to reverse immediately once they start, I encourage women to try the pill first, unless they can't remember to take a daily pill or can't tolerate the estrogen. I worry about bone loss in young women on DMPA during the years bone is supposed to be made.

Overall, I ask women to assess how they feel on oral hormonal contraceptives. Some women are moody, some are less so. Some women love the regularity of their menses, and their reduced pain; others feel nauseous and bloated. Some love that their acne improves; others fret about breast cancer. Some women feel great, and have low risks for most diseases; for them, the hormones can fit into a healthy life.

∽ *Abortion*

Unfortunately, all methods of birth control can fail. Humans make mistakes. Women have sex against their wills. For all these reasons and more, abortion will always be with us, and it bears a mention in a discussion of fertility control. Women practiced abortion long before they practiced birth control, because that's what was available to them. The last measurable drop in maternal mortality in this country occurred with the legalization of abortion in 1973. Abortion has never been safer, with mortality at 0.25/100,000 women—about 20 times safer than childbirth.[9] Unfortunately, the political fracas around abortion—and the real risk to workers and patients of clinic violence—has made access to abortion more rather than less difficult in recent times. We must recall that the battle for birth control was nearly as emotional; perhaps someday we will see this struggle resolved as well.

In the interim, if you need an abortion, consult your regular provider first. Gynecologists and family doctors need to realize how many women (1.5 million per year) in all walks of life need this service, and how judged they feel by their pro-choice doctors who send them across town to a clinic just because it's easier for the provider. If your gynecologist won't help, go to one of the wonderful women-run and supported clinics that provide the service out of love and respect for women. Their doctors are very experienced with extremely low complication rates. Emergency contraception can be obtained at most clinics as well in the form of three 0.035-mg estrogen birth control pills taken twice, 12 hours apart. When this regimen is taken within 72 hours of unprotected sex, the risk of pregnancy drops 75 percent.

Medical abortion with mifepristone (Ru-486) is on the horizon and offers a method of abortion that aligns much more naturally with our bodies. The medical abortion is just like a miscarriage. There is more bleeding and cramping than a period, but it occurs within a 4- to 24-hour period, and 98 percent of the time avoids surgery all together. The infection rate is lower, and the chance of significant uterine injury, already miniscule, is further lowered. Many women are quite pleased with this method, and if the political obstacles to women's health ever cease, this state of the art in abortion will be available.

CONTRACEPTIVE CHOICE SUMMARY

Birth Control Pill

Advantages:	Continuous contraceptive protection when taken correctly
	Reversible
	Other possible health benefits
Disadvantages:	Has to be taken daily
	Increases the risk of blood clots, heart attack, stroke, especially in smokers over age 35
	Side effects such as nausea, weight gain, headaches
Effectiveness:	99% or greater

Depoprovera Injections

Advantages:	Continuous contraceptive protection for up to 5 years
	Reversible
	Don't need to remember to take a daily pill or use a device
Disadvantages:	Requires a visit to a practitioner for quarterly injections
	Delayed fertility after stopping the injections
	Side effects such as weight change, irregular bleeding
Effectiveness:	99% or greater

Tubal Ligation

Advantages:	Continuous contraceptive protection
Disadvantages:	Permanent
	A surgical procedure
Effectiveness:	99% or greater

Intrauterine Device (IUD)

Advantages:	Continuous contraceptive protection for up to 8 years
	Don't need to remember to take a daily pill or use a device
	Reversible
Disadvantages:	May be expelled by the uterus; may perforate the uterus
	Increases the risk for PID
	May cause heavy bleeding
Effectiveness:	97–99%

Condom (alone)

Advantages:	Easily obtained
	Inexpensive
	Best method for protection against STDs
	Good results when used with a spermicide

Disadvantages: May reduce sexual sensation
Less sexual spontaneity
Condoms may break
Male partner must agree

Effectiveness: 88–98%

Diaphragm (with spermicide)

Advantages: Insert up to 6 hours before
intercourse
Noninvasive method
Inexpensive

Disadvantages: Must leave in for at least 8 hours
after intercourse
Must reapply spermicide for
repeat intercourse
Discomfort
Must be able to insert oneself
Increases the risk of urinary tract
infections

Effectiveness: 82–94%

Cervical Cap

Advantages: Insertion 30 minutes to 48 hours
before intercourse
Inexpensive

Disadvantages: Increased risk of trauma to cervix
and changes in cervical cells
Vaginal odor and discharge
May be uncomfortable to
insert

Effectiveness: 82–94%

Spermicide (alone)

Advantages: Easy to obtain and use
Good results when used with
cervical caps, condoms, or
diaphragms
Inexpensive

Disadvantages: Insertion within half hour of
intercourse
Reapplication necessary for
repeated intercourse
May be messy
Allergies in some people
May increase the risk of urinary
tract infections, especially
with diaphragms

Effectiveness: 79–97%

ENDOMETRIOSIS

 ## *Overview*

Endometriosis, one of the most common yet misunderstood diseases to date, affects 10–15 percent of menstruating women between the ages of 24 and 40 years. In some cases, symptoms begin with the onset of menstruation. In others, symptoms begin later and progressively become worse until menopause. The triad of symptoms include: dysmenorrhea (pain with menses), dyspareunia (pain with vaginal intercourse), and infertility. Acute pain occurs before menses and can last for a day or two during menses or throughout the month. This pain can be a life-disrupting experience, affecting a woman's social relationships, work, school, and well-being. For some women, vomiting, diarrhea, and fainting can occur along with intense labor-like pains. Other pain is described as chronic bearing-down pain and pressure on the lower back and pelvis, sometimes radiating down the legs. Other less common complaints include pain with urination and bowel movements and bleeding from the nose, bladder, and/or bowels. Endometriomas, enlarged areas of ectopic endometrial involvement on the ovaries, are found in two out of three patients with endometriosis.[1]

Early research as to the source of infertility initially led to the concept that endometriosis was a "working woman's disease." Women who delayed pregnancy until later in life and were found to have endometriosis were told to "just get pregnant." Current research does not support this concept. However, research as to increased immune action within the pelvic cavity and the possibility of antibody reactions to sperm has prompted recognition of an immunological basis for endometriosis. Other studies suggest that infertility is a cause of endometriosis, due to the unruptured follicle, rather than a result.[2] Whether endometriosis causes infertility or infertility causes endometriosis, tubal scarring, adhesions, and unruptured follicles are common with women having endometriosis and infertility problems.

The main risk factor for endometriosis is heredity. The likelihood for a mother to also have endometriosis is 8.1 percent and a sister 5.8 percent.[3] Women with menstrual cycles that are shorter in time between cycles and longer in length have been found to be of higher risk for endometriosis.[4] Increased or unbalanced estrogen levels, lack of exercise from early age, high fat diets, and use of intrauterine devices have also been found to be risk factors. Even natural-red hair color was found in one study to be a factor in the development of endometriosis.[5]

Baboons who developed endometriosis in captivity were found to have higher stress levels and a decreased ability to react to stress compared to those in the wild, suggesting a stress factor.[6] Individuals who exercised consistently from an early age reported a decreased risk for endometriosis, while those who began a program later on experienced less painful periods. Although not all women with endometriosis have a childhood history of abuse, a greater number of individuals with adhesions and/or endometriosis have reported abuse in their history.[7] Additional possible risk factors include prenatal exposure to high levels of estrogen and pelvic contamination with menstrual products, although these issues are largely theory, and research is needed.

Physical examination reveals one or more of the following: tenderness of the pelvic area and/or cul-de-sac; enlarged or tender ovaries; a uterus that tips backward and lacks mobility; fixed pelvic structures; and adhesions. Endometrial tissue can be found on surgical scar tissue, in the vagina and on the cervix. Physical examination during the first or second day of menses highlights tender areas in the septum between the rectum and vagina, most likely correlated with deeply infiltrating endometriosis.[8]

An ultrasound study can determine the consistency of the endometriomas. Evidence of endometriosis other than on the ovaries cannot be seen on the ultrasound. Although magnetic resonance imaging (MRI) can detect endometriomas, cost prevents widespread use. A blood test called a CA-125 can have positive results in endometriosis. The problem is that a high CA-125 cannot completely differentiate endometriosis from uterine fibroids, cancerous growths, and normal tissue. High levels of CA-125 have been found in stages III and IV of endometriosis, which are the diagnosis for more advanced endometriosis.[9] The CA-125 test may, however, help in monitoring treatment and progression once endometriosis has been confirmed. However, this test is not used by many practitioners.

Definitive diagnosis of endometriosis can only be accomplished with a biopsy using either of the following two surgical procedures. A laparoscopy is a surgical procedure in which the surgeon inserts a scope through one of two very small pelvic incisions. More invasive, a laparotomy consists of major pelvic and/or abdominal surgery.

Endometrial implants or lesions are known to have similarities to uterine tissue—featuring endometrial glands, endometrial stroma, and hemorrhage into adjacent tissue. Growth of this tissue is thought to be stimulated by estrogen. Therapeutic treatment aimed at manipulating the body's own level of hormones as in menopause or pregnancy has had a positive effect. In some individuals, the implants have their own cycle, with an ebb and flow that differ from the estrogen binding during the menstrual cycle.[10]

Although the most commonly accepted theories of origin today vary and sometimes seem contradictory, they all have their place in holistic approaches to the treatment of endometriosis. The predominant theory first proposed by Sampson in 1927 is the theory of retrograde flow—that during menses, blood flows backward and becomes seeds of implants in the pelvic cavity.[11] This theory and research showing that over 90 percent of menstruating women without endometriosis have retrograde flow have raised questions as to the biochemical and immunological differences causing implantation within the pelvic environment.[12] Endometrial implants from women with endometriosis compared with normal women have been found to be biochemically different.[13] Other studies suggest that cells may only implant in women with altered cell immunity.[14] As implants are found in the nose, lungs, and other organs far from the uterus, transportation through lymphatic channels and blood vessels has been suggested. Still other researchers believe the implants to be of embryological origin, pieces of the uterus left behind during development which, when activated, secrete a chemical causing the nearby capillaries to bleed.[15] Research on baboons with endometriosis suggests activation by environmental toxins that mimic estrogens.[16]

Whether implants are caused by retrograde flow, decreased immune function, or embryological development or are stimulated by high estrogen levels from the environment or within the body, the worsening of symptoms prompts individuals to seek medical help. Pain and the extent of the disease correlate poorly. Women with fixed ovaries and large endometriomas may only report mild discomfort, while those with visibly smaller lesions may report severe and chronic pain. Upon surgery, these lesions are found to extend more deeply; they are possibly more influenced by circulating estrogens.[17] Research has found that the severity of symptoms is correlated with the depth of the lesions rather than the number of lesions.[18]

Studies on the immunological functions of baboons with spontaneous (noninduced) endometriosis have led researchers to find a correlation between suppressed immunity and a higher number and greater area of lesions.[19] Both types of immunity, cell mediated and humoral, have been implicated in endometriosis with immunological defects present even in the mildest forms of the disease.[20] Macrophages that scavenge other microbes, debris, and aberrant tissue are found in greater numbers in the early stages of endometriosis.[21] This increase in macrophage activity may correlate with decreased fertility and possible reaction to sperm perceived by the woman's body as "foreign."[22] In the peritoneal fluid of women with severe endometriosis, natural killer cell activity has been found to be suppressed.[23, 24] Natural killer cells release cell toxins and thus help keep tumor and other abnormal cells in check. By a decrease in natural killer cells, the immune defense against the growth of tissue is decreased. Interestingly, studies suggest a correlation between high estradiol levels and decreased killer cell activity.[25]

Humoral immunity involves antibodies, more specifically immunoglobulins, that are produced by B-cells, activated macrophages, and endometrial implants. These immunoglobulins provide protection to the body by their attachment to foreign substances called antigens. Patients with endometriosis have been found to have high levels of immunoglobulins IgG and IgM when compared with normal controls.[26] Higher than normal amounts of immunoglobulins cause destruction of the body's own tissue as seen in autoimmune conditions. Evidence of high levels of autoantibodies against ovary and endometrial cells is consistent with the finding of individuals who have both endometriosis and autoimmune diseases.[27, 28]

As mentioned earlier, irregular cycles are common among women with endometriosis. Anovulatory cycles, premenstrual spotting, luteal phase defects, and salivary progesterone secretion are altered in women with endometriosis.[29] Since higher estrogen levels are implicated in endometriosis, it is not surprising that heavy smokers have a decreased risk for endometriosis if they began smoking earlier in life. (Smoking is known to decrease estrogen levels.)[30] In addition, an increased body fat placement indicative of increased estrogen levels was also found to be correlated with a higher incidence of endometriosis.[31] Since estrogens are known to stimulate endometrial implants, women on hormone replacement therapy have been known to experience a recurrence of endometriosis not unlike others who are not on hormone therapy.[32]

Current research suggests a connection between the immune and endocrine systems and environmental estrogens that is being linked to endometriosis.[33] The presence and severity of endometriosis in Rhesus monkeys exposed to long-term high dioxin (TCDD) levels have helped shape the concept of environmental endocrine disrupters.[34] Researchers for the last 50 years have been reporting that chemicals from the environment—effective because they disrupt the reproductive cycles of unwanted pests—are now affecting the reproduction of other animals such as mink, sheep, alligators, and birds. Evidence for higher concentrations of dioxin in women with endometriosis is beginning to surface.[35] Substances that have been shown to have estrogenic effects in the body include polychlorinated biphenyls (PCBs), weed killers, substances that line cans, plastics, detergents, and household cleaners.[36]

The liver has the enormous task of breaking down estrogen and secreting metabolites through the bile into the large intestine. Whether hormones are produced naturally within the body, are provided through medication, or enter the body as substances from the environment that mimic estrogen, optimal functioning of the liver is imperative in maintaining a healthy balance.[37] Inappropriate breakdown of estrogen can result in local liver damage, continual recycling of estrogens, and alterations in immune function. Since the liver is involved in breaking down 80–90 percent of the hormones in the body, it follows that optimal liver function can be of benefit in treatment.

Containing different types of microflora or gut organisms, the large intestine has a unique role in the excretion and recycling of estrogen. The liver inactivates estrogen by attaching a bond between glucuronic acid and the estrogen molecule and excreting this substance with the bile. Some "unfriendly" bacteria in the large intestine, however, secrete an enzyme called beta-glucaronidase that breaks down these bonds, releasing a strong estrogen that is then recycled back through the body. In order to produce the enzyme beta-glucaronidase, these bacteria feed on fat taken in by the body. However, the balance can be restored by greater numbers of the "friendly" bacteria that feed on fiber and crowd out the "unfriendly" bacteria. With a balance of the "friendly" bacteria in the large intestine, a higher amount of inactivated estrogen metabolites leave the body through the large intestine, preventing their reactivation and movement back through the body.[38]

Endometriosis is a complex disease with a variety of interconnecting influences. Enhancing the immune system, the endocrine system, and the liver's detoxification of hormones, and providing optimal health in the large intestine represent innovative and effective approaches to the treatment of endometriosis. Considering the long-term consequences of endometriosis—those of pain, disability, and disruption in personal, family, and work activities—innovative approaches that treat the whole body and remove the cause promise a light at the end of the tunnel.

✺ Overview of Alternative Treatments

While analgesics and estrogen-blockers temporarily relieve symptoms, the need for a long-term definitive treatment that involves removal of the cause is imperative. A systemic approach to treatment that takes into consideration a multifaceted cause with long-term and acute symptomatic relief is the goal of alternative therapy. While late-stage endometriosis may only be addressed by radical surgery, early treatment, in the form of stimulation of the body's inherent ability to heal through enhancing the immune system, balancing hormones, and aiding in the liver's ability to break down environmental and naturally occurring estrogen, is worthy of consideration.

KEY CONCEPTS

- A gynecological checkup is imperative with any type of pelvic pain to rule out any pelvic or abdominal abnormality.
- Provide symptom relief for acute pain.
- Provide removal of cause (endocrine, immune, liver).
- Create a plan for treatment of the chronic problem.
- Optimize nutritional intake and delete environmental toxins.

PREVENTION

- Nutrition from whole foods.
- Regular exercise.
- Avoid pesticides.
- Drink filtered water.
- Maintain good digestion and regular bowel habits.
- Avoid alcohol.

Certain foods and supplements aid in enhancing the body's own ability to mount a natural immune response. Optimal liver function involves enhancing the liver's ability to detoxify hormones, excess medicines, and toxins through two main phases. Individuals who have decreased function of the first pathway continue to recycle hormones, toxins, and other products harmful to the body. If the second detoxification pathway is dysfunctional, the metabolic products of the first pathway build up and can become even more toxic, decreasing immune response and accumulating as oxygen free radicals. These metabolites can cause tissue injury and formation of adhesions.[39] Healthy elimination of broken-down metabolites assures that the body doesn't get a chance to reabsorb products that are ready for release from it.

Nutrition, exercise, and healthy lifestyle practices play a preventive role in providing immune support and a healthy body's response to added stressors and imbalances of hormones. Women who exercise and eat less fat and sugar produce less estrogen. Vegetarian women excrete two to three times more estrogen in their feces and have half as much mean plasma level of unconjugated estrone and estradiol than meat-eaters.[40] Additional approaches in the area of mind-body medicine recognize that belief systems and emotional health affect optimal physical health.

Nutrition

Foods high in fiber are associated with optimal transit time in the intestines and an optimal balance of friendly microorganisms within the large intestine.[41] These microorganisms, better known as gut flora, crowd out the other types of flora that deconjugate estrogens and allow estrogens to recycle back through the body. Studies suggest that an intake of less protein and high fiber or a vegetarian diet lead to a decrease of biologically active unconjugated estrogens in blood plasma.[40] While higher protein diets are found to provide enzymes for the detoxification pathways of estradiol,[42] vegetarian diets are of greater value due to their lower fat content. Animal protein diets, especially red meat, contain large amounts of arachidonic acid, which promotes inflammatory prostaglandins and thus inflammation and pain. By enhancing your diet with vegetable protein, soy, almond and other nut butters, and salmon, you tip the inflammatory pathway toward anti-inflammatory prostaglandins that inhibit tumor growth—and possibly endometrial growth.

By increasing intake of vegetables, specifically those that enhance liver function, the buildup of toxins and metabolites that produce cell damage is prevented. Liver-friendly foods to increase are carrots, kale, and the cabbage family vegetables due to their known help in phase two of the liver's detoxification pathway. Indole-3-carbinol, found in broccoli, Brussels sprouts, cabbage, and cauliflower, favors the less active metabolite of estrogen.[43] Other liver-cleansing foods include beets, carrots, artichokes, lemons, dandelion greens, watercress, and burdock root. Onions, garlic, and leeks contain organosulfur compounds that enhance the immune system and induce enzymes that detoxify in the liver. In addition, they contain the bioflavonoid

quercitin, which is known to stimulate the immune response, protect against oxidation, block the inflammatory response, and inhibit tumor growth.[44] By eating as many of your vegetables in as organic a form as possible, you cut down on your intake of pesticides that may also mimic estrogen.

Use seasonings such as turmeric (curcumin) that protect against environmental carcinogens, decrease inflammation, and increase bile secretion. Ginger is helpful with joint stiffness and other types of inflammation—and helps with liver detoxification. Adding a tablespoon of milk thistle seeds each day that have been soaked and ground can also help with liver function. Grind a tablespoon of fresh flaxseeds and place on cereals or salads. The increase in lignans from these seeds aids in providing fiber as well as an oil that helps in the anti-inflammatory pathway. Seasoning with fucus (a seaweed) helps stimulate T-cell production and absorb toxins.[45]

Foods to omit or decrease include sugar, caffeine, dairy, red meat, and alcohol. Sugar is known to increase estrogen levels in men; presumably the effect is similar in women.[46] Endometriosis is found to be correlated with caffeine consumption. Women consuming 5–7 grams of caffeine per month had a 1.2 times incidence of endometriosis, while those consuming over 7 grams had a 1.6 times increase.[47] One cup of coffee contains 120 mg of caffeine; one cup of black tea contains 60 mg; one cup of decaffeinated contains about two mg of caffeine. The EPA estimates that 90 percent of human dioxin exposure is through food, primarily meat and dairy products.[48] Cheese, milk, and cottage cheese cause the lipid pathway to be tipped toward prostaglandins and leukotrienes that cause inflammation, smooth muscle contraction, and vascular constriction. Alcohol use depletes stores of B vitamins in the liver and also has estrogenic effects on the body.

Nutritional Supplements
Vitamin C

Studies with the use of vitamin C show increase in cellular immunity, and decreases in autoimmune progression and fatigue.[49] In addition, vitamin C

DIETARY RECOMMENDATIONS

- High fiber.
- High protein vegetarian diet.
- Increase intake of vegetables.
- Use turmeric, ginger, milk thistle, and flaxseeds.
- Omit or decrease alcohol, dairy, red meat, sugar, and caffeine.

---

enhances immunity and decreases capillary fragility and tumor growth, all of which are involved at various levels in women with endometriosis. Studies on autoimmune progression indicate the effectiveness of high levels of vitamin C.[50]

Vitamin C

6–10 grams in divided doses daily, starting with 1,000 mg a day, increasing to bowel tolerance. Decrease amount if diarrhea occurs.

Beta Carotene

Beta carotene helps enhance immunity. Studies show that use of beta carotene increased T-cell levels after seven days.[51] In addition, beta carotene was shown to be protective against early stages of tumor growth.[52] Impairment of phagocytosis is seen in vitamin A–deficient states.[53] Although vitamin A was used in the latter study, one-third of beta carotene is converted to the active form of vitamin A, that of retinol. Additional studies suggest that immune function is due to carotenoids rather than vitamin A.[54]

Beta carotene

50,000–150,000 IU daily

Vitamin E

Vitamin E helps to correct abnormal progesterone/estradiol ratios in patients with mammary dysplasia (increased growth of cells).[55] Since parallels have been found between abnormal tumor growth in can-cer and abnormal growth of lesions in endometriosis, vitamin E supplementation may be advantageous. While secondary dysmenorrhea is usually involved with endometriosis, studies on the use of vitamin E with primary dysmenorrhea[56] show benefit perhaps through the inhibition of the arachidonic lipid pathway. Inhibiting the arachidonic pathway helps prevent the release of chemicals that would normally cause edema, inflammation, and smooth muscle contraction.

Vitamin E

400–800 IU daily

Essential Fatty Acids

Gamma linoleic acid (borage, black currant, evening primrose oils) and alpha-linolenic acid (flaxseed, canola, pumpkin seed, soy, walnut oils) help decrease the inflammatory response on the tissue level through pathways that produce prostaglandins in the body. Depending on one of three main pathways of prostaglandin production, the effects can be helpful or harmful to the body. Animal fats produce a pathway of prostaglandin products that increase inflammation, muscle constriction, and edema. However, gamma linoleic acid and alpha linolenic acid produce the opposite effects. These fatty acids taken in supplemental form can produce the prostaglandins that are involved in inhibiting tumor growth, dilating smooth muscle, and decreasing inflammation.[57] Since endometriosis implants are thought to secrete chemicals that cause leakage from nearby capillary beds, decreasing the permeability of these vessels could help control the tissue destruction and adhesions, decreasing irritation in the pelvis.

Alpha linolenic or Gamma linoleic acid

300 mg daily

B Vitamins

B vitamins help the liver to inactivate estrogen. Studies suggest that supplementation of B vitamins may cause the liver to become more efficient in processing estrogen.[58]

B vitamins
50–100 mg B vitamin complex;
B-6 should not exceed 200 mg daily

Selenium

Selenium aids in the synthesis of antioxidant enzymes responsible for detoxification reactions within the liver. In addition, selenium stimulates white blood cells and thymus function.[59] Individuals with decreased selenium levels have sub-optimal cell-mediated immunity, decreased numbers of T-cells, and associated inflammation.[60]

Selenium
200–400 mcg daily

Lipotropics

Lipotropics aid in promoting liver function and detoxification reactions. Supplements that contain choline (a B vitamin), betaine, and methionine promote the flow of fat and bile (containing estrogen metabolites) from the liver out through the large intestine.[61]

Lipotropics
1,000 mg choline and 1,000 mg methionine
or cysteine, 3 times a day

Botanicals

Herbal Medicines for Pain Relief

The herbs appropriate for acute pain relief in endometriosis are the same herbs used for menstrual cramps. Valerian, crampbark, black cohosh, and other helpful herbs are discussed in Chapter 11.

Traditional Herbal Therapies

Chaste tree (*Vitex agnus castus*) has traditionally been used as a treatment for hormone imbalances in women. Through action on the pituitary gland, chaste tree has a progesterone effect by increasing leuteinizing hormone (LH). Useful for fibroids, premenstrual syndrome, perimenopause, and various menstrual cycle disorders, it also has an indication in endometriosis, perhaps because less estrogen is available to stimulate endometrial tissue.[62]

Dandelion root (*Taraxacum officinale*) is one of nature's most detoxifying herbs. It works principally on the liver and gallbladder to help remove waste products. By supporting the liver, excessive estrogens and toxins can be deactivated. Researchers in Japan have found a link between dandelion and antitumor activity.[63] In addition, dandelion leaf contains vitamins A, C, and K and calcium, as well as choline, a lipotropic substance.

Prickly ash (*Xanthoxylum americanum*) is known for its specific action on capillary engorgement and sluggish circulation. Through its stimulation of blood flow throughout the body, prickly ash helps enhance the transport of oxygen and nutrients in addition to the removal of cellular waste products. For women with pelvic congestion, this herb enhances circulation throughout the pelvis.

Motherwort (*Leonurus cardiaca*) is antispasmodic and gently soothes the nerves. As women with endometriosis generally experience uterine cramps and pain, motherwort is useful in promoting relaxation during times of extreme "bearing down" pain in the uterus and other regions.[64] As a mild sedative, motherwort helps with the needed rest during menstrual cramps.

Herbal tincture for chronic treatment
Chaste tree, dandelion, prickly ash, motherwort
combination: ½ tsp, 3 times daily for 3 months

Turska's Formula

Turska's formula is a favorite old naturopathic treatment for decreasing aberrant cancer cell growth. A tincture of this formula is useful in endometriosis due to the similarities of cancer to cell growth found in the pelvis. This formula contains monkshood (*Aconite napellus*), yellow jessamine (*Gelsemium sempervirens*), bryony (*Bryonia alba*), and poke root (*Phytolacca americana*). Monkshood and yellow jessamine contain various alkaloids that have been known to disrupt the assembly of micro-tubules which eventually help in the formation of cells that differentiate and give rise to connective tissues, blood, lymphatics, bone, and cartilage. Quite possibly, these herbal alkaloids interfere with the induction of abnormal ectopic lesions within the pelvis (consistent with the theory of cells left be-hind in embryonic development). Bryonia is also known to provide antitumor effects. Poke root con-tains glycoproteins known to stimulate lymphocyte transformation for immune enhancement. Poke root also has anti-inflammatory properties. Due to its potential toxicity, however, this tincture can only be provided by a licensed health professional.

Turska's formula (see Resources)
5 drops 3 times daily

Natural Progesterone

Progesterone has been known to modify the action of estradiol by decreasing the retention of recep-tors, causing a fall in serum estradiol levels. Women without enough progesterone are unable to bal-ance out estrogen, which can then lead to problems that result from a relative excess of estrogen. In ad-dition, progesterone has the effect of sedating painful uterine contractions. Chapter 11 discusses in more detail how progesterone inhibits uterine contractions and reduces pain. It is possible that this uterine sedative effect extends to pain relief in the pelvic region in general. I have not used natural progesterone alone as a treatment for endometrio-sis, but it has been my observation that proges-terone as part of a comprehensive treatment plan is an important piece of the puzzle.

Natural progesterone creams can be applied in various regimens. For some women I recommend ¼ tsp two times a day for three weeks on and the week of menses off. Other women just need to use it the week before their menses is due. Still other cases require higher doses of natural oral mi-cronized progesterone in a cyclic dosing pattern.

SAMPLE TREATMENT PLAN FOR ENDOMETRIOSIS

Nutrition
- Increase
  Veggies (especially cauliflower, Brussels sprouts, carrots)
  Protein (tofu, beans, salmon, soy nuts, low amounts of turkey and chicken)
  Fiber (whole grain breads, rice, raw vegetables, flax seeds)
- Decrease or eliminate
  All animal fats
  All foods containing **sugar, caffeine, chocolate, alcohol**
- Avoid pesticides and heating food in plastic containers
- Drink filtered water

Daily Supplements
- Vitamin C: 6–10 grams
- Vitamin E: 400–800 IU
- Gamma linoleic or alpha linolenic oil: 300 mg
- Beta carotene: 50,000–150,000 IU
- Selenium: 200–400 mcg
- Lipotropics: 2–4 capsules

Botanicals
- **Acute tincture:** ½–1 tsp every 2–4 hours for acute pelvic pain
  Black cohosh 1 oz
  Wild yam   1 oz
  Cramp bark   1 oz
  Valerian   1 oz
- **Chronic tincture:** ½ tsp, 3 times a day
  Chaste tree   1 oz
  Dandelion   1 oz
  Prickly ash   1 oz
  Motherwort   1 oz
- **Turska's formula:** 5 drops, 3 times daily

Progesterone cream

Option #1	Day 1–7	no cream
	Day 8–28	¼–½ tsp, twice a day
Option #2	Day 1–14	no cream
	Day 15–28	¼–½ tsp, twice a day
Option #3	Day 1–21	no cream
	Day 22–28	¼–½ tsp, twice a day

⪼ *Conventional Medicine Approach*

Although appropriate treatment varies from case to case, initial treatment usually involves the use of nonsteroidal anti-inflammatory drugs such as acetaminophen and aspirin. As symptoms progress, patients usually resort to prescription analgesics and/or hormones. Since estrogen is known to stimulate the growth of endometriosis, treatment is aimed at suppression of estrogen synthesis. By achieving states of pseudo-pregnancy (through birth control pills) or pseudo-menopause (through cessation of the body's own production of estrogen and progesterone), women have found significant symptom relief. Benefit from birth control pills is thought to be due to reduced menstrual bleeding, anovulation, and lesion regression. However, stimulation of the lesion does occur, possibly due to a decrease in concentration of progesterone receptor sites in the lesions.[65]

In the past, danazol was regarded as a highly effective drug due to its suppression of the pituitary and inhibition of estrogen and adrenal hormone production. Relief quite possibly is due to action on reducing endometriosis associated with autoimmune abnormalities.[66] However, male hair pattern growth, irreversible low voice, hot flashes, depression, weight gain, acne, reduced breast size, muscle cramps, fatigue, and other symptoms have caused danazol to become a less popular alternative, and, for the most part, it has fallen out of use.

Prescription drugs called gonadotropin-releasing hormone agonists such as Lupron are used to induce a menopausal state. Upon stimulation of the receptors of the brain by these hormones, a decrease in production of LH (luteinizing hormone) and FSH (follicle -stimulating hormone) is achieved causing the individual to achieve a low estrogen state within two weeks. This state causes dramatic relief of symptoms within two to three months. However, side effects similar to those accompanying natural menopause (insomnia, hot flashes, vaginal dryness, osteoporosis) do occur. Current "add-back therapy" with low-dose estrogen without progestin or low-dose estrogen plus progesterone might reduce these risks while maintaining suppression of the lesions. After the Lupron is discontinued, recurrence of endometriosis frequently occurs.

Treatments with progestins help endometrial tissue to atrophy. However, side effects include nausea, weight gain, fluid retention, breakthrough bleeding, and sometimes depression. Progestins do not cause the disappearance of endometriosis lesions but do provide significant pain relief.[67]

Combinations of estrogen and progestin such as are found in low-dose birth control pills suppress FSH and LH. Mild to moderate pelvic pain relief is achieved because the body's own estrogen production is decreased. In addition, since the volume of menstrual flow is also decreased, theoretically less blood is available for reflux into the pelvic cavity.

Current research shows promising results in use of the antiprogesterone RU-486 due to the regression of endometriosis and possible absence of significant side effects.[68] The use of medications that enhance the immune system is also being studied.

Laparoscopy continues to be the diagnostic procedure of choice to definitively diagnose endometriosis. Laparoscopic surgery has the advantage of extensive use of microscopic imaging so that surgeons can view lesions in greater detail. In addition, laparoscopy allows for a shorter recuperation time when compared to a laparotomy. During a laparotomy the surgeon makes a larger incision in the abdomen, allowing for larger endometriomas to be excised. Recovery takes longer with a laparotomy, but it can be a better option depending on the size of the lesions.

Definitive surgery has produced cure for some individuals, while it has proved to be disappointing to others. Whether laparotomy or laparoscopy, surgical treatment varies as to type of surgery (conservative versus radical) and technique (burning by laser or excision by electrocautery). Surgery that is conservative removes the endometrial lesions and/or endometriomas while leaving the uterus and ovaries intact. Recurrence rates vary from 5–20 percent per year with a rate of 40 percent after five years (74 percent for severe cases).[69] Differences in recurrence rates with surgery may be due to the method of endometriosis implant removal and the skill of the surgeon.[70] Laser surgery is able to penetrate deeply but without the possibility of biopsy, while excision by electrocautery allows for meticulous biopsy but takes time and additional effort. The knowledge and experience of the surgeon are important in the identification of implants since color, consistency, appearance, and location of implants can be variable. In addition, some surgeons remove the clear peritoneal covering because they believe that implants reside in this tissue.

Radical surgery consists of removing implants, ovaries, and uterus. While surgery removes implants that adhere to the ovaries, uterus, and other pelvic organs, the effects of ovary removal and the resulting abrupt cessation of hormone production have to be taken into consideration. While beneficial for some individuals, medical or surgical management is not effective in all circumstances.[71]

❧ Seeing a Licensed Primary Health Care Practitioner*

As with any pain of unknown origin, a licensed primary health care practitioner should be consulted to rule out other causes of pain before extensive use of analgesic medications, botanical formulas, or supplements. The cultural bias that menstrual periods are supposed to be painful—as well as a reluctance to seek help due to past abuse, trauma, or fear—can be a detriment to healing. Although the norm is changing, in the past many women with endometriosis were

*N.D. = Naturopathic Doctor; M.D. = Medical Doctor; D.O. = Osteopathic Doctor; N.P. = Nurse Practitioner; P.A. = Physician's Assistant

told that the pain was "in their head" and psychosomatic. An increased understanding of the pain, pattern of symptoms, and loss of quality of life for those who experience endometriosis has drawn attention and research to this disruptive problem.

Abnormal bleeding, pain that increases in intensity, continued pain with or without menses, lower back pain, pain with urination, bowel movements, and vaginal intercourse should be brought to the attention of your health care practitioner, who will listen to your symptoms, take a medical history, and do a pelvic exam. This physical exam is valuable in determining whether there are masses, areas of sensitivity, or abnormal findings suggestive of endometriosis. Depending on the exam, an ultrasound, MRI, and/or blood work may be recommended. In addition, depending on these results, further recommendations may be made (such as a laparoscopy that can diagnose and potentially treat the endometriosis at the same time).

If you are reluctant to seek out help due to past trauma or just a feeling of discomfort, it is essential that you find a health care practitioner you can trust. Have a friend (or even therapist) come with you to the office and even to the exam room to hold your hand, ask questions, and be there for you. Since the key to prevention of further pain is early diagnosis, prompt medical intervention can lead to more effective assistance in supporting your body's own ability to heal itself.

CHAPTER SEVEN

FIBROCYSTIC BREASTS

Overview

Virtually all knowledgeable health care providers agree that the term fibrocystic breast "disease" or "condition" should be abandoned in favor of a more accurate physiologically based description. First of all, the benign breast conditions that are present in almost all of us to some degree should never have been given the "disease" label in the first place.[1] Moreover, the widespread misconception that women with painful or lumpy breasts are at increased risk of breast cancer borders on the tragic. Unfortunately, our health care system requires a "diagnostic code" to reimburse services, and "fibrocystic breast disease" has one, even though the medical literature is replete with reasons why it shouldn't. This reinforces misinformation and fear and obscures the safe and simple means that exist for obtaining relief and reassurance.

Tender or lumpy breasts are one of the most common reasons why women consult their gynecologists for assessment and treatment. Since painful breasts are not always lumpy, and lumpy breasts are not always painful (and neither is usually abnormal), it is useful to create descriptive categories of symptoms and conditions to replace the generic term "fibrocystic."

Physiological, Cyclical Pain and Swelling

Many women notice painful or sensitive breasts just prior to menstruation. This has been attributed to a more prominent estrogen than progesterone effect on breast tissue at this time. Sometimes less progesterone is made late in the cycle, as in irregular ovulation ("inadequate luteal phase"). Other women may have average amounts of progesterone but increased tissue sensitivity to estrogen with related fluid retention. Most of us tolerate this well enough once reassured it is normal, and the symptoms always resolve with menses. Women who take exogenous estrogen, such as oral contraceptives or estrogen replacement therapy during menopause, may be similarly affected.

Mastalgia

Mastalgia refers to any breast pain severe enough to interfere with the quality of a woman's life, causing her to seek treatment. Physiologic cyclical mastalgia is this severe about 15 percent of the time, and comprises the bulk of this group. Women who suffer from noncyclical pain are rarer, and the pain is less likely to be hormonal in cause. Pain may be due to old trauma, acute infection, or sometimes something related to the chest wall. In contrast, breast cancer presents as a unilateral painful firm lump about 5 percent of the time. Painful swellings that flux with the cycle unchanging over time are not worrisome as cancer signals.

Breast Nodularity or Diffuse Lumpiness

Breast lumpiness—the most worrisome category in most women's minds—may be either cyclic or noncyclic, and might or might not include pain. The distinction between these and normal breasts is often simply a matter of degree. Normal breasts are always irregularly textured because the tissue they are made of is not homogeneous. It is a mix of glands, fat, and connective tissue. Glands can be more or less prominent and more or less obscured by fat or fluid, so all breasts feel different. Symmetry is important; finding a mirror-image thickening in the opposite breast indicates a normal condition.

Non-Dominant Masses

Even densities that are not symmetrical are largely due to benign non-progressive causes but do require careful distinction from dominant masses. When careful palpation around the edges of a non-symmetrical lump reveals that the density merges in one or more places with the surrounding breast tissue, it is considered non-dominant and may be comfortably observed for change over time. When these lesions are biopsied or, preferably, a sample of cells is taken in the office through a needle to be looked at microscopically (fine-needle aspirate), some 70 percent will show "non-proliferative" changes (adenosis, fibrosis, microcysts, mild hyperplasia, and more); some 20 percent will show "proliferative changes without atypia"—mostly epithelial hyperplasia. None of these conditions places one at increased risk for cancer, and all are self-limited. Only a fraction, roughly the 5 percent that show atypical hyperplasia, carry a significantly increased risk of breast cancer, especially when coupled with a positive family history.[2] (The relative risk is 4 percent and 9 percent, respectively.) It was this tiny sub-group that led to the original cancer scare attached to "fibrocystic breasts" in the first place.

The most useful tool a woman can bring to her own breast health is her knowledge and familiarity with the architecture of her own breasts, particularly as it varies over time. Nothing is more helpful in avoiding an unnecessary biopsy than a self-knowledgeable woman who has observed the monthly variation in her own breasts and knows which tissue thickens cyclically. Think of the self-exam as a familiarization process, not a diagnostic one. The majority of cancer occurs in women over age 60, and most women don't get breast cancer at all. We all have plenty of time to learn our textures, so that our own hands are the most sensitive to any changes that may occur. This will occur effortlessly over time with regular self-exams.

Dominant Masses

These outright noncyclical unilateral lesions are clearly distinct on all sides from the surrounding breast tissue. They persist over time, and except in the very young demand some kind of assessment. Most commonly they are either fibroadenomas or "gross" (obvious) cysts. A fibroadenoma is a rubbery, smooth, benign, fibrous tumor common in younger women. In women under age 25, it can be observed over time. They generally do not grow bigger. Large cysts are more common in women aged 25 to 50—an age group when cancer just begins to appear. They are softer, usually squishier, and can be made to disappear by draining them through a needle in the office; unless they recur frequently, no further treatment is necessary. Recurrent large cysts have been shown to slightly increase cancer risk in some studies but not in others;[3, 4] fibroadenomas do not. Unfortunately, noncyclical unilateral dominant masses can sometimes be cancerous.

❧ *Overview of Alternative Treatments*

Women with fibrocystic tissue causing breast pain, discomfort, and lumpiness will find comfort in an alternative perspective on their situation. Given that this

KEY CONCEPTS

- Practice monthly breast self-exams; know your breasts; be able to detect new and unusual changes, thickenings, and lumps.
- Have a yearly breast exam from a licensed physician.
- Relieve symptoms.
- Have changes, if any, evaluated by a physician.

PREVENTION

- Avoid caffeine (black tea, coffee, decaffeinated coffee, cola, chocolate, medications with caffeine).
- Assure regular, daily bowel movements.
- Eat a whole food, natural diet.

condition is not really a disease, a woman can direct her energies toward relieving symptoms and optimizing breast health, as well as increasing her motivation toward general health practices and self-care.

The liver is the primary site for estrogen clearance or estrogen metabolism. A compromised liver function can lead to a state of estrogen dominance, contributing to texture and density changes in the breast. To assure that estrogens are being metabolized properly, it may be necessary to provide nutritional and herbal support for the liver.

Digestion and elimination are fundamental factors involved in hormone-related health problems. Women having fewer than three bowel movements per week have a risk of fibrocystic breasts four to five times greater than women having at least one movement per day.[5] The longer it takes food to move through the colon, the more waste products pass into the bloodstream, creating a potentially toxic physiological environment. Bacterial flora in the large intestine, such as *Lactobacillus acidophilus*, improve the transit time of bowel toxins, as well as improving the excretion and detoxification of estrogens. Women on a vegetarian diet excrete two to three times more detoxified estrogens than women on an omnivorous diet.

Nutrition

Methylxanthines (caffeine)

Removal of caffeine from the diet, an idea that originated with an Ohio surgeon named Dr. John Minton, is probably the most well-known alternative treatment for fibrocystic breasts. Of the 20 uncomfortable women who followed his advice to stop all caffeine intake, 13 said their breasts felt better as a result.[6]

Dr. Virginia Ernster conducted the first randomized study of a larger number of women, in which for four months 158 women eliminated caffeine (coffee, tea, cola, chocolate) from their diets as well as caffeinated medications (theophylline and theobromine). She found a significant reduction in clinically palpable breast findings in the abstaining group compared with the control group, although the absolute change in the breast lumps was quite minor and considered to be of little clinical significance.[7]

Several other studies have been done, leaving us with mixed reports: three studies show no association between methylxanthines and benign

CAFFEINE CONTENT OF COMMON ITEMS

Beverage	Serving size	Caffeine (mg)
Coffee, drip	5 oz	110–150
Coffee, perk	5 oz	60–125
Coffee, instant	5 oz	40–105
Coffee, decaffeinated	5 oz	2–5
Tea, 5-minute steep	5 oz	40–100
Tea, 3-minute steep	5 oz	20–50
Hot cocoa	5 oz	2–10
Coca-Cola	12 oz	45

Food	Serving size	Caffeine (mg)
Milk chocolate	1 oz	1–15
Bittersweet chocolate	1 oz	5–35
Chocolate cake	1 slice	20–30

Over-the-counter drugs	Dose	Caffeine (mg)
Anacin, Empirin, or Midol	2	64
Excedrin	2	130
NoDoz	2	200
Aqua-Ban	2	200
Dexatrim	1	200

breast disease,[8–10] and two studies show a correlation with caffeine consumption.[11, 12] Such is the way of science.

In clinical practice, I always recommend avoiding caffeine. Many women gain mild to dramatic results with this simple approach, and some women receive no benefit. A fair experiment would be to completely abstain for three months and observe any changes in the pain, swelling, and discomfort. A decrease in the nodularity will generally take longer, as long as eight months of complete abstention.

Dietary Fat

How dietary fat affects the human breast is still confusing and controversial, although some research has looked at low fat diets in relation to women with fibrocystic breasts, and at how low fat diets affect the hormone levels in these women. Reducing the fat content of the diet to 15 percent of total calories (in contrast to the average American diet of 40 percent fat), while increasing complex carbohydrate consumption, has been shown to reduce the severity of premenstrual breast tenderness and swelling, as well as reducing the actual breast swelling and nodularity in some women.[13] Reducing the dietary fat intake to 20 percent of total calories results in significant decreases in circulating estrogens in women with benign breast disease.[14]

Since fibrocystic breasts are a result of estrogen dominance, it is logical that decreasing estrogens in the body would improve the symptoms of breast pain and swelling. However, only a slight reduction in fat intake has repeatedly showed very little, if any, effect on breast problems, including breast cancer. A more rigorous approach to lowering the amount of fat in the diet is clearly needed.

The simplest way to accomplish the necessary levels of fat reduction is to avoid animal fats in all forms; a vegan diet (vegetarian, without any animal products at all, including dairy or eggs) is naturally a very low fat diet. Of course, vegetarians, and even strict vegans, can succumb to fat in other forms like french fries, potato chips, and other greasy fried foods. A vegan diet rich in whole grains, legumes, fruits, vegetables, seeds, nuts, olives, seafood, seaweed that is enriched with oils for stir-frying and in

DIETARY RECOMMENDATIONS

- Avoid methylxanthines (caffeine).
- Lower dietary fat to 20 percent of calories.
- Increase dietary fiber (whole grains, legumes, fruits, vegetables).
- Increase seafood and seaweed.

salad dressings result in a diet that derives about 15–20 percent of its calories from fat.

Nutritional Supplements

Vitamin E

For more than 35 years, clinicians have used vitamin E in the medical management of benign breast disease. This practice was initially based on positive reports from small numbers of patients as far back as 1965, and in subsequent studies in 1971, 1978, and 1982.[15–18] When larger numbers of women were studied, vitamin E did not fare so well, showing no significant effects either subjectively or objectively,[19, 20] and the earlier results have never been duplicated.

However, this is not to say that some women don't find symptom relief from taking vitamin E. Two studies demonstrated that vitamin E is clinically useful in relieving pain and tenderness, whether cyclical or noncyclical.[18, 21] The studies have been done with varying dosages: 150, 300, or 600 IU daily. In clinical practice, practitioners generally recommend from 400–800 IU of D-α-tocopherol with a minimum trial period of two months. Since vitamin E in these dosages is completely safe to use, this is a simple and appropriate self-treatment method for a benign breast condition.

Vitamin E (natural)
400–800 IU daily

Omega-6 Fatty Acids

The pain and tenderness of benign breast disease associated with "cyclic mastalgia" have been alleviated with evening primrose (*Oenothera biennis*) oil, the only one of the many essential fatty acids to be scientifically studied in relation to fibrocystic breasts. In 1985, when 291 women took three grams per day of evening primrose oil for three to six months, almost half of the 92 women with *cyclic* breast pain experienced improvement (either no pain or easily bearable pain), compared with one-fifth of the patients who received the placebo. For those women who experienced breast pain *throughout* the month, 27 percent (just over one-fourth of the 33 women) responded positively to the evening primrose oil, compared to 9 percent on the placebo.[22] Another 73 women with breast pain with or without lumpiness randomly received three grams per day of evening primrose oil or placebo. After three months, pain and tenderness were significantly reduced in both cyclical and noncyclical groups, while the women who took placebo did not significantly improve.[23] Although symptom relief can be achieved through the use of evening primrose oil, it should not be relied on to actually reduce the number of developing cysts.

Note: Other omega-6 fatty acids that may have beneficial effects but have not been studied in relation to fibrocystic breasts are flaxseed oil, black currant oil, and borage oil.

Evening primrose oil (omega-6 fatty acids)
1,500 mg, twice daily

Vitamin A

Of 12 patients with fibrocystic breast disease who were treated with 150,000 IU of vitamin A daily for three months, 5 of the 9 women who completed the study showed complete or partial response.[24] Some of the patients experienced mild side effects.

Although the potential toxicity of vitamin A in doses this high makes it an impractical approach to fibrocystic breast disease, it is possible that beta carotene could be substituted, since it has a similar activity without the side effects of vitamin A, or, a diet high in yellow and orange fruits and vegetables.

Beta carotene
50,000–150,000 IU daily

Iodine/Thyroid Hormone

It has been known for a long time that for the thyroid gland to secrete thyroxine (its hormone), it requires iodine. Thyroid hormone with low or even normal thyroid function may result in improvement of fibrocystic breasts.[25, 26] These results suggest that iodine deficiency may be a causative factor in fibrocystic breasts.

Although the exact mechanisms of action on breast tissue are not known, the breast has an affinity for both thyroid hormone and iodine. The only areas of the breast in which iodine can be found are in the terminal and interlobular duct cells, which are also the areas primarily involved in cystic changes. Without iodine, the breast tissue becomes more sensitive to estrogenic stimulation, which in turn produces microcysts high in potassium. The potassium is believed to be an irritant that produces fibrosis and eventually cyst isolation.

Four types of iodine have been studied in the treatment of fibrocystic breasts, only one of which has been truly effective and free of side effects on the thyroid gland. According to the research by Dr. William Ghent, although all forms of iodine relieve subjective clinical symptoms, the fibrocystic breast reacts differently to these different forms of iodine: sodium iodide (Lugol's solution); potassium iodide; caseinated iodine (protein-bound); and aqueous (diatomic) iodine. Symptom relief varied a great deal with the different iodines, but only the aqueous or diatomic iodine achieved both symptom relief in 74 percent of the women and also objective reduction in nodules and resolution of fibrosis in 65 percent of the patients, without adverse effects on the thyroid gland.[27]

Note: Women get different amounts of iodine in their diets, depending on the iodine content of the soil and water, as well as the types of food they prefer to eat. Plant foods grown in the so-called "goiter belt" areas of the country lack iodine, because the soil and water are iodine-deficient. Certain foods, such as seafoods and seaweeds, are naturally high in iodine and might be used to supplement a diet low in iodine.

Aqueous iodine
3–6 mg daily (prescription item)

Additional Supplements

- **B-complex:** 10 times the recommended daily dietary allowance
- **Methionine:** 1 gram per day
- **Choline:** 1 gram per day
- **Lactobacillus acidophilus:** 1 tsp, 3 times per day
- **Flaxseed oil:** 1 tbs per day

Botanicals

Herbal therapies for addressing the symptoms of breast pain, swelling, and cystic nodules in the breast are largely arrived at from traditional uses of herbal medicines and from observational experience in clinical practice. Herbal diuretics are useful in decreasing breast swelling and the discomfort associated with it. The most effective of these is dandelion leaf (*Taraxacum officinale*). Unlike synthetic diuretics, dandelion leaf does not deplete potassium; instead, it actually contains a high percentage of potassium. However, since potassium is possibly implicated in fibrosis and potential cyst isolation, dandelion may not be the ideal diuretic to use. Diuretics effective for fibrocystic breasts include cleavers (*Galium aparine*), yarrow (*Achillea millefolium*), and uva ursi (*Arctostaphylos uva-ursi*).

Additionally, poke root (*Phytolacca americana*), an herb used in traditional naturopathic medical practices, can be applied as an oil to the breasts and rubbed in like a lotion, reducing painful lumpiness and nodularity.

Herbal support for the liver improves how the liver metabolizes hormones. In this case, our goal is to encourage the normal pathways for the metabolization, excretion, and recirculation of estrogens. Traditional herbs that support the liver include burdock root, dandelion root (not leaf), and milk thistle.

HERBAL RECOMMENDATION

- Yarrow leaf capsules: 2–6 per day or yarrow leaf liquid tincture or extract: ¼–1 tsp per day.
- Phytolacca oil: Apply to breasts nightly for two weeks; then reduce to three times per week.

Additional Natural Therapies

Natural Progesterone

Once we agree that fibrocystic breasts are, at least in part, due to a high-estrogen/low-progesterone problem, then it is logical to use progesterone therapy as a treatment. Specifically, many practitioners and women patients have experienced that the application of natural progesterone in a cream or gel form routinely resolves the problem. Dr. John Lee, the leader in the use of natural progesterone, states that he cannot recall a single case in his own practice in which the results were not positive.[28] Lee suggests using the natural progesterone cream or gel as prescribed by a health care practitioner until the cysts are gone, and then reducing the dose to the smallest amount that is still effective, to be continued monthly as needed through menopause.

Natural progesterone cream
¼–½ tsp applied to breasts and palms twice a day from ovulation to menses.

SAMPLE TREATMENT PLAN FOR FIBROCYSTIC BREASTS
Three-month period

- Avoid methylxanthines (caffeine).
- Lower dietary fat to 20 percent and increase dietary fiber (whole grains, legumes, fruits, vegetables); increase seafood and seaweed.
- Vitamin E: 400 IU, twice per day.
- Evening primrose oil: 1,500 mg, twice per day.

If there is no change after three menstrual cycles, then incorporate a more assertive approach utilizing some of the other therapies listed, or see a naturopathic physician for individualized recommendations.

❧ *Conventional Medicine Approach*

Conventional medical literature has tended to focus more on pathologic descriptions of disease and on verifying or disproving related cancer risk rather than on exploring therapeutic options for symptom relief. In spite of conflicting data in the 1980s, many women added vitamin E and eliminated coffee from their diets with noticeable subjective improvement and no side effects—other than those imparted by caffeine withdrawal. Low-fat, high-carbohydrate diets can reduce cyclical pain, and the results of studies with evening primrose oil have been mixed.

Cyclic breast pain and swelling is felt to be hormonal, so treatment is aimed at hormonal manipulation, usually by suppression. More often than not, oral contraceptives help to relieve mild or severe premenstrual pain, although for smaller numbers of women the pain is worsened by this treatment. This paradox is explained by the fact that oral contraceptives suppress ovarian production of hormones and replace it with an average synthetic dose of both estrogen and progesterone. If the replacement level is higher than the natural one, sore breasts may result; usually the replaced level is lower, and then pain is relieved.

Individual sensitivity to chemical compounds also varies among women, and hormonal therapy necessarily involves a lot of trial and error. Sometimes synthetic progesterone, usually medroxyprogesterone acetate (5–10 mg daily), is used, although it lacks contraceptive benefit and causes the same potential side effects as the pill, such as bloating and mood changes. Micronized natural progesterone can be tried as well. Women vary significantly in their ability to tolerate exogenous hormones; many do extremely well. Diuretics are not used much any more, but can be a nonhormonal option at times.

Many so-called effective conventional treatments cause such serious side effects that it is hard to imagine any cases that would warrant their use. Danazol, which interrupts LH and FSH secretion from the pituitary gland (and drives ovarian hormone production), has been touted as the most effective breast pain reliever. Because it is a male hormone, it can

cause facial hair, frequent voice deepening, and other androgenic changes—quite unacceptable side effects for most women. Moreover, it can cost $200 a month. In the past, many women have used danazol for severe pain with endometriosis and many found it tolerable.

Similarly, GNRH (gonadotropin-releasing hormone) agonists work at the hypothalamic level to eradicate estrogen via a temporary-induced menopausal condition. This class of drugs may make danazol obsolete but again do not present a good long-term solution due to the side effects, including reversible bone loss. They cost even more.

Tamoxifen, an antiestrogen (with some estrogen-like effects as well) is used to treat breast cancer and works for cyclic breast pain 90 percent of the time. However, it can cause menopausal side effects such as hot flashes. Long-term effects are unknown, with potential bone loss as one worrisome possibility in young women. Some postulate that it may decrease breast cancer risk. Tamoxifen also increases the incidence of endometrial cancer. For benign breast changes it is difficult to imagine a situation where the benefits would outweigh the risks and side effects. However, a recent study reported that the use of tamoxifen reduced the development of breast cancer in women who are in the high-risk group (two or more first-degree relatives with breast cancer).[29]

Bromocriptine is a nonhormonal drug therapy that lessens the levels of prolactin, the hormone that manages lactational changes, and seems to work well, although it is often not tolerated because of nausea or dizziness in so many.

Iodine therapy, an old European treatment, is regaining interest in the United States and Canada, although not rapidly. It tastes nasty, but the molecular iodine form is safe, fairly symptom-free, and inexpensive. Educating conventional physicians about this therapy would surely lead to its use by more.

The side effects of most of the expensive drugs used to eliminate breast pain and lumpiness are probably too extreme to warrant their use for most women, until the simpler remedies have proven inadequate. If elimination of caffeine, adding vitamin E, and switching to a low-fat, high-carbohydrate diet doesn't bring results, the next logical step would be a trial of oral contraceptives.

❧ *Seeing a Licensed Primary Health Care Practitioner**

A woman might decide to see a licensed health care practitioner (HCP) because she needs a breast exam or wants to determine the exact nature of her breast pain/tenderness or lumps. The HCP will ask about her symptoms as well as other pertinent factors in her medical history, and will perform a physical examination.

*N.D. = Naturopathic Doctor; M.D. = Medical Doctor; D.O. = Osteopathic Doctor; N.P. = Nurse Practitioner; P.A. = Physician's Assistant

If the HCP considers it necessary, she might recommend a mammogram and/or ultrasound to determine the nature of a specific lump, and may encourage aspiration of a mass to determine whether it is cystic or solid. The HCP will no doubt recommend that highly suspicious lumps be surgically biopsied.

A lump that is new or one that is increasing in size, or a lump that does not change over the course of the menstrual cycle, are all causes for concern and might lead to a professional evaluation.

CHAPTER EIGHT

GENITAL HERPES

Overview

The prevalence of genital herpes in the United States increased by more than 30 percent between 1978 and 1991.[1] There are six members of the herpesvirus family that are known to infect humans: HSV type 1 (HSV-1) and HSV type 2 (HSV-2), varicella zoster virus, human cytomegalovirus, Epstein-Barr virus, and herpesvirus type 6. Today, HSV-2 is the leading cause of genital ulcer disease in the United States. As many as one in five Americans is believed to be infected with HSV-2—the virus type more closely associated with genital herpes. Six hundred thousand new cases are anticipated every year. Another virus type, HSV-1—the type more closely associated with infections of the mouth, lips, pharynx, and eyes earlier in life—through oral/genital contact is believed to be responsible for 10–50 percent of new cases of genital herpes.[2] About 80 percent of people with their first episodes of genital herpes are 18 to 36 years of age. The highest annual incidence of genital herpes among women occurs at 20 to 24 years of age and is estimated to be 210 per 100,000 women.

The diagnosis of typical genital herpes is fairly straightforward most of the time but involves local and systemic signs. There are three distinct syndromes: primary herpes, first-episode nonprimary herpes, and recurrent herpes. There are, however,

atypical manifestations, and these are the ones that are not so straightforward.

The severity of symptoms varies in extent and duration according to whether the episode is the patient's first infection with either HSV-2 or HSV-1; initial genital infection in a woman who has already had an infection with the other HSV type (initial, or first-episode nonprimary herpes); or a recurrence of a genital infection with either type. A woman's first episode of genital herpes (primary herpes) is usually the most severe form of the disease. Symptoms usually start appearing within a week after infection, if they are going to appear at all. However, symptoms can start one day and up to twenty-six days after exposure to the virus. Typically, infection is characterized by extensive, multiple clusters of painful lesions involving the genitals, anus, perineum, or surrounding areas. Primary genital herpes is usually the most severe form of the disease, but symptoms and lesions vary in severity, extent, and duration. The classic herpes lesion begins as a red papule, evolving within two to three days to a vesicle containing clear fluid, and then progressing to a pustule. When the surface breaks open, a tender ulceration occurs that may explain the burning pain. Lesions ulcerate more rapidly in moist areas than on dry skin, so that painful genital ulcerations are more apt to occur on the external vulva area. Several successive lesions may appear in the first three

97

to four weeks of primary herpes. The lesions of primary herpes may heal in one to six weeks.

In more than two-thirds of women, primary herpes is accompanied by systemic symptoms that may include fever, malaise, body aches, headaches, and nausea. Meningitis-like symptoms, such as stiffness of the neck and a sensitivity to light, are also common.

Nearly three-quarters of women will also suffer from herpetic cervicitis, with vaginal discharge and intermenstrual spotting. Swollen lymph nodes in the groin area are also a common finding. Discomfort with urination is also common, sometimes as a result of herpes in the urethra and in other cases because the urine comes into contact with lesions on the labia.

DIAGNOSTIC CRITERIA

Three of the following criteria must be present to confirm a diagnosis of genital herpes:

- Multiple genital sores or eruptions with severe local pain and inflammation
- Persistent genital eruptions
- Simultaneous presence of herpes lesions at nongenital sites (fingers, mouth)
- Two or more systemic symptoms such as fever, headache, body aches, or malaise

A practitioner can often make a diagnosis of herpes based on the medical history and inspection of the area. Laboratory testing to confirm the diagnosis is indicated for most people who are having their initial genital eruption. Some lesions are classic in appearance, and perhaps a laboratory test is not necessary. Viral cultures are the most sensitive and commonly available test for confirming the diagnosis of genital herpes. Cultures also permit viral typing, which provides useful information about the predicted recurrence rate. Individuals with a genital infection with HSV-1 (about 20–30 percent of people with first-episode herpes) have a much lower risk of symptomatic recurrent outbreaks. Other testing methods include direct fluorescent antibody test, techniques that detect herpes' viral DNA, and blood tests for HSV antibodies. Most of these additional methods do not adequately distinguish HSV-1 infection from HSV-2.

Some women already have oral herpes or herpes in some other nongenital site, and then acquire their first-episode of genital herpes (nonprimary genital herpes). These are most often caused by HSV-2 in women with a history of HSV-1 infection, often dating back as far as childhood. These cases of genital herpes tend to have fewer eruptions than those with primary herpes, and healing time occurs in one to three weeks. Systemic symptoms are generally not seen in these cases.

About half the women who sustain a first episode of genital herpes will have another episode within six months, and more than 80 percent will have a recurrence within a year. In the first year following symptomatic primary genital herpes, women experience an average of five recurrences; about 40 percent will have six or more occurrences, and about 20 percent will have ten more outbreaks. Recurrent outbreaks are usually milder and shorter in duration and usually resolve within ten days. Systemic symptoms are rare, but many women with recurrent herpes experience prodromal symptoms of local tingling or burning, itching, or pain a few hours to a few days prior to an eruption.

One of the most frustrating areas of herpes infections is the uncertainty of knowing when you are contagious. Many outbreaks of herpes, and in fact probably a majority, occur with no apparent warning without symptoms prior to the onset of the eruption. In these prodromal states, virus can be shed, and it is easy to infect another individual during sexual contact. Shedding of the virus without any apparent symptoms is commonplace in the majority of individuals who have had herpes for some time. It is important that individuals learn to recognize even subtle symptoms that may warn of an outbreak. The safest method of protecting a sexual partner is to use some sort of barrier method to prevent contact (e.g., female and male condoms).

The most serious and feared complication of genital herpes is the transmission from an infected pregnant mother to her newborn child. Consultation with a health care practitioner during the pregnancy is advisable both in women with recurrent genital herpes and in women who may uncommonly acquire their primary infection during pregnancy. Viral cultures late in the pregnancy may be advised and consultations about a delivery by Cesarean section may be justified. Other complications for the infant include meningitis, urinary or rectal dysfunction, infection in the eye, and erythema multiforme (a skin disease).

The impact of genital herpes on a person's psychological and sexual health can be quite intrusive and profound. Many people withdraw from interpersonal relationships because of stress related to their infection or because of fear of spreading the disease to others. Disruption of one's sexual life can also manifest as a significantly reduced sexual pleasure and a strong sense of sexual inhibition. Many people also worry that they would be rejected by future partners and are pessimistic about the possibility of establishing normal sexual relationships. Since many people become emotionally upset upon learning of

the diagnosis, a health care provider can be extremely valuable in helping to deal with anger, guilt, or anxiety. Education and counseling include information about the nature of HSV infection, most importantly prevention of its transmission. It is important that patients also understand that the primary infection may have been asymptomatic and that even an initial outbreak may be a reactivation of an infection acquired months or even years previously.

〰 Overview of Alternative Treatments

A susceptible host plus exposure to the herpes simplex virus adds up to acquiring the disease. Improving the health of the host and enhancement

KEY CONCEPTS

- Genital herpes is most commonly associated with HSV-2.
- Approximately 80 percent of primary genital herpes infections are asymptomatic or unnoticed.
- All HSV infections establish latency and are considered incurable. The present infection may actually be a recurrence of an asymptomatic infection acquired some time in the past.
- Systemic symptoms are more common with primary infections, and symptoms are generally more severe in women than in men.
- Seek the advice of a health care practitioner in diagnosing an initial genital lesion; differentiate herpes from other causes of genital ulceration.
- Recurring eruptions are common and are generally less severe than initial episodes.
- Treating acute episodes can reduce symptoms and shorten the duration of the eruption.
- Immune supportive therapy and antiviral therapy can reduce the frequency of recurrences and can reduce symptoms in acute episodes.
- The individual with herpes, the sexual partner, and the health care practitioner all need to realize that genital herpes is a sensitive issue. Open communication, trust, and respect are essential for an informative dialogue and effective management of genital herpes.

PREVENTION

- Genital herpes is a sexually transmitted disease. Education about recognizing the disease and its prodromal symptoms, protection during sexual contact, or abstaining during outbreaks are important in preventing transmission.
- The virus can shed; thus, transmission of the disease to another individual is possible even without symptoms. The use of barrier methods is recommended for any person who has evidence of prior infection with HSV-2.
- Informing one's sexual partner of a history of herpes is the responsible thing to do.
- A willingness to practice "safer sex" techniques is an important health issue to discuss with a sexual partner. One should understand that HSV infection can be spread by orogenital contact as well as genital-genital sexual contact. The use of male condoms, female condoms, dental dams or household plastic wrap are all recommended options.
- Transmission from one body site to another is possible, and infected areas should be patted, rather than wiped, dry. Be especially careful about transmitting the infection from another part of the body to the eye.
- Enhance the immune system.

of the immune system is essential in preventing and controlling herpes. There is some evidence that some defect in the immune system is present even in otherwise healthy individuals who have recurrent HSV infection. Support of the immune system, dietary factors, stressors, skin health, and preventing and treating other nonherpes infections are all avenues for using natural therapies in reducing the likelihood of contracting herpes and in reducing the frequency and intensity of recurrent herpes infections.

Nutrition

A health-supportive diet is fundamental to good health and an optimal immune system. Although biochemical differences may require that some of us eat more of some foods and less of others, health-supportive diets are based on the guidelines listed below.

More specifically, a dietary approach for preventing recurring herpes outbreaks that reduces high-arginine foods and increases high-lysine foods has become quite popular. This concept arose out of two findings. First, we know that the replication of the herpes simplex virus requires the manufacture of proteins rich in arginine, and arginine itself may be a stimulator of HSV replication. Second, laboratory research has shown that lysine has antiviral activity which blocks arginine.[3] Thus, theoretically, reducing one's intake of arginine and increasing one's intake of lysine should be effective in reducing HSV replication. In fact, many people do observe an increased susceptibility to outbreaks if they eat chocolate or peanuts, foods which are high in arginine. Other high-arginine foods include almonds, cashews, and sunflower seeds. Foods high in lysine include most vegetables, beans, fish, turkey, and chicken.

Nutritional Supplements

L-Lysine

Scientific studies on the effectiveness of lysine supplementation have not shown consistent results. One study that did show positive results was done in 52 patients with recurrent (oral, genital, or both)

DIETARY RECOMMENDATIONS
• Maximize your intake of vegetables, whole grains, legumes, and fruit. • Drink 4 to 8 glasses of water daily. • Reduce fat intake. • Eliminate refined sugar and chocolate. • Avoid food additives, coloring agents, pesticides, and herbicides. • Reduce salt and alcohol intake. • Reduce almonds, cashews, sunflower seeds, and peanuts.

infections. Test subjects received L-lysine, 1 gram three times daily, or a placebo. They also avoided nuts, chocolate, and gelatin. After six months, the treatment was rated as effective or very effective by 74 percent of those receiving the lysine, compared to 28 percent of those receiving placebo. Mean number of herpes outbreaks was 3.1 in the lysine group compared to 4.2 in the placebo group, and lysine-treated patients reported milder symptoms. There were no significant side effects reported in either group.[4] Another experimental study was done with 41 patients who took a daily dose of 1,248 mg of lysine. This demonstrated a decreased recurrence rate and a decreased severity of symptoms during recurrences, but not a reduced healing time.[5]

For people who want to rely on lysine supplementation alone, my recommendation is to take one gram daily for maintenance and one gram three times daily during acute outbreaks.

Lysine can also be found in topical ointments to be applied directly to herpes eruptions. These may be helpful in reducing symptoms but have not been adequately studied to prove their effectiveness.

Lysine *Acute: 1 gm, 3 times daily;* *Maintenance: 1 gm daily*

Vitamin C

Supplementation with vitamin C may have therapeutic value in the treatment of recurrent external genital herpes eruptions. Using 600 mg of vitamin C and 600 mg of bioflavonoids three times daily for three days after the initial onset of symptoms (in the prodromal phase) was found to be the optimal dosage for the most rapid disappearance of symptoms.[6]

Vitamin C
Prodromal period: 600 mg with 600 mg bioflavonoids 3 times daily for 3 days

Vitamin E

Applying topical vitamin E to a lesion may provide pain relief.[7] Although clinical observations have been made of only four published cases (in oral primary herpes, not genital), it would seem logical that vitamin E applied to genital eruptions may provide a similar benefit. Dry the area around the lesion with warm air and apply vitamin E oil with a Q-tip. Leave in place for 15 minutes. After the 15 minutes, pain relief should be evident. Repeat as needed.

Vitamin E
Dry area around lesion; apply vitamin E oil; leave in place for 15 minutes. Repeat as needed.

Zinc

Supplementation with zinc has been observed to reduce the frequency, duration, and severity of genital herpes eruptions. A compound of zinc (25 mg) and vitamin C (250 mg) was given twice daily for six weeks. In some cases, the eruption was completely suppressed, and in others the eruptions disappeared within 24 hours of their onset.[8]

Zinc
25 mg with 250 mg vitamin C twice daily for 6 weeks.

Botanicals

Lemon Balm

Lemon balm ointments have been used topically in Germany for oral cold sores, and products are now available in the United States. The German cream (*Lomaherpan*) is a concentrate of 70:1 lemon balm extract. Several clinical studies have shown impressive results. One such study demonstrated that when the lemon balm cream was used on patients with an initial herpes infection, not a single recurrence occurred. Not one patient using the cream developed another cold sore. The cream was also shown to be effective in reducing the healing time in cases of genital herpes.[9] The cream should be applied two to four times a day during an active eruption. No side effects have been observed.

Lemon balm
Apply topically 2–4 times a day.

Licorice

In clinical practice, I have observed that topical preparations of licorice containing glycyrrhetinic acid have helped to reduce both healing time and uncomfortable symptoms associated with genital herpes. Apply the ointment or gel several times daily.

Licorice
Apply ointment or gel several times daily.

Myrrh and Goldenseal

I am not aware of any research studies using myrrh and goldenseal for genital herpes eruptions, but the traditional use of both of these herbs is longstanding. As an antiseptic and as an anti-inflammatory for inflammations and sores of the mucous membranes, these two herbs have been very reliable and may go a long way not only toward improving the health of the epithelial tissue of the mouth and genital region but also stimulating an immune response locally in that tissue.

Myrrh

Oral tincture 10–30 drops, 3 times per day.

Goldenseal

Oral tincture 10–30 drops, 3 times per day.

Additional Botanicals

Many botanicals have the ability to provide immune support through various mechanisms. Other plants have very specific antiviral properties as well. The antiviral activity of St. John's wort (*Hypericum perforatum*) has been demonstrated. Laboratory studies have shown that two constituents in St. John's wort, hypericin and pseudohypericin, exhibit strong antiviral activity against herpes simplex virus I and II as well as influenza types A and B, in addition to a virus in the mouth that causes vesicular stomatitis.[10] Botanicals such as echinacea, thuja (*Thuja occidentalis*), lomatium (*Lomatium disectum*), astragalus (*Astragalus* spp.), and licorice have been traditionally used by naturopathic physicians, herbalists, and other health care practitioners to support the body's immune system and to defend against the effects of disease-causing viral infections. These herbs are typically administered in liquid extracts, capsules or tablets, or teas. Lomatium may cause a temporary skin rash if used in an improper dose, and licorice, if used daily over several weeks or months, may cause fluid retention and thereby raise blood pressure in certain individuals.

✳ *Conventional Medicine Approach*

Many patients prefer to use antiviral therapy to suppress infections and to reduce recurrent episodes. The primary goals of antiviral therapy are to limit the severity of the infection and to give the patient a sense of control over the disease process. Antiviral therapy is offered to normal immunocompetent patients with either primary or nonprimary genital herpes. In the vast majority of cases, oral antiviral therapy is sufficient, although more severe cases may require hospitalization and intravenous acyclovir.

The value of episodic therapy is debatable because the reductions in healing time and symptom

SAMPLE TREATMENT PLAN FOR GENITAL HERPES

During an acute episode:

- Apply ice preferably during the prodrome stage or even after the eruption has appeared for 10-minute applications several times during the day. This limits the discomfort and swelling and can keep an outbreak from fully erupting.
- Apply lemon balm ointment twice per day.
- Apply licorice ointment (glycyrrhetinic acid) twice per day.
- Lysine: 1,000 mg, 3 times per day.
- Vitamin C: 600–800 mg and 600–800 mg bioflavonoids per day.

Prevention:

- Follow a diet that is high in lysine foods (vegetables, beans, fish, turkey, and chicken) and avoid foods high in arginine (chocolate, all nuts and seeds).
- Lysine: 1,000 mg per day.
- Safe sex protection.

duration are of relatively minor benefit. Patients who have a clearly identifiable prodrome are better candidates for episodic therapy. Patients who desire continuous suppressive therapy need to discuss with their physician the advantages and disadvantages of this regimen. Medical considerations, psychosocial needs, and cost are all factors influencing the wisdom of such a regimen.

The most effective class of agents possessing antiviral activity are the nucleoside analogs: acyclovir, famciclovir, and valaciclovir. Acyclovir was the first antiviral agent approved by the Food and Drug Administration for the treatment of herpes simplex. This drug is indicated for the treatment of initial episodes and the management of recurrent episodes of genital herpes in selected patients. Acyclovir is available in capsules, tablets, and suspension for oral administration, ointment for topical therapy, and sterile powder for intravenous infusion. More than a decade of clinical experience confirms that acyclovir is safe and effective in the treatment of patients with genital herpes infections.[11] In clinical trials, the most common adverse reactions associated with oral acyclovir were nausea and/or vomiting and headache. Caution is warranted when administering acyclovir to patients taking agents that are potentially toxic to the kidneys because of the potential risk of renal dysfunction and impaired elimination of acyclovir.

To improve bioavailability, a host of acyclovir derivatives were investigated. One such drug is valaciclovir. The drug is available in two dosage forms: caplets containing valaciclovir hydrochloride equivalent to 500 mg and 1,000 mg of valaciclovir. Studies of valaciclovir have demonstrated that a therapeutic drug level equivalent to a standard treatment regimen of acyclovir (800 mg five times daily) can be achieved with a valaciclovir regimen of 250 mg four times daily.[12] The most common side effects associated with valaciclovir are nausea and vomiting, headache, and diarrhea. Check with your pharmacist about potential drug interactions.

Famciclovir is also effective in treating and suppressing recurrent genital herpes infections and in suppressing viral shedding. Many herpes experts believe that famciclovir is also effective in treating primary episodes of genital herpes, although the drug is not labeled for that purpose. No studies comparing famciclovir and acyclovir have been done. Famciclovir is available in 125, 250, or 500 mg tablets. The most frequent adverse events reported are headache, nausea, and dizziness.

Herpes simplex viruses may develop resistance to antiviral agents, although this seems to be rare in normal immunocompetent patients who receive acyclovir for episodic treatment or suppression of herpetic eruptions. Immunocompromised patients who receive antiviral therapy for extended periods of time may be at risk for developing resistance; thus, judicious use of antiviral agents is advisable. The development of an effective HSV vaccine is a future strategy for the prevention and treatment of HSV infections.

❧ *Seeing a Licensed Primary Health Care Practitioner**

The most appropriate method for accurate diagnosis of a genital lesion is to see a licensed health care practitioner qualified to perform a gynecological exam. Accurate diagnosis of genital lesions is not only an important key to effective and appropriate treatment but also a key to determining sexual behavior and habits with sexual partners. Laboratory testing using viral cultures and blood tests for antibodies are the most common methods that may be recommended by your practitioner.

A qualified health care practitioner can be extremely helpful in providing education and counseling to the person who has newly acquired herpes. Education includes information about the nature of HSV infection, various treatment options, effect on pregnancy, and prevention of transmission. Counseling includes helping patients to deal with fears, shame, guilt, and feelings of social isolation as well as developing strategies for communicating with present and future sexual partners.

Women who are pregnant need to inform their practitioner of their history of herpes. Any outbreaks during the pregnancy should be recorded and reported so that appropriate testing, treatment, and management can be done during the pregnancy and delivery. Whether your practitioner is a midwife, alternative practitioner qualified to perform home births, obstetrician, or family physician, she or he needs to know your infection status to make appropriate recommendations for the health of you and your baby.

Women with recurrent genital herpes infections may need to seek more aggressive or individualized care from an alternative practitioner than the therapies discussed in this chapter. Homeopathy, additional herbal/nutritional combination products, or Chinese herbal medicine may be more effective in an individual case.

Some women may choose to use conventional pharmaceutical antiviral therapy, although this is not usually medically necessary. There are cases of primary or nonprimary genital herpes, however, when antiviral therapy is indicated for immunocompromised individuals. Cases where symptoms and complications are severe enough to warrant hospitalization may require intravenous antiviral therapy.

---

*N.D. = Naturopathic Doctor; M.D. = Medical Doctor; D.O. = Osteopathic Doctor; N.P. = Nurse Practitioner; P.A. = Physician's Assistant

CHAPTER NINE

HEART DISEASE

⪼ *Overview*

While most of us are aware that heart disease is a primary affliction for men, it seems that women and even their health care practitioners are inadequately aware that coronary heart disease is the leading cause of death in women. Two hundred and fifty thousand women die annually in the United States from heart attacks. If one includes other atherosclerotic disorders such as strokes, almost four of every ten women will die of these diseases. Approximately 100,000 of these deaths are premature.[1] Starting at age 50, more women die of cardiovascular diseases than of any other condition.[2] The lifetime risk for developing cardiovascular disease is two out of three. Not only is cardiovascular disease a major cause of death but is also the major cause of disability in older women. For black women, the concern is even greater. Black women between the ages of 35 and 74 encounter a two-fold risk of coronary death as compared to white women.[3]

Even though heart disease is the leading cause of death in both men and women, the rates of coronary disease at virtually every age are higher in men than in women.[4] When women are in their thirties and forties, the difference between men and women is four- to five-fold. After that, the difference shrinks with increasing age. Why are men at higher risk right from the start? One reason is that sex hormones alter the pattern of fat distribution. Male hormones cause a higher amount of abdominal fat (apple shaped), and female sex hormones lead to a predominance of fat in the thighs and hips (pear shaped).

Overweight women and those with the apple fat distribution are at greater risk for developing coronary artery disease than are slim women and those with the pear fat pattern.[5] This abdominal obesity also increases the risk of high blood pressure and diabetes and may lower the HDL-cholesterol level and raise the triglyceride level.

A desirable ratio of waist-to-hip for middle-age women is <0.8. Measure your abdomen at the largest point, and divide it by your hip measurement. This is called the waist-hip ratio. Overall weight is also an important tool for assessing one's risk for coronary artery disease (CAD). It is usually calculated in terms of body mass index (BMI). Body mass index is calculated as weight in kilograms divided by the square of the height in meters. A desirable body mass index is <25. The body mass index according to the height and weight table found in the chart on page 307 will help you to determine your body mass index. The Nurses' Health Study found that women with a BMI of >29 had triple the risk of coronary heart disease (CHD) compared with women who were lean and with a BMI of >21.[6] Women with a BMI of 25–28.9 and only moderately overweight had almost double

105

the risk. As many as one-third of white women and one-half of black women are 20 percent or more over their desirable body weight. While men have more of an apple shape due to male hormones and premenopausal reproductive-age women have more of a pear shape due to estrogen, postmenopausal women fall somewhere in the middle.

A second possible explanation is that men have differences in lipid (fat) composition. High-density lipoprotein (HDL) levels decline steeply in young men as they go through puberty. Their blood vessels then spend their lifetime exposed to higher levels of low-density lipoprotein (LDL) due to a poorer ability to remove LDL from the vessel wall. As a consequence, men essentially undergo premature atherosclerosis. After menopause, even in women who don't take hormone replacement therapy, women's levels of HDL are higher than men's. Nevertheless, HDL levels do decrease and LDL levels do increase in women after menopause. This change in the blood lipids in women after menopause may be one reason why the differences in rates of cardiovascular disease between men and women start to narrow beginning around age 50, which is the average age of menopause. Overall, the rates of cardiovascular disease increase in both men and women as they grow older.[7] In women, coronary disease occurs largely in the older population, and increases significantly after age 70.[8] Because more women are living to older ages when they are more likely to get coronary artery disease (CAD), there are now more women than men who die of CAD in the United States each year.[9]

Between the ages of 30 and 60, and in each of the decades in this age group, women who have had either surgical or natural menopause have twice the rate of CAD when compared to women in their age group who still have premenopausal ovarian function.[10] Women who have had both ovaries removed (oophorectomized) have a higher rate of CAD at an earlier age than women who undergo natural menopause.[10] This is most likely explained by the fact that menopausal women with ovaries continue to secrete small amounts of estrogens for several years after menopause has actually occurred. Women who have been oophorectomized stop secreting ovarian estrogens abruptly.

Menopausal and postmenopausal women are the recipients of one of the most heavily promoted medications in medical practice, namely, conventional hormone replacement therapy (HRT). This has not always been the case. In fact, a hormonal connection with decreased cardiovascular disease was viewed with skepticism just a few years ago. Now, cardiologists, internists, gynecologists, and family practice physicians are largely convinced that taking estrogen should be a first-line treatment for cardiovascular disease. However, a growing number of conventional practitioners and most alternative practitioners see a more limited role of estrogen replacement therapy in cardiovascular disease. The conventional "party line" on HRT is that the risk for myocardial infarction is reduced by about 50 percent.[11] About three dozen epidemiological studies have shown fairly consistent results in demonstrating a reduced incidence of coronary heart disease based on either reduced heart attacks (MIs) or reduced atherosclerosis in HRT users.

Although it may seem blasphemy to some, there is reason to question these results. Selection bias is the most common criticism. All of these studies are observational—the women and their physicians selected estrogen therapy. Since a certain number of women elect to take estrogen and others don't, it might be the case that the healthier women were taking estrogen and the women with risk factors were not. There is general agreement that women who take estrogen are healthier.[12] Estrogen users tend to be leaner, are of higher socioeconomic status, exercise more, tend to be nonsmokers, have a healthier diet and lifestyle, have better access to health care, and have additional characteristics that are associated with a lower risk of heart disease. Also, they tend to visit their doctor more frequently than their counterparts. As a consequence, they will then get a physical exam, have their blood pressure checked, cholesterol testing, and other parameters directly or indirectly related to CAD, on a regular basis. This leads to medical recommendations, other therapies that may benefit them, and routine evaluations.

Other experts question that menopause plays a leading role in the increased incidence of heart disease in women.[13] They argue that the increased rates of heart disease have more to do with simple actuarial tables. For example, by the age women reach menopause, many men in their same age group have already died of CAD. Therefore, as the group ages, women become more numerous. The resulting calculations give the appearance that there are more of them dying of heart disease. The facts, however, do not support this conclusion. If one looks at the CAD death rate for women, from birth to age 90, one finds it steadily increasing. In other words, it does not rise any faster after menopause than before.[13] This is a very important concept: HRT therapy is promoted on the assumption that it reduces the risk of cardiovascular disease by 50 percent postmenopausally. This erroneous view is the foundation why conventional hormone replacement therapy is recommended to virtually every woman after menopause. This perspective raises the issues of individualized assessment of a woman's risk for heart disease in opposition to the conventional syndrome that one size fits all.

As this book goes to print, the very first double-blind placebo controlled trial has now been completed on the effects of HRT in preventing heart attacks in postmenopausal women. This study, called the Heart and Estrogen/progestin Replacement Study (HERS),[14] is now one of the most damaging pieces of research to date that seriously calls into question the value of HRT in preventing heart attacks. The results of this study, explained in more detail in Chapter 10, concluded that post-menopausal women with established coronary heart disease who use estrogen-progestin therapy are not at lower risk of CHD-related death or nonfatal heart attacks than control subjects. Shockingly, women who took hormones were not protected from heart attacks, as most would have predicted. In fact, more women in the hormone group died in the first year than women not on hormones, and women in the hormone group were 2.89 times more likely than women in the placebo group to experience venous thromboembolic events. Having said that, I must hasten to state that some women do in fact benefit from hormone replacement therapy and, as a result, have significantly reduced risk for cardiovascular disease. Continued research on CAD and HRT will illuminate the truth for the vast number of menopausal-aged women trying to make educated, non-biased decisions.

Cardioprotection from HRT has several possible mechanisms: HRT increases HDL cholesterol; decreases LDL cholesterol; reduces oxidation of LDL cholesterol; lowers uptake of LDL in blood vessels; binds to vascular estrogen receptors; reduces vascular tone; preserves endothelial function; increases prostacyclin release; decreases thromboxane A2 formation; decreases fibrinogen; reduces plasminogen activator inhibitor; and decreases fasting blood glucose and insulin.[15] Although some of these effects of estrogen may be unfamiliar, I think that we can better appreciate the fact that our ovarian production of estrogen is beneficial to our cardiovascular system. The question really is, does hormone replacement therapy benefit women, and, if so, which hormones, in what form, in what dose, and in whom is it beneficial? I will be discussing this topic in more detail in the hormone section of this chapter.

In determining the best plan of action, it is important that each woman is individually assessed for her heart disease risk. Utilizing subjective and objective information, it can be determined with reasonable accuracy what the risk for heart disease is for an individual woman. Criteria must be developed to facilitate advise, intervention, and follow-up of the individual woman: (1) when to recommend lifestyle interventions only; (2) when to recommend lifestyle plus botanical and nutritional regimens: (3) when to recommend lifestyle, botanical and nutritional regimens plus natural hormone therapy, and; (4) when to recommend lifestyle, nutritional, and botanical therapies in combination with conventional HRT and/or pharmaceuticals. To assess each woman individually, to advise and make decisions based on thorough singular evaluation utilizing a holistic and integrative therapeutic base, is a long overdue alternative approach to management of the menopausal woman.

What Is Heart Disease?

Before we go too far here, let's clarify what we mean by heart disease. Generally, when we refer to the risk of heart disease in menopausal women we are including coronary artery disease due to atherosclerosis, hypertension, and hyperlipidemia. The term "heart disease" is most often used to describe coronary atherosclerosis, which is hardening of and deposition of atheromas in the arteries of the blood vessels that supply the heart. Coronary artery disease in women is associated with elevated serum total cholesterol (>200 mg/dL), elevated low-density lipoprotein (LDL) cholesterol levels (>130 mg/dL), low high-density lipoprotein (HDL) cholesterol (<55 mg/dL), and elevated triglyceride levels (>400 mg/dL). One of the strongest predictors of coronary heart disease in women is a low HDL cholesterol.[16] There is some evidence suggesting that blood levels of vitamin E may be even more predictive.

Other forms of heart disease include congestive heart failure, arrhythmias, mitral valve prolapse, and cardiomyopathy, but these are unrelated to issues of menopause and hormones. The focus of this chapter is the prevention and treatment of coronary artery disease and atherosclerosis, hypertension, hyperlipidemia, and myocardial infarction.

When determining one's risk for heart disease, there are some critical things to look for. Women whose father had a heart attack or stroke before age 50, or a mother before age 65, are at a genetic disadvantage. It's important for these women to work harder in the areas of prevention because they are at increased risk just by virtue of their family history. If the parents also smoked cigarettes and died at a young age, their premature death was probably due to smoking and not genetics, and inherited risk is not apparent.

Hypertension is the most common chronic disease in older women and a significant risk factor for stroke, congestive heart disease, and kidney disease. Beginning at age 50, hypertension is more common in women than in men and even more so in black women. The most recent national recommendations define incipient hypertension at readings of 140/90 mm Hg. Blood pressure readings fairly consistently above these require treatment. Isolated systolic hypertension (systolic BP of 160 mm Hg or greater) or combined hypertension (systolic BP of 160 or greater and diastolic BP of 90 or greater) is directly related to increased death rates from cardiovascular disease (see Table 9.1).

Cholesterol numbers are a little more complicated. It is important to know more than just the total cholesterol. Consistently low HDL and/or high LDL correlates with increased coronary artery disease risk even if serum total cholesterol is 200 mg/dL or less: total cholesterol readings are not very significant in the presence of high HDLs and low LDLs. The ratio of serum total cholesterol to HDL cholesterol is probably more useful in predicting coronary artery disease risk than either total cholesterol or HDL cholesterol levels alone. In women, the cholesterol/HDL risk ratios[17] are as follows:

Below average	<3.9
Average (normal)	3.9–5.7
Above average (moderate)	5.8–9.0
Above average (high)	>9.0

Triglyceride levels:[18]

Normal	<200
Borderline-high	200–400
High	401–1,000
Very high	>1,000

The average amount of HDL-cholesterol in women is approximately 55–60 mg/dL, about 10 mg/dL higher than in men. In women, an increase in HDL of 1 mg/dL is associated with a 3.2 percent decrease in the risk of heart disease.[19] Women with very high HDL levels (over 55–60 mg/dL) have virtually no increased risk of heart disease even in the presence of elevated concentrations of total cholesterol. It is appropriate to be concerned when HDL cholesterol levels are less than 50 mg/dL.

Reviews of clinical trials indicate that there is a 20 percent decrease in cardiac mortality for every 10 percent fall in total cholesterol levels. There is a 2–3 percent decrease in coronary heart disease risk in men and women for each 1 mg/dL increase in HDL cholesterol.

Triglycerides probably also are an important risk factor for coronary heart disease in women, but an increased incidence of heart disease occurs only when increased triglycerides are present in association with low HDL levels. If the triglyceride level is greater than 400 mg/dL and HDL cholesterol is less than 50 mg/dL, the risk of heart disease is significantly increased.[20] Patients with elevated triglycerides and a family history for heart disease most likely have familial hyperlipidemia. Women under age 40 who have heart disease most likely have this disorder. Triglyceride levels from 200–400 mg/dL

TABLE 9.1   Classification of Blood Pressure for Adults Age 18 Years and Older*

Category	Systolic (mm/Hg)		Diastolic (mm/Hg)
Optimal	<120	and	<80
Normal	<130	and	<85
High-normal	130–139	or	85–89

Hypertension (based on the average of two or more readings taken at each of two or more visits after an initial screening).

Stage 1	140–159	or	90–99
Stage 2	160–179	or	100–109
Stage 3	>189	or	>110

* *The Sixth Report of the Joint National Committee on Prevention, Detection, Evaluation, and Treatment of High Blood Pressure.* Bethesda, Md.: National Heart, Lung, and Blood Institute; 1997. NIH publication 98–4080.

are considered elevated but borderline. Weight loss alone can return elevated triglyceride levels to normal. Smoking, obesity, and lack of exercise are all related to elevated triglycerides.

Research has also shown that the sugars in fruit (fructose) significantly raise blood triglyceride and cholesterol levels. If your triglycerides are above 150 mg/dL, or if you have additional significant risk factors for heart disease such as elevated blood pressure or diabetes, avoid too much fruit, fruit juice, and other simple sugars. Limit them to one serving per day. Sugar can be eaten in small amounts only if your triglyceride level is below 150 mg/dl. All sugars can increase triglycerides, but fructose is actually more damaging than sucrose and glucose. It gets even worse if you eat high-fructose corn syrup, a very common sweetener used in packaged foods. Fructose increases LDL and does not improve HDL. If you have elevated triglycerides, you can eat all the whole grains that you want, although some diets, such as the popular Zone diet, present some provocative controversial ideas that may be contrary to this. Alcohol also raises the blood levels of triglycerides.

Impaired tolerance to glucose is another risk factor for heart disease. Women with higher than normal blood sugar or who are clinically diabetic are at increased risk. The diabetic woman has three to seven times the risk of coronary disease and of dying prematurely from atherosclerosis than a non-diabetic woman.[21] Diabetes seems to lessen any gender advantage women may have. It is a stronger predictor of coronary disease in women than in men.[22] Women are more prone to suffer unrecognized or "silent" events related to ischemia.

In this country, we have two Syndrome Xs. The first one was named by Dr. Harvey Kemp of Harvard in 1967 to describe women with normal coronary angiograms who had anginalike chest pain with or without positive treadmill tests.[23] Some of these women turned out to have abnormal circulation in the small coronary arteries, and their coronary flow didn't adjust itself appropriately. Since Syndrome X is more frequent in women, some investigators have speculated that hormonal factors may influence these vascular changes.

The second Syndrome X, also called Reaven's Syndrome,[24] was coined Syndrome X in 1988 by Dr. Gerald Reaven of Stanford University. It is a syndrome of increased truncal (mid-section) obesity—a waist-to-hip ratio greater than 1:1. It is defined as a cluster of symptoms that appear to occur secondarily to cellular resistance to insulin. Individuals who secrete larger amounts of insulin, because the normal insulin action is impaired, are at increased risk for a number of health problems. They are predisposed to glucose intolerance, hyperinsulinemia, dyslipidemia, and hypertension. The relationship between resistance to insulin, non-insulin dependent diabetes mellitus, hypertension, and coronary heart disease has been extensively documented.[25] Evidence suggests that hyperinsulinemia may be seen in as many as 25 percent of the normal non-diabetic population. As many as 50 percent of individuals with high blood pressure may have Syndrome X.[26] In the past, insulin resistance has been linked to obesity. Overweight individuals are more susceptible to this condition, but many obese patients do not have insulin resistance. It is also clear that insulin resistance is not limited to obese individuals; as many as 50 percent of hyperinsuline-mic patients may be of normal weight.[27] Individuals who have this glucose intolerance and hyperinsuline-mia should eat a diet lower in carbohydrates, whether simple or complex. A diet that is 40 percent carbohy-drates, 30 percent fat, and 30 percent protein may help to correct the hyperinsulinemia.

After the age of 45, a woman's annual exam should include a careful examination of the heart; carotid, abdominal, and femoral arteries; the pe-ripheral pulses; and a blood test checking blood sugar, total cholesterol, HDL, LDL, ratio of total cho-lesterol to HDL, and triglycerides. For menopausal women, I recommend an annual fasting lipid pro-file in addition to the annual physical/pelvic exam. It is common practice for physicians to order cholesterol testing as little as every five years, but this is strikingly inadequate for individ-ualized decisionmaking and effective prevention and interventions.

RISK FACTORS FOR CORONARY ARTERY DISEASE

Medical Conditions

Hypertension
Diabetes mellitus
Lipid abnormalities
Syndrome X
Obesity

Lifestyle

Sedentarism
High-fat diet
Cigarette smoking

Family History

Coronary artery disease

There are heart disease risk factors unique to women. These include oral contraceptive use, preg-nancy, having had both ovaries removed, and pre-mature menopause. Additional risk factors not related to gender include increased body fat, espe-cially if it is in the abdominal area, history of smok-ing, being sedentary, diabetes mellitus, high blood pressure, poor lipid ratios, and family history.

❧ Overview of Alternative Treatments

One issue that conventional and alternative medi-cine can agree on is that, in most cases, atheroscle-rosis and cardiovascular disease are directly related to diet and lifestyle. While family history and ge-netic predisposition play an important role in CAD, risk factors such as cigarette smoking, exercise, di-etary habits, and stress can be modified to reduce a person's risk.

Dr. Dean Ornish and his team of researchers conducted the first significant clinical trial to de-termine whether comprehensive lifestyle changes affect coronary atherosclerosis. In his landmark study, called the Lifestyle Heart Trial, published in 1990, patients who had proven coronary artery dis-ease were prescribed a program that included a low fat vegetarian diet, moderate aerobic exercise, stress management training, stopping smoking, and group support. The changes in serum lipids resulting from this protocol were similar to those seen with cholesterol-lowering drugs, without, of course, the undesirable side effects. After one year in the program, patients also showed significant overall regression of their coronary atherosclerosis when measured by arteriography.[28] It is interesting to note that patients who made less comprehensive changes in lifestyle showed significant progression of their atherosclerosis. These results suggest that the conventional 30 percent fat diet recommenda-tion made to patients with coronary heart disease is not low enough. Those who make the greatest changes benefit the most, although it seems that women may show benefit and actual regression of atherosclerotic lesions with modest lifestyle changes, while men do not.

Smoking is the most important risk factor for coronary heart disease. Smokers have three to five times the risk of coronary artery disease as non-smokers. Tobacco smoke contains chemicals that damage the lining of the arteries, raises the cho-lesterol level, promotes the ability of platelets to clump together, elevates fibrinogen levels (a clot-forming protein), and elevates the blood pres-sure. The good news is that women who stop smoking can reduce their risk of coronary artery disease to that of a nonsmoker within two years of quitting.

Exercise is a vital part of a lifestyle routine that can have lifelong benefits in preventing premature heart disease and strokes. Regular exercise lowers cholesterol levels, improves the blood supply and therefore the oxygen delivered to the heart, increases the strength of the heart muscle and thus improves the volume of blood it can move, reduces blood pressure, helps to inhibit blood clots, reduces overall body fat, and minimizes damage from stress.

In many women, stress is the major cause of their high blood pressure. Relaxation techniques such as deep breathing, biofeedback, meditation, yoga, progressive muscle relaxation, and hypnosis have all been shown to have some value in lowering blood pressure.[29] Enough interest and effect exist in these techniques as therapeutic tools that

the Office of Alternative Medicine has funded several studies involving meditation and stress reduction techniques in order to study their effects on blood pressure.

A fundamental tenant of alternative medicine is that lifestyle changes that include smoking cessation, appropriate exercise, diet, and the use of dietary ingredients, nutritional supplements, and herbal extracts can treat CAD in addition to providing cardioprotective effects. Considerable scientific research exists that demonstrates the effect of these natural therapies and interventions in lowering cholesterol, improving blood lipid ratios, lowering blood pressure, preventing clots and strokes, inhibiting fibrinogen, lowering homocysteine levels, strengthening the cardiac muscle, and preventing the oxidative damage to vessel walls, all of which are implicated in CAD risk. Ingredients, such as fiber, soy, antioxidants, folic acid, vitamins B_6 and B_{12}, fish oils and flax oil, garlic, hawthorn berry, and others are just some of the many natural therapies that give alternative practitioners a great deal of confidence in their ability to help women to prevent and treat heart disease.

Most alternative practitioners employ a diverse, holistic health plan in their approach to preventing and treating cardiovascular disease. A comprehensive plan that includes dietary changes, regular exercise, smoking cessation, stress reduction, nutritional supplementation, botanical therapies, and possibly natural or conventional hormonal therapies yields outcomes that present a serious and viable option in managing high blood pressure, poor cholesterol levels, atherosclerosis, and the individual who has or is at high risk for heart disease.

Nutrition

Dietary Factors

Dietary habits are an important area where we can exert a great deal of influence on our heart health. Lowering the level of dietary fat has been in the news for a long time now. The American Heart Association says that 30 percent or less of our total calories should be from fat. Many alternative practitioners advise even lower intakes because of some of its additional benefits, such as reduction of breast, ovarian, and uterine cancer risk. The kinds of fats are also important. Basically, it comes down to less animal fat and more vegetable fats.

Fats

Understanding the harmful effects of some fats and the beneficial effects of others can be confusing. A little explanation of terms and concepts may go a long way in clarifying the issue. Fats are the most concentrated source of food energy. Each gram of fat provides nine calories, compared with only 4 calories per gram for carbohydrates or protein. All fats are made from carbon, oxygen, and hydrogen. These elements are arranged in molecules called fatty acids. The three major classes of dietary lipids are triglycerides, phospholipids, and sterols (e.g., cholesterol). Ninety-five percent of the dietary fats are triglycerides. A triglyceride is a glycerol molecule with three fat molecules. These fat molecules are called fatty acids. Lipase enzymes, found in our bile, break apart the triglyceride molecule. The triglyceride is converted into a monoglyceride which the body can then absorb, along with the individual fatty acids and the glycerol.

Fatty acids and monoglycerides are absorbed and transported by lipoproteins. These lipoproteins are the very low-density lipoproteins (VLDL), low-density lipoproteins (LDL), and high-density lipoproteins (HDL) that we have discussed earlier in the chapter. VLDL and LDL transport the fats from the liver to the cells in the body, and HDL returns the fats to the liver.

A distinction should be made between different types of fatty acids. Saturated fatty acids are solid at room temperature and are typically animal fats (beef, lamb, butter, cheese, lard). They are usually referred to as saturated fats. "Saturated" refers to the fact that their carbon molecules are saturated with hydrogen molecules. Unsaturated fats have some of the hydrogen molecules missing. Unsaturated fats are liquid at room temperature and, therefore, are called oils. Most vegetable oils contain mainly unsaturated fats. Oleic acid is a monounsaturated fat. It contains approximately 76 percent monounsaturated fatty acids.

Vegetable oils can be used either for cooking or as medicine. Oils used medicinally do not maintain their stability as well as cooking oils when exposed to heat and, therefore are not advisable to use as cooking oils. Medicinal oils contain gamma-linolenic acid and include evening primrose, borage, and black currant seed oils, or alpha-linolenic acid that is found in flaxseeds and their oil. Monounsaturated oils like canola and olive are made chiefly of oleic acid that is more resistant to damage from the heat from cooking and light from storage. The high content of oleic acid make these two oils far superior to the highly polyunsaturated oils like corn, safflower, and soy that are easily damaged by heat and light. The fatty acids in these less desirable oils are changed to lipid peroxides with cooking, which have a toxic effect on the inside of the arteries. In a healthy cardiovascular prevention regime, one would, therefore, preferentially eat the seeds, grain, and fruits of the oils, use canola and olive oil for cooking, and leave the rest of the oils on the supermarket shelves.

Margarine is an unsaturated oil that has been hydrogenated (i.e., made into a saturated fat). Margarine raises LDL, lowers the protective effects of HDL, and can in fact increase the incidence of heart disease. Foods such as margarine, cakes, cookies, candies and doughnuts typically contain partially or totally hydrogenated oils. This is also true of most oils sold in supermarkets; in order to prolong their shelf life, hydrogenated fats are used in many so-called cooking oils.

Cholesterol is a waxy substance found in animal tissue. It is produced by the liver (about 1,000 mg/day) and is a component of all cell walls. Blood circulating cholesterol is supplied by the liver and the intake of animal foods.

The body can make most of the fatty acids it needs from the carbon, hydrogen, and oxygen provided by food. These have been arbitrarily classified as nonessential fatty acids.* Essential fatty acids are polyunsaturated fats that must be obtained from the foods that actually contain them. The two main groups of essential fatty acids are omega-3 and Omega-6 fatty acids. Linoleic acid is the main omega-6 fatty acid. Alpha linolenic acid is the main omega-3 fatty acid, which the body can convert to eicosapentaenoic acid (EPA) and docosahexaenoic acid (DHA).

The body uses the omega fatty acids to create eicosanoids. One of the most important eicosanoids are the prostaglandins. Prostaglandins exert a local hormonelike effect on target cells and tissues. For example, in the cardiovascular system, they affect dilation or constriction of blood vessels and clot formation.

The omega-6 and omega-3 fatty acid groups each produce separate, distinct prostaglandins. Both types of fatty acids are needed, but in the right ratio. There is some disagreement as to the right ratio between omega-6 and omega-3 oils. Our early ancestors probably ate roughly equal amounts of omega-6 and omega-3 essential fatty acids (EFs). In the modern industrialized countries, most people eat from 10:1 to as high as 30:1 omega-6 to omega-3. Overall, we want to reduce omega-6 fats and increase omega-3 fats in our diet.

Dr. Michael Murray, a noted naturopathic physician and author, recommends a 4:1 ratio, based on the scientific research of Yehuda and Carasso.[30] This dietary ratio of fatty acids will produce a favorable production of the friendly prostaglandins, series 1 and series 3, and a limited amount of the unfriendly series 2 prostaglandins. It would then be prudent to increase our intake of omega-3 oils such as those found in flaxseeds, walnuts, and fish. The omega-6 to omega-3 ratio in flax is 1:3.

Diets that are high in cholesterol and saturated fats (beef, pork, lamb, butter, cheese, palm oil, coconut oil) contribute to the poor lipid ratios and ele-

vated cholesterol that we discussed earlier. Lowering the cholesterol in the diet will lower the blood cholesterol in most individuals.[31] Replacing saturated fatty acids in the diet with polyunsaturated fatty acids (PUFAs) from vegetable oils will lower both total cholesterol and LDL levels. However, it may also lower HDL. Monounsaturated fatty acids, as found in olive oil, show either no effect, or an increase in HDL, thereby promoting a better effect than either PUFAs or saturated fats (see Table 9.2).[32]

Fish oils contain omega-3s that the body converts to EPA and DHA. These eicosanoids are also associated with cardioprotective effects. Coldwater fish such as salmon, tuna, mackerel, herring, and halibut are excellent sources of omega-3 fatty acids. Fish oils prevent clots, inhibit inflammation in the vessel walls, cause vasodilation, and promote a regular cardiac rhythm. Similar to aspirin, fish oils block the production of thromboxane A2, which is a potent vasoconstrictor and promoter of the stickiness of blood.[33] Fish oils may also lower blood pressure and triglycerides, but they may raise LDL.[34] In a recent human study, fish oil, given with a garlic supplement, lowered both total cholesterol and LDL.[33] In another recent study that spanned 11 years, the diets of 22,000 male physicians was tracked to see if eating fish decreased the abnormal heart rhythms that often precede sudden cardiac death. During the study period, 133 men died suddenly of heart attacks within one hour of the onset of symptoms. Compared to men who ate fish less than once per month, those who ate at least one serving per week had a 52 percent lower risk of sudden cardiac death.[35] However, fish intake was not associated with a decreased risk of total heart attacks, nonsudden cardiac death, or total deaths from cardiovascular disease.

Fiber

Increasing the fiber in the diet is another important nutritional habit to acquire. Fiber sources that form a gel such as psyllium seed or oat bran bind bile and cholesterol in the intestines and promote their excretion. This action improves the cholesterol by decreasing LDL levels while increasing HDL levels.[36] A diet high in whole grains, fruits, vegetables, and legumes is the optimal high fiber diet. Soluble

---

*This is a most unfortunate classification. It tends to mask the fact that the so-called "nonessential" fatty acids are as critical to cellular life and metabolism as are the so-called "essential." A similar observation can be made in relation to the classification of essential and nonessential amino acids. The nonessential fatty and amino acids are manufactured by the cells from raw materials. The others must be supplied by food. We cannot survive without both.

FIVE OMEGA-6 AND OMEGA-3 FATTY ACIDS TO REMEMBER

LA: Linoleic acid. An omega-6 fatty acid found in vegetable oils, nuts, and seeds. Given the proper conditions, the body converts LA to GLA and eventually into prostaglandin 1.

GLA: Gamma-linolenic acid. LA gets converted to GLA by enzymes in the body. Certain foods and habits and events (saturated fat, partially hydrogenated oils, stress, aging, drinking alcohol) disrupt this conversion so that only 5–10 percent LA gets converted to GLA. It may be better to get GLA directly from evening primrose oil, black currant oil, or borage oil supplements.

ALA: Alpha-linolenic acid. This is an omega-3 fatty acid not commonly found in foods. Seven seed oils contain some ALA, with flax oil being the richest natural source. Through several biochemical steps, the body converts ALA to EPA and then to Prostaglandin 3.

EPA and **DHA:** Eicosapentaenoic acid and docosahexaenoic acid. These two omega-3 fatty acids are found in cold-water fish oils. EPA is a building block for the body to make prostaglandin 3; DHA is important for the brain, nervous system, and vision.

fibers, such as pectin or oat bran have the most consistent beneficial effects on cholesterol levels.[37] A review of 20 scientific trials on the effect of oat products on cholesterol demonstrates that a modest reduction in blood cholesterol can be achieved by eating oat products daily.[38] Most studies have shown rather impressive lipid reductions, but few have demonstrated virtually no benefit. At least some of the variability in results from one study to the next can be accounted for by differences in study subjects and the protocols and oat products that were used. It also seems that there is an age-gender interaction and that older women have the most marked total cholesterol reduction. Also, the higher the initial cholesterol, the greater the benefit is apt to be. Fiber also helps to increase the rate at which food passes through the digestive tract, thereby increasing the loss of cholesterol in the

stool. Eating one bowl of oat bran cereal or oatmeal daily (3 grams of oat fiber) lowers the total cholesterol by 8–23 percent. These results have been achieved in as little as three weeks.

One of the best ways to achieve a high fiber and low fat diet is the vegan diet. This is a vegetarian diet in which absolutely no animal products are consumed. Strict vegan diets, which are typically very low in saturated fat and dietary cholesterol and high in fiber, can help maintain or achieve desirable blood levels by especially lowering the total cholesterol and the LDL cholesterol.[39]

Specific fruits or vegetables may also have a particular positive effect on serum lipids. Raw carrots may have a more potent effect on lowering cholesterol than do oat products. Eating a raw carrot at breakfast every day for 3 weeks has been shown to significantly reduce serum cholesterol by 11 percent and increase fat excretion by 50 percent.[40]

Evidence also exists demonstrating that people with a low intake of fruits and vegetables have an increased risk for heart disease.[41] Numerous studies have continued to show that a diet high in carotenes and flavonoids found in fruits and vegetables reduces the risk of heart disease and strokes.[42] It is thought that the antioxidants (C, E, carotenes, flavonoids) found in fruits and vegetables reduce the risk of cardiovascular disease by scavenging free radical species. The antioxidants protect the unsaturated fatty acids from peroxidation, thus preventing atherosclerosis. Lipid peroxide concentrations are in fact higher in individuals with atherosclerosis.[43] Good dietary sources of carotenes as well as vitamins C and E are green leafy vegetables, yellow-orange fruits and vegetables, red and purple fruits and vegetables, legumes, grains, and seeds. Good dietary sources of flavonoids are citrus fruits, berries, onions, parsley, legumes, green tea, and red wine.*

Soy

Another effective cholesterol-lowering strategy is to consume more soy protein and less animal protein. This is perhaps my most favorite recommendation

---

*Evidence on the cardioprotective effects of red wine is contradictory. At present, the use of any alcoholic beverage as part of a healthy diet is questionable.

TABLE 9.2 **Fatty Acid Composition of Different Dietary Oils**

Oil	GLA (Omega-6) %	LA (Omega-6) %	ALA (Omega-3) %	Oleic (Omega-9) %	Saturated Fat %
Flax	0	14	55	20	9
Safflower	0	75	0	13	12
Soy	0	50	9	26	15
Olive	0	8	0	76	16
Coconut	0	3	0	6	91
Corn	0	59	0	24	17
Canola	0	30	7	49	7

to women because soy offers many other potential benefits (e.g., reduction of menopausal symptoms and prevention of breast or uterine cancer). The evidence that soy lowers cholesterol is substantial. Many studies have demonstrated this effect. Perhaps the best evidence comes from a review of 38 scientific studies. This meta-analysis concluded that consumption of soy protein rather than animal protein significantly decreased serum concentrations of total cholesterol, LDL cholesterol (LDL-C), and triglycerides.[44] The soy intake averaged 47 grams per day. The average decreases were: in total cholesterol 9.3 percent, in LDL-C 12.9 percent, and in triglycerides 10.5 percent. HDL cholesterol increased by 2.4 percent. In order to fully appreciate what this means, for every 1 percent reduction in total cholesterol there is a 2 percent reduction in heart disease.[16]

The use of soy for menopausal symptoms and heart disease protection continues to receive great interest from women, practitioners, and scientists. Investigators at Bowman-Gray Medical Center in North Carolina are currently conducting a three-year study on the effects of phytoestrogens in soy products on menopausal symptoms, plasma lipids, thickness of the carotid artery, bone density, and mood. Called the Soy Estrogen Alternative Study (SEAS), this randomized double-blind study will be completed in late 1999.

Good Carbs, Bad Carbs

It seems we all love carbohydrates. Complex carbohydrates, such as found in brown rice, whole wheat, rye, oats, barley, millet, whole fruits, and vegetables are both high in fiber and vitamin content. They are highly recommended. Refined carbohydrates, on the other hand, must be placed in the group of unhealthy foods. Sugar, a refined carbohydrate, is a significant factor in the development of atherosclerosis.[45] High sugar diets lead to elevations in triglycerides and cholesterol and also to an increase in insulin production. Elevations in insulin levels are associated with risk of cardiovascular disease by increasing cholesterol, triglycerides, and blood pressure. The prudent woman would decrease all sources of refined sugar in the diet by avoiding candies, pastries, and desserts; she would also avoid sweetened cereals, white breads, or any food containing refined carbohydrates. Reading labels on packaged foods is another strategy in reducing intake of refined sugars. Any label that says sucrose, glucose, maltose, lactose, fructose, sugar, corn syrup, and white grape juice concentrate is a source of added dietary sugar.

The most important strategy to improving heart health, lowering cholesterol levels, and improving our good and bad cholesterol ratios is a healthful diet and lifestyle. The fundamental message here is to eat less animal products and more fruits, vegetables, whole grains, and legumes. Other important strategies in this regard are the elimination of caffeinated and alcoholic beverages and smoking. In many cases, diet therapy alone can satisfactorily normalize the blood lipid profile.

With all this talk of lowering cholesterol and improving the cholesterol ratios, it is easy to forget how important it is to balance the blood pressure and how foods may have a positive or a negative

TABLE 9.3 **Effects of Foods on Cholesterol Levels**

Positive	Negative
Oats	Saturated fats
Olive oil, canola oil, flax oil	Beef, pork
Other vegetable oils	Butter, cheese,
Fish (salmon, tuna, sardines, herring, makerel, halibut, swordfish)	Milk (other than low fat)
Whole grains	White flour products
Vegetables (especially carrots)	Sugar
Fruits	Coconut oil, lard
Garlic	Eggs
Onions	Coffee
Soy products	Ice cream, pies, cakes, cookies, etc.

effect on this (see Table 9.3). For example, a diet low in potassium and high in sodium is associated with high blood pressure. By contrast, a diet high in potassium and low in sodium can protect against elevation of blood pressure as well as lower elevated blood pressures.[46, 47] It has become common knowledge that too much salt in our diet may contribute to high blood pressure. Not so commonly known is that high blood pressure is also related to too little potassium in our diet. In fact, restricting salt alone may not be enough to lower the blood pressure. Potassium must be increased. Most Americans eat a standard American diet in which they ingest twice as much sodium as potassium. Nutrition researchers recommend a 5:1 potassium: sodium ratio that is easily accomplished by a diet high in fresh fruits and vegetables, which are rich in potassium.

Caffeine

So far, I'm the only adult I know who has never had a cup of coffee. The peer pressure to become a coffee drinker is no greater than the conflicting evidence around the health impact of coffee. Some studies say it raises cholesterol; some do not. Some say caffeinated is the problem but decaffeinated is not; others show no difference between the two. What if it's boiled versus filtered versus instant? What if its naturally decaffeinated, filter-brewed coffee? There is no one consistent answer here on the effect of coffee on coronary heart disease. What does seem to be true is that caffeinated coffee drinkers drink more alcohol, consume more

dietary saturated fats and cholesterol, are more likely to be smokers, and less likely to be current exercisers.[48]

I encourage all my patients to decrease their coffee intake (that's after they have parked their car in the Starbuck's parking lot next to my office). Avoidance of any stimulant to falsely raise energy and obscure the fact that we are tired or stressed or doing just plain too much in our lives does not seem consistent with respecting our normal bodies' rhythms.

For those women who have elevated cholesterol, elevated blood pressure, or generally higher risks for heart disease, the number of studies that do show a connection between coffee and hyperlipidemia, hypertension, and coronary heart disease seem to deliver an obvious message: just say no.

In hypertensive individuals, the use of caffeinated beverages is questionable. Two recent studies showed slight elevations in blood pressure or a potentiation of the stress-related rise in blood pressure in hypertension-prone males. In a third study, caffeine (75 mg/day) had no effect on blood pressure of young, healthy subjects.[49]

Caffeine also appears to have adverse effects on serum lipid profiles. In men, coffee intake induced hypercholesterolemia.[50, 51] Moreover, when hypercholesterolemic men refrained from coffee for five weeks, their serum cholesterol dropped by 10 percent. Those who continued to abstain from coffee showed a 13 percent average drop at ten weeks and those who returned to coffee gradually reached pre-study levels of total cholesterol.[52] In women, plasma cholesterol has increased with increasing coffee drinking as follows: 0–7 oz, 214 mg/dL; 8–32 oz, 222 mg/dL; and 33+ oz, 234 mg/dL.[53] Almost all of the difference was due to an increase in low-density lipoprotein cholesterol. Plasma cholesterol was not affected by decaffeinated coffee in this study.

Unfiltered coffee seems to be responsible for the effect of coffee on serum cholesterol[54, 55] and its increase of coronary artery disease risk and mortality in men and women.[55, 56] The presence of the diterpines (removed by filtering), cafestol, and possibly kahweol in unfiltered coffee has been offered as an explanation for these effects of coffee.

Another, albeit stronger, explanation came to light in a recently published Norwegian study.[57] Sixteen thousand 40- to 67-year-old women and men showed a dose-response between average coffee consumption and blood homocysteine levels: the larger the coffee intake, the greater the homocysteine levels.

Homocysteine is formed during the breakdown of certain amino acids and is known to increase the risk of heart disease when it accumulates in the blood. It may do so in smokers and in people who eat diets low in fruits and vegetables, presumably because of inadequate levels of B vitamins, which function to breakdown the homocysteine and inhibit its accumulation in the blood.

Alcohol

Many sweeping statements have been made about the benefits of alcohol in preventing heart disease. If we look at the connections between heart disease and alcohol more closely, we will find that these general statements are in fact inappropriate and misleading. Heavy use of alcohol causes damage to the heart muscle and is also related to high blood pressure, strokes (hemorrhagic), and arrhythmias (irregular heart beats). On the other hand, people who abstain from alcohol, when compared to those who drink, are at greater risk of major coronary heart disease events such as heart attacks.

One of the problems in understanding the alcohol-heart connection is that the question of "light," "moderate," or "heavy" alcohol use is often ignored or unknown. A working definition is helpful: "Heavy" use is three or more drinks per day.

One to two drinks per day is "moderate," and "light" would be something less than one daily drink. Another factor in these definitions is that people often underestimate, or actually lie, about drinking.

All the excitement and rationale about the positive benefits of alcohol is that there is now strong evidence that light-to-moderate alcohol drinking is protective against coronary heart disease. It is not clear whether there are any significant differences between red wine, white wine, liquor, or beer, although a phenomenon called the "French paradox" has been observed. In France, saturated fat intake and mean cholesterol levels are high, but coronary heart disease mortality is low. Wide publicity about this paradox has asserted that red wine consumption in France is high and is responsible for the unexpected results. As a consequence, a general perception exists that red wine is especially beneficial. Non alcoholic ingredients in the red wine may in fact be responsible, including antioxidants and flavonoids. There is evidence that the observations that have been made of red wine actually have to do with the antioxidant capacity of the red grape to prevent the oxidation of LDL cholesterol. Other French lifestyle factors may also play a role. The most plausible mechanism by which alcohol drinking might protect against coronary heart disease is that alcohol tends to raise HDL cholesterol. Other areas of importance may be that alcohol has a beneficial effect on Apo A lipoproteins, as well as an anti-thrombotic action.

Alcohol ingestion, however, harbors potential dangers that probably outweigh its alleged benefits. In my opinion, daily ingestion of alcohol cannot be responsibly recommended to women. Well-documented evidence indicates that alcohol may increase serum estradiol by 300 percent in postmenopausal women who were taking hormone replacement.[58] Alcohol also increases the incidence of breast cancer,[59–61] osteoporosis,[62] depression,[63] pancreatitis, liver cirrhosis, gastritis, degenerative nervous system conditions, fetus damage, substance abuse, and cancers of the mouth, pharynx, larynx, esophagus, and liver.[64] These, and the harmful cardiovascular consequences of heavy drinking, add up to considerable increase in disease and death. In addition, behavioral problems, violence, and crime are also contributions of drinking alcohol to vast public health nightmares.

From a medical perspective, all heavy drinkers should reduce their intake. It is my opinion that moderate drinkers should also reduce to light intake or even abstinence. Alcohol probably does not belong in a healthful life.

The potential heart benefits of alcohol can be achieved through much safer methods with all of its benefits and none of its drastic consequences. It is better to drink red grape juice daily than drink red wine. Even better perhaps: eat the red grapes themselves.

Nutritional Supplements

Scientific research supports the use of several herbs and supplements for the prevention and treatment of heart disease. Although dietary changes alone can have a powerful effect in reducing heart disease, they may not be enough for everyone. Lowering cholesterol, lowering blood pressure, inhibiting blood clots, preventing oxidative damage to the vessel walls, and several other mechanisms are all effects that can be achieved with the therapeutic use of nutritional supplements. This is an exciting and successful area for alternative medicine to make an impact on a large segment of the population. Given that heart disease is the number-one cause of death in men and women in America, these concepts deserve the attention and respect of individuals and practitioners of all disciplines and all schools of thought.

Vitamin E

Of all the antioxidants, and I would even go so far as to say of all the vitamins or minerals, vitamin E may offer the greatest protection for women against heart disease because of its ability to be easily incorporated into the LDL-cholesterol molecule and prevent free radical damage and, as a result, prevent atherosclerosis and CAD.[65]

A number of clinical trials have shown that vitamin E supplementation (alone or in combination with other antioxidants) leads to increased resistance of LDL to oxidation. Doses between 500 IU and 1,500 IU have shown significant reduction in LDL oxidation.[66] In an eight-year study of 87,245 healthy female nurses in the United States age 34 to 59, the risk of coronary heart disease was 36 percent lower in women taking vitamin E supplements of more than 100 mg per day as compared to women who did not use supplements. Women who took vitamin E supplements for over two years had about half the risk. No protective effect was seen in women whose only source of vitamin E was from their dietary intake.[67] The *New England Journal of Medicine* published a report showing that women who took at least 100 IU of vitamin E per day for several years had 40 percent decreased likelihood of having a coronary event when compared with non-vitamin E users.[68] Continued research has now demonstrated that doses between 400 and 800 IU per day dramatically reduces the risk of nonfatal heart attacks. This same study, however, did not show any reduction in the number of deaths from CAD.[69] Doses of 400–1,000 IU per day provide additional cardiovascular benefit by inhibiting platelet aggregation, increasing HDL-cholesterol, and stimulating the breakdown of fibrin (a clot-forming protein).

Blood vitamin E levels may be more directly related to the development of a heart attack or stroke than total cholesterol levels. Whereas high blood pressure was predictive of a heart attack 25 percent of the time, and high cholesterol 29 percent of the time, low blood levels of vitamin E was predictive almost 70 percent of the time.[70]

Vitamin E
400–1,000 IU per day

Vitamin C

Several mechanisms by which vitamin C has a positive effect on the cardiovascular system have been identified. It protects LDL cholesterol from oxidation[71] raises HDL cholesterol, and lowers total cholesterol triglycerides.[72] It appears that blood vitamin C levels correlate inversely with serum total cholesterol and triglycerides, and directly with higher HDL levels. A mere 0.5 mg/dL increase of vitamin C in the blood increased HDL by 14.9 mg/dL in women that were studied.

Vitamin C may also have a beneficial effect on blood pressure. One study demonstrated a five-point reduction in blood pressure in people with mildly elevated blood pressure.[73]

Vitamin C
1,000 mg, 3 times per day

Niacin

Conventional practitioners and alternative practitioners alike acknowledge that several grams of niacin per day will lower total cholesterol and LDL cholesterol and raise HDL.[74] The main drawback to using this much niacin (500 mg three to six times per day) is that it may cause undesirable side effects. These range from acute flushing, appropriately called a "niacin flush," stomach irritation, nausea, glucose intolerance, elevations in serum uric acid levels, visual disturbances, and liver damage. Manufacturers have produced time-release or sustained-release forms of niacin that minimize some of its side effects (i.e., the skin flushing). However, these products are more toxic to the liver. Inositol hexaniacinate (IHN) is a form of niacin proven to be safe and not linked to serious side effects. Hexaniacinate is therefore the recommended form used to lower cholesterol. In order to improve the tolerance of niacin, start with a dose of inositol hexaniacinate 500 mg three times a day for two weeks and then increase the dose to 1,000 mg three times per day.

Niacin has been compared to several conventional pharmaceutical drugs used to reduce cholesterol levels. A study published in 1994 compared niacin and lovastatin over a period of 26 weeks in 136 patients who were at high risk for coronary heart disease.[75] Lovastatin produced a greater effect on reducing LDL cholesterol, but niacin provided better overall results. Niacin far exceeded lovastatin in increasing HDL cholesterol, which is a more significant indicator in reducing the risk for coronary heart disease.

Inositol hexaniacinate
500–1,000 mg, 3 times per day

Pantethine

Pantethine is the activated form of vitamin B_5 (pantothenic acid) and is a key component of coenzyme A (CoA). CoA plays a significant role in lipid metabolism and is involved in the transport of fats. The cells of our body need CoA to utilize the fats in the form of energy. Pantethine, at the typical dose of 300 mg three times per day, has been shown to significantly reduce serum triglycerides, total cholesterol, and LDL cholesterol, while also increasing HDL cholesterol.[76, 77]

Pantethine
300 mg, 3 times per day

Coenzyme Q10

The primary uses of CoQ10 is in high blood pressure control, atherosclerosis, angina, mitral valve prolapse, congestive heart failure, and cardiomyopathy. As an antioxidant, CoQ10 protects against atherosclerosis by preventing the oxidation of LDL. It also works together with vitamin E in preventing damage to lipids and to the vessels.[78]

CoQ10
50–150 mg per day

Magnesium

Many scientists and health practitioners believe that magnesium is one of the most important nutrients for cardiovascular protection and treatment. Drs. Burton and Bella Altura of NY Health Science Center have done some of the most consistent research in magnesium over the last 30 years. They, and others, assert that magnesium contributes to the strength of contraction of heart muscle,[79] increases HDL levels,[80] inhibits platelet aggregation, and prolongs the clotting time.[81–83] Stickiness of blood platelets (platelet aggregation) is an independent risk factor for heart disease and strokes. When platelets stick to each other, they release compounds that promote the formation of atherosclerotic plaque. They may also form a clot that can get stuck in small arteries, and, if these are located in the heart or brain, the result is a heart attack or stroke.

At least 10 independent clinical studies show that patients with hypertension exhibit serum and/or tissue hypomagnesemia. On the average, patients with long-term hypertension have at least a 15 percent deficit in total magnesium.[84] Pregnant women, with labor-induced hypertension have decreased blood levels of magnesium.

Evidence from both animals and humans suggests that magnesium levels in diet and blood may affect blood lipids; the lower the magnesium intake, the higher the serum lipid levels.

In diabetic patients with hypertension, elevated insulin levels, and insulin resistance are often associated with decreased HDL cholesterol, increased LDL cholesterol, and increased triglyceride levels. Some of the mechanisms underlying these biochemical effects still are not adequately understood. However, there is strong evidence suggesting a relationship between uncontrolled diabetes and magnesium deficiency. Both insulin-dependent and non-insulin dependent diabetes are associated with reduced serum total magnesium and intracellular magnesium as well as increased urinary loss of magnesium.[84] In the few published studies, magnesium improves control of both types of diabetes. It is thus reasonable to conclude that magnesium deficiency may predispose diabetic patients to an increased incidence of cardiovascular disease and death.

Magnesium also improves cardiac performance by enhancing blood flow in the coronary arteries. It also prevents oxidation of lipoproteins and subsequent atherosclerosis.

Magnesium
400–1,200 mg per day in divided doses

Potassium

In addition to increasing the potassium foods in our diet, several studies now show that potassium supplementation can reduce blood pressure. It has been shown that potassium supplementation of 2.5 grams per day can lower the systolic blood pressure an average of 12 points and diastolic blood pressure an average of 16 points.[85] Potassium supplementation may be even more beneficial in people over age 65 who often do not respond well to anti-hypertensive drugs. Potassium supplements are available by prescription and over the counter. The FDA restricts the potassium over-the-counter dose per tablet to 99 mg due to potential problems with nausea, vomiting, diarrhea, and ulcers that may result from higher doses of the mineral. The frequency and severity of side effects associated with potassium supplementation are negligible when compared with the frequency and severity of side effects associated with conventional antihypertensives.

Potassium
2.5 grams per day (most likely a prescription item)

Folic Acid, Vitamin B$_6$, Vitamin B$_{12}$

Some recent research has focused on homocysteine and its role in heart disease. Results associate elevated plasma levels of this amino acid with significant increases in coronary artery disease,[86, 87] myocardial infarction,[88] peripheral occlusive disease, and cerebral occlusive disease.[89, 90] A deficiency of folic acid, vitamin B$_6$ or vitamin B$_{12}$ will lead to an increase in the level of homocysteine, and homocysteine levels are highest among individuals with low levels of folic acid. Folic acid, vitamin B$_6$, vitamin B$_{12}$ and betaine either alone or in combination have demonstrated the ability to normalize homocysteine levels.[91–93] However, in one study, the optimal concentration of homocysteine was not reached until the folic acid intake was around 400 mcg per day. In a study of 100 men, 650 mcg folic acid, 400 mcg vitamin B$_{12}$, and 10 mg B$_6$ were used separately or in combination daily for six weeks. Homocysteine levels were reduced 41.7 percent by the folic acid alone and 49.8 percent by the combination.[94] In another study, supplementation with 2.5 mg folic acid per day reduced hyperhomocysteinemia in 94 percent of patients.[88]

High consumption of foods containing folate and vitamin B_6 may reduce the risk of heart attack in women by nearly 50 percent.[95] A study of 80,000 female nurses showed a direct link between the ingestion of these two B vitamins and reduced coronary disease. The results suggested that eating more fruits, vegetables, and whole grains or obtaining these vitamins through supplementation may be as important as quitting smoking, lowering cholesterol, or controlling high blood pressure in lowering heart disease risk. The highest cardiac protection was achieved with daily intakes from either food or supplementation of more than 400 mcg of folic acid and more than 3 mg of vitamin B_6. The RDA for folic acid is only 180 mcg of folic acid and 1.6 mg of vitamin B6.

Folic acid
400 mcg–2.5 mg per day

Vitamin B_6
10–25 mg per day

Vitamin B_{12}
400 mcg–1,000 mcg per day

Essential fatty acids

As I discussed in the nutrition section, observations of large populations of people have demonstrated that people who eat a diet rich in omega-3 oils from either fish or vegetable sources have a much lower risk of developing heart disease. Observing numerous cultures from around the world teaches us that diets high in omega-3 oils such as the native Eskimo and numerous island cultures are associated with less heart and coronary artery disease.

Besides changes in diet, supplementation of various oils for prevention and treatment is also warranted for many individuals. The daily consumption of fish oils can significantly lower blood pressure in people with hypertension. A group of researchers at the Johns Hopkins Medical School evaluated the results of 17 clinical trials using fish oil supplementation. They found that the consumption of 3 grams or more per day of fish oil led to reductions in blood pressure of individuals with hypertension.[96] Systolic pressure was lowered by an average of 5.5 mm Hg, and diastolic pressure was lowered by 3.5 mm Hg. The effect was found to be greater at higher blood pressures, and no significant effects were noted in people with normal blood pressure.

Norwegian researchers concluded that eating fish like mackerel, herring, and salmon will significantly reduce the risk of heart disease. As little as one serving of 300 grams of fish per week will provide the benefit. They suggested that the minimal dietary requirement for EPA and DHA should be about 200 mg/day.[97]

Flax oil, nature's richest source of omega-3 fatty acids, is the vegetable alternative to fish oil. It contains twice as many omega-3s and is usually less expensive. Flax oil provides the body with alpha-linolenic acid (ALA) which it uses to make EPA, whereas fish oil provides EPA directly. Studies on supplementation with flaxseed oil have provided evidence that consumption of alpha linolenic acid-rich oils may offer protective effects against cardiovascular disease by decreasing the tendency of platelets to aggregate.[98]

Lastly, evening primrose oil rich in gamma-linolenic acid (GLA) may also have a role in prevention of heart disease. Nineteen hypercholesterolemic patients were given evening primrose oil in a placebo-controlled crossover design over six weeks with safflower oil as the placebo.[99] There was a significant decrease in LDL cholesterol compared with the levels observed during safflower oil administration.

Fish oil
EPA and DHA, 200 mg per day or more

Flax oil
1 tbsp per day

Evening primrose oil
3–4 grams per day

All supplemental oils should be taken with meals.

Botanicals

Garlic (*Allium sativum*)

Garlic is one of the key herbal ingredients shown to have remarkable benefits in cardiovascular health. Garlic has the ability to lower cholesterol and triglycerides while increasing HDL levels.[100] Since 1975, over 32 human studies have been published demonstrating the lipid-lowering effects of garlic.[101] The majority of these studies utilized a garlic powder tablet with a daily dosage from 600–900 mg and provided 5,000 mcg (5 mg) of allicin. Two meta-analyses of these studies indicate that one to three months of treatment using 600–900 mg of garlic powder tablets reduced total serum cholesterol an average of 9–12 percent and triglycerides from 8–27 percent.[102, 103] Garlic is not as aggressive at lowering serum cholesterol and triglycerides as some of the newer pharmaceuticals, but it also does not have any of their side effects. For women with a modest elevation of cholesterol, it will provide a safer and effective alternative. For women with severe hypercholesterolemia, appropriate drugs may be used and later replaced by garlic when the desired drug effect is complete.

Garlic mildly lowers blood pressure in women with hypertension. Studies have shown that garlic can lower systolic pressure by 20–30 mm Hg and the diastolic pressure by 10–20 mm Hg.[104] Garlic is also fibrinolytic and inhibits platelet aggregation,[96, 105] an effect theoretically anti-stroke.

Garlic is not contraindicated during pregnancy and lactation. Problems with ingestion of garlic are usually minor. In sensitive individuals they may include heartburn and flatulence. Some people do not appreciate the odor or taste of garlic. Odor-free or enteric-coated products may avert these undesirable effects. Individuals are rarely allergic to garlic. However, people taking anticoagulant drugs should take garlic with caution and be monitored by a health care practitioner.

> **Garlic**
> *1 fresh raw clove of garlic per day or a garlic pill providing a minimum of 4,000 mcg allicin daily*

Ginger (*Zingiber officinale*)

The same ginger that is used in cooking and ginger ale has been shown to inhibit platelet aggregation, perhaps even better than garlic,[106] and to lower cholesterol.[107] Ginger stimulates the conversion of cholesterol to bile acids and increases bile secretion, thereby lowering cholesterol by promoting its excretion and impairing its absorption. Most research studies have used 1 gram of dry powdered ginger root, which is a small amount of ginger.

> **Ginger**
> *1 gram per day*

Gugulipid (*Commiphora mukul*)

The mukul myrrh tree is native to India and is the source of gugulipid, the standardized extract obtained from this medicinal tree. The extract is further concentrated in order to isolate compounds known as guggulsterones. The two guggulsterones important in the management of hyperlipidemia are Z-guggulsterone and E-guggulsterone. Gugulipid has a significant ability to lower total cholesterol, triglycerides, and LDL cholesterol, and raise HDL cholesterol.[108, 109] Total cholesterol levels can drop from 14–27 percent within one to three months of therapy. LDL cholesterol will drop 25–35 percent and triglycerides from 22–30 percent. HDL levels usually increase by about 20 percent. Clinical studies have indicated that gugulipid is effective in treating cases with total cholesterol greater than 220 mg/dL and triglycerides greater than 170 mg/dL. The effective therapeutic dose of gugulipid is based on its guggulsterone content. The recommended dose is 25 mg of guggulsterones per 500 mg tablet three times per day. Look for extracts that contain 5–10 percent guggulsterones. When using the standardized extract preparations, only mild abdominal discomfort is reported in a small number of people. Crude extracts, previously used, were associated with diarrhea, anorexia, abdominal pain, skin rash, and heavier menstrual flow.

Gugulipid
500 mg with 25 mg guggulsterones,
3 times per day

Hawthorn (*Crataegus oxyacantha*)

Hawthorn leaves, berries, and blossoms contain flavonoids. One of these, proanthocyanidin, is largely responsible for the cardiovascular effects of hawthorn. Hawthorn preparations are clinically effective in reducing blood pressure,[110] in the prevention and treatment of atherosclerosis, lowering cholesterol, and preventing the oxidation of LDL.[111] Hawthorn preparations improve the blood supply to the heart by dilating the coronary arteries, increase the force of contraction of the heart muscle, and regulate cardiac rhythm.[110]

Hawthorn

Tincture
(1:5) 405 milliliters per day or

Freeze-dried berries
1–1.5 grams per day or

Flower extract
(standardized to contain 1.8 percent vitexin or 20 percent procyanidins): 100–250 mg per day or

Berries or flowers, dried as a tea
3–5 grams of dried herb per day

Flavonoids

Flavonoids are a group of compounds found in many fruits, vegetables, nuts and seeds, and numerous medicinal plants. Over 4,000 different flavonoids have been identified in foods and plants. Quercetin, rutin, catechin, and hesperidin are the most frequently used in medicine.

Flavonoids inhibit the peroxidation of lipids by acting as free radical scavengers.[112] Quercetin specifically has been shown to inhibit LDL oxidation.[113] In addition to these direct antioxidant effects, flavonoids inhibit platelet aggregation, protect vitamin E from oxidation, and chelate iron. Their association with cardiovascular disease reduc-

tion is substantiated in dietary studies. In one study, 805 Dutch men who consumed more than 30 mg per day of flavonoids largely from tea, onions, and apples had approximately one-third the risk of cardiovascular disease as compared to men with the lowest intake.[114] In another study involving the dietary analysis of over 12,000 men in seven different countries, flavonoid intake was again lower in the men who had the highest risk of dying from coronary artery disease.[115]

Flavonoids

Quercetin
200–400 mg, 3 times per day

Citrus bioflavonoids
1,000–6,000 mg per day

Grape Seed and Pine Bark Extracts

Extracts from grape seeds and the bark of the maritime pine tree are high in a group of flavonoids called proanthocyanidins, also called procyanidins. Mixtures of proanthocyanidin molecules are referred to as procyanidolic oligomers, PCO for short. These commercially prepared extracts of grape seeds and pine bark, or PCO extracts, possess potent antioxidant activity that is far stronger than even vitamin E or vitamin C. In animal studies, PCO extracts have been shown to prevent damage to the arterial lining, lower blood cholesterol levels, and shrink cholesterol deposits in the arteries.[116, 117] PCO extracts may also inhibit the constriction of arteries and inhibit the formation of platelets. These benefits may also occur in humans and many individuals; especially those women who have high cholesterol, atherosclerosis, or a family history of premature CAD should consider supplementation of PCO extracts.

PCO
50–300 mg per day

Additional Botanical Therapies

A vast range of herbs have been used for decades, or even centuries, to treat heart and vascular system conditions. Some of these herbs are categorized below according to their dominant action:

Diuretics: dandelion leaf, lily of the valley, parsley

Heart tonics: broom, bugleweed, figwort, hawthorn, lily of the valley, motherwort, night-blooming cereus

Aids to circulation: broom, cayenne, ginger, hawthorn, horsechestnut, lime blossom, mistletoe, yarrow

Nervines (reduce anxiety and stress): lemon balm, hops, lime flowers, motherwort, passion flower, skullcap, valerian

Antihypertensives: hawthorn, mistletoe, garlic, yarrow, cramp bark

Anti-atherosclerosis: lime blossom, hawthorn, mistletoe, yarrow

Exercise

Review of Selected Recent Research[118-144]

In women of all ages, exercise has been shown to reduce the risk for cardiovascular disease (CVD) by altering CVD risk factors.

In fact, recent studies show that exercise decreases blood pressure generally and in adolescent girls and young women; and reduces body fat in elderly women, in female children and adolescents, and in young women. It also reduces BMI in adolescent girls and middle-aged women and controls weight in obese African-American girls. In addition, it diminishes central arterial stiffness in highly physically active pre- and postmenopausal women and decreases atheromatous plaque in blood vessels and sympathetic activity in baroreceptors in women. Finally, exercise reduces the risk of arrhythmias, normalizes blood lipids, and increases insulin sensitivity.

Williams found an average 0.13 mg/dL plasma HDL increase for each additional km run by female runners per week. Similarly, other studies have reported modest-to-significant increases in HDL cholesterol following aerobic training. In one of these studies, the increase in HDL was measured at 7.6 mg/DL when exercise was combined with smoking cessation in women. Gibbons' and Mitchell's clinical experience at the Cooper Clinic in Dallas, Texas, corroborates these findings. They feel that plasma HDL is the "most powerful cholesterol fraction in predicting CAD risk" in women and men (p.68e). Their experience suggests that:

1. Aerobic exercise raises HDL independent of diet.
2. Five exercise sessions per week are more effective in raising HDL than three sessions.
3. Nine months of consistent aerobic exercise represent the minimum necessary to raise HDL significantly.
4. Aerobic exercise reduces the risk of CVD independent of HDL plasma levels, which appears to indicate that exercise might be an even more powerful predictor of cardiovascular health than HDL.

Moreover, the type of exercise chosen appears less significant that its intensity or duration on its effects on CVD risk factors. Thus, reduction in CVD risk factors in women is reported for fast walking and tennis playing. Sacco and colleagues found an inverse dose-response relationship between stroke and intensity and duration of exercise.

This study also found decreased risk of CVD and premature death with increased physical activity.

It should be noted here that the effects of exercise on CVD risk factors are not permanent. Code and colleagues found that, in both men and women, the effects of exercise on blood pressure disappeared within weeks after the return to a sedentary lifestyle.

The effects of aerobic exercise in female CVD risk factors constitute no surprise. Surprising are the beneficial results obtained from strength training in some of these same parameters. Thus, previously inactive women performed 12 resistance exercises for one hour, three times per week. After five months of exercise, they showed decreases of 13 and 14 points in total cholesterol and low-density lipoprotein cholesterol (LDL-C), respectively, from baseline values. Another study noted that previously hypertensive adolescents who reduced their blood pressure by aerobic exercise were able to maintain blood pressure control by taking weight-lifting exercise after discontinuing aerobic exercise. These results are even more surprising when one considers the lack of effect noted for aerobic exercise in plasma total and LDL and triglycerides in women.

Until 1990, exercise was considered an absolute contraindication for heart failure. In that year, however, Coats and colleagues' landmark study found increased exercise tolerance and beneficial changes in pathophysiological parameters characteristic of chronic heart failure (CHF) in 11 patients with CHF secondary to ischemic heart disease after eight weeks of home-based bicycle training. Since then, other studies have confirmed their findings.

Regular exercise and physical fitness reduce all-cause mortality, including CVD, in women and men. Blair and colleagues' longitudinal study of 10,224 men and 3,120 women, whom the authors followed for eight years, revealed a significant inverse dose-response relationship between physical fitness and CVD. In women, the age-adjusted all-cause mortality rates per 10,000 person-years were 7.4, 2.9, and 0.8 for least-, moderate-, and highest-fit individuals, respectively.

For several decades, exercise has been advocated for the treatment of men who have had a heart attack or stroke. Recent encouraging results suggest that it should also be prescribed for women in similar situations. Lavie and Milani found nonsignificant changes, but all in the right direction, in blood lipids, BMI, and exercise capacity in women following a three-month, formal, outpatient phase-two cardiac rehab supervised training program. Ades and colleagues studied 60 older patients (41 men and 19 women) who had had previous MI or bypass surgery and participated in a rehab program that included treadmill running for 25 minutes, stationary biking for 15 minutes, and machine rowing for 10 minutes for three and twelve months. The results showed improved fitness and increased quadriceps capillary density and size.

In conclusion, regular, lifelong exercise offers women with CVD risk factors benefits that far exceed those of drugs. Exercise:

1. Normalizes blood lipids
2. Elevates protective HDL levels in dose-response fashion
3. Significantly reduces LDL
4. Reduces and stabilizes blood pressure
5. Increases insulin sensitivity
6. Stabilizes weight and decreases fat mass and BMI
7. Is beneficial in congestive heart failure

EXERCISE RECOMMENDATIONS

Prevention of CVD

Follow guidelines in "General Exercise Instructions" and "General Exercise Program" (see Appendix A).

Treatment of existing CVD

1. Consult a health care provider.
2. Use caution and moderation. Note that in men who seldom exercise, cardiac arrest is 56 times more likely during vigorous exercise than at rest. In men who exercise frequently, the risk is 5 times.[145]
3. Walking program for heart patients:[146]

Weeks	Distance (miles)	Time (min/mile)
1–2	1	20
2–3	1	17–20
5–6	1	15
7–8	1.5	15
9–10	1.5	14

To maintain the conditioning effect, exercise 20 to 30 minutes three to five times a week. If you stop exercise for more than two weeks, start again at a lower level and gradually build back up to your original program.

Examples of moderate exercise for mild CAD:[147]

- 30 minutes of brisk walking each day
- 10 minutes of brisk walking 3 times a day
- Swimming, biking, or working out on an exercise machine such as a treadmill, stair-climbing machine, rowing machine, or stationary cycle at moderate intensity for 30 minutes daily

Note: Begin slowly and increase speed gradually over time. If you have never exercised before, start with a few minutes each day and increase time gradually every week until you reach 30 minutes.

8. Reduces CVD mortality
9. Is an essential adjuvant to rehabilitation after heart attack, stroke, or bypass surgery
10. Alleviates stress
11. Helps women achieve control of their lives

Stress Management

Women's hearts appear more vulnerable to stress than men's. Arnold[148] suggests that women's general lack of social support and inability to take charge of their lives are important factors in CAD risk. A similar inference is possible to make from the data obtained by Blumenthal and colleagues.[149] In patients with CAD or ischemia, these authors found that a stress management program was approximately three times more effective at reducing cardiac events than exercise.

If we perceive certain events in our lives as stressful, if this perception is extended over time and we have not learned to cope with it, stress will eventually produce outward manifestations in our health, e.g., elevated blood pressure. Many simple techniques can be effective in managing our stress and reducing its baleful influence. Techniques such as deep-breathing exercises, biofeedback, transcendental meditation, yoga, progressive muscle relaxation, and hypnosis have all been shown to reduce stress and lower blood pressure.[150] The antihypertensive effect of these techniques is not dramatic. However, they constitute an important adjuvant in a holistic program to lower blood pressure and treat and prevent heart disease.

Natural Hormone Replacement Therapy

Whether a woman can live through the menopausal years without hormone therapy or whether she should use natural or conventional hormone therapy is a complex decision. The decision is especially difficult when one considers the many unanswered questions about menopause, cardiovascular disease, and natural and conventional hormones. The method I follow is to systematically evaluate each woman with a thorough medical history, physical exam, and laboratory testing. The information retrieved from these sources, in concert with her preferences and concerns, and a willingness and commitment on the part of both patient and practitioner to monitor and evolve the plan in an ongoing manner, is the key to find out what is right for that particular patient.

A woman's risk (mild, moderate, or severe) for cardiovascular disease changes over time. The plan needs to change accordingly. To treat menopause as a disease and use a one-size-fits-all approach are errors of conventional medicine that unnecessarily expose many women to HRT and its pernicious side effects, for example, increased risk of breast cancer. In contrast, naïveté and blind faith in the "natural" and the often inadequately known outcomes of alternative management of menopause unnecessarily exposes many women to undertreatment and increased risk of heart disease and osteoporotic fractures. It is essential to keep an open mind and carefully balance the benefits versus the risks of both therapy and outcomes. Both practitioner and patient need to be open-minded, so that informed and appropriate decisions are reached.

Conventional HRT may be appropriate for some women. When it is appropriate, it behooves physicians to advise the use of the least objectionable options. Phytoestrogens and natural hormone therapy are perhaps the most appropriate for some other women. No single protocol or approach is equally appropriate for all women. Determining if my patient is a low, medium, or high risk for CAD has been a critical tool in the path to the recommendations I finally make.

Natural Progesterone

The use of natural progesterone creams and oral micronized natural progesterone has grown in popularity over the last several years. However, it was only recently that natural progesterone creams have been shown to have biological activity. Progesterone is synthesized from diosgenin or stigmasterol found in Mexican wild yams and soybeans. This hormone end product has come to be known as natural progesterone, both because it is plant derived, but more important, because it is biochemically identical to the progesterone that is produced by the human ovary. It should be stated that wild yam or soy does not contain progesterone. These plants contain the diosgenin and stigmasterol that must be extracted from the plant and then converted in the manufacturing laboratory to the hormone end product. Natural progesterone is biochemically different than progestin, commonly misstated as progesterone. The most common progestin used for menopausal women is medroxyprogesterone acetate (MPA), better known as Provera.

There are few studies on natural progesterone. However, the development of oral micronized progesterone (OMP) in the last 10 to 15 years and the release of natural progesterone vaginal gel Crinone in September 1997, together with the few side effects and popularity of natural progesterone, have encouraged scientific research and medical interest in this natural hormone. For more information on the indications and effects of natural progesterone, please refer to Chapter 10 on menopause.

To date, unfortunately, very few studies have addressed the possible cardiovascular effects of these preparations in postmenopausal women. The study with the biggest impact on the perception of natural progesterone was the Postmenopausal Estrogen/ Progestin Interventions (PEPI) trial.[151] Although the postmenopausal women in this study were also given estrogen, the PEPI trial demonstrated similar lipid changes for estrogen and progesterone that are known to occur with administration of estrogen alone, except for HDL-C, which was significantly reduced. Natural progesterone alone has been used in only one study. The author reported the lipid impact of 10 days of oral micronized natural progesterone at doses of 300 mg, 200 mg, and placebo in 60 premenopausal women, who either had no menses or very few menses in a year.[152] Although there was no statistical significance, the results suggest that LDL cholesterol may vary with different progesterone doses. Perhaps what merits reflection here is that, despite its other undesirable effects, estrogen alone has the most favorable effect on lipids. When combined with progesterone, natural HDL cholesterol does not improve as much and, much less so, when given with progestin, HDL improves even less.

Very recent information in a new study comparing the effects of natural progesterone and synthetic progestin did not fare so well for the natural progesterone advocates. The conjugated equine estrogen (CEE) alone group had an increase in HDL levels of 14.4 percent after six months, the estrogen plus progestin had an increase in HDL of 4.58 percent, and the estrogen plus natural progesterone had an increase in HDL of 5.44 percent.[153] Total cholesterol levels were significantly decreased only in the estrogen plus progestin group, and triglyceride levels were increased only in the estrogen plus natural progesterone group. The authors of this study concluded that micronized progesterone was not superior to medroxyprogesterone acetate.

The effects of natural progesterone on hypertension merit discussion. Oral micronized progesterone (OMP) may cause less fluid retention than the synthetic progestins. However, perhaps because of some of its metabolites, it may still have a negative impact on fluid retention. It is a mixed bag: its diuretic effects could lower blood pressure, but its fluid retention effects could have the opposite outcome. There is, however, some evidence showing that OMP may lower blood pressure. In fact, OMP administered in doses of 200, 400, and 600 mg/day to hypertensive postmenopausal women and older men significantly reduced systolic blood pressure as compared to placebo in a two-week treatment trial.[154] With the maximum dose, systolic blood pressure was decreased approximately 19.7 mm Hg and diastolic blood pressure about 9.6 mm Hg. At the lower doses, the decreases in systolic blood pressure were less significant.

Two studies have demonstrated a markedly different effect of synthetic progestins, as opposed to natural progesterone, on the coronary vessels[155] and on their wall smooth muscle cells.[156] The results of these two studies indicate that synthetic progestins may induce vasospasm of the coronary arteries, whereas estrogen and/or natural progesterone promoted vasodilation.

Although many women are presently using natural progesterone creams as an alternative to conventional HRT, relatively little research has been done on these products—none on their potential impact on cardiovascular risk factors. For more information on the use of natural progesterone alone or in combination with different estrogens in menopause, please refer to Chapter 10.

Natural Estrogens

Natural estrogens are what we have come to call plant-derived bio-identical hormones. They include estradiol, estrone, and estriol. "Bio-identical" estrogens from the Mexican wild yam and the soybean can be synthesized in a laboratory. Mexican wild yam contains diosgenin and soy contains stigmasterol. Both diosgenin and stigmasterol can then be converted in the laboratory into a biochemically identical estrogen to that produced by our ovaries. In his book *Natural Woman, Natural Menopause,* Dr. Marcus Laux refers to them as "the naturals."[157] These hormones are available in standardized dosages and are obtainable by prescription from pharmacists who still know the art of compounding. There exists approximately 1,500 compounding pharmacists in the United States. (See the Resources section for a partial list of compounding pharmacies.) Natural estrogens have been produced since the 1930s, used in Europe since the 1950s, and have been available in the United States since the 1970s. The advantages of natural estrogens over HRT are presented in Chapter 10. This section will focus on their effect on the cardiovascular system.

Theoretically, if we have a dose of natural estrogens that is equivalent in strength to the dose of the conventional estrogen, the cardiovascular benefit should be the same. Nonetheless, any hormone therapy that is considered to be an alternative to the leading form of therapy (conjugated equine estrogens, i.e., Premarin) must at some point be compared in order to prove its worthiness and acceptability among patients and health care practitioners. A few studies have looked at oral micronized estradiol alone or in combination with micronized progesterone and compared it to conjugated equine estrogens (CEE) plus medroxyprogesterone acetate (MPA) to evaluate possible effects on CAD parameters. Ten menopausal women, administered the natural estrogen/progesterone combination, experienced a decrease in total cholesterol. In contrast, this parameter did not change significantly at 12 months over the initial cholesterol readings in the five women who were given CEE and MPA. Both groups experienced an increase in HDL cholesterol.[158]

SAMPLE TREATMENT PLAN FOR CARDIOVASCULAR DISEASE

- Reduce dietary saturated fat by minimizing or eliminating beef, pork, lamb, cheese, butter, milk, chocolate, and fried foods.
- Increase intake of fruits, vegetables, whole grains, and legumes, especially soybean products, nuts, seeds, and fish.
- Avoid smoking.
- Practice regular aerobic exercise (30 minutes or more, 3–7 times per week).
- Reduce or eliminate coffee (caffeinated and decaffeinated).
- Strive for ideal body weight.
- Daily supplements
  Vitamin E: 400–800 IU per day
  Flaxseed oil: 1 tbsp per day
  Garlic: 1 capsule per day containing 4,000–5,000 mcg allicin
- Women with high blood pressure or elevated cholesterol should receive additional herbal or nutritional supplementation.
- The use of natural hormones should be customized to each individual woman.
- Stress management: meditation or relaxation exercise 15 minutes each day.

Another study reported the results of a combination pill containing 2 mg of oral micronized estradiol, 1 mg of estriol, and 1 mg of a synthetic progestin in 265 women, who were followed for over 4 years; serum cholesterol and triglyceride levels decreased significantly, but HDL levels were not measured.[159] In yet another study, the same formula resulted in decreased triglycerides after 3 months of therapy and a subsequent increase after 12 months; LDL levels decreased both at 3 and at 12 months of treatment. Unfortunately, HDL levels also were decreased at 3 and at 12 months. The authors speculated that this latter effect was due to the synthetic progestin used in the study.

Natural estradiol is thus a viable alternative to conventional HRT, with the potential for less undesirable side effects. It seems reasonable to state that natural estradiol in combination with natural progesterone is the preferred form of administering HRT.

Estriol is the other natural estrogen that can be used either alone or in combination with estradiol (called bi-est), or with estradiol and estrone (called tri-est). Estriol is discussed in more detail in Chapter 10: its potential protective properties against uterine and breast cancer; treatment of vaginal atrophy; and dryness; and menopause symptoms in general. When one turns to cardiovascular disease, little is known about what estriol may or may not do. However, two studies indicate positive effects of estriol administration on lipid profiles and cardiac function. Japanese researchers found that 2 mg/day of estriol was effective in decreasing total cholesterol and triglycerides and increasing HDL levels in elderly women (age 70 to 84), but not in middle-aged postmenopausal women (age fifty to sixty-five).[160] The other study followed postmenopausal women using estriol and found an increase in their cardiac function and improved blood flow in the extremities.[161] I would not currently consider estriol, used above, as a viable substitute for the other modalities in preventing coronary artery disease.

❧ Conventional Medicine Approach

It must be remembered that there is still much that is unknown about cardiovascular disease, hormone replacement, natural menopause options, and the aging process in women. June 1998 will see the completion of the first double-blind placebo-controlled trial on HRT and coronary heart disease and mortality, stroke, peripheral arterial disease, lipid levels, and quality of life. Prior to the establishment of the Office of Research on Women's Health in 1990 and the availability of funding from the Women's Health Initiative (WHI), research in diseases related to women was rarely done. Women, moreover, were seldom research subjects. These two factors remained a significant problem in health research until Congress mandated the National Institutes of Health (NIH) to develop a research agenda for women's health. This historical decision has begun to eradicate this research disparity. The WHI, the research project born of it, is currently underway. The WHI will be addressing some of our dilemmas about the use of conventional estrogen (Premarin) and synthetic progestins (Provera) and evaluating preventive approaches to coronary artery disease in women. The results will be made available in 2008. The Heart and Estrogen-Progestin Replacement Study (HERS) is investigating the use of estrogen and/or progestin replacement in 2,340 premenopausal women with current coronary artery disease who have not had a hysterectomy.

Conventional practitioners are as eager to educate their patients on the importance of preventing heart disease as are holistic care providers. For several years now, patients have been encouraged by their conventional physicians to stop smoking, increase exercise, lower their dietary fat, increase fruits and vegetables, lose weight, and reduce their stress. Increasingly, though, estrogen replacement therapy has become the number-one preventive measure. It is routinely suggested to most menopausal women. It has become much more common than diet and lifestyle education and prescription.

The concept of a hormonal connection with CAD in women was viewed with a great deal of skepticism just a few years ago. In the last three to five years, most cardiologists have been presenting estrogen to their female patients as a first-line drug for cardiovascular disease. The efficacy of postmenopausal administration of estrogen on reducing CAD risk in women is well documented. More than 30 studies (case-control and cohort) consistently have shown a decreased incidence of coronary heart disease in women undergoing HRT therapy as evidenced by either reduced heart attacks or reduced atherosclerosis.[11] Different study designs and populations of menopausal women have elicited similar findings: HRT reduces CAD risk by 50 percent. Therein lies the basis for HRT recommendation to almost every postmenopausal woman by internists, family practitioners, ob/gyns, and cardiologists: your risk for a heart attack will be cut in half.

However, the results of these studies are open to question. The most common criticism leveled at them is that they were obtained from only observational studies. What this means is that a certain number of women elect to take estrogen while others do not. A selection bias exists: women participating in these studies were not randomly chosen and, therefore, cannot represent the general population. Typically, they were healthier, leaner, of higher socioeconomic status, and had additional characteristics associated with lower risk of heart disease. Even if the difference between the estrogen users and nonusers is not that great to begin with, we see that women who take estrogen over time tend to alter their lifestyles in a healthier direction. In addition, they tended to smoke less, exercise more, eat a lower-cholesterol diet, and weigh less than their counterparts. Moreover, women who are taking estrogen also interact with their physicians more often and regularly receive information about preventive health care. Selection bias notwithstanding, most conventional practitioners still are convinced that estrogen replacement makes sense.

In fact, various possible biological mechanisms may explain the beneficial effects of estrogens on CAD in postmenopausal women. HRT, even at low levels, has been shown to increase HDL cholesterol and decrease LDL cholesterol back toward premenopausal levels.[150] Also, HRT reduces high blood pressure.[162] Other possible mechanisms include the ability of HRT to increase antioxidant activity in the blood, prevent cholesterol deposits in damaged blood vessels, and increase the production of nitric oxide within the vessel wall which translates into potent vasodilation.

Now that large study analyses have demonstrated that HRT is causally related to breast cancer[163] in postmenopausal women, the decision on whether to use HRT has been illuminated. As with all therapies, HRT must be examined against the backdrop of benefit versus risk. The Colditz study has heightened its risk. However, until at least some of the double-blind, placebo-controlled studies underway on HRT and women and heart disease are completed, doubts about the advisability of using HRT will persist. Unfortunately, these data will not be available for 8 to 10 years. No single study to date, even the observational studies, is completely convincing. If you look at all the evidence, both the results of those studies and the known biologic effects of estrogen, it is reasonable to understand the value of HRT, at least in women who remain at higher risk for heart disease. The nagging questions for women continue to be, "Should I or shouldn't I?" and "Is it worth the risk?" The questions remain, Do natural estrogen and natural progesterone replacement therapies also pose the same risk, and are they causally related to breast cancer, or is there something different enough in how the body metabolizes these hormones? Further discussion of these concerns is presented in Chapters 3 and 10. Hopefully, this discussion will help both patients and practitioners facing these important and pressing questions.

It seems likely that women should derive the similar benefits from medical interventions for coronary heart disease as do men. In fact, biological differences between the two sexes preclude this conclusion. Women are at a disadvantage here because large scientific trials to assess the efficacy of various therapies have included either none or few women. For example, a recent meta-analysis of the literature on hyperlipidemia in women shows no evidence that lowering cholesterol improves total mortality in women, but that treating women with existing CAD may decrease mortality.[164, 165] Most trials of aspirin therapy have excluded women. The Aspirin Myocardial Infarction Study[166] addressed secondary prevention in survivors of heart attacks. There were 4,021 men and 503 women studied for an average of 38 months. There were no significant survival differences between the groups, although women showed a slight increase in mortality with treatment. Only one of three multicenter trials on the role of coronary bypass surgery has included women.[167] Analyses of this treatment modality have consistently shown higher mortality rates among women as compared to men after the surgery.[166] Relief from angina chest pain after surgery is less frequent among women than men. The results of several recent studies involving significant numbers of women show that lipid-lowering drugs prevent both CAD and stroke in women.[168, 169]

The significance of high blood pressure as a coronary risk factor in women is currently controversial. While women have hypertension less often, it is also more benign.[170] These two factors may explain the apparent lack of benefit from lowering blood pressure.[171] For example, the Hypertension Detection and Follow-up Program[171] demonstrated that treatment of mild hypertension reduced the death rate from heart disease but a sub-analysis of white women suggested not only no benefit but possibly a negative effect of the therapy. The British Medical Research Council Trial[172] contained 8,000 women between the ages of 35 and 64 years. Antihypertensive treatment resulted in a 25 percent reduction in cardiovascular events and a 48 percent reduction in strokes. The Systolic Hypertension in the Elderly Program[173] observed a 36 percent reduction in strokes and a 25 percent reduction in coronary heart disease. A meta-analysis of randomized drug treatment trials in which 47 percent of the patients were women showed decreases in stroke of 42 percent and 14 percent in coronary disease.[174] Based on these trials, women with a systolic blood pressure over 160 mm Hg and a diastolic pressure over 90 mm Hg should begin lifestyle changes of exercise and stress reduction. If the blood pressure does not improve, then conventional practitioners would recommend drug treatment.

Pharmaceutical Interventions

Even with conventional practitioners, dietary and lifestyle modifications are the initial treatment steps. In postmenopausal women, HRT is one of the primary treatment interventions. The major classes of lipid-lowering agents used in conventional medicine include HMG-CoA reductase inhibitors (statins), which primarily decrease LDL cholesterol levels; fibric acid derivatives, which primarily decrease triglyceride levels; and nicotinic acid, which can decrease both LDL cholesterol and triglyceride levels. The latter, however, is associated with side effects that are often severe enough to warrant discontinuance of the treatment.

Of all available major lipid lowering agents, the statins provide the most effective pharmacologic therapy. All statins lower LDL cholesterol and total cholesterol and have a variable effect on lowering triglycerides. Of all the statins currently available, atorvastatin has demonstrated the most powerful cholesterol- and triglyceride-lowering effect.[175]

The treatment of high blood pressure is responsible for more primary care visits than any other chronic medical condition. However, approximately 75 percent of treated hypertension patients are receiving inadequate care, as defined by their inability to achieve and maintain their target blood pressure.[176] Blood pressures above 140/90 mm Hg are thought to increase cardiovascular death rates by twofold over normal blood pressure. The Joint National Committee on Prevention, Detection, Evaluation, and Treatment of High Blood Pressure (JNC VI) has reached a consensus that medical practitioners should advise all hypertension patients to attain ideal weight, refrain from using tobacco products, drink alcohol only moderately, partake of regular aerobic exercise, and maintain a diet low in saturated fats and sodium. The committee advises using this conservative approach for up to 12 months before considering medication therapy in patients with Stage I hypertension (140–159 mm Hg systolic over 90–99 mm Hg diastolic) in the absence of other risk factors or target organ damage. Although lifestyle modifications alone may not be enough to control blood pressure, they may help limit pharmacologic intervention.

Two classes of agents are recommended for initial antihypertensive therapy: diuretics and beta-blockers. Thiazide diuretics may be preferred for women affected by osteoporosis, since their effects on sodium excretion lead to a retention of serum and spinal calcium. Thiazide-type diuretics are the most commonly prescribed diuretics for hypertension; loop diuretics, however, are more appropriate for the elderly and others with compromised kidney function.

Beta-blockers, the other class of antihypertensives recommended for initial therapy in patients who do not have other illnesses that might require a different drug, are often prescribed for systolic hypertension and for hypertension in the elderly. They are also preferred in people who have experienced a heart attack, since beta-blocker therapy limits subsequent cardiovascular events and lowers cardiac and overall mortality.[177] Beta-blockers can alleviate symptomatic chest pain and anxiety states, and may have the side benefit of preventing migraines. They can be difficult to prescribe and use due to adverse effects and sensitive dosing regimens.

Calcium antagonists, another class of antihypertensive agents, can be divided into two major subclasses: the dihydropyridine agents, including Adalat and Procardia, and the nondihydropyridines including Covera, Calan, and Cardizem. New subclasses of drugs are available, such as Posicor. Other agents are still being developed. Although controversial,[†] calcium antagonists continue to be the most widely prescribed class of antihypertensive medications. Calcium antagonists are well-tolerated and are available in one-per-day doses. Some of them may cause constipation or edema (swelling of the lower legs/feet). Diuretics should not be used to solve the edema caused by these medications. The edema is due to the profound vasodilating effects of the drug. The solution is to lower its dose or try another agent. Advantages and disadvantages are ascribed to different drugs, and the expert advise of a cardiologist or internist is necessary.

Alpha-blockers are as effective as other antihypertensive agents but are not well accepted by clinicians. Thus, they constitute less than 10 percent of the hypertension treatment market. Confusing dose regimens and fears of adverse side effects may be at the root of this phenomenon. There are select patients where this drug regimen is preferred, however—patients with insulin resistance and abnormal blood lipids.

ACE inhibitors are the preferred antihypertensive class of drugs in patients with type 1 and type 2 diabetes, congestive heart failure, and certain kidney diseases. ACE inhibitors are often not used in African-Americans and Latinos, based on the presumption that they will be less efficacious in lowering elevated blood pressures in these minority populations. Higher doses may be needed that could lead to greater side effects. Ace inhibitors most common adverse effect is a persistent, dry, hacking cough. A much rarer adverse effect is angioedema that manifests as swelling of the lips or tongue accompanied by

difficulty in breathing. Any of these symptoms warrants immediate medical attention. Ace inhibitors are contraindicated in the second and third trimesters of pregnancy, since they have been associated with the development of fetal abnormalities, and they should be prescribed with caution in women of childbearing age for the same reasons.

Combination medications are being increasingly used in treating hypertension. A lower dose of two medications may achieve the desired effect with fewer adverse effects.

The use of pharmacologic agents to lower lipids and/or blood pressure are appropriate regimens for patients who have not responded to a rigorous lifestyle modification program and nutritional and/or herbal supplementation. It is important to recognize, however that despite the effectiveness of alternative therapies, not all patients are able to make the necessary changes or comply with the supplementation regimen. A minority of patients have conditions that will resist their own and their physician's best efforts.

Seeing a Licensed Primary Health Care Practitioner[*]

The signs and symptoms of coronary heart disease in women can be different from those found in men. Most notable is that women more often have cases of silent myocardial infarction, have chest pain while having normal coronary vessels, and have a higher incidence of mortality with their first incidence of chest pain due to coronary artery spasm. Diagnostic testing in women may not be as reliable either. Exercise stress testing is less predictive, and angiograms reveal less extensive disease in women than in men.

One's risk of heart disease changes with time. Risk assessment must be done periodically. For menopausal women, it needs to be done annually and include a thorough medical history, physical exam, blood pressure checking, weight, listening to heart and lungs, checking pulses, and other physi-

---

[†] Ten days after the Food and Drug Administration took the heart medication Posicor off the market, a new warning has been issued about the drug. A team of doctors in Oregon has reported that four patients who stopped taking Posicor went into shock after switching to other drugs, and that one died as a result. *The New York Times,* June 19, 1998.

[*]N.D. = Naturopathic Doctor; M.D. = Medical Doctor; D.O. = Osteopathic Doctor; N.P. = Nurse Practitioner; P.A. = Physician's Assistant

cal findings, (and more often if abnormal); lipid panels checking for total cholesterol, HDL, LDL, triglycerides, and the cholesterol/HDL ratio. If deemed necessary, EKG, stress test, and other laboratory tests such as homocysteine levels may also be recommended. The evaluation of the results of these tests will help determine the most appropriate intervention.

For women with abnormal findings, it is important to seek the advice of someone who can help determine if therapeutic doses of some of the natural therapies discussed in this chapter are suitable and sufficient for success. A treatment plan can be agreed on; then, with follow-up evaluation and testing after an appropriate interval, the next step in the process can be determined. Some women may need to take cholesterol- or blood-pressure lowering pharmaceutical agents if an aggressive natural treatment plan has not brought adequate results, at least on an interim basis, and with appropriate monitoring and follow-up. The determination of whether to use natural or conventional HRT and its dosage can best be made by a practitioner who appreciates the role and value of each.

Menopause

 Overview

There are currently 40 million American women who are postmenopausal, and their numbers are expected to increase to 60 million by the year 2010. By the year 2015, nearly 50 percent of the women in the United States will be menopausal. This rapid expansion in the menopausal population is related both to an increase in longevity (mean life expectancy of approximately 84 years) and to the maturation of the baby boom generation into the menopausal age group. We might call it "boomerpause."

The term "menopause" is derived from *meno* (month, menses) plus *pausis* (pause, cessation), i.e., a pause in menstruation. The menopause is the permanent cessation of menstruation following the loss of ovarian activity. Several other terms are used when describing menopause. The "perimenopause" is the period immediately before and after the menopause. The "climacteric" indicates the period of time when a woman passes from the reproductive stage of life to the postreproductive stage of life.

Menopause should be regarded as a normal, natural event of aging except when it is brought about by surgery, medications, or radiation. As we discuss problems that can be associated with menopause for some women, it can quickly be viewed as a disease process and a sign of pending fragility, disability, and even death. It is important to appreciate that the menopause is or can be the beginning of a new phase of life, with fewer family obligations, new options, new learning opportunities, and new adventures. With a proper understanding of menopause and an adequately informed and respectful health care practitioner, the majority of menopausal women can be healthy and happy and use this time period as an opportunity to foster a preventive health care plan and lifestyle.

The average age of menopause has been estimated to be between 50 and 52.[1] In the Massachusetts Women's Health Study, the largest and most comprehensive prospective, longitudinal study of middle-aged women, the median age for menopause was 51.3 years.[2]

Women can enter menopause by several different routes and pass through more than one phase. Premature menopause is a combination of secondary amenorrhea, menopausal (climacteric) symptoms, and a persistent elevation in follicle-stimulating hormone (FSH) levels greater than 20 ml IU/ml before 40 years of age. One in 100 women between the ages of 15 and 40 will spontaneously develop premature menopause.[3] In two-thirds of cases no apparent cause for the premature ovarian failure will be found.[4] These cases are called "idiopathic." In one-third of cases, causes of premature menopause include metabolic and systemic disease, chromosome abnormalities, immunologic disorders, infections, lack of blood supply to the ovaries, cigarette smoking, ovariectomy (both ovaries removed), pelvic irradiation, and chemotherapy.

Probably the most dramatic entry into menopause is to have both ovaries removed. This is referred to as a bilateral oophorectomy. A hysterectomy is actually only the surgical removal of the uterus. These surgeries can be done separately or together. The incidence of hysterectomy and oophorectomy in the United States is substantial. Women who undergo a bilateral oophorectomy have an increased risk of developing osteoporosis, coronary artery disease, and/or atrophy of the genital area at a younger age. Approximately 1.7 million hysterectomies were performed between 1988 and 1990; both ovaries were also removed in 49.6 percent of the surgeries performed. Both procedures were performed in 37 percent of women younger than 45 years of age and 65 percent in women 45 years or older.[5]

When the ovaries are removed, the onset of menopause is immediate. The sudden onset of hot flashes, mood changes, sleep disturbances, and loss of sexual arousal is accompanied by a slower onset of fatigue, headaches, dry skin, bone and joint pain, loss of vaginal lubrication, and painful vaginal sex. This overwhelming barrage of symptoms results from the sudden drop in hormone production—estrogen, progesterone, testosterone, and DHEA.

Fortunately, all of the sex hormones are not lost. For example, about 50 percent of our testosterone comes from the ovaries and adrenal glands; the other 50 percent comes from many different parts of the body, including the liver, the skin, and the brain. These tissues manufacture testosterone from precursor hormones that are made in the ovaries and the adrenals. In other words, the ovaries and the adrenal glands are responsible for producing all of a woman's testosterone, either directly or indirectly. The adrenal glands also produce androstenedione. Androstenedione is converted to estrogen (estrone) in the body fat and to a lesser degree in some other tissues and organs including the muscle and skin. For some women, this source of estrogen is adequate to counter some of the menopausal symptoms, and they have an easier time.

Women who have more body fat or more muscle mass may likely do a little better. Although this

adrenal source of hormonal support is a blessing, the adrenal glands produce their maximal amount of androgens in the presence of fully functioning ovaries. The function of the cortex of the adrenal glands is linked to the functions of the ovaries due to their shared original group of cells in the developing embryo. If you don't have your ovaries, then the adrenal glands will not produce their potential amount of androgens. In natural menopause, the ovaries continue producing androgens (typically referred to as male hormones) that help maintain the potential for sexual arousal.[6] Several studies have shown that surgically-induced menopausal women have lower sexual desires and subjective arousal as compared to women who have retained their ovaries; treating these post-oophorectomy women with estrogen and androgens results in a greater sexual response than treatment with estrogen alone.[7] Surgical menopause may also have a psychological impact on women. Not only is this related to the sudden change in hormone status, but the severity of depression that develops can often be correlated to body image, sexual identity, cultural background, and family issues.[8]

Women who have had a hysterectomy but still retain one or both ovaries will go through menopause more naturally most of the time, although sometimes earlier than they would have. Without the uterus and the monthly bleeding, it may be harder to know when menopause arrives. All the typical symptoms can occur, though. If you are fortunate to not have any of the overt menopausal symptoms, you can estimate that you'll have gone through menopause somewhere between ages 48 and 53. The FSH blood test may be used to determine menopausal status.

Another form of menopause is a medically-induced menopause. Women who have been treated with chemotherapy may go into menopause either temporarily or permanently. About 30 percent of these women will have a return of their menses sometime within the first year. Irradiation of the pelvic or abdominal area can also induce menopause. Tamoxifen, another cancer drug used mostly for women who have breast cancer, can either induce menopause in premenopausal women or increase menopause symptoms in postmenopausal women.

Several drugs can induce menopause that is reversible once the drugs are discontinued. These include Lupron and Synarel, which are usually given to suppress menses in the case of endometriosis and to shrink fibroids before surgery. Menopausal symptoms tend to be not as severe as in surgical menopause but worse than natural physiologic menopause.

The natural transition from the reproductive years to the postmenopausal years is not necessarily a smooth one, even though it is a normal process of aging. Though not a disease, there can be health problems associated with menopause. For many women, symptoms of these hormonal changes occur intermittently for a number of years. Dr. Susan Love calls this period "puberty in reverse." Just like the hormonal highs and lows of puberty brought sleepiness, acne, mood swings, and unpredictable menses, this end of the spectrum with its own hormonal fluctuations may bring hot flashes, insomnia, mood swings, acne, poor concentration and memory, and unpredictable menses again.

No two women's menopause transition is alike. Many women begin to experience an array of physical, mental, and emotional symptoms long before they meet the definition of menopause. These changes, which can occur over many years (usually from around age 40 to 51), are a transition period called "perimenopause."

A narrower definition is the transition from regular to irregular menses. On average, the onset of perimenopause occurs around age 47, and the average duration is 4–5 years. Menopause is the proper term used after 12 months have elapsed since the last menstrual period.

During perimenopause, several biological changes occur:

- The number of ovarian eggs (oocytes) reaches very low levels, from 1–2 million at birth to only a few thousand.
- The menstrual cycle begins to vary, usually shortening from one menses to the next.
- The levels of FSH in the body increase. This rise is one of the first signs of an aging reproductive system. Health care practitioners often measure FSH levels to determine if one's symptoms are related to menopause. There are two problems with

this test, however: 1) varying patterns of FSH may occur even in the same woman, and 2) the FSH is often normal even in a perimenopausal woman.
- Ovarian production of estradiol, progesterone, and testosterone decreases with the onset of true menopause.
- Although hormone levels will eventually decrease, lower estrogen levels aren't experienced until six months to one year before true menopause. It's only in the last year of perimenopause that estrogen levels begin to decrease. Near menopause, estrogen levels rise very high and then drop very rapidly. Declining progesterone levels precede declining estrogen levels. Some of the perimenopause symptoms may in fact be due to lowered progesterone levels or a relative change in the relationship of estrogen to progesterone.
- Eventually, the lower levels of estrogen are no longer adequate to cause a buildup of the uterine lining, and there is not enough tissue to produce a menses.
- The specific reason why menopause occurs is the ultimate loss of follicles in the ovaries. This leads to the loss of progesterone production and declining estrogen influence. This coincides with an increase in FSH and LH (luteinizing hormone). (See page 17 for normal menstrual cycle and hormones.)

The symptoms of decreased hormone levels and perimenopause are varied, unpredictable, and often go unrecognized as perimenopausal symptoms. The signs and symptoms of perimenopause can include menstrual irregularities, hot flashes, vaginal dryness and thinning, skin changes, fatigue, decreased libido, mood swings, depression, changes in memory and cognition, sleep disturbance, hair loss on the head, hair growth and acne on the face, palpitations, nausea, headaches, urinary tract infections, joint pains, and the beginning stages of osteoporosis and heart disease.

Menopausal Symptoms

The changes associated with menopause can be mild, moderate, or severe. Some women may have no significant menopausal symptoms, and others will have symptoms that are progressive and problematic for many years to come. Let's talk a little more about some specific menopausal symptoms.

Hot Flashes, Night Sweats, Insomnia, and Palpitations

These four problems in menopausal women are often referred to clinically as vasomotor symptoms. The traditional vasomotor symptoms reported by about 85 percent of menopausal Western women are related to the decline in ovarian function.[9] Hot flashes, known as "hot blooms" in the 1800s, are the most common symptom associated with the menopausal period. Despite the large numbers of women in Western societies who are affected by hot flashes, we know little about the natural course of this symptom. We still do not understand the physiology of hot flashes, the mechanism of lowered estrogen levels and hot flashes, the average age of onset, triggers, duration, frequency, or why they are prominent in some cultures and absent in others. The number of women who are affected by hot flashes in the United States is remarkable. About 75 percent of women will experience hot flashes, and 15 percent are severely affected.[10] The occurrence of hot flashes is highest in the first two years postmenopause, although information is scanty on the total time over which hot flashes are experienced. Women with surgically-induced menopause often report particularly persistent, more intense, and more frequent hot flashes. It has been determined by one large interview study in 1933 that for most women hot flashes last about two years, although some women experience them for 5–10 years.[10] As many as 15 percent of women may still report hot flashes 16 years after menopause. Hot flash frequency is particularly variable and ranges anywhere from several episodes in a year to every hour throughout each day.

Perhaps the most intriguing observation about hot flashes is how cultural attitudes toward menopause may affect the incidence of hot flashes as well as other menopausal symptoms. For example, Japanese and Indonesian women report far fewer hot flashes than do women from Western societies.[11] Mayan women in the Yucatan do not report any symptoms at menopause other than menstrual cycle irregularity.[12] Many researchers have attributed these differences to biological, psychological, social, and cultural factors, but I would speculate that there are significant dietary factors influencing the experience of menopause symptoms, largely due to a diet high in phytoestrogens. More about that in the nutrition section.

The clearest explanation for hot flashes is that they appear to be the body's response to a sudden but transient downward resetting of the body's thermostat, which is located in the hypothalamus.[13] This temporary alteration of the set point would cause the sensation of intense heat and flushing. What we don't know is what initially triggers this event. A logical correlation between low estrogen levels and hot flashes exists. Estrogen levels have been found to be lower in premenopausal women with hot flashes than in those without hot flashes.[14] However, there are observations that are not consistent with the association between low estrogen levels and hot flashes. Postmenopausal women have estrogen levels that remain low, yet some women never have hot flashes, while others have persistent ones, and yet others have them only sporadically. Prior to puberty, girls have low estrogen levels, but not hot flashes. Also, hot flashes are reported during pregnancy, when the estrogen level is high. Although estrogen does play a role in internal temperature regulation, the specific effect of estrogen on the body's thermoregulation remains unknown. Some researchers believe that hot flashes are due to an imbalance in beta-endorphins and other opiates in the brain which in turn may influence the temperature regulation center.[15] Estrogen and progesterone may alter the activity of these naturally occurring opiates, and it is possible that lower levels of estrogen and progesterone cause a withdrawal of opioids, triggering a hot flash.

A primary problem for many women with hot flashes and nighttime sweats is sleep disruption. Some women are awakened during sleep due to a night sweat, but sleep disturbances are not always a result of hot flashes, and not all hot flashes disrupt sleep. Most nighttime hot flashes are associated with waking up, but almost half the time a waking episode is not associated with hot flashes. Sleep disturbances and early morning awakenings are also signs of depression and anxiety. These emotional changes are also associated with menopause for some women.

Depression and Anxiety

The psychological conditions associated with menopause have been a source of conflicting scientific data and controversy. Even though the relationship between menopause and depression has been extensively studied, the results have been inconsistent. Some studies have shown more frequent depressive moods among peri- and postmenopausal women as compared to premenopausal women, while other studies have not. It may be that the psychosocial and cultural factors that influence variations in moods affect women more at the time of menopause.[16]

Data from the Massachusetts Women's Health Study were used to address the effect of change in menopause status on depression, while controlling for prior depression.[17] The study concluded that women who were depressed premenopausally had higher rates of depression in perimenopause; for the women who were not depressed during the premenopause years, the rate of depression was slightly increased during the perimenopause and was highest for women who remained perimenopausal for at least 27 months. Researchers observed that the rate of depression begins to decrease as women move from peri- to postmenopause, and is lowest for those women who have been postmenopausal for at least 27 months. These results show that depression is moderately associated with the perimenopause and that the depression is transient. As women move through perimenopause and become postmenopausal, their rates of depression decline. As mentioned earlier, the women who had a history of prior depression were the most likely to be depressed during the perimenopause, but symptoms of hot flashes, night sweats, and menstrual problems may actually have triggered the depression.

A 1997 study was able to demonstrate that depression and anxiety were higher in post- than in perimenopausal women.[18] The researchers were able to further confirm their hypothesis by showing that depression and anxiety scores were reduced to values below those of perimenopausal women when subjects took hormone replacement therapy (HRT).

Any mood disorders that had become fully manifest during and after menopause were fully reversed with HRT. The estrogen used was a transdermal estradiol patch. However, adding synthetic progestin to the estrogen could reduce the mood-elevating effects of estrogen. Women who take estrogen alone seem to do best mood-wise, as compared to women who take estrogen plus synthetic progestins.[19]

Loss of Memory and Cognition

Many of us experience some degree of change in memory and concentration and clarity of thinking as we age. There are specific cognitive changes that occur when estrogen is rapidly withdrawn from the system, most commonly short-term memory loss. This is most dramatic after childbirth or after oophorectomy. Short-term memory impairment is also a common cognitive change in women with natural menopause. Difficulty concentrating, difficulty with previously simple technical tasks, decrease in memory, and lack of mental clarity are typical states that can then be worsened by difficulty sleeping and sleep interruptions.

An observant health care practitioner can evaluate cognitive impairment throughout a routine medical history by looking for appropriateness of responses, short-term recall of test questions, a medication history, alcohol history, and substance abuse history. When necessary, a neurological exam may be conducted. Many perimenopausal and menopausal women are on thyroid medication, and a thyroid imbalance can cause problems in cognition. It may be a matter of the wrong thyroid dose or an as yet undiagnosed thyroid condition. Antihistamines, caffeine, and daytime sedatives may also affect cognition. For those women on hormone therapy, adjustments may improve mental function.

There are different types of memory, and these involve different brain structures. Usually when we speak of memory, we are referring to "episodic memory." This type of memory enables us to learn and recall events or information that happened in the last few days. "Verbal memory" often refers to the episodic information that is verbally learned. "Semantic memory" refers to the memory for information from the distant past and for what is called "over-learned information." This is information that is not associated with particular life events. Examples of semantic memory would include memory for how many cups in a quart, how many inches in a foot, or the names of things. In the early post-menopause, when women complain of memory problems, they're referring to episodic memory dysfunction. A decrease in estrogen seems to cause some deficits in verbal or episodic memory, although estrogen declines in women with Alzheimer's disease may be more evident in the area of semantic memory.[20]

Alzheimer's disease (AD) is the most common cause of dementia. It affects 1.5–3 times more women than men.[21] The overall severity of dementia is similar between men and women, but women with AD dementia have more difficulty with naming and other semantic memory tasks.[22] The potential mechanisms by which the body's own estrogens (endogenous) or estrogen medications (exogenous) affect cognition are diverse and complicated in some cases. Some of these include potentiating the growth of nerves and nerve cells, increasing the blood flow in the brain, aiding the brain's use of glucose, reducing the negative effects of stress, and preventing the formation of free radical nerve toxins. One of the growing considerations for women around taking HRT is not only short-term improvements in memory but also the potential to reduce the incidence of AD. We will discuss this further in the HRT treatment section.

Vaginal Dryness and Thinning and Urinary Dysfunction

Vaginal dryness, vaginal thinning, and what is called "atrophy" are very common problems for menopausal women but usually do not become troublesome until several years after the menopause. Estrogen is responsible for the thickened, elastic, lubricated tissue of the vagina and vulva (external genital area). When estrogen levels decline, the vulva loses its collagen, fat, and water-retaining ability. As a result, it becomes flattened, thin, and dry and loses tone. With estrogen loss, the vagina also shortens and narrows, and the vaginal walls become thinner, less elastic, and pale in color. Problems of vaginal

dryness, vaginal discharge, and pain with vaginal sex are reported by two out of three women at the age of 75.[23] The change that is usually noticed first is a feeling of dryness of the vagina. The cause is atrophy of the mucus-producing glands of the vaginal wall. With a loss in lubrication and a thinning of the tissue, the vagina is more prone to infections and mechanical injury from vaginal penetration. Small pinpoint bleeding, itching, and burning can result. Other tissue in the same area also becomes thin and atrophied. The urethral tissue (exit route for urine), the labia (the "lips" of the external genital region), and the vaginal wall can all atrophy. These changes can result in increased bladder infections, involuntary loss of urine (incontinence), and prolapse of the bladder, rectum, or uterus. As the atrophy progresses, women may experience an increase in urinary urgency or difficulty holding the urine. A full bladder, laughing, coughing, or exercise can then trigger incontinence.

Change in Sexual Response and Sex Drive

Changes in sexual response and libido are common throughout life, can be due to a host of influences, and tend to increase with aging. With an increasing number of menopausal women, an aging population, and an increased openness about the topic of sexuality, women are increasingly coming to their health care practitioners wanting help in this area. The role of androgenic hormones in female physiology has not been extensively studied until very recently, but we know that throughout a woman's life, hormonal, psychosocial, and medical factors are critical influences.

In women, as noted earlier, the androgens androstenedione and testosterone are synthesized and secreted by both the adrenal glands and the ovaries. The ovaries also synthesize and secrete a small amount of dehydroepiandrosterone (DHEA), although the adrenals are the main source of DHEA, as well as DHEA-sulfate. At the menopause, even though the cyclic hormonal activity of the ovaries has stopped, the ovaries do continue to secrete significant amounts of androgens, mainly testosterone and, to a smaller extent, androstenedione. A woman's total estrogen production decreases by

70–80 percent, while androgen production decreases by about 50 percent. The total amount of testosterone produced after menopause is subsequently reduced; however, it is not due to decreased secretion by the ovaries. If one has a surgical menopause, the plasma levels of testosterone are decreased (about 12 ng/dL) significantly more than in women in natural menopause (about 25 ng/dL).[24] If we compare the plasma levels in naturally menopausal women, four years or more after the last menstrual period, with women of similar ages who have had both ovaries removed, we can show that the ovaries secrete only a minimal amount of estrogens, if any, and small amounts of androstenedione and DHEA, but they continue to secrete testosterone.[25] These androgens are the precursors of estrogens in postmenopausal women although the ovaries within the first four years after menopause have not completely stopped producing estrogen. Within those first four years they secrete small amounts of estrogens, and the plasma levels during this time are only slightly lower than the levels in the early part of the menstrual cycle. Thus, the ovaries continue to be a significant source of both estrogens and androgens within those first four years after the menses have stopped.

So what do all these hormone changes have to do with sexuality? Most, but not all, sexual problems in postmenopausal women are related to estrogen loss to the genitals. This can manifest as a lack of adequate vaginal lubrication with sexual arousal, bleeding after vaginal sex, and pain with vaginal sex. Vaginal dryness is not only associated with painful vaginal sex, but also with a decrease in sexual desire.[26] It is not hard to understand why anticipation of painful sex would dampen one's desire for sex. With a loss of estrogen, relaxation of vaginal tissue and decreased muscle tone also occur, which leads to a decrease in sexual response.

Any relationship between a hormonal cycle and sexual interest, sexual response, or sexual behavior is difficult to assess. In eight studies, increased sexuality was noted around ovulation; in seventeen, during the premenstrual phase; in eighteen, after menses had ceased; and in four, during menses. It is difficult for most women to determine a clear cyclic pattern, but the research seems to reveal that

there is a tendency for women's interest in sexual activity to be most pronounced shortly after, shortly before, or during menstruation.[27]

As many as 86 percent of postmenopausal women experience some form of decreased libido,[28] and it is now generally accepted that androgens play a key role in the sexuality of adult women. As early as 1939, reports were being made that testosterone was responsible for an increased sexual urge in women. At that time, an investigator reported that external daily use of a testosterone ointment in a previously anorgasmic woman enlarged her clitoris enough for her to achieve orgasm.[29] Two sources of information provide the evidence for the testosterone and female sexual behavior connection. One body of evidence comes from studies where testosterone is given as a medication, and the other from studies where levels of androgens in the blood are correlated with sexual behavior. The most convincing evidence of a testosterone medication effect was found in studies where women were given testosterone after both ovaries were removed.[30, 31] Women with medium or high testosterone levels in the blood without taking a testosterone medication reported higher sexual arousal than those with the lowest levels of testosterone.[32] Another study has concluded that postmenopausal women treated with a combination of estrogen and testosterone showed a greater improvement in "sexuality" (sexual activity, satisfaction, pleasure, and orgasm) than was observed with estrogen supplementation alone.[33] Additional studies looking at normal menopausal women have failed to corroborate the statistical improvement with testosterone supplementation over estrogen alone. This again brings up the dynamic nature of the female libido. The addition of estrogens may alleviate vaginal dryness and pain, thereby increasing libido; however, in the absence of true androgen deficiency, testosterone administration may not be helpful.

Acne, Facial Hair, and Hair Loss

Many peri- and postmenopausal women have problems related to an excess in androgens, usually testosterone. Remember that there is a change in the relationship of estrogen to testosterone in peri- and postmenopausal women as compared to premenopausal women. In addition to this relative increase in testosterone, women have individual sensitivities to androgens. Some women only react to very high levels, while others are especially sensitive to what are considered normal androgen levels. In addition, women have different kinds of end-organ sensitivity. Some will develop acne, some thinning hair, and some excess body/facial hair. Acne is always triggered by androgens. The best predictor of acne is early acne, and the best predictor of severe acne is severe early acne.

Excessive hair growth occurs in areas where hair follicles are the most androgen-sensitive. These include the face, chin, skin under the jaw bone, upper lip, sideburn area, and cheeks. Other sensitive areas include the area below the belly button, the lateral pubic area, midline of the chest, around the nipple area, and the low back over the sacrum. Hirsutism is most notably correlated with elevated free testosterone, but testosterone must be converted by an enzyme in the skin to be fully active in the skin. This enzyme is probably higher in women who have excess body and facial hair. These enzyme levels may change in postmenopausal women, or the hair follicle may become more sensitive to the activated testosterone in some postmenopausal women.

Hair thinning and hair loss are often traumatic for women and cause a great deal of anxiety. Androgenetic alopecia is the most common alopecia in humans and is genetically determined. Androgens modulate hair growth. The follicle responds to the androgens and is dependent on the amount present and the presence and number of androgen receptors. The thinning of hair that can be seen in menopausal women is more likely to be diffuse but is most common on the top of the head called the vertex, and next most common at the crown. Some women have a receding hair line and thinning at the temples. Again, the relative increase in testosterone, higher skin enzyme levels that convert one form of testosterone to another, and a change in the receptor sensitivity explain these effects on the hair of menopausal women.

Irregular Bleeding

Perimenopausal women account for approximately 50 percent of abnormal bleeding cases due to the waning function of the ovaries. As the ovary ages, it becomes less efficient in completing the ovulatory process. Initially there is a decrease in progesterone production, which causes shorter cycles. As the aging process progresses, ovulation becomes less frequent, resulting in a variable length of the menstrual cycle and a variation in the duration of the flow. Eventually, the longer a woman goes without ovulating, she ends up with an estrogen-dominant state in the presence of too little progesterone. Ovulation must occur in order to produce progesterone. Women who are in a state of chronic anovulation tend to have an excess of estrogen in the body. This excess estrogen is what disrupts the normal pattern of menstruation.

Even though these hormonal changes are normal, the woman with abnormal uterine bleeding needs to be evaluated by a licensed health care practitioner. Fortunately, in the vast majority of cases there is nothing serious, and the solutions are straightforward and effective. Although perimenopausal women are at risk for endometrial hyperplasia (a thickening of the lining of the uterus), the majority with abnormal perimenopausal bleeding do not have hyperplasia. In postmenopausal women who bleed and who are not taking HRT, it is generally due to atrophy. In those women on HRT, abnormal bleeding can be due to too little estrogen, too much estrogen, too little progesterone, or too much progesterone. It is important to see your licensed health care practitioner in order to determine the correct hormonal solution and also to determine if further testing with a pelvic ultrasound and/or uterine biopsy is necessary. These issues are discussed further in Chapter 1.

Osteoporosis

Osteoporosis is a serious and disabling disease and the most prevalent metabolic bone disease in Western societies. Osteoporosis affects 75 million people in Europe, the United States, and Japan. In the United States alone, it affects 25 million people and causes 1.5 million fractures annually.[34] Osteoporosis is defined as a skeletal disease characterized by low bone mass and a deterioration in bone microarchitecture leading to bone fragility and susceptibility to fracture.[35] Osteoporosis-related fractures will develop in half of all women and one-fifth of all men older than 65 years.[36] Within the first year following a hip fracture, the mortality rate is increased by up to 20 percent, and as many as 25 percent of the survivors will be confined to long-term care facilities one year after the fracture.[34] Fortunately, osteoporosis can and should be prevented and, when present, treated.

The three most common fracture sites are the spine, hip, and forearm. Vertebral fractures of the spine are twice as common as either hip fractures or wrist fractures. The most visible sign of vertebral fractures is a stooped posture that is new or worsening over time, and loss in height.

Menopause is generally considered the reason why women suffer from osteoporosis more than men. However, there are other contributing factors. Men generally have a higher bone mass because of a tendency to have a greater body size and muscle strength. This greater bone mass in turn provides greater stimulation of bone formation. Young women also generally have less calcium intake than do males, which may limit the bone mass women accumulate during early adulthood. The role that estrogen plays in the rate of bone loss perhaps contributes the greatest difference between men and women. Women who have undergone early menopause, late onset of menses in adolescence, and periods of amenorrhea or infrequent menses have a higher incidence of osteoporosis. Women who missed up to half of their expected menstrual periods had 12 percent less vertebral bone mass than did women with normal menstrual cycles; those who missed more than half had 31 percent less bone mass than healthy women.[37]

Many factors have been observed to identify those women who are at greatest risk for osteoporosis. Postmenopausal women; short, slender, fair-skinned, blonde, blue-eyed; a family history of osteoporosis; and early menopause are just some of the key risk factors. Medical history, physical examination, laboratory testing, and bone density testing are the methods used to determine one's risk of osteoporosis and future fractures.

For a thorough discussion on the causes, risks, diagnosis, and treatment of osteoporosis, refer to Chapter 12.

Heart Disease

While most people are aware that heart disease is a primary affliction for men, it seems that women and even health care practitioners don't realize that coronary heart disease is the leading cause of death in women. Two hundred fifty thousand women die annually in the United States of heart attacks. If one includes other atherosclerotic disorders such as strokes, almost 4 of every 10 women will die of these diseases. Approximately 100,000 of these deaths are premature.[38] Starting at age 50, more women die of cardiovascular diseases than of any other condition.[39] Even though heart disease is the leading cause of death in both men and women, the rates of coronary disease at virtually every age are higher in men than in women.[40] When women are in their thirties and forties, the difference between men and women is four- to fivefold. After that, the difference shrinks with increasing age. Distribution of body fat, differences in lipid composition in the bloodstream, and sex hormones are the main factors that account for the gender differences in heart disease.

The generally accepted school of thought is that the incidence of heart disease in women increases after menopause due to a drop in estrogen levels. Many experts question that menopause plays a leading role in the increased incidence of heart disease in women in this age group.[41] The facts actually show that if one looks at the coronary artery disease death rate for women from birth to age 90, one finds it a steady straight line increase. In other words, it does not rise any faster after menopause than before.[11] I discuss this in more detail in Chapter 9.

The other generally accepted dominant school of thought is that conventional HRT reduces the risk for a heart attack by about 50 percent.[42] About three dozen epidemiological studies have shown fairly consistent results in demonstrating a reduced incidence of coronary heart disease based on either reduced heart attacks or reduced atherosclerosis in HRT users. Although it may seem blasphemy to some, there is reason to question these results. We will discuss this more in the treatment sections of this chapter, but it is also addressed comprehensively in Chapter 9.

Several critical issues determine a woman's risk for heart disease. These include a father who had a heart attack or stroke before age 50 or a mother before age 65; high blood pressure; consistently low high-density lipoprotein (HDL) levels and/or high low-density lipoprotein levels (LDL); elevated triglyceride levels in association with low HDL levels; smoking; obesity; sedentary lifestyle; and higher than normal blood sugar levels.

Medical history, physical examination, and laboratory testing are the basic methods of evaluating one's individual risk for heart disease.

For a thorough discussion on the causes, risks, diagnosis, and treatment of heart disease, refer to Chapter 9.

Overview of Alternative Treatments

The fundamental goals of an alternative approach to menopause are to provide relief from common menopausal symptoms and to prevent osteoporosis, heart disease, and other diseases of aging. The goal is to do this with methods that do not increase the risk of other life-threatening diseases such as breast cancer.

In order to accomplish these fundamental goals, a very individualized approach must be embraced by both the menopausal woman and her practitioner. An alternative approach is distinct from the conventional medical approach in that each woman should be evaluated not only for her individual menopause symptoms but also for her individual risks for future diseases. This requires a more comprehensive health history, judicious use of tests to assess her risks for osteoporosis and heart disease, an appreciation of her risk factors for breast cancer, and a willingness to individualize her treatment very carefully. Although more conventional HRT regimens are becoming available and new nonhormonal drugs are being de-

> ### KEY CONCEPTS
>
> - In sorting out treatment options, the management of menopause symptoms should be distinct from disease prevention.
> - Determine individual risks for significant diseases—osteoporosis, heart disease, Alzheimer's, breast cancer. Knowing your subjective and objective risks will help to determine your treatment options.
> - Utilize current testing methods to evaluate and monitor bone and heart health.
> - Be well informed about the process of menopause.
> - Be well informed about the spectrum of alternative and conventional treatment options.
> - Seek the advice of practitioners who can inform you about the spectrum of options.
> - Realize that menopause and aging are processes that evolve over time.
> - What you decide today is not permanent; you can change your treatment decisions based on your changing health, changes in medical understanding and research, and newly available treatment options.

veloped, a practitioner who has an understanding of the whole spectrum of options from the most natural to the most conventional is in the ideal position to properly advise and prescribe a customized optimal treatment and prevention plan. A licensed naturopathic physician is currently the only primary health care provider trained in all the options, although they may have to refer for some selected medications. Conventional medicine still largely approaches the situation as "HRT for all and forever."

At the other extreme is the woman who prescribes for herself. A weakness of self-prescribing over-the-counter natural substances for ongoing menopause management is that this may just treat symptoms like hot flashes or mood swings but often does not adequately address greater long-term concerns such as bone density, blood pressure, cholesterol levels, or vaginal tissue health. Other women self-prescribe mineral supplements, vitamin E, garlic, and others to prevent osteoporosis and heart disease, but their risks have not been identified with

---

PREVENTION

- Do regular aerobic and weight-bearing exercise.
- Eat a healthy diet: low fat, especially lower saturated fat; increase soy foods, fish, whole grains, fruits, vegetables, legumes, nuts and seeds; avoid sugar and refined carbohydrates; small amount of low-fat dairy, if desired.
- Maintain ideal body weight.
- Stop smoking.
- Utilize stress management techniques such as meditation and yoga.
- Have regular annual physical exams.
- Avoid alcohol.
- Request bone density testing if you are concerned about your risk for osteoporosis.
- Request blood lipid panels at least yearly.
- Utilize nutritional/herbal supplement recommendations for prevention of heart disease and osteoporosis.
- Carefully consider risks and benefits of HRT for your situation now and over a long duration of use.

---

objective testing, and they do not monitor changes in bone and heart health over time. The identification of disease risks may not be very important in the early perimenopausal years, but they acquire increasing importance as the postmenopause years accumulate. This is why I recommend that women seek the advice of a naturopathic physician.

Foremost in the evaluation of a potentially menopausal woman is to determine if the symptoms and changes being reported are indeed due to menopause. For example, hot flashes can also be due to hyperthyroidism; night sweats can be due to Hodgkin's disease; mood swings might be a sign of clinical depression or thyroid problems; heart palpitations might be distinctly cardiac in origin rather than a symptom of menopause. Significant errors can also be made in misdiagnosing abnormal menstrual patterns: thyroid conditions, polycystic ovaries, endometriosis, uterine fibroids, ovarian cysts, pituitary tumors, endometrial hyperplasia, and uterine cancer can all present with variations in bleeding patterns. Variations can range from spotting to heavy bleeding or even hemorrhage, from

frequent menses to infrequent, or a complete absence of menses.

Licensed primary health care alternative practitioners such as licensed naturopathic physicians are trained to evaluate these changes and investigate or diagnose all concerns relative to menopause, much as a licensed conventional practitioner would. Sometimes, alternative practitioners might have additional tests that are not yet in common use by conventional practitioners such as salivary hormone testing or urinary peptides of bone turnover. Often, a naturopathic physician is more likely to recommend a bone density test or a blood lipid panel, because we are eager to identify problems early and institute lifestyle and natural supplement preventive measures that do not involve using HRT.

The Naturopathic Approach

In my approach to menopause, therapeutic intervention is determined following an assessment of symptom severity and scope and an evaluation of risk factors for osteoporosis, heart disease, Alzheimer's, and breast cancer. A determination of low risk, medium risk, and high risk, especially for osteoporosis and heart disease, is especially directive in providing choices regarding alternative therapies and/or conventional therapies. Once the symptoms have been pinpointed and the risk for osteoporosis and heart disease has been assessed, then treatments are recommended. Treatment considerations include a spectrum of options from the least intervention to the most intervention. The six treatment considerations are:

1. Diet, exercise, lifestyle, stress management
2. Nutritional supplementation
3. Botanical therapy
4. Natural hormone preparations
5. Friendlier conventional HRT
6. Less-friendly conventional HRT and nonhormonal drugs

You may be surprised to see the inclusion of conventional hormone replacement therapy in my list of options. Choosing to use hormones, whether "natural" or conventional pharmaceutical preparations, is a matter of risk weighed against benefit. My opinion is, if we don't have to use hormones, don't; if we do, let's use them for the shortest amount of time possible and in the safest form or manner possible. These issues are addressed in my discussion of hormones.

Diet changes and/or nutritional supplements and/or botanical therapies will be effective for the management of menopause symptoms in most women. When these are not adequate, then natural hormone options are utilized. If these are not adequate, then friendlier hormone therapy is preferred over less-friendly HRT. Determining risk is a combination of subjective and objective findings resulting from the medical history, physical exam, and any lab or diagnostic imaging tests. General treatment strategies for prevention of osteoporosis and heart disease are as follows:

Low risk:

- Diet changes
- Aerobic and weight-bearing exercise
- Nutritional supplementation
- Botanical therapies

Moderate risk:

- Diet changes
- Aerobic and weight-bearing exercise
- Nutritional supplementation
- Natural hormone options with varying dosages

High risk:

- Diet changes
- Aerobic and weight-bearing exercise
- Nutritional supplementation
- Friendlier conventional hormones or less-friendly conventional hormone and non-hormonal drugs

The specifics of these options and therapies will be expanded on as we discuss nutrition, exercise, nutritional supplementation, botanicals, natural hormones, conventional HRT, and nonhormonal drugs.

Nutrition

An alternative approach to menopause isn't complete without proper nutrition. This includes general considerations such as a diet rich in whole "natural" and unprocessed foods, with an emphasis on fruits, vegetables, whole grains, beans, seeds, nuts, and healthy oils, and low in animal fats.

However, the most important dietary recommendation for all menopausal women may be to increase foods that are high in phytoestrogens. A large number of plants, especially legumes, contain compounds called phytoestrogens. Phytoestrogens are mainly, but not exclusively, nonsteroidal in structure and are either of plant origin or derived from the body's metabolism of precursors present in dietary components. In terms of dietary sources of phytoestrogens, the most important class of these compounds are the phenolic phytoestrogens that contain the isoflavones and the lignans. Phytoestrogens have a unique ability to weakly bind to estrogen receptors in the body and seem to have both a weak estrogen effect as well as an antiestrogen effect.

The Value of Soy

Soybeans are the richest food source of isoflavones, containing 1–2 mg of isoflavones per gram of soy protein. The isoflavones of soy are genistein, daidzein, and glycitein. Not all soy protein products contain phytoestrogens. Some soy protein isolates have been processed with an alcohol extraction that removes the phytoestrogens.[43] When eating soy foods, this is not really a concern, but when using a soy powder or soy capsule, be careful to look for the isoflavone content on the label. Soy protein that has not had the phytoestrogens removed usually contains about 1.2 mg/gram of protein as genistein, 0.5 mg/gram protein as daidzein, and small quantities of glycitein.

The benefits of soy for menopausal women are diverse. Soy appears to have an effect on hot flashes, vaginal dryness, lipids and coronary arteries, bone, mental function, and the prevention of breast and uterine cancer. It's almost as if soy is a miracle food for women, although I'm sure not all would agree. The miracle might be if you actually like soy foods!

The effects of a 12-week diet high in phytoestrogens on menopausal symptoms were studied in 145 women with menopausal complaints.[44] The phytoestrogen diet consisted of daily soybean foods and flaxseeds as approximately one-fourth of the caloric intake. The group of women who ate this diet had an overall greater (although not statistically significant) improvement in their symptoms than that of the nonphytoestrogen diet group. However, when symptoms were evaluated separately rather than all together, the reductions in hot flashes and vaginal dryness were more significant.

Dietary soy supplementation was studied for its effect on hot flashes in postmenopausal women.[45] Fifty-one women were given 60 grams of isolated soy protein daily (76 mg of isoflavones), and 53 women took 60 grams of placebo (casein) daily for 12 weeks. The soy group was significantly superior to the placebo group in reducing the number of hot flashes: a 26 percent reduction by week 3, a 33 percent reduction by week 4, and a 45 percent reduction in daily hot flashes versus a 30 percent reduction with the placebo by week 12.

Other studies have included giving 160 mg of isoflavones daily for three months, which significantly reduced several menopausal symptoms, especially hot flashes,[46] and the use of a soy bar containing only 40 mg isoflavones which showed a small decrease in menopausal symptoms over a 12-week period.[47]

Not all studies show that soy fares quite as well. In another study, women were given a high soy foods diet with a daily intake of 165 mg/day of isoflavones for four weeks.[48] Investigators found no significant estrogen effect on blood measurements of LH, FSH, and sex-hormone-binding globulin (SHBG) such as were found when 0.3 mg/day of Premarin was given. Once again, though, there was a small estrogenic effect on the vaginal tissue.

Other evidence for the use of soy isoflavones in menopause comes from observations of Japanese women, whose menopausal complaints such as hot flushes or flashes are much less prevalent than in Western women.[49] Probably the most famous researcher in soy, Herman Adlercreutz, his colleagues in Helsinki, and Japanese scientists have further studied the diet and phytoestrogen excretion in Japanese women (and men and a few children).[50] The excretion of isoflavonoids in the urine of the Japanese women was much higher than in American and Finnish women. These compounds were excreted in 100-fold to 1,000-fold higher amounts than

those of normal women who consumed a Western diet. The soy foods eaten by Japanese women in high amounts include tofu, miso, aburage, atuage, koridofu, and boiled soybeans in the pod. These high levels of isoflavonoid phytoestrogens may partly explain why hot flashes and other menopausal symptoms are infrequent in Japanese women.

This and other convincing information on large populations of women, called epidemiologic data, imply that the lower incidence of menopausal symptoms may be related to enhanced dietary intake of soy food isoflavones. These observations support the potential role of soy foods and soy supplements in controlling at least some menopausal symptoms. There are newer controlled clinical studies in several countries that demonstrate the benefits of soy isoflavones in the control of menopausal symptoms without negative consequences.[51, 52]

Two questions that arise are: (1) How much soy should one consume? and (2) Are soy supplements as beneficial as soy foods? The digestion and absorption of soy is quite variable among individuals. In fact, some people may have very poor absorption of soy isoflavones. This will be a limiting factor for some women, and I would suggest that if you have indigestion, irregular bowel habits, constipation, or even a soy allergy, higher amounts of soy may not be well tolerated or may not be adequately metabolized and absorbed. The optimal dose of isoflavones has not been determined, and, although there is always a reason to be cautious about things we don't know enough about, the overuse of soy foods is probably not possible, unless you are allergic.

When it comes to taking concentrated dietary soy supplements, however, we should be aware that a different biologic activity and effect may be possible. The decision about the amount is then not clear. A reasonable approach would be to take a daily level of isoflavones that does not exceed the amount consumed in ethnic diets that contain high amounts of isoflavones. From a review of those diets, it appears that this amount is somewhere between 50–150 mg of isoflavones per day for adults.

The isoflavone content of soy foods varies with the form. A listing of the isoflavone content of some of these soy foods will offer some help in calculating your daily intake (see Table 10.1).

TABLE 10.1   **Isoflavone Content of Soybeans**

Soy Food	Amount	Isoflavones (mg)
Textured soy protein granules	¼ cup	62
Roasted soy nuts	¼ cup	60
Tofu, low fat and regular	½ cup	35
Tempeh	½ cup	35
Soy beverage powders	1–2 scoops	25–75 (varies with manufacturer)
Regular soy milk	1 cup	30
Low fat soy milk	1 cup	20
Roasted soy butter	2 tbsp	17
Cooked soybeans	½ cup	150

The relief of menopausal symptoms is not, however, our only concern in menopause. What about bone effects, heart disease, mental function, and the two cancers that are most on the minds of menopausal women: uterine and breast?

In some experiments, soybean phytoestrogens appear to have some estrogen effect on bone. So far, we have our most encouraging data from animal studies, but research on osteoporosis and women and soy foods is in progress. In animal studies, the addition of soy to the diet was able to inhibit bone loss,[53] although not to the extent of estradiol treatment. Another study reported that the effect of soy in ovariectomized rats suppressed bone-losing cell activity.[54]

A heart disease prevention strategy also involves the use of increasing soy in the diet. The evidence that soy lowers cholesterol is substantial. Many studies have demonstrated this effect. Perhaps the best evidence comes from a review of 38 scientific studies. This meta-analysis concluded that consumption of soy protein rather than animal protein significantly decreased serum concentrations of total cholesterol, LDL cholesterol, and triglycerides.[55] The soy intake in these studies averaged 47 grams per day. The average decrease in total cholesterol was 9.3 percent, with a decrease in triglycerides of 10.5 percent, and an increase in HDL cholesterol of 2.4 percent.

While evidence is increasing that HRT has a favorable influence on both memory and cognitive function,[56, 57] there is very little information to suggest that soy isoflavones have either proestrogen or antiestrogen effects on the brain. We will have to await further research.

One of the greatest fears for women contemplating menopause treatment options is the concern about estrogen replacement therapy and breast cancer. Although we will be addressing this in the hormone and conventional medicine sections of this chapter, there are several lines of evidence and logic that support the conclusion that soy is not only safe, but that there is actually a relationship between increased soy intake and breast cancer prevention. Several studies have observed and concluded that Asian women who consume a traditional low fat, high soy diet have a four- to sixfold lower risk of developing breast cancer.[58] The soy-derived isoflavones, i.e., genistein and daidzein, protease inhibitors, phytosterols, and saponins are remarkable in their activities against a variety of cancers. Biochemical mechanisms that explain the anticancer action of genistein are numerous and include antiestrogenic effects, induction of cell differentiation (the more differentiated a cell, the less likely it is to become cancerous), inhibition of several enzymes that induce cancers, antioxidant effects, and antiangiogenesis (limiting the blood supply to cancer cell sites and tumors). Dietary phytoestrogens also inhibit cancer cell growth by competing with estradiol for the type II estrogen binding sites.[59] Even more convincing evidence for the breast cancer protection benefit of soy comes from animal studies.[60] Soy supplementation has reduced the number and size of tumors that were induced with a carcinogenic substance. Doubts as to the significance of the breast cancer protective effects of soy will remain until there has been a prospective study on soy comparing women on a high soy diet with women on a low soy diet over the span of many years with identical risk factors in other areas.

This exciting research on soy is just one more reason why this simple bean has so much appeal for the menopausal woman. Two questions remain: (1) Does soy have a different breast-protective effect in the premenopausal woman as compared to the postmenopausal woman? (2) Because soybeans are high in phytoestrogens, and because these phytoestrogens do weakly stimulate the estrogen receptor in the breast, would this effect be different in women who still produce significant amounts of their own estrogen versus women who are now postmenopausal and have a low estrogen output? To put it another way, premenopausal women normally have higher estrogen levels than postmenopausal women. In premenopausal women who eat a diet or take supplements high in phytoestrogens, these weak plant "estrogens" stimulate estrogen receptors and perform some of the same functions as our own body's stronger estrogens. Our chemical messenger system then says, well, we already have enough total estrogen here, so I'll tell my ovaries to produce less estrogen because I just don't need that much more. By doing so, the rate of production of the body's stronger estrogen declines, and the total estrogen effect on the body (lower internal estrogen production plus weak plant estrogens) is now lower. This mechanism is in part what earns phytoestrogens the characteristic of being called both a "proestrogen" and an "antiestrogen."

But with postmenopausal women, the result of these mechanisms may be different. Postmenopausal women produce less estrogen, and the total level is low. Eating a high phytoestrogen diet or soy supplement boosts the total estrogen levels, even though these estrogens are far weaker. Now, it would seem that because we have a higher total estrogen effect, it may affect the breast differently when the breast is prepared for less estrogen stimulation at this time in life. The problem is this: we have many facts about women who eat soy throughout their lifetimes starting at an early age, we have animal studies, we have laboratory studies about the mechanisms and some of the antitumor effects of soy. But, what we don't have yet is a large body of information on women who begin to take large amounts of soy

later in life starting after menopause, and we don't have information on the effects of soy in women who already have breast cancer. Especially with breast cancer, there is some disagreement about the safety of eating soy.

As a practitioner who advises many postmenopausal women and many pre- and postmenopausal women who have breast cancer, I have had to come to some decision about this now while waiting for more scientific information to unfold. Here's what I tell my patients:

1. We know that women who eat high soy diets during their lifetime have significantly less breast cancer.[58]
2. We know that soy phytoestrogens are significantly weaker, to the order of 10^{-3} times that of estradiol.[61]
3. Phytoestrogens compete with estradiol for the binding of estrogen receptor sites.[59]
4. A review of the biological effects of soy, the mechanisms of action and metabolism of soy, and a review of the epidemiologic and animal studies of soy all provide evidence as to the cancer prevention effects of phytoestrogens.[62]
5. We also have seen soy inhibit tumor growth in animal studies.[60]
6. Three epidemiological trials have reported a protective effect of soybean products against the development of breast cancer.[63–65]

These studies and clinical observations give me great reassurance not only as to the benefit of soy for breast cancer survivors, but to the safety of soy as well. Looked at in another way, the benefits of soy in the areas of hot flashes, vaginal dryness, cholesterol lowering, and possibly bone density far outweigh any speculative insignificant potential risk. We must, however, continue to keep an open mind and extend our science and our scrutiny to the benefits as well as the potential risks of natural therapies.

Another potential question to ask is: How do soy phytoestrogens affect the uterus? We know that estrogen replacement therapy, when given without a progestin or progesterone, increases uterine cancer, but do the phytoestrogens in soy have a negative effect on the uterus as well? The evidence is very clear here regarding soy, although later on we will discuss some of the phytoestrogens in other plants. If we look at data from cultures with high soy diets just as we have done with breast cancer, we find that soybean foods are not stimulatory to the endometrium and are in fact probably an estrogen antagonist, associated with low rates of endometrial cancers.[66] An animal study has evaluated the effect of estradiol versus soybean extract on the endometrial cells.[67] Just as we would expect, estradiol showed a marked effect in causing a proliferation of cells, while there was no effect with the soy and even strong evidence for soy having an antagonistic effect and thereby inhibiting the effect of estradiol. Another piece of reassuring and exciting news has come out of Hawaii. The researchers conducted a case-control study among the multiethnic population of Hawaii to examine the role of dietary soy, fiber, and related foods and nutrients on the risk of endometrial cancer.[68] Using diet history questionnaires, authors found that a high consumption of soy products and other legumes was associated with a decreased risk of endometrial cancer. Similar reductions in risk were found for increased consumption of other sources of phytoestrogens such as whole grains, vegetables, fruits, seaweeds, and fiber.

Many women will be encouraged by this information and insights on soy and will plan to utilize a high soy diet and/or soy isoflavone supplements as a replacement for conventional HRT. Some perspective may be helpful in anticipating their results. It has been estimated that 200 mg of isoflavones are approximately equivalent to 0.3 mg of conjugated equine estrogens (Premarin). Continued research will provide further insight and direction on how and in whom to use soy. Investigators at Bowman-Gray Medical Center in North Carolina are currently conducting a three-year study on the effects of phytoestrogens in soy products on menopausal symptoms, plasma lipids, thickness of the carotid artery, bone density, and mood. Called the Soy Estrogen Alternative Study (SEAS), this randomized double-blind study will be completed in late 1999.

To conclude our discussion on soy, the optimal use of soy would be to start earlier in life and eat a diet utilizing a diverse array of soy foods with a total dietary intake of 50–150 mg per day of soy isoflavones. If you haven't been eating soy, start now.

If you don't like soy foods, take one of the high quality soy isoflavone products on the market—either in the form of a powder or a capsule. Again, a guideline would be 50–150 mg per day of soy isoflavones. More information about different kinds of soy products that are available can be found in the Resource section.

Flaxseeds

Another significant dietary source of phytoestrogens to consider is flaxseeds. Flaxseeds contain a class of compound called lignans. Two lignans, matairesinol and secoisolariciresinol, are known to have estrogenic activity. Other lignans are modified by intestinal bacteria to form enterolactone, enterodiol, and a few other estrogenic compounds. Lignans from plants such as flaxseeds are absorbed in the circulation and have both estrogenic and antiestrogenic activity,[69] much like soy, although to a lesser degree.

Flaxseed flour and its defatted meal (flaxseed meal) are the highest plant producers of lignans and are several magnitudes greater than any other foods.[69] The lignan production from the flaxseed meal is 75 times higher than that of seaweeds (second highest lignan-producing group) and 804 times higher than that of fruits (the lowest lignan-producing group).[69]

The evidence that lignans can reduce the risk for cancer is still unclear, although the biologic properties of lignans and data from various cultures suggest that they do. Many lignans have antitumor, antioxidant, weak estrogenic, and antiestrogenic characteristics.[70–74] Adding to the evidence, urinary excretion of lignans has been found to be lower in nonvegetarians and in postmenopausal women with breast cancer as compared with healthy women.[75–77]

Foods for Bone Health

At the time of perimenopause and the menopause transition, women have a bone mass that is a consequence of family history, medical history, and their lifestyle before menopause. Peak bone mass occurs at age 35–40 in white women. After that, there is a slow downward trend of bone mass which is then followed by an abrupt decline of bone mass around the time of menopause. We have thoroughly addressed the lifestyle and nutritional issues of menopause and osteoporosis in Chapter 12, so we won't reiterate these same concepts here except to offer some reminders. Several dietary factors affect bone health and are involved in the development of osteoporosis: insufficient calcium intake, vitamin D deficiency, low calcium and high phosphorus intake, high protein diet, excess salt intake, and other mineral deficiencies. Studies have shown that excessive dietary animal protein may promote bone loss.[78] High phosphorus beverages are also implicated in osteoporosis development. Studies have shown that the more soft drinks that are consumed, the lower the calcium level in the blood.[79] Other nutritional factors accelerate calcium loss and may be implicated in osteoporosis. These include refined sugar, salt, and refined grains and flours. The refining process produces white flour stripped of vitamin B_6, folic acid, calcium, magnesium, manganese, copper, and zinc. One of the best general dietary preventive habits to acquire is to eat a lot of dark green leafy vegetables. Kale, collard greens, romaine lettuce, spinach, Swiss chard, and more are a rich source of vitamins and minerals including calcium, vitamin K, and boron. As you will learn in Chapter 12, these nutrients also have very specific roles in the achievement of optimal bone health. Low fat dairy products, baked beans, soy beans, sesame seeds, salmon, tofu, the grain amaranth, and numerous calcium-fortified foods are also rich sources of calcium. As we age, we need to feature these calcium-rich foods in our diet.

Foods for Heart Health

Heart disease is the other major concern in the postmenopausal years. Again, let's briefly review a few issues from Chapter 9 as reminders of the key points. The prevention of heart disease is largely determined by diet and lifestyle, so these concepts are extremely significant. Those women who make the necessary dietary changes have a significant advantage in being able to age healthfully as well as to reduce the potential need to take conventional HRT. Lowering the level of dietary fat, particularly

animal fat and saturated fats, is the key to a nutritional preventive approach to heart disease. Diets that are high in cholesterol and saturated fats (beef, pork, lamb, butter, cheese, palm oil, coconut oil) contribute to poor fat ratios and elevated cholesterol. Lowering the cholesterol in the diet will lower the blood cholesterol in most individuals.[80] Most experts recommend lowering total fat intake to below 30 percent of total calories. Even though we want total fat intake to be reduced, switching from saturated fats to vegetable oils will lower total cholesterol levels. Olive oil is your best choice for salads and cooking.

A diet high in cold-water fish such as salmon, tuna, mackerel, herring, and halibut provide an excellent source of omega-3 fatty acids, which are linked to the prevention of heart disease. Fish oils prevent clots, inhibit inflammation in the vessel walls, cause vasodilation, and promote regular cardiac rhythm. Fish oils also block vasoconstricting chemicals in the blood.[81]

Increasing the fiber in the diet is another important nutritional habit to acquire. A diet high in whole grains, fruits, vegetables, and legumes is the optimal high fiber diet. Soluble fibers, such as the pectin in apples or oatbran, have the most consistent beneficial effects on cholesterol levels.[82] Specific fruits or vegetables can also have a positive effect on blood levels of fat. Raw carrots, for example, may have a more potent effect in lowering cholesterol than oat products.[83] Evidence also exists which shows that people with a low intake of fruits and vegetables have an increased risk for heart disease.[84]

The subject of alcohol has been addressed in the chapters on heart disease, osteoporosis, and cancer prevention. My preferred advice, when all the information is taken into account, is to recommend none. An occasional social drink should not be considered a health risk, but a few drinks a week will have adverse health consequences for many women. There are healthier ways to relax, and other ways to get some of the heart benefits without getting all the health risks.

In the menopausal years, there is little doubt that a healthful diet rich in whole unprocessed foods will reap rewards for the years to come. A diet high in fruits, vegetables, whole grains, beans, seeds, and nuts not only contains important nutrients, but is also high in fiber and low in fat. The primary guideline for most menopausal women is to increase the amount of plant foods and reduce the amount of animal foods.

DIETARY RECOMMENDATIONS

Reduce

Total fat
Animal fat
Refined grains and flours
Sugar and salt
Use only a modest amount of low fat dairy
   products

Increase

Fruits
Vegetables
Legumes and especially soy
Whole grains
Nuts and seeds
Olive oil, canola oil
Cold-water fish (salmon, tuna, mackerel,
   herring, halibut, sardines)

Nutritional Supplements

Following are the nutritional supplements that are used to treat some of the symptoms of menopause. For an in-depth look at some of the nutritional supplements used to treat and prevent osteoporosis and heart disease, consult Chapters 9 and 12.

Bioflavonoids

Bioflavonoids, such as rutin, hesperidin, and quercetin, are usually known for their antioxidant and anti-inflammatory properties and their ability to strengthen capillaries. Some evidence exists to show that giving bioflavonoids in combination with vitamin C will help to relieve menopausal hot flashes.[85] Ninety-four women who suffered from hot flashes were given a combination of 900 mg hesperidin, 300 mg hesperidin methyl chalcone, and 1,200 mg of vitamin C every day for four weeks. At the end of that

month, symptoms of hot flashes were relieved in 53 percent of the women and reduced in 34 percent.

Bioflavonoids
1,000 mg per day plus 1,000–1,500 mg vitamin C

Vitamin B$_6$

Vitamin B$_6$, or pyridoxine, plays a critical role in the manufacture of serotonin as well as other amino acid neurotransmitters. Vitamin B$_6$ levels are typically quite low in depressed patients, especially women taking birth control pills or conjugated equine estrogens (Premarin).[86–88] An insufficiency of vitamin B$_6$ may also cause insomnia and irritability. Since depression, insomnia, and irritability are typical menopausal symptoms, this vitamin may be a helpful addition to a supplement program.

Vitamin B$_6$
50–200 mg per day

Note: *Chronic intake of dosages greater than 500 mg per day can be toxic over a period of many months or years.*

Evening Primrose Oil

Currently, natural products for menopause often include evening primrose oil (EPO) because it has a reputation for alleviating vasomotor symptoms such as hot flashes. However, a study on the effects of gamma linolenic acid (GLA) from evening primrose oil found it to offer no benefit over placebo in treating menopausal flushing.[89]

Cyclic breast pain is a common symptom in menstruating women before their period. In perimenopausal women, this symptom can be exacerbated or can occur in women who have not had the problem in the past. This breast pain, or mastalgia, is a disorder precipitated by ovarian hormones, yet no consistent abnormalities of circulating ovarian hormone levels have ever been detected. The conclusion has been that women with breast pain have breast tissue that is unduly sensitive to normal amounts of ovarian hormones. Because perimenopausal women have fluctuations in their hormone levels and there is a change in the relationship of estrogen to progesterone production, it is easy to understand why some perimenopausal women report these breast symptoms. Results of research and clinical trials have consistently shown that EPO is effective in relieving breast pain and premenstrual cyclic breast pain.[90–92] In the course of treatment, it has been detected that women with breast pain have unusually low concentrations of GLA metabolites. However, they increase while the concentration of saturated fats in the breast decreases when supplemented with EPO, a particularly concentrated source of GLA.

Evening primrose oil
1,500–3,000 mg per day

Gamma-oryzanol

Gamma-oryzanol is a substance in grains and is isolated from rice bran oil. This ferulic acid compound is present in rice, wheat, barley, oats, tomatoes, asparagus, olives, berries, peas, citrus fruits, and other foods. The concentrations are higher in whole grains than in refined grains and flours.

Gamma-oryzanol was initially shown to be effective in relieving menopausal hot flashes in the early 1960s,[93] and at least one additional study has confirmed that finding.[94] The initial research studied eight naturally menopausal women and thirteen surgically induced menopausal women. They were given 300 mg of gamma-oryzanol daily for 38 days. Over 67 percent of the women had a 50 percent or greater improvement in their menopausal symptoms. In the later study, a 300-mg daily dose was effective in 85 percent of the menopausal women. The typical dosage of gamma-oryzanol is 100 mg three times daily.

Gamma-oryzanol
100 mg, 3 times per day

Vitamin E

The considerable reputation of vitamin E for hot flashes comes from studies done as far back as 1945. Vitamin E was first used by Evan Shute in 1937 to control hot flashes,[95] and several confirmatory reports and studies have followed. The first preliminary study in 1945 reported that vitamin E was useful in controlling some of the symptoms of menopause, including hot flashes.[96] The entire group of 25 patients showed either complete relief or very marked improvement with less frequency and less severity of the hot flashes and perspiration, in addition to an improved mood. In 1948, a study of 66 women was undertaken where the women were given between 20–100 mg of vitamin E daily.[97] The average was 30 mg. Thirty-one patients, or 47 percent, obtained good to excellent results; sixteen, or 24.2 percent, obtained fair relief, and nineteen, or 28.8 percent, were not benefited. Five patients had an aggravation of their symptoms. A study in 1949 also attempted to assess the value of vitamin E on menopausal flushing and sweating.[98] Doses ranged from 1,400 mg per day to 60,000 mg per day, but the average was 18,500 mg per day over 37 days. Twenty-three cases were completely cured, seven were markedly improved, and seventeen were failures. This same study demonstrated that about 400 IU of vitamin E per day and one to four months of use was effective in treating about 50 percent of postmenopausal women who had atrophic vaginal tissue.

So, as you can see, the use of vitamin E for hot flashes and vaginal dryness has scientific backing. The problem is that vitamin E has received very little scientific attention for use in alleviating menopausal symptoms since those early studies. Only recently has there been renewed research interest, largely born of the need to provide menopausal breast cancer patients with safe and effective medicines for symptom relief. Vitamin E therapy for hot flashes in breast cancer survivors was recently studied in a double-blind, placebo-controlled, randomized, and crossover design, i.e., the gold standard of scientific research.[99] After a one-week baseline period, patients received four weeks of vitamin E (800 IU per day), then four weeks of an identical placebo, or vice versa. Symptom diaries were used to measure the hot flashes. The 105 patients who finished the first treatment period showed a minimal decrease in hot flashes per day when compared with the placebo group. Hot flash frequency decreased by 25 percent in the vitamin E group and 22 percent in the placebo group. Although this is considered a statistically significant difference, the clinical impact of this reduction was marginal, and the patients did not particularly show a preference for vitamin E over placebo.

Vitamin E
400–800 IU per day

Botanical Medicines

Phytoestrogens

As discussed earlier in the diet section, phytoestrogens are plant-derived substances that are able to activate the estrogen receptors in mammals. They are classes of compounds that are mainly, but not exclusively, nonsteroidal in structure and are either of plant origin or derived by the body's metabolism of precursors present in dietary components. Phytoestrogens are present in virtually every plant even though in some it may be in very small amounts, while others have particularly high levels. Overall, phytoestrogens are only a fraction of the strength of true estrogen; some estimates place them at 1/100th the strength and others at 1/1,000th the strength. Phytoestrogens, whether from edible plants or from medicinal plants, have the ability to act as both estrogen agonists (proestrogen) and estrogen antagonists (antiestrogens). These characteristics appear to be dependent on the target organ, the dose, the kind of phytoestrogen, and the total estrogen levels in the body. It can be a confusing area of medicine, in part because we don't yet fully understand all the mechanisms and all the implications.

Phytoestrogens are capable of exerting weak estrogenic effects, but are also referred to as "antiestrogens." These antiestrogenic effects are due to their ability to occupy estrogen receptor sites and then block the estrogen produced from our own body from binding at those same sites. Since the phytoestrogens are so much weaker, the net effect is significantly less estrogenic stimulation in that particular target organ. However, if the total body's estrogen level is low, as in menopause, the phytoestrogens will have a net increase in estrogen effect since they have some weak estrogenic activity, although far less than if it were estrogen from the body or estrogen from a manufactured steroid.

There are three types of these naturally occurring estrogenlike compounds found in plants: resorcylic acid lactones, steroids, and phenolics.

Resorcylic acid lactones are not true phytoestrogens but are the mycotoxins produced by molds found in the soil. Basically, they are the moldy contamination of the stored plant. They contain 0.1–15 percent the estrogenic potency of beta estradiol depending on the animal or route of administration.[100, 101]

Steroids are the classic steroidal estrogens—estradiol and estrone—which when found in a few plants, are identical to those produced by the body.

Phenolics are the dominant phytoestrogen. Different classes of phenolics make up this category, and the estrogenic potency of these substances varies between about 0.01–0.5 percent compared to estradiol.[102] Phenolic estrogens are present in almost all plants to some degree and are members of the largest single family of plant substances—the flavonoids. The principal estrogenic phenols come from seven subfamilies: flavones, flavonols, flavanones, isoflavones, coumestans, lignans, and chalcones.

Resorcylic acid lactones are mostly found in cereals such as rice, barley, corn, and wheat. Only a few plants actually contain steroidal estrogens. Rice, apple seed, date palm, licorice, pomegranate seed, and French beans contain levels of these estrogens in the range of 1–10 ppb.[103, 104]

Phenolic phytoestrogens undergo several structural changes as they are metabolized within the body. They are first hydrolyzed to some extent in the stomach as a result of stomach acid hydrolysis but then mostly in the colon where the gut flora contains an enzyme that facilitates absorption. Some of the phytoestrogens are absorbed intact and then conjugated to glucuronides and sulphates, and some of them are further metabolized by fermentation, mostly with the flora of the gut. Dietary phytoestrogens have a very high bioavailability and circulate in the blood in both conjugated and free structural forms. Some of them are excreted in the bile via the same enterohepatic pathways as the body's own steroidal estrogens and pharmaceutical estrogens. Most of the excretion is in the urine with half of it being excreted within the first 24 hours.[105]

The dietary intake of all flavones, flavonols, and flavanones in the United States is estimated to be about 160 mg per day,[106] and the richest sources of flavonols are onions, apples, and red wine.[107]

The richest source of isoflavones are the leaves of subterranean clover and red clover, and the second highest levels are found in soybeans. As mentioned in the diet section, intake of estrogenic isoflavones in Asian communities with a diet high in soy products is estimated to be about 50–100 mg per day.[108] Many vegetarians such as the Seventh Day Adventists also eat these same amounts. Isoflavones are largely found in the legume family of plants, which have a very clever characteristic: they attract bacteria in the soil to attach to the plant roots. These bacteria fix nitrogen from the air and the soil, which the plant converts into protein. This is why these foods have a higher protein level than other plants. Legumes such as chickpeas, lentils, soybeans, red beans, lima beans, and pinto beans are foods that contain isoflavones and are a major source of dietary proteins. The major estrogenic isoflavones are formononetin, biochanin, daidzein, and genistein, the latter two being the main dietary isoflavones.

Coumestan levels in the sprouts of beans and young plants can be considerably high and coumestrol is approximately six times more estrogenic than the isoflavones. If you eat a diet high in bean shoots and bean sprouts you may get some coumestrol in the diet; otherwise, the dietary intake of coumestans is extremely slight.

Lignans are widely found in nature in most fruits, vegetables, and cereals but are highest in flaxseeds, although rye, buckwheat, millet, sesame seeds, sunflower seeds, legumes, and other whole grains also contain reasonable quantities. Lignans are phenolic compounds that form the building blocks in plant cell walls, but some types of lignans are modified by intestinal bacteria to form enterolactone and enterodiol, the two estrogenic compounds that are found highest in vegetarians. Only two lignans actually found in the plants, matairesinol and secoisolariciresinol are known to have estrogenic activity. Lignans are considerably weaker than isoflavones.

Phenolic phytoestrogens bind to estrogen receptors in humans and vary in their affinity, effect, and potency. With the exception of coumestrol, the phenolic phytoestrogens have a significantly lower ability to bind to the human estrogen receptor than does estradiol and are much weaker in their potency. If taken in very high dosages, beyond what we would take in food or in a medicinal herb, or perhaps in the case of higher doses of coumestrol, phytoestrogens may be comparable in their estrogen effect to beta17 estradiol. The problem is, we don't know clearly what that dose is in enough circumstances, which phytoestrogens do what in which target organ (although we do know some target-organ effects), and how this response varies with the estrogen status of the individual. It has been estimated that about 200 mg of isoflavones are approximately equivalent to 0.3 mg of conjugated equine estrogens (half-strength Premarin).

The main concern with phytoestrogens for women has to do with their effects on the breast and the uterus. Do they protect against cancers of these organs? Are they contraindicated in women who are at high risk for these cancers or who have had or currently have these cancers?

We've addressed some of these questions in the discussion on dietary intake of soy and flaxseeds, but in the black cohosh and red clover section we will address this same issue.

Black Cohosh (*Cimicifuga racemosa*)

The term "black" refers to the dark color of the rhizome, and the name "cohosh" comes from an Algonquin word meaning "rough," referring to how the rhizome or root structure feels. The rhizomes with their side roots are the medicinal plant material we call black cohosh. The primary constituents in the rhizome of black cohosh are triterpenoid glycosides, specifically actein and cimicifugoside. Other characteristic constituents are the flavonoids. Black cohosh was traditionally used for many different indications, including pain relief during menses and childbirth, rheumatism, general malaise, kidney ailments, malaria, and, externally, for rattlesnake bites. Use and research in Germany since the 1940s has had a great influence recently on our uses for black cohosh. A special extract of black cohosh used in Germany is the most widely used and thoroughly studied natural alternative to hormone replacement therapy in menopause. Clinical studies have shown that this black cohosh extract relieves not only hot flashes but also depression and vaginal atrophy. As early as 1960, an essay on the clinical effectiveness of black cohosh was published in a German medical journal.[109] At least six well-publicized studies have been conducted on the standardized extract of black cohosh.

In one of the largest studies, 629 women with menopausal complaints were seen by 131 general practitioners.[110] The participants fell into one of several categories: 367 women previously who had not been treated, 204 women who had been treated with HRT, 35 who were treated with psychopharmaceuticals, 11 who were treated with a combination of HRT and psychopharmaceuticals, and 12 who lacked specific treatment data. All of the 629 women received a liquid standardized extract of black cohosh at 40 drops twice per day for six to eight weeks. As early as four weeks after beginning the therapy, a clear improvement in the menopausal ailments was seen in approximately 80 percent of the women. After six to eight weeks, complete disappearance of symptoms occurred in approximately 50 percent.

In a second study, 60 patients were given either a standardized extract of black cohosh tablets (80 mg twice daily), conjugated estrogens (.625 mg daily), or diazepam (2 mg daily) for 12 weeks.[111]

An estrogenlike stimulation of the vaginal mucosa occurred with the black cohosh group and the estrogen group as early as four weeks. No such changes were seen with the diazepam group, as would be expected. All three forms of therapy produced a significant reduction in the mood symptoms, as reported in the Self-Assessment Depression Scale, and in hot flashes, night sweats, nervousness,

headaches, and heart palpitations. This study was impressive in that black cohosh was on a par with estrogen in the ability to improve these typical menopausal symptoms.

Black cohosh has fared well in other studies, too. In a randomized, double-blind study, black cohosh extract was compared to estrogen and placebo in 80 patients over the course of 12 weeks.[112] What we see especially interesting here is that the herbal extract increased the degree of proliferation of the vaginal tissue. This means that there is some kind of estrogenlike effect on this tissue which will then manifest as a decrease in vaginal dryness, improved vaginal tone and elasticity, and an increase in vaginal lubrication. These 80 women were divided into three groups where one group received 80 mg twice daily of a black cohosh standardized extract, one group received 0.625 mg of conjugated estrogens, and the last group received a placebo. In this study, the women who took black cohosh had better results in all parameters that were studied using the Kupperman menopause index, the Hamilton Anxiety Scale, and the maturation index of the vaginal epithelium.

At least two other studies have also documented the ability of black cohosh extract to decrease hot flashes, melancholy, fatigue, irritability, and other menopausal indices.[113, 114] Although I have not reviewed all the studies done on black cohosh and menopausal women, there is certainly sufficient evidence to warrant its growing popular use. What everyone needs to realize, however, is that herbs such as black cohosh are meant to relieve common and uncommon menopause symptoms but should not be considered a substitute for the prevention of osteoporosis, heart disease, or other significant diseased states associated with low estrogen. An herbal treatment such as this can be very helpful for the perimenopausal woman who is at the peak of many of her symptoms. For the woman who is at low risk for osteoporosis and heart disease but just looking for management of some of her day-to-day menopause changes, black cohosh is an ideal choice with very few downsides to consider.

The side effects of black cohosh that have been reported are occasional gastrointestinal disturbances, headaches, heaviness in the legs, and possible weight problems. Drug interactions are not known, and the only contraindication is pregnancy, because an overdose may cause premature birth.[115]

Although we don't yet understand the exact mechanism of the effects of the black cohosh extract, investigations in 1944 showed a stimulation of ovarian activity and normalization of the menstrual cycle.[116] Since the triterpene glycosides in black cohosh are phytoestrogens, it is assumed that they affect receptors in the pituitary gland and the hypothalamus. Animal studies have been able to document that actein (a phytoestrogen found in black cohosh as well as other plants) suppresses the secretion of the pituitary hormone LH but does not affect prolactin and FSH.[117] In menopausal women, black cohosh also reduces LH but not FSH.

There are several different forms of black cohosh just as is the case with many other herbs. Different delivery systems of tablets or capsules, tinctures, or standardized extracts have different concentrations of herb as well as active ingredients of the plant. Variability is also seen from manufacturer to manufacturer. Most of the studies on black cohosh have been done with either a liquid standardized extract or a standardized extract tablet, and the total day's dose was 160 mg per day (or 4 mg of triterpenes per day). In tablet form or capsule form (usually 40 mg per tablet/capsule), the dosage would be two capsules twice daily. Recently, one manufacturer has decreased the dose to 20 mg per tablet and recommended one tablet twice per day. This is essentially one-fourth the original dose. This change was not based on any evidence of toxicity or negative side effects. In my experience, this lower dose clearly does not work as well. My advice is to start with two 40-mg capsules/tablets twice per day. Results should be evident within two to four weeks. The dose may be able to be reduced in the future, and women should feel free to experiment with the dose that is right for them. There is no danger of taking this dose of black cohosh for the long term, even though there has been some very generic, unsubstantiated counsel about not taking it longer than six months. There have been no adverse reactions with long-term use.

For a liquid standardized extract, look for an equivalent strength to the 160-mg total day's dose. Some may prefer tinctures or crude herb capsules and tablets or even freeze-dried herbs. Although some of these products may also be effective, there may be more variability in reliable strengths and the results may be less predictable.

Patients with a history of breast cancer or uterine cancer who are now menopausal have had questions and concerns about the safety of black cohosh. If estrogen replacement therapy is contraindicated, then what about black cohosh? Several studies give a great deal of reassurance about the safety of black cohosh in these circumstances. One of these studies demonstrates that black cohosh does not have estrogenlike effects in established estrogen-receptor-positive breast cancer cell lines whose growth is estrogen dependent and actually markedly inhibits the proliferation rate of the breast cancer cells.[118] In laboratory experiments, the estrogen-induced stimulating effect of estradiol can be inhibited by black cohosh extract.[119] In these same experiments, the combined effects of tamoxifen (an antiestrogen drug used to treat breast cancer) plus black cohosh were even higher than those of the individual substances.

Very recently, the relative effects of different herbs on estrogen receptor-positive breast cancer cells were tested in vitro (the laboratory).[120] When comparing the effects of estradiol with the effects of black cohosh, estradiol had almost a 3,000-fold greater effect than that of black cohosh. Although earlier we mentioned that black cohosh caused vaginal cell proliferation and improved vaginal dryness in studies of menopausal women, a recently published experiment showed that black cohosh liquid extracts did not exert an estrogenic effect on the vagina and uterus of ovariectomized rats and mice.[121] Experimental studies indicate no toxic, mutagenic, carcinogenic, or teratogenic properties of black cohosh. Thus, in my clinical advice to women with a history of hormone-dependent cancers, I consider black cohosh a safe and appropriate treatment for menopausal complaints of hot flashes, night sweats, insomnia, mood swings, and vaginal dryness.

Black cohosh
Standardized extract capsules, 40 mg per cap
One to two capsules, twice per day
Standardized liquid extract,
½–1 tsp twice per day

Chasteberry (*Vitex agnus castus*)

The chaste tree is a plant of paradoxes. While one of its uses is to promote ovulation and fertility, the English name, "chaste tree," is derived from the belief that the plant would suppress the libido of women taking it. The Catholic Church in Europe also placed the blossoms of the tree next to the clothing of young monks to supposedly suppress their libido, hoping that this would help to maintain their vow of chastity.

As an herb for the management of menopausal symptoms, I believe its use has been overstated and overpromoted. The fruits of chaste tree contain essential oils, irridoids, pseudoindicans, and flavonoids. The effect of chaste tree is on the hypothalamus-hypophysis axis. One of the mechanisms is it increases secretion of LH and also has an effect that favors progesterone.[122–124] The result is a shift in the ratio of estrogen to progesterone and consequently a "progesteronelike" effect. One of the most common changes that occurs in the menopause transition is irregular bleeding. Whether it be frequent or infrequent, heavy or light, ultimately a change and cessation will occur. In the process, some will experience significant bleeding problems because of menses that are either too frequent or too heavy. These problems are some of the most convincing indications for chaste tree berry.

The first major study on chaste tree was published in 1954.[125] Although this study was predominantly treating women with amenorrhea (lack of menses), a dramatic improvement was seen in 40 patients with cystic hyperplasia of the endometrium (excessive thickening of the uterine lining). The impressive effect lends credence to its progesterone effect.

Chaste tree was also studied in 126 women with frequent menses and heavy menses, although they were not perimenopausal.[126] In 33 women who had frequent menses, the duration between periods lengthened from an average of 20 to 26 days. In 58 patients with excessive bleeding, a shortening of the number of heavy bleeding days occurred.

Chaste tree is the most important herb to normalize and regulate the menstrual cycle. It is not a fast-acting herb, so do not hesitate to use it over a long period of time. Results may not be achieved until after four to six months.

As far as its libido-lowering effects, I have only rarely seen this. However, in a perimenopausal woman who already has low libido, it would seem counterproductive to prescribe this herb and probably wise to choose another.

> **Chaste tree**
> *Standardized extract capsules (175 mg),*
> *one capsule or per day*
> *Standardized liquid extract, 30–60 drops per day*

Dong Quai (*Angelica sinensis*)

Dong quai, also known as tang-kuei, dang-gui, and Chinese angelica, is an aromatic herb widely used throughout Asia. In Asia, dong quai is to women's health what ginseng is to men's. It has predominantly been used as a female remedy to treat menopausal hot flashes, menstrual cramps, lack of menstruation, or frequent menstruation, and to promote a healthy pregnancy and easy delivery. The coumarins in dong quai are found largely in the root, which is the medicinal part of the plant that is commonly used. The potential estrogenlike activity of dong quai has been assumed because of some of its observed traditional uses and clinical effects, but the evidence for this has been based on references to its ability to cause an initial increase in uterine contraction, followed by relaxation[127] and its effect in increasing uterine weight when given to mice.[128] These observations seem to be a stretch of an explanation as to why dong quai may be useful in menopause, although clearly there is some benefit at least for issues related to missed menses or frequent menstruation.

In a 12-week study conducted by Kaiser Permanente in Oakland, California, using dong quai as a solo agent for the relief of menopausal symptoms such as hot flashes and sweats, did not prove to be effective.[129] Seventy-one postmenopausal women with hot flashes were randomized to receive 4.5 grams per day of dong quai or placebo. Women kept daily diaries of their hot flashes, and their menopausal symptoms were assessed according to the Kupperman index where the range and severity of 11 menopausal symptoms are rated from 0 to 3. Hot flashes dropped from 47 to 35 per week in the dong quai group while these symptoms declined from 33 to 27.5 per week in the placebo group, a statistically insignificant difference. Thirty-three percent of the women taking dong quai reported that they had achieved a good or excellent control of their hot flashes, compared with 29 percent of women on placebo. Other findings included no change in vaginal cells or maturation (usual estrogen effects) and no thickening of the uterine lining (also seen in the presence of an estrogen effect). The authors' conclusions were that "dong quai does not show appreciable estrogenic effects in menopausal women." Comments from Chinese herbalists have noted that dong quai is usually used in combination with other Chinese herbs and not used as a solo agent. A misconception may have been perpetrated by Western herbalists when we concluded that because Chinese herbalists use it for women's reproductive problems it must work via hormones. More research with dong quai is needed, and it should not be discounted just on the basis of this one study, especially when it was used as a solo herb and not in combination with other herbal preparations.

Dong quai may increase the flow of a period or bring on a menses. In a perimenopausal woman who is either already having heavy flow problems or may have missed a menses for several months, this may be alarming. If you already have heavy and/or frequent menses, dong quai is probably not the best herbal choice for your menopausal symptoms.

Dong quai

*Dry herb is generally used in combination
with other herbs in capsule form
Tincture: ½–1 tsp, 1–3 times per day*

Ginkgo (*Ginkgo biloba*)

Ginkgo is the world's oldest living species of tree with fossil records as old as 200 million years. It is the leaves of younger, cultivated trees that are used in modern herbal preparations. Two groups of active constituents—the terpene lactones and the ginkgo flavone glycosides are the most critical compounds of modern standardized herbal products. Again, many forms and methods of preparation of ginkgo are available, although a high quality of *Ginkgo biloba* extract is typically standardized to 24 percent ginkgo flavone glycosides and 6 percent terpene lactones. The actions of these constituents include improving vascular flow of blood to the brain[130] and improving blood flow to the hands and feet.[131, 132] Although ginkgo extract has not been specifically studied in menopausal women with memory or cognition problems, it has repeatedly been used to improve memory.

Clinical studies have demonstrated the efficacy of ginkgo biloba extract (GBE) for the treatment of memory loss, depression, and disorientation associated with cerebrovascular insufficiency in geriatric patients.[133–135]

Two studies have shown gingko to be effective for patients with mild to moderate primary dementia of the Alzheimer's type or multi-infarct dementia. Patients in the first study were age 50–75 and had a diagnosis of senile dementia of the Alzheimer's type.[136] Patients were given either 240 mg of GBE (80 mg three times daily) or placebo for three months. Results showed memory and attention improvements in the ginkgo-treated group at one month that continued at two and three months. There were also reported improvements in mental clarity, memory, mood, appetite, orientation, anxiety, depression, and motivation. The second study enrolled 222 patients with mild to moderate multi-infarct dementia in a double-blind, placebo-controlled trial for six months.[137] Patients were randomized to receive either GBE 120 mg twice daily or placebo daily. Of the 156 patients who completed the study, there was a significant improvement in cognitive function tests and depression for the gingko group. Relative differences for dementia were not observed.

I think it is important to include ginkgo for menopausal women because changes in mental clarity, memory, and concentration are common, and it may be that ginkgo will have an increasing role in improving these symptoms for this group of women.

Another commonly reported change in peri- and postmenopausal women is a drop in their sex drive. This is an area where some extrapolation is required, but since there are no great solutions to this troubling problem, it's worth being liberal with our ideas. In fact, it's not such a stretch to include ginkgo as a treatment for a decreased libido or decreased orgasmic response. Extract of ginkgo appears to be remarkably effective in reversing antidepressant-induced sexual dysfunction in women as well as men.[138] Thirty-three women and 30 men were given GBE after having erectile dysfunction, anorgasmy, or diminished libido after the onset of using antidepressants. Ginkgo alleviated these problems in 30 of 36 women (91 percent) and 23 of 30 men (76 percent). The overall efficacy, based on patient self-reporting, was 84 percent. Although this report is preliminary and limited by the reliability of patient self-reports, the high rate of response is attractive. Doses were given in the range of 60–120 mg, twice daily for four to six weeks. Nearly all the patients from the original trial are still taking the ginkgo on a daily basis; some have taken it for 2.5 years with continued sex-enhancing effects. It is not known whether this effect would persist after discontinuing the ginkgo. Although this was a case of treating a drug induced sexual dysfunction, not a change in hormone status-induced sexual dysfunction, I recommend trying this safe and simple approach.

Ginkgo biloba
Standardized extract capsules (40–80 mg),
3 times per day
or
Tincture: ½ –1 tsp, 3 times per day

Ginseng (*Panax ginseng*)

Panax ginseng, also known as Korean or Chinese ginseng, contains at least 13 different triterpenoid saponins, collectively known as ginsenosides. There are many types and grades of ginseng and ginseng extracts that also include other related species: *Panax quinquefolium* (American ginseng), *Panax japonicum* (Japanese ginseng), *Panax pseudoginseng* (Himalayan ginseng), and *Panax trifolium*. *Panax ginseng* is the most widely used.

Whether it involves reducing mental or physical fatigue,[139–142] enhancing your ability to cope with various physical and mental stressors by supporting your adrenal glands,[143] or treating the atrophic vaginal changes due to lack of estrogen,[144] ginseng is a valuable tool for many menopausal women.

Panax ginseng
Standardized extract capsules:
If 5% ginsenosides, 200 mg per day

If 10% saponin ginsenoside, 100 mg per day
High quality root: 4–6 grams per day

Licorice (*Glycyrrhiza glabra*)

The major active constituent in licorice root is glycyrrhizin, although for menopausal symptom relief, we are more interested in some of its phytoestrogen components including beta-sitosterol, formononetin, coumarin, and others. Although much of the attention on licorice root has centered on its anti-inflammatory, antibacterial, antiviral, and expectorant properties, we are interested here in its estrogenic activity, which is predominantly due to the presence of beta-sitosterol, which is 1/400th as active as estradiol.[145] However, the glycoside of glycyrrehetinic acid has been shown to have an antiestrogen activity, inhibiting the effect of estradiol on uterine growth in ovariectomized animals.[146] It may be that licorice has both hormone and antihormone effects or it may in fact lower estrogen levels while simultaneously raising progesterone levels. This creates some confusion in thinking about why and when to take it, and at this time we cannot really clear up the confusion because there is insufficient research to account for its use as a single menopausal herb. The section on combination herbal products, however, presents licorice in combination with

---

Licorice
Dry form used in combination with
other herbs in capsules
or
Tincture: ½–1 tsp 1–3 times per day

---

other herbs as part of an effective formulation for symptom relief.

Red Clover (*Trifolium praetense*)

Red clover is a member of the legume plant family and is widely used in agriculture as a crop to improve the soil in preparation for other crops. Considerable research has been carried out on the constituents of red clover because of its role as a major forage plant for agricultural rather than medicinal purposes. Most of these investigations are of the leaves, stems, or seeds, and very few investigations have concentrated specifically on the flowerhead, the part used medicinally. The known constituents of the flowerhead are the flavonoids, including the isoflavone formononetin, daidzein, genistein, and quercetin glycosides. Phenolic acids, including coumaric and salicylic acids, volatile oils, and sitosterol are also found in the flowerheads of red clover. The coumestans are a small group of flavonoids, with only one known estrogenic member—coumestrol. Coumestrol stands out among the phytoestrogens because it is approximately six times more estrogenic than the isoflavones.[147] Coumestrol is found in only trace amounts in the leaves and flowers of red clover (the part of the plant most often used for medicinal purposes). It is found in the highest amounts in the young sprouts of the plant.

Red clover can be used alone or in combination with other botanicals and phytoestrogen-containing plants for the relief of menopause symptoms. Although it has been used for centuries, it has largely been studied in animals due to its agricultural use and has only recently been studied in menopausal women. Standardized extracts of red clover are now on the market and one in particular contains between 200–225 mg of dried, aqueous-alcoholic extract of red clover containing 40 mg of the four isoflavones—formononetin, daidzein, biochanin, and genistein. This final extract is a blend of extracts from three different red clover sources selected for their high isoflavone levels and proportions of different isoflavones. This dose of isoflavones is reported to be equivalent to a cup of soy milk and four cups of chickpeas every day.

As of this writing, two unpublished clinical trials have been conducted in postmenopausal women who had symptoms of menopause, using a standardized extract of red clover. Trial #1 was a double-blind, randomized, placebo-controlled trial of 37 postmenopausal women that consisted of three arms: placebo; one tablet of standardized extract of red clover, 40 mg; and four tablets of the same extract totaling 160 mg. The women were treated over a 12-week period. There was no difference between the groups in the vaginal pH or blood tests that included FSH, sex-hormone-binding globulin (SHBG), total cholesterol, and liver function. A statistically significant increase in HDL cholesterol of 18.1 percent occurred in the 40-mg group. There was no significant difference in the menopause symptom scores or incidence of flashes between the three groups at the trial conclusion. Urinary isoflavone levels tended to be higher in the individuals on the red clover extract.

Trial #2 was of 51 postmenopausal women who were randomized to receive either placebo or one tablet of a 40-mg red clover extract for 12 weeks and then were crossed over into the opposite treatment arm for another 14 weeks. There was no significant difference between active and placebo groups in the reduction in hot flashes between start and finish time points. There was a substantially greater reduction in flushing in the active group than the placebo at 4 and 8 weeks after beginning treatment, but this was not statistically significant. There were no significant differences between the groups for other menopause symptom scores, SHBG, vaginal swabs, or additional blood parameters. There was a strong correlation between the level of urinary isoflavone excretion and the incidence of hot flashes. The higher the isoflavones that showed up in the urine, the greater the reduction in hot flushes.

The curious thing about this new standardized extract of red clover and the promotion it is receiving is that both of these studies appear to lay the groundwork for a weak case in using red clover high-isoflavone extracts to treat menopausal symptoms. Safety data were particularly comforting, however. There was no adverse or intolerant reactions, there was no significant change in blood parameters used to measure toxicity, and there was no evidence of uterine bleeding or increased endometrial thickness over the course of the study.

I cannot offer women who have a history of breast cancer or uterine cancer the same degree of reassurance about using red clover as I can with black cohosh. It's not that I consider it definitely contraindicated, because in fact red clover has a rich history in herbal medicine as a treatment for cancers of all kinds. Red clover is a prominent ingredient in the Hoxsey formula, a combination herbal extract used in its original formulation at the Hoxsey Clinic in Mexico. One can see the logic of its use in cancer because of its genistein and daidzein constituents, both known inhibitors of tumor growth and cancer cell division. What leaves room for concern is the effect of red clover on the reproductive tract of some animals.

In the 1940s, an outbreak of permanent as well as temporary infertility was observed in sheep grazing on red clover in western Australia.[148] The abnormalities observed in the affected sheep were similar to those observed in animals exposed neonatally to estrogens.[149] Another study showed a notable increase in uterine weight in ovariectomized ewes following administration of red clover.[150] Although sheep are considerably more sensitive to phytoestrogens than humans, it does create some reason for doubt in using red clover in cancers that are known to be caused by or adversely affected by estrogens. Another point worth bringing up again is that coumestrol (found especially in red clover) is six times more potent than isoflavones. One last concern is the results of the black cohosh experiment that compared the relative effects of several different herbs on estrogen-receptor positive breast cancer cells in vitro.[120] Surprisingly, the breast cancer cells in the laboratory responded the same to red clover as they did to estradiol.

To argue the counter opinion that red clover is safe, it could be said that the mechanism of action of the red clover on the uterus and the breast is the same as for other soy isoflavones. Red clover has an affinity for estrogen receptors, and by occupying those receptor sites it may have an antiestrogen effect by blocking the binding of the body's own estradiol and thereby have a net decreased estrogen effect.

Red clover
*Standardized extract of 40 mg total isoflavones,
1 tablet per day; or dry herb capsule (500 mg),
1 per day*

So, is red clover safe and appropriate for women who have a history of breast cancer or uterine cancer? Arguably yes. Arguably no.

St. John's wort

St. John's wort is the most thoroughly researched natural antidepressant. Twenty-five double-blind controlled studies have shown an improvement in many psychological symptoms, including depression, anxiety, sleep disturbances, and insomnia.[151–153] Although none of these studies specifically involved peri-and postmenopausal women, St. John's wort is an excellent addition to be used in combination with other menopausal herbs for the psychological changes some women experience.

St. John's wort
*Standardized extract of 3 percent hypericin;
300 mg, 3 times per day*

Combination Herbal Product for Menopause

The natural food stores and drug stores are brimming with herbal menopause products these days. You will find the herbs we have discussed in most of them in one combination or another, and perhaps in combination with some nutritional supplements, soy, or additional herbs that contain phytoestrogens or have some other therapeutic benefit specific to menopause. Most all of these combination products have not been researched, even though an individual ingredient has been. I am aware of only one herbal combination product that has been researched in a double-blind, placebo-controlled trial. I was one of two principal investigators on this study. This study set out to research the effects of a botanical formulation containing phytoestrogens on menopausal symptoms, serum lipids, and some of the hormone indicators of menopause.[154]

Thirteen peri- and postmenopausal women were randomly assigned to a treatment group or a placebo group. The treatment group received capsules of burdock root, licorice root, motherwort, dong quai, and wild yam root and took two capsules three times per day. After three months, women receiving the herbal product showed a greater response rate than women in the placebo group. Response rate was calculated as the percent of patients in each group who showed a decrease in either the number or severity of symptoms. One hundred percent of women taking the botanical formula had a reduction in their symptom severity, while only 67 percent of women receiving placebo showed a decrease. Seventy-one percent of women taking the herbal formula reported a reduction in the total number of symptoms, while only 17 percent of the women taking placebo reported a decrease in the total number of their symptoms. The botanical formula was most effective in treating hot flashes, mood changes, and insomnia. There were no clear effects of blood levels of estradiol or total estrogens, although there was actually a trend for a decrease in the treatment group. Serum progesterone levels also appeared to decrease in the herbal group. No clear effects of the botanical formula were apparent in HDL cholesterol, triglycerides, or total cholesterol.

This combination of herbs is an example of an herbal formulation that can be used very effectively by many women to manage either their perimenopausal symptoms or their symptoms after menopause. However, it should only be considered for relieving the symptoms of menopause, not as a substitute for dietary and lifestyle changes or nutritional supplements meant for the prevention or treatment of heart disease or osteoporosis. Not should it be seen as a replacement for hormone therapy in the prevention of these diseases. (See Appendix B for further information about this formula.)

Natural Hormones

One of the greatest areas of confusion in natural medicine today is the subject of natural hormones. Consumers, practitioners, educators, manufacturers, and the media all contribute to some of the misinformation and misunderstanding. Some would contend that "natural hormones" are no different than any other hormones, but I would disagree, so let me explain. Up to now, I have discussed diet and exercise, the first step in the intervention options; nutritional supplements, the second step; and botanicals (including phytoestrogens), the third step. Now we're up to the fourth step, natural hormones.

I'm not exactly sure where the term "natural hormones" originated, but it has come to be defined in this way: a hormone that is biochemically and molecularly identical to the human hormone form and has been derived from plants. The two most common examples are estrogen and progesterone. There are three dominant estrogens within the human body: estradiol, estrone, and estriol. All of these can be manufactured from plant-derived substances in the laboratory. The two plants utilized in this process are soybeans and the Mexican wild yam. Plant-derived biochemically identical hormones can be made from either plant. With soybeans, beta-sitosterol is extracted, and then with various enzymatic reactions, a hormone is made—either estradiol, estrone, estriol, progesterone, or even DHEA and testosterone. The hormone endproduct that they term "natural" is biochemically identical to the corresponding human hormone.

With Mexican wild yam, diosgenin is extracted, and in the manufacturing laboratory and with various enzymatic reactions these same hormones are made. Either plant can be used to make any of these bioidentical hormones. What is the difference between a natural hormone and conventional hormone replacement such as conjugated equine estrogens (Premarin) or a synthetic hormone such as medroxyprogesterone acetate (Provera)? Natural hormones are biochemically identical to ours and match the hormone molecules produced by our own ovaries and adrenal glands. Synthetic hormones or hormones from the urine of pregnant mares are not the same hormone molecules as ours. They do not match and are not natural to what our body is familiar with. The arguable contention is that this difference contributes to some of the short-term and long-term problems of HRT. The assertion further goes that women may metabolize these foreign hormones differently, taxing their metabolic pathways and producing more harmful metabolites and interactions with their own physiology. Foreign hormones may be excreted more slowly, and, by lingering in the body longer, they may have an opportunity to affect receptor sites in a negative way. In clinical practice and my own observations, women by and large tolerate natural progesterone better than the synthetic counterpart. To a lesser degree but still to a significant degree, women who are having trouble on a foreign estrogen do much better on a natural estrogen, especially when a balance of estrogens that more closely mimics the human estrogen milieu is used.

Natural hormones deserve the attention and research as well as the scrutiny of modern conventional medicine. Women want them, women like them, and they offer not only a potentially safer and more comfortable alternative but also one with many more options for individualized dosing and formulations to meet the unique needs of each menopausal woman.

Natural Progesterone

Progesterone is synthesized in the body from cholesterol and is secreted by the ovary, mainly from the corpus luteum, during the second half of the menstrual cycle. Secretion actually starts just before ovulation in the ovarian follicle that has become dominant and is destined to ovulate. Progesterone is also synthesized in the testes, the adrenal cortex, and the placenta. In the adrenal glands, progesterone is the precursor of testosterone, estrogen, estradiol, and corticosteroids. Progesterone secreted by the corpus luteum is responsible for the development of what is called the secretory endometrium. The abrupt drop in progesterone secretion at the end of each menstrual cycle is the main determining factor in the onset of menstruation, (i.e., the sloughing off of this secretory endometrium). If the egg is fertilized, then this drop in progesterone does not occur and the fertilized ovum implants about seven days later, and thanks in large part to the effects of progesterone, the lining of the uterus has been prepared for the embryo implantation. During the second or third month of pregnancy, the placenta is developing and begins to secrete progesterone as well as estrogens, and the endometrium remains stable during pregnancy. Progesterone and estrogens continue to be secreted in large amounts by the placenta up to

the time of delivery. Progesterone has many other functions and activities in the body: it functions as an antiestrogen, it helps to normalize water balance, it is a precursor to making other hormones, it helps in thyroid function and blood sugar metabolism, it has a direct effect on breast growth, it exerts various effects on the central nervous system, and it is involved in skeletal growth and weight regulation.

When progesterone is used as a medicinal or cosmetic agent, some people make the mistake of using the term *progesterone* when they really mean the synthetic analogue, *progestin*. In order to better understand the different hormone products, it is important to make a distinction between progesterone, progestin, and progestogen. *Progesterone* is a natural hormone found in a woman's body and is the principal progestational hormone of the body. *Progestin* is the term applied to the synthetic derivatives, which differ in biochemical structure from progesterone. Progesterone can also be made from plant-derived constituents. *Progestogen* is a term applied to any substance possessing progestational activity. It can refer to progesterone or progestin. Progestins, which are the synthetic form used in conventional hormone replacement therapy and birth control pills, are often what account for the irritability, depression, bloating, swelling, and mood swings experienced by women when taking these medications.

As a medicinal agent, progesterone has many uses, some of which we have discussed in other chapters of this book, including PMS, preterm labor, recurrent miscarriage, irregular menses, fibrocystic breasts, and menopause. In menopause, progesterone can be used for the relief of many menopausal symptoms and to balance the effects of estrogen on the uterus. Its role in regulating the menses and preventing endometrial hyperplasia and uterine cancer associated with estrogen is discussed in Chapter 1. Its role in the prevention and treatment of osteoporosis is debated in Chapter 12. Its role in inhibiting coronary artery spasms with other implications in the prevention of heart disease is discussed in Chapter 9. Here, we will address the rationale for using progesterone to manage general menopause symptoms.

However, I can't stress enough that if you are peri- or postmenopausal with an intact uterus and taking any kind of estrogen, you must also take a proven form and dosage of progesterone (or progestin) to protect your uterus from hyperplasia and uterine cancer. All progestins have undesired side effects.[155] Premenstrual symptoms such as increased breast tenderness, edema, irritability, and abdominal cramps are fairly frequent, and as many as 40 percent of women often do not take their progestin prescription. More serious side effects are rare but more life-threatening and include cancer, high blood pressure, blood clotting dysfunction, and altered carbohydrate and lipid metabolism.[156] If you do not tolerate synthetic progestins, then natural progesterone is an excellent option. If you are one of the small numbers of women who do not even tolerate natural progesterone, and you are taking an estrogen, then you and your uterus must be regularly monitored by a primary care practitioner.

Progesterone is available for over-the-counter use as a cream and for prescription use, as an oral micronized (improves oral absorption) capsule, sublingual drops, sublingual pellets, lozenges, transvaginal, rectal suppositories, and even injection.

A very popular form of progesterone is the topical cream that is actually sold as a cosmetic cream by law. Here is another maze of confusion and misinformation. There are basically two categories of creams on the market—ones that only contain wild yam and no progesterone and ones that contain wild yam but have had the diosgenin in the wild yam extracted and converted in the laboratory to bio-identical natural progesterone. Most manufacturers use Mexican wild yam, but there are actually over 600 species of wild yam. The species that we can easily acquire with the greatest concentration of diosgenin seems to be Mexican wild yam, or *Dioscorea barbasco*. Unfortunately, manufacturers are not always clear about into which category their cream falls. The confusion is further exacerbated by the varied strengths of a particular cream. Wild yam extracts with no progesterone could be a 3 percent, 7 percent, or 10 percent extract of wild yam. However, the main thing you need to know is that it's still just wild yam. The wild yam creams that now also have had natural progesterone derived from the diosgenin added to the cream also come in a wide range of dosages. Some of these products will have less than 2 mg of progesterone per ounce of cream, some may have between 2–15 mg per ounce, and some may have as much as 400 mg per ounce.

All of these creams have value, but it is best to know exactly what you are getting because their effects and how to use them are very different. As a practitioner, I largely use the creams that have more than 400 mg per ounce, because they yield the clinical results that I am seeking.

Dr. Katherina Dalton was the first person to popularize the use of natural progesterone, and, since then, Dr. John Lee has been the most outspoken advocate of progesterone. Although Dr. Lee can be criticized for his steadfast position and perhaps overstated claims about the medical uses of natural progesterone creams, he does offer women additional insight into what's happening in their bodies and options for how to address those troubles. The purpose of supplying natural progesterone as a sole agent is to correct what he calls an "estrogen dominance."[157] Due to months or years of irregular ovulation in the perimenopausal years, our production of progesterone is the initial hormone that declines, not estrogen. Progesterone falls to almost zero, while estrogen levels decline to about 40–60 percent of premenopausal levels. This relative progesterone deficiency explains many of the perimenopausal changes such as mood swings, hot flashes, vaginal dryness, and irregular menses. The goal of natural progesterone cream is to support the waning daily production of progesterone in the body and accomplish physiologic levels of progesterone. The goal is not to supply pharmacological levels, which can be accomplished with higher doses of oral micronized progesterone.

Absorption of progesterone via the transdermal method of the creams is variable from person to person. Studies evaluating different concentrations of progesterone creams are currently under way to document how much progesterone can be measured in the serum if the cream is applied on a regular basis. This documentation will pave the way for a broader understanding of transdermal progesterone therapy and reliable indications for its use. We do know that some gets absorbed into the serum, but we do not know yet if this is an adequate level to offer endometrial protection if estrogen is also being given.

Adequate scientific documentation on the use of natural progesterone creams to effectively treat menopause symptoms is lacking, although its consumer use and its use in a clinical environment by alternative practitioners are extensive. Side effects of this form of cream have been reported to be less than 4 percent by manufacturing companies. In a very small group of women, side effects may include breast tenderness, drowsiness, depressive moods, headaches, and irritability. In general, women tolerate natural progesterone cream extremely well and find it a very satisfactory solution to their menopausal symptoms.

NATURAL PROGESTERONE CREAM
(400+ mg per ounce)

Perimenopausal women

Days 1–7: do not use progesterone cream (during menses).
Days 8–21: use ¼ tsp, twice a day.
Days 22–28: use ¼–½ tsp twice a day.
Apply the cream to the palms, inner arms, chest, or inner thighs.

Postmenopausal women

Days 1–7: do not use progesterone cream.
Days 8–30 (or 31): use ¼ tsp once or twice a day.

With the current state of research, I recommend natural progesterone creams only for the management of menopause symptoms. I do not recommend them as an agent with the expressed purpose of preventing heart disease, osteoporosis, or breast cancer or to oppose estrogen to prevent endometrial hyperplasia and uterine cancer. More time for observation and scientific research is needed to demonstrate the indication of progesterone for these uses.

While natural topical progesterone creams are popular with the female menopause health care consumer, only oral, transvaginal, and intramuscular routes have been proven to deliver suitable serum concentrations and protect the uterus from hyperplasia. Initial attempts to make progesterone as an oral delivery product showed that oral absorption was quite poor. Since the discovery of micronization, these problems have been solved, and oral absorption has been improved such that adequate serum concentrations are achieved.[158] Subsequent studies demonstrate that oral micronized progesterone (OMP) is effective in preventing endometrial hyperplasia associated with estrogen;[159–163] it does not negate the bone-sparing effects of estrogen (nor does it improve bone density when it is added to estrogen replacement)[164, 165] and it does not have as negative an effect on lipids.[166–168]

In fact, progesterone is preferred to progestins in this regard because progestins do have more of a negative effect on blood lipids.[169] This fact is overshadowed by the positive effects of estrogen replacement therapy, so conventional medicine does not consider it significant, but this is still an advantage for using the oral micronized progesterone instead of Provera. Oral micronized progesterone is available by prescription from a compounding pharmacy in any dose imaginable. One pharmaceutical company has just come out in the U.S. market with prescription oral micronized progesterone in 100-mg capsules.

ORAL MICRONIZED PROGESTERONE (OMP)

1. For a perimenopausal woman who is taking continuous estrogen and/or when a monthly menstrual cycle is desired: 100 mg twice daily (or 200 mg once daily), 12 days per month, *or*

2. 1 mg estradiol (or equivalent) + OMP 50 mg twice daily (or 100 mg once daily), three weeks on and one week off (during menses).

3. For a postmenopausal woman who is taking continuous estrogen and a monthly cycle is *not* desired: 1 mg estradiol (or equivalent) + OMP 50 mg twice daily (or 100 mg once daily) continuously.

Dosing note: 10 mg medroxyprogesterone acetate (synthetic progestin) is equivalent to approximately 200 mg OMP. There are many different dosing options, depending on the individual need and on the dose of estriol, estradiol, and/or estrone that is being used. See the natural estrogens section and Appendix B for further formulating guidelines.

OMP appears to be well tolerated in doses of 200 mg or less but adverse reactions increase when higher doses are used, especially if greater than 400 mg per day. These higher doses are used largely for the treatment of amenorrhea or the management of severe acute heavy uterine bleeding. Adverse effects that have been reported include dizziness, abdominal cramping, headaches, breast pain, nausea, diarrhea, fatigue, irritability, and abdominal bloating.[172]

Intramuscular (IM) administration of progesterone in oil has several drawbacks including discomfort for the patient and serious side effects such as sterile abscess formation and allergic response. The usual dosing is from 25–100 mg daily, sometimes in divided doses. IM progesterone achieves supraphysiological progesterone levels and is largely used to assist infertility and miscarriage problems.

One of the newest systems for delivering vaginal progesterone is a bio-adhesive vaginal gel containing micronized progesterone in an emulsion system that has been developed specifically for this use. A polymer is infused with an oil-water mixture that in turn contains progesterone. The oil component acts as a reservoir while the water makes progesterone available for diffusion into the vaginal tissue. This delivery method provides a sustained and controlled delivery of progesterone into the circulation. This now-patented progesterone delivery method received FDA approval in the United States in April 1997 as part of an assisted reproductive technology treatment for infertile women with progesterone deficiency.[173] It is supplied in a disposable applicator for single-dose use. It is available in 8 percent, which is 90 mg progesterone, and 4 percent, which is a 45-mg dose. Some practitioners may want to use this form of progesterone in a menopausal patient who is on estrogen as part of her hormone replacement regimen. This method of delivering progesterone produces subphysiologic serum levels of progesterone[174] but appears to be adequate in stabilizing the endometrium.[175] Dosing is the same for the 4 percent and the 8 percent: one applicator every other day for twelve days (a total of six doses). Vaginal delivery methods for progesterone have not been approved by the FDA for use in menopause and hormone replacement therapy regimens, although practitioners can use them for that purpose.

Sublingual micronized progesterone can be absorbed in sufficient quantity to achieve physiologic serum levels. Typically, tablets must remain under the tongue for 20 minutes before they can be fully absorbed. An advantage of sublingual tablets, creams, and vaginal and rectal deliveries is that, in these methods, progesterone does not pass through the enterohepatic circulation first and is not subject to the massive first-pass metabolism in the liver, as is the case with oral progesterone. Although alternative practitioners often site this as a logic for using these forms versus the oral form, this advantage does not outweigh the current lack of information we have on the other delivery methods and their unknown ability to protect the endometrium from the effects of estrogen.

Rectal administration of progesterone has not been well studied. Nasal sprays of progesterone (in oil) produce relatively low serum levels, which are sustained for only a few hours.[176] Even though these levels are low, it can produce some secretory changes in the endometrium and may prove sufficient with further study to reverse endometrial hyperplastic effects of estrogen replacement therapy.

The issue of progesterone and breast cancer is complex and not very well understood. There is encouraging evidence to infer that progesterone has a protective effect on the breast, but there is also a disturbing body of evidence (at least with synthetic progestins) to show that not only is there no protective effect but it also actually increases the risk. It is difficult to come to a comfortable conclusion on this matter. One of the largest studies to date, the Nurses' Health Study, showed that adding a synthetic progestin to estrogen failed to reduce the incidence of breast cancer and actually increased it.[177] Women taking estrogen alone had a 36 percent increase in their risk of breast cancer; those on estrogen plus progestin had a 50 percent increase; those on progestins alone had a 240 percent increase, although this number may be misleading because the number of women on only progestins was very small. The Nurses' Health Study also was able to report on duration of use. For those women who had been taking estrogen and progestin for five to ten years, there was a 46 percent increase in their risk of breast cancer.

Another study done in Seattle had contradictory findings to the Nurses' Health Study.[178] This study found no effect on the risk of breast cancer from either estrogen alone or estrogen and progestins together. The Seattle study included 1,000 women and the Nurses' study almost 122,000 women. Statistically, the Seattle study may not have been able to detect an increased risk because it didn't have enough women. Keep in mind that this was a synthetic progestin, not natural progesterone.

Would the results be the same for natural progesterone? This is a difficult question to answer with any certainty. Some evidence does exist that progesterone creams might help to prevent breast cancer. In a 1995 study, women who were scheduled for breast reduction surgery applied progesterone cream to their breasts for two weeks before the surgery.[179] The cells in the removed breast tissue were looked at to see how progesterone affected their multiplication. The researchers found that there was less cell division and concluded that progesterone applied directly to the breast might even help prevent breast cancer.

For women already at risk for breast cancer or who have had breast cancer, no good studies exist on the effects of progestins or progesterone.

My current position is that if you don't need to take hormones, don't. For women who are at low risk for breast cancer, I assess for osteoporosis and heart disease risks, and follow my six-step treatment model. For women at higher risk for breast cancer or who have had breast cancer, I prefer not to recommend hormones, even natural progesterone. It always requires weighing the benefits versus the risks. Some women suffer so much with their menopause symptoms, even though they have tried numerous herbal, nutritional, and even nonhormonal drug therapies. For those women, I will recommend natural progesterone, and if that is not adequate, then I use estriol and progesterone. I consider these two hormones a far safer option than the stronger estradiol and estrone.

Natural Estrogens

There are three dominant estrogens in the body: estriol, estradiol, and estrone. This is an important concept because these estrogens are different from each other, and estriol is particularly different from estradiol and estrone. The bio-identical estrogens can then be formulated either alone or in combination with each other, with progesterone, or even with DHEA and testosterone. The combinations and strengths and variability in formulations allow for a great many options to suit the individual needs of the menopausal woman. Estrogens are prescription medications and are not available over the counter. Practitioners who use alternative therapies can make them available and can write prescriptions to pharmacists who do "compounding." There are approximately 1,500 compounding pharmacists in the United States. If there is not a compounding pharmacist in your town or city, a licensed practitioner can write a prescription to one of the many pharmacies that do mail-order business. A partial list is available in the Resources.

The rationale for the preferred use of natural estrogens over patented "friendlier" conventional hormone replacement therapy (HRT) and patented "less-friendly" conventional HRT is based on some unique characteristics of estriol, a greater variability in dosing and formulating, and a desire for "purity." Natural estrogens, as stated earlier, are biochemically identical to human estrogens. "Friendlier" conventional HRT agents in fact also contain natural estrogens. These drugs, which are reviewed in the next section, also contain the bio-identical form of the estrogen. The difference is the additives, binders, preservatives, excipients, or delivery method for these hormones. These patented drugs are also constrained by a limited number of products.

The distinctions between natural estrogens and "less-friendly" conventional HRT are more clear. As stated earlier, these "less-friendly" estrogens contain hormones that are foreign to human estrogens. Whether they are the conjugated estrogens from the urine of pregnant mares or a synthetic estrogen, or a combination of those, they are not exclusively estrogens that are biochemically identical to human estrogen. These foreign estrogens have an exaggerated potency in the liver relative to their inherent estrogenicity.[180, 181] In effect, they may upregulate and become stronger in potency rather than down-regulate. The advantage of conventional HRT agents, especially the "less friendly," is that their benefits are documented with a significant body of scientific research.

I admit that the preference of a biochemically identical hormone over a "foreign" hormone is largely theoretical. But theory is the foundation of science. Some of the perceived advantages of natural estrogens have to do with combining the estradiol and estrone with estriol. This can be done as a bi-estrogen (estriol + estradiol) or a tri-estrogen (estriol + estradiol + estrone).

Theoretically, if we have a dose of natural estrogens that is equivalent in strength to the dose of the conventional estrogen, the benefit should be similar. Nonetheless, any hormone therapy that is considered to be an alternative to the leading form of therapy (conjugated equine estrogens, i.e., Premarin) must at some point be compared in order to prove its worthiness and acceptability among patients and health care practitioners. A few studies have looked at oral micronized estradiol alone or in combination with micronized progesterone and compared it to conjugated equine estrogens (CEE) plus medroxyprogesterone acetate (MPA) to evaluate possible effects on coronary artery disease parameters. In one study, the natural estradiol/natural progesterone combination lowered cholesterol, where the CEE/MPA combination did not. Both groups experienced an increase in high-density lipoprotein cholesterol.[182] Another study reported the results of a combination pill containing 2 mg of oral micronized natural estradiol, 1 mg of estriol, and 1 mg of a synthetic progestin over four years; serum cholesterol and triglyceride levels decreased significantly, but HDL levels were not measured.[183]

The studies we have on micronized estrone and estradiol relative to bone mineral density seem to have similar but not identical bone density effects to those of CEE. A study of postmenopausal women compared 0.625 mg CEE/5.0 mg MPA with 1.0 mg micronized estradiol (considered to be an equivalent dose to 0.625 mg CEE) and 200 mg OMP administered daily and continuously for 13 cycles.[184] Lumbar spine bone density improved by 5.0 percent in the CEE/MPA group and 3.8 percent in the micronized estradiol/OMP group. Hip bone density improved by 2.6 percent in the CEE/MPA group and

3.1 percent in the micronized estradiol/OMP group. These numbers are considered similar due to a lack of statistical difference and the margin of error in the bone density measuring test itself. Half-dose (0.5 mg) of estradiol, equivalent to 0.3 mg of CEE, has also been shown to be effective in maintaining spinal bone mass.[185] Although the authors of this study were able to show that 0.5 mg of estradiol effectively preserved spinal bone density, the usual dose, 1.0 mg, and a higher dose, 2.0 mg, of estradiol actually increased spinal bone mass by 1.8 percent and 2.5 percent, respectively. These studies support the efficacy of using natural estrogens, whether the patented "friendlier" form or the "purer" compounded form, in the menopausal patient.

Estriol is an estrogen used largely by practitioners of alternative medicine. Currently, there is no available patented product, and all formulations of estriol require a prescription that is filled by a compounding pharmacist. Estradiol, made from androgens, is the principal estrogen secreted by the ovaries in premenopausal women. Estradiol is oxidized to estrone, and both estradiol and estrone can be metabolized to estriol primarily in the liver. Estriol is in lower concentrations than estradiol and estrone in the postmenopausal woman, but because estriol does not bind very strongly to a carrier protein, sex-hormone-binding globulin, a greater percent is available for biological activity.[186]

One of the believed preferences of estriol over estradiol and estrone is that it appears to have both pro- and antiestrogenic effects. Remember, this is what was true for soy phytoestrogens. When estriol is given alone, it generally exerts an estrogenic effect. The strength of this estrogenic effect depends on the dosage. When given in combination with estradiol, a bi-estrogen formula, it appears to exert antagonistic effects.[187] Estriol has also been found to compete with estradiol binding in vitro, further demonstrating its antagonistic effects.[188]

Several researchers have studied the use of estriol in postmenopausal women. One such study was of 52 postmenopausal women with severe menopausal symptoms.[189] The women were divided into four dosage groups: 3 mg/day, 4 mg/day, 6 mg/day, and 8 mg/day. Menopause symptoms were decreased in all patients, the degree of improvement depending on the dosage used. Those taking 8 mg/day had the most dramatic improvements. No signs of endometrial hyperplasia were found in any of the groups as determined by an endometrial biopsy.

Another study reported on 20 women who had either natural or surgical menopause and were given 2 mg/day of estriol for two years.[190] Symptoms of hot flashes and insomnia were effectively treated in 86 percent of the women within three months. Atrophic vaginal changes were also improved with satisfaction.

A study of 1 mg of estriol given to 150 menopausal women for two years showed continual and significant improvement in subjective symptoms during the first, second, and third months on the estriol. The Kupperman index was used to measure the subjective symptoms.[191]

In a study of 26 postmenopausal women in Australia, each was given a dose of 1mg of estriol. If symptoms did not improve, the dosage of estriol was doubled for the following month, until satisfactory control of symptoms was achieved or until the dosage of estriol reached 8 mg/day.[192] Seventeen women had hot flashes, and nine (53 percent) reported an improvement on 1 mg/day of estriol. Six women reported no change in hot flashes, and two stated they were worse. Increasing the dose of estriol controlled the hot flashes in four of the eight women. Sixteen women presented with a dry vagina and pain with vaginal penetration. All had atrophic vaginal tissue. After one month of taking 1 mg/day of estriol, six had a moist and estrogenized vaginal tissue. When estriol was increased to 2 mg/day, six more improved but four still complained of a dry vagina. This study, along with at least two others, also provides evidence that oral estriol, given over a prolonged period of time, will not stimulate the endometrium and does need to be given with a progestational agent.[193] The effect of vaginal estriol on the endometrium does yield mixed results, and there are studies showing a stimulatory effect.[194] However, the dominant data on intravaginal estriol show no effect to the endometrium and therefore no need for a progestational agent. A meta-analysis of 12 studies concluded that daily use of intravaginal estriol is safe and without risk of endometrial proliferation or hyperplasia.[195]

A common problem associated with menopause is atrophic vaginitis, experienced as vaginal dryness, pain with vaginal penetration, increased frequency of vaginal and urinary tract infections, urinary incontinence, and urinary frequency and urgency. Estriol has been used orally to show an estrogenic effect on the vaginal tissue;[196, 197] used as vaginal tablets with *Lactobacillus acidophilus* it has provided complete homeostasis to the vaginal environment[198] and has been used intravaginally as a treatment for menopause-related urinary incontinence, urgency, and persistent urinary tract infections.[199, 200] I often prescribe estriol vaginal cream for atrophic tissue, urinary incontinence, and recurrent urinary tract infections.

The intravaginal administration of estriol prevents recurrent urinary tract infections in postmenopausal women, probably by restoring the vaginal flora, and it improves the additional problems by increasing lubrication, elasticity, and thickness of the vaginal epithelium due to its local estrogen effect.

Estriol
*Oral estriol dosing typically ranges
from 1–8 mg per day*

Estriol vaginal cream
*Estriol (0.5mg/gram of cream): Insert 1 gram every
night for 2 weeks, then twice weekly for 8 months*

If one is considering estriol as an option for menopause, symptom relief is not the only issue. How does estriol affect heart disease risk factors, and how does it affect bone density? Two studies indicate positive effects of estriol administration on lipid profiles and cardiac function. Japanese researchers found that 2 mg/day of estriol was effective in decreasing total cholesterol and triglycerides and increasing HDL levels in elderly women (ages 70 to 84), but not in middle-aged postmenopausal women (ages 50 to 65).[201] The other study followed postmenopausal women using estriol and found an increase in their cardiac function and improved blood flow in the extremities. A synthetic estriol derivative was tested in 2-mg doses every two weeks. Results revealed an increase in

HDL and a lowering in LDL and no change in total cholesterol and trigylcerides.[202] In another study, estriol did not fare so well; it was found to have no effect on cholesterol.[203]

Estriol has been just as minimally studied regarding its effects on bone loss, yet some of those studies have been encouraging nonetheless. Seventy-five postmenopausal women with bone densities at least 10 percent or more below peak bone density were given estriol 2 mg/day with 800 mg daily of calcium lactate. After 50 weeks, an average increase in bone mineral density of 1.79 percent was seen on the routine DEXA scan.[204] Another group of 17 Japanese women, who were 10 years postmenopause, were given estriol 2 mg/day and 2 gm/day of calcium lactate for one year. Another group was given only the calcium lactate. Bone density was significantly reduced after one year in the calcium-only group, while the estriol-plus-calcium group had a 1.66 percent increase in bone density, using the DEXA scan.[205] A third Japanese study compared 50–65-year-old women and elderly women who received either estriol 2 mg/day plus 1 gm/day calcium lactate or 2 mg/day of estriol alone for 10 months.[206] Increases of about 5 percent in the lumbar spine were seen in both groups of women who took the estriol and the calcium. Women of both age groups in the calcium-alone group had a decrease in bone mineral density of the lumbar spine. Studies in Scotland using doses of 4–6 mg of estriol and another as high as 12 mg/day did not find any protection from bone loss.[207]

These studies of estriol leave us with some encouragement, yet lack of sufficient confirmation about its bone protective and heart disease prevention benefits. However, for women looking for symptom relief, when herbs and nutritional supplements do not work, for women who are at mild risk for osteoporosis and heart disease, or for women who are at higher risk of breast cancer and still need some bone density effects and heart disease prevention hormonal benefits, estriol is a viable option in addition to other lifestyle changes and natural therapies.

What about estriol and breast cancer? Many women decline the use of conventional HRT due to the fear of breast cancer, and many practitioners and researchers have joined them in a search for safer hormone replacement options. This has led some to the study and use of estriol. Several reasons have been used as a rationale for the preference of estriol over all forms of estradiol, estrone, CEE, and synthetics, but none so appealing as its possible safety in regard to breast cancer risk. Animal studies have demonstrated a protective effect of estriol when rats were also given a tumor-inducing carcinogen.[208] A decreased urinary excretion of estriol has been reported in women with breast cancer when compared to women without.[209] Six epidemiological studies found more estriol in relation to estrone and estradiol in populations with lower risks of breast cancer.[210] Not all studies, however, have confirmed this association. One such researcher has not found a correlation between the levels of urinary metabolites of the various estrogens and breast cancer risk, or a correlation between the ratio of these hormones.[211] Henry Lemon, a leading researcher on estriol, has hypothesized that estriol is a safer form of estrogen replacement when it comes to the risk of breast cancer. His reasoning is based on several reasons:

1. In laboratory studies, estriol, when given with estradiol, accelerates the removal of estradiol that is bound to protein receptors (an estrogen antagonist effect).
2. Estriol is associated with very little carcinogenesis in animal studies unless huge doses are given on a continuous basis.
3. Estriol has been found to prevent carcinogen-induced breast tumors in rats.
4. Estriol metabolism does not result in the formation of large numbers of potentially carcinogenic substances, whereas estrone and estradiol do.

Clinical results in breast cancer patients were reported by Lemon where he prescribed 5–15 mg to 24 patients with existing metastases.[209] He found an increased growth of metastases in 6 patients. He hypothesized that lower doses and a noncontinuous dosing schedule would provide more protection from breast cancer. Additional research by Lemon reported by a colleague was also carried out on postmenopausal women with breast cancer. They were given 2.5–5 mg per day of estriol, although a few were given as much as 15 mg daily. Thirty-seven percent had remission or arrest of metastatic lesions.[212] Additional in vitro studies have not been reassuring. Estriol, estrone, and estradiol all had stimulatory effects on human breast cancer cells in tissue cultures, and estriol was able at least in part to overcome the antiestrogen effect of the antiestrogen drug tamoxifen.[213]

Although at least some of these characteristics and observations of estriol may provide some basis to believe it is safer for the breast, it is not convincing, and each breast cancer survivor must weigh the benefits and risks for herself after being provided with well-balanced information.

A popular practice for prescribing compounded natural estrogens is to combine the perhaps safer effects of estriol with the more certain osteoporosis and heart disease prevention benefits of estradiol and estrone. The current common practice is for a tri-estrogen compound to be composed of 80 percent estriol, 10 percent estradiol, and 10 percent estrone. This is based on a laboratory determination made by Dr. Jonathon Wright; he has unpublished reports that this is most similar to normal body physiology. There is some question as to the basis of this formulation, and further study and research are needed to determine the accuracy of these percentages.

The calculation of a formulation is based on approximate and estimated equivalencies to either 1 mg of estradiol or 0.625 mg of CEE. A compounded tri-estrogen formulation considered to be equivalent is estriol 1 mg/estradiol. 0125 mg/estrone. 0125 mg; the dosage is one cap twice daily. This formula of tri-estrogen actually then delivers 2.5 mg of total estrogens per day. Estriol is estimated to have between 25–40 percent of the activity of estradiol. Progesterone (OMP) is added to the formula and should be a minimum of 40 mg twice daily to adequately oppose the estrogen and protect the uterus from estrogen effects.

The postmenopausal estrogen/progestin intervention (PEPI) trial used 200 mg OMP for 12 days per month, which is a total of 2,400 mg per month. Eighty mg of OMP daily for 30 days is a total of 2,400 mg. This formulation would then look like estriol 1 mg/estradiol 0.125 mg/estrone 0.125 mg/progesterone 40 mg. Dosage: one cap twice daily continuously. If a monthly cycle is still appropriate, then the formula would be given three weeks on and one week off. An alternative would be the tri-estrogen formulation one cap twice daily for 30 days and the OMP 100 mg twice daily for 12 days per month prior to menses.

Tri-estrogen formulation *considered equivalent to 0.625 mg Premarin/2.5 mg Provera: Estriol 1 mg/estradiol 0.125 mg/estrone 0.125 mg/OMP 40 mg Dosage: 1 cap twice daily*

A **bi-estrogen formulation** *is increasingly popular because of concerns that estrone may have more unwanted metabolites and possible negative breast effects*

Bi-estrogen formulation *considered equivalent to 0.625 mg Premarin/2.5 mg Provera: Estriol 1 mg/estradiol 0.250 mg/OMP 40 mg Dosage: 1 cap twice daily*

There is much to be learned about natural hormones, and further studies are needed to document any clear and certain advantage over the use of "friendlier" and "less-friendly" conventional HRT. But the logic for using sex steroids that do occur naturally in women is compelling to many women and their practitioners. A review of some of the distinctions may be helpful:

1. Preparations containing estrogens that do not occur naturally in women have an exaggerated potency in the hepatic system relative to their estrogen effect.
2. Preparations of synthetic progestins have negative effects on lipoproteins.[214–216]
3. Synthetic progestins also decrease sex-hormone-binding globulin, resulting in an increase in free sex hormone levels and potentially increased androgen (male hormone) effects.
4. Hormones that are administered are degraded and eliminated, but all produce metabolites. Some of these metabolites are active and may have metabolic consequences that are independent of the parent hormone. If a hormone is given that is not natural to a woman's body, the metabolites of these foreign estrogens may pro-

duce amplified effects or effects different from that of native and bio-identical sex steroids leading to a variety of side effects.[217]

5. Nature has painstakingly allowed our natural sex steroids to evolve with us over a much longer period of time than we could ever hope to research. If given at physiologic replacement levels if and when necessary in an individual woman, the use of hormones that occur naturally in women represents a logical approach to menopause management that is consistent with what nature intended.

Friendlier and Less-Friendly Conventional HRT

Friendlier conventional HRT includes all estrogens that are made with micronized estradiol or estrone and are derived and manufactured in the same manner as the natural estrogens. As stated earlier, the differences are the binders, fillers, preservatives, and additives used in the pills, and the additional adhesive substances used in the patches. The 0.05 mg estrogen patch (Estraderm) is considered to be equivalent to 0.625 mg CEE (Premarin); 1 mg estradiol (Estrace) is equivalent to 0.625 mg of CEE; 0.75 mg estrone pipate (Ortho-est and Ogen) is equivalent to 0.625 mg CEE. Many new patches of estrogen that contain micronized estradiol are now on the market. Some of these newer patches have the advantage of offering additional doses and lower-dose estrogen delivery. A micronized estradiol estrogen cream that delivers 0.1 mg per gram is also available.

Less-friendly conventional HRT has been described earlier as drugs that are composed of foreign estrogens and are not identical to a woman's own estrogen. Conjugated equine estrogens are derived from the urine of pregnant mares. Esterified estrogens are in part estrone sulfate and in part equilin sulfates. (See Appendix B for a chart on conventional hormone options and equivalents.)

Androgens

As we have noted earlier in this chapter, the normal postmenopausal ovary produces testosterone as well as androstenedione and small amounts of estrogen. Following menopause, a woman's androgen (male hormone) production decreases by as much as 50 percent. The total amount of testosterone produced after menopause is subsequently reduced. Ovarian androgen production stops abruptly with surgical menopause and more gradually with natural menopause. A substantial number of menopausal women who are given estrogen replacement at standard dosages continue to have menopause symptoms such as hot flashes, night sweats, and insomnia. These women who seem to be nonresponsive to estrogen alone may have enhanced symptom relief when they are switched to estrogen plus androgen, usually testosterone. Data have shown that testosterone increases the bioavailable androgen, both that produced by the body and that given in a pill and estrogen.[218]

Estrogen and testosterone therapy has been explored not only for its ability to improve vasomotor symptoms but also to improve sexual desire and sexual satisfaction. For example, a double-blind study of women who were dissatisfied with their HRT regimen showed that sexual desire, satisfaction, and frequency of sexual activity were increased when they used the estrogen/testosterone combination.[219] A nurses' study conducted a retrospective review of symptoms among 148 healthy, early postmenopausal women, both natural and surgical, who switched from estrogen alone to estrogen/testosterone therapy.[220] Overall symptom relief was greater with estrogen/testosterone therapy than with estrogen-only therapy. Sexual drive and satisfaction increased. Results of other studies have shown that the combination of 1.25 mg of esterified estrogen and 2.5 mg of methyltestosterone given daily for two years significantly reduced the intensity of hot flashes and vaginal dryness in 81 percent and 73 percent of women, respectively, with surgical menopause.[221] Comparing the effect of estrogen and an estrogen/testosterone combination on sex drive may bring about improvement in 50 percent of women on estrogen alone, but 90 percent of women when testosterone is added.[222]

There have been some concerns about estrogen/testosterone therapy reversing the increased HDL cholesterol achieved with estrogen alone. The combination of esterified estrogens and methyltestosterone has been shown to decrease triglycerides, LDL, HDL, and total cholesterol in postmenopausal women. However, a two-year study of estrogen/testosterone therapy produced no change in LDL levels but did show significant reductions in triglycerides, very low-density lipoprotein, and also reduced HDL levels. So the story is mixed, and further studies are needed to determine the actual impact of these changes on cardiovascular disease. If testosterone is being used, it would be prudent to monitor blood lipid levels for any adverse effects.

For treatment of osteoporosis, adding testosterone therapy to estrogen therapy appears to produce a greater increase in bone density compared with estrogen therapy alone. In a double-blind study, 66 surgically menopausal women without osteoporosis received either 1.25 mg of esterified estrogen alone or 1.25 mg of esterified estrogen and 2.5 mg of methyltestosterone daily for two years. Both groups already had bone loss at the spine, hip, and wrist. Only the combination of estrogen with testosterone significantly increased spinal bone density after one year and two years, respectively.

Standard formulations of CEE and methyltestosterone combine either 0.625 or 1.25 mg of CEE with 5 mg of methyltestosterone. Others come with estrogen, as either 1.25 or 0.625 esterified estrogens, combined with 2.5 mg or 1.25 mg of methyltestosterone, respectively.

Through a compounding pharmacist, one can obtain oral nonmethylated testosterone. I generally use 0.5–1 mg of testosterone formulated into the bi-estrogen or tri-estrogen formulation, and the pills are taken one capsule twice daily. Testosterone cream applied to the genital region recently received mass media attention on *The Oprah Winfrey Show*. It is used as an alternate method of delivering the testosterone. This topical method can enhance local sexual response if used prior to sex. Common prescriptions are either 0.5 percent, 1 percent, or 2 percent testosterone creams. Apply to the genital region daily for two weeks, then use twice a week. The twice weekly dosage will avert local testosterone side effects that can occur if used daily and in the stronger dosages. These may include enlargement of the clitoris. A good resource for both menopausal women in need and their health care practitioners is a book called *The Hormone of Desire*.[223]

Another androgen that warrants attention as a potential benefit in postmenopausal women is dehydroepiandrosterone (DHEA), the most abundant circulating steroid in humans. The adrenal gland is the source of 90 percent, and the ovary contributes the remaining 10 percent of circulating DHEA. Ninety-nine percent of DHEA is converted to DHEA-S, which lasts longer before being degraded than does DHEA.

Peak levels of DHEA occur at age 25 and then decline gradually to only 15–20 percent of the maximum by the time one is 70 years old. DHEA has many claims regarding immune status, age-related physiologic changes, bone density, cancer prevention, brain function, and cardiovascular disease. A daily oral intake of 50 mg of DHEA for a postmenopausal woman restores levels to a young adult value. At this dose, DHEA is converted to other more potent androgens, including testosterone. In pharmacologic doses of 1,600 mg, DHEA will be converted to estrone and estradiol. Unfortunately, there are only a handful of randomized placebo-controlled studies examining the effects of giving DHEA to humans. Although animal studies are promising, they may not transfer to humans.

Animal studies have shown that DHEA may have a cholesterol-lowering effect, but this has not been shown in human studies with low doses. At physiologic doses (e.g., 50 mg in women), DHEA reduced HDL cholesterol in postmenopausal women.[224] At higher doses, it raised serum cholesterol and lowered HDL and VLDL cholesterol.[225]

DHEA has conflicting evidence in its association with bone mineral density. In a study that showed a positive correlation, it was hypothesized that DHEA is converted to estrogen in the bone tissue.[226] Studies in which DHEA was given in a dose of 50–100 mg per day for three or six months respectively showed no improvements in bone density in postmenopausal women.[227] One could point out that three and six months is too short a period of time to detect any effect on bone density. DHEA seems to have no benefit as an anti-obesity drug in humans,[227] and should be contraindicated in women who have hormonally responsive tumors such as breast and endometrial.

One of the most significant effects of DHEA may be its ability to enhance a sense of general

TABLE 10.2   **Comparison of Menopausal and Premenopausal Women**

	Menopausal women	Premenopausal women
Fat-free mass	−3.0 kg	−0.5 kg
Resting metabolic rate	−103 kcal/day	−17 kcal/day
Exercise	−127 kcal/day	64 kcal/day
Fat mass	2.5 kg	1.0 kg
Fasting insulin	11 pmol/L	9 pmol/L
Waist:hip ratio	0.04	0.01

well-being. This effect was found at doses of 50 mg and 100 mg daily.[227] Few adverse effects have been reported with DHEA, although in women, androgenic side effects such as facial hair growth and acne can occur with doses as low as 50 mg. A dose of 25 mg daily may be more appropriate.[228] I typically give 5–20 mg per day to women who are either low in DHEA according to test results or to women with fatigue, loss of vitality, and/or low sex drive.

DHEA
5–25 mg per day

Ural Natural Testosterone
.5–1 mg; one capsule twice daily; furmulate with or without the natural estrogens/progesterone

Testosterone Cream
.5%, 1% or 2% cream; apply to vulva twice weekly

❦ *Exercise*

Menopausal symptoms have been categorized into primary and secondary. Primary symptoms include vasomotor symptoms (e.g., hot flashes), osteoporosis, and atrophic vaginitis. Among the secondary symptoms are fatigue, depression, tension, insomnia, irritability, headaches, and weight gain.[229]

In addition, postmenopausal women experience reduced resting metabolic rates that may be responsible for weight gain and increased body fat,[230] high plasma levels of fibrinogen,[231, 232] increased insulin resistance,[233] low heart rate variability,[234, 235] elevated serum total cholesterol and LDL cholesterol,[236] and decreased HDL cholesterol.[237]

All of these factors combine to dramatically increase the risk of coronary artery disease (CAD) and accelerate the risk of cardiac sudden death (CSD) to such an extent that, from mild contributor to women's demise in premenopausal years, CAD becomes the leading cause of death among postmenopausal women.[238]

A longitudinal study by Poehlman and colleagues[239] of 35 late-premenopausal women summarizes the above information succinctly. The authors followed these women for six years and compared 18 women who had stopped menstruating with 17 who remained premenopausal in the course of the study. The results were enlightening (see Table 10.2).

The reader may ask, What does exercise have to do with menopausal symptoms? This array of symptoms listed in Table 10.2 cannot be ascribed solely to the lack of hormones occasioned by the shutdown of ovarian function at menopause.[240] Moreover, study after study shows that regular exercise that begins at any point in a woman's development continues for the rest of her life, ameliorates, and, in some cases, completely prevents any of these changes.

Hammar and colleagues[241] studied the occurrence of hot flashes in postmenopausal women and reported that 21.5 percent of physically active women experienced hot flashes as compared to 43.8 percent of age-matched sedentary controls. They further noted that the physically active women who had no flashes exercised at least 3.5 hours/week. Those who exercised 2.6 hours/week had moderate to severe hot flashes. Recent studies find concurrence with Hammar. Lucerno and McCloskey[242] conclude their study by remarking that physical activity, balanced diet, stress reduction, and avoidance of alcohol and caffeine can reduce hot flashes in postmenopausal women.

EXERCISE RECOMMENDATIONS

Physical exercise that includes strength, cardiac, and flexibility modalities (consult "General Exercise Programs" and "General Exercise Instructions" in Appendix A) ensures a menopause without exaggerated symptoms and protects against heart disease and osteoporosis when it is initiated early in life, is appropriate and moderate, and lasts as long as life.

However, if the reader has reached menopause and has been sedentary, several cautions apply to the initiation of a rest-of-life exercise program:

1. Start slowly and progress very gradually.
2. Begin with strength exercises that engage all muscle groups. "The first task is gaining strength to prevent falls during aerobic exercise."[263] "In general the older and more frail a person is, the more important muscle strengthening and improving flexibility becomes."[264]
3. At first, practice the strength exercises under the supervision of a qualified exercise consultant.
4. Do these strength exercises 3 times per week on alternate days, for a minimum of 10–12 weeks, at which point you may reduce strength exercises to 2 times per week and add an aerobic dimension (e.g., walking, rowing, cycling, etc.) to the exercise program.

SAMPLE TREATMENT PLAN FOR MENOPAUSE

1. For symptom relief, low risk for osteoporosis and heart disease:

   Diet: Whole foods diet high in fruits, vegetables, whole grains, legumes

   Emphasize soybean products and flaxseeds

   Reduce total fat, animal fats, simple carbohydrates; modest amounts of low fat dairy

   Exercise: Regular weight-bearing, strengthening, and aerobic exercise with light weight training

   Supplements: Vitamin E, 400–800 IU per day

   Calcium/magnesium/vitamin D/ trace mineral supplement (see Chapter 12 for guidelines)

   Folic acid, B_6 and B_{12} (see Chapter 9 for guidelines)

   Herbal: Black cohosh; standardized extract capsules of 40 mg per cap, 2–4 caps per day; *or* herbal combination product containing phytoestrogens; or

   Natural hormones: Natural progesterone cream ¼–½ tsp twice daily, 3 weeks on and 1 week off

2. Symptom relief, moderate risk for osteoporosis or heart disease:

   Diet and exercise: Same as #1

   Nutritional supplements: Same as #1, plus supplements recommended in Chapters 9 and 12

   Natural hormones: Bi-estrogen/progesterone formulation (to be prescribed by practitioner); formulation will vary depending on circumstances. See Appendix B.

3. Symptom relief, high risk for osteoporosis or heart disease:

   Diet and exercise: Same as #1

   Supplements: Same as #2, or consider a more aggressive supplement plan as outlined in Chapters 9 and 12

   Friendly conventional HRT: Estradiol/ progesterone (OMP) *or* estradiol patch/ progesterone (either to be prescribed by practitioner). See Appendix B.

Similar conclusions have been reached by studies that looked at the other menopausal signs and symptoms. Thus, exercise improves the lipid profile—it decreases serum total cholesterol, LDL, and triglycerides and, generally, increases HDL cholesterol.[243, 245] It reduces depression[246, 247] and mild insomnia[248] with certain limitations.[249] In general, morning exercise of any intensity and duration does not disturb sleep, late afternoon moderate exercise improves sleep, and close-to-bedtime exercise of high intensity and long duration will disrupt sleep.[250]

Resistive or aerobic exercise of adequate intensity and duration reduces serum fibrinogen and ferritin[251] levels, elevates heart rate variability, increases insulin action and reduces hyperinsulinemia, and increases resting metabolic rate,[252] all of which translate into a

50 percent reduction in heart attacks[253] and substantial CHD risk reduction in postmenopausal women.

Physically active postmenopausal women have decreased central arterial stiffness (thought to contribute to the increased incidence of cardiovascular disease noted with age) when compared with sedentary counterparts. This effect of exercise was equally detectable in exercising pre- and postmenopausal women despite increased systolic and diastolic blood pressures in the latter group.[254]

Other benefits of exercise, particularly of resistive exercise, in postmenopausal women are significantly increased muscle strength and size, protection against osteoporosis and fractures, greater mobility and freedom, reduced morbidity and mortality, extended disease-free life,[255–260] and maintenance of optimal weight and percent body fat.[261, 262]

❧ Conventional Medicine Approach

Women take and are prescribed conventional HRT to alleviate menopausal symptoms (especially hot flashes) to prevent osteoporosis and fractures and to prevent heart disease. The FDA has approved four estrogen drugs—Premarin, Estraderm, Estrace, and Ogen—for long-term use to prevent osteoporosis. Other approved uses for estrogen drugs include the treatment of vaginal atrophy, abnormal bleeding conditions due to hormonal imbalance, and for comfort in the treatment of certain advanced cancers. Many health care practitioners prescribe HRT because of the data showing that estrogen may prevent heart disease by lowering cholesterol, lowering LDL, raising HDL, and strengthening the lining of the blood vessels, but this effect has yet to be clearly proven. Details on the scientific evidence and the weaknesses of that evidence have been discussed extensively in Chapter 9 and we will not duplicate that information. Simply put, the dominant number of conventional practitioners believe that HRT reduces coronary artery disease risk by 50 percent.[42] The results of these studies are open to question, and there is a momentum of criticism leveled at these studies. The results of several ongoing studies with heart disease as a major endpoint began to be concluded at the end of 1998. The Heart and Estrogen-Progestin Replacement

Study (HERS), the Women's Health Initiative (WHI), the Estrogen in the Prevention of Reinfarction Trial (ESPIRIT), and the Women's International Study of Long-Duration Oestrogen after Menopause (WISDOM) study are all randomized, double-blind, placebo-controlled trials that will clarify this growing controversy. Dr. Susan Love, in her book *Susan Love's Hormone Book*,[265] is the most outspoken conventional medical doctor critical of the logic of giving a drug that may prevent heart disease or osteoporosis in a woman's seventies and eighties but that can cause breast cancer in her fifties or sixties.

Reports from the HERS study have just been announced. This is now one of the most damaging pieces of research to date that seriously calls into question the value of HRT in preventing heart attacks in postmenopausal women.[266] A total of 2,763 women with coronary disease, aged 44–79, with a mean age of 66.7 years, were given either Prempro, which contains 0.625 mg of CEE plus 2.5 of MPA, or a placebo for an average of 4.1 years. Eighty-two percent of those assigned to the hormone group were taking it at the end of one year, and 75 percent at the end of three years.

The primary outcome that was measured was the occurrence of nonfatal myocardial infarction (MI) or death from coronary heart disease. Overall, after an average of 4.1 years, there were no significant differences between groups in the rate of nonfatal MI or CHD death. One hundred and seventy-two women in the HRT group and 176 women in the placebo group had MI or CHD death. This lack of difference in the HRT group occurred despite a net 11 percent lower LDL cholesterol level and the 10 percent increase in HDL cholesterol level in the hormone group.

Although the overall effect between the two groups was not apparent, there was a statistically significant trend according to time. More CHD events occurred in the first year in the hormone group than in the placebo group, and fewer in years four and five. Women in the hormone group were 2.89 times more likely than women in the placebo group to experience venous thromboembolic events. Women in the hormone group also had more gallbladder disease.

This study is overwhelmingly significant for those who question the standard recommendations of conventional medicine for postmenopausal women. The HERS study now offers evidence to support the practice of refraining from routinely starting HRT for the purpose of secondary prevention of CHD.

Estrogen therapy is also used to prevent or treat osteoporosis by retarding the rapid loss of bone that occurs in the early years following menopause. The degree of this loss has been estimated to be 2–3 percent per year without estrogen.[267] Most conventional practitioners continue to practice as if the minimum effective dose of estrogen for the prevention of osteoporosis were 0.625 mg/day of CEE, 1.0 mg/day of micronized estradiol, 0.75 mg of estropipate, or 0.05 mg/day of transdermal estradiol. Results from studies indicate that estrogen reduces the risk of hip fractures by about 35 percent[268] and increases bone density from 5–15 percent after one year of CEE therapy.[269]

The number-one fear for women about HRT is a concern about the risk of breast cancer. Although most conventional practitioners still consider the benefits to outweigh the risks, most women see it differently. Numerous meta-analyses of the published studies concerning the use of postmenopausal hormones provide a summary indicating that there is a relationship between the duration of use of HRT and the risk of breast cancer.[270, 271] When previous data from 51 epidemiologic studies have been reanalyzed, a review of 52,000 patients with breast cancer and more than 100,000 women without breast cancer indicates that the risk of breast cancer increases by 2.3 percent for each year of HRT use.[272] In the most recent review of the existing English language literature on hormones and breast cancer, Colditz found evidence of a causal relationship between postmenopausal HRT and breast cancer.[273] Women and practitioners might best heed the advice of Dr. Susan Love who advocates taking HRT if you need it only for the menopause transition and symptoms that are not relieved with nonhormonal methods, and then later on around age 70, so that the total duration of use does not exceed five years. Most studies have shown that estrogen taken for more than five years postmenopausally increases the risk by about 30 percent.[270] Compared with women who have never used hormones, it is estimated that for every 1,000 women who begin to take postmenopausal HRT at age 50 and take it for 10 years, there are six more cases of breast cancer; at 15 years, there are 12 more cases.[272] Indeed, it is a risk versus

benefit issue and we cannot neglect that women who are at high risk for osteoporosis and heart disease will receive great benefit from HRT.

While the estrogen and breast cancer controversy rolls on, one issue that is not argued is that longer-term estrogen therapy is associated with endometrial cancer (the lining of the uterus). Endometrial cancer is influenced by genetics, just like breast cancer. Some women may have an abnormal gene that is either inherited or becomes damaged. Estrogen can cause gene mutations, but mostly estrogen increases cell division. If there is already a damaged gene, then estrogen can cause the multiplication of that gene. Risk factors for endometrial cancer include medications and health problems that leave women with a higher estrogen state. Taking estrogen without a progesterone or progestin that opposes the stimulatory effect of estrogen is one of the more obvious situations that leaves a woman at higher risk for endometrial cancer. When estrogen is given to a postmenopausal woman without an adequate progestin or progesterone added, the risk of endometrial cancer increases significantly.

A meta-analysis of studies on endometrial cancer clarifies the effect of estrogen on this risk.[274] Women who had used estrogen at any point in their lives, whether for only 1 year or for as much as 30 years, had 2.3 times the risk for endometrial cancer. For women who took it for less than 1 year, who the risk was 1.4 times, but for those took it for more than 10 years the risk was almost 10 times greater than normal and, after 20 years, 20 times greater than normal. Women who took Premarin had a greater risk than women who took an estrogen like Estrace. Women who are 20–50 pounds overweight have three times the normal risk of endometrial cancer because body fat contains an enzyme that converts some of our other hormones into estrogen. Women who are more than 50 pounds overweight have 19 times the risk of endometrial cancer. Women with diabetes have 3 times the risk of endometrial cancer. This may be related to being overweight, but there may be some other mechanism at work as well.

A drug called tamoxifen is used to treat some women with breast cancer because it blocks the estrogen effect in the breast. The problem is, it has an estrogen-stimulating effect in the uterus, and it, too, can increase the risk of endometrial cancer.

The good news is that these risks are relatively small, and the lifetime risk of developing endometrial cancer is about 3 percent. Also, risk of endometrial cancer can actually decrease with some other medications or modifications in one's habits. If you take an estrogen of any kind, and have a uterus, the most important prevention method is to take an adequate dose of a progestin or progesterone a minimum of 10 days per month, and preferably 12 days per month is necessary to have a preventive effect. Either 10 mg of MPA (the synthetic progestin) or 200 mg of oral micronized natural progesterone 12 days per month is required. Oddly enough, premenopausal women who take birth control pills have a lower incidence of endometrial cancer that lasts for at least 15 years after they've discontinued taking them. Regular exercise will also decrease the risk of endometrial cancer because it helps to regulate and lengthen the menstrual cycle. The less often a woman menstruates, the fewer hormones her uterus is exposed to. Eating a diet high in soy protein will also lower one's risk of endometrial cancer, which was discussed in more detail in the nutrition section of this chapter.

Another potentially deadly but thankfully rare disease is ovarian cancer. Ovarian cancer is most common in women who have a mother, sister, or daughter with it. The risk of ovarian cancer also increases the more a woman ovulates. If she started her menses at a younger age and reached menopause at an older-than-average age, then the risk is higher. Certain fertility drugs that increase ovulation may possibly be linked to ovarian cancer as well. Birth control pills actually decrease the risk of ovarian cancer because they decrease ovulation. Observational studies have suggested that estrogen replacement therapy may increase the chance of getting ovarian cancer.

Women who took estrogen after menopause for more than six years increased their risk by 72 percent.[275] It may be that adding progestin to the regimen decreases this effect, but as yet we have no way of knowing. Although progestins and progesterone decrease the risk of endometrial cancer and there is evidence to show that both may increase or de-crease the risk of breast cancer, we do not know the effect on the ovaries.

When all is said and done, there is good news and bad news about conventional hormone replacement therapy. Just as in life, there's no free lunch. There are clearly important benefits and a potential for disease prevention due to HRT for some women. There are also important downsides and risks. Always remember that the decision whether or not to use HRT is not permanent. Newer nonestrogen therapies are increasingly available that have an antiestrogen effect or no estrogen effect in the breast or endometrium while offering potential health benefits for the heart and bones. Bisphosphonates to prevent and treat osteoporosis and selective estrogen receptor modulators (SERMs) head the list of the rapidly expanding nonhormone options.

Each woman must make an educated choice. If you choose a conventional practitioner as part of your health care team, choose one who is willing to learn about the spectrum of natural, hormonal, and nonhormonal therapies. Having a practitioner that respects your choices is not too much to ask.

〜 *Seeing a Licensed Primary Health Care Practitioner**

Most women who are perimenopausal can feel comfortable starting on their own with the diet, exercise, herbs, nutritional supplements, and natural progesterone creams described in this chapter for the relief of menopause symptoms. Women who do not find adequate relief from these therapies will need to see a licensed primary care provider who preferably is educated in the range of hormone options, not just conventional HRT.

At some time, however, my advice to all women is to have full evaluation by a practitioner who is educated in all the natural, hormonal, and pharmaceutical nonhormonal options. The only primary care practitioners that are trained in the medical school setting about all of these options

*N.D. = Naturopathic Doctor; M.D. = Medical Doctor; D.O. = Osteopathic Doctor; N.P. = Nurse Practitioner; P.A. = Physician's Assistant.

are licensed naturopathic physicians. The purpose of this evaluation, as discussed in the overview section and overview of alternative medicine, is to take a medical history, physical exam, and necessary laboratory and imaging studies to determine the risk for osteoporosis and heart disease. After a determination of whether you are at low risk, medium risk, or high risk for both of these conditions, a treatment plan will be recommended that will use one or more of the six treatment options. For a further comparison and description of some of these therapies, see Appendix B.

Using natural therapies versus using conventional HRT or some combination of both is a very personal decision. A well-informed patient who also has the good fortune of having a well-informed, respectful, open-minded practitioner is in the best position to make appropriate decisions. Remember that any decision you make is reversible. There is nothing permanent here. Decisions can and do change over time. Menopause, aging, and our concerns about long-term health problems evolve over time. A balance is necessary. Naïveté is inappropriate, and overmedicalization of menopause is inappropriate. Menopause is a normal and natural event of aging. It can be a time of strength, empowerment, personal growth, and positive, life-changing insights and decisions.

MENSTRUAL CRAMPS

 Overview

Menstrual cramps are one of the most common problems that women face, affecting over 50 percent of menstruating women. The term "dysmenorrhea," derived from the Greek and meaning difficult monthly flow, is commonly used to refer to painful menstruation. Dysmenorrhea is best classified as primary or secondary. In primary dysmenorrhea, painful menstrual cramps occur that have nothing to do with any physical abnormalities or identifiable pelvic disease. Secondary dysmenorrhea is painful menstrual cramps due to some specific pelvic abnormal condition such as endometriosis, pelvic inflammatory disease, adhesions, ovarian cysts, congenital malformations, narrowing of the cervical opening, polyps, or uterine fibroids. We will be focusing on primary dysmenorrhea in this chapter. Treatment for secondary dysmenorrhea is directed to treating the underlying cause of the condition, whether it be endometriosis or fibroids. The treatments in this chapter can be used to alleviate acute menstrual-related painful episodes in both primary and secondary dysmenorrhea.

Menstrual cramps are a significant personal and public health problem for women. Of the 50 percent of menstruating women who are affected by menstrual cramps, about 10 percent have severe pain that renders them incapacitated for one to three days each month.[1] It is estimated that 600 million work hours are lost in a year in the United States because of untreated and incapacitating dysmenorrhea. Social and family life is also disrupted by the painful episodes.

Dysmenorrhea occurs most commonly between the ages of 20–24. Women in this age group experience the most severe pain. Women older than 24 have less painful cramping, and the overall incidence of primary dysmenorrhea tends to decrease with age—more rapidly in married women than in unmarried ones, possibly due to childbearing. Women who begin to menstruate at a younger age and have longer menstrual periods have increased severity of pain and more days of pain. In smokers, cramps tend to last longer. Being overweight is also an important risk factor for menstrual cramps, and it doubles the odds of having a long painful episode.[2]

Primary dysmenorrhea usually appears within 6 to 12 months after the first menstrual period. The pain usually begins several hours before or just after the onset of menstruation and is often the most severe the first or second day of menstruation. It tends to be spasmodic and is strongest in the lower part of the abdomen above the pubic hairline, although it can often radiate to the back and along the inner aspects of the thighs. More than 50 percent of women with menstrual cramps also have additional symptoms including nausea and vomiting, fatigue, diarrhea, lower backache, and headache. Women with severe cases may also become dizzy and even faint. The symptoms may last from a few hours to one day but seldom last longer than two to three days. Some women have more congestive symptoms that are characterized by a dull aching in the low back and pelvis, bloating and weight gain, along with some systemic symptoms including breast tenderness, headaches, and irritability.

Primary dysmenorrhea is diagnosed when other causes of pelvic pain have been excluded. Certain characteristic clinical features distinguish the diagnosis with several important hallmarks.

CLINICAL FEATURES OF DYSMENORRHEA

- The initial onset is at or shortly after the first menstrual period (menarche). If dysmenorrhea starts two years or more after menarche, then other causes and secondary dysmenorrhea should be considered. Endometriosis is difficult to distinguish from primary dysmenorrhea because they produce similar symptoms.
- Duration of the pain is usually 48–72 hours, starting a few hours before or just after the onset of the flow. Pain that starts several days before is less likely to be primary dysmenorrhea.
- The pain is cramping, or laborlike, although some women have more congestion and bloating.
- Findings on pelvic exam are normal.

The cause of primary dysmenorrhea may be attributed to one of several factors, including behavioral and psychologic causes; lack of blood flow, and therefore oxygen, to the uterus (ischemia); and increased production and release of uterine prostaglandins. Increased prostaglandins, specifically PgF2-alpha and PgE2, cause uterine contractions that lead to ischemia and pain. The levels of both PgF2-alpha and PgE2 are low during the first half of the cycle and early part of the second half, but then rise sharply and reach their highest levels shortly before and during the onset

of menses. Studies have found that women with dysmenorrhea produce 8–13 times more PgF than do women without dysmenorrhea.[1] This increase in prostaglandin production may be related to the decline in progesterone levels toward the end of the cycle just before the onset of menses. Dysmenorrhea occurs only in cycles where ovulation has occurred. In cycles without ovulation, there is no increase in progesterone production in the second half of the cycle and then decline, as in a normal cycle, and there is subsequently no increase in the prostaglandin concentrations in the lining of the uterus. These mechanisms form the basis for many of the therapies used, both natural and conventional.

◈ Overview of Alternative Treatments

An alternative approach to menstrual cramps needs to provide effective pain relief while at the same time correcting the underlying dysfunction that is creating the cyclic menstrual pain. Because we are dealing with a functional problem and not a disease state that is causing the pain, we can truly focus on a holistic approach by looking for aggravating factors in the diet, lifestyle, and emotional environment. Dietary principles emphasizing good nutritional habits, eliminating junk foods and saturated fats, and increasing whole grains, fruits, and vegetables provide a range of nutrients needed to prevent menstrual cramps. Stress reduction can help relieve tension in the lower back and pelvic area that can worsen cramps. Improvements in posture improve the positioning of the spine and promote proper circulation and nerve stimulation to the pelvic organs.

Providing acute pain relief is one of the greatest challenges for natural medicine. Mild and moderate levels of pain are more treatable with natural therapies than is acute severe pain, although some women with severe pain will experience relief from the therapies that follow. Even when acute pain relief is not accomplished with alternative therapies, a treatment plan for the interim days of the month is important to follow in order to reduce the severity of

KEY CONCEPTS

- Primary dysmenorrhea should be distinguished from secondary dysmenorrhea.
- Provide adequate acute pain relief in addition to trying to correct the underlying mechanism that is causing the problem.
- About half of all women experience menstrual cramps.

PREVENTION

- Good posture and spinal alignment may decrease the tendency toward menstrual cramps.
- Stress reduction may help to relax the pelvic and low back muscles.
- Some women may find that their menstrual cramping is worsened when they use tampons; these women should switch to sanitary napkins.
- An IUD for contraception may worsen spasmodic menstrual cramping, and an alternative may need to be chosen.
- Maintain a healthy weight.
- Avoid smoking.
- Food allergies may contribute to water retention, gas, and bloating which may contribute to congestive menstrual pain.
- An increase in exercise may improve blood flow to the uterus and create an optimal pelvic musculature that will tend to reduce the incidence of menstrual discomfort.
- Maintain optimal digestive function. Irregular bowel habits may be correlated to primary dysmenorrhea.
- Avoid foods that may aggravate an excess of the prostaglandins that cause uterine contractions: dairy products, beef, pork, lamb, and poultry.

the recurring menstrual cramp episodes over time. Having a natural therapeutic treatment plan for the chronic problem and using over-the-counter or prescription conventional medicines for acute pain relief can turn out to be the most effective plan. Over time, the need for pain medications will decrease.

Many alternative practitioners have experience with other natural therapies not included in this book such as acupuncture, homeopathy, and hands-on techniques that also may offer effective help for many women with mild, moderate, and even severe menstrual cramps. I often encourage women to try the herbal or nutritional product for a couple of hours during acute pain. If no relief is accomplished within that amount of time and the pain is severe enough (based on one's own personal judgment), then switch to a pharmaceutical method of pain control. As each successive month of treating the chronic problem goes by, a measure of the success of that treatment will be a decreased need to use the acute pain relief medication.

We don't want to overlook the role of stressors in our personal lives that can be at least part of the cause of our pain and can also impact our ability to deal with pain. Psychotherapy can help one to gain insight into these influences and learn how to reduce and manage these stressors. Research has shown that behavior therapy has been highly effective in reducing the symptoms of spasmodic dysmenorrhea.[3] Biofeedback treatment with a relaxation practice has also proven to be significant in reducing dysmenorrhea.[4] After two months of biofeedback treatments, sufferers of menstrual cramps had dramatic declines in the severity and duration of their symptoms as well as a decline in the amount of medication they were taking. Meditation, visualization, and relaxation techniques are used by many women both as a primary form of pain management and also in combination with other therapies. My advice would be to seek the advice of a trained person to teach you which method may be most appropriate and effective for you.

Nutrition

A healthy diet is fundamental to an effective menstrual cramp treatment program. Many women experience relief from cramps just by switching to good nutritional habits. There are two basic aspects to making changes in the diet. One is to decrease the intake of foods that may be contributing to the condition, and the other is to increase the intake of foods that provide a wide range of important nutrients necessary to bring about a functional change in the pelvic area.

The most important foods to avoid are those that are high in arachidonic acid. This is the fat that the body uses to produce the series-2 prostaglandins (PgE2)—the ones that cause muscle and uterine contractions. Dairy products are the main source of arachidonic acid. In addition, many people are allergic to dairy products or lack the enzymes to digest them. Digestive problems such as bloating and gas can intensify with menstrual cramps, which adds to the overall discomfort. Reducing or even eliminating the intake of milk, cheese, cottage cheese, butter, ice cream, and yogurt may be enough to have a significant impact for as many as one-third of women with menstrual cramps. Saturated fats from nondairy sources can also intensify menstrual cramps by stimulating the PgE2 series. Most of our saturated fats come from animal products, although a few are from vegetable sources such as palm oil or coconut oil. Animal foods to reduce or avoid that contain saturated fat include beef, pork, lamb, and even chicken and turkey. Even though chicken and turkey are lower in saturated fat, they are actually higher in arachidonic acid than red meats.

Salt can be another aggravating factor for women with menstrual cramps. Too much dietary salt can increase fluid retention and worsen bloating that contributes to the congestive symptoms of menstrual cramps. Canned and frozen foods, fast foods, and processed/packaged foods are all suspect for high amounts of salt. Read the labels carefully. You may be surprised to find that some of the things you thought were healthy, such as certain salad dressings, are actually loaded with salt. Even a bean burrito at a fast-food restaurant will be high in salt. Look for "no salt" labels on your packaged foods, and go light on the salt shaker in the kitchen and at the table.

Although sugar in the diet may not be directly related to menstrual cramps, sugar does interfere with the absorption and metabolism of some B vitamins and minerals. Deficiencies or less than optimal amounts of some of these nutrients may worsen muscle tension and increase the contractile nature of the uterus. High-sugar foods are often the same foods that are high in saturated fats.

Women with monthly menstrual cramps run the risk of overusing alcohol because of its sedative and pain-relieving effects. This overuse then may lead to other problems, including alcoholism and substance abuse. Other pain relief medications that are non-addictive would be far preferable. Alcohol also depletes the nutrient status of many B vitamins and minerals such as magnesium. These deficiencies and nutritional imbalances can then lead to a difficulty in regulating muscle function and worsen muscle spasms during menstruation. Alcohol may also interfere with the liver's ability to metabolize hormones effectively and efficiently. This may lead to heavier flows. A heavier amount of blood then creates more clots, and the passage of clots will trigger an increase in the uterine muscle spasms.

The best medicinal foods for menstrual cramps are those foods that increase the antispasmodic prostaglandins, the PgE1 and PgE3 series. Certain fish, like salmon, tuna, halibut, and sardines, contain linolenic acid, a fatty acid that helps to relax muscles by the production of these prostaglandins.[5] There are many seeds and nuts that are sources of linoleic acid and linolenic acid, also precursors to these muscle-relaxing prostaglandins. The best sources of both these fatty acids are flaxseeds and pumpkin seeds. Sesame seeds and sunflower seeds are excellent sources of linoleic acid. The oils from the seeds of flax, pumpkin, sesame, and sunflower are the best oils to use in salad dressings. Flax and pumpkin oils should not be heated, but sesame and sunflower are acceptable cooking oils. In all likelihood, the seeds, nuts, and fruits from which these oils are extracted are healthy choices as well.

To round out the healthy changes in the diet, emphasize whole grains, legumes, vegetables, and fruits. Whole grains such as brown rice, oats, millet, barley, rye, amaranth, and buckwheat provide sources of magnesium, calcium, potassium, fiber, vitamin E, B-complex vitamins, and protein. Both calcium and magnesium reduce muscular tension, fiber will help to regulate the bowel function, and potassium has a diuretic effect that can then aid in reducing bloating. Beans are also good sources of calcium, magnesium, potassium, and protein. Many vegetables are high in the calcium, magnesium, and potassium that help to relieve and prevent muscle spasms. Fruits are an excellent form of natural inflammatory substances like bioflavonoids and vitamin C. These nutrients not only strengthen the blood vessels that can aid circulation to areas of muscle tension in the pelvis but also reduce the pain from menstrual cramps through their anti-inflammatory effect.

Nutritional Supplements

Vitamin B₃ (Niacin)

Niacin or vitamin B₃ has been shown in clinical research to be effective in 87.5 percent of women with menstrual cramps.[6] Niacin was given in 100-mg doses twice daily throughout the month, and then every two to three hours during the periods of menstrual cramps. Although a sometimes uncomfortable niacin flush could easily occur at the escalated dosing, none of the women in the study stopped the medication due to the flushing. Interestingly, the women who received no real relief of their menstrual cramps were frequently the women who reported no flushing. This vasodilating effect of niacin may indeed be the main treatment effect. It may still be important to consider the theory that vasospasm of the uterine arteries may be responsible for the menstrual pain.

Niacin
100 mg, twice daily throughout the month;
100 mg, every 2–3 hours during episodes
of menstrual cramps

Vitamin C and Rutin

In a follow-up study, the same author of the niacin study found that rutin with ascorbic acid increased the effectiveness of niacin in the treatment of menstrual cramps.[7] In twice as many women as the niacin-only study, the same dose of niacin (100 mg twice daily regularly and every two or three hours during menstrual cramps) was given while also adding 300 mg of vitamin C and 60 mg of rutin daily. These additions slightly improved the response in up to 90 percent of the women. This increased effectiveness was thought to be due to improving the permeability of the capillaries, thus potentiating the vasodilating effect of the niacin. In most cases, niacin was not effective unless it had been taken 7–10 days before the onset of the menstrual flow.

Vitamin C
300–3,000 mg per day

Rutin
60–1,000 mg per day

Vitamin E

Vitamin E was studied back in the 1950s for the treatment of spasmodic dysmenorrhea. It was used in doses of 150 IU ten days premenstrual and during the first four days of the menstrual period. In approximately 70 percent of the women tested, it helped to relieve menstrual discomfort within two menstrual cycles.[8] I generally recommend higher amounts of vitamin E because there are so many other benefits for women, including relieving cyclic breast pain, raising beneficial HDL cholesterol, and providing antioxidant protection.

Vitamin E
150–800 IU per day

Calcium

Calcium supplementation for menstrual cramps has been used by women as a self-care treatment for many years. Muscles need calcium to maintain their normal muscle tone; and if they are deficient in calcium, they can more easily cramp. This is true of the uterine muscle as well. Low calcium intake is associated with menstrual water retention and greater pain during the menses.[9] The typical American diet supplies about 450–550 mg per day, falling short of the recommended daily allowance of 800 mg per day in menstruating women.

Calcium
800–1,000 mg per day

Omega-3 Fatty Acids

Essential fatty acids are the raw materials from which prostaglandins, beneficial hormonelike substances, are made. There are two essential fatty acids: linoleic acid (omega-6 family) and linolenic acid (omega-3 family). Linoleic and linolenic acids cannot be made by the body and must be supplied daily in the diet from either food or supplements. The typical American diet is often much higher in omega-6 oils than it is in omega-3 oils. As a result, we end up with the PgE2 prostaglandins that cause muscle contractions and pain. Another problem is that our bodies need a certain amount of linoleic acid to convert to gamma linolenic acid (GLA), which leads to the production of the PgE1 prostaglandins (the antispasmodic and anti-inflammatory effect). The conversion of linoleic acid to GLA and the beneficial prostaglandins require the presence of magnesium, vitamin B_6, zinc, vitamin C, and niacin. Women who are deficient in these nutrients won't adequately be able to make this conversion. Supplementation with flax oil (high in omega-3 fatty acids) or borage oil, black current oil, and evening primrose oil (all high in linoleic acid and GLA) is one way of favorably altering the synthesis of the beneficial prostaglandins; the end result likely will be fewer uterine contractions and menstrual pains.

As mentioned earlier, after the rise of progesterone in the second half of the menstrual cycle followed by its decline right before menstruation, omega-6 fatty acids, particularly arachidonic acid, are released. Subsequently, an increase in PgF2-alpha and PgE2 occurs, causing uterine contractions leading to ischemia and pain. Instead of inhibiting ovulation and therefore the progesterone effect, or inhibiting the synthesis of prostaglandins with nonsteroidal anti-inflammatory agents, the omega-3 fatty acids, eicosapentaenoic acid (EPA), and decosahexaenoic acid (DHA) compete with omega-6 fatty acids and result in the production of the friendlier antispasmodic and anti-inflammatory prostaglandins, series 1 and 3.

Based on these observations, using fish oil containing omega-3 fatty acids as a supplement seems logical. Dietary supplementation with fish oils was tested in 42 adolescent girls with dysmenorrhea.[5] The first group of 21 girls received fish oil (1,080 mg EPA and 720 mg DHA) and 1.5 mg vitamin E daily for two months followed by a placebo for an additional two months. In the second group, 21 girls received placebo for the first two months, followed by fish oil for two more months. At the conclusion of the study, on a 7-point scale, a score of 4 being moderately effective and a 7 meaning totally effective, 73 percent of the girls rated it greater than or equal to 4.

Fish oils
1,080 mg EPA and 720 mg DHA per day

Evening primrose oil (EPO)
500–1,000 mg up to 3 times per day

Melatonin

I have no personal experience prescribing melatonin for menstrual cramps, but I think it has potential based on some of its known biochemical effects. It has been proposed that insufficient melatonin secretion during the second half of the menstrual cycle (luteal phase) is a factor in primary dysmenorrhea.[10] This hypothesis is based on several factors: (1) melatonin levels are low at ovulation and increase premenstrually three- to sixfold and reach their peak at menstruation;[11] (2) melatonin decreases uterine contractility;[12] (3) melatonin exerts analgesic effects;[13] (4) melatonin stimulates progesterone secretion;[14] and (5) melatonin inhibits uterine prostaglandin synthesis and release.[15]

Since melatonin has been shown to have all these effects, supplementation in order to achieve high concentrations during menstruation may serve to oppose the effects of prostaglandins and therefore prevent the occurrence of dysmenorrhea.

Melatonin
2.5 mg per day, taken
3–4 days prior to onset of menses

Botanicals

Valerian (*Valeriana officinalis*)

Valerian has been used traditionally primarily as a sedative and antispasmodic for the treatment of anxiety disorders, sleep disorders, and a diverse array of conditions associated with pain. Valerian contains an important class of compounds called valepotriates and valeric acid, which are found exclusively in this perennial plant native to North America and Europe. It is not difficult to see how valerian would help to relieve pain, anxiety, and insomnia because both valepotriates and valeric acid are capable of binding to the same receptors in the brain as the pharmaceutical drug Valium.[16] Although valerian has not been scientifically studied for menstrual cramps, it has been shown to relax the spasmodic contractions of intestinal muscles.[17] Both the uterus and intestines are smooth muscles. In clinical practice, valerian is usually a significant feature of an alternative medicine approach to painful menstruation. It is most practical to take valerian in tincture form or capsules. Many people prefer valerian capsules because the tincture has a very bitter taste. Attempts to disguise the taste can be made by placing the tincture in a small amount of fruit juice and then following that with several swallows of plain juice. Valerian may make you tired and sleepy, so it is advisable to stay home and rest or take a nap.

Valerian tincture
1 tsp, every 3–4 hours as needed for pain or

Valerian capsules
1–2 capsules, every 3–4 hours as needed for pain

Crampbark (*Viburnum opulus*) and Black Haw (*Viburnum prunifolium*)

Both of these species of *Viburnum* are mentioned repeatedly in the traditional botanical reference books as uterine relaxants and general antispasmodics.[18] They have been used mainly for menstrual cramps, bearing-down uterine pains, and chronic uterine and ovarian pains. Animal studies have confirmed that both species have an antispasmodic effect on the uterus.[19] Laboratory studies on human uterine tissue also have confirmed that *Viburnum prunifolium* exhibits a relaxant effect on the uterine tissue.[20]

When the menstrual pains are of either a congestive or spasmodic nature and include low back pains, especially if the pains radiate down the thighs, there is no better herbal choice than crampbark.

The root bark of black haw is reported to contain several active constituents that are uterine relaxants, one of which is scopoletin. It has been historically used as a specific medicine for menstrual cramps with severe low back and bearing-down pelvic pains. For menstrual pains associated with a profuse menstrual flow and intermittent severe pains, black haw would probably be a more specific choice than crampbark. American Indians used the root and/or stem for the treatment of painful menses, to prevent miscarriage, and as a postpartum antispasmodic.

Crampbark tincture
½ tsp, every 2–3 hours or

Crampbark capsules
1 capsule, every 2–3 hours

Black haw tincture
¼ tsp every 2–4 hours or

Black haw capsules
1 capsule, every 3–4 hours

Caution: *Both* Viburnum *species should be avoided during pregnancy except in the hands of an experienced herbal practitioner.*

Ginger (*Zingiber officinale*)

Ginger is typically known for its stimulatory effects on digestion and easing the nausea of an upset stomach. The pungent constituents in ginger, shagaol, and gingerol also have an inhibitory effect on inflammatory and spasmodic prostaglandins. Although ginger has not been studied specifically in relation to menstrual cramps, it does have antispasmodic effects on the smooth muscle of the intestines. Given that the uterus is also made up of smooth muscle, and ginger has a long history of traditional use for the purpose of treating spasmodic dysmenorrhea, I use it in clinical practice with great confidence in combination with other herbs .

Black Cohosh (*Cimicifuga racemosa*)

Black cohosh has gained increased attention in the last few years largely as an herb for the relief of menopause symptoms. However, when I was first studying botanical medicine, this herb was known more for its relaxant effect on the uterus in dysmenorrhea, false labor pains, and threatened miscarriage. It can be helpful in both congestive or spasmodic menstrual cramps of even a severe nature. If the menses is also associated with PMS irritability and anxiety, delayed or irregular menstrual cycles, or scanty flow, then black cohosh would be an even more indicated herbal choice for menstrual cramps.

> **Black cohosh tincture**
> *¼–½ tsp, every 2–4 hours* or
>
> **Black cohosh capsules**
> *1–2 capsules, every 2–4 hours*
>
> ***Caution:*** *Avoid during pregnancy except when prescribed by a trained herbal practitioner.*

Other Traditional Herbs to Consider

Herbs such as false unicorn root (*Chamaelirium luteum*), wild yam (*Dioscorea villosa*), passionflower (*Passiflora incarnata*), German chamomile (*Matricaria chamomilla*), blue cohosh (*Caulophyllum thalictroides*), and hops (*Humulus lupulus*) have an independent antispasmodic or sedative effect on the uterus in their own right. They are often used in combination with each other or in formulations with some of the more dominant choices such as crampbark, black haw, valerian, and black cohosh.

Additional herbs may also be considered for their different actions. For example, herbs that have an anti-inflammatory effect, such as white willow and ginger; diuretic herbs that decrease the pelvic congestion such as parsley, dandelion leaf, or horsetail; and herbs that promote circulation such as ginkgo may also have a role in reducing the pain experienced from dysmenorrhea.

Natural Progesterone

As we discussed earlier, it is believed that the drop in progesterone premenstrually results in an increased production of arachidonic acid from the endometrium. This stimulates PgE2 release and uterine contractions. If we can temper or delay this drop in progesterone premenstrually, then, in effect, natural progesterone can be used to inhibit the uterine contractions, ischemia, and pain during menstruation.

Remember, though, that some decline in progesterone is necessary in order to trigger the onset of blood flow. Natural progesterone may allow a slower decline or a delayed decline.

Thus, some women do indeed find that a natural progesterone cream, applied topically for 3–12 days prior to onset of menses, will reduce menstrual cramps.

> **Natural progesterone cream** (>400 mg/1 oz):
> *Apply ¼ tsp 2 times per day for 3–12 days before the expected onset of menses.*

Exercise

The effects of both special exercises[21–23] and general regular physical exercise on primary dysmenorrhea have been studied. No discrepancies exist in the results from the first group of studies—special exercises are reported consistently to reduce, or "cure," menstrual pain. For example, one researcher found symptom reduction in 89.3 percent of 129 dysmenorrheic women who adhered to his program of special exercises. Similarly, another researcher, investigating 141 dysmenorrheic girls 14–18 years of age from two different high schools, found that 92 percent of participants were "cured"* or improved in one of the schools after being given a set of specific exercises to reduce menstrual pain.[24] The experiment was con-

---

*A girl was considered cured "if she was free of pain for at least three menstrual periods" following the performance of the prescribed exercises.

ducted from mid-September 1956 to mid-June 1957. The results for the second school were 76 percent.

The three studies included in the latter group offer conflicting results. One group of investigators[25] conducted a twelve-week experiment that compared two groups of dysmenorrheic women who volunteered to either walk/jog or to act as sedentary controls. The experimental group reported significantly less severe menstrual symptoms than the controls. In contrast, another group of investigators reported a 30 percent increase in menstrual symptoms in regularly exercising over sedentary student nurses.[26] However, a more recent, controlled study again validated the hypothesis that regular exercise decreases menstrual symptoms in finding that "high exercisers experienced the greatest positive effect and sedentary women the least."[27]

SAMPLE TREATMENT PLAN FOR DYSMENORRHEA

Dietary recommendations
- Increase salmon, tuna, halibut, sardines, herring, fruits, vegetables
- Decrease dairy, salt, sugar, red meat, poultry

For acute pain management
- Calcium carbonate, 1,000–1,500 mg during pain
- Valerian tincture, 1 tsp every 3–4 hours *or* Valerian capsules, 1–2 every 3–4 hours
- Crampbark and/or black haw, 1 capsule every 3–4 hours
- Relaxation techniques

Use throughout the month
- Niacin, 100 mg twice daily
- Borage/flax oil, 2 caps twice daily
- Vitamin E, 200–400 IU daily
- Crampbark and/or black haw and/or black cohosh, 1–2 capsules daily

---

 ## Conventional Medicine Approach

Two groups of drugs are highly effective against dysmenorrhea: the oral contraceptives and prostaglandin synthetase inhibitors. The choice of

---

EXERCISE RECOMMENDATIONS FOR MENSTRUAL CRAMPS

If not exercising regularly, incorporate exercise into daily routine. Consult "General Exercise Instructions" and "General Exercise Program" in Appendix A.

Special exercises for moderate to severe dysmenorrhea (adopted from Haman[21] and Golub[24]): Do the following exercises twice a day for 10 consecutive days before menses:

Exercise #1
- [ ] Stand at right angles to the wall with left elbow on the wall on a level with the left shoulder.
- [ ] Tilt pelvis forward.
- [ ] Keeping knees straight, move left hip until it touches wall.
- [ ] Return to original position.
- [ ] Repeat 5 times.
- [ ] Repeat sequence with right elbow on the wall.

Exercise #2
- [ ] Stand facing the wall with both elbows on wall on a level with shoulders.
- [ ] Without moving elbows or feet and keeping knees straight, move pelvis away from wall and then toward it until pelvis touches the wall.
- [ ] Return to original position.
- [ ] Repeat 5 times.

Exercise # 3
- [ ] Stand with feet 12 inches apart and arms raised to the side at shoulder level.
- [ ] Keeping knees straight, twist trunk to the right and bend forward attempting to touch the right ankle with the left hand.
- [ ] Return to original position.
- [ ] Repeat sequence in the opposite direction.
- [ ] Repeat 5 times.

Exercise #4
- [ ] Stand with feet a few inches apart and arms at the sides.
- [ ] Swing arms forward and upward, simultaneously raising the right leg backward.
- [ ] Return to the original position.
- [ ] Repeat with the left leg.
- [ ] Repeat 5 times.

Note: For mild menstrual pain, do only one or two of the above exercises.

medication depends on whether the woman also wants oral contraceptives for birth control and whether there is any medical reason that she should not take oral contraceptives or prostaglandin synthetase inhibitors or chooses not to. If the woman desires birth control, the combined oral contraceptive is the agent of first choice. Combination-type oral contraceptives reduce the prostaglandin levels, and 80 percent of patients achieve complete relief of dysmenorrhea with oral contraceptives.[28, 29] This pain reduction is most likely the result of two mechanisms: (1) reduced volume of menstrual fluid, and (2) the suppression of ovulation, which results in an anovulatory cycle and low uterine prostaglandin levels. A trial of oral contraceptives is often initiated for three to four months. Women who respond to oral contraceptive therapy can be maintained on that regimen throughout their reproductive years. If the dysmenorrhea is not adequately relieved, a prostaglandin synthetase inhibitor can be added. These inhibitors are often changed or increased in dosage if complete relief is not achieved during the first few cycles of treatment. It is important to remember that when oral contraceptives are discontinued, there is a return to the previous state of elevated levels of menstrual fluid prostaglandins, and the dysmenorrhea will return.

For women who do not need contraception or who do not tolerate or choose to take oral contraceptives, prostaglandin synthetase inhibitors can be used. These agents reduce menstrual fluid prostaglandins and their metabolites, resulting in decreased uterine contractility and menstrual pains. They also decrease the amount of menstrual flow. They are most effective if given as soon as the menses begin, but before the cramping begins. They are taken for only the two to three days of the acute pain.

There are five major groups of prostaglandin synthetase inhibitors and include medications such as aspirin, ibuprofen, and indomethacin. The indole-acetic acid derivatives (indomethacin) and the aryl-propionic acid derivatives (ibuprofen and naproxen sodium) have all been shown to be highly effective in relieving primary dysmenorrhea. The success rate for these two classes of prostaglandin synthetase inhibitors is in the range of 60–90 percent.[30] Aspirin

in doses of 500–650 mg four times per day has been shown to be no better than a placebo except in one study.[31] Side effects of prostaglandin synthetase inhibitors include headaches, stomach or intestinal upset, and occasional "spaciness." More serious complications may lead to kidney disease, interstitial cystitis, and acute papillary and tubular necrosis. Most of these more serious complications only occur in older women who take these medications for a long period of time.

Other forms of treatment may also be considered if the patient has not responded to either or both of the above regimens. Narcotic pain relievers and newer prescription analgesics may be additional pharmaceuticals necessary in the management of dysmenorrhea. Psychotherapy interventions may help in learning how to deal with the pain as well as to uncover stressors that may influence the pain. Various meditation techniques are increasingly used by women as part of their menstrual pain management.

For those who do not respond to the oral contraceptives or other medications, it is appropriate to reconsider whether the problem really is primary dysmenorrhea. In this case, your doctor may recommend a laparoscopy to rule out or confirm pelvic disease. If pelvic disease is discovered, then it may need surgical intervention. It is important to discuss the possibilities and treatment options prior to the laparoscopy. Many women have had hysterectomies for primary dysmenorrhea. It may be that they were at the end of their options, and this was the wise choice. However, it is also true that many women have had hysterectomies unnecessarily. Do not be shy about having a second or even third opinion when contemplating a hysterectomy as a treatment for menstrual pains. If discussing possibilities and treatment options prior to a laparoscopy, be sure that you and your surgeon clearly understand each other and that you clarify your wishes regarding the circumstances under which you would choose a hysterectomy and other circumstances in which you would not. Preserving the ovaries, even when doing a hysterectomy to remove the uterus, should be a priority, and bilateral ovarian surgery should be considered only when the disease that is present truly warrants it. Removing healthy ovaries will reduce surgical menopause, and most likely, a more difficult menopause to manage satisfactorily.

The progesterone-medicated IUD has been found in one study to reduce menstrual fluid, inhibit the spasmodic prostaglandin 2 series, and relieve primary dysmenorrhea.[32] However, the IUD itself can cause dysmenorrhea and is probably not an appropriate treatment, in very many women.

✺ *Seeing a Licensed Primary Health Care Practitioner**

If we remember that primary dysmenorrhea is pain during menses that exists without any identifiable pelvic disease, then the only reason to seek a licensed health care practitioner is for conventional pain medications that are not available over the counter, or for more expertise in using effective alternative therapies and higher doses of natural medicines. The most important issue is worth repeating: you must be certain that your menstrual pain is indeed primary dysmenorrhea and not pain due to pelvic disease such as endometriosis, adenomyosis, uterine fibroids, an IUD, pelvic infection, cervical polyps, or ovarian tumor. These conditions can be diagnosed by a licensed primary health care practitioner, be it an alternative practitioner such as a naturopathic physician or a conventional practitioner such as a medical doctor, nurse practitioner, or physician's assistant.

*N.D. = Naturopathic Doctor; M.D. = Medical Doctor; D.O. = Osteopathic Doctor; N.P. = Nurse Practitioner; P.A. = Physician's Assistant.

OSTEOPOROSIS

≋ *Overview*

As the U.S. population ages, certain diseases and medical conditions more common among aging Americans are gaining greater public attention. Osteoporosis, a serious and disabling disease and the most prevalent metabolic bone disease in Western societies, is one such condition. Fortunately, osteoporosis can and should be prevented and, when present, treated. Osteoporosis affects 75 million people in Europe, the United States, and Japan. In the United States alone, it affects 25 million people and causes 1.5 million fractures annually.[1]

Osteoporosis is defined as a skeletal disease characterized by low bone mass and a deterioration in bone microarchitecture leading to bone fragility and susceptibility to fracture.[2] The World Health Organization has defined osteoporosis as a bone mineral density (T-score) that is 2.5 standard deviations (SD) below the mean peak value in young adults.[3] This definition is useful because it provides objective criteria, but it has limitations because it ignores the importance of other determinants of bone strength. In addition, it also ignores other risk factors for fractures in elderly women such as a maternal history of hip fracture.

Although low bone mass, as measured by bone density, is important in determining a person's risk of fracture, there are other equally important risk factors. These include maternal history of a hip frac-ture, previous vertebral fracture, previous hip fracture, high fall risk, and so forth.[4] Assessing a person's likelihood of a fall (use of sedative medications, inability to stand unaided from a sitting position) is very important. Low bone mass may be due to osteoporosis and/or poor bone quality. Vitamin D deficiency and other causes of secondary hyper-parathyroidism can lead to poor bone quality. Clinically, the term "osteoporosis" is used in reference to loss of bone associated with relatively atraumatic fractures of the ribs, spine, wrist, and hips.

Osteoporosis-related fractures will develop in half of all women and one-fifth of all men older than 65 years.[5] Within the first year following a hip fracture, the mortality rate is increased by up to 20 percent, and as many as 25 percent of the survivors will be confined to long-term care facilities one year after the fracture.[1]

Fractures associated with osteoporosis are distin-guished by three characteristics:[6]

- Greatly increased incidence with aging, with fractures occurring 2–100 times more among adults over age 75 than younger people.
- Greater incidence among women than men.
- Associated with modest trauma.

The three most common fracture sites are the spine, hip, and forearm. Vertebral fractures are twice as common as either hip fractures or distal radius fractures (wrist area). The incidence of wrist fractures starts to rise immediately after menopause with an incidence of about 15 percent by age 80. Each year, 172,000 wrist fractures occur and are the result of moderate trauma and rapid postmenopausal bone loss. The female to male ratio is 5:1. Wrist fractures are rarely fatal and cause much less disability than do hip and spinal fractures.[7, 8]

The majority of women with vertebral fractures suffer from compression fracture syndrome with a peak incidence between the ages of 50–70. Osteoporosis causes 500,000 vertebral compression fractures annually and is at least 10 times more common in women than in men.[8, 9]

Hip fractures tend to occur later in life with a cumulative prevalence of about 6 percent by age 80. A 20- to 25-year delay occurs between the peak incidence of wrist fractures and hip fractures. Hip fractures are twice as common in women as in men, and approximately 200,000 occur annually in the United States. Adult Caucasian women who live to age 80 have a 15 percent lifetime risk of suffering a hip fracture. As stated earlier, hip fractures are associated not only with high rates of complications and disability but also with high mortality.

There are two types of bone: trabecular and cortical. The trabecular bone is the inside part of the bone where the bone marrow is. It is comprised of a network of bone that prevents it from compressing with pressure (for example, from a fall). The cortical bone is the hard circular bone covering the bone that protects the bone from external trauma. Vertebrae are made up of 90 percent trabecular bone and only 10 percent cortical bone; the hip is 50:50, and the extremities are 90 percent cortical bone. The skeleton is living tissue composed of about 75 percent cortical bone and 25 percent trabecular bone. Cortical bone has a slower turnover rate than trabecular bone. Trabecular or cancellous bone is concentrated in the vertebrae, pelvis, other flat bones, and at the ends of long bones like the upper and lower leg. Trabecular bone is metabolically much more active and has a higher turnover rate than cortical bone. To provide support, bone is continuously rebuilding to maintain an optimal structure. Any damage or fatigue effect is constantly repaired through remodeling, a process of bone breakdown (resorption) and rebuilding (formation).

Certain problems cause different types of bone loss. Trabecular bone loss occurs with low estrogen levels, steroid use, and immobilization. So, when women choose not to take estrogen after menopause, they are more likely to lose trabecular bone and therefore may be at higher risk for vertebral and hip fractures. Cortical bone loss occurs with calcium and vitamin D abnormalities such as vitamin D deficiency. An extreme form of this is rickets, which presents with bowing of the femurs (small microfractures of those bones). Therefore, cortical bone loss leads to an increased risk of extremity fractures. These differences in the cortical bone and trabecular bone are why we prefer to measure both the hip and the spine when doing bone density testing.

In childhood, bone formation far exceeds bone remodeling, leading to longer, denser bones. During the adult years, bone resorption and bone formation are in balance, and total bone mass remains relatively stable. An increase in the rate of bone remodeling is the basis of many bone diseases including osteoporosis, hyperparathyroidism, hypercalcemia associated with cancer, Paget's disease, and bone loss in rheumatoid arthritis. Bone resorption is carried out by osteoclasts derived from stem cells in the bone marrow. Osteoblasts are bone-forming cells that originate from another kind of stem cell. They participate in bone mineralization and the regulation of bone turnover.

In the younger adult years prior to age 30–35, bone mass is maintained through a balance between bone resorption and formation. Bone formation and resorption are interdependent processes; if one is altered, it directly affects the other. As we age, the osteoblasts and osteoclasts may no longer function in a balanced fashion, and osteoporotic bone destruction may occur. Bone loss can be osteoclast-mediated, as seen in osteoporosis, or osteoblast-mediated, as seen in bone cancers. Increased bone resorption continues as we age and is worsened by a decrease in bone formation in women after menopause. Five to ten years after menopause there is an acceleration of bone loss that slows after age 65 when bone loss occurs at a slower rate. In osteoporosis, osteoclast-mediated bone loss outpaces the ability of osteoblasts to fill in the empty spaces.

Normal bone metabolism is dependent on hereditary, nutritional, and lifestyle factors, hormonal influences, and regulatory functions of the liver and kidneys. Genetic predisposition contributes significantly to bone mass and to the development of osteoporosis later in life. Female children of women who experienced an osteoporotic fracture were found to have 3–7 percent lower bone mass than would be expected for their age.[10] Additional studies have shown that relatives of women with osteoporosis tend to have lower bone mass.[11] The racial differences observed in bone mass also suggest the role of a genetic factor.

Dietary factors and nutrient deficiencies alter bone growth and remodeling and may result in lower bone mass. Girls/women with a dietary abnormality such as anorexia nervosa have significantly lower bone mass than healthy counterparts.[12] Calcium is needed to maintain the strength and integrity of the skeleton throughout our lives. The intake of calcium is most important during the bone-building years of childhood through adolescence and in old age. During puberty, calcium is required for bone growth and for the achievement of maximal calcification. Postmenopausal women and men over 65 require a greater intake of calcium because absorption of calcium is less efficient, and the dietary intake of calcium is usually lower because of intolerance to dairy products or elimination of dairy products as part of a low fat diet.

Bone metabolism is affected by hormonal factors, and the most important hormone in this regard is estrogen. What you may not know is that the bones are also influenced by progesterone, testosterone, parathyroid hormone, calcitonin, growth hormone, and insulin. The commonly held view is that low levels of estrogen at menopause or low body weight are associated with accelerated bone loss in women. With declining estrogen levels in the postmenopause, bone resorption is increased dramatically. Chronically high levels of parathyroid hormone (PTH) stimulate bone resorption by acting directly on osteoblasts, which then secrete factors that contribute to osteoclast-mediated bone resorp-

tion. PTH also inhibits and stimulates osteoblast collagen synthesis. Thyroid-produced calcitonin has some effect on calcium metabolism, and the osteoclasts do have a calcitonin receptor. This may explain why synthetic salmon calcitonin is an effective treatment for osteoporosis. However, a calcitonin deficiency that may occur after the removal of the thyroid gland has not been shown to cause bone loss.

Lifestyle factors, such as the level of physical activity, cigarette smoking, and alcohol consumption can profoundly impact bones. Generally, physical exercise increases osteoblast function, and bone formation and immobilization lead to substantial bone loss. Smokers have a lower bone mass, and alcohol consumption promotes bone loss. Alcohol also increases the metabolism of estrogen, leading to decreased action of estrogen on bone.

No one test or risk factor, alone or in combination, will accurately predict which patients will or will not experience osteoporotic fractures. In general, the more risk factors present, the greater the potential for lower bone mass and the higher the risk of fracture. However, predictions from risk factors cannot pinpoint all persons who will be affected. Risk factors for osteoporosis account for only 20–40 percent of bone mass variance.[13] Therefore, risk factors alone do not provide adequate assessment of low bone mass, but rather are important guides in the clinical assessment of osteoporosis risks that contribute to optimal preventive management. Ultimately, an individual woman's risk of fracture is the most relevant parameter for her future health care. Many factors have been observed to identify those at greatest risk. These are:

- Gender: female
- Age: postmenopausal
- Characteristics: short, slender, fair-skinned, blonde, blue-eyed
- Family history of osteoporosis
- Early menopause (physiologic, surgical, or drug-induced)
- History of amenorrhea, infrequent menses, late menstrual onset, anovulation
- History of anorexia nervosa, diabetes mellitus, Cushing's disease, hyperthyroidism, hyperparathyroidism

- Digestive problems: gallbladder disease, primary biliary cirrhosis, fat malabsorption, hypochlorhydria, lactose intolerance
- History of chronic low back pain for more than 15 years
- History of stress fractures
- Prolonged bedrest, paralyzed, or wheelchair bound
- History of other fractures after the age of 45
- Kidney disease and kidney stones, rheumatoid arthritis, multiple myeloma, COPD, scoliosis, underweight
- Dental conditions: bone loss in the jaw, dentures before age 60, increased tooth loss
- Nulliparous (never had a full-term pregnancy; i.e., no periods of sustained high estrogens)
- Inadequate calcium and vitamin D intake during pregnancies and nursing
- Dietary factors: high caffeine, high animal protein, high sodium, high phosphate, low calcium
- Lifestyle factors: sedentary, moderate (or more) alcohol intake, cigarette smoking
- Medications: isoniazid, furosemide, heparin, tetracycline, anticonvulsants, cortisone or prednisone, and aluminum-containing antacids
- Surgeries: total thyroidectomy, removal of part or all of intestines, intestinal bypass surgery for weight control

The strongest risk factors for hip fracture include current use of an anticonvulsant, the inability to get up from a chair without using one's arms, and maternal history of hip fracture.

Osteoporosis is more common in Caucasian and Asian women than in African-American women.[14] Non-Hispanic white women older than 50 years have a 1.3- to 2.4-fold higher prevalence of low hip density than non-Hispanic black women.[15] While hip fracture rates are higher in whites than blacks, both races experience a rise with aging.[16] African-American women are less prone to osteoporosis because they achieve a higher peak bone mass in their thirties, before the onset of bone loss.[17, 18] Ranked in order of bone density, African-Americans are highest; Asians and Northern European whites are lowest.[19]

The risk for osteoporosis and osteoporotic bone fracture increases with aging. Although bone mass clearly declines with age, the results of some studies of the radius suggest that the rate of bone loss slows or even stops after the age of 70.[20, 21] Most researchers agree that age-related bone loss begins around 40 years of age, with a loss of approximately 0.5–1.0 percent of bone mass per year. As women enter menopause, this age-related bone loss accelerates to 2–5 percent per year for the next 8–10 years.[22] The rate of hip fracture rises exponentially with age until the tenth decade, but there is variation in the incidence of fracture with age, depending on the fracture site. In older white women, fracture rates for the hip, pelvis, spine, and rib steadily rise with age. The fracture rates for the wrist and distal extremities do not appear to increase with age.

A drop in estrogen levels after menopause is generally considered to be the explanation for why women suffer from osteoporosis more than men. However, there are other contributing factors. In the United States, middle-aged and elderly Caucasian women have a three to five times greater incidence of fractures of the wrist, pelvis, humerus (upper arm) and spine compared to age-matched men.[23] Men generally achieve a higher bone mass than women prior to the time of age-related bone loss.[24–26] This greater bone mass is a result of lifelong testosterone production that provides greater stimulation of bone formation. The gender differences in risk of fracture may result from the smaller size of the bones in women. Also, young females generally take in less calcium than do males, which may limit the bone mass women accumulate during early adulthood. The underlying mechanisms of bone loss in men and women vary in that women tend to lose more structural trabecular bone, and at a faster rate, than do men.[27] The role that estrogen plays in the rate of bone loss contributes perhaps the greatest difference between men and women. Women who have undergone early menopause, late onset of menses in adolescence, and periods of amenorrhea or infrequent menses have a higher incidence of osteoporosis. Women who missed up to half of their expected menstrual periods had 12 percent less vertebral bone mass than did women with normal menstrual cycles; those who missed more than half had 31 percent less bone mass than healthy controls.[28]

The evaluation of risk and diagnosis of osteoporosis is made by a careful medical history, a thorough physical examination, laboratory analysis, and measuring bone density.

History should include family history of osteoporosis and fracture; any periods of immobilization, particularly in childhood, which can affect the eventual maximum bone mass; surgeries/hospitalizations; medical conditions that can lead to bone loss such as hyperthyroidism, Cushing's disease, hypogonadism, and hyperparathyroidism; dental conditions; medications that can lead to bone loss such as steroids, excessive thyroid hormone, and anticonvulsants; menstrual history, menopausal history, contraception, term childbearing and nursing history; and lifestyle habits (nutrition, exercise, smoking history, and alcohol consumption).

Physical exam should assess central (abdominal area) obesity, thyroid size, spinal contours and deformities, localized muscle spasms, decreasing height, nail and tooth health, and general characteristics (slender, short, fair-skinned, blonde, blue eyes). Laboratory studies are done on an individual basis. Some women may need some or all of these tests initially because their risk is determined to be high from the history and physical exam. Other women will want or need these tests because their bone density is significantly low, and further possible metabolic causes will be important to determine. Tests may need to be repeated over time in order to monitor the effectiveness of the treatments that have been employed.

Laboratory studies may include:

- Routine chemistry profile, i.e., serum calcium, creatinine, liver enzymes, alkaline phosphatase, thyroid-stimulating hormone
- Osteocalcin levels
- Hyperparathyroid testing
- Twenty-four hour urine for total urine calcium and creatinine
- Estradiol levels
- Salivary hormone studies, i.e., estradiol, estrone, progesterone, testosterone
- Evaluation of bone absorption: Urinary pyridinoline cross-links, i.e., urinary pyridinoline and deoxypyridinoline

Bone mineral density testing is a very underutilized test in my opinion. I am not ready to say that all menopausal women should be routinely screened, but it has a very definite role in determining a rational treatment program. As women increasingly make careful decisions about whether they use hormone replacement therapy (HRT), whether they use natural treatments, or whether they use some of the increasing array of non-estrogen osteoporosis prevention and treatment drugs, bone density testing is an extremely valuable tool in selecting the most appropriate therapy. While conventional medicine tends to err in overtreating and overmedicalizing menopause and aging by recommending HRT, alternative medicine tends to err in undertreating women and being unrealistic in its expectations for what diet, exercise, and nutritional/herbal supplements can accomplish in a woman with low bone density. Bone density testing can clarify an already difficult decision and can optimize the use of both conventional and natural medicine therapies.

Imaging techniques may include:

- **Radiographic techniques**, i.e., dual energy X-ray absorptiometry (DEXA), CT scan, X rays, dual photon absorptiometry (DPA), single-photon (SPA), and X-ray absorptiometry (SXA). DEXA is the most precise of the commonly used densitometry techniques and is more accurate in measuring bone density of the lumbar spine and proximal femur. DEXA offers a lower dose of radiation and a shorter examination time than other imaging methods. Because of its enhanced precision and accuracy, DEXA has become the "gold standard" for bone densitometry.
- **Ultrasound of the heel**, a newer test, is less expensive, easily administered, and uses no radiation. The heel bone is 100 percent trabecular bone, the same type of bone that makes up 90 percent of the vertebrae and 50 percent of the hip. Ultrasound measurement of the heel bone may provide an excellent, less expensive screening test. Recent reviews have concluded that ultrasound of the heel was a good predictor of fractures of the spine.[29] This simple, portable, inexpensive method may be a good screening device for osteoporosis. Its limiting factor is that

the scans are not useful in detecting small changes in density over time and therefore cannot be used to monitor the effectiveness of treatment of osteoporosis. Women with abnormal results would then be referred for DEXA testing to more precisely assess bone mineral density. Optimal prevention and treatment methods could then be recommended individually. We could then avoid overtreatment with long-term HRT in women who don't need it and improve the education and compliance for women who really do need it. However, this method is currently still less precise than DEXA.

WORLD HEALTH ORGANIZATION DEFINITIONS

1. **Normal bone mineral density (BMD):** Within +/−1 standard deviation (SD) of young adult gender-matched means
2. **Osteopenia:** BMD between 1–2.5 SD below young adult means
3. **Osteoporosis:** BMD more than 2.5 SD below young adult means
4. **Severe Osteoporosis:** BMD more than 2.5 SD below young adult means and the presence of one or more fragility fractures

---

It may be that ultrasound could be used for general screening and the DEXA test used as a more precise and expanded diagnostic technique. The reporting of bone mineral density varies with the facility performing the test. It may include standard deviations below the norm, in gm/cm^2, or percentages compared to normal young adults. The key is to compare the results to normal young adults and not to age-matched controls. Fracture risk interpreted by percentages is the easiest to comprehend:

- Mild if bone density is 75–85 percent of that found in young adults
- Moderate if bone density is 65–75 percent of young adults
- Moderate/severe if bone density is 55–65 percent of young adults
- Severe if bone density is less than 55 percent of young adults

It may not be appropriate to use the SD number as a sole criterion for treatment. For example, if an 80-year-old woman has an SD score of 2 and a vertebral fracture, she should strongly consider treatment, whereas a 50-year-old with the same SD may not need treatment immediately, just long-term follow-up.

✒ Overview of Alternative Treatments

Osteoporosis is far easier to prevent than to treat. An osteoporosis prevention perspective needs to start in the teenage years. Education should include several key areas: 1) medical problems early in life that can lead to osteoporosis; 2) medications that can interfere with calcium metabolism; 3) the role of nutrition and exercise early in life and their necessity in achieving peak bone density; 4) awareness of the long-term consequences for bone health, if anorexic.

For women in their forties, fifties, and older who have just begun to think about osteoporosis, the time for reaching peak bone density at age 30–35 is already past. We all lose bone density as we age, and if you achieved 100 percent or more at around 30–35 and you do not have a condition or genetics that cause rapid bone loss, then all is well. If your peak bone density was only 85 percent, then you can't afford as much normal age-related bone loss before your bone density becomes osteopenic and then osteoporotic.

Several approaches are available to prevent osteoporosis and to treat both those who are at high risk and those who have developed the condition. Natural medicines are especially key in prevention. Once osteoporosis has been diagnosed, many of the natural interventions such as diet, exercise, nutritional supplementation, and herbal medicines could be used aggressively in milder cases to slow bone loss and possibly improve bone density. In more serious osteoporosis cases, the natural intervention will become adjunct to a primary antiresorptive therapy (a therapy that stops or slows the rate of bone loss). Natural hormone replacement therapy may be used as a substitute for conventional hormone replacement therapy in selected individuals with monitor-

---

KEY CONCEPTS

- Osteoporosis-related fractures will develop in half of all women older than age 65.
- Osteoporosis is a serious and disabling disease, a disease far easier to prevent than to treat.
- Women with a family history of osteoporosis are at the highest risk of developing the condition. Eighty to ninety percent of the determination of the development of osteoporosis is a family history of osteoporosis.
- Fracture risk can be determined from a medical history, physical exam, laboratory testing, and a DEXA bone density test.

PREVENTION

- Stop smoking.
- Reduce alcohol.
- Do regular weight-bearing exercise, especially comprehensive weight lifting throughout life.
- Ensure proper nutrition; take in adequate calcium and vitamin D levels during pregnancy and breast feeding.
- Avoid being underweight (which can lead to a lack of or infrequent menses).
- Avoid caffeine.
- Reduce animal protein in diet as well as salt and simple sugars.
- Avoid falls and injuries.
- Get regular annual health checks; laboratory testing and bone-density testing may be appropriate.
- Consider hormone replacement therapy (natural hormones or conventional hormones) if you have several risk factors.
- Nutritional supplementation.

---

ing. This is an important area and will be carefully addressed in the discussion on treatment options and criteria for treatment. Natural hormone replacement therapy is still relatively unknown in this country, and the even more controversial issue of whether natural progesterone creams prevent and reverse osteoporosis is indeed a hot one.

Natural interventions for osteoporosis include dietary and lifestyle factors, exercise, nutritional supplementation, the use of phytoestrogens, and natural hormone replacement therapy. Each of these areas deserves special attention.

Nutrition

Several dietary factors affect bone health and are involved in the development of osteoporosis: insufficient calcium intake, vitamin D deficiency, low calcium, high phosphorus intake, high protein diet, excess salt intake, and other mineral deficiencies.

Studies have shown that excessive dietary protein may promote bone loss. Animal protein particularly causes an increase in urinary excretion of calcium. Raising daily protein intake from 47–142 grams doubles the excretion of calcium in the urine.[30] Calcium is mobilized from the bone to buffer the acidic breakdown products of protein. In addition, the amino acid methionine, found highest in meat, dairy products, and eggs, is converted to homocysteine, which in high amounts may also cause bone loss. All of these mechanisms of a high protein diet contributing to calcium and bone loss should raise a serious concern about high protein diets now popular such as the Zone diet, Atkins diet, and 40-30-30 diet plans. All of these diets are high protein diets.

A vegetarian diet, on the other hand, is associated with a lower risk of osteoporosis,[31] even though vegetarians do not have greater bone mass in their twenties, thirties, and forties. Several studies have shown that vegetarians do have significantly higher bone mass later in life which would indicate that vegetarians lose bone more slowly than nonvegetarians.[32, 33] Many high protein animal foods also contain high amounts of phosphorus, which mobilizes calcium from the bones in order to maintain homeostasis in the bloodstream.

High phosphorus beverages are also implicated in osteoporosis development. A study in children demonstrated a severe impact of soft drinks on calcium levels. Fifty-seven children with low blood calcium levels were compared to 171 children with normal calcium levels.[34] Of the 57 children who had low blood calcium levels, 66.7 percent drank more than four 12 to 16-ounce bottles of soft drinks per week. Only 28 percent of the 171 children with normal serum calcium levels consumed that many soft drinks per week. For all 228 children, a strong correlation was seen in the serum calcium level and the number of bottles of soft drinks consumed each week. The more soft drinks consumed, the lower the calcium level in the blood. Due to the high intake of soft drinks in the United States, we can probably expect to see increased osteoporosis in the "Pepsi" generation for many years to come. The American per-capita consumption of soft drinks is about three quarts per week.

Other nutritional factors accelerate calcium loss and may be implicated in osteoporosis. Refined sugar may impact the risk for osteoporosis by increasing the loss of calcium from the body and by causing a significant increase in the fasting serum cortisol levels. A serving of refined sugar increases the urinary excretion of calcium,[35] and an excess of corticosteroids can cause osteoporosis. High sodium intake can also cause an increase in urinary excretion of calcium in some individuals.[36] Refined grains and flours may also play a part in the development of osteoporosis. Due to their lack of nutrient-rich germ and bran, there is a significant loss of vitamins and minerals in these foods. The refining process produces white flour stripped of B_6, folic acid, calcium, magnesium, manganese, copper, and zinc.

One of the best general dietary preventive habits to acquire is to eat a lot of dark green leafy vegetables. Kale, collard greens, Romaine lettuce, spinach, Swiss chard, and other dark greens are a rich source of vitamins and minerals including calcium, vitamin K, and boron. As you will learn in the supplement section, vitamin K is involved in the mineralization of bone, and boron decreases the urinary excretion of calcium and magnesium.

One of the most exciting items of nutritional news in women's health today is the health benefits of soy foods. As discussed in the heart disease, cancer prevention, and menopause chapters, soy foods have a very definite and specific role in preventing and treating some of women's most common concerns. Soy contains a class of compounds called phytoestrogens. The phytoestrogen especially high in soy is isoflavone. Phytoestrogens and isoflavones are discussed in more detail in Chapter 10.

Osteoporosis is an area where soy isoflavones may also benefit women. So far, the most reassuring data come from animal studies, but research on osteoporosis, women, and soy foods is in the works. In animal studies, the addition of soy to the diet was able to inhibit bone loss.[37]

The soybean protein diet was most effective in preventing bone loss in the lumbar vertebrae (bones in the center of the low back) and somewhat in the right femur (upper leg bone). The soybean protein apparently has more of an effect on trabecular bone than on cortical bone. One might question why a diet high in soy protein does not cause the same problems as a diet high in animal protein. As mentioned earlier, a diet high in animal proteins can cause greater calcium loss. However, calcium loss is thought to be minimized by plant-based diets, because unlike animal-based diets, soy-based vegetarian diets are low in the sulfur-containing amino acids. This type of diet also significantly reduced the abdominal fat in the animal study, an interesting finding because it may indicate that soybean protein stimulates the synthesis of growth hormone, which is known to decrease adipose tissue mass[38] and increase bone mass.[39]

Soy foods come in a diverse array of options, some of which taste great and some of which are for the truly committed: soy milk, soy flour, dried soy beans (cooked in soups), tofu, tempeh, soybean ice cream, soy cheese, soy yogurt, soy burgers, roasted soy nuts (one of my favorites), soy candy bars, fresh soybeans in the pod (ask at your Japanese grocery or restaurant), miso, and soy sauce (not much soy protein in this). My recommendation for routine prevention would be an intake of about 50 mg per day of isoflavones (the phytoestrogen compounds found in soy foods). See Table 10. 1 on page 148 of Chapter 10 for the isoflavone content of various soy foods.

Alcohol and Smoking

Consumption of alcohol also appears to promote bone loss. Scientific evidence links excessive alcohol (seven ounces or more per week) with lower bone mass, increased bone loss, and a higher incidence of fracture.[40] However, in another study, moderate alcohol intake, less than seven drinks per week, was found to be associated with a lower risk of hip fractures in women, compared to women who did not drink.[29]

The results of most studies show that smokers lose bone more rapidly and have a lower bone mass than nonsmokers.[41] In female smokers, the risk of hip fracture is increased by 1.5–2.5-fold.[14] Smoking tobacco increases estrogen metabolism by the liver and consequently increases bone loss in women taking estrogen replacement therapy.[42]

Nutritional Supplements

Calcium and Vitamin D

When women think about what they can do to prevent osteoporosis, most women think of calcium supplementation. Indeed, calcium supplementation has been shown to decrease bone loss in postmenopausal women.[43] The effects have been greatest in women whose baseline calcium intake was low, in older women, and in women with osteoporosis.[44] Many studies have been done to better understand the effect of calcium and vitamin D supplementation both as a preventive measure and as an additional treatment intervention. In a study of 3,270 institutionalized women in France who were treated with calcium (1,200 mg per day) and vitamin D (800 IU per day) for three years, the risk of hip fractures was 30 percent lower than in the placebo group.[45] This form of supplementation also resulted in a reversal of secondary hyperparathyroidism and an increase in the bone mineral density of the femoral neck (hip). In another study of 2,578 elderly women of a similar age in the Netherlands who were treated with 400 IU vitamin D per day or placebo for three and a half years, the rate of hip fracture in the two groups was similar.[46] The difference in the results of these two studies may obviously be that one study included calcium and the other did not; but the French women also had lower dietary calcium intakes, were more frail, had lower serum 25-hydroxyvitamin D concentrations, and supplemented twice as much vitamin D.

A more recent study demonstrated that 389 men and women over age 63, who were treated with 500 mg calcium per day and 700 IU vitamin D per day, had a decrease in the rate of nonvertebral fractures.[47] This study stands out because, although the fracture rate was decreased, the bone mineral density of the femoral neck increased only 1.2 percent and the total body, 1.2 percent. This is considered a very small increase.

Calcium supplementation alone may be only partially effective in preventing bone loss, especially in older women and in women with a low calcium intake. In a study of 86 women given 1,000 mg of calcium per day or placebo for four years, experienced in the calcium group was sustained reduction in the loss of total-body bone mineral density, a reduction in the lumbar-spine loss, and a reduction in the loss of density in the upper part of the femur bone mineral density. Most of the benefit occurred during the first year of supplementation.[48] Even though there was a reduction in bone loss, there was not much reduction in the rate of fractures in the calcium group. In another study, women over age 60 who consumed less than 1,000 mg of calcium per day were given a supplement of 1,200 mg per day for four years. The researchers found that bone loss was prevented in the forearm and there was a 59 percent reduction in the rate of vertebral fractures in the women who had such fractures before the study began.[49]

Vitamin D enhances intestinal calcium absorption, thereby contributing to a favorable calcium balance. Those who lack adequate exposure to the sun's ultraviolet rays do not get the sterols within the skin converted into vitamin D. This population must obtain their vitamin D from food including vitamin D-fortified dairy products, fish, eggs, and liver. Supplementation with 700 IU vitamin D daily has shown that it can reduce the annual rate of hip fracture from 1.3–0.5 percent.[50] In another study, 348 women age 70 and older were given either 400 IU of vitamin D_3 or a placebo for two years.[51] Bone density at the hip increased from 1.9–2.6 percent in the vitamin D group. The placebo group showed decreased bone density in the same site.

Although calcium alone or vitamin D alone appear to be beneficial to bone health, better results are achieved with a combination of both nutrients.

Foods high in calcium include kelp, Swiss and cheddar cheese, carob flour, dulse, collard greens,

TABLE 12.1   **Calcium Content of Selected Foods**

Food	Mg per 3½-oz serving	Food	Mg per 3½-oz serving
Kelp	1,093	Soybeans, cooked	73
Cheddar cheese	750	Pecans	72
Carob flour	350	Wheat germ	72
Dulse	298	Peanuts	69
Collard leaves	250	Miso	68
Kale	249	Romaine lettuce	68
Turnip greens	246	Apricots, dried	67
Almonds	234	Rutabaga	66
Yeast, brewer's	210	Raisins	62
Parsley	203	Black currants	60
Dandelion greens	187	Dates	59
Brazil nuts	186	Green snap beans	58
Watercress	151	Globe artichoke	51
Goat's milk	129	Prunes, dried	51
Tofu	128	Pumpkin/squash seeds	51
Figs, dried	126	Beans, cooked dry	50
Buttermilk	121	Cabbage	49
Sunflower seeds	120	Soybean sprouts	48
Yogurt	120	Wheat, hard winter	46
Wheat bran	119	Orange	41
Whole milk	118	Celery	41
Buckwheat, raw	114	Cashews	38
Sesame seeds, hulled	110	Rye grain	38
Olives, ripe	106	Carrot	37
Broccoli	103	Barley	34
English walnuts	99	Sweet potato	32
Cottage cheese	94	Brown rice	32

Source: USDA Nutritive Value of American Foods in Common Units, Agricultural Handbook No. 456.

turnip greens, molasses, almonds, brewer's yeast, parsley, corn tortillas, dandelion greens, Brazil nuts, watercress, goat's milk, tofu, dried figs, buttermilk, sunflower seeds, yogurt, beet greens, wheat bran, whole milk, buckwheat, sesame seeds, olives, broccoli, walnuts, cottage cheese, and spinach (see Table 12.1).

There is a great deal of confusion and controversy about which form of calcium is best. I discourage women from using either oyster shell or bone meal calcium. These calcium supplements may contain substantial amounts of lead. In 1981, the FDA cautioned the public to limit their intake of calcium supplements made from either dolomite or bone meal because of the potentially high lead levels. Other sources of calcium from various chelates may also contain lead. A study of lead content in 70 brands of calcium supplements was conducted in 1993.[52] Lead was the highest in bone meal, unrefined calcium carbonate, and dolomite.

Lead was the lowest in calcium chelate supplements and refined calcium carbonate. Calcium chelates are bound to citrate, fumarate, malate, succinate, and aspartate. These forms of calcium are better absorbed than calcium carbonate.

To illustrate the difference between calcium citrate absorption and calcium carbonate absorption researchers demonstrated that at dosages from 200–2,000 mg calcium, absorption from calcium citrate was superior to that from calcium carbonate. They demonstrated that calcium absorption following a 500 mg load of calcium as calcium citrate was higher than after a 2,000 mg load of calcium from carbonate.[53] Calcium citrate bound to malate has also demonstrated significantly improved solubility and absorption when compared to other calcium salts.[54–56] A popular calcium supplement is calcium hydroxyapatite, which is a purified bone meal. Not only is it more poorly absorbed than calcium carbonate or citrate, it is derived from bone meal which has a high amount of lead. Because of a lower content of lead, improved absorption, and therefore a need for lower amounts, I recommend using calcium citrate and/or calcium malate.

The Institute of Medicine of the National Academy of Sciences (NAS) released new calcium recommendations in 1997. These new guidelines call for increased intakes for most age groups. The previous recommendations were last updated in 1989. New RDAs, now called Dietary Reference Intakes (DRIs), were also established for other bone nutrients, including vitamin D, phosphorus, magnesium, and fluoride. The new calcium recommendations were set at levels associated with maximum retention of body calcium, because bones that are calcium-rich are known to be less susceptible to fractures. For most adults, the new guidelines say that 1,000 mg of calcium a day is needed, rather than 800 mg per day. Women over age 50 need even more calcium: 1,200 mg per day if taking estrogen and 1,500 per day if not, according to the 1994 National Institutes of Health Consensus Panel. Guidelines for adolescents ages 9–18, whose growing bones need adequate calcium to reach peak bone density, call for 1,300 mg per day. Pregnant and breast-feeding women should get the amount recommended for their age group, rather than an increased amount as previously advised. Hormonal changes during pregnancy and lactation boost a woman's ability to absorb calcium. The NAS panel also created a category called Tolerable Upper Intake Levels (UL). This is the maximum intake that is unlikely to pose risks of adverse health effects. For calcium, the UL is 2,500 mg/day.

These figures are total calcium intake, whether from diet or supplements, or a combination of both. The average adult consumes 500–700 mg of calcium per day in the diet. Supplementation should then make up the difference, not be an additional 1,000–1,200 mg in a supplement in addition to the diet. This is an important concept in determining the necessary amount needed in a supplement in addition to one's dietary intake.

Not all researchers and clinicians agree on what kind of calcium is best, what dose is best, and what ratio of calcium to magnesium is best. Some studies have even associated calcium supplementation with an increased fracture risk. One large cohort study, involving 9,704 U.S. white women aged 65 years or older, found no association between dietary calcium intake and the risk of several different types of fractures. Calcium supplements were actually associated with increased risk of hip and vertebral fractures; Tums antacid tablets was associated with increased risk of fractures of the proximal humerus (upper portion of the upper arm).[57] One of the most striking aspects of this study was that this increased fracture rate occurred in women with a total intake of 700 mg per day. As you can see, this is barely half the recommended amount for postmenopausal women.

Another issue that makes it difficult to determine the optimal dose of calcium is that higher doses of calcium may interfere with the absorption of other nutrients. In two separate studies, researchers have shown that a high dietary calcium intake adversely affects zinc absorption and balance in humans.[58, 59]

This may be especially important in elderly women due to their compromised zinc absorption, their possible marginal zinc status to begin with, and their high risk of osteoporosis. A zinc deficiency can result in skin changes, growth retardation, loss of appetite, changes in vision, decreased insulin function, dysfunction in prostaglandin synthesis, and immunologic abnormalities. Zinc is also essential for normal bone formation; it enhances the biochemical actions of vitamin D, is required for the formation of osteoblasts and osteoclasts, and is required for the synthesis of various proteins found in bone tissue. Zinc levels have been found to be low in the serum and bone of elderly people with osteoporosis,[60] and also in people with bone loss at the alveolar ridge of the mandible.[61] This negative interaction between calcium and zinc absorption raises concerns about how higher calcium intakes may affect the absorption of other minerals needed for bone health.

Some researchers and clinicians recommend twice as much calcium as magnesium; others recommend equal parts calcium and magnesium; others recommend 1.5 parts calcium and 1 part magnesium; and still others recommend twice as much magnesium as calcium. Most support exists for two parts calcium to one part magnesium.

The optimal time to take calcium supplementation is the last confusion to consider. The absorption of calcium is dependent on its becoming ionized in the intestines. Calcium carbonate has to be solubilized and ionized by stomach acid in order to be absorbed. Many people have insufficient stomach acid, and, most important, stomach acid secretion decreases with age. In studies of postmenopausal women, about 40 percent are severely deficient in stomach acid.[62] For this reason, I recommend taking a form of calcium that is already in a soluble and ionized state, such as calcium citrate, calcium lactate, or calcium gluconate. In these ionized products, about 45 percent of the calcium is absorbed from calcium citrate in patients with reduced stomach acid, as compared to 4 percent absorption for calcium carbonate.[63] If you decide to take calcium carbonate, it is best to take one dose with food and the other before bedtime to assure optimum effect on the bones.

All of these issues make it difficult to choose from the myriad options of form and dosing in calcium supplementation. Although my recommendations are arguable and certainly will vary from person to person, in general they can be summarized the following way.

TOTAL DAILY INTAKE IF USING CALCIUM CARBONATE

Age 9–18	1,300 mg
Age 19–50	1,000 mg
Age 51+	1,200 mg (if also using estrogen replacement)
	1,500 mg (if not taking estrogen replacement)

Pregnant or lactating women

18 or younger	1,300 mg
19–50	1,000 mg

If using calcium citrate or citrate with malate, comparable doses may be anywhere from 20 percent less to one-fourth the dose of calcium carbonate. In fact, I recommend calcium citrate or malate that is about one-half the carbonate doses.

Magnesium

The conventional scientific view is that magnesium is essential for parathyroid hormone (PTH) produc-

tion and release. PTH is essential for the activation of vitamin D and therefore absorption of calcium across the gut wall. However, magnesium is an intracellular ion and difficult to measure. A magnesium level is a reflection of extracellular magnesium. There are several conditions that can lead to magnesium deficiency and therefore hypoparathyroidism and vitamin D deficiency. These include diuretic use (urinary loss), alcohol abuse (nutritional deficiency), diabetes (urinary loss), and chronic diarrhea (malabsorption). Otherwise, magnesium deficiency is rare. From the conventional scientific viewpoint, the main reason why magnesium is part of calcium supplements is that carbonates are constipating and magnesium has a laxative effect and therefore the combination is usually better tolerated.

Even though calcium has received the most attention, alternative medicine views the importance of magnesium in skeletal metabolism and calcium regulation in a little bit different and perhaps broader context. Magnesium influences both matrix and mineral metabolism in bone. Magnesium depletion causes cessation of bone growth, decreased osteoblastic and osteoclastic activity, osteopenia, and bone fragility.[64] Adequate serum magnesium levels are necessary for proper calcium metabolism; however, adequate calcium intake may not ensure proper bone health if magnesium status is abnormal. Magnesium deficiency has been shown more than once to be related to osteoporosis. Magnesium status appears to have a major influence on the type of calcium crystals present in the bones, and therefore its deficiency is associated with abnormal calcification of the bone.[65] This may in part explain why some women who have reduced bone mineral density do not have an increase in fracture rates. These women may have a lowered bone mass, but they have excellent structural calcification, due in part to adequate levels of magnesium. In order to assess the effects of magnesium on bone density, a group of osteoporotic postmenopausal women were given magnesium over a period of two years. At the end of the study, magnesium therapy appeared to have prevented fractures and resulted in a significant percent increase in bone mass density after the first year of treatment. There was, however, no change in density from then on to the end of the study.[66] The finding that magnesium supplementation actually caused an increase in bone density rather than just a stabilization of current bone density is significant. Other factors may have influenced the increase in bone density, but the results of this study warrant further investigation into the potential effect of magnesium on bone density.

Dr. Guy Abraham published a study supporting the importance of magnesium above that of calcium. His study demonstrated an 11 percent increase in bone density in the group that was given dietary advice, hormones, and nutritional supplements (500 mg calcium citrate, 600 mg magnesium oxide, vitamin C, vitamin B-complex, vitamin D, zinc, copper, manganese, and boron). The group that received the dietary advice plus the hormones but no supplementation had an average increase of only 0.7 percent.[67] An 11 percent increase in bone density is greater than in studies of calcium or hormone replacement therapy taken either separately or together. Continued research to elucidate magnesium's role in bone metabolism and calcium-magnesium interactions needs to be done as well as clinical treatment trials that vigorously evaluate magnesium as a potential treatment for postmenopausal osteoporosis.

Foods high in magnesium include kelp, wheat bran, wheat germ, almonds, cashews, molasses, brewer's yeast, buckwheat, Brazil nuts, dulse, filberts, peanuts, millet, whole wheat, pecans, walnuts, rye, tofu, beet greens, and coconut.

Magnesium citrate/malate
200–400 mg per day

Manganese

Manganese may be one of the most important trace nutrients related to osteoporosis. Manganese deficiency causes a reduction in the amount of calcium laid down in the bone and thereby an increased susceptibility to fracture. Manganese stimulates the production of mucopolysaccharides that provide a structure on which calcification takes place.[68]

Manganese
15–30 mg per day

Boron

Dr. Forrest Nielsen studied the effect of boron on bone loss in postmenopausal women. Published in 1988, his results indicated that boron supplementation reduced the urinary excretion of calcium by 44 percent, reduced urinary magnesium excretion, and markedly increased the serum concentrations of 17 beta-estradiol and testosterone.[69] These findings definitively implicate boron in calcium and magnesium metabolism, hormonal stabilization, and the subsequent prevention of bone loss.

Boron
3 mg per day

Zinc

Zinc is essential for normal bone formation,[70] enhances the biochemical actions of vitamin D,[71] and is required for the formation of osteoblasts and osteoclasts and for the synthesis of various proteins found in bone tissue. Zinc levels have been found low in the serum and bone of elderly people with osteoporosis.[60]

Zinc
15–20 mg per day

Copper

Copper deficiency may be a related cause of osteoporosis. Copper deficiency is known to produce abnormal bone growth in growing children. Copper supplementation has been shown in laboratory studies to inhibit bone resorption.[72] Its supplementation is deemed necessary in women at risk or with diagnosed osteoporosis.

Copper
1.5–3.0 mg per day

Folic Acid

Accelerated bone loss in menopausal women may in part be due to the increased levels of homocysteine, a breakdown product of methionine. Homocysteine has the potential to promote osteoporosis if it is not eliminated adequately. Since folic acid is involved in the breakdown of homocysteine, supplementing postmenopausal women with this nutrient results in significant reductions in homocysteine levels,[73] which at the same time is also associated with greatly reduced incidences of heart attacks.

Folic acid
400–800 mcg per day

Vitamin B$_6$

Vitamin B$_6$ also plays a role in homocysteine metabolism. In genetic homocystinuria, B$_6$ supplementation has been shown to reverse the elevated levels of homocysteine.[74] Vitamin B$_6$ has been studied and prescribed for its role in osteoporosis prevention in other capacities as well. Animal studies have shown B$_6$ deficiencies to cause increased fracture healing time,[75] impaired growth of cartilage and defective bone formation,[76] and more rapid development of osteoporosis.[77] Vitamin B$_6$ may also stimulate the production of progesterone and, through this hormone's activation of osteoblasts, have a distinct role in preventing osteoporosis.

Vitamin B$_6$
50–100 mg per day

Vitamin C

One of the actions of vitamin C is to promote the formation and cross-linking of some of the structural proteins in bone. Also, animal studies have shown that vitamin C deficiency can cause osteoporosis.[78] Moreover, it has been known for decades that scurvy, a disease caused by vitamin C deficiency, is associated with abnormalities of bone.

Vitamin C
500 mg or more per day

Vitamin K

Vitamin K is a strong contributing factor in the prevention of osteoporosis. It is required for the production of osteocalcin, the protein matrix on which mineralization occurs. Osteocalcin attracts calcium to bone tissue, enabling calcium crystal formation to occur. Vitamin K plays a key role in the formation, remodeling, and repair of bone by helping the calcium adhere to the site of this protein matrix.

Vitamin K
150–500 mcg per day

Botanical Medicine

Phytoestrogens

Phytoestrogens are compounds present in over 300 medicinal plants and edible foods. There has been a great deal of confusion about phytoestrogens, and it starts with their name. The term implies that there are plant estrogens or estrogens in plants. In fact, with a few and minor exceptions, that is not the case at all. Phytoestrogens are classes of compounds that are mainly, but not exclusively, nonsteroidal in structure and are either of plant origin or derived by the body's metabolism from precursors found in the plants. There are three main classes of phytoestrogen compounds, the most important being the phenolics, which include isoflavones and lignans. These are found in high amounts in soy and flaxseeds. Phytoestrogens are more extensively discussed in Chapter 10. Here, we will comment on their impact on bone density and osteoporosis.

What we currently know about phytoestrogens and osteoporosis is in fact very little, although this area is of great interest to menopausal women, practitioners of alternative medicine, and a few researchers around the country. In the next few years, we will likely know a lot more. Although phytoestrogens have a positive effect on many menopausal issues, it is not certain yet whether they have a role in preventing or reversing osteoporosis. In the nutrition section of this chapter, the possible role of soy in preventing osteoporosis was briefly mentioned.

Several animal and human studies have provided further insight and comfort in the possible role of soy in our bone health. A study conducted at the University of Illinois found that menopausal women had an increase in mineral levels and density in their lumbar spines after taking 55–90 mg of isoflavones for six months.[79] The placebo group showed the lowest bone density and the greatest bone loss, while the estrogen group showed the highest bone density and the slowest bone loss. What was surprising was that the soybean protein diet was effective in preventing bone loss in the fourth lumbar vertebra and, although less so, in the right hip as well. Soybean protein seems to have more of an effect on trabecular bone (more predominant in the spine) than on cortical bone (more predominant in the hip). The soybean protein did not show as great an ability in preventing bone loss as the estrogen group, but the positive effect it showed is encouraging. Further studies are needed to clarify whether this protective effect on bone is due to the protein itself or to the presence of the phytoestrogen isoflavones in soybean protein.

Soy isoflavones can be acquired in capsule or powder form. Each manufacturer will label how much isoflavones per capsule is contained in their product. I would recommend 50–100 mg per day.

It is not yet known whether phytoestrogenic herbs, such as black cohosh, ginseng, licorice, red clover, hops, Dong quai, and others have any effect on increasing bone density or on slowing bone loss in postmenopausal women.

Isoflavones
50–100 mg per day

A synthetic derivative of isoflavones, ipriflavone, until recently was only available in Italy and a handful of other countries. It is now available over the counter in natural food stores or from alternative practitioners. Two multicenter, two-year clinical trials evaluated the efficacy and bioavailability of ipriflavone in postmenopausal women with low bone mass.[80] Women were randomly selected to receive either oral ipriflavone (200 mg three times daily) or a placebo, plus 1 gram oral calcium daily. Both studies

were reported in the same paper. Study A showed a bone-sparing effect of 1.6 percent in the spine, and study B, 3.5 percent in the wrist after two years. A significant difference was found between the treatment groups and the placebo groups in both studies.

It seems as though ipriflavone has a direct ability to inhibit the osteoclastic (bone-losing) cell activity, but how it does this is unknown. Although all the effects on bone density using ipriflavone tend to be small, between 1.15–3.7 percent, these results provide yet another option for many women. It remains to be seen whether ipriflavone can have a positive effect on the hip, a far greater concern. Although the effect on the spine and wrist is encouraging, these small increases in bone density do not necessarily mean there is a reduced fracture rate, the true test of an effective treatment for the prevention and treatment of osteoporosis.

Ipriflavone
200 mg 3 times per day

Herbs High in Mineral Content

Throughout the centuries of traditional herbal medicine, many herbs have been known for their high mineral content. It is difficult to use herbs as a substitute for mineral supplementation because we know so little about the precise mineral content of a given herb. However, using these high-mineral herbs to augment mineral supplementation may not only improve one's mineral status but also offers other health benefits. High-mineral herbs include nettles, oatstraw, red raspberry leaves, chamomile, horsetail, and dandelion greens.

Natural Progesterone

The term "natural progesterone" refers to progesterone produced by the body itself, or progesterone derived from Mexican wild yam or soybeans. It is important to realize that the latter is made in a manufacturing laboratory by extracting diosgenin from either Mexican wild yam or beta sitosterol from soybeans which is then converted, through various enzymatic and biochemical reactions, into progesterone. This progesterone is biochemically identical to the progesterone produced by a woman's ovaries. Because of this, it is often called bio-identical progesterone or natural progesterone. This is distinctly different from numerous synthetic progestins, the most common of which is medroxyprogesterone acetate (MPA).

We know that accelerated bone loss has been shown to occur after menopause, but evidence also exists indicating that normal menstruating women begin to lose spinal bone prior to menopause.[81–85] Evidence also exists that this bone loss prior to menopause is related to progesterone deficiency and that progesterone, like estrogen, plays an important role in bone metabolism.[86–88] Dr. Jerilyn Prior postulated a hypothetical relationship between phases of the bone remodeling cycle and the normal menstrual cycle. Ovarian steroid levels are low at menstruation, so increased bone resorption occurs at this time. As estrogen production increases before ovulation, resorption begins to reverse. Finally, bone remodeling begins as progesterone levels peak in the mid part of the second half of the menstrual cycle.[89]

Dr. Prior and colleagues went on to study 66 premenopausal women over one year.[86] In these women, 29 percent of all menstrual cycles were disturbed by a lack of ovulation or short luteal phases (number of days between ovulation and onset of menses) even though nearly all of these women continued to have regular 30-day cycles. These subtle ovulatory disturbances did not result in any symptoms, but they did correlate with decreases in spinal bone density. The women with the shortest luteal phases, and therefore with decreased progesterone production, had the greatest decline in spinal bone density, losing 2–4 percent of bone per year. These results have been cited as a strong suggestion that the maintenance of peak bone density throughout a woman's adult life requires normal ovarian production of progesterone as well as estrogen.

Dr. Prior and colleagues also studied the effects of synthetic progesterone, medroxyprogesterone acetate (Provera), 10 mg for 10 days each month, in athletic women who had stopped having a menstrual cycle. The regimen led to significant increases in spinal bone density.[90] These studies basically indicate that progesterone and MPA appear to have osteotropic (bone-building) effects. This is some of the research that alternative practitioners cite when making a case for administering natural progesterone for the treatment and prevention of osteoporosis. An error is often made when we assume that administering natural progesterone is the same as administering the synthetic analogue MPA, and this often occurs when advocates of natural progesterone attempt to make a case for its use in osteoporosis management. There is good theoretical evidence from these studies and additional laboratory and animal studies that the body's progesterone and MPA have a stimulatory effect on bone formation and reduce bone turnover. What is not clear is whether giving natural progesterone in a pill or cream has similar effects.

When it comes to preventing or reversing osteoporosis, no other product has been the subject of as much controversy as the use of topically applied natural progesterone. A large segment of women seeking alternatives to conventional hormone replacement therapy and many alternative practitioners have accepted the premise, most often promoted by Dr. John Lee, that topically applied natural progesterone cream will not only prevent osteoporosis but will actually increase bone mineral density and prevent fractures. In his publications, Dr. Lee has become the strongest advocate of the role of progesterone in preventing and reversing osteoporosis. He asserts that almost all women can successfully prevent and reverse osteoporosis and improve their bone density by as much as 15 percent with this cream and that estrogen replacement therapy is very seldom a necessary component.

Although I know that Dr. Lee will disagree, this premise is based almost exclusively on a hypothesis that lacks conclusive scientific evidence and is based on an often-cited collection of 100 cases from his private practice over a period of several years. Visionaries, inventors, explorers, doctors, and scientists who hold positions that stray from the conventional viewpoint are often ahead of their time. Perhaps that will prove to be the case with Dr. Lee and natural progesterone. But, for now, it is important to separate fact from hypothesis and possibility from reality. If alternative medicine is to gain its rightful place in the system of health care, practitioners need to discriminate clearly between hope and theory and the body of knowledge that actually exists. After all, women's lives are literally at stake. Negative experiences or objections to the conventional hype about hormone replacement therapy must not be replaced by naïveté or blind faith in the alternatives.

Dr. Lee's optimism and position about natural progesterone comes from studying the work of Dr. Ray Peat and the general physiological role of progesterone, the research of Dr. Jerilyn Prior about the role of progesterone and bone metabolism,[91] and his often cited collection of 100 cases from his family practice.[92] Those who have been influenced by Dr. Lee's passionate enthusiasm perhaps do not realize the full scope of treatment used in those 100 cases. Dr. Lee's treatment program included the following:

- Many leafy green vegetables in the diet
- Avoidance of all carbonated sodas
- Red meat limited to three times or less per week
- Limited alcohol use
- Vitamin D, 350–400 IU daily
- Vitamin C, 2,000 mg daily
- Beta carotene, 25,000 IU daily
- Calcium, 800–1,000 mg daily (from diet and/or supplements)
- Estrogen, 0.3–0.625 mg daily of conjugated equine estrogens (Premarin), 3 weeks per month, unless contraindicated
- Progesterone, 3 percent cream of natural progesterone applied daily, 12 days each month or during the last 2 weeks of estrogen use (about ½ tsp applied topically each day)
- Exercise, 20 minutes daily or ½ hour 3 times a week
- No smoking

Dr. Lee reports that he saw women ranging in age from 38 to 83 years, with an average age of 65. The average time from menopause was 16 years. He further reports that (1) he commonly saw a 10 percent bone density increase in the lumbar spine in the first 6–12 months and an annual increase of 3–5 percent until stabilizing at numbers equivalent to those of healthy 35-year-olds; (2) the occurrence of osteoporotic fractures dropped to zero (although three women did have fractures associated with trauma). He further reports that there was no difference in results relative to concomitant estrogen use (although in his published study he does not show any kind of breakdown separating the results from the few patients who did not take estrogen from the rest who did). From my perspective, it is odd to conclude that natural progesterone was the one part of the plan that was responsible for his results.

The study incorrectly states that estrogen replacement therapy (ERT) does not increase bone density but merely slows the rate of bone loss. In general, antiresorptive drugs such as ERT result in a 5–10 percent increase in the bone mineral density of the lumbar spine in two years in women with postmenopausal osteoporosis. This change is associated with a decrease in the fracture rate by approximately 50 percent.[93] What may be true is that in women who take ERT and who are also highly motivated to follow the rest of the regimen of diet, exercise, and supplementation, in addition to using topical natural progesterone, will experience greater improvements in bone density than women who do not follow the full regimen.

Too many women are inappropriately selecting natural progesterone cream as their main and possibly only treatment intervention. Often these women are at high risk for osteoporosis, have documented osteoporosis, or even have had a fracture already. It greatly concerns me that decisions and choices are being made based on inaccurate information about natural progesterone and inadequate information about their health problems and additional treatment options that they also need to consider. So many women have been alienated by their conventional medical doctor, have been the recipients of disrespect and mistreatment by conventional medicine, or recognize the opportunism of the pharmaceutical industry that they are left with mistrust, suspicion, and rejection of all things associated with conventional medicine. A careful process of sifting through the benefits of alternative and conventional medicine and the weaknesses or downside of any natural or conventional therapy is especially warranted when it comes to osteoporosis.

Natural progesterone cream deserves a fair and unbiased look by consumers, practitioners, and researchers. What can it do? What can't it do? In what situations is it appropriate and adequate, and in what situations is it insufficient to address a particular woman's case? Research conducted within controlled parameters and which follows scientific guidelines will begin to clarify the situation. Dr. Lee should be commended for his contributions to the expanded understanding of menopausal issues and his willingness to be an advocate for an underutilized product as well as his promotion of the concept that estrogen is not all that it's cracked up to be. My main concern is that we don't equally promote the concept that progesterone is the new savior for women's aging and menopausal health concerns.

Another form of natural progesterone, oral micronized progesterone (OMP), is also often used in menopause management, although it has not received the attention and commercial interests for general consumer use because it is available only by prescription. Results from the Postmenopausal Estrogen/Progestin Interventions Trial (PEPI) have also provided us with some insight on natural progesterone and bone density.[94] Researchers were able to demonstrate that participants in the placebo group lost an average of 1.8 percent of spine bone density and 1.7 percent of hip bone density by the 36-month visit, while those assigned to one of the four treatment groups gained bone density at both sites ranging from 3.5–5.0 percent and a total increase of 1.7 percent bone density in the hip. Although the changes in bone density were significantly greater in the treatment groups when compared to placebo, the results among the treatment groups were not significantly different from each other.

Treatment groups were either (1) conjugated equine estrogens (CEE) 0.625 alone;(2) CEE, 0.625 + MPA, 10 mg/day for 12 days per month; (3) CEE, 0.625 + MPA, 2.5 mg/day daily; or (4) CEE, 0.625 mg/day + OMP, 200 mg/day for 12 days per month. I am presenting this in some detail because, in this study, it appears that it was the estrogen therapy component that increased bone density and not various different progesterone regimens, either synthetic or natural.

So, does natural progesterone, without estrogen, either topically or orally, have an ability to increase bone density? We just do not know yet. What we do know is that when an oral natural progesterone is given with estrogen, there is no increase in bone density when compared to the other regimens.

Natural Estrogens

Natural estrogens are made in the same way as natural progesterone. However, instead of the end product being bio-identical progesterone, the end product is either estrone, estradiol, or estriol. Estrone used by alternative practitioners is the same hormone that is used in at least two prescription conventional estrogens (Ogen and Ortho-est) with the caveat that the prescription drug has fillers, binders, preservatives, and/or excipients. These are added in order for the particular product to receive a patent; a particular individual may absorb and tolerate one form better than another. "Natural estrone" is also available only by prescription, but from a compounding pharmacy. These pharmacies are able to formulate the dose requested by the practitioner and adjust the dosing and the delivery method based on very individual needs. Bio-identical estrogens are free of unnecessary fillers and available in individualized doses and delivery forms (capsules, tablets, sublingual tablets, lozenges, creams, gels), an important advantage in using natural estrogens. In addition, estrone can be used either alone or in combination with estradiol and estriol as is appropriate to each woman and each set of circumstances.

Bio-identical estradiol is also available from a compounding pharmacist and also individualized by dose and delivery for each woman. "Natural estradiol" is the same hormone as the estradiol that is used in many conventional estrogens (Estrace and all the current estrogen patches on the market such as Estraderm, Climara, Allesse, Vivelle, Alora). Again, the difference in the compounded natural estradiol is that it is devoid of the binders, fillers, preservatives, and adhesives that we find in the patented product. As with compounded natural estrone, compounded natural estradiol also carries with it the extra advantage of very individualized dosing, combined options with estriol or estrone and estriol, and numerous delivery methods depending on patient preference or tolerance.

The studies we have on estrone and estradiol are actually on the patented form of the hormone and not on the nonpatented compounded form. It appears as though micronized estrone and micronized estradiol have similar bone mineral density effects to those of conventional CEE. A study of 32 post-menopausal women compared CEE, 0.625 mg, and MPA, 5.0 mg, with micronized estradiol, 1.0 mg (considered to be an equivalent dose to 0.625 CEE) and OMP, 200 mg, administered daily and continuously for 13 cycles.[95] Lumbar bone density improved by 5 percent in the CEE/MPA group and 3.8 percent in the micronized estradiol/OMP group. Hip bone density improved by 2.6 percent in the CEE/MPA group, and 3.1 percent in the micronized estradiol/OMP group. When it comes to statistical significance and percent error in the DEXA measurement device itself, these numbers are considered similar in both groups. Low-dose (0.5 mg) of estradiol, equivalent to 0.3 mg of CEE, has also been shown to be effective in maintaining vertebral mass.[96] Although the authors of this study were able to show that 0.5 mg of estradiol effectively preserved spinal bone density, more traditional (1.0 mg) and higher dose (2.0 mg) estradiol actually increased spinal bone mass by 1.8 percent and 2.5 percent, respectively. Based on this information, it seems that 0.5 mg estradiol can be used to maintain bone mass whereas 1.0 mg of micronized 17-beta estradiol is considered the optimal dosing for enhancement of bone mass in postmenopausal women. No significant differences were seen with using the synthetic progestin (MPA) compared with the natural progesterone (OMP).

Most people have not heard much about estriol, and I discuss it in quite a bit more detail in the preceding chapter about menopause. A question for us in this chapter is whether estriol will effectively prevent bone loss. A few studies done in the last couple of years in other countries have been able to shed some light on the effects of estriol on bone. Although not all estriol studies have shown positive results with bone mass, several Japanese studies have. Seventy-five postmenopausal women with bone densities at least 10 percent or more below peak bone density were given estriol, 2 mg/day, with 800 mg daily of calcium lactate. After 50 weeks, an average increase in bone mineral density of 1.79 percent was seen on the routine DEXA scan.[97] In another Japanese study, 17 women who were 10 years postmenopause were given estriol, 2 mg/day, and 2 gm/day of calcium lactate for one year. Another group was given only the calcium lactate. Bone density was significantly reduced after one year in the calcium-only group, while the estriol-plus-calcium group had a 1.66 percent increase in bone density, using the DEXA scan again.[98] A third Japanese study compared 50 to 65-year-old women and elderly women who received either estriol, 2 mg/day, plus 1 gm/day calcium lactate or 2 mg/day of estriol alone for 10 months.[99] Increases of about 5 percent in the lumbar spine were seen in both age groups of women who took the estriol and the calcium. Women of both age groups in the calcium-alone group had a decrease in bone mineral density of the lumbar spine. High doses of estriol, one at 4–6 mg/day and one as high as 12 mg/day were studied in Scotland, but they were not proved protective against bone loss.[100]

As with natural progesterone, studies about estriol also leave us with some encouragement yet lack of sufficient confirmation about its bone-protective benefits. For women who are at mild risk for osteoporosis but not at moderate or high risk, or for women who are at moderate to higher risk but cannot tolerate or cannot take other forms of estrogen, estriol could be considered part of a comprehensive plan.

Exercise

When bones are stressed by weight, the bone cells (osteocytes) sense it. Osteocytes, in cooperation with other bone cells, initiate a cascade of events leading to increased bone mass which limits the deformation to a predetermined setpoint (0.1–0.5 percent) in any given dimension. When the load on bone exceeds the setpoint, more bone is deposited than removed. When it is below, the opposite effect takes place.[101, 102]

This statement explains why swimming and moderate walking generally do not lead to increased bone mineral density (BMD),[103] but weight lifting,[104–106] jogging/running,[107] gymnastics,[108, 109] and certain sports like basketball do. The setpoint theory of bone mass increase in response to strain also explains why a few studies showed no effect[110] or a negative effect[111] of exercise on BMD—a load below the setpoint fails to trigger a response.

Regular physical exercise of appropriate intensity and duration that overloads the skeletal system above its setpoint increases BMD in women of all ages within the limits set by hereditary factors, nutrition, and the hormonal status of the individual. In children and adolescents;[112] in college-age women;[113, 114] in women in their forties; and in young,[115, 116] older,[117, 118] and very old[119] postmenopausal women, exercise has been shown to be essential to the developing and maintaining of bone health.

In sedentary women, trabecular bone loss begins to occur in the third decade of life and cortical bone loss in the sixth.[120, 121] The 35–45 percent reduction in muscle strength observed in women at age 80 years parallels the observed bone loss at that same age.[122] Conversely, the age-related loss of bone parallels decreased physical activity.[123] Moreover, women who exercise retain bone mass throughout life,[124] achieve greater peak bone mass which contributes to the consolidation and strength of bone following the end of linear growth,[125] and have significantly lower risk of fractures in later life.[111, 126]

Furthermore, Recker and associates demonstrated that, independent of calcium intake or oral contraceptive use, the more college-age women exercised, the greater BMD they achieved. These increases were highly significant despite relatively small increments on exercise. A 1996 review of the literature on peak bone mass and exercise[127] confirms these results and adds that exercise can maintain normal bones sufficiently strong until very old age and can strengthen weak bones when used in concert with adequate nutrition. The author of this review concludes that even small increases in initial bone mass—as is the case in many studies—grow to a substantial difference if the increased bone mass is maintained by a lifetime of regular exercise.

Finally, at least one study[117] found significantly increased BMD from non-weight-bearing exercise in postmenopausal women. An eight-month bicycle ergometer exercise trial at 60–80 percent of maximum heart rate resulted in a BMD increase of 3.55 g/cm^2 in the participants and a decrease of 2.44 g/cm^2 in the sedentary controls. The differential favoring exercisers was 5.99 g/cm^2.

To develop and maintain bone health, the choice for women is not among exercise, HRT, or calcium. Appropriate nutrition is critical to bone health. Some women may need hormonal replacement to avoid osteoporosis. However, exercise throughout life is as critical as a lifetime of adequate nutrition. The decision, apparently, needs to focus on types, intensity, and duration of exercise.

The important question for doctors is not to help their female patients of any age decide whether or not to exercise. It is rather to study ways to personalize the exercise prescription and motivate the patient to begin and continue exercising for life.

Note: The problem of exercise-induced amenorrhea and consequent bone loss is discussed in Chapter 2.

EXERCISE RECOMMENDATIONS

If not already exercising regularly, consult with your licensed health care professional in cooperation with a qualified exercise expert. Together with them establish:

- Schedule of exercise
- Types, intensity, and duration of exercise

Consider the following guidelines:

- Begin slowly
- Increase intensity very gradually
- Train with weights for 6 weeks before introducing intensive aerobic exercise (e.g., running, speed walking) into your program
- Begin each exercise session with joint-warming exercises (see Appendix A) for 5 minutes
- End each exercise session with 5–10 minutes of stretching exercises
- Use caution and moderation throughout your lifetime of exercise

---

Mary Larkin's "Bone Up"[128] provides an excellent introduction to your lifetime of exercise. Use simple low-impact exercises and stretching for two or three months before you branch out into the more comprehensive exercise program described in Appendix A, under "General Exercise Program."

If already exercising regularly, consider introducing into your program:

- The principle of "pyramiding" (explained in Appendix A).
- Variations of speed in your aerobic exercises.
- Different exercise positions, particularly in weight training, that challenge your bones from different angles.
- Alternating practicing sports, e.g., basketball, volleyball, tennis, etc., with regular exercise routine.

THERAPEUTIC SCHEME FOR MANAGEMENT OF OSTEOPOROSIS

A. Determine risk for osteoporosis: mild, moderate, severe.

B. Be aware of six levels of intervention that cover the majority of clinical situations:

Level 1: Diet, exercise, lifestyle, stress management
Level 2: Nutritional supplementation
Level 3: Botanicals
Level 4: Natural estrogens and natural progesterone
Level 5: Friendlier conventional hormones (estrogen patches, estradiol); use with oral natural progesterone
Level 6: Less-friendly conventional hormone replacement therapy (conjugated estrogens such as Premarin, ethinyl estradiol, esterified estrogens, medroxyprogesterone acetate [Provera])

C. Recommendations according to risk:

Level	Mild	Moderate	Severe
1)	X	X	X
2)	X	X	X
3)	X		
4)		X	
5)			X*
6)			X**

* use with oral micronized progesterone if uterus is still intact.
** in cases that do not respond to other medicines.

SAMPLE TREATMENT PLAN FOR OSTEOPOROSIS

Dietary recommendations

- High soy diet: 50–100 mg isoflavones per day
- High in dark leafy greens: 1–2 servings per day
- Low fat dairy, especially low fat cultured yogurt
- Reduce animal products, promote vegetarian choices, but with adequate protein
- Avoid alcohol, caffeine, sugar

Regular weight-bearing exercise

30–60 minutes, 4 or more times weekly

Nutritional supplementation

- Calcium carbonate: 1,000–1,500 mg/day *or* Calcium citrate/malate: 500–750 mg per day
- Magnesium oxide: 400–800 mg per day *or* Magnesium citrate/malate: 200–400 mg per day
- Vitamin D: 400 IU per day
- Trace minerals: boron (3 mg), zinc (15 mg), chromium (100 mcg), manganese (15 mg), copper (1.5 mg)
- Other nutritional cofactors such as vitamin K (200 mcg)

Natural hormone recommendations

1) Women at low risk: recommended diet, regular weight-bearing exercise, nutritional supplementation, no natural hormones necessary; Soy: 50–100 mg isoflavones daily

2) Women at medium risk: recommended diet, daily weight-bearing exercise, nutritional supplementation, natural hormones (estriol + estradiol + progesterone, or estriol + estrone + estradiol + progesterone); dose equivalent to 0.3 mg or 0.625 mg Premarin, depending on individual. See Appendix B.

3) Women at high risk: recommended diet, daily weight-bearing exercise, nutritional supplementation, conventional estradiol (1mg/day) and oral micronized progesterone, 200 mg per day for 12 days per month or 100 mg daily

Most importantly, keep finding ways to motivate yourself:

- Form the habit of regularly reading about the benefits of exercise.
- Be moderate—avoid burnout.
- Form a circle of friends who also love to exercise.

✦ Conventional Medicine Approach

Estrogen and estrogen/progestin combinations are currently the conventional treatments of choice for the prevention and treatment of postmenopausal osteoporosis. Estrogen will slow bone loss, preserve bone mass, and increase bone density. Estrogen has been shown to reduce the risk of osteoporotic fractures by approximately 50 percent.[97] The greatest benefit from estrogen is seen when it is started in the early menopause when the rate of bone loss is greatest and then continued for at least six to nine years.[129] Even women who begin estrogen replacement therapy later in life may still experience a beneficial effect on their bone density[93, 129] although the benefits are not quite as great as those in women who start at menopause and continue lifelong. The discouraging news for women is that once hormone replacement therapy (HRT) is discontinued, bone loss resumes. Despite these benefits of HRT on the prevention and treatment of osteoporosis, compliance among women is very low. Only 15–25 percent of women eligible for HRT actually fill their prescriptions. Of those who do, the overall compliance rate may be as low as 30 percent.[130] Women are wary of side effects and fear breast and uterine cancer. They should be reminded that the addition of the progestin greatly reduces this risk of uterine cancer.[131] Studies have fostered much controversy about whether HRT promotes breast cancer. Most evidence shows that an increased risk for breast cancer does exist with long-term (more than five years) use of HRT.[130] An article in the June 1998 issue of the *Journal of the National Cancer Institute* reviewed the existing literature on hormones and breast cancer.[132] They concluded that existing evidence supports a causal relationship between use of estrogens and progestins for longer than five years and breast cancer

incidence in postmenopausal women. This is clearly a difficult area of choice for women. It becomes a matter of weighing the benefits of HRT against its risks. Decisions are best made when fully informed and educated; when risks for osteoporosis, heart disease, and breast cancer are known; and when personal concerns, choices, and preferences are respected.

Bisphosphonates are nonhormonal inhibitors of bone resorption and are specific to their target, the osteoclast in the bone. Since the bisphosphonates act only on bone, they do not offer the cardiovascular benefits that can be gained from HRT. The effect of bisphosphonates on bone resorption varies considerably from compound to compound. Alendronate (Fosamax), a new drug for the prevention and treatment of osteoporosis, is given at a dose of 10 mg per day for the treatment of osteoporosis in postmenopausal women. The administration has resulted in an increase in bone mineral density of 8.8 percent in the lumbar spine and of 5.9 percent in the femoral neck in three years.[133] This increase in bone mineral density was matched by a decrease in biochemical markers of bone turnover, with the markers of bone resorption decreasing maximally at two months and the markers of bone formation decreasing maximally at six months. Other results of alendronate therapy include a 48 percent decrease in the proportion of women with new fractures; it also prevents height loss.[133] Alendronate is also increasingly being used for prevention at a lower dose of 5 mg per day. Among 2,027 women with vertebral fractures in the Fracture Intervention Trial[134] who were treated with 5 mg of alendronate daily for two years, with an increase to 10 mg per day for the last nine months of the study, the rate of new vertebral fractures decreased by 47 percent when compared to the women who took only the placebo. There were also similar decreases in the frequency of hip and wrist fractures.

Alendronate has poor absorption and has been associated with gastrointestinal irritation.[135] Side effects such as esophagitis are common if the exact recommendations are not strictly followed. It must be taken on an empty stomach with a full eight-ounce glass of water, and the woman must remain upright for at least 30 minutes after ingestion. For the woman in whom estrogen is contraindicated, who cannot tolerate its side effects, or who prefers not to take it for her own personal reasons, alendronate may offer a viable option if her osteoporosis is significant enough.

Interest in the potential of androgens as a therapy for osteoporosis has been based on two observations: (1) androgen levels are lower in postmenopausal women with osteoporosis, and (2) androgens have been shown to stimulate osteoblasts in laboratory research.[136] Although studies have been of short duration, data suggest that androgen derivatives, such as anabolic steroids, may be associated with protection against vertebral fracture.[137] The only randomized study that looks at the possible benefit in osteoporosis of using testosterone medication was done in 1986.[138] This study was designed to evaluate the effect on overall bone density when implants of 50 mg of estrogen alone were compared with the same amount of estrogen plus 100 mg of testosterone. After three years, the estrogen-alone groups showed no change, whereas the group receiving the combined therapy showed an increase in bone mass of 2.5 percent. It is important to note that the study used the measurement of a bone in the hand, which is a bone not at risk for osteoporosis. A subsequent study in 1992 looked at overall bone density of the skeleton between those women on oral estrogen only, as compared to subcutaneous estrogen and testosterone implants.[139] The results showed a significant increase in bone density by 5.7 percent in the spine, and 5.2 percent in the hip with subcutaneous estrogen and testosterone implants. The bone density of the women who remained on the oral estrogen alone remained unchanged. Even though these studies point to the role of testosterone in bone density, conventional medical practitioners by and large do not use testosterone therapy as part of a regimen for preventing or treating osteoporosis.

Calcitonin therapy is a lesser known medication used (although not extensively) in the treatment of osteoporosis. It is a peptide hormone that inhibits bone resorption.[140] Calcitonin therapy results in a modest increase in bone mineral density, and in one study it resulted in a decrease in the rate of vertebral fracture.[141] Problems with calcitonin are that

it is available only by injection; some people may become resistant; and it can cause nausea, flushing, and diarrhea. A newer intranasal salmon calcitonin with few side effects has been developed that may make it more acceptable, although intranasal calcitonin is not effective in preventing bone loss in early-postmenopausal women. It may be that it will be used in older women, where it has had a small impact on decreasing the vertebral fracture rate.[142]

A new class of drugs called selective estrogen receptor modulators (SERM) is the latest in the attempt to provide women with more choices within the conventional medical model. A SERM is a compound that produces estrogenlike effects in select tissues (e.g., bone) while not having an estrogen effect or even an antagonistic activity in other tissues (e.g., breast or endometrium). Tamoxifen (Nolvadex) was the first SERM to be marketed and has been used for many years as a breast cancer therapy. Tamoxifen appears to have estrogenlike effects on the skeleton in terms of maintaining bone mass in postmenopausal women.[143] One of the main concerns about tamoxifen is that it has an estrogenlike effect on the endometrium and therefore can increase the risk for endometrial cancer.

The new SERM on the block is raloxifene (Evista). Raloxifene appears to have estrogenic activity on the skeleton and serum lipids without stimulating the endometrial or breast tissue. In a two-year study in postmenopausal women, raloxifene therapy resulted in a decrease in bone resorption[144] and an increase in bone mineral density in the lumbar spine (2.4 percent), total hip (2.4 percent), and total body (2.0 percent).[145] Raloxifene decreases serum low-density lipoprotein (LDL) cholesterol concentrations but does not stimulate endometrial growth. These bone studies have not yet been supported by fracture studies, but pharmaceutical companies are continuing to develop other SERMs (droloxifene, idoxifene, and levormeloxifene). Conventional medicine sees these as alternatives to HRT, and many women will consider them an option because of their antiestrogen effect on breast tissue.

Because osteoporosis is such a significant health problem, conventional practitioners see these pharmacologic therapies as essential for the prevention of osteoporosis and fractures and in the treatment of osteoporosis. Even though there is an increasing array of pharmacologic options, HRT remains the mainstay in osteoporosis treatments and is currently the first-line therapy for the prevention of osteoporosis. That's not to say that medical doctors ignore some of the basic lifestyle issues. Many are recommending increasing dairy products (the hallmark of the dietary advice), regular weight-bearing exercise, and calcium supplementation to round out the preventive recommendations.

Seeing a Licensed Primary Health Care Practitioner*

Osteoporosis is one of the most important age-associated disorders and should be considered a potentially disabling disease that warrants substantial preventive efforts and management interventions. Early identification of risk factors for osteoporosis, prevention strategies, and assessment of calcium metabolism and bone density provide the basis for determining what is appropriate for each woman. A licensed health care practitioner who is educated about the importance of early identification, prevention, and treatment and who is also aware of the spectrum of alternative and conventional options is especially crucial for women who are at higher risk or who already have osteoporosis.

*N.D. = Naturopathic Doctor; M.D. = Medical Doctor; D.O. = Osteopathic Doctor; N.P. = Nurse Practitioner; P.A. = Physician's Assistant.

Be cautious about practitioners who only discuss short-term physical symptoms of menopause such as hot flushes and irregular bleeding. They often fail to address the primary long-term concern, which is osteoporosis. One-third of physicians do not discuss osteoporosis at all. You may have to insist on your request for a DEXA scan to measure your bone density. The newer, less comprehensive but less expensive ultrasound tests of the heel may prove to have an increased role in identifying those women who are at higher risk. Ultrasonometry of the heel provides excellent diagnostic sensitivity for both spine and hip fracture. Recent reviews[146, 147] concluded that ultrasound of the heel was as strong a predictor of osteoporotic fracture as a bone density test of the spine. Using this method for screening purposes can be an important tool for identifying those women who are at increased risk for osteoporosis

The more risk factors you have for osteoporosis, the greater the need to have laboratory and bone density testing. If you had a mother or sister or maternal grandmother with osteoporosis, or you remember them having had a hip fracture or being very stooped in their posture, you are automatically in a higher-risk category. Women in this category are especially encouraged to seek a licensed health care practitioner who is well educated in the diagnosis and management of osteoporosis. One of the most important things to remember is that every woman is different and that osteoporosis and fractures are affected by many factors.

PELVIC INFLAMMATORY DISEASE

 ## Overview

Pelvic inflammatory disease (PID) includes a spectrum of infections of the upper genital tract. These include endometritis (infection of the lining of the uterus), salpingitis (infection of the fallopian tubes), tubo-ovarian abscess, and pelvic peritonitis (infection of the serous membrane lining the abdominal and pelvic walls. More than one million women in the Unitd States develop PID each year, and one-fourth of them require hospitalization. The infection typically results from the spread of microorganisms that ascend from the endocervix to the upper genital organs. The most common organisms are *Neisseria gonorrhoeae* and *Chlamydia trachomatis.* Chlamydia causes 50 percent of PID in Europe and 20–30 percent of cases in the United States, though the real incidence may be even higher. Additional organisms implicated in PID include *Mycoplasma* species, *Haemophilus influenzae, Streptococcus agalactiae,* and *Ureaplasma urealyticum.* PID is considered a polymicrobial infection due to the many organisms involved. One in four women diagnosed with PID may develop complications, including ectopic pregnancy, infertility, recurrent pelvic pain, and recurrent PID.

It is important to recognize the possibility of PID due to its potential for developing into a lethal condition, a more complicated condition, or a condition with long-term consequences. It is also important to be alert to possible surgical emergencies. Sometimes PID can be elusive and there is little clinical evidence to support a suspicion of PID, especially when the symptoms are mild and insidious. The classic presentation of lower abdominal pain and tenderness with examination or motion of the cervix occurs in fact in only 20–25 percent of patients. A much more common presentation is often a mild or subtle pelvic pain. Some women with PID will have discomfort with urination and urinary frequency as well as other urinary tract symptoms. An increased number of risk factors for PID increases the suspicion. These may include:

- Age 14 to 24
- Heterosexual and sexually active
- Multiple sex partners
- New sex partner
- History of sexually transmitted disease
- History of PID
- Use of IUD for contraception
- Never having been pregnant
- Onset of pain during or within one week of menses
- Cigarette or alcohol or illicit drug use
- Surgical abortion, or pelvic or bowel surgery

Adolescents and young single heterosexual adults have the highest incidence of gonorrhea. This organism is believed to be the cause in 33–80 percent of the PID cases, although mixed gonorrhea and chlamydial infections occur frequently. About 15 percent of endocervical gonorrhea infections result in PID. A diagnosis of PID in children warrants an evaluation for child abuse.

PID symptoms more often begin during or within one week of menses because the opening of the cervix is wider due to menstruation. Microorganisms can then more easily ascend into the upper genital region and use the flow of blood as fresh nutrition for their growth.

Women with new heterosexual partners within the last 30–60 days or multiple sex partners are more likely to develop PID. If a woman's partner is not monogamous, then she is also at increased risk. A history of a sexually transmitted disease (STD) increases the likelihood of contracting subsequent STDs, as does a history of PID.

Barrier contraceptive methods such as condoms, diaphragms, and cervical caps reduce the risk of PID while IUDs are associated with an increased risk of PID, particularly in the first four months after insertion. The incidence of PID in IUD users is three to five times that of nonusers in most populations of women studied. If a woman with suspected PID has an IUD, it must be removed.

Use of illicit drugs (especially crack cocaine), alcohol, or cigarettes has been associated with an increased risk of STDs and PID. Substance abuse also increases the potential for HIV infection. Women with HIV are far more likely to have PID.

PREVENTION

- Use barrier methods of contraception.
- Avoid illicit drugs and cigarettes, and limit alcohol.
- Treat previous STDs with appropriate therapy and be certain of resolution.
- Avoid douching.
- Know the sexual history of your partner.
- Heterosexual women who have multiple partners and do not use condoms, cervical caps, or diaphragms are at higher risk for PID.
- Women with HIV are at even higher risk and need to practice even greater caution.

KEY CONCEPTS

- Acute or chronic pelvic pain warrants a visit to a qualified licensed health care practitioner for diagnosis.
- PID must be differentiated from other causes of pelvic and abdominal pain.
- PID should be primarily treated with antibiotic therapy, while alternative medicine can offer supportive and adjunct therapies to conventional treatment.
- Seek prompt medical attention if you have the symptoms described in this chapter or suspect you have PID.
- The sex partner must be evaluated and treated. Re-infection will almost certainly occur if the sex partner is not treated.

✤ Overview of Alternative Medicine

Gonorrhea is a reportable disease. This means that a practitioner must call the public health department and report the disease if this organism has been cultured. Due to the potential complications and seriousness of PID, in concert with a lack of proven therapeutic results in using natural treatments for this disorder, alternative therapies should be seen as secondary to conventional treatment. Women who suffer from PID and have strong opinions about not being treated with antibiotics should be fully educated and informed, so that their decision to decline antibiotic therapy is not naïve. A short course of antibiotic therapy is rarely detrimental to one's health. In this case, the benefit of the therapy far outweighs the risk of its use. Likewise, alternative practitioners should not be naïve about the scope of their treatments and should understand that the integration of antibiotic therapy for the benefit of the patient is not a failure of natural medicine. There are old texts that make reference to treating PID with natural therapies, but they lack modern methods of evaluation and follow-up. It could be that botanicals used in India, China, or elsewhere have a tradition substantiated by modern confirmation testing, but I am not aware of these treatments.

Using alternative therapies to support the immune system, assist in managing pain and discomfort, and counteract some of the side effects of the antibiotics are the main priorities. Drinking plenty of water, getting rest, eating simple light foods, and avoiding stimulants are basic guidelines during any acute infection, including pelvic infections.

General immune support to complement conventional antibiotic treatment is just good plain common sense. Nutritional and botanical support can stimulate white blood cells that engulf and destroy bacteria. Herbs and nutrients can enhance the function of T-cells, B-cells, and natural killer cells that support the immune system's response to bacteria. Vitamin A, vitamin C, the carotenes, vitamin E, zinc, and the B vitamins all play an important role in immune enhancement. Increasing antibody response, stimulating helper T-cells, enhancing white blood cell response and function, and directly killing the virus or bacteria are just some of the ways in which these supplements can be helpful during an infection of any kind. Many herbs have also been shown to have antimicrobial and immunostimulating effects. The most commonly used herb for immune support is echinacea. Echinacea can increase the production of T-cells, stimulate the white blood cells that engulf and destroy bacteria, stimulate natural killer cell activity, and increase the number of circulating white blood cells in order to deal with the infection.[1] The end result is a strengthened immune system.

The best complement to counteract the side effects of antibiotic use is to add or increase the intake of *Lactobacillus acidophilus* to help prevent a vaginal yeast infection. This can be accomplished by eating yogurt daily or by taking oral capsules of *Lactobacillus acidophilus*. Four to eight ounces of unsweetened acidophilus yogurt or at least three capsules of *Lactobacillus acidophilus* daily for two weeks should prevent the overgrowth of vaginal yeast that often occurs when taking antibiotics. Additional dietary advice, plus botanical and nutritional therapies for the prevention and treatment of yeast vaginitis, are discussed in Chapter 18.

Ice packs over the pelvic region can reduce inflammation and pain in cases of acute PID. Cold or

---

SAMPLE TREATMENT PLAN FOR PELVIC INFLAMMATORY DISEASE
(to be used as a complement to antibiotic therapy)

- Eat a light diet during acute infection: vegetable broths, steamed vegetables, salads, fruits
- Acidophilus yogurt, 4–8 oz per day as a preventive of yeast vaginitis
- Vitamin E: 400 units twice daily
- Vitamin C: 1,000–2,000 mg 3 times daily
- Vitamin A: 25,000 units per day and up to 50,000 units for a maximum of 2 weeks
- Zinc: 45–60 mg per day
- Ice pack over the uterus with a hot foot bath
- Echinacea: Liquid extracts (½ tsp every 3 hours) or capsules/tablets (2 every 3 hours) during course of infection
- Garlic: 1 capsule twice daily

---

ice packs placed over the region of the uterus while putting the feet in a tub of hot water can further assist in reducing the inflammation, congestion, and pain in the pelvic area. Alternating hot and cold sitz baths can also be used to improve circulation in the pelvic area and improve the healing time from the infection. This is done by sitting in a bath of hot water, with the water level just above the waist, for three minutes, followed by sitting in a small second portable metal or plastic tub of ice cold water for one minute. This procedure is repeated three times in succession, once or twice daily throughout the course of the pain and infection.

≈ Conventional Medicine Approach

Conventional practitioners rely on their own judgment in assessing the severity of the disease and the ability of the patient to carry out the treatment successfully. It is essential for the practitioner to educate the patient about the exact treatment regimen. If she is able to comply with the recommendations, she may be a candidate for outpatient treatment. Infertility may be more successfully prevented by prompt administration of intravenous (IV) antibiotics, even if the woman is not acutely ill. In the case of outpatient treatment, once antibiotics are administered, the patient must have a follow-up visit within 72 hours. Other treatments are used to assure that the patient stays hydrated, fever is managed, and discomfort and pain relieved.

PID therapy must provide broad-spectrum coverage of the most likely-offending organisms. Although several antimicrobial regimens have been effective in achieving cure in randomized clinical trials, few studies have been done to assess and compare elimination of infection of the lining of the uterus and the fallopian tubes or the incidence of long-term complications such as infertility and ectopic pregnancy. No single antibiotic regimen has been established. Health care providers select treatment regimens based on drug availability, cost, the patient's tolerance of the drug, and other individuating factors.

Doxycycline is the treatment of choice for chlamydial infections and is included in both inpatient and outpatient regimens. Ofloxacin is effective against both gonorrhea and chlamydia. Because ofloxacin is limited in its antimicrobial effect, it is important to add clindamycin or metronidazole. Ofloxacin should not be used by pregnant women or girls younger than age 18.

Two main antibiotic regimens are used for outpatient management of PID. Most conventional practitioners follow these Centers for Disease Control (CDC) treatment guidelines.[2]

- *Regimen A:* Defoxitin, 2 g IM (intramuscular injection); plus probenecid, one by mouth, concurrently; or ceftriaxone sodium, 250 mg IM, plus doxycycline, 100 mg twice daily for 14 days
- *Regimen B:* Ofloxacin, 400 mg by mouth twice daily for 14 days; to this add clindamycin, 450 mg four times daily for 14 days or metronidazole, 500 mg twice daily for 14 days

Research conducted at several different medical facilities has shown that ampicillin/sulbactam regimens are equally as effective as cefoxitin/doxycycline in the treatment of PID[3] and are better tolerated.

It is important for the patient to realize how critical it is to follow her doctor's directions and complete the drug regimen as described on the bottle. There may be side effects from the medication that she should be informed about as well. If hospitalization occurs, a more complex regimen is administered with several combinations of IV antibiotics. After the patient leaves the hospital, two weeks of doxycycline is given. It is important that patients follow these recommendations and then return for follow-up.

Treatment of PID should eliminate signs and symptoms of the infection and eradicate the microorganisms while minimizing the damage to the fallopian tubes as well as long-term complications. Follow-up for outpatient treatment is crucial within 72 hours to assure that the patient is taking the medicine accurately and to evaluate the effectiveness of the treatment. If the infection is not responding to treatment, further cultures may be done to determine whether the antibiotic selected is the appropriate one. Hospitalization may be necessary at that time. Hospitalized patients receiving IV therapy should show substantial improvement within three to five days after beginning the therapy. Patients who do not improve within this time usually require further diagnostic testing, surgical intervention, or both.

Pregnant women with suspected PID should be hospitalized and treated with IV antibiotics. Women with HIV must be managed more aggressively and are more likely to require surgical intervention. Hospitalization and IV antimicrobial therapy are recommended for HIV-positive patients.

Conventional practitioners take great care in educating the patient about the disease, the importance of treatment, the possible consequences, the importance of treating her male partners, and the importance of barrier contraceptives and other methods to reduce the risk of STDs. To a patient not accustomed to dealing with severe infections and the need for antibiotics, some practitioners may seem overly aggressive in their recommendations and insistence. Although this may offend some women, it is important that they do not let a less-than-optimal bedside style distract their attention from the value of what physicians know and have to offer.

❧ *Seeing a Licensed Primary** Health Care Practitioner*

Women with pelvic pain need to consider not only PID but also other conditions that can present with similar discomfort. Ectopic pregnancy, tubo-ovarian abscess, ruptured ovarian cysts, appendicitis, inflammatory colitis, pancreatitis, cholecystitis (inflammation of the gallbladder), cystitis (inflammation of the bladder), diverticulitis (inflammation of a small pouch along the border of the colon), hepatitis, and a twisted fallopian tube are among the other potentially serious disorders that require differentiation from PID.

Women with PID typically describe pain that is sharp, localized, and bilateral. They may also have an oral temperature above 101 degrees. Ectopic pregnancy typically presents with one-sided pain, but no fever.

If you are a woman reading this with these symptoms, call your doctor immediately. A licensed health care practitioner will proceed with a history, physical examination, and diagnostic testing including blood work, cultures, and possible pelvic ultrasound. Laparoscopy and culdocentesis are infrequently used in the diagnosis and management of PID unless the diagnosis is uncertain or a serious complication is suspected. An abdominal exam will be done to check for pain in various locations. A pelvic exam will check the external genital region; a speculum exam will check for inflammation and discharge. A thick, transparent, yellow, gray, or brown discharge coming through the cervix suggests a chlamydial or gonococcal infection. An internal exam will check for an enlarged uterus or pain and tenderness. Cultures for the infectious agents require two to three days to process and are important in confirming a diagnosis, but severe symptoms and the potentially serious consequences of acute PID require immediate treatment even if confirmation has not yet been obtained.

Since PID can be caused by more than one organism, a negative culture result can be misleading.

*N.D. = Naturopathic Doctor; M.D. = Medical Doctor; D.O. = Osteopathic Doctor; N.P. = Nurse Practitioner; P.A. = Physician's Assistant.

Newer and more accurate tests using antigen detection methods or fluorescence antibody marker techniques are available for the rapid detection of chlamydial infection. They can be especially useful in detecting mild cases or cases that have no symptoms at all. Pelvic ultrasound examinations are performed when a pelvic mass or abscess is suspected. They may be able to reveal a cyst, an ectopic pregnancy, an abscess, or an enlarged tube.

Laparoscopy is considered to be the gold standard for diagnosing PID. Because diagnostic laparoscopy is expensive and invasive, requires special training, and may not affect the decision to treat the patient for pelvic infection, it is not routinely used in the emergency management of patients with PID. A procedure called culdocentesis aspirates fluid that has collected behind the uterus. The removal of blood suggests an ectopic pregnancy or a ruptured ovarian cyst. The removal of cloudy or purulent fluid suggests an infection, and the fluid is then tested with cultures. If the culture is positive for PID, the practitioner will most likely recommend antibiotics and, in more severe cases, hospitalization for IV antibiotics and monitoring.

About 25 percent of women with PID will require hospitalization. Criteria for hospitalization

---

DIAGNOSTIC CRITERIA FOR PELVIC INFLAMMATORY DISEASE

All three criteria must be present for clinical diagnosis:

- Lower abdominal tenderness
- Bilateral adnexal tenderness
- Cervical motion tenderness

Additional criteria useful in diagnosis:
- Oral temperature > 101 degrees F
- Abnormal cervical or vaginal discharge
- Elevated sedimentation rate or C-reactive protein
- White blood cells > 10,500 mm^3
- Evidence of cervical infection with *Neisseria gonorrhoeae* or *Chlamydia trachomatis*
- Tubo-ovarian abscess on pelvic ultrasound
- Laparoscopic abnormalities consistent with PID

have been established by the CDC. If your practitioner recommends that you be admitted to the hospital, I would urge you to entrust yourself to his or her care. You can always use natural therapies to augment the treatment. The CDC criteria for hospitalization include:

- Adolescent patient
- HIV infection

- The diagnosis of PID is uncertain
- The patient has not responded to outpatient treatment
- The patient has not been able to tolerate or follow the outpatient regimen
- A surgical emergency is possible
- Ectopic pregnancy
- Severe illness or nausea and vomiting
- Suspected pelvic abscess

PREGNANCY

Overview

All women want to do everything they possibly can to optimize the health and well-being of themselves and their coming offspring. There is simply no other condition that inspires women to care for themselves as well. That said, Mother Nature's talent in producing healthy babies is awesome indeed, and no matter the range of one's individual decisions regarding optimal health care, most babies arrive intact and healthy. It is true that the United States has a disturbingly high incidence of infant mortality, given the high standard of care that is available. However, it is women who do not have access to care, volitional or otherwise, who are most apt to lose their babies. Women who receive prenatal care enjoy the lowest risk of maternal and infant mortality in history. It is important to recognize those things we have control over and those we don't. While women should do their best to take excellent care of themselves during pregnancy, they must struggle against assuming personal responsibility for the vagaries of biology—like miscarriages and rare abnormalities. Ninety-eight percent or more of babies are born healthy. Keep that number in mind as you read through this information . . . remembering that fetuses are strong little parasites. They pull what they need from our bodies pretty effectively. It is the woman carrying the child, in all but extreme cases, who suffers subsequent deficiencies in her health—the fetus gets preferential treatment. Welcome to motherhood!

Pregnancy and birthing are normal physiological processes that can be positively supported through adequate rest, preventive nutrition, and the avoidance of harmful substances. Minimizing stress, getting plenty of low-impact exercise and fresh air, and sleeping well are important factors leading to a positive overall experience of pregnancy and birth. The important thing to remember is that each pregnancy is unique, and although there are certain universal factors to consider, the most important preventive medicine is the mother's positive own relationship to her body and her emotional and physical connection to the child she is carrying.

During pregnancy, hormone secretion changes radically, causing the physical and emotional changes experienced by most women fairly early in the first trimester. Estrogen levels are about 10–70 times higher than prepregnant luteal phase levels, and progesterone is 10 times higher than nonpregnant luteal phase levels.[1] These levels drop immediately after birth to prepregnancy levels, as prolactin (the pituitary hormone) is produced to stimulate the production of breast milk. Throughout pregnancy, the placenta produces a hormone called relaxin, which softens the connective tissues and ligaments that support the uterus, allowing it to expand. The production of endorphins (morphinelike hormones that are the body's natural painkillers and tranquilizers) is increased during pregnancy and continues to rise during labor when it reaches peak levels.[2] It has been suggested that morning sickness problems are related to an increase in thyroid hormone or relaxation of smooth stomach muscle.

❦ Overview of Alternative Treatments

Nearly all pregnant women can benefit from nutritional and multivitamin supplementation one year before, all during pregnancy, and throughout labor, delivery, and breast-feeding. The effects of poor nutrition during pregnancy can be seen in the increase of birth defects during times of famine.[3] A standard Western diet (high in fats, salt, and sugar, and low in complex carbohydrates) lacks the essential vitamins and minerals needed during pregnancy and breast-feeding, and thus may lead to a "compromise in an offspring's health."[4] The appropriate diet is well balanced and varied and includes fresh fruits, vegetables, whole grains, legumes, beans, and fish, with a limit on refined sugars, processed foods, and saturated fats. Organically grown produce, meats, and poultry are preferable to those grown with the use of pesticides/herbicides. If one chooses to use non-organically produced foods, these must be carefully washed with soap to remove agricultural chemicals.[5]

In an observational study involving 76 healthy pregnant women, 78 percent had "one or more

glaring nutritional deficiencies."[6] Another study showed an "overall apparent protective effect of periconceptual multivitamin use" for prevention of certain pregnancy-related illnesses and birth defects.[7] Of special importance is folate (folic acid), which is the only vitamin whose requirement doubles in pregnancy.[8] This is essential not only for a healthy fetus but for the pregnant woman and the newborn as well. Vitamin B_{12} is also essential to a good outcome.[9] Nutrients such as folic acid and vitamins B_6 and B_{12} have been correlated with prevention of the more common negative pregnancy outcomes, such as spontaneous abortion, placental abruption, preterm delivery, low infant birth weight, and neural tube defects (e.g., spina bifida and anencephaly).[10] Supplementation with calcium has been positively correlated with prevention of pregnancy hypertension[11] and pre-eclampsia,[12, 13] preterm delivery,[14] and low birth weight.[15] Magnesium supplementation has also been shown in studies to reduce the complications of pregnancy and improve the health of the infant.[16]

Certain substances should be avoided in preparation for and during pregnancy. Smoking during pregnancy increases the incidence of premature labor,[17] low birth weight,[18] and infant complications.[19] These complications may not be alleviated by increased maternal caloric intake. In addition, women who abuse alcohol and use illicit drugs are more likely to have inadequate nutrition as well as birth abnormalities and developmental problems.

Nutrition

During pregnancy, a woman's physiology changes dramatically to allow for the development of a healthy fetus. To support the rapidly growing fetus, changes in metabolism, biochemistry, and hormone status are needed to provide the environment and energy required. Appropriate nutrition greatly improves pregnancy outcomes when used wisely during the prenatal nine months and is an important factor affecting the pregnancy outcome. Members of the health care team assess maternal nutritional risk, assign goals for weight gain, and recommend dietary changes to achieve those goals. Prenatal evaluation and continued health care are important in monitoring the progress of the pregnancy and intervening with corrective changes when needed.

The nutritional assessment includes information about diet, eating habits, daily activities, medical and medication history, and the use of tobacco, alcohol, and recreational drugs. An initial physical examination followed by ongoing exams throughout the pregnancy are essential in assessing the mother's body mass index (BMI) and appropriate weight gain and fetal growth. BMI relates weight to height and thus provides a better estimate of body fat distribution than weight alone. BMI calculated from the prepregnant weight is then used to categorize weight into underweight, normal weight, overweight, or obese. Weight is a very important indicator of fetal health and requires precise and regular measurement. At each visit with your prenatal health care worker, you should be weighed and have that figure recorded on a grid to facilitate assessment of your rate of weight gain compared to the target goals.

Low prepregnant weight and inadequate weight gain during pregnancy are dominant contributors to intrauterine growth retardation[20] and low birth weight.[21] Maternal prepregnant weight and weight gain in pregnancy also have an impact on early infant death rates. For women who are underweight prior to pregnancy, the perinatal mortality risk at birth is lowest when their weight gain is greater than 37 pounds. For women who had normal weight prior to pregnancy, the lowest risk is with a weight gain of between 30–37 pounds.[22] Women who are obese prior to pregnancy need to gain less weight for an optimal fetal outcome. Significant risk occurs in obese women if there is a greater than 25-pound weight gain during the pregnancy.[23] Weight loss in obese women is not recommended during pregnancy. Teenagers often need careful education about the importance of nutrition, nutritional choices, the importance of healthy weight gain, and guidance throughout the pregnancy.

Women with limited or potentially imbalanced dietary habits (vegetarians, vegans, anorexics, and women consuming macrobiotic, high-protein, weight-loss, high-fat, or high–junk food diets) should receive special attention and be educated on the potential complications and risks of these habits to both the mother and the fetus. Vegetarian, vegan, and macrobiotic diets are not necessarily inappropriate as long as certain parameters are monitored. These include regular physical exams and prenatal checks, appropriate weight gain, and laboratory testing. Even women that have done well or seemingly well on these diets prior to pregnancy may not do well when pregnant or nursing. Other women may suffer from an inadequate caloric intake because of their fear of weight gain, inadequate education about pregnancy, or insufficient money to purchase enough nutritious food.

Some women are potentially at nutritional risk. These include women who have had several full term pregnancies, previous low-birth-weight deliveries, and short intervals between births. Women with medical conditions such as diabetes mellitus, chronic renal disease, anemia, and phenylketonuria all require special attention to dietary counseling. Use of prescribed medications, over-the-counter drugs, vitamin and mineral supplements, laxatives, and diet aids should all be reviewed by a qualified health care practitioner.

The average amount of weight gain is 28 pounds. The maternal component of weight accumulation starts in the first trimester and is most prominent in the first half of the pregnancy. The growth of the fetus is most rapid in the second half of the pregnancy. In the last 12 weeks, the weight of the fetus more than triples.

Optimal health during pregnancy not only helps to ensure a healthy baby but also helps to determine the health of the mother after the birth. A foundation well laid during the pregnancy can provide the necessary support in the postpartum period, throughout breast-feeding, and during the years to come when the demands of raising young children are high. When contemplating pregnancy, the first step that needs to be taken is a commitment to eat healthfully throughout that period. Support of family and friends during days of not feeling well along with assistance with shopping and cooking can help in keeping that commitment. Almost every pregnant woman will experience cravings. The main problem with cravings arises when cravings for chocolate, sodas, sweets, and ice cream become substitutes for nutritious foods. Cravings often can also be clues about specific nutritional needs. A craving for ice cream may indicate an increased need for protein, fat, or calcium. A craving for acid foods like pickles may be a clue to increased need for calcium or salt. A craving for sweets may indicate a physical need for more protein in the diet. Cravings for chips can indicate a need for more salt and even fats. A continued effort should be made to replace these junk foods with healthier nutritious choices.

The best way to ensure that you are eating well is to establish a balanced, wide variety of foods, including whole-grain cereals and breads, vegetables and fruits, nuts, seeds, legumes, and complementary amounts of dairy products and meats, especially fish and poultry. If you are unfamiliar with natural foods, try to find a nutritional practitioner who can advise you and begin to make appropriate changes in your diet. Books on nutrition and cooking also can be of help as you try to incorporate healthy foods into your diet. If you already eat a very healthy diet, then it is important to ensure that you are eating adequate amounts of food. If you are on a restricted diet or follow a specific dietary system, I would advise you to seek the advice of a knowledgeable health care practitioner in the area of nutrition. Generally this would be a licensed naturopathic physician or a nutritionist/dietitian. The following general guidelines for daily food servings have been proposed as the "daily dozen" in *What to Eat When You're Expecting*.[24]

- Calories: plenty of healthy foods to ensure adequate calories (2,300) daily

- Protein: 4 servings (either vegetable or animal sources—74 grams total)
- Calcium foods: 4 servings daily (dairy and non-dairy sources)
- Vitamin C–rich fruits and vegetables: 2 servings
- Green leafy vegetables and yellow fruits and vegetables: 3 servings
- Other veggies and fruits: 1–2 servings
- Whole grains and other complex carbohydrates: 4–6 servings
- Iron-rich foods daily
- High fat foods: 2 servings
- Salt: in moderation, to taste
- Fluids: at least 6–8 glasses
- Supplements: nutritious herbs, highly concentrated food supplements (soy or green drinks), and a vitamin/mineral supplement

The Food and Nutrition Board of the Institute of Medicine has published Recommended Dietary Allowances (RDAs) periodically since 1943. The RDAs are listed by nutrient in the nutritional supplement section following this section.

The question of how many calories per day to consume is dependent upon many variables. The input portion of the energy equation includes the consumed food plus the amount of stored fuel in the body. The output variable in the equation includes the metabolic rate, thermogenesis, and physical activity. The caloric content of the diet required to supply daily energy needs and achieve optimal weight gain can be estimated by multiplying one's optimal body weight in kilograms by 35 and adding 300 to the total.

All pregnant women will benefit from prenatal nutritional education that focuses on healthy nutritional practices. Some women will require specialized instruction about food content, meal planning, and dietary requirements. Women with a history of anorexia, bulimia, obesity, diabetes, chronic kidney disease, chronic gastrointestinal diseases, or extreme diets may need more individualized education and nutritional therapy. Some women will lack the financial resources to purchase sufficient amounts of nutritious food. For low-income pregnant and postpartum lactating women, for infants, and for children up to the age of five years at nutritional risk, assistance is available through the federal Supplemental Food Program for Women, Infants and Children (WIC). Food stamp programs and Aid to Families with Dependent Children may also be available for women. Other local, private, church, county, and state organizations may also be a source of assistance.

The postnatal period is another time period where the physiological demands of lactation and breast-feeding put continued and additional nutritional strain on the mother. The production of breast milk requires an additional average of 640 calories per day. Optimal milk production requires a total daily caloric intake of at least 1,800 calories. The energy sources are fat stores and diet that need to supply an additional 500 calories per day. Intake of water, juice, and milk (cow, goat, almond, soy, oat, or rice) to satisfy thirst is sufficient for breast milk production needs. The well-balanced, varied, whole foods diet that was consumed prenatally should be maintained postnatally. The monthly loss of iron with breast-feeding is about half that of regular menstruation, and because women do not menstruate during breast-feeding, their iron stores are usually replenished. Some vitamins and other minerals, however, may be depleted during lactation. Continued nutritional supplementation with a prenatal vitamin or, even better, a postnatal vitamin can prevent deficiencies and is even important if the diet is sufficient. After rapid weight loss in the first month, the lactating mother of normal weight may lose weight at a rate of about two pounds a month without affecting milk volume. For the obese woman, losing four pounds a month is also safe. Intentional weight reduction diets or rapid weight loss during lactation are not advisable. At one year after delivery, a two-pound residual additional weight is considered average.

Nutritional Supplements

Vitamin B Complex

Folic Acid

Folate is the only vitamin whose requirement doubles in pregnancy.[8] Deficiencies of folic acid have been linked to low-birth-weight infants and neural tube defects. According to one controlled study, women at high risk (having previously given birth to babies with neural tube defects) were given folate supplementation and showed a 72 percent protective effect compared to the placebo group.[25] In another study, a group of pregnant women given folate supplementation gave birth to infants with increased birth weight and Apgar scores and had a decreased incidence of fetal growth retardation and maternal infections.[26] Other studies also showed significant prevention with supplementation.[27–30] Because of firmly established connections between deficiencies of folic acid and low-birth-weight infants and neural tube defects, the U.S. Public Health Service recommends that all women of childbearing age take daily folic acid supplementation to reduce their risk of congenital birth defects.

Dietary folic acid is a mixture of folates in the form of polyglutamates, which are readily destroyed by cooking. Higher levels of dietary folate intake have been shown in some cases to decrease the incidence of neural tube defects, but women hereditarily predisposed to such defects may need to take in more folic acid through supplements in order to reach optimal levels.[31] Folic acid can be found in green leafy vegetables, nuts, whole grains,[32] liver, watercress, parsley, and dandelion.[33] With artificial supplementation, care must be taken, because large doses of folic acid have been associated with maternal infection, abnormally slow fetal heart rate,[34] and a decrease in zinc absorption, a mineral required for proper fetal growth and immunity.[35]

Folic acid
Pregnant: 800 mcg per day
Nursing: 500 mcg per day
Food sources: *green leafy vegetables, nuts, whole grains, liver, watercress, parsley, dandelion*

Niacin (*Nicotinic acid*)

Niacin supplementation in the first trimester has been positively correlated with higher birth weight, longer length, and appropriate newborn head circumference (all signs of healthier infants).[36]

> **Vitamin B₃ (niacin)**
>
> *Pregnant: 17mg per day*
>
> *Nursing: 20 mg per day*
>
> *Food sources: wheat germ, fish, garlic*
>
> *Herbal sources: alfalfa, burdock root and seed, dandelion, parsley*

Riboflavin (Vitamin B₂)

Studies show that riboflavin depletion is common during pregnancy (up to 40 percent less at term than nonpregnant women and men), so riboflavin supplementation is recommended to prevent metabolic disturbances.[37]

> **Vitamin B₂ (riboflavin)**
>
> *Pregnant: 1.6 mg per day*
>
> *Nursing: 1.8 mg per day*
>
> *Food sources: watercress, brown rice*
>
> *Herbal sources: rose hips, parsley, saffron, dandelion, dulse, kelp, fenugreek*

Thiamin (Vitamin B₁)

Direct correlation has been shown between supplementation of thiamin early in pregnancy and higher infant birth weight and size.[36] Thiamin depletion is common during pregnancy. Supplementation, therefore, is recommended.[38]

> **Vitamin B₁ (thiamin)**
>
> *Pregnant: 1.5 mg per day*
>
> *Nursing: 1.6 mg per day*
>
> *Food sources: green peas, bell peppers, sunflower seeds*
>
> *Herbal sources: alfalfa, dandelion, fenugreek, raspberry leaf, red clover, seaweed*

Vitamin B₆ (Pyridoxine)

Vitamin B₆ is "marginally deficient" in about 50 percent of pregnant women.[39] Supplementation has been linked to relief of nausea and morning sickness, especially in extreme cases that include vomiting.[40, 41] In one experimental study, 75 percent of women taking vitamin B₆ experienced complete relief from symptoms of morning sickness.[42] Higher doses were used for treatment of first trimester morning sickness (25–200 mg, 3 times daily) but are not recommended before delivery, as higher doses may shut off breast milk in nursing mothers or cause the baby withdrawal seizures if commercial formula is given that does not include enough pyridoxine (B₆).[43-4] However, when given during labor, vitamin B₆ may prevent many postnatal adaptation problems by increasing the oxygen-carrying capacity of the blood.[45] Supplementation may also prevent toxemia of pregnancy (pre-eclampsia).[46]

> **Vitamin B₆ (pyridoxine)**
>
> *Pregnant: 2.2 mg per day*
>
> *Nursing: 2.1 mg per day*
>
> *Food sources: whole grains, wheat germ, egg yolks, peas, carrots*

Vitamin B₁₂

The coenzyme form of vitamin B₁₂ is a very complex molecule containing cobalt, designated in humans as cobalamin, which is required for proper homocysteine metabolism. At least 12 different inherited inborn errors of metabolism related to cobalamin are known; low plasma vitamin B₁₂ levels were shown to be an independent risk factor for neural tube defect in one study.[47] B₁₂ may also help to prevent anemia. Supplementation is recommended. A study published in 1982 reported that 92 percent of vegans in the United States had serum B₁₂ levels below normal range.[48] The reason for this is that vitamin B₁₂ generally is absent from plant/vegetable foods. Vitamin B₁₂ is produced by microorganisms (e.g., actinomycetes). Therefore, fermented soybeans and some legumes and seaweeds (including spirulina), which have symbiotic microorganisms, can be a good source of this vitamin.

> **Vitamin B$_{12}$ (cobalamin)**
>
> *Pregnant: 2.2 mcg per day*
>
> *Nursing: 2.6 mcg per day*
>
> *Food sources: fermented soybeans, legumes, seaweeds, spirulina*

Vitamin A

The consumption of too much vitamin A by pregnant women may cause birth defects. In 1987, the Centers for Disease Control, the Teratology Society, and the Council for Responsible Nutrition independently published recommendations in order to reduce pregnant women's exposure to excessive amounts of vitamin A in supplements.[49–51]

Daily doses of 40,000 units or more of vitamin A during pregnancy may be toxic.[52] A study of 22,000 pregnant women who consumed more than 15,000 units of vitamin A per day from food and supplements, or 10,000 units as a supplement, showed a significant increase in birth defects associated with cranial-neural-crest tissue.[53] Most of these women consumed the vitamin A before the seventh week of pregnancy. Elevated blood levels of vitamin A have also been correlated with low birth weights.[54]

The recommendations issued in 1987 by the Centers for Disease Control, the Teratology Society, and the Council for Responsible Nutrition were the result of teratogenesis that was thought to occur at some level above 8,000 IU of vitamin A per day. The recommendations included limiting supplemental vitamin A for pregnant women to 5,000–8,000 IU per day. Other researchers have tried to clarify the situation further and report that the consumption of less than 10,000 IU of vitamin A per day from a vitamin supplement is safe.[53] They also report that more than 10,000 IU of vitamin A per day from a supplement is associated with an increased risk of birth defects in the infant. So here we have a little gap—is it less than 8,000 IU or less than 10,000 IU that is safe? I recommend the cautious route, less than 8,000 IU. It is worth considering the avoidance of vitamin A altogether during pregnancy and just supplementing with beta carotene.

Preterm infants have been shown to be deficient in vitamin A, which may predispose them to developing chronic lung disease.[55] In addition, healthy pregnant women who developed pre-eclampsia also were shown to be deficient in vitamin A (but not beta carotene).[56] Pre-eclampsia is a potentially dangerous condition characterized by high blood pressure, swelling, and/or protein spilling into the urine. Supplementation with no more than 6,000 units of vitamin A is recommended.[57] Beta carotene, which has the same positive effects as vitamin A, has not been associated with toxicity or teratogenicity in humans or animals,[58] and many supplement companies now put beta carotene into their prenatal supplements instead of vitamin A.

Plant sources of the nontoxic "provitamin A" beta carotene are organic fruits and vegetables, especially yellow and orange ones; for example, one sweet potato or one cup of carrot juice contains 25,000 IU of beta carotene.[59]

> **Vitamin A**
>
> *Do not exceed 6,000 IU daily*
>
> or
>
> **Mixed carotenoids**
>
> *Pregnant: 10,000 IU per day*
>
> *Nursing: 10,000 IU per day*
>
> *Food sources: yellow and orange fruits and vegetables*
>
> *Herbal sources: alfalfa, cayenne, comfrey, dandelion, elderberries, lamb's quarters, seaweed*

Vitamin C

Vitamin C plays a vital role in the formation of collagen—a major protein found in connective tissue, cartilage, and bone—and is chronically deficient. It is essential to the nerves, healthy gums, and teeth, and prevents infection. Although one study showed that women who took 5,000 mg of vitamin C daily during pregnancy delivered healthy infants who developed scurvy,[60] this "rebound scurvy" is very rare, and the affected infant recovers quickly without treatment. Supplementation with vitamin C may be as effective as calcium for leg cramps during pregnancy.[61]

Vitamin C

Pregnant: 70 mg per day

Nursing: 95 mg per day

Food sources: cabbage, cucumbers, all fruits (especially citrus), green chilies, honey, tomatoes, prunes

Herbal sources: alfalfa, cayenne, dandelion greens, elderberries, nettles, parsley, rose hips

---

Vitamin D

The absorption of vitamin D (as well as calcium, which vitamin D helps metabolize) is enhanced during pregnancy. Since vitamin D tends toward toxicity, supplementation should be moderate to prevent excessive amounts of it from accumulating. Fish oil and sunshine are good sources of natural vitamin D, which benefits the development of good teeth and bones.

Vitamin D

Pregnant: 10 mcg per day

Nursing: 10 mcg per day

Source: sunshine

Food sources: fish, fortified milk

Herbal sources: alfalfa, nettles

Vitamin E

Vitamin E status declines during pregnancy, creating deficiencies, and fetal vitamin E levels are usually low.[62] Lower plasma levels in the mother may be associated with increased risk of pre-eclampsia, as well as premature and low-birth-weight infants.[63] Supplementation has been shown to be effective in preventing habitual or chronic abortion.[64]

Vitamin E

Pregnant: 10 mg per day

Nursing: 12 mg per day

Food sources: brown rice, parsley, wheat germ

Herbal sources: alfalfa, dandelion, raspberry leaf, rosehips, seaweed

---

Vitamin K

Necessary for bone metabolism, vitamin K is required by law in most states to be given to newborns in the hospital by injection in the foot immediately after birth, or a shot of the vitamin is given during labor to prevent hemolytic disease in the newborn. This condition is characterized by anemia, jaundice, enlargement of the liver and spleen, and generalized edema. Naturopathic doctors recommend checking the pregnant mother's diet for vitamin K deficiency (to see if she is getting enough of the vitamin through her intake of squash and dark leafy vegetables). If needed, oral supplementation of vitamin K would be added in the last month of pregnancy rather than automatically giving the shots, which in some studies have been linked to childhood cancer.[65]

Vitamin K (along with vitamin C) is effective in preventing the nausea and vomiting of early pregnancy and may reduce the risk of intraventricular hemorrhage in premature infants.[66] Nettle or alfalfa leaf tea taken throughout the pregnancy will increase available vitamin K and hemoglobin in the blood.

Vitamin K

Pregnant: 65 mcg

Nursing: 65 mcg

Food sources: parsley, brown rice, leafy green vegetables, kelp

Herbal sources: alfalfa, nettles

Calcium

Women are often advised to consume additional calcium during pregnancy and lactation. The assumption has been that calcium intake should be increased from 800–1,200 mg/day during both pregnancy and lactation.[67] In recent years, more has been learned about the changes in calcium homeostasis that occur during pregnancy and lactation. Calcium absorption studies, bone density testing, and blood and urinary markers of bone metabolism have enabled us to view pregnancy and calcium needs differently. One recent study was able to show that the calcium required for fetal bone mineralization is obtained by an increased efficiency of maternal calcium absorption in pregnancy, with no detectable increase in mobilizing calcium from the mother's bone to her blood.[68] This study, as well as a British study,[69] both show that calcium mobilization to the fetus and to breast milk was the result of changes in maternal metabolism, which were not influenced by the amount of dietary calcium consumed. These studies also support the recently revised recommended U.S.-Canadian dietary guidelines that no increase in calcium intake is required for either pregnant or lactating women.[70] Lactating adolescents may need more calcium, and breast-feeding more than one infant could cause more bone calcium loss and thus put one at greater risk of calcium deficit.[71]

A deficiency of calcium can pose health risks for pregnant women. Low dietary intake is associated with pre-eclampsia,[72] a potentially dangerous (but preventable) condition characterized by high blood pressure, swelling, and/or protein spilling into the urine. Supplementation with calcium may reduce the risk of preterm delivery and may also prevent the hypertensive disorders of pregnancy.[73] Calcium supplementation can also help to ease leg cramps during pregnancy.

Excessive levels of calcium in the body, however, can result in spillage into the urine and kidney stones. Supplementation with calcium must be done with efficient forms of the mineral, such as calcium citrate or citrate/malate, which are the more absorbable forms. Also, attention must be paid to the relationship between calcium and other minerals, such as magnesium and zinc.

Raspberry leaf tea contains calcium in its most absorbable form, as do nettle tea, fresh parsley, and watercress. Other food sources of calcium include milk products (although consumption of these can

lead to an allergic condition in the baby), dark green leafy vegetables, asparagus, and pumpkin seeds. Avoid bone meal or oyster shell calcium tablets, which have been found to be high in lead, mercury, cadmium, and other toxic metals.

Chromium, Cobalt, and Copper

These three trace minerals were positively associated in studies with higher infant birth weights, and supplementation is therefore recommended.[73]

> **Chromium**
> *120 mcg*
> **Cobalt**
> *presumably, as part of B_{12}, 2 mcg*
> **Copper**
> *2 mg*

Iron

Some researchers have concluded that iron supplementation is essential during pregnancy in order to maintain adequate maternal iron stores. But iron supplementation can exacerbate zinc depletion by blocking absorption of that mineral, so any supplementation should be warranted only after tests that show a deficiency in the mother's hemoglobin. Routine iron supplementation during pregnancy is not clearly indicated.[74] One textbook has stated that "women who are not anemic at the beginning of pregnancy and who do not receive iron supplementation have a significant drop in hemoglobin concentration, serum iron, chelated serum ferritin levels at term, whereas such changes do not occur in women supplemented with iron."[75]

For women who get sufficient iron in the first trimester of pregnancy, studies show a definite

> **Calcium carbonate**
> *Pregnant: 1,000 mg per day if age 19–50, 1,300 mg per day if under age 18; or half as much calcium citrate/malate*
> *Nursing: same as for pregnancy*
> *Food sources: asparagus, dairy products, dark green leafy vegetables, pumpkin seeds, parsley*
> *Herbal sources: raspberry leaf tea, nettle tea*

> **Iron**
> *Pregnant: 30 mg per day*
> *Nursing: 15 mg per day*
> *Food sources: almonds, beets (including greens), egg yolks, honey, organ meats (liver, kidney, heart)*
> *Herbal sources: alfalfa, dandelion, nettles, kelp*

positive association with infant birth weight and size (but not in the second and third trimesters).[36]

Magnesium

Magnesium deficiencies are associated with pre-eclampsia[76, 77] and preterm labor.[78] Supplementation must be in the first trimester to positively affect birth weight and size. Researchers think that magnesium may act by opposing calcium-dependent arterial vasoconstriction. Magnesium also prevents cell damage and death. For alternative practitioners, it may be the first thing to try in the treatment of pre-eclampsia.[79] Magnesium supplementation may reduce the complications of pregnancy and improve the health of the infant. The effect of magnesium was studied in 568 women who received a supplement of magnesium aspartate for 16 weeks.[16] Magnesium supplementation was associated with significantly fewer maternal hospitalizations, a reduction in preterm delivery, and less frequent referral of the newborn to the neonatal intensive care unit. The results suggest that supplementing pregnant women with magnesium has a significant influence on fetal and maternal health both before and after delivery.

Magnesium

Pregnant: 300 mg per day

Nursing: 355 mg per day

Food sources: almonds, barley, dried fruits, honey, potatoes

Herbal sources: alfalfa, dandelion, dulse (seaweed)

Potassium

Supplementing with potassium is probably not necessary in pregnant or nursing women.

Potassium

Food sources: bananas, bran, green leafy vegetables, olives, potatoes (especially peels)

Herbal sources: alfalfa, chamomile, dandelion, nettles

Zinc

Zinc is required for proper fetal growth and immunity. Plasma zinc levels decline about 30 percent during pregnancy,[80] and low zinc intake in animal studies is associated with spontaneous abortion and premature delivery.[81] In human studies, low zinc was also associated with complications and labor abnormalities[82] as well as the specific complication of fetal distress.[83] It may also be associated with central nervous system abnormalities in infants, including neural tube defects[84, 85] low-birth-weight infants,[86–88] and toxemia of pregnancy.[89] Supplementation, especially if zinc levels are low, is recommended to reduce the risk of fetal and maternal complications.[90] In one study, complications during labor (vaginal bleeding, fetal acidosis, uterine inertia) were improved.[91]

Another study showed a lower incidence of pregnancy induced hypertension (which is associated with pre-eclampsia and preterm labor).[92]

Zinc

Pregnant: 15 mg per day

Nursing: 19 mg per day

Food sources: beets, broccoli, fish, lentils, oysters, wheat bran and germ

---

Bioflavonoids

When women who chronically abort were placed on citrus bioflavonoids daily as soon as a period was missed, many stopped aborting.[93] There is no RDA for bioflavonoids, but this nutrient can be found in grapefruit, oranges, apricots, tomatoes, currants, strawberries, onions, apples, and many other familiar fruits and vegetables.

Essential Fatty Acids (EFAs)

Evening primrose oil has been shown effective in preventing pregnancy induced hypertension.[94] The main food sources of essential fatty acids are raw seeds and nuts or fish. Whole and ground flaxseeds or the purified flaxseed oil are excellent sources of the two essential oils, linoleic and linolenic acid.

Borage oil and black currant oil can be taken in capsule form as nutritional supplements. There is no RDA for EFAs.

CoQ10

Coenzyme Q10 is a fat soluble quinone occurring in the mitochondria of every cell whose primary biochemical action is as a cofactor in the electron transport chain on which most cellular functions rely. Thus it is essential for the health of virtually all human tissues and organs. Plasma levels of this enzyme rise during normal pregnancy, reaching highs of 50 percent above normal by the 36th week. Decreased levels have been linked to spontaneous abortion and threatened abortion, particularly before 12 weeks.[95]

Every plant and animal cell contains CoQ10, but vegetarians absorb double the amount that omnivores do. There is no RDA for this nutrient.

Methionine (SAM)

Methionine, a sulfur-containing amino acid, is a component of many proteins, serving as a source of available sulfur for synthesizing both cysteine and taurine, crucial to cellular metabolism. Supplementation with methionine in mice reduced neural tube defects by 47 percent,[96] and also positively affected birth weight and size.[97] There is no RDA for methionine.

Phosphatidylcholine (PC)

PC is one of the major phospholipids in the cell membrane. It is commonly called lecithin. It represents a large proportion of the body's store of choline, a very important precursor for neurotransmitters and a critical nutrient for brain and nerve development and function. Most lecithin taken orally is broken down in the small intestine by lecithinase. Lecithin itself is produced in the liver from its elements. In mammals, amniotic fluid has a ten-fold greater concentration of choline than that of maternal blood[98] and, at birth, all mammals studied have plasma choline concentrations much higher than those found in adults.[99] When rats were supplemented with choline, the spatial memory of their offspring was permanently enhanced, and they showed more accurate performance on both working and reference memory components of tasks. These studies[99, 100] suggest that choline is critical for optimal brain development, and therefore supplementation is suggested.

Soybeans and eggs are excellent sources of lecithin. Other sources include liver, wheat germ, peanuts, and all plant-ripened vegetables in trace amounts. There is no RDA for PC.

Taurine

Taurine is an amino acid found widely distributed in foods of animal origin (but not in milk or milk products). Taurine is biosynthesized from methionine or from cysteine. Disturbances in the enzymatic reactions of taurine synthesis can lead to mental retardation. Vegetarian mothers who consume no meat products during their pregnancy and therefore have low taurine intakes, and others on a protein-, methionine-, or B_6-deficient diet might be at particular risk.[101] Although dietary deficiency of taurine has not been demonstrated to impact fetal development in humans, vegetarian women who intend to have children should consider taking an amino acid supplement, since there is no taurine present in plants.

Botanicals

There are many herbs that can be used safely during pregnancy. Some herbs are characterized as tonics, others are spices that improve taste and digestion, other herbs contain specific vitamins and minerals that aid different organ systems, and still others can be used as medicines to intervene and treat certain conditions or illnesses related to the pregnancy. However, there are some herbs that are commonly contraindicated for use during pregnancy. Although even some of these herbs may be used in very small amounts for specific conditions, it is prudent to avoid them unless under the supervision of an expert in herbal medicine. Some of these contraindicated herbs can be used safely late in the pregnancy or during labor with the guidance of an experienced practitioner (see Table 14.1).

TABLE 14.1   **Herbs Contraindicated During Pregnancy**

Common Name	Latin Name	Common Name	Latin Name
Alder buckthorn	Rhamnus frangula	Ipecac	Ipecac ipecacuanha
Aloes	Aloe vera	Juniper berries	Juniperis communis
Angelica	Angelica archangelica	Licorice	Glycyrrhiza glabra
Arnica	Arnica montana	Lily of the valley	Convallaria majalis
Autumn crocus	Colchicum autumnale	Lobelia	Lobelia inflata
Barberry	Berberis vulgaris	Male fern	Dryopteris filix-mas
Bethroot	Trillium spp.	Mandrake	Podophyllum peltatum
Black cohosh	Cimicifuga racemosa	Mistletoe	Viscum album
Blessed thistle	Carbenia benedicta	Mugwort	Artemesia vulgare
Blood root	Sanguinaria canadensis	Nutmeg*	Carum petroselinum
Blue cohosh	Caulophyllum thalictroides	Pennyroyal	Mentha pulegium
Broom	Sarpthamnus scoparius	Periwinkle	Vinca spp.
Butternut	Juglans canadensis	Peruvian bark	Cinchona spp.
Calamus	Acorus calamus	Pleurisy root	Aesclepius tuberosa
Calendula	Calendula officinalis	Poke root	Phytolacca decandra
Cascara sagrada	Rhamnus purshiana	Rue	Ruta graveolens
Coltsfoot	Tussilago farfara	Rhubarb	Rheum palmatum
Cowslip	Primula veris	Sage*	Salvia officinalis
Damiana	Turnera aphrodisiaca	Sarsaparilla	Smilax officinale
Dong quai	Angelica sinensis	Senna	Cassia senna
Ephedra (Ma huang)	Ephedra vulgaris	Shepherd's purse	Capsella bursa-pastoris
Feverfew	Tanacetum parthenium	Stillingia	Stillingia sylvatica
Ginseng	Panax quinquefolium	Tansy	Tanacetum vulgare
Goat's rue	Galega officinalis	Thuja	Thuja occidentalis
Goldenseal	Hydrastis canadensis	Wormwood	Artemesia absinthinum
Gotu kola	Hydrocotyle asiatica	Yarrow	Achillea millefolium

*Small amounts of nutmeg and sage used in cooking are okay.

Note: Some of the herbs listed above may be recommended by a licensed practitioner with expertise in the use of botanicals during pregnancy and labor.

The following herbs are some of the most common medicinal plants used in traditional herbal practice for promoting and maintaining health during pregnancy.

Dandelion Leaf and Root

Dandelion is a potent source of vitamins and minerals, especially vitamin A, calcium, potassium, and iron. Mildly diuretic and stimulating to bile flow, dandelion leaf helps with the inevitable digestive complaints of pregnancy, and its root cleanses and tones the liver.[102] In early pregnancy, dandelion can help to alleviate nausea, upset stomach, and indigestion. As a diuretic, the most active part of the plant is the leaf. The root or the leaf can be taken as a tea, in capsule form, or as a liquid tincture (a mixture of plant/alcohol/water). It can be safely taken throughout pregnancy as a tonic or to address one of the indicated specific problems associated with pregnancy.

False Unicorn (*Chamaelirium luteum*)

False unicorn has traditionally been used as a uterine tonic before, during, and after pregnancy, especially for women who have had a history of miscarriage. Similar to dandelion, it is used to support liver and digestive function. Due to its bitter taste, this herb is probably best tolerated in capsule or tincture form, rather than as a tea.

Ginger Root (*Zingiber officinale*)

Ginger root is probably best known for its treatment of nausea and vomiting, whether pregnancy or not. Ginger has even been studied in *hyperemesis gravidarum*, the most severe form of pregnancy-related nausea and vomiting. In a double-blind, randomized, crossover trial, 250 mg of ginger root powder taken four times a day significantly reduced the severity of the nausea and the number of attacks of vomiting in 19 of 27 pregnant women, who were in an early stage of pregnancy.[103] Ginger is safe to use at any time during the pregnancy and is a welcome alternative to some of the antinausea pharmaceuticals that may be associated with teratogenicity.

Nettle (*Urtica dioica*)

Nettle is one of the best herbs to use in pregnancy due to its appreciable amounts of vitamins and minerals, including calcium and iron. Used throughout the pregnancy, nettles can help to improve energy, strengthen the blood vessels, reduce varicose veins, alleviate leg cramps, prevent anemia, and decrease the likelihood of hemorrhage during childbirth. This is an herb that can be taken in all forms, including freshly picked young leaves from the forest as a leafy green addition to steamed vegetables or salads.

Partridgeberry (*Mitchella repens*)

Partridgeberry or squaw vine is considered one of the best uterine tonics. It should be taken for several weeks before the due date. Squaw vine is often used in combination with raspberry leaf. It can be taken as a tea, in capsule form, or as a tincture.

Red Raspberry (*Rubus idaeus*)

Red raspberry leaf is the most-often mentioned traditional herbal tonic for general support of pregnancy and breast-feeding. Rich in vitamins and minerals, especially high in naturally chelated iron (well assimilated), it tones the uterus, increases the flow of milk, and restores the reproductive system after childbirth. Raspberry leaf contains fragrine, an alkaloid that gives tone to the muscles of the pelvic region including the uterus itself. In addition to tonifying the uterus, raspberry is used to prevent hemorrhage and is rich in iron and vitamins C and E. It deserves its reputation as a pregnancy herb par excellence.

Wild Yam (*Dioscorea villosa* and *barbasco*)

Wild yam can be used to help prevent miscarriage due to its calming and antispasmodic action on the uterus. Even though wild yam has acquired a considerable reputation as a "female herb," perhaps its most traditional uses are as a digestive aid in treating nausea, an antispasmodic for intestinal and gallbladder colic, and as a liver herb. This herb is best used in capsule or tincture form. To help prevent miscarriage, higher doses of the tincture can be used, ¼–½ tsp every 3–4 hours.

Exercise

Sternfeld[104] concludes her excellent 1997 review on "Physical Activity and Pregnancy Outcome" stating that "the appropriate public health message, based on research to date, is probably not that women *should* exercise during pregnancy, but that they *may*." The cautious "permission" given pregnant women to exercise if they so choose echoes previous efforts at regulating a behavior that is potentially dangerous, not to the woman, but to the fetus she carries. In some segments of the American population, observed James Clapp in 1984,[105] 25 percent of exercising pregnant women planned to keep on exercising throughout their pregnancies.

The possible public health impact of increasingly larger numbers of exercising pregnant women likely prompted the publication of the *Guidelines for Exercise During Pregnancy and Postpartum* by the American College of Obstetricians and Gynecologists (ACOG) in 1985.[106]

Evaluation of the 1985 ACOG guidelines has suggested that they may be "too stringent" for well-conditioned women.[107, 108] Mona Shanghold, a physician and director of the Sports Gynecology Center at Georgetown University, raised the concern that the guidelines were primarily written by a male physician[109] and needlessly restrictive. She, therefore, published her own guidelines in which she advises the pregnant woman to "continue the same sport or activity at the same level of perceived exertion." The word "perceived" puts the responsibility where it belongs—on the woman who chooses to exercise during pregnancy.

If she elects to exercise during pregnancy, a woman may want information. Fortunately, information on exercise and pregnancy, despite conflicting opinions, is plentiful and its message clear: there is no evidence for any harmful effects of exercise on pregnancy.

Since the publication of the ACOG guidelines in 1985 (revised less conservatively in 1994),[110] research efforts at substantiating the potential harmful effects of exercise on pregnancy outcomes have greatly intensified as is seen in the large number of reviews of the literature on the subject published in just four years. Our search detected seven review articles published between 1994 and 1997.[111–115] The intensive search for answers notwithstanding, the hypothetical dangers of maternal exercise to the fetus have remained just that, hypothetical.

However, the concern that exercise in pregnancy might harm the fetus is justifiable. Studies in rats and ewes have shown increased plasma corticosterone in maternal and fetal blood immediately following treadmill running,[116, 117] and decreased uteroplacental blood flow and incidence of live births in rats, sheep, and pygmy goats.[118]

Moreover, among humans, work-related physical exertion appears detrimental to the fetus, particularly in late pregnancy. Thus, some studies have reported significantly increased observed to expected (O/E) ratios for abortion in women exposed to occupational high levels of physical stress, particularly weight lifting, other physical effort, and standing, as well as increased ratios for stillbirth from other physical effort and vibration in the work place.[119] Epidemiological studies have negated this effect of work-related weight lifting, but have corroborated the observed positive relationship between long hours of job standing and/or walking and preterm labor.[120]

A case report of 3,174 (cases and controls) nulliparous pregnant women who received prenatal care and delivered a live baby at the University of Pavia, Italy, between 1990 and 1994, observed a twofold increase in the risk of severe pre-eclampsia with work-related moderate to high physical activity, as compared to mild physical activity in pregnancy.[121] Finally, a prospective study of 2,743 pregnant women found only small differences in pregnancy outcome and related occupational physical demands.[122] Similar findings were observed by Schramm and colleagues.[123]

Several reasons may account for these differing results: self-selection, lack of randomization, and variation between species. The principal contrast between job-related physical exertion and recreational exercise is that the first is mandatory and of much longer duration per session than the latter. Voluntary and mandatory physical exertion have been shown to have disparate effects in breast cancer development in animals: voluntary exercise was protective, whereas forced exercise was not.[124–126]

Results of recent studies indicate, in essence, that in healthy pregnancies, exercise significantly reduced length of hospitalization and incidence of cesarean section and increased Apgar scores.[127, 128] Exercise also increased birth weight[108] (although duration and intensity of exercise beyond a certain point may decrease birth weight),[129] reduced hypoxic stress,[130] and elevated maternal blood volume.[131] Also, it did not interfere with fetal fat mass[132] and caused no change in fetal heart rate.[133] Finally, women who exercised during pregnancy reported less discomfort,[134–136] maintained ideal body weight,[137] and showed no hypoglycemia despite decreased blood sugar.[138, 139]

Stretching and Breathing Exercises[140]

The Speak Pregnancy Exercises described in Appendix A may be used alone if the reader is beginning an exercise program during pregnancy. If the reader intends to continue an already existing exercise program, this sequence may be added at the close of the exercise session.

Weight Training Guidelines

1. Do not compete, not even with yourself.
2. Begin with very light weights, so that you can perform 12–15 repetitions of the exercise easily.
3. Avoid holding your breath while lifting. Breathe in during relaxing part of exercise and breathe out during effort part of exercise.
4. Rest between exercises.
5. Take a mouthful of pure water between exercises.

EXERCISE RECOMMENDATIONS

Contraindications

Pregnancy-induced hypertension, toxemia, pre-eclampsia, preterm rupture of membranes, history of preterm labor, persistent second or third trimester bleeding, incompetent cervix, or signs of intrauterine growth retardation are conditions in which exercise may be contraindicated.

Safety Tips[141]

1. Fluid intake during and after exercise should be adequate to prevent dehydration and hypovolemia.
2. Clothing worn during exercise should allow for adequate ventilation and prevention of hyperthermia.
3. Do not exercise if you have a fever.
4. Supine exercise should be avoided, especially in the third trimester.
5. Exercises that require repetitive bouncing and jerky movements should be avoided, especially in the third trimester.
6. Recommended exercise regimens should emphasize low-impact activities, such as stationary bicycling, swimming, walking, and low-impact aerobics.
7. Activities that involve potential low-oxygen states, such as scuba diving and mountain climbing, are contraindicated.
8. The exercising pregnant woman should be encouraged to follow a diet that emphasizes complex carbohydrates to replace muscle glycogen lost during exercise, thereby minimizing the risk of fetal ketosis.
9. Participation in competitive team sports is acceptable in the first 15 weeks of pregnancy, if the woman understands that there are potential but unproved risks for fetal loss from pelvic trauma, abdominal trauma, or both.
10. Exercises requiring significant use of Valsalva's maneuver, such as weight lifting, should be avoided, especially in the third trimester.

Summary of 1994 ACOG Guidelines[110]

1. Regular frequency of exercise is preferable to sporadic physical activity.
2. Exercise in the supine position should be avoided after the first trimester.
3. Intensity of exercise should be monitored according to symptoms, and exhaustive exercise should be avoided.
4. Exercises requiring balance should be avoided, particularly in the third trimester.
5. Adequate caloric and nutrient intake should be maintained.
6. Adequate hydration, proper clothing, and avoidance of hot, humid environments should augment heat dissipation, especially in the first trimester.

Georgetown University Sports Gynecology Center Guidelines[109]

1. Continue the same sport or activity at the same level of perceived exertion. Since exercise becomes more difficult as pregnancy progresses, the required level of perceived exertion will occur sooner at a lower level of intensity.
2. Body temperature should not exceed 101 degrees.
3. Maximal heart rate should be between, but not exceed, 140–160 beats/min.
4. Total weight gain should be 20–30 pounds.
5. Adequate consumption of calories, vitamins, iron, and calcium is important.
6. Drink plenty of fluids.
7. Do not exercise at high altitudes or in high temperatures.
8. Consult a physician immediately if pain, bleeding, rupture of the membranes, or lack of fetal movement occur.

6. Do not lift while lying on your back. ACOG recommends that pregnant women not lie on their backs while exercising, especially after the fourth month. Blood supply may be reduced to the fetus.

7. Stay cool. Exercise increases body temperature, which may threaten the health of the fetus. Keep your temperature below 100 degrees. Dress lightly in warm weather.

8. Warm up before performing weight lifting exercises for three to five minutes. See "Joint Warming Exercises" in Appendix A.

9. Perform a few basic stretches of muscles used during the exercise session at the end of the workout.

❧ Substances to Avoid During Pregnancy

Besides supplementing with multivitamins, minerals, and other appropriate nutrients, a pregnant woman improves her chances for a complication-free pregnancy and birth by avoiding harmful substances, such as alcohol, caffeine, nicotine, recreational and prescription drugs. Teratogens are substances that cause birth defects when a pregnant woman is exposed to them, especially in the early stages of pregnancy. Pesticides and other contaminants found in the environment (including our food and water) can disrupt the hormonal and chromosomal cycles, leading to breaks in the DNA and a wide range of deformities and abnormalities in all animal species, including humans.

Alcohol

Even mild alcohol ingestion during pregnancy is said to result in hyperactivity, short attention span, and emotional problems in children.[142] Alcohol consumption during pregnancy contributes to birth abnormalities whether the mother drinks a little or a lot.[143] There are two periods of pregnancy when the maternal consumption of alcohol is particularly threatening to the development of the fetus: from the 12th to the 18th week and from the 24th to the 35th week. Three or four beers or glasses of wine a day can cause any one or more of the following defects: mental retardation, hyperactivity, a heart murmur, facial deformity such as a small head, or low-set ears.[144]

Cigarettes

Cigarette smoking is known to cause lower birth weight and size; mothers who smoke thirteen or more high-tar cigarettes a day have smaller babies in poorer condition than those of nonsmoking mothers.[145] Smokers have a miscarriage rate twice as high as that of nonsmokers,[146] and babies born to mothers who smoke have more than double the risk of dying of sudden infant death syndrome.[147] Women who smoke may experience more ectopic pregnancies (a potentially dangerous situation in which the fertilized egg attaches to, and grows on, the fallopian tube outside the uterus). Children of smokers may have far more respiratory illnesses (like asthma) than those of nonsmokers. Even secondhand smoke is seriously harmful to mother and baby and should be avoided when possible.

Caffeinated Beverages

Caffeine has been shown to contribute to growth-retarded or low-birthweight infants.[148] Researchers have suggested that women limit their intake of caffeine to approximately 300 mg per day during pregnancy, and since caffeine is known to enter breast milk, that level might be appropriate for nursing mothers as well.[149] One cup of regular coffee contains about 120 mg of caffeine. Even with this limited amount, the coffee or tea should be organic, in order to avoid the pesticides used in agricultural processes.

Pesticides and Environmental Hazards

Environmental factors are becoming more and more problematic to each generation of pregnant women, as many artificial compounds (e.g., PCBs from plastics) build up in the environment over time without degrading, become part of the food chain, and are incorporated into our bodies. Theo Colburn's ground-breaking study of the links between pesticides, PCBs, and other organochlorides in the food chain and hormonal disruption and birth defects makes clear that whatever an individual woman can do to avoid these compounds in her food and water is well worth doing.[150] Because humans are high on the food chain, the effects of these compounds on human reproduction are potentially exponential and devastating.

Hazardous substances, such as pesticides, lead, and other chemicals, brought home from the work environment on a parent's clothing, can harm an unborn child.[151] Also potentially harmful to the fetus are the mother's exposures to X rays during pregnancy or the father's preconception exposure to X rays.[152] One study showed that excessively high amounts of lead and barium in drinking water caused an increased risk of miscarriages.[153] Elevated lead in the body has also been linked to pre-eclampsia[154] and lower birth weight. A study of women in an Italian factory showed that daily inhalation of mercury vapors caused more menstrual difficulties, infertility, bleeding during pregnancy, miscarriages, preterm deliveries, and fetal malformations than were experienced by nonexposed women.[5]

Because so many of the artificial compounds in the environment mimic estrogen and other hormones in their actions on the human system, part of good prevention before and during early pregnancy might be to regularly eat plant foods called phytoestrogens that contain small amounts of natural estrogen. These natural sources of estrogen bond with the cells in the body and prevent the dangerous artificial substances from doing so in their place. Organic soy products (tofu, soybeans, soy milk) are rich in phytoestrogens as are sweet potatoes.

Over-the-counter and Prescription Drugs

Seemingly harmless over-the-counter drugs like aspirin, taken by mothers in the first half of the pregnancy, have been linked to lower-than-average IQs in their offspring.[155] Valium oil administered to egg-laying chickens induced impaired muscle cell development, suggesting potential harm from its use in pregnancy.[156] Medications such as lithium (antidepressant) and tetracycline (antibiotic) can harm the fetus; if at all possible, avoidance of these substances is recommended. Some

antiseizure medications are folate antagonists and, as such, can increase the risk for fetal neural tube defects, unless folic acid supplementation is implemented along with the medication.[157, 158]

In addition to the products mentioned above, herbalist Susun Weed provides the following list of products to avoid: DES (diethylstilbestrol), laxatives, pHisoHex (or anything else containing hexachlorophene), hair dyes, phenobarbital, barbiturates, tranquilizers, epinephrine (adrenaline) shots, sulfa drugs, antibiotics, vaccines, anesthetics, mercury vapors in dentists' offices, steroids, hormones, and Acutane (acne medication).[33]

James and Phyllis Balch further recommend avoiding food products containing the sweetener aspartame (Equal, NutraSweet), which contains high levels of phenylalanine; Tylenol, Datril, Alka-Seltzer, Di-Gel, Gelusil, Maalox, Pepto-Bismol, Rolaids, Tums; cold pills, cough remedies, decongestants, and mineral oil (which blocks the absorption of the fat-soluble vitamins); and preparations containing shark cartilage and estrogens. They also suggest not using electric blankets, which increase the risk of miscarriage and developmental problems.[159]

Recreational Drugs

Before conception and during pregnancy, especially the first trimester, it is important to avoid using recreational drugs, even those that may seem harmless at other times: consequences to a developing fetus may be serious. Genetic material can be damaged by marijuana, for example; in animals, it has been linked to an increase in fetal deaths and malformations.[160] Cocaine may decrease sperm concentration in semen, may induce deformities in the shape of the sperm, and reduce the speed at which it swims after ejaculation.[161] Men's preconceptual use of cocaine has been linked to cases of neurological damage in children.

❧ Common Complaints and Disorders of Pregnancy

Most problems experienced during pregnancy are a result of the immense hormonal changes, nutritional deficiencies, and the shift in weight distribution that happens as a result of sudden weight gain.[159] Backache, digestive discomfort, fatigue, swelling, and mood changes are almost inevitable. With the judicious use of rest, exercise, and nutrition, most women can successfully weather the hormonal roller-coaster ride of pregnancy. Walking a mile a day is unanimously recommended by researchers and birth supporters, as is eating healthy organic foods every day (including protein, whole grains, fruits, and vegetables). If a pregnant woman eats meat and/or dairy products, these should be "free range" and organic, or at least free from the artificial hormones and pesticides used in the agricultural processes. Dairy products have some of the highest concentration of estrogen-mimicking artificial compounds. These xenoestrogens may then augment the body's own estrogen levels, thereby causing elevations of estrogen beyond what nature intended. Xenoestrogens from pesticides are also suspected of causing genetic damage.

Morning Sickness

One of the first and perhaps most annoying complaints of pregnancy is the nausea (and vomiting) of "morning sickness," which generally stops being a problem after the first trimester. No one really knows what causes morning sickness, although it may be linked to an increase in thyroid hormone (T_4) effects on smooth muscle relaxation in the stomach. Physical exercise, especially walking, is recommended. Low blood sugar is implicated in the nausea of early pregnancy and can be regulated by eating smaller meals more often, eating high-protein snacks before sleeping, and eating unsalted crackers or matzo before getting out of bed in the morning.

Insufficient B vitamins may be associated with morning sickness; pregnant women are often deficient in B_6 as well as folic acid (the need for which increases during pregnancy). Foods rich in B vitamins—such as nutritional yeast, yogurt, bee pollen, spirulina, wheat germ, whole grains, egg yolk, cabbage, and organ meats (organic)—might be sufficient to alleviate morning sickness; if not, a B-50 vitamin supplement may be needed during the first trimester.

Anise, fennel, peppermint, chamomile, or spearmint teas are all helpful; raspberry leaf tea,

sipped before getting out of bed in the morning, may help. Wild yam root, according to herbalist Susun Weed, is "specific and powerful for nausea of pregnancy."[33] Studies have shown ginger root to be extremely effective in the treatment of the nausea and vomiting of severe morning sickness. These include a double-blind, randomized crossover trial done in England, in which ginger root scored significantly greater results for relief of morning sickness symptoms than placebo.[162] Start with 250 mg of ginger root powder four times daily; increase if necessary. Fresh ginger root tea can be made by simmering slices of ginger root in boiling water for 15 minutes. Add honey to taste.

Chronic Miscarriage/Abortion

Ten percent of first trimester pregnancies end in spontaneous abortion or miscarriage. Women who miscarry always feel guilty; they often feel responsible for the miscarriage. The fact is, however, that nature is not perfect; all conceptions are not destined to become a child. Two miscarriages—even in a row—is not necessarily abnormal. The causes of miscarriage include environmental factors (toxic substances in food, water, air, and pollutants in the workplace), smoking, drinking alcohol, dietary deficiencies, and fetal abnormalities. Low zinc intake has been associated with spontaneous abortion and premature delivery.[81] Prevention of miscarriage may be achieved with vitamin E supplementation (although no specific dose has been proven to do so),[64] or the use of bioflavonoids (200 mg, three times daily), which have been shown to help "chronic aborters" to stop aborting.[93] The following are traditional herbal supports for preventing miscarriage:[33]

- **Black haw root** (especially effective): Drink one or two cups of tea or one-half cup of infusion daily as soon as pregnancy is known; use throughout entire pregnancy if desired.
- **False unicorn root** (especially for women who have experienced repeated miscarriages): Take 3 drops of tincture 4–5 times daily from preconception through the first trimester.
- **Wild yam root:** For threatened miscarriage, make a strong tea by steeping 1 tsp of wild yam

root in 2 cups hot water for 15 minutes; take 2–4 ounces every 30 minutes. The tincture is less effective and may induce nausea or vomiting.

Pre-eclampsia or Eclampsia (Toxemia)

Pre-eclampsia is a dangerous condition that may develop in the third trimester of pregnancy. It includes hypertension (high blood pressure), edema, and protein in the urine. About 6 percent of all pregnant women will develop pre-eclampsia sometime after completing 20 weeks of gestation; eclampsia occurs in 0.1 percent of cases.[75]

Western medicine believes that there is no way to prevent pre-eclampsia but that it can be kept from progressing to eclampsia with good prenatal care. Herbalist Susun Weed disagrees, calling pre-eclampsia "the result of malnutrition during pregnancy," and says it is easily prevented by eating 60–80 grams of protein daily, getting enough salt, foods high in calcium, adequate calories, and nourishing herbal supports like raspberry, nettle, and dandelion leaves throughout pregnancy.[33] The *Harvard Guide to Women's Health* links pre-eclampsia to very young or much older women (over 45), women with underlying medical problems (high blood pressure, kidney disorders, autoimmune disorders, and diabetes), and multiple births.[163]

Once pre-eclampsia is diagnosed, a skilled professional must be called in to help manage the treatment, since the condition is serious enough to threaten the mother's life and damage the fetus. Potassium levels must be increased (eating potato peels and bananas help; also mint, chicory, and dandelion leaves). The sodium-potassium ratio needs balancing (drink raw beet juice, up to four ounces daily); supplement with B_6 in conjunction with a high-potency B complex vitamin; eat spirulina and add seaweed to your daily diet. Dandelion leaves are effective in prevention and treatment of pre-eclampsia, as well as for strengthening the liver, which is implicated in the condition.[33]

The *Harvard Guide* expresses the current allopathic medical perspective when it states unequivocally: "The only definitive cure for pre-eclampsia is delivery of the baby."[163] However, women with pre-eclampsia are generally sent to bedrest unless the diastolic blood pressure is greater than 100 with bedrest. If significantly preterm, efforts are made to confirm fetal maturity or mature fetal lungs medically before delivery. Usually the earlier in the pregnancy that pregnancy induced hypertension occurs, the more severe it becomes. The majority of cases at term are usually benign and easily managed. Catastrophic outcomes of toxemia include seizures, strokes, and failure of the heart, liver, lungs, or kidneys.

Since pre-eclampsia is characterized by high blood pressure, it stands to reason that yoga, meditation, and stress reduction techniques would be a useful complement to nutritional, botanical, and other treatments.

Heartburn, Gas, and Constipation

Hormonal imbalances during pregnancy may result in the softening of the smooth muscle found in the wall of the digestive tract. The consequent reduction in peristaltic movement causes food to pass more slowly through the esophagus, stomach, and small and large intestines to the rectum, inducing gas and constipation. Heartburn can be caused by the softening of the muscular valve between the esophagus and the stomach, so that partially digested, acidic food may leak back up into the esophagus, causing a burning sensation in the chest. Heartburn and constipation are generally experienced in the later stages of pregnancy.

Susun Weed[33] and Rosemary Gladstar[102] emphasize eating small meals frequently, chewing food carefully, and avoiding acid-causing and greasy foods. Both recommend papaya (especially raw, but also in tablets and papaya leaf) for the enzymes, fennel, and anise seeds; Gladstar adds cumin and dill seeds, suggesting an old-fashioned remedy for digestive disturbances: combine these four seeds and chew them before and after meals.

Be aware that coffee and cigarettes increase heartburn by irritating the stomach, and remember that whole grains, fresh fruits, and vegetables combined with nonstressful exercise are the best solutions to constipation.

Varicose Veins

Varicosities can occur in the legs, or in the anal or vulvar areas in pregnancy, due to hormonal softening of the muscular walls of the veins, combined with the extra weight. Simple yoga (and other nonstressful exercise) can help by improving circulation from the lower body up to the trunk; it is also good to get your weight off the legs as much as possible and put your feet up whenever possible.

A lack of nutritional elements in the diet, especially vitamin C, rutin, and other bioflavonoids, combined with the extra stress on the circulatory system, can cause the fragile capillaries to break. A tendency toward varicose veins and hemorrhoids may also be inherited. Eat foods high in vitamin C and bioflavonoids, such as buckwheat, nettles, rose hips, oranges, lemons, grapefruit, peppers, whole grains, hibiscus flowers, and the white rinds of organically grown citrus fruits; also include garlic, onion, chives, and leeks. These help maintain elasticity in the veins and capillaries. Lecithin, vitamin E, and rutin supplements are also recommended for preventing and repairing varicose veins.

Backache

Herbalist Susun Weed points out that there are no drugs safe to take for backache during pregnancy, not even aspirin, and she recommends gentle yoga stretches; chiropractic adjustments; sleeping with pillows to support the legs, back, and belly; wearing flat heels; and getting plenty of minerals; lemon juice in water, up to six glasses daily, benefits the kidneys, easing backache. An excellent guide to safe, effective yoga during pregnancy is *Preparing for Birth with Yoga* by Janet Balaskas.

Bladder Infections

Blood volume increases 50 percent during pregnancy, causing the kidneys to work harder and making the urinary system more vulnerable to stress and infection. Especially in the last trimester, burning or frequent urination or cramping in the abdomen may indicate a bladder infection. Many herbs and nutrients can be used to treat urinary tract infections, although not all of them are safe while pregnant. Uva ursi is safe and is one of the most effective herbs to prevent recurrent bladder infections while also having antimicrobial activity in acute infections. Used in leaf form, place the leaf in a tea ball and place in water that has already come to a boil. Let it steep for five minutes, then drink one cup every three hours for two days, then one cup three times a day for an additional week. Vitamin C can also be used to acidify the urine and fight the infection. Take 1,000 mg of vitamin C three to four times per day for up to one week. Unsweetened cranberry juice will also acidify the urine, making it a less friendly environment for bacteria, interfering with the ability of the bacteria to stick to the bladder wall. Eight to 16 ounces per day is recommended.

❦ Conventional Medicine Approach

Nothing would please me better than for peace to be made between those who endorse modern obstetrics and hospital births, and those who applaud the naturalness of pregnancy and labor and prefer that it occur at home when uncomplicated. There is merit in both. Like all options in health care, only the pregnant woman can decide which is right for her—but with better cooperation between the sides, her choice would be easier. When childbirth goes normally—which is most of the time—it can be safely managed at home. Unfortunately, we are not privy to knowing beforehand when births among healthy low-risk women will go awry, and there are some conditions—like profound fetal distress, prolapsed umbilical cords, and maternal hemorrhage—that can be significantly worsened during the time it takes to transport to the hospital.

Modern obstetrics was born after a time when all births occurred at home, no matter what, and maternal mortality was substantially higher than now. Forceps—we now groan at their mention—were a lifesaving invention for mothers as well as their babies—who otherwise died of the "obstructed" pelvis, often after laboring for days. Life without Cesarean sections was life with many more maternal deaths.

Where is the happy medium? How can we avail ourselves of the truly lifesaving aspects of obstetrics and eliminate the excess? The best answer I have is to be as educated as possible about options—and be open to the obstetrical reality that things do not always go as we hope and plan. Be flexible. If possible, have a relationship with a conventional provider you can call if needed. One good option is to consider hospital-based midwife services. The midwives are very committed to natural childbirth and, unlike a physician, are present and supportive throughout your labor. They work with a back-up physician, someone presumably of their choosing. Even if the physician is called, they will continue to attend you as their primary patient and advocate for your wishes. Their c-section rates are low, their respect for the birthing process high. If you choose an out-of-hospital birth, be aware that the main reasons women eventually come to the hospital are for prolonged labor and/or pain—not emergencies. Have a plan worked out for what you will do in that situation.

Conventional obstetrics need not be as off-putting as many assume. There are a number of providers who support a woman's wish to have her birth naturally. They also support women who choose to have their labor pains assuaged. Women are offered the choice of intravenous medication or epidural medication if they choose. When an epidural is given at no sooner than 4–5 cm dilation in a woman delivering her first child, the Cesarean section rate is not increased over the rate of those women who go without epidural anesthesia.

Cesarean section rates vary among physicians and institutions; it is reasonable to ask a provider for numbers. Around 15 percent is acceptable, although some will be as high as 20 percent; it depends somewhat on how "high-risk" the practice is. Sicker moms have sicker babies that may need to be delivered more urgently, and therefore more often by c-section. Most doctors do not take the decision to operate lightly and should always discuss the issues with you clearly. Nothing will ever happen without your informed consent. You never need to have the drug Pitocin or any adjunct to labor unless you are in agreement. I encourage women to make their needs and wishes known in all aspects of their health care. That is the only way

the system can become responsive to the evolving and varied needs of women.

≈ Seeing a Licensed Primary Health Care Practitioner*

Healthy women with normal pregnancies have the lowest risk of complications, so medical management choices are largely personal. Most non-MD providers use a list of criteria to determine the low-risk or high-risk status of a pregnant woman. The list should address the following:

Blood pressure: Hypertensive disorders are the most common disorder of pregnancy—affecting as many as 5–10 percent.[164] One of the main reasons practitioners see pregnant women so often is to check their blood pressure. Most women's blood pressures goes way down in pregnancy. Women with chronic hypertension, which does not stabilize at a safe level during pregnancy, have a higher risk of smaller, more at-risk babies. They, themselves, are at risk of developing the complications of hypertension, such as renal disease. Labor is sometimes induced at term—38 weeks or so—to lighten the load on mother and baby.

Pre-eclampsia is a different hypertensive disorder of pregnancy. It is most often a mild disease, characterized by the development of hypertension toward the end of pregnancy. At its worst, it can cause seizures or eclampsia and significant hematological abnormalities, including loss of the ability to clot blood. Kidney failure can occur. Usually none of these things happens, but because severity of disease does not predict seizures, women with pre-eclampia require protection against this risk with magnesium sulfate that is given during labor and for 24 hours afterward. Mild forms of pre-eclampsia are treated with bedrest. Severe forms—which often come earlier in a pregnancy—are treated with bedrest in the hospital. All efforts are made to avoid delivering babies very prematurely. However, when maternal health is significantly compromised, this measure

---

*N.D. = Naturopathic Doctor; M.D. = Medical Doctor; D.O. = Osteopathic Doctor; N.P. = Nurse Practitioner; P.A. = Physician's Assistant.

may need to be taken. When severe, there is no cure for this disorder but delivery. It is felt to be an immunologic intolerance of the particular genetic load of first births. It is extremely rare to have a second severe case in subsequent pregnancies with the same partner.

Bleeding: Bleeding is never normal in pregnancy. Although it doesn't necessarily indicate a serious problem, it must be assumed so until proven otherwise. Placental abruption is a disorder in which the placenta pulls away from the uterus prematurely, causing bleeding and contractions that can be life-threatening to women and their fetuses. Because the placenta is so large, a lot can pull away before things are hugely compromised, but an evaluation is in order. Placenta previa—in which the placenta covers the cervical os—can also cause significant hemorrhage, and is classically heralded by a small, otherwise insignificant "sentinel bleed." Ultrasound can diagnose this easily. No pregnant woman should have a vaginal exam in the third trimester without first ultrasounding to locate the placenta. Digital exploration can cause significant blood loss in the case of previa.

Abnormal lie (usually breech): Many hospitals will support the vaginal birth of a healthy frank breech infant (butt first). Footling breech—with the feet presenting—is unsafe vaginally, because the feet can come down through the partially dilated cervix—as can the cord—before the entire infant will fit. Another alternative to delivering a frank breech vaginally is a version in which the fetus is rotated or rather coaxed to rotate from outside. The success rate is about 50–50. Either way, neither of these procedures should be undertaken at home.

Measuring significantly large or small at any point should prompt at least an ultrasound. Fetal abnormalities associated with poor growth or too much or too little fluid can present this way, and are best prepared for in advance of delivery. Size discrepancy is often as simple as an error in dating—but figuring out the right due date is still very helpful.

Women with any major underlying health problem—such as diabetes or heart or respiratory disorders significant enough to require ongoing surveillance in the non-pregnant state—should be managed with input from a licensed provider. So should women with kidney disease or autoimmune disorders like lupus or rheumatoid arthritis. All these conditions can make a pregnancy much riskier for both mother and child. Ultrasound can be invaluable in assessing fetal growth and well-being. Ongoing surveillance of the pregnant woman can alert her to any medical problems as early as possible.

Premenstrual Syndrome

⤳ *Overview*

When finally we understand premenstrual syndrome (PMS) we will have gone a long way toward understanding the interplay between the cultural, physiologic, and emotional factors that regularly affect women's lives during the premenstruum. A huge piece of work will have been done toward improving women's health.

Maria Gurevich has written, "The persistence of PMS as a medical category despite the inconclusiveness of the research, suggests that PMS is not simply a biomedical entity . . . it is also a complex, ideologically and culturally constructed category . . . predicated on a number of unarticulated, well-entrenched beliefs about the nature of science, biology, health and femaleness."[1]

Maintaining good health and attitude through all phases of the menstrual cycle is just not as simple as correcting female physiology gone awry but also involves on some level transforming our cultural image of women's reproductive health, specifically menstruation, from negative (the "curse") to positive.

However far-reaching these ideals, what we are after is practical help for the woman who suffers premenstrually. While precisely defining PMS remains scientifically challenging, any woman can tell you what it is, and a great many will tell you that they have it. Defining terms carefully helps to extract "pure" PMS—the syndrome as defined—from an assortment of overlapping conditions.

Eighty percent of women experience premenstrual emotional or physical changes, whereas only about 20–40 percent of these women have difficulties as a result. A much smaller number, about 2.5–5 percent,[2] feel it has a significantly negative impact on their lives, to the point where work, relationships, or home life are jeopardized. Most women who have symptoms do not seek medical care but instead self-treat, making this an ideal arena for natural self-care.

There are some 150 symptoms that have been ascribed to PMS—most commonly feelings of anxiousness (premenstrual tension was the first name given to this syndrome), irritability, and anger or moods vacillating unpredictably among the three. Some women feel predominantly sad or self-deprecating, others simply fatigued and lethargic. Physical changes include bloating, breast tenderness, food cravings, headache, and gastric upset. No particular assortment is diagnostic; it is the regular recurrence of symptoms on a monthly basis, just before menses occur, that matters. Symptoms usually last a few days to a week before menses, sometimes beginning at mid-cycle precisely with ovulation.

As important as the regular timing of the arrival of these symptoms is the predictable relief and complete resolution experienced with the onset of menses or within one to two days of the menstrual

245

flow beginning. PMS symptoms, whatever they may be for a particular woman, completely go away just as regularly as they arrive. Most who study this entity require that a woman be able to predict in advance for at least a couple of cycles when symptoms will come and when they will leave to warrant a diagnosis of PMS.[3] It is important to eliminate other possible sources of the symptoms that might indicate medical conditions a woman may suffer from even more dramatically in the premenstruum. Women who are afflicted with asthma, migraines, epilepsy, or herpes, for example, often note a cyclic worsening, a premenstrual magnification, if you will, but this is not considered to be PMS. Treatment for the underlying condition is more likely to eliminate the premenstrual aggravation than is treatment aimed solely at PMS.

Among women self-presenting to PMS clinics for medical care, fully 75 percent had another diagnosis that contributed significantly to their symptoms—major depressive or other mood disorders being most prominent.[4] About 10 percent had early menopausal symptoms, 10 percent were affected by hormonal contraceptives, and about 5 percent each were found to have eating disorders or substance abuse issues predominating. Anyone who considers her PMS to be significantly bothersome might be wise to check with her practitioner should her efforts with self-care fail. There may be other more effective treatments.

Most women feel different emotionally and physically during the premenstruum. The term "molimina" refers to those changes women notice that let them know their menses are approaching: appetite changes, swelling, or menstruallike cramps. A recurrent pattern of mild but noticeable changes provides evidence that cycles are ovulatory. Some women enjoy positive changes: enhanced creativity, heightened sexual desire, intellectual clarity, and feelings of happiness and well-being.[5]

It is difficult to identify "cause" in a condition that overlaps so broadly with normal physiology, affects so many, and has such a wide array of symptoms. Many theories have been explored and none found completely satisfying. Most likely this is because it is such a complex interaction of factors both physiologic and social. While absolute levels of es-

trogen and progesterone are no different in PMS sufferers, we know that in women in whom both hormones are pharmaceutically blocked, PMS diminishes by 75 percent.[3] Blocking progesterone only using Ru-486 did not have this effect, nor did it worsen symptoms.[6] It is likely that ovarian hormones affect the neurotransmitter, neuroendocrine, and circadian systems that influence mood and behavior differently in each of us.

It is interesting to look at the work done on serotonin to appreciate the role our social environment may have on PMS. Anita Rapkin, M.D., studied serotonin levels in women with PMS and those without, and found that serotonin levels fell after ovulation in women with PMS.[7] Those without PMS had much higher levels of serotonin during the last half of the menstrual cycle. Abnormal serotonin metabolism has long been linked to depression. Elevating serotonin levels is how the wildly popular antidepressant Prozac works. There is evidence that estrogen levels affect the serotonin system. More interestingly, studies in animals and humans have demonstrated how social interactions in groups can affect our serotonin levels. Dominant animals in groups have higher levels of serotonin, which then fall if they are removed from their prominent position. Serotonin levels rise in the animals that replace them in dominance.[7] Rapkin postulates that women without PMS may offset ovulation-induced susceptibility to low serotonin/isolation behavior through interacting more with "desirable others." In other words, women able to manipulate their social environment successfully are less susceptible to the mood consequences of low serotonin. One begins to see how our culture's historical attitude of embarrassment or distaste around menstruation might contribute to susceptible women's neurotransmitters being adversely affected at a physiologically critical time, resulting in mood swings, anger, and irritability. This is congruent with the views of feminist writers who criticize the medicalization of PMS symptoms as disease, arguing that medicine has tended to pathologize behaviors that do not conform to the unnatural yet pervasive female stereotype. Certainly, no other named condition in women is so common, so little understood, and yet contains so many significant pieces to our lives.

KEY CONCEPTS

- No clear cause despite its obvious existence.
- Cyclic symptoms during the second half of the menstrual cycle with a symptom-free phase during the first half of the cycle.
- Medical evaluation revealing concurrent disorders of depression and anxiety.
- Provide symptom relief while also addressing need for lifestyle changes.

PREVENTION

- A whole foods diet with minimal intake of sugar, refined carbohydrates, dairy products, caffeine, and saturated fats.
- Stress management.
- Regular exercise.

 Overview of Alternative Treatments

Historically, conventional mainstream medicine has not been able to offer women a known cause for PMS nor has it been able to offer a management approach short of pharmaceuticals with as many side effects as relief. Self-care with natural therapies has been the dominant method of how women manage PMS. Women have clearly taken this monthly recurring familiar problem into their own hands and more often than not have determined what works for them. Fortunately, PMS is a condition where inadequate self-treatment yields dissatisfaction rather than dangerous side effects or progression of a serious disease.

In an attempt to offer women viable natural treatments for the relief of PMS and explain their rationale, many theories have been offered. While comforting in their attempt to organize the syndrome, these theories are poorly confirmed in research studies yet still used as a basis for using these many natural therapies. Even though a given therapy may work for a number of women, its mechanism still eludes our true understanding.

Models of therapeutics based on hormonal patterns like elevated estrogen levels and reduced progesterone levels, elevated prolactin and increased aldosterone, are not adequately confirmed in research. These models are tidy and convenient for a logical train of thought, but, due to their limited ability to help many women, they distract us from potentially having a more accurate understanding and more effective treatment options. Clinically, I have not usually found it useful to use these models, nor do I usually classify PMS with some of the commonly used classification systems used by alternative practitioners like PMS-A (anxiety), PMS-C (carbohydrate craving), PMS-D (depression), or PMS-H (hyperhydration). Yes, women may have one or more of these symptoms characterized in the particular classification, but treating women with the correlating hormonal imbalance has not typically been productive in my experience. In the more difficult cases, it is often necessary to expand one's thinking, however, and explore some of these theories.

Another basic foundation for many alternative practitioners in treating PMS is the concept of the liver's role in the detoxification process. If the liver function is compromised, then estrogen metabolism is inadequate, leading to excess estrogen levels and an estrogen-dominant state. A "sluggish liver" is then addressed with various dietary, nutrient, and herbal interventions. It is important to understand that this is a theory with much speculation and minimal scientific support. One cannot argue, however, about the central role of the liver and its varied metabolic processes with subsequent influence on the biochemistry of hormone and enzymatic pathways. There may in fact be a role for liver function in PMS, but what that is remains unknown. However, improving liver function pays off down the road, like exercise does, with many positive health benefits to numerous body systems.

Numerous natural alternative therapies are available including lifestyle changes, vitamin and mineral supplementation, herbal medicines, and natural hormones. Many of these have demonstrated their effectiveness in standard scientific studies. But at least an equal number have either shown no effect or an effect that was not significantly greater than the placebo effect. Herein lies one of the curiosities of medicine, elegantly portrayed with PMS: Why do conventional scientific studies fail to demonstrate success with many of these natural therapies that women consistently rely on for their monthly successful treatments?

Perhaps the answer is as simple as what works for one person is different than what works for another. We are truly individuals with our own unique physiology, stressors, psychological makeup, etc. Double-blind, placebo-controlled, scientific studies attempt to find what works for as many people as possible, not what works best for an individual.

Even in studies where the placebo response is given credit, perhaps the belief that the mind can heal the body is the real explanation. The interaction between neurotransmitters, the body's steroids, circadian systems, mood, behavior, plus plants and nutrients from nature may remain scientifically elusive, but, to the credit of women, we have instinctually come upon safe and effective natural solutions.

Treating PMS naturally serves as a touchstone for motivating women to make lifestyle changes that have a positive cascade effect on their general health.

Nutrition

Women who have PMS typically have dietary habits that are worse than the standard American diet. In a nutritional analysis published in 1983, Guy Abraham, M.D., reported that PMS patients consumed 62 percent more refined carbohydrates than women who did not have PMS, 275 percent more refined sugar, 79 percent more dairy products, 78 percent more sodium, 53 percent less iron, 77 percent less manganese, and 52 percent less zinc.[8] A diet higher in dairy products can also contribute to PMS symptoms such as anxiety, irritability, and nervous tension. A dietary survey of 39 patients with PMS and 14 women with no PMS was done which found that the women with PMS consumed five-fold more dairy products and three-fold more refined sugar than those women without PMS.[9] Dairy products and calcium interfere with magnesium absorption, and refined sugar increases the urinary excretion of magnesium.[10] Another nutritional factor in PMS is the effect of refined sugars on the retention of sodium. After a large intake of sugar, insulin increases quickly, which causes sodium and water retention due to insufficient ketoacid formation. Symptoms such as swelling in the hands and feet, abdominal bloating, and breast engorgement and tenderness result. Complex carbohydrates (whole grains such as brown rice, whole wheat, oats, barley, etc.) are preferred over simple sugars (white sugar, white flour, white rice, etc.), because they stimulate insulin release much more slowly and in a more sustained manner, thereby preventing many of these water-retention symptoms.

Excessive and incorrect prostaglandin (PG) synthesis has been implicated in the pathogenesis of PMS, and a deficiency of prostaglandin E1 (PgE1) at the central nervous system has been proposed to be involved in PMS.[11] There are many nutrients important for the synthesis of PgE1. These include magnesium, linoleic acid (an essential fatty acid), vitamin B_6, zinc, vitamin C, and vitamin B_3. On the other hand, arachidonic acid is a precursor to PgE2, which has antagonistic effects with regard to PgE1. Think of PgE1 as the good guy and PgE2 as the bad guy. Vegetable oils are rich sources of linoleic acid, and animal fats are the main dietary sources of arachidonic acid; therefore, patients with PMS would be wise to decrease their consumption of animal fats and increase their consumption of vegetable oils so that they have more of the good guy, PgE1. Obviously, a diet high in the other nutrients mentioned would also promote the synthesis of PgE1. We will discuss these more in the nutritional supplement section.

Limiting the dietary intake of salt can be helpful to some women. Table salt enhances the response to the ingestion of glucose, consequently increasing the insulin response. As mentioned earlier, an increase in insulin causes swelling through water retention.

Many women with breast symptoms in their premenstrual phase benefit from avoiding caffeine. Even though scientific studies are controversial on this subject, the practical results speak for themselves. Restricting the intake of coffee (caffeinated and decaffeinated), black tea, chocolate, and caffeine-containing soft drinks will especially benefit those with fluid-retention symptoms.

See Chapter 7 for more information about the detrimental effects of caffeine.

It is estimated that there are two million alcoholic women in the reproductive-age group in the United States.[12] Sixty-seven percent of these women relate their drinking to their menstrual cycles, and drinking bouts occur usually during the premenstrual phase.[13] Alcohol may also play a role in the reactive hypoglycemia of PMS.

Dietary Recommendations

- Reduce the intake of alcohol, caffeine, salt, sugar, refined carbohydrates, and dairy products.
- Increase the intake of fruits, vegetables, legumes, nuts, seeds, fish, and flax oil.

Nutritional Supplements

Nutritional supplements are widely used in the treatment of PMS despite the inconsistent evidence to support their use. Again we have this discrepancy between scientific information and what a significant number of women report. A possible explanation for this discrepancy might be that vitamin and mineral levels in the peripheral blood (which is measured in a laboratory) do not parallel those levels found in the central nervous system (CNS). Researchers J. C. Chuong and E. B. Dawson have written, "It is possible that the bioavailability of vitamins and minerals in the CNS, which is related to the activities of several neurotransmitters (including serotonin), could change during the luteal phase in some patients with PMS. As a result, premenstrual symptoms occur. However, these changes in vitamin and mineral levels in the CNS may not show up in the peripheral blood levels."[14]

Multiple vitamin and mineral supplements may be helpful for women with PMS. A study was done in 1985 of Optivite, a rather typical multiple vitamin/mineral supplement. The quantities and proportions of vitamins and minerals in this supplement either met or exceeded the recommended daily allowances except for calcium and vitamin D. In a double-blind, placebo-controlled, crossover study,[15] 16 of 23 subjects reported feeling better during the cycles in which they took the supplement, and 7 reported feeling better during the placebo cycles. These researchers also classified the patients into four different subgroups (PMS-A, PMS-C, PMS-D, PMS-H) and found that only two of the four subgroups responded to this particular supplement. When selecting a multiple vitamin and mineral supplement, I recommend one that has been formulated especially for women. These formulations take into account some of the special nutritional needs of women.

Vitamin B$_6$

A rational basis for the use of pyridoxine in the treatment of PMS was first indicated by the work of Adams and his colleagues in 1973[16] although it had been prescribed since the 1940s. They reported on the successful treatment with vitamin B$_6$ of patients complaining of depression associated with oral contraception. Since that time there have been over one dozen studies on vitamin B$_6$ and PMS. Some of these have shown no effect from vitamin B$_6$, but most of the studies have shown that there was a substantial and broad effect on the whole range of PMS symptoms. An overview of these studies has been published in the *British Journal of Obstetrics and Gynaecology*.[17] The studies have used anywhere from 50–500 mg per day. Vitamin B$_6$ is thought to be unique in its ability to increase the synthesis of several neurotransmitters in the brain. These neurotransmitters include serotonin, dopamine, norepinephrine, epinephrine, taurine, and histamine.[18] Lower levels of brain neurotransmitters such as serotonin and dopamine have been implicated in the etiology of PMS.[19]

Vitamin B$_6$ supplementation is generally considered safe in dosages of 50–100 mg daily. When using dosages greater than 50 mg, it may be important to divide it into 50-mg dosages throughout the day to assure appropriate utilization by the liver. Vitamin B$_6$ is one of the few water-soluble vitamins that is associated with some toxicity when taken in large doses or in more moderate dosages over long periods of time. Chronic intake of dosages greater than 500 mg per day can be toxic if taken daily for many months or years. There are also a few rare reports of toxicity at chronic long-term dosages of 150 mg per day.[20] Toxicity symptoms are called sensory neuropathies that present as tingling, numbness, and a decrease in sensation, generally in the hands or feet. The toxicity is thought to be a result of supplemental pyridoxine overwhelming the liver's ability to add a phosphate group to form the active form of vitamin B_6, called pyridoxal-5-phosphate. The pyridoxine itself then most likely becomes toxic to the nerve cells. The safest method of taking vitamin B_6 supplementation is to take dosages of 50 mg at a time spread throughout the day; one should not exceed 200 mg total in one day.

Vitamin B_6
50 mg, 2–4 times per day

Vitamin E

Vitamin E is probably not a big player in PMS relief, although studies have demonstrated a reduction in premenstrual nervous tension, headache, fatigue, depression, insomnia, and breast tenderness.[8, 21] Aberrant prostaglandin (PG) synthesis has been implicated in PMS, and a deficiency of prostaglandin E1 (PgE1) has been proposed to be involved in PMS as well as an increase in another prostaglandin called PgF2-alpha. It has been hypothesized that vitamin E inhibits the negative prostaglandin (PgF2) and increases the PgE1. Women continue to use vitamin E to relieve the symptoms of breast tenderness before the period. Despite science that does not confirm a statistically significant benefit, vitamin E remains an important part of self-care. This is discussed more in Chapter 7.

Vitamin E
400–800 IU per day

Essential Fatty Acids

The main strategy of supplementing with essential fatty acids is an attempt to raise the body's own formation of PgE1. The most popular method of doing so has been to supplement with evening primrose oil (EPO) products in order to supply increased levels of gamma linolenic acid. Although there are several studies that show positive results, some of the studies did not include a placebo group, and other studies did not show a statistically significant difference between the treatment group and the placebo group. Four double-blind, crossover, controlled trials of EPO have demonstrated a significant effect over the placebo group.[22–25] One of these studies used 3 grams of EPO per day; the others used 4 grams per day. EPO has been shown to be most effective for relieving clumsiness and headaches, although all symptoms including depression, irritability, bloatedness, and breast tenderness showed a marked improvement. Other sources of oils that contain gamma linolenic acid and raise PgE1 levels include borage oil, black currant oil, and rapeseed oil.

Gamma linolenic acid
3–4 grams per day

Magnesium

Magnesium has shown some beneficial effect in the treatment of PMS. In a 1991 study involving 32 women with PMS, 360 mg of magnesium three times daily was given from mid-cycle to the onset of menstrual flow.

In menstrual distress questionnaire scores, relief of premenstrual mood fluctuations and depression during magnesium treatment was significant. Although blood serum levels of magnesium are not found to be different between women who have PMS and women who don't, it seems there is a significant decrease in red blood cell magnesium levels in PMS patients. The mechanism of magnesium and its possible role in PMS are not well understood, but we do know that magnesium is involved in essential fatty acid metabolism and pyridoxine (vitamin B_6) activity.

Magnesium
300 mg, 1–3 times per day

Calcium

Reports have suggested that problems in calcium regulation may underlie some of the symptoms of PMS and that calcium may have a therapeutic benefit. A very recent randomized, double-blind, placebo-controlled, multicenter clinical trial was conducted to test this hypothesis.

Four hundred ninety-seven women were enrolled and given either 1,200 mg of calcium carbonate or placebo for three menstrual cycles.[26] During the luteal phase of the treatment cycle (from ovulation to menses), a significantly lower symptom complex score was observed in the calcium group for both the second and third months. By the third month, calcium effectively resulted in a 48-percent reduction in total symptom scores from baseline compared with a 30-percent reduction in the placebo group. All four symptom factors (i.e., negative mood affect, water retention, food cravings, and pain) were significantly reduced by the third treatment cycle.

> **Calcium carbonate**
> *1,200 mg per day*

Botanicals

Chaste Tree (*Vitex agnus castus*)

The single most important plant for the treatment of premenstrual syndrome is *Vitex agnus castus,* also known as chaste tree. The fruits of chaste tree contain essential oils, irridoids, pseudoindicans, and flavonoids. The effect of chaste tree is on the hypothalamus-hypophysis axis. It increases secretion of luteinizing hormone (LH) and also has an effect which favors progesterone.[27–29] Chaste tree has also been substantiated in its ability to inhibit prolactin.[30] Elevated prolactin levels may be a factor in PMS.

Two surveys were done covering 1,542 women with premenstrual syndrome who had been treated with a German liquid extract of chaste tree for periods of up to 16 years. The mean duration of treatment was 166 days, and the average dose was 42 drops daily. Effectiveness as recorded by the patients' doctors was either very good, good, or satisfactory in 92 percent of the cases.[31] Only 2.1 percent of the women noted side effects during treatment, and 1.1 percent of them discontinued the medicine because of them.

> ***Vitex agnus castus* (chaste tree)**
> *40 drops liquid*
> or
> *extract per day; standardized extract:*
> *175 mg per day*

Ginkgo (*Ginkgo biloba*)

A double-blind, placebo-controlled study was done in 1993 to determine the effectiveness of ginkgo extract on PMS symptoms. One hundred sixty-five women between the ages of 18 and 45 years who had fluid retention, breast tenderness, and vascular congestion were studied. The patients were assigned to receive either a ginkgo extract of 24 percent ginkgo flavonglycoside content at 80 mg twice daily or a placebo from day 16 of their cycle to day 5 of the next cycle. Based on symptom evaluation by both patient and doctor, ginkgo extract was effective against the congestive symptoms of PMS, particularly breast pain or tenderness.[32]

> **Ginkgo (*ginkgo biloba*)**
> *80 mg standardized extract twice daily*

Additional Herbs

Many other herbs that have not been subjected to scientific research have also been used successfully by women and practitioners for decades. These include many species of wild yam, licorice root, dong quai, black cohosh, and more. Other plants are used because of their benefit with specific symptoms; for example, kava extract for anxiety, St. John's wort for depression, dandelion leaf for water weight gain, valerian for sleep problems, and lemon balm for herpes eruptions. You will often find one or more of these herbs in a combination herbal and nutritional product that has been specifically formulated for PMS symptom relief. Many of these herbs do have scientific research in their specific area of use, for example, St. John's wort and depression.

Exercise

Specific exercises are conspicuously absent from scientific studies looking at the effects of exercise on PMS. In contrast, although mechanisms of action remain elusive, general regular physical exercise has been the subject of several controlled trials. In all of these, the results show that women who exercise regularly have less strong or fewer PMS symptoms.

Aerobic training (walking, jogging, swimming, cycling) appears more effective at reducing PMS symptoms than strength training (weight lifting);[33] frequency of exercise, but not intensity, relates to decreased rating of selected menstrual distress symptom clusters;[34] gradual increase in running distances correlate directly with greater reductions in PMS symptoms;[35] regular exercisers show improvement in all PMS parameters, e.g., concentration, affect, pain, water retention, as well as hostility, fear, guilt, and sadness.[36]

Regularly exercising women, but not nonexercising women, report significant decrease in anxiety following baseline relaxation but show greater increase in anxiety during a stress task than nonexercisers.[37]

Finally, two recent reviews of the literature on exercise and PMS emphasize the obvious fact that controlled trials of exercise training and PMS cannot be performed under double-blind conditions, a fact that somehow places exercise research outside the realm of the scientific, making it difficult to formulate probable mechanisms for the observed effects of regular training on PMS symptoms. According to L. Gannon,[38] exercise may reduce PMS symptoms by (1) decreasing estrogen levels, (2) improving glucose tolerance, (3) decreasing catecholamines, and (4) elevating endorphins. Gannon concludes, "If PMS symptoms are caused or exacerbated by dramatic variations in endorphin levels, exercise may serve to prevent exaggerated elevations and abrupt declines and, ultimately, to reduce symptoms."

Other Therapeutic Agents

Natural Progesterone

Perhaps no other PMS therapy has been the target of so much controversy as natural progesterone. This has as much to do with the lack of agreement

---

EXERCISE RECOMMENDATIONS

- Follow the "General Exercise Programs" and "General Exercise Instructions" outlined in Appendix A.
- The key words are *regularity* and *diversity*.
- It is important to schedule exercise along with the other vital activities of the day—meals, sleep, and rest.
- Equally important is to enjoy the exercise you choose, remembering that best results are obtained from a combination of types of exercise—flexibility, stretching, strength, and cardiovascular.

---

and scientific research to support a unified theory as to the cause of PMS as it has to do with the efficacy of natural progesterone itself. Dr. Raymond Green and Dr. Katharina Dalton advanced a theory in the 1950s that PMS was caused by unopposed estrogen during the luteal phase (second half) of the menstrual cycle. Dr. Dalton's original work with progesterone therapy is the historical root on which the use of natural progesterone is based today. Research scientists and therefore the majority of the conventional medical community ultimately did not embrace Dr. Dalton's conclusions about the efficacy of progesterone therapy and PMS. This was largely based on what they thought to be inadequate scientific research studies. I think it is also fair to speculate that other matters of medical politics and the business of medicine were at play here as well. The fifties, sixties, and seventies were crucial times in the development of hormone therapy for contraception. Many careers, patents, and investments were at stake. Natural progesterone, an item not available in patent form for reasons which I do not fully understand, was therefore not something that pharmaceutical companies would deem desirable for investment of their considerable resources.

Natural progesterone is a white crystalline powder derived from extracts of the Mexican wild yam or soybean. This requires laboratory manufacturing processes and is something altogether different than what we know as botanical medicine. What makes natural progesterone natural is not so much the original plant material but rather that the progesterone molecules that result are chemically identical to the progesterone hormone produced by a woman's own ovaries and adrenal glands. Confusion exists when people think that natural progesterone is found in wild yam and soybeans or that the human body can convert wild yam and soybean extracts to natural progesterone. Neither of these is true. Further confusing the issue is that many people mistakenly call synthetic progestogens or progestins, progesterone. Progestins are chemically different than progesterone and therefore chemically different than the progesterone the body produces and also chemically different than natural progesterone.

Dr. Dalton reports that she has used natural progesterone via injections (25–100 mg daily), vaginal and rectal suppositories (400–1,600 mg daily), and subcutaneous pellets (500–1,600 mg every 3–12 months) with results as good as complete relief of PMS symptoms in 83 percent of women.[39] There have been several studies that demonstrate a lack of efficacy of rectal and vaginal suppositories in the treatment of PMS. Sampson and Freeman found these forms of progesterone to be no better than placebo.[40, 41] Although the suppository method of delivering natural progesterone for PMS has not held up to scientific scrutiny, oral micronized natural progesterone has. A study by Dennerstein and colleagues in 1985 found an overall beneficial effect using 300 mg/day (100 mg, A.M., 200 mg, P.M.) for 10 days of each menstrual cycle starting 3 days after ovulation.[42] After only one month of treatment, those receiving progesterone could be clearly distinguished from those receiving placebo on measures of stress, anxiety, and concentration. Most all other symptoms also continued to improve with each menstrual cycle. The only premenstrual complaint not consistently improved by progesterone was arousal. A 1993 study also reported successful use of progesterone in doses of 300 mg oral micronized progesterone daily or 3 cc rectal solution twice daily.[43]

More recently, Dr. John Lee has become the most outspoken proponent of the use of natural progesterone by using transdermal creams that are applied to specified areas of the skin. He reports significant success in his medical practice and has written about it in his treatise on natural progesterone.[44]

The availability of natural progesterone in transdermal creams in the retail over-the-counter market has created perhaps the greatest confusion yet in the use of this valuable medicine. It is important for the consumer and practitioner to understand the difference between wild yam extracts versus natural progesterone products derived from extracts found in wild yam (and soy). Wild yam extracts do not contain natural progesterone unless they say that natural progesterone has been added. Also, different products contain different amounts of progesterone in their product. The range is as little as 2 mg per ounce to more than 400 mg per ounce. User beware and be educated. They all have their value, but not necessarily for the treatment of PMS.

In my clinical practice, I largely use the transdermal creams that contain more than 400 mg per ounce of cream. For severe PMS symptoms that have not responded to nutritional, botanical, and lifestyle changes, and for those whose symptoms start from a few days to one week before the menses, I recommend applying ¼ tsp natural progesterone cream twice daily starting at mid-cycle and stopping the day before the menses is due. For women whose significant symptoms begin at ovulation, I recommend ¼ tsp per day from day 8 to day 14 (do not use during days 1–7 while bleeding), and then ¼ tsp twice daily until the menses begin, as described above. The best sites for rubbing in the cream include the palms, inner forearms, chest, and inner thighs. Also, it is best utilized when rotating sites of application. Individual uses may vary depending on symptoms or menstrual pattern.

Since natural progesterone is a hormone, I think it is best to seek the advice of a qualified health care practitioner who is experienced with its use. This assures proper usage and therefore maximum results. Some of the companies that sell over-the-counter natural progesterone have very qualified physician staffing available as a resource to customers and practitioners. Oral micronized progesterone and some of the other delivery methods of progesterone are prescription items. These products are used mainly by licensed naturopathic physicians, but also by progressive medical doctors and a growing number of chiropractors and acupuncturists.

NATURAL PROGESTERONE CREAM

- If symptoms start from a few days to 1 week before the menses, apply ¼ tsp twice daily beginning at mid-cycle and stopping the day before the menses is due.
- If symptoms begin at ovulation, apply ¼ tsp per day from day 8 to day 14 (do not use during days 1–7 while bleeding), and then ¼ tsp twice daily until the menses begin.

SAMPLE TREATMENT PLAN FOR PREMENSTRUAL SYNDROME

Three-Month Plan

- Reduce the intake of alcohol, caffeine, salt, sugar, refined carbohydrates, and dairy products.
- Increase the intake of fruits, vegetables, legumes, nuts, seeds, fish and flax oil.
- Exercise regularly.
- Take a combination nutritional/botanical PMS product (available at natural food stores or alternative health practitioners). It should include B_6; magnesium; borage, flax, or evening primrose oil; vitex; vitamin E; dong quai; wild yam.
- Take a multiple vitamin/mineral supplement, 1–6 caps per day.
- If the above plan doesn't relieve PMS after 3 cycles, then use natural progesterone creams with greater than 400 mg per ounce or prescription oral micronized progesterone.

❦ Conventional Medicine Approach

In perhaps no other diagnostic category has the advice of conventional physicians so overlapped with that of their naturopathic colleagues. All are searching! Basic lifestyle issues such as exercise, diet, nutritional supplements, and stress/mood assessment have all been studied[45, 46] and are always the starting point of treatment. Probably in part because we had no consistently effective therapy, conventional physicians borrowed eagerly from natural medicine, and enthusiastic interest in natural progesterone occurred several years ago. Several studies on natural progesterone were undertaken, and these were discussed earlier in this chapter. Because patients in slightly more than half the studies failed to show significant improvement over those taking placebo—and despite the fact that patients in about half the studies did demonstrate improvement—natural progesterone has fallen far from favor, and most now recommend against using it.[47] Theoretical concern exists around exacerbating rather than relieving symptoms, although this has not been reported. It is interesting to note that oral contraceptives have virtually the same—or a slightly worse—track record in studies[48] and experience, and yet they are offered as an option that is reasonable to try. The bias shows! It is unfortunate that one of our few forays into documenting natural medicine's power "scientifically" failed, even though many of us continue to use natural progesterone because it works—in some women.

The main pharmaceutical recommended presently is Prozac, the ubiquitous drug which has been studied with good success.[49] This makes logical sense given the serotonin-based physiology we discussed above. Side effects include headaches and weight loss as well as a high incidence of orgasmic dysfunction, despite which huge numbers of prescriptions are written every day. Similarly, gonadotropin-releasing hormone agonists (Synarel, Lupron) that induce a pseudo-menopause, bone density loss, and which, for obvious reasons, cannot be used long term, are recommended. These are powerful drugs that work in large part by eliminating cyclicity altogether, a heavy price that I have yet to meet the woman whose PMS warranted. Alprazolam (Zanax), a short-acting benzodiazepine, is also suggested, although this too seems unwise for most women given its addictive potential. It is basically a shorter-acting Valium, and you would think we would have already learned our lesson here. Spironolactone, a diuretic that spares potassium, is a great option for those most bothered by fluid retention and bloatedness, but this is rarely the most aggravating symptom.

While much attention has been directed at PMS, the multifactorial nature of this discomfort only becomes more and more obvious. I do not yet know what to make of the recent popularity of Prozac and similar drugs to improve our collective mood, but I do know a lot of PMS sufferers are among the many who partake. I know many are grateful. I also know that if this were a culture that honored women's power and sexuality in a more healthy way, then perhaps PMS would fade into the realm of the rare rather than the common.

≈ Seeing a Licensed Primary Health Care Practitioner*

PMS is the perfect condition for self-treatment. Mild to moderate PMS is well addressed by lifestyle changes and safe and effective nutritional and botan-

---

*N.D. = Naturopathic Doctor; M.D. = Medical Doctor; D.O. = Osteopathic Doctor; N.P. = Nurse Practitioner; P.A. = Physician's Assistant.

ical supplements most of the time. When these measures are not effective or when the symptoms are severe, a licensed naturopathic physician can readily utilize natural progesterone therapy or more aggressive dosing of nutritional and botanical supplements. Few conventional medical doctors are trained in these therapies, although increasing numbers are integrating them into their practice. Severe symptoms of depression, headaches, breast pain, or others may require the use of pharmaceutical intervention, although this is rarely necessary. In these cases, temporary use of such drugs must be recommended judiciously, while the continued use of natural medicines is integrated into the long-term plan. Only rarely will PMS not respond to a comprehensive natural medicine approach.

CHAPTER SIXTEEN

SEXUALLY TRANSMITTED DISEASES

❧ Overview

Sexually transmitted diseases (STDs) and their complications continue to infect women at epidemic rates. Each year, more than 13 million American men and women contract an STD. Worldwide, the estimated incidence of STDs is 250 million cases per year. All women who are sexually active are at risk for acquiring infection and related reproductive tract problems, although heterosexual women are at substantially increased risk as compared to lesbian women. Gonorrhea and chlamydial infections may produce urethritis, cervicitis, and pelvic inflammatory disease (PID). Human papillomavirus (HPV) is the cause of genital warts and cervical dysplasia. Syphilis is responsible for myriad systemic and tissue abnormalities. Herpes simplex virus (HSV) infection is associated with small blisterlike skin eruptions and ulcerations. Scabies and pediculosis are fraught with itching of the skin. Sexual contact is the leading method of transmitting hepatitis B (HBV). HIV infection and AIDS (the most advanced stage of HIV infection) are sexually transmitted diseases as well. Less common STDs, such as lymphogranuloma venereum and chancroid, present as pimple-like or ulcerative genital lesions.

The purpose of this chapter is to discuss some of the alternative approaches and conventional therapies used in the treatment of chlamydia, gonorrhea, and hepatitis B. Please refer to Chapter 18 (Vaginitis),

Chapter 4 (Cervical Dysplasia), Chapter 8 (Genital Herpes), and Chapter 13 (Pelvic Inflammatory Disease) for further information and treatment recommendations regarding other conditions that can be transmitted through sexual contact.

Chlamydia trachomatis infection is the most common STD in the United States. The infection rate is considered epidemic in women and is estimated at four million new cases each year. Chlamydia is evident in about 20–40 percent of sexually active women in the United States.[1] Chlamydia can be deceptive because as many as 70 percent of women with this infection do not exhibit symptoms. When symptoms do occur, it commonly causes urethritis, cervicitis, and PID in women. Common symptoms that occur include uncomfortable urination, frequency of urination, vaginal spotting, increased discharge that may be yellowish, pelvic pain, and pain or spotting with intercourse. Chlamydia is diagnosed on physical examination, with a smear of the discharge from the urethra and cervix viewed under a microscope and with special tests and cultures of the same discharge. Untreated infection can lead to PID involving the uterus (endometritis) and/or the fallopian tubes (salpingitis), ectopic pregnancy, and infertility. About 60–70 percent of untreated cases in pregnant women result in neonatal infection in the eyes or lungs.[1] Because of the number of women who have contracted chlamydia and do not exhibit symptoms, many women go untreated. Unfortunately, many of these women find out later that their fallopian tubes have been scarred, which leads to infertility.

Gonorrhea is caused by *Neisseria gonorrhoeae* and is responsible for at least half a million cases of infection in both males and females yearly. Approximately 40 percent of the cases occur in women, and the highest risk is among women aged 15–19 years. The incubation period of gonococcal infection averages three to five days, with a range of one to fourteen days. The majority of women with gonorrhea present with no symptoms, but one-third of women observe a vaginal discharge. Urethritis with uncomfortable urination and frequency, cervicitis, a puslike discharge, abdominal/pelvic pain, vaginal spotting, and pain with intercourse are symptoms that warrant a suspicion of gonorrhea. Symptoms often do not present until PID develops. Abdominal pelvic pain is generally an indication of endometritis, salpingitis, or an abscess, and gener-

ally develops a few days following the onset of menses. Infected mothers during pregnancy or at the time of delivery may transmit gonorrhea to neonates. It most commonly causes conjunctivitis. Gonorrhea can also cause blindness in newborns. Other complications can include increased risks of spontaneous abortion, premature labor, early rupture of the fetal membranes, and perinatal infant mortality. Gonorrhea is diagnosed on a physical exam and confirmed with cultures. As many as 30–60 percent of women with gonorrhea are also infected with chlamydia[2] and therefore both gonorrhea and chlamydia should be tested together.

Hepatitis B (HBV) is a virus that infects more than 300,000 Americans annually. It is estimated that 1.5 million people in the United States are carriers of the disease but experience no symptoms at all. Sexual contact, especially anal sex, is the leading method of transmitting HBV. Other methods of transmission include the sharing of needles among drug users, exposure to infected body tissues or fluids through an open cut or sore, and infected mothers who pass the virus on to their babies. The most common early symptoms are flulike. Symptoms that arise later include jaundice (yellowing of the skin and whites of the eyes), abdominal

KEY CONCEPTS

- Any sexual contact with a person with gonorrhea, chlamydia, or hepatitis B warrants a visit to the doctor where a physical exam and tests will likely be performed.
- Antibiotic treatment of chlamydia and gonorrhea should be considered the primary treatment with alternative treatments used as complements.
- Complications of gonorrhea, chlamydia, and hepatitis B can be serious and even life-threatening and can infect the newborn.
- Symptoms of chlamydia and gonorrhea include vaginal discharge, difficult or painful urination, bleeding between periods or after intercourse, pain in the pelvic area during sex, and acute or chronic pelvic pain. However, many women have no symptoms at all.
- Appropriate management of an STD includes seeing a health care practitioner that can identify, screen, and treat the woman and her current sexual partner.

PREVENTION

- Know the sexual disease history of your potential sexual partner.
- The best protection against acquiring a sexually transmitted disease is for the male partner to use latex condoms.
- All heterosexual women who engage in unprotected sex with one or more men are at risk for STDs. Women with frequent partners or multiple partners have more STDs.
- Oral contraceptive use may predispose women to chlamydial infection.[3]
- Patients diagnosed with one STD should be screened for other common STDs.
- IV drug users should avoid sharing needles.
- Health care workers should be focused, careful, and practice universal precautions in their workplace.

pain, and dark and foamy urine. With treatment, most people begin to feel better within two to three weeks and recover within four to eight weeks. A very small percentage of people who are chronic carriers of HBV will develop potentially severe and fatal liver diseases such as active hepatitis, cirrhosis, or cancer. Blood tests are used to diagnose both the active form of HBV and the carrier state. Pregnant women can be screened for the virus during their prenatal care.

❦ Overview of Alternative Medicine

Due to potential infertility from the scarring of acute PID as well as some of the other complications of chlamydial infection and gonorrhea, my advice is to consider alternative medicine as an adjunct to conventional antibiotics. Using alternative therapies to support the immune system, to assist in managing pain and discomfort, and to counteract some of the side effects of the antibiotics are the main priorities. Drinking plenty of water, getting enough rest, eating simple light foods, and avoiding stimulants are basic guidelines during any acute infection, including pelvic infections.

General immune support to complement conventional antibiotic treatment is just good plain common sense. Nutritional and botanical support can stimulate the white blood cells that engulf and destroy bacteria and enhance the function of T-cells, B-cells, and natural killer cells that modulate the immune system in reaction to bacteria and viruses. Such supplements as vitamin A, vitamin C, the carotenes, vitamin E, zinc, and the B vitamins play an important role in immune enhancement. Increasing antibody response, stimulating helper T-cells, enhancing white blood cell response and function, and directly killing the virus or bacteria are just some of the ways in which these supplements can be helpful during an acute infection of any kind.

Many herbs have also been shown to have antibacterial, antiviral, and immunostimulating effects. The most commonly used herb for immune support is echinacea. Echinacea can increase the production of T-cells, stimulate phagocytosis of bacteria, stimulate natural killer cell activity, and multiply the numbers of white blood cells that circulate in order to

deal with the infection.[4] The end result is a strengthened immune system.

The best complement to counteract undesirable intestinal side effects of antibiotic use is to add or increase the intake of *Lactobacillus acidophilus* to help prevent a vaginal yeast infection. This can be accomplished by eating yogurt daily or by taking oral capsules of lactobacillus. Eating four to eight ounces of unsweetened acidophilus yogurt daily or taking at least three capsules of lactobacillus acidophilus daily between meals for two weeks should prevent the overgrowth of vaginal yeast that often occurs when taking antibiotics. Additional dietary advice and botanical and nutritional therapies for the prevention and treatment of yeast vaginitis can be gleaned by reading Chapter 18.

Ice packs over the pelvic region can reduce inflammation and pain in cases of acute PID. Placing cold or ice packs over the region of the uterus and putting the feet in a hot foot bath or placing a hot water bottle on the feet can further assist in reducing the inflammation, congestion, and pain in the pelvic area.

Nutrition

The nutritional goals during an active STD infection are to eat health-promoting and immune supportive foods. Generally, this refers to a diet high in fiber, plant-based foods, essential fatty acids, and antioxidant nutrients, and low in saturated fat and refined sugar.

The best dietary sources of antioxidants and especially the carotenes are green leafy vegetables and yellow-orange fruits and vegetables such as carrots, apricots, peaches, mangoes, yams, and squash. Beans, whole grains, and many seeds are also good sources of carotenes.

Eliminating refined sugar and simple sugars (corn syrup, honey, fructose, maple syrup, white grape juice concentrate, etc.) will help to assure optimal immune function. Eliminating saturated fats such as red meat, butter, cheese, and ice cream, even in the short run, will enable the body to utilize essential fatty acids such as the fats from olive oil, canola oil, and ocean fish. These essential fatty acids are important in the promotion of the anti-inflammatory prostaglandins, PgE1 and PgE3; reducing inflammation is a primary goal in healing an STD infection.

Keeping the digestion in order with regular bowel habits and free of constipation can be accomplished with a high fiber diet rich in whole grains, fruits, vegetables, and beans. This will not only minimize digestive side effects, if antibiotics are used in the STD treatment, but will also maximize the elimination of the body's metabolic toxins that are increased during the infection.

Some naturopathic physicians advocate a very light diet or even fasting during an active acute infection. The rationale is to minimize the burden on the body so that all of its resources can be utilized for an immune response and for fighting the infection. Fasting is also presumably a more efficient way of eliminating the metabolic toxins. If you're not used to fasting, I would not suggest trying this approach for any longer than three days on your own. Drink plenty of water as well. Better yet, you may want to seek advice from a knowledgeable practitioner about this approach.

If you are taking antibiotics, then be sure to eat eight ounces of unsweetened lactobacillus yogurt daily to prevent the possibility of a yeast vaginitis infection caused by the antibiotics.

Nutritional Supplements

Alpha Lipoic Acid

Alpha lipoic acid (ALA) is an excellent antioxidant and is an important coenzyme for the production of acetyl coenzyme A. Dihydrolipoic acid (DHLA) is the reduced form of ALA and functions as a donor of electrons that helps to recycle other important antioxidants. For example, vitamin C is recycled by DHLA, and subsequently vitamin E is recycled by vitamin C. In Europe, lipoic acid is often used as a treatment for all types of liver disease. Currently, there is a lack of research on the use of lipoic acid in liver disease. However, some noted physicians, such as Dr. Burton Berkson, have a great deal of experience in using lipoic acid in severe liver disease. The few studies that have been done report conflicting results. In one of these

studies, lipoic acid enhanced the regeneration of liver cells and function in persons who had chronic alcoholic and viral liver disease.[5] Lipoic acid is administered both intravenously and orally. Patients with hepatitis are often given 200 mg orally three times daily, as noted by Dr. Berkson.[6]

Alpha lipoic acid
200 mg, 3 times daily

Vitamin C

According to one study, vitamin C has been effective in reducing the incidence of hepatitis B infections acquired in hospitalized patients.[7] Patients who received two grams or more of vitamin C per day did not contract hepatitis B, while 7 percent of the patients who received less than 1.5 grams did. Based on this finding, it would seem logical to give vitamin C to patients with HBV, and even in higher doses. Vitamin C in general protects the liver from free radical damage and stimulates its mechanisms of detoxification.

Vitamin C
2 grams per day or more

Botanical Medicine

Phyllanthus Species

This Ayurvedic remedy has been used by traditional practitioners in India for decades. It has also been subjected to scientific scrutiny in the study of hepatitis B patients. In one study, 60 patients with HBV were given 200 mg capsules of *Phyllanthus amarus* powdered extract or placebo three times daily for one month. Researchers reported 59 percent of the subjects receiving the herbal extract had responded by testing negative for the antigen to HBV at the first follow-up visit. Only 4 percent of the patients on placebo had that response. The bad news was that the carriers of HBV, not those with active hepatitis B virus, were less likely to respond to the herbal therapy than those who received the placebo.[8] Other studies of *Phyllanthus amarus* have not demonstrated this same success in eliminating the viral hepatitis markers. Another species of *Phyllanthus* may be more effective. *Phyllanthus urinaria* has elicited a response in patients who received 300 mg three times daily for one month, then 600 mg three times a day for one month, and 900 mg three times a day for one month. 60 percent were positive for the HBV antigen at the beginning of the trial, and only 40 percent remained positive at the end of the treatment.[9] In this same study, a group of patients took *Phyllanthus amarus* and *P. niruri*. No patient receiving the *P. amarus* extract converted from a positive antigen marker to a negative, and there was only minimal response to *P. niruri*.

Phyllanthus spp

Month one: 300 mg, 3 times per day

Month two: 600 mg, 3 times per day

Month three: 900 mg, 3 times per day

Licorice (*Glycyrrhiza glabra*)

Glycyrrhizin, the most active constituent of the root of *Glycyrrhiza glabra*, has been used by both Western and Eastern herbal practitioners and alternative practitioners in the treatment of chronic fatigue syndrome, stomach and duodenal ulcers, eczema, and chronic inflammatory conditions, as an immune modulator, and in the treatment of acute and chronic upper respiratory infections. In Japan, glycyrrhizin has been used for its hepatic actions, specifically in the treatment of chronic hepatitis B and C.[10] One such preparation used was an intravenous formulation of glycyrrhizin, cysteine, and glycine in saline. The standard dose is 40 ml that includes 80 mg of glycyrrhizin per day.

Licorice (*glycyrrhiza glabra*)

80 mg glycyrrhizin per day

Milk Thistle (*Silybum marianum*)

Silymarin, or milk thistle, is a powerful antioxidant and is even more potent in that regard than vitamin E and vitamin C. Milk thistle prevents the depletion of glutathione, and glutathione levels in the liver are critically linked to the liver's ability to detoxify. A reduction in glutathione makes the liver cells susceptible to damage, and thus liver function wanes.

Milk thistle has been used for centuries in folk traditions and by herbalists who considered it to be a liver-protective agent. Silymarin, the active flavonoid component of the herb, is made up of potent flavanoligans that serve to improve and/or restore liver function by preventing and reversing liver damage. It has been used in alcoholic liver disease, liver toxicity from poison mushrooms, and in acute and chronic viral hepatitis. In a study of 25 patients with acute hepatitis B, a dose of 140 mg of silymarin was given three times a day.[11] Liver enzymes and serum bilirubin regressed significantly after five days of treatment, and after three weeks the liver enzymes were normal in many more patients than in the placebo group. Silymarin did not, however, cause the hepatitis antigen to turn negative as in the *Phyllanthus* study reported earlier. So while milk thistle may not be able to influence the growth and replication of the hepatitis B virus, it does have a significant effect in protecting the liver from damage, scarring, and tissue death. Milk thistle is therefore a key player in preventing future complications from hepatitis B.

Milk thistle (*silybum marianum*)

140 mg silymarin, 3 times a day

Other herbs that may be helpful:

- *Azadirachta indica* (neem seed oil), *Sapindus mukerossi* (reetha saponin extract), and quinine. An Indian study of these herbs included 58 women who presented to a gynecology clinic in India with an abnormal discharge. They were tested and were found to have either chlamydia, *Candida albicans*, *Trichomonas*, bacterial vaginosis, or mixed infections.

    The women were randomized to receive either a cream containing neem seed oil, reetha saponin extract and quinine, or a placebo cream. The creams were applied intravaginally at bedtime for

---

SAMPLE TREATMENT PLAN FOR CHLAMYDIA AND GONORRHEA

*To be used as a complement to antibiotics

- **Vitamin A:** 50,000 IU per day for up to 1 week and 25,000 IU for 1 additional week. (Do not exceed 5,000 IU if pregnant.)
- **Vitamin C:** 500 mg every 2 hours for 2 days followed by 1,000 mg 3 times daily for 2 weeks.
- **Carotenoids:** 50,000 IU per day for 2 weeks
- **Zinc:** 30 mg per day for 2 weeks.
- **Echinacea:** 2 capsules every 2 hours for 2 days followed by 2 capsules 3 times daily for 2 weeks, or ¼ tsp of tincture every 2 hours for 2 days followed by ½ tsp 3 times daily for 2 weeks,
- *Lactobacillus* **spp:** 4–8 oz of *Lactobacillus acidophilus* yogurt daily for 2 weeks or 3 capsules of *Lactobacillus acidophilus* daily for 2 weeks.
- **Ice packs** over the uterus with a hot foot bath or hot water bottle to the feet. Repeat twice daily as needed.

SAMPLE TREATMENT PLAN FOR HEPATITIS B

- **Diet:** Eat lightly for the acute phase of the infection. Limit foods to brown rice, steamed vegetables, moderate intake of low fat animal protein, vegetable broths, vegetable juices (carrot, beet, greens) diluted with half as much water, avoid sugars, white flour, and all alcohol. Eat increased amounts of foods that help protect the liver from damage and/or improve liver function: garlic, onions, cabbage-family vegetables, legumes, oat bran, carrots, artichokes, and beets. Eat foods that are high in water-soluble fiber that promote increased secretion of bile: apples, legumes, pears, oat bran.
- **Vitamin C:** From 1,000 mg 3 times daily up to bowel tolerance. Bowel tolerance is achieved with the onset of diarrhea, gas and bloating, and intestinal cramping. At that point, reduce dosage slightly until these symptoms subside.
- **Lipoic acid:** 200 mg oral lipoic acid, 3 times daily.
- **Phyllanthus:** 200 mg, 3 times daily.
- **Silymarin:** 140–300 mg, 3 times daily.
- **Lipotropic agents:** Take enough of the combination formulation to achieve 1,000 mg of choline and 1,000 mg of methionine or cysteine.
- **Detoxification program:** May include fasting, hydrotherapy techniques, and supplementation with magnesium, zinc, vitamin C, glutathione, vitamin B_6, fish oils, and lipotropic nutrients.

---

14 days. Ten of the 12 patients with chlamydia who received the treatment cream recovered within two weeks. Ten of the 17 women with bacterial vaginosis who received the treatment cream recovered within two weeks. There was no benefit in women with *Candida* or *Trichomonas*. There was no improvement in symptoms or lab test results in any of the women in the placebo group. Although there were not enough women to achieve statistical significance, the cream showed encouraging results and should clearly be investigated further. It would be very appropriate to try this cream in bacterial vaginosis. In chlamydia infection, it could be used as an adjunct treatment along with antibiotics, or following the antibiotics to help prevent recurrence.[12]

- *Cynara scolymus* (Globe artichoke) has been found to be similar to silymarin in its hepatoprotective effects.
- *Bupleurum falcatum* contains saponins that are particularly active in lowering the liver enzymes GOT and GPT.
- *Shizandra chinensis* has been useful in preventing liver toxicity in laboratory rats that were exposed to toxic chemical substances that normally induce hepatitis.[13] Other studies clearly show its ability to protect against hepatotoxicity by lowering liver enzymes, accelerating recovery rate, or reducing the inflammatory response.

Other Agents That Might Be Helpful

For over 100 years, liver extracts have been used to treat chronic liver disease. These extracts promote the regeneration of normal healthy liver cells. Liver enzymes have been significantly lowered versus a placebo in patients with chronic hepatitis by giving 70 mg of liver extracts three times daily for three months.[14] Although lowering liver enzymes is not necessarily a sign of cure, it is indicative that the agent was effective in stopping and preventing further damage to the liver.

Lipotropic agents, which include choline, betaine, methionine, vitamin B$_6$, folic acid, and vitamin B$_{12}$, have been a mainstay of many natural medicine treatment practices for liver disorders. These compounds promote the flow of fat and bile to and from the liver. They produce a kind of decongesting effect on the liver by improving liver function and fat metabolism. Lipotropic formulations seem to increase S-adenosylmethionine (SAM) and glutathione, two important liver compounds that promote liver detoxification pathways. Methionine, choline, and betaine increase the levels of SAM.

⧼ *Conventional Medicine Approach*

The primary treatment of chlamydia infection and gonorrhea is a course of antibiotics. The Centers for Disease Control (CDC) has recently published new guidelines for treating STDs, the first since 1993. In many cases, more than one therapeutic strategy is endorsed and carries a positive recommendation. Antibiotics can be used to treat both chlamydia and gonorrhea and have a cure rate greater than 95 percent. Penicillin, however, often used for treating syphilis, is not effective against gonorrhea and chlamydia. For the treatment of chlamydia infection in women, the CDC recommends a single, 1-gram oral dose of azithromycin, or a seven-day regimen of oral 100-mg doxycycline twice daily; alternative treatment options are ofloxacin (300 mg, twice daily for seven days), erythromycin base (500 mg, four times daily for seven days), erythromycin ethylsuccinate (800 mg orally, four times daily for seven days), and sulfisoxazole (500 mg, four times daily for seven days).[15] The single dose regimen of azithromycin makes it an appealing choice for many women and practitioners. The CDC recommends that the practitioner administer this single-dose medication, because a single-dose agent ensures better compliance, which is especially important in treating asymptomatic patients and patients who are inconsistent with their health care. In a study conducted at several facilities of women with evidence of chlamydia infection, single-dose azithromycin was shown to be as effective as one week of doxycycline.[16] The women who received the single dose of azithromycin had a 98 percent clinical response; for those treated with doxycycline, it was 95 percent. Diagnosis and treatment of chlamydia infections are especially important in pregnant women. The CDC recommends screening all pregnant women for chlamydia and treating infected women with 500-mg oral erythromycin administered four times a day for seven days. One of the problems with erythromycin, however, is that it is well known for its negative effects on the gut. It can cause nausea and vomiting, which may already be a problem in a pregnant woman. Azithromycin may be an appropriate alternative for pregnant women.

The CDC urges that most women treated for gonococcal infection also be treated for chlamydia infection. However, there may be circumstances where a coinfection with chlamydia is a minimal risk, and it may be preferable to test for chlamydia rather than presume and treat. When patients are seen who are unlikely to return for follow-up, they should be treated for both infections. Gonococcal infections can be treated with regimens of cefixime, ceftriaxone, ciprofloxacin, or ofloxacin in conjunction with doxycycline. As stated above, new guidelines recommend azithromycin (one gram orally in a single dose) as an alternative to doxycycline.

The CDC recommends that all sex partners of persons with STDs be treated, and patients should be advised to abstain from intercourse until their partners are treated to avoid re-exposure. Follow-up tests of cure are advisable to ensure the effectiveness of the treatment. Tests of cure for chlamydial infection or gonorrhea should be performed approximately one week after treatment if culture or antigen tests are used and three weeks after treatment if nucleic acid-based tests are used (polymerase chain reaction and ligase chain reaction). These highly sensitive and specific nucleic acid testing techniques offer the best assurance that treatment has been effective and that re-infection from an untreated or under-treated partner has not occurred.

The CDC offers recommendations on who should be vaccinated for hepatitis B. In addition to infants and adolescents, the list now includes sexually active homosexual and bisexual men; sexually active heterosexual men and women, including those recently diagnosed with an STD, those with more than one partner in the previous six months, clients seen in STD clinics, prostitutes, illegal drug users (including those who do not inject drugs), health care workers, recipients of certain blood products, household and sexual contacts of people with chronic hepatitis B virus infection, adoptees from countries where hepatitis B virus infection is endemic, certain international travelers, clients and staff members of institutions for the developmentally disabled, and hemodialysis patients.[17] This list is quite extensive and probably exceeds the willingness of many patients in these categories. Each patient should be educated about the pros and cons, including the benefits of the vaccine versus the risks of the vaccine, and then weigh that against the risks of having the disease. In cases of exposure to HBV, a solution of hepatitis B immunoglobulins is given by injection, and two doses are given within two weeks of the exposure.

Alpha interferon has been utilized in over half a million people in the United States since its approval in 1991, with limited success. Alpha interferon therapy is expensive and results in many side effects, some of which are serious. Side effects include flulike symptoms, irritability, depression, interstitial pneumonia, thyroid dysfunction, and bone marrow suppression. Currently, alpha interferon is the best medicine conventional treatment has to offer for hepatitis B, but, unfortunately, it is not that effective. Liver transplants are expensive and hard to come by.

An entirely new consideration has been given to hepatitis A. Transmission of this form of hepatitis is most commonly fecal-oral, but the virus may be transmitted to sexual partners through oral-anal contact. Treatment is generally supportive because the infection resolves on its own with few complications. Some people require hospitalization because they become dehydrated or have a very severe case. Hepatitis vaccines are available and may be appropriate for women who are at high risk for being exposed to the virus. A two-dose series of vaccine provides long-term protection.

Seeing a Licensed Primary Health Care Practitioner*

If you have unprotected sexual contact with someone who has chlamydia, gonorrhea, or hepatitis B, I strongly urge you to see a practitioner trained and qualified to perform a physical exam and take samples for testing, and capable of administering or making available the prescription antibiotics and vaccine. This does not necessarily require a gynecologist or other conventional practitioner. Licensed naturopathic physicians are trained to perform and provide these services. State law determines which antibiotics naturopathic physicians may be able to prescribe. If they cannot prescribe a particular antibiotic, they can either refer you to a conventional practitioner or work in cooperation with a conventional practitioner who can make a prescription available to you. Nutritional and herbal supplements can then be used in addition to your conventional treatment. A naturopathic physician can also provide additional natural therapies to augment your immune support, prevent side effects from the medications, and help you to recover optimally from the infection.

Deciding to use alpha interferon is a much more significant decision due to its relatively poor cure rate as weighed against the side effects. If you have severe liver disease due to hepatitis B, I would strongly consider the alternative treatments as the primary treatment, with careful monitoring of liver enzymes, and liver biopsy with the help of a specialist.

---

*N.D. = Naturopathic Doctor; M.D. = Medical Doctor; D.O. = Osteopathic Doctor; N.P. = Nurse Practitioner; P.A. = Physician's Assistant.

UTERINE FIBROIDS

 Overview

Uterine fibroids (also known as *leiomyomas* or *myomas*) occur in 20–25 percent of women by age 40,[1] more than 50 percent of women overall, and are the most common indication for major surgery in women. Some studies have shown that in black women the incidence of fibroids is three to nine times higher and the fibroids' rate of growth is increased.[2, 3] They are the most common solid pelvic tumors in women. You would think with something as common as this that we would have a good understanding of their cause and cure. Nevertheless, the cause of fibroids remains poorly understood.

Uterine fibroids are not actually fibrous but consist of muscle, probably uterine smooth-muscle cells but possibly from connective tissue or the smooth-muscle cells of uterine arteries. The growth of fibroids is thought to be stimulated by estrogen. The tendency of fibroids to arise during the reproductive years, grow during pregnancy, and to regress postmenopausally does implicate estrogen as one factor in the cause and growth of fibroid tumors. A growth spurt in the fibroids is frequently seen in the perimenopausal period and is likely due to anovulatory cycles with a relative estrogen excess that commonly occurs during this period. Pregnancy is a condition of both elevated estrogen and progesterone, and even though progesterone is an antiestrogen, the increased blood supply during the pregnancy leads to an overall stimulating effect on the uterine fibroids.[4]

There have been reports that fibroids have a significantly higher concentration of estrogen receptors than does normal uterine muscle.[5] Although these findings may help to explain why fibroids are sensitive to estrogen, they have not been substantiated by some other researchers.[6, 7] There may be a local hyperestrogenic effect via alterations in estrogen metabolism within the fibroid itself. Pollow and colleagues[7] demonstrated a significantly lower conversion of estradiol into estrone in fibroids than in the myometrium. This suggests that increases in local estradiol concentration within the fibroid itself may play a role in the cause and growth of fibroids. The prevalence and size of fibroids are greater in women who do not ovulate or have endometrial hyperplasia or a granulosa cell tumor of the ovary. Even though fibroids do not lead to cancer and are not a cause of uterine cancer, they are associated with a fourfold increase in the risk of endometrial carcinoma. This is probably because too much estrogen without any or enough progesterone (i.e., unopposed estrogen) is a contributing factor in both conditions. Concentrations of estrogen receptors in fibroid tissue are higher than in the surrounding uterine muscle tissue (myometrium) but lower than in the uterine lining (endometrium).

Fibroids come in all sizes and shapes and usually occur as multiple tumors, although each fibroid is discrete. Most discernible fibroids are between the size of a walnut and the size of an orange, but unusual tumors have been reported up to 100 pounds. The classification of fibroids is according to their location. They are either submucosal (just under the endometrium), intramural (within the uterine muscle wall), or subserosal (from the outer wall of the uterus). They can also be intraligamentous (in the cervix between the two layers of the broad ligament) or pedunculated and dangling from a stalk into the uterine cavity (pedunculated submucous) or pedunculated on the outside of the uterine wall (pedunculated subserous). The pedunculated submucous fibroids can on occasion protrude through the cervix and appear in the vagina. Other pedunculated fibroids on a long stalk outside the uterus can be mistaken for an ovarian mass or attach to the bowel.

The majority of fibroids (an estimated 50–80 percent)[8] don't cause any symptoms but when symptoms do occur they often begin as a vague feeling of discomfort and may include a feeling of pressure, congestion, bloating, heaviness, pain with vaginal sex, urinary frequency, backache, abdominal enlargement, and abnormal bleeding. Abnormal bleeding occurs in 30 percent of women with fibroids. Heavy bleeding (menorrhagia) results when intramural tumors enlarge the endometrial cavity and increase the surface area of endometrium and blood supply to the uterus. Intermenstrual bleeding (metrorrhagia) results when submucous fibroids ulcerate through the endometrial lining or cause congestion of the surrounding blood vessels.

Fibroids can undergo degenerative changes. One type of degenerative change is when the continued growth of the fibroid outgrows the blood supply. A more common type of degenerative change is when there is a loss of cellular detail (hyaline degeneration) as a result of a decrease in the vascularity of the tumor. Necrosis results in cystic degeneration, which lends itself to a softer than usual consistency and can be confused with an ovarian mass on exam or pelvic ultrasound. Calcification can occur over time and is usually seen in postmenopausal women.

Fibroids are not usually associated with pain except when degeneration occurs within a fibroid or when the uterus contracts in its efforts to expel a submucous fibroid. Feelings of pressure pains may develop if the uterus becomes excessively enlarged with fibroids. Some of the urinary complications that occur in 5 percent of fibroids are cause for concern because they may be due to compression of the ureter (outflow tract from kidney to bladder), which can then cause enlargement of the kidneys and compromise of kidney function.

Fibroids are thought to be the cause of 2–10 percent of cases of infertility. There are several proposed mechanisms by which this may occur. The tumors may interfere with implantation of the fertilized ovum, they may cause compression on the fallopian tubes and interfere with motility of sperm or egg, or they may cause early miscarriage. They may also cause periodic anovulation or abnormal uterine blood flow and may interfere with transport of sperm. Large fibroids can interfere with a normal pregnancy by interfering with the growth of the fetus, which may lead to intrauterine growth retardation, premature rupture of membranes, retained placenta, postpartum hemorrhage, abnormal labor, or an abnormal lie of the fetus. Not all practicing obstetricians would agree with these reports, and their main observations with pregnant women and large fibroids are an abnormal lie or postpartum hemorrhage. The incidence of miscarriage due to fibroids is unknown but estimated to be two to three times greater than normal.

If a fibroid uterus is present, it can often be felt during a pelvic examination. It usually feels firm but can vary from soft to rock-hard. The uterus can be irregularly shaped, irregularly enlarged, and often feels like it has protrusions. Most of the time it is not painful during the exam.

Many times women don't realize they have a fibroid until the practitioner completes the exam and feels the enlarged uterus or irregularly shaped uterus. This is not cause for alarm. Fibroids are benign growths most all the time. The worrisome fibroid is a rapidly growing one; the rare malignant uterine sarcoma may have to be considered in these cases.

A pelvic ultrasound is the most useful tool in diagnosing a fibroid after the pelvic exam. This imag-

KEY CONCEPTS

- Uterine fibroids are benign and common.
- We do not know what causes fibroids.
- Fibroids are estrogen dependent.
- Usually there are no symptoms.
- Abnormal bleeding may be caused by uterine fibroids.
- Abnormal bleeding warrants a visit to your health care practitioner.
- There are several kinds of fibroids that have to do with where they grow.
- An enlarged uterus or abnormal finding on a pelvic exam may require further testing to determine the diagnosis.
- Less than 1 percent of fibroids are malignant, but rapidly growing fibroids warrant further exploration.

PREVENTION

- Ensure regular ovulation.
- Avoid situations that promote lack of ovulation, such as stress.
- Avoid estrogen medications.
- The more estrogen your body produces, the more the fibroids are likely to grow.
- Dietary phytoestrogens (soy, flax) do not stimulate the growth of fibroids.
- Practice good nutritional habits with a diet that is low in saturated fats, alcohol, or other foods that interfere with the liver's role in metabolizing hormones.
- Maintain a healthy weight. Obesity can lead to higher estrogen effects on the uterus.

ing test is able to identify fibroids, delineate the size and to some degree the location, as well as identify that the ovaries are normal in size. The ultrasound detects the contours of the uterus, what are called hypechoic masses (i.e., the fibroid), compression of the ureters, and any potential enlargement of the kidneys caused by the compression, and of course the presence of an enlarged uterus. It is difficult for the ultrasound to detect fibroids smaller than 2 cm. A magnetic resonance imaging (MRI) test is more accurate in assessing the number, size, and location of fibroids, but it does not provide significant enough additional information to be worth the cost. A hysteroscopy can detect submucous tumors. An X ray can diagnose fibroids that have become calcified.

The main diagnostic consideration that the practitioner will be considering is differentiating a possible fibroid from the following conditions: ovarian malignant tumor, an abscess in the fallopian tube/ovarian region, a diverticulum from the colon, a pelvic kidney (rare), endometriosis, adenomyosis (endometriosis within the muscle wall of the uterus), congenital anomalies, adhesions in the pelvis, or a rare retroperitoneal tumor. Not all of these considerations can be distinguished from the medical history, physical exam, and pelvic ultra-sound. Surgery may be required to distinguish one condition from the other. Laparoscopy is the definitive method of excluding these other diagnoses from fibroids, even though laparoscopy is not typically done to diagnose fibroids. Only when there is great concern or lack of clarity about the diagnosis might the procedure be warranted.

❧ Overview of Alternative Medicine

Over the more than 14 years I have been in clinical practice, not many health problems have eluded successful treatment as consistently as uterine fibroids. Women who are seeking an alternative to the drug or surgical treatment for uterine fibroids will not find an easy, reliable alternative to shrink the tumors within natural medicine. Using my protocol we are usually able to successfully resolve or improve most symptoms that relate to the fibroids such as abnormal bleeding, pelvic pain/pressure, and backache. In addition, there are natural therapies that may be able to slow the growth of the fibroids to avoid further problems. When it comes to shrinking fibroids, especially the large ones, we can expect to actually shrink those in any significant way only a minority of the time. Many alternative practitioners and women who use alternative medicine have reported individual case histories that create some optimism for reducing the size of fibroids. They report reduction in size on pelvic ultrasound, disappearance of symptoms, and even total disappearance of any evidence of fibroids. I myself can report cases where the fibroid growths and the size of the uterus have been significantly reduced. The problem is that the results are very inconsistent and random. Often the cases that have shown the most dramatic improvements are the women who are in their forties and early fifties and are in fact perimenopausal or postmenopausal. The fibroids of these women will tend to shrink because of the natural decrease in their estrogen levels regardless of any natural therapies.

It may be possible to reduce uterine fibroids and avoid a surgery or drug treatment that your gynecologist has recommended; but, more likely than not, large fibroids that are causing symptoms that have not been successfully dealt with will indeed require some kind of conventional intervention. My main goals with women who have large fibroids are to (1) deal with problem symptoms, (2) try to stabilize the situation and hold out until menopause, and (3) recognize the clinical situations when conventional treatment intervention is appropriate and reasonable.

One aspect of being a naturopathic physician is to more fully educate patients about their health and their health problems so that they can make informed decisions about their health care. With uterine fibroids, I have often been in the position of discussing "alternative surgeries" or procedures that their gynecologist has not discussed with them. There are many new therapies that I will discuss in the conventional medicine section that can be an alternative to a hysterectomy in many cases. Educating the woman with fibroids who is faced with a possible hysterectomy and finding a surgeon/gynecologist who is knowledgeable about these hysterectomy alternatives and willing to consider that their patient may be a candidate for these alternatives may be the most important service an alternative provider can offer. Hysteroscopic resection, embolization, and laparoscopic surgery are some of the new therapies that may be possible in individual cases. However, not all cases of fibroids may be successfully treated with these alternate methods.

Nutrition

Even though simply changing one's diet is unlikely to shrink one's fibroids, good dietary habits are still important. Clinical observation has taught me that all natural therapies work best in the context of a healthy lifestyle including dietary changes. Improving one's diet can help to decrease heavy bleeding or the pain and discomfort caused by the fibroids. Besides these potential benefits, dietary improvements will improve your general well-being. Also, women with uterine fibroids may be at higher risk for endometrial cancer in the future due to the estrogen effect on the uterus.

Poor nutritional habits can elevate estrogen levels by inhibiting the body's ability to break down and excrete excess estrogen. The tradition of naturopathic medicine holds that the health and vitality of an individual depend on the health of the liver. The liver's basic functions are vascular, secretory, and metabolic. As a vascular organ, the liver is a major reservoir of blood and filters over one quart of blood per minute. The liver removes bacteria, endotoxins, antigen-antibody complexes, and other particles from the circulation. The liver's secretory functions are the synthesis and secretion of bile. The liver manufactures about one quart of bile on a daily basis. Bile is required for the absorption of fat-soluble substances including some of the vitamins. The majority of the bile secreted from the liver into the intestines is reabsorbed by the many toxic substances that are eliminated from the body by the bile. The metabolic functions of the liver are involved in carbohydrate, fat, and protein metabolism; the storage of vitamins and minerals; the formation of numerous biochemical factors; and the detoxification or excretion into the bile of hormones such as estrogen as well as histamines, drugs, and pesticides.

The liver not only has to process the foods that we eat on a daily basis, but also serves as the great detoxifier of harmful substances (both internal and external) and metabolizes and deactivates hormones. The liver metabolizes estrogen so it can be eliminated from the body by converting it to estrone and finally to estriol, a weaker form of estrogen that has very little ability to stimulate the uterus. If the liver cannot effectively metabolize estradiol, this may be one mechanism by which the uterus becomes overestrogenized and responds with fibroid growths.

Saturated fats, sugar, caffeine, alcohol, and junk foods are presumably problematic in two main ways: (1) they interfere with the body's ability to metabolize estradiol to estrone to estriol, and (2) some of these foods are deficient in vitamin B or interfere with B-vitamin metabolism. If B vitamins are lacking in the diet, the liver is missing some of the raw materials it needs to carry out its metabolic processes and regulate estrogen levels.

Whole grains such as brown rice, oats, buckwheat, millet, and rye are excellent sources of B vitamins. Whole grains also help the body to excrete estrogens through the bowel. The role of whole grain fiber in lowering estrogen levels was first reported in 1982.[9] This study found that vegetarian women who eat a high fiber, low fat diet have lower blood estrogen levels than omnivorous women with low fiber diets. Once again, we can see why a high fiber diet might prevent and perhaps reduce uterine fibroids. It's the estrogen connection, and we know that estrogen is involved in the growth of fibroids.

A high fiber diet may also help relieve some of the bloating and congestion associated with some fibroids. By bulking up the stool and regulating the bowel movements, some of these symptoms may improve. Some women have a hard time tolerating increased fiber in their diet because they have some other compromise in their digestive function. In these cases, go slow with the increase in fiber; other digestive support may be necessary such as enzymes or acidophilus.

Because there is an association between having uterine fibroids and a fourfold increase in the risk of endometrial cancer,[1] three dietary considerations stand out above all else: increase the fiber, lower the dietary fat, and increase the soy products and other legumes. Researchers at the Cancer Research Center at the University of Hawaii published a case-control, multiethnic (Japanese, Caucasian, Native Hawaiian, Filipino, and Chinese) population study to examine the role of dietary soy, fiber, and related foods and nutrients on the risk of endometrial cancer.[10] Over 300 women with endometrial cancer were compared with women in the general multiethnic population, and all women were interviewed with a dietary questionnaire. The researchers found a positive association between a higher level of fat intake and endometrial cancer as well as a higher level of fiber intake and a reduction in risk for endometrial cancer. They also found that a high consumption of soy products and other legumes was associated with a decreased risk of endometrial cancer. Similar reductions in risk were found for increased consumption of other sources of phytoestrogens such as whole grains, vegetables, fruits, and seaweeds. The authors of the study concluded that plant-based diets low in calories from fat, high in fiber, rich in legumes (especially soybeans), whole grain foods, vegetables, and fruits reduce the risk of endometrial cancer. These dietary associations may explain at least in part the reduced rates of uterine cancer in Asian countries compared with those in the United States.

I can't say that lowering the fat and increasing the soy and fiber will definitely prevent or treat fibroids, but there is a relationship between these foods and lowering the risk of endometrial cancer. Since uterine fibroids are associated with an increase in the risk of endometrial cancer, hopefully you can see the logic in eating a diet with these recommendations in mind if you have fibroids.

Some people have raised the question that since soy foods are high in phytoestrogens (specifically isoflavones), and if phytoestrogens have the ability to have a weak estrogenic effect, then shouldn't patients with uterine fibroids or endometrial cancer avoid phytoestrogens? My answer is no. Soy phytoestrogens do not have an estrogenic effect on the uterus. They appear to be selective in terms of which tissues they have an estrogenic effect on and which tissues or organs they have an antiestrogenic effect. Soy foods may be analogous to a new class of drugs called Selective Estrogen Receptor Modulators (SERMs). They act one way in one part of the body and another way in a different part of the body. It seems that, in the uterus, soy isoflavones have an antiestrogen effect. The subject of phytoestrogens is discussed in more detail in Chapter 10.

Nutritional Supplements

As mentioned earlier, many of the symptoms of enlarged fibroids can be effectively treated using natural therapies. For abnormal bleeding problems and pelvic pain problems, refer to Chapters 1 and 11. In this section, I will largely be discussing the traditional naturopathic method of trying to reduce the size of uterine fibroids or to inhibit their growth. These recommendations are based more on tradition, theory, logic, and clinical experiences than on scientific evidence. Those of you who need scientific documentation may be disappointed, but when it comes to uterine fibroids, we usually have the time to be creative in our attempt to discover something that works.

Lipotropic Factors

Supplements such as inositol and choline exert a "lipotropic" effect. This means they promote the removal of fat from the liver. Lipotropic supplements are usually a combination vitamin and herbal formulation and sometimes an animal liver extract designed to support the liver's function in removing fat, detoxifiying the body's wastes, detoxifying external harmful substances (pesticides, fossil fuels, etc.), and metabolizing and excreting estrogens. These lipotropic products vary in their formulations depending on the manufacturer, but they are all similar and have the same uses in mind. Because the liver is the most important organ of metabolism, naturopathic physicians believe that when the liver function improves, metabolism improves; this is fundamental to the treatment of many chronic diseases.

Lipotropic factors
1–4 tablets per day with meals

Pancreatic Enzymes

There are three categories of pancreatic enzymes:

- *Lipases:* enzymes that help digest fats along with bile. A deficiency of lipase results in malabsorption of fats and fat-soluble vitamins.

- *Amylases:* enzymes that break down starch molecules into smaller sugars.
- *Proteases:* trypsin, chymotrypsin, and carboxypeptidase break down protein molecules into single amino acids.

Supplementation with pancreatic enzymes is usually done to treat pancreatic insufficiency. Symptoms of abdominal bloating, gas, indigestion, undigested food in the stool, malabsorption, and nutrient deficiencies are the usual manifestations of pancreatic insufficiency. Other clinical uses of pancreatic enzymes include cystic fibrosis, rheumatoid arthritis, athletic injuries, and, one of the most controversial uses, the treatment of cancer.

The logic for the treatment of uterine fibroids is similar to the logic for the treatment of cancer. Enzyme preparations have been used at the Contreras Clinic in Mexico and by Drs. William Kelley and Nicholas Gonzalez as part of a cancer treatment protocol. There is little evidence in the scientific literature to support their use, but the logic is that the pancreatic enzymes will digest the protein cell membrane surrounding the malignant cells. By doing so, the natural killer immune cells will then be able to enter the cancer cells and alter the abnormal cell division occurring in the cancer cells. In the case of uterine fibroids, the belief is that the pancreatic enzymes will help to digest the fibrous/smooth muscle tissue and dissolve the fibroids. When used for this purpose, the pancreatic enzyme supplement must be taken between meals rather than with meals.

Pancreatic enzymes
2–4 capsules, 3 times per day between meals

Botanical Medicines
Traditional Herbs

Many plants have been used in traditional herbal medicines in an attempt to treat women with uterine fibroids. The plants and herbal formulations talked about here are used to try to shrink uterine fibroids; herbs used to deal with abnormal bleeding and uterine cramping are discussed in Chapters 1 and 11.

Rik Scalzo, a well-known herbalist, has developed a uterine fibroid protocol that he reports has achieved modest success in reducing the size and number of uterine fibroids. I have used many herbs and herbal formulations over the years in an attempt to shrink fibroids, and most of those herbs are found in Scalzo's protocol. I present the protocol here as an option for your consideration. See Appendix B for listing of herbal resources.

Herbal Phytoestrogens

There are three types of naturally occurring estrogen-like substances called phytoestrogens found in plants: resorcylic acid lactones, steroids and sterols, and phenolics. Phytoestrogens are present in virtually every plant in at least modest levels, with some plants having particularly high levels. Resorcylic acid lactones are not true phytoestrogens but are included because they are mycotoxins produced by soil-dwelling molds. Their presence in plants is the result of contamination with molds. Steroids are the classic steroidal estrogens (estradiol and estrone) and are found in very minute amounts in a few plants such as apple seed, date palm, and pomegranate seed in the range of one to ten parts per billion.[10–12] Diosgenin is a steroid derivative and is found in at least 20 plants including wild yam species. Beta-sitosterol is the most common phytosterol and hence is distributed widely through the plant kingdom. It is found in plant oils, such as wheat germ oil, cotton seed oil, and soybean oil. Beta-sitosterol is the dominant phytosterol found in garlic and onions. Herbal sources include licorice root, saw palmetto, and red clover. Stigmasterol is closely related to beta-sitosterol. Soybean oil is an important source of stigmasterol and is a better source for laboratory synthesis of progesterone than is beta-sitosterol. Some herbal sources include burdock, fennel, licorice, alfalfa, anise, and sage. The phenolic phytoestrogens are members of the flavonoids, the largest single family of plant substances, which has over 4,000 individual members. The term "flavonoid" derives from the Latin "flavus" meaning "yellow" because

SCALZO'S PROTOCOL

Scudder's Alterative

Corydalis tubers	*Dicentra canadensis*
Black alder bark	*Alnus serrulata*
Mayapple root	*Podophyllum peltatum*
Figwort flowering herb	*Scrophularia nodosa*
Yellow dock root	*Rumex crispus*

Add 30–40 drops to a small amount of warm water and take 3 times daily.

Echinacea/Red Root Compound

Echinacea	*Echinacea* spp
Red root	*Ceanothus americanus*
Baptisia root	*Baptisia tinctoria*
Thuja leaf	*Thuja occidentalis*
Stillingia root	*Stillingia sylvatica*
Blue flag root	*Iris versicolor*
Prickly ash bark	*Xanthoxylum clava-herculus*

Add 30 drops to a small amount of warm water and take 3 times daily.

Fraxinus/Ceonothus Compound

Mountain ash bark	*Fraxinus americanus*
Red root	*Ceanothus americanus*
Life root	*Senecio aureus*
Mayapple root	*Podophyllum peltatum*
Helonias root	*Chamaelirium luteum*
Goldenseal root	*Hydrastis canadensis*
Lobelia	*Lobelia inflata*
Ginger root	*Zingiber officinalis*

Add 30 drops to a small amount of warm water and take 3 times daily.

Turska Formula

Gelsemium root	*Gelsemium sempervirens*
Poke root	*Phytolacca americana*
Aconite	*Aconitum napellus*
Bryonia root	*Bryonia dioica*

Add 5 drops to a small amount of warm water and take 3 times daily.

Other herbal extracts to consider

Chaste tree	*Vitex agnus castus*
Nettles	*Urtica dioica*
Burdock root	*Arctium lappa*
Dandelion root	*Taraxacum officinalis*
Oregon grape	*Berberis aquifolium*

Topical preparations

Poke root oil: Rub onto the belly over the uterus nightly before bed.

Castor oil packs: Apply over pelvis 3–5 times per week. See Appendix B for instructions.

the flavonoids are responsible for the yellow, red, white, and blue pigments in plants. Phenolics include isoflavones, higher in legumes and especially soybeans than any other plants; coumestans, with one known estrogenic member (coumestrol) that is approximately six times more estrogenic than the isoflavones;[13, 14] and lignans, high in grains and cereals and highest in flaxseeds.

There has been some concern and controversy about how phytoestrogens affect the uterus and if they have an estrogenic effect, in which case they should be avoided by women with uterine fibroids or endometrial cancer. We talked earlier about soybeans and how they are actually associated with a reduced incidence of uterine cancer.[10] I do not believe that eating a high soy diet is something to be concerned about; in fact I recommend increasing the soy foods in the diet.

Most of the research of the effects of phytoestrogens on the uterus is found in relationship to the agricultural industry and the health of grazing animals. In the 1940s, it was reported that the red clover sheep grazed on in Australia was responsible for their infertility.[15] A Finnish study of pasture legumes identified red clover as containing the highest concentrations of phytoestrogens[16] and showed that abundant intake of red clover resulted in fertility problems in cattle.[17]

In one study on the effects of phytoestrogens in sheep, it was noted that both coumestans and isoflavones produce changes in the typical stimulation with steroidal hormones such as estradiol in all of the target organs.[18] Among these changes was an increase in uterine weight. Other investigators have examined the binding of phytoestrogens to the uterus and vagina. Coumestrol has temporarily enhanced the uptake of estradiol by the uterus and vagina only one hour after being injected into mice.[19] What they also noted was that coumestrol actually inhibited the uptake of estradiol by the uterus in a prolonged manner, and they postulated that there was actually an inhibitory effect at the estradiol receptor sites. Other researchers have noted that coumestans and isoflavones compete with estradiol for uterine receptor sites but have less affinity for them than does estradiol.[20]

Coumestrol has been found to increase uterine weight at a 100 mcg dose when given to rats at a certain time in the development of glands.[21] It appears as though the estrogenic effect of phytoestrogens is dose dependent. When given in high enough doses, they will have estrogenic effects on all the same target tissues as estradiol. The question is, What is an excessively high dose, and are the observations in animals translatable to humans? One way of answering the former is to note that in countries with a high intake of phytoestrogens (Japan, Thailand, China), women do not have an increase in uterine fibroids. However, they do have a four- to sixfold lower incidence of breast cancer[22] (also an estradiol target tissue), although how a substance affects one tissue is not necessarily translated to how it affects another.

Again though, I must come back to the effects of soy on the endometrium, which may be different than some of the other plants, most notably red clover. Like data on breast cancer, data on women of different cultures support the conclusion that soy phytoestrogens are not an estrogen stimulus for the endometrium. Rather, they probably act as an estrogen antagonist and are associated with low rates of endometrial cancer in countries where soy phytoestrogen intake is high.[23]

Based on these studies, my recommendation to those with uterine fibroids is to eat a diet high in soy products; however, my current cautionary advice would be to avoid the use of red clover.

Natural Progesterone

Several old studies have suggested that progesterone may inhibit growth of uterine fibroids. A. Lipschutz[24] demonstrated that progesterone administered to guinea pigs prevented formation of tumors that had been induced by estrogen. In 1946, A. Goodman[25] reported six cases of clinically diagnosed uterine fibroids that regressed after using progesterone therapy.

Dr. John Lee poses that because uterine fibroids are a result of estrogen stimulation and what he calls "estrogen dominance," the corrective solution is to use progesterone. He asserts that estrogen dominance is a much greater problem than recognized by conventional medicine. "Since many women in their mid-thirties begin to have nonovulating cycles, they are producing much less progesterone than expected, but still producing normal (or more) estrogen. They retain water and salt, their breasts swell and become fibrocystic, they gain weight (especially around the hips and torso), they become depressed and lose sex drive, their bones suffer mineral loss, and they develop fibroids. All are signs of estrogen dominance relative to a progesterone deficiency. When sufficient natural progesterone is replaced, fibroid tumors no longer grow in size (they generally decrease in size) and can be kept from growing until menopause, after which they will atrophy. This is the effect of reversing estrogen dominance.[26]

The preferred form of natural progesterone for treating fibroids (unless there is heavy bleeding involved) is a topical cream with about 400 mg of progesterone per one ounce of cream.

Be advised, however, that there is another theory and counter-opinion about the relationship of progesterone to uterine fibroids. Dr. Mitchell Rein and his colleagues at Brigham and Women's Hospital published a report in 1995 stating that not only is there no evidence that estrogen directly stimulates myoma growth, but that it is actually progesterone and progestins that promote the growth of fibroids.[27] The authors site the biochemical, histologic, and clinical evidence that supports an important role for progesterone and progestins in the growth of uterine myomas. Their comprehensive hypothesis is based on an analysis of many different technical studies which they conclude suggest that the development and growth of myomas involves a multistep chain of events.

Since both these schools of thought involving the pros and cons of using progesterone are based on

NATURAL PROGESTERONE CREAM (400+ MG/OZ)

¼ tsp one to two times daily for one week after menses; ¼ to ½ tsp twice daily for the next two weeks. Discontinue for one week during menses. Apply the cream to the inner arms, chest, inner thighs, and/or palms.

SAMPLE TREATMENT PLAN FOR UTERINE FIBROIDS

Diet

- Eat a high fiber, low fat diet.
- Eat a diet high in whole grains (brown rice, oats, buckwheat, millet, rye, whole wheat).
- Eat a diet high in flaxseeds, particularly ground flaxseeds.
- Eat a diet high in legumes, especially soy products.
- Avoid saturated fats, sugar, caffeine, alcohol, and "junk foods."

Nutritional Supplementation

- Lipotropic factors — 1–2 tablets twice per day with meals
- Pancreatic enzymes — 2–3 capsules three times per day between meals

Botanicals (see Resources)

- Scudder's Alterative: 30 drops 3 times per day
- Echinacea/red root compound: 30 drops 3 times per day
- Fraxinus/ceonothus compound: 30 drops 3 times per day
- Gelsemium/phytolacca compound: 5 drops 3 times per day

Turksa Formula

- See Chapter 1 for abnormal bleeding problems.
- See Chapter 11 for pelvic and menstrual pains.

theories, I encourage all women and their health care practitioners to educate themselves and make the best decision for themselves. Most situations where fibroids are involved are not urgent and can allow for experimentation and then observing the response.

Conventional Medicine Approach

Small fibroids that cause no symptoms require no treatment, only observation of growth. Pelvic examinations to follow the size of the uterus/tumors should be done as often as every 6 months with a pelvic ultrasound possibly recommended every 6–12 months. In postmenopausal women with uterine fibroids, estrogen replacement therapy should be prescribed with care and the lowest dose possible needed to control menopause symptoms. In premenopausal women, oral contraceptives are used with caution,[1, 2] although sometimes estrogens are used to control bleeding.

In cases of fibroids where heavy bleeding exists, progestogens or estrogen are used to manage the bleeding, and any anemia is treated with iron supplements. Treatment of fibroids with progestational agents (norethindrone, medrogestone, medroxyprogesterone acetate) has been used, but there is no consensus regarding routine use of these drugs to shrink fibroids. Progestational drugs produce a hypoestrogenic effect by inhibiting gonadotropin secretion and suppressing ovarian function. They may also have a direct antiestrogenic effect. Even though estrogen and progestins may be necessary to control bleeding from fibroids, most practitioners do not consider them useful in shrinking fibroids, however, their necessity may preclude any small concern about increasing the size of the fibroid uterus.

Agents such as leuprolide acetate (Lupron) have been used to temporarily control bleeding and shrink tumors. This practice is often used today to shrink a large tumor so that surgery will be easier and with less risks. When the drug is used preoperatively, a vaginal hysterectomy with a shorter hospital stay and a smaller scar is more likely to be possible. Lupron, a GnRh analogue, suppresses ovarian estrogen secretion, thereby causing temporary and reversible medical castration. In a number of studies of women with symptomatic fibroids,[26, 28–30] the use of GnRh analogues has successfully reduced uterine and tumor size by 40–65 percent.[26] Most reduction in size occurs within 8 weeks,[29] and maximum reduction occurs within about 12 weeks.[26, 28] After the treatment with the drug is discontinued, the uterus and fibroids return to 88 percent of their original size within three months.[26] On occasion, the use of Lupron may make surgical treatment unnecessary, but usually the solution is temporary and surgery is inevitable. By and large, Lupron is not a permanent solution. One of the most significant

disadvantages of Lupron is that it's expensive, somewhere around $300–$400 per month. The other is that it puts you into instant menopause with hot flashes being the main effect. The GnRh analogues cannot be used long-term because they can lead to bone loss and an elevation of total cholesterol. The elevated blood cholesterol reverses after the Lupron is discontinued.

The standard surgical treatments for uterine fibroids are either a hysterectomy or a myomectomy. Hysterectomy, the removal of the uterus, is the only approach that provides a permanent solution for fibroids. An alternative hysterectomy much more common in Europe but gaining popularity in this country is a supracervical hysterectomy. With an abdominal incision, the body of the uterus is removed but the cervix is spared. By leaving the cervix, the vagina is unaffected, and the normal length and sensations of the vagina are maintained. The most important concern about a hysterectomy is preserving the ovaries. In premenopausal women, the ovaries should definitely be left in place unless the ovaries are severely affected or diseased in some way. In postmenopausal women or in women ages 45 and older, the doctor will often recommend removing the ovaries to reduce the risk of ovarian cancer. What if we started removing all our organs to reduce the risk of ovarian cancer? How ridiculous! Special circumstances might warrant the removal of the ovaries, including a mother or sister with ovarian cancer, but as a routine preventive I don't recommend it. The lifetime risk of ovarian cancer is 1 in 70 women.

Myomectomy is abdominal/pelvic surgery where just the fibroids are removed but the uterus is spared. Many women prefer this surgery, and I encourage women to find a surgeon who will agree to this surgery if it is appropriate. However, compared with hysterectomy, some myomectomies may be associated with more blood loss and more complications, and 15–30 percent of women who have a myomectomy eventually require further surgery because the fibroids recur. Even if you do not want to retain your fertility, myomectomy should be seriously considered. Dr. Vicki Hufnagel, a surgeon in California, is considered a progressive surgeon by some and a risky renegade with bizarre surgical techniques by others; in any case, she is far from conventional. In her book *No More Hysterectomies*,[31] Dr. Hufnagel promotes reconstructive surgical techniques that avoid the need for a hysterectomy. Some of these techniques and recommendations are very controversial. Perhaps her greatest contributions have been to point out more clearly for women some of the potential complications from a hysterectomy and how it may affect future quality of life. She also stresses the number of unnecessary hysterectomies that are performed in the United States each year.

A number of newer therapies have more recently become available at least by some doctors and in some hospitals. A hysteroscopic resection has been used to remove fibroids within the uterine cavity. A hysteroscope, an instrument that is inserted through the vagina into the uterus, provides a view of the interior of the uterus. The surgeon may use a laser or an electrical knife to remove the fibroids and cauterize the endometrium. Submucous fibroids or pedunculated submucous fibroids are the fibroids that lend themselves to this kind of surgical treatment. Subserosal fibroids cannot be reached with this procedure.

Uterine embolization is designed to reduce fibroids by obstructing the blood supply that nourishes them. It entails making a small incision in the groin and threading a small catheter into the femoral artery. The doctor works the catheter up to the vessels that supply the fibroid with the help of a dye and X ray. Microscopic plastic particles are injected into the catheter to close off those vessels. The fibroid shrinks because it is deprived of its blood flow. In a study of 88 women between the ages of 34 and 51 with one or more symptomatic uterine fibroids who failed drug treatment, arterial embolization was done as an alternative to the scheduled hysterectomy.[32]

Out of the 80 patients that investigators were able to interpret data on, there was a 69 percent reduction in the size of the fibroids; the menstrual periods returned to normal in 89 percent of the 67 menorrhagic (heavy menstrual bleeding) patients; and further surgery was avoided in 71 of the cases. Nine cases were considered failures. Pelvic pain and severe cramping after the embolization lasting 12–18 hours were the most commonly re-

ported side effects. Embolization is considered a very new experimental treatment, and more research is needed. It is a procedure that is not commonly available.

Laparoscopic surgery is the least invasive approach for removing subserous and subserous peduculated fibroids. It is similar to the hysteroscopic resection. With a laparoscopy, the scope and surgical instruments are inserted through two small incisions in the abdomen. When the fibroid is small, the surgeon removes the fibroid using the myomectomy technique (i.e., cut out the fibroid and suture up the uterus where the fibroid was plucked out). For fibroids that are larger or inaccessible, the surgeon may use myolysis. Using a laser or electrical needles, the fibroids are cauterized, and they shrink. I've even heard of a large fibroid uterus being removed using laparoscopy. This is basically a hysterectomy through a laparoscope. Since there is no major abdominal incision through all the muscles of the abdomen, the recovery time is much shorter and the cosmetic advantages are obvious. However, a laparoscopic hysterectomy is much more time-consuming and may take as long as seven hours to perform.

❧ *Seeing a Licensed Primary Health Care Practitioner**

Four clinical problems that require special consideration are the relationship of fibroids to heavy, prolonged, or frequent bleeding, infertility, and the management of pregnancy complicated by big fibroids.

Menstrual flows that are longer than 7 days in duration, more frequent than every 21 days, or that involve more than 80 ml of blood loss (the normal averages 33 ml) deserve a visit to your licensed primary care practitioner. It is difficult to quantify the number of pads or tampons used as a criterion for determining excessive blood loss. Bleeding that meets or exceeds saturation of a super tampon or heavy pad every hour for six to eight hours or more

---

*N.D. = Naturopathic Doctor; M.D. = Medical Doctor; D.O. = Osteopathic Doctor; N.P. = Nurse Practitioner; P.A. = Physician's Assistant

requires immediate intervention. Some women tolerate excessive blood loss better than others. A hemoglobin and hematocrit can determine if you are anemic from blood loss. Additional tests may be done to determine if your iron stores are low.

Infertile women who have uterine fibroids may need to consider the causal relationship. Even though fibroids may be a cause of only a small percentage of infertility cases, if it is the cause, the solutions aren't particularly optimistic. It is reported that only a 16 percent pregnancy rate follows myomectomy for infertility.[33] Postoperative adhesions and the low return question the value of myomectomy for this set of circumstances.

Pregnancy in women with uterine fibroids is generally problem-free, but each situation is different. Even though fibroids can grow under the hormonal conditions of pregnancy, some clinicians have reported that a review of consecutive ultrasounds in 89 women found that only 6 of them had continued growth of the fibroid during the pregnancy.[34] Six weeks after delivery, they reviewed ultrasounds on 31 of the women and all of them had a decrease in their tumor size similar to the prepregnancy size. That said, some complications can occur during pregnancy. An enlarging fibroid during pregnancy can degenerate and cause pain, infection, and fever. Though debatable, the presence of fibroids can also affect implantation of the fertilized egg with the potential for an early miscarriage, bleeding later in the pregnancy, premature rupture of membranes, and postpartum hemorrhage. Other potential complications include a decrease in the ability of the uterus to contract during labor, or obstruction of the birth canal with the fibroid itself. In women who have previously had a myomectomy, the safety of a vaginal delivery is controversial.

One school of thought believes that if there has been an incision into the uterine cavity, you must get a cesarean section. Other practitioners believe that if there was no infection after the myomectomy, the incision into a nonpregnant uterus is of no concern in subsequent vaginal deliveries.

Remember, the mere presence of uterine fibroids does not require treatment. If you have symptoms, then these can most often be managed with alternative therapies with a realization that excessive bleeding may require drug or surgical intervention. Even if you have no symptoms, a licensed primary health care practitioner should examine you every six months to rule out rapid enlargement. This is especially true for women who are planning pregnancies or who are approaching menopause. Rapidly enlarging fibroids warrant special attention because of the potential for malignancy. A young woman who is several years prior to menopause with a uterus that is larger than a 12–14 week pregnancy should stay watchful of the growth and be open to considering the need for some kind of surgical intervention. The reason is that there are many more years for potential further growth, and the bigger the uterus and fibroids, the more technically difficult the surgery.

Not often do women have to rush to any decisions about surgical interventions. Excessive bleeding problems, a rapidly enlarging fibroid uterus, and prolonged or severe pain are the motivating circumstances. If surgical intervention becomes appropriate, remember that you may have options there as well. Explore some of the newer surgical techniques that we have discussed. If a hysterectomy is indeed the best option, and sometimes it is, then discuss with your surgeon your desire to keep your ovaries; most of the time, there is no pressing medical need to remove them.

CHAPTER EIGHTEEN

VAGINITIS

 ## *Overview*

Vaginal infections are responsible for an estimated 10 percent of all visits by women to their health care practitioners. There are three general categories of vaginitis: hormonal, irritant, and infectious. Hormonal vaginitis includes the atrophic vaginitis usually found in postmenopausal or postpartum women, but occasionally in young girls before puberty. Irritant vaginitis can be due to allergies to such substances as condoms, spermicides, deodorants, soaps, perfumes, semen, or douches. Irritation may also be due to hot tubs, mechanical abrasion, sanitary napkins, tampons, toilet tissue, or topical medications. All of these may cause vaginitis.

However, more than 90 percent of vaginitis in reproductive-age women is due to an infectious cause of one of three types: bacterial vaginosis, candidiasis, or trichomoniasis. We will be discussing these most common types in this chapter. There are other less common infectious causes like gonorrhea, chlamydia, mycoplasma, herpes, campylobacter, and even parasites like pinworms and giardia. Atrophic vaginitis in postmenopausal women is discussed in Chapter 10.

Bacterial Vaginosis

Bacterial vaginosis (BV) is the most common vaginal infection and accounts for approximately 40–50 percent of all cases in women of childbearing age.

In the past, BV has been known by several other names: *Gardnerella vaginalis*, nonspecific vaginitis, hemophilus, and *Corynebacterium vaginale*. The term BV was introduced to describe increased vaginal discharge without signs of clinical inflammation and in the absence of white blood cells under the microscope as well as the absence of fungi and parasites. This form of vaginitis is characterized by a decrease in aerobic lactobacilli (normal flora in the vagina) and an increase in anaerobic lactobacilli and gardnerella and mycoplasma bacteria.

Four diagnostic criteria, of which three must be present, confirm a diagnosis of bacterial vaginosis.

Symptoms experienced include an odorous discharge and mild itching or burning of the external

---

DIAGNOSTIC CRITERIA

Three of these criteria must be present to confirm a diagnosis of bacterial vaginosis.

1. A thin, frothy, gray, odorous discharge.
2. Vaginal pH greater than 4.5 with pH paper.
3. A wet-mount lab sample that reveals "clue cells."
4. A positive "whiff" test (a fish odor detected when 10 percent potassium hydroxide is added to the discharge).

genitalia (vulva). One of the difficulties in self-diagnosis of BV is that these symptoms could be absent in approximately 50 percent of the women who actually have BV. Women often self-diagnose BV when they actually have candida vaginitis, or candida when they actually have BV. Accurate diagnosis is made by viewing the discharge under a microscope and looking for white blood cells and something called clue cells.

The natural history of BV is poorly understood. It is unclear if it is sexually transmitted, what the triggers are for the change in the vaginal flora, and just how many microbes are actually involved. Because it is still unclear whether bacterial vaginosis is sexually transmitted, treatment of the male partner who does not have any symptoms is controversial. In stubborn, recurring, or severely symptomatic cases it would be prudent to practice safer sex and treat the partner, whether the partner is male or female.

There are some potential consequences of an untreated or undertreated infection.[1] The bacteria can migrate into the uterus and the upper genital tract and cause pelvic inflammatory disease in a minority of women who have the infection. In pregnant women, BV can cause premature rupture of membranes and premature labor and is responsible for 70 to 80 percent of all perinatal deaths.[2] BV is also responsible for approximately one-third of postpartum endometritis (infection of the uterus).[3] Unfortunately, BV can be the most difficult vaginal infection to treat satisfactorily with alternative treatments. However, even conventional treatments can be insufficient without a lot of patience and time.

Candida Vaginitis

In the United States, candida is currently the second most common cause of vaginal infections and will affect an estimated 75 percent of women at least once in their life. Between 40–50 percent of these women will experience at least one repeat episode, and 5 percent will develop chronic recurrent vulvovaginal candidiasis (VVC).

Candida albicans is the most common organism in vulvovaginal candidiasis (VVC). There are more than 150 species of candida, although only 9 are

considered to be clinically significant in humans. In recent years, the non-albicans species seem to be occurring increasingly, and this may be due to the one-to-three-day drug treatments that effectively suppress *Candida albicans* but may facilitate the overgrowth of non-albicans species.[4, 5] In the end, this may make it more difficult to treat VVC. Some women who culture positive for candida do not have any symptoms of vaginitis. Candida may be a normal part of the vaginal flora until some mechanism triggers the process into a symptomatic condition.

Acute itching and vaginal discharge are the usual presenting symptoms of VVC. The discharge is typically described as cottage cheeselike in character, but it may actually vary from watery to thick. Symptoms may also include vaginal soreness, irritation, vulvar burning, inflammation and swelling of both the internal and external genital tissue, redness, pain with vaginal sexual activity, and urinary discomfort. The symptoms are often worse the week preceding the onset of menses with some relief after the menstrual flow.

Most women with symptomatic vaginitis can be diagnosed with a simple microscopic examination of vaginal secretions. Yeast can be seen with this method. The vaginal pH is normal (4.0–4.5) in candidal vaginitis. Sometimes more reliable cultures need to be obtained, especially when the routine wet mount is negative but the symptoms are highly suspicious for candida. Unfortunately, self-diagnosis of VVC by women is unreliable too much of the time; thus it is unfortunate that so many over-the-counter self-treatments are available. In a study assessing the ability of women to accurately self-diagnose yeast infections without the benefit of potassium hydroxide or culture confirmation, two out of three women misdiagnosed vulvovaginal candidiasis.[6] The most candida-specific symptom is itching without discharge, and even this criterion correctly predicts VVC in only 38 percent of patients.[7]

The greatest concern in self-diagnosing and self-treating VVC is in women who have recurrent VVC, which is defined as four or more candida-confirmed episodes of symptomatic infection within one year. This occurs in approximately 5 percent of women.[8] Recurrent VVC commonly affects women who are immunocompromised as the result of AIDS or other predisposing conditions such as diabetes, Cushing's disease, Addison's disease, hypo- or hyperthyroidism, or leukemia. The danger then is that the underlying condition goes undiagnosed because the woman is repeatedly treating herself for what she thinks are simple vaginal yeast infections. There are other predisposing factors in recurrent infections that may also need to be addressed: high-estrogen medication, antibiotics, hormones, contraceptive devices, cytotoxic drugs, immunosuppressive drugs, radiotherapy or chemotherapy, tight clothing, nylon underwear, pregnancy, and excessive sugar in the diet. Re-infection may also come from extravaginal sources. Although the sexual transmission of candida is still considered controversial, there is evidence that sexual transmission might be a likely source of recurrent infection. In one such study, the researchers found identical strains of candida in the male sexual partners of 48 percent of women with recurrent VVC.[9, 10] Reservoirs of infection were found in the oral cavities of 36 percent of 33 heterosexual couples, the rectums of 33 percent, and the ejaculate of 15 percent of the men.[11] The data in these studies suggest that oral-genital contact constitutes a probable mode of sexual transmission; however this remains controversial.

Even more controversial is whether re-infection can occur from an intestinal reservoir. Many alternative practitioners address chronic candida vaginitis by also addressing the possibility of migration from rectum to vagina and therefore treating the overgrowth of candida in the digestive tract. Although numerous studies have failed to yield definitive results, it may provide a useful avenue of treatment in especially chronic and resistant cases.[12]

The diagnosis of candida vaginitis is made most commonly from a slide of the vaginal discharge called a wet prep or wet mount that is viewed under the microscope looking for yeast. Even though it is the most widely used method of diagnosis, it is actually accurate, at best, only 50 percent of the time. A more accurate diagnosis is made using a culture method.

Trichomonas Vaginalis

Trichomonas vaginalis is a motile, flagellate, anaerobic protozoan and is the most prevalent nonviral sexually transmitted disease. Worldwide, there are approximately 180 million cases with 2.5–3 million infections occurring annually in the United States.[13] The prevalence of disease varies widely in different populations. Multiple sexual partners, black race, previous history of sexually transmitted diseases, coexistent infection with *Neisseria gonorrhoeae*, and nonuse of either barrier or hormonal contraceptives are known risk factors for acquisition of trichomonas.[14] The sexual transmission rates are higher from man to woman than from woman to man, and transmission is considered rare from woman to woman. It is rarely transmitted to infants born to infected mothers, and although the trichomonas organism can survive for short periods on moist objects (toilet seats, benches, towels) or exposed bodily fluids (urine, vaginal exudate, semen), no cases of transmission by indirect or inanimate exposure have been documented.

The most common complaints associated with trichomoniasis are vaginal discharge and vulvovaginal irritation including itching. Discharge is present in 50–75 percent of infected women and is classically described as frothy or bubbly and yellow-green. Other associated symptoms include dyspareunia (pain with vaginal sexual activity), dysuria (painful urination), and in a small number of patients, some degree of lower abdominal pain. Vulvar redness is an uncommon finding, but vaginal redness is noted in as many as 75 percent of patients. A "strawberry cervix" is created by dilatation of capillaries on the cervix with small hemorrhages and is seen through a magnification device called a colposcope in as many as 90 percent of cases.[15] With the naked eye it is seen in only 2 percent of cases, but when it is seen it is almost a sure sign of trichomoniasis.

The time-honored method for diagnosing trichomonal infections has been the microscopic (wet prep) evaluation. The diagnosis is made by directly observing the motile parasite. This procedure detects 60–80 percent of cases and is even more sensitive when symptoms are present. Other laboratory methods can be added to improve detection up to 100 percent of the time. Newer, more sophisticated methods of testing have also been developed so that the practitioner can quickly, inexpensively, and accurately make the diagnosis.

KEY CONCEPTS

- Diagnosis is necessary to determine the cause of the vaginal infection.
- Be aware of underlying metabolic or immune incompetence problems in chronic resistant cases of candida vaginitis.
- In recurrent cases of candida vaginitis and bacterial vaginosis, the sexual partner should be treated.
- Consider additional testing methods such as cultures and DNA probes in cases that elude diagnosis.
- Self-diagnosis is considered an inaccurate method.

PREVENTION

- Tight clothing can predispose the wearer to candidiasis.[16]
- Women who wear pantyhose have about three times more yeast vaginitis infections than nonwearers.[17]
- Safer sex may be helpful in preventing even infections not clearly considered to be sexually transmitted such as yeast and bacterial vaginosis.
- Support a healthy vaginal ecosystem and immune system by having a generally whole foods diet and very little to no sugar and refined carbohydrates.
- Consider food, pollen, clothing detergent, and semen allergies.
- Increase intake of acidophilus yogurt and/or take supplemental lactobacillus supplements when using antibiotics.
- Consider using condoms to prevent all types of vaginitis and using condoms until treatment regimen is complete to prevent recurrence.

Overview of Alternative Treatments

An important aspect of treating vaginal infections is looking at the problem more holistically and systemically rather than just finding drug alternatives for killing unwanted organisms. To this end, the alternative practitioner tries to improve the vaginal immune system, support the systemic immune system, restore the proper balance of normal microflora in the vagina, restore the normal pH of the vagina, decrease the inflammation and irritation of the tissue itself, provide symptomatic relief, and, when necessary, also curb the population and overgrowth of the offending organism.

Although this approach sounds basic and logical, it is radically different than the conventional approach, which is essentially to kill the overgrowth of the causative organism. Although in severe acute cases, pharmaceutical antifungals and antibacterials may ultimately be necessary, there is evidence that the organisms are becoming resistant to overuse of these products, and newer and stronger ones continually need to be developed in order to deal with these resistant strains. This is not unlike what is happening with antibiotic overuse for simple ear infections and upper respiratory infections and what has happened with mosquito repellents for an increasingly uncanny resistant mosquito population. So, even when the pharmaceutical over-the-counter medications or prescription medications need to be used, the principles and methods of some of the natural treatments can be an important part of a healthy vaginal ecosystem and immunity for the future.

Perhaps no other concept is as important as the health of the ecosystem of the vagina. The flora that colonizes the vagina does so in the birth canal during delivery, and the flora that is established in the newborn girl must therefore consist of the same strains as in the mother. The vaginal environment of a newborn changes during the first month, then again at pre-puberty, puberty, during the reproductive years, and postmenopausally. Additionally, the cyclic hormonal changes of the menstrual cycle also influence the vaginal ecosystem. It is a variable state throughout a woman's lifetime, but nothing is more key to this ecosystem than lactobacillus.

The vaginal microflora of healthy asymptomatic women consists of a wide variety of anaerobic and aerobic bacteria dominated by lactobacillus. The first extensive study of the human vaginal microflora was published in 1892 by Doderlein.[18] During the next 100 years, the presence in the normal vagina of a wide variety of microorganisms has been recognized. The range of bacterial types isolated is immense, including *Staphylococcus* species, *Gardnerella vaginalis*, *Streptococcus* species, *Bacteroides* species, *Lactobacillus* species, *Mobiluncus*, even *Candida* species (most commonly *Candida albicans*), and more. Again, the predominant organisms isolated from the normal vagina are members of the *Lactobacillus* genus.

The body's ability to control the vaginal microflora is no easy feat. The premise is that the normal vaginal microflora defends the host against abnormal vaginal colonization. Factors controlling this defense system include the content of the vaginal tissue itself (called the squamous epithelium), the dominance of lactobacilli, and the subsequent low or acid pH balance and hydrogen peroxide production, hormonal activity (over one's lifetime as well as monthly cyclic changes), pregnancy, contraceptive devices, feminine hygiene products, and vaginal sexual activity including friction, lubricants, and semen.

Nutrition

It cannot be overemphasized how the health of the entire body affects the internal ecosystem of the vagina. The pH of the vagina, the microflora that lives there, the hormonal cycles, and the immune tissue in the vagina are all influenced by our general health and our dietary habits, and this in turn determines how susceptible we are as a host for the overgrowth of the unfriendly organisms that cause vaginitis. A generally healthy diet assures our body's defense system. A diet low in sugars and refined carbohydrates is particularly important in preventing candida vaginitis. In general, a well-balanced whole foods diet that is low in fat, sugars, refined foods, and alcohol is optimal in preventing all infections. Some women who have severe stubborn cases of chronic candida vaginitis may benefit from stricter diets that avoid fermented foods.

However, many "anti-candida" diets can be rigorous and unnecessarily stressful in my opinion. Some of these diets are so restricted that they actually cause other health problems. Women who have self-diagnosed or who have been diagnosed with systemic candida by an alternative practitioner might want to make sure of this popular diagnosis by testing the stool, the blood, and the vaginal secretions for the candida antigen. In fact, using all three of these tests provides the best hope for accurately diagnosing true systemic candida infections.

> ### NUTRITION
> - Avoid sugar, refined carbohydrates, and alcohol.
> - Eat eight ounces of unsweetened acidophilus yogurt daily.

Nutritional Supplements

Vitamin E

We most often think of using nutritional supplements orally, but in this case I recommend the use of vitamin E intravaginally and topically. This use of vitamin E dates back at least to 1954, when it was used to treat diabetic patients with yeast vulvovaginitis.[19] As demonstrated back then, as well as in my own practice, the use of vitamin E as either a suppository or from a gelatin capsule that is inserted into the vagina once or twice daily for seven or more days provides a very soothing effect. The tissue becomes less irritated with a decrease in redness, swelling, and congestion. The patient experiences relief of burning and itching usually within one to three days. Vitamin E oil or ointment can also be applied externally to the vulvar tissue to relieve discomfort there as well. Vitamin E is especially useful in cases of allergic and irritant-induced vaginitis because it is so soothing.

> ### Vitamin E
> *Intravaginal suppository or gelatin capsule once or twice daily for 7 or more days*

Vitamin A and Beta Carotene

Both vitamin A and beta carotene are necessary for the normal healthy growth of epithelial tissues. Epithelial cells make up the vaginal mucosa. Vitamin A and beta carotene enhance the immune response in epithelial tissues and thereby help in the resistance to infection of mucous membranes. Vitamin A and beta carotene can be used orally to enhance the immune response, and vitamin A can be used intravaginally to stimulate the local immune tissue of the vaginal mucosa. Vitamin A in a capsule can suffice, but there are companies that make vitamin A suppositories that are available in higher doses than a standard vitamin A capsule. Vitamin A intravaginally is useful in cases of infectious vaginitis as well as allergic and irritant-induced vaginitis. Daily use for up to one week is typical. It can be repeated after one week without suppositories or one week of some alternate like vitamin E, lactobacillus, or mixed herbal. This is to avoid any possible side effects from the vitamin A dosage itself.

Vitamin A
Intravaginal suppository or gelatin capsule once daily for 7 days; use vitamin E, lactobacillus, or mixed herbal suppository daily for one week before repeating this dosage.

Botanical Medicines

Garlic (*Allium sativum*)

Garlic extracts have been shown to inhibit the growth of *Candida albicans* by blockage of lipid production which thereby inhibits growth.[20] The major growth inhibitory component in garlic extract is allicin; therefore, garlic products that have the highest amount of allicin are the most desirable. Garlic is diverse in its uses for vaginitis because it is both antibacterial and antifungal.[21, 22] Although I am not aware of any research on the use of garlic inserted into the vagina, this consistently has been one of my recommendations for women over the years for both candida (yeast) vaginitis and bacterial vaginosis. A carefully peeled clove (don't nick the garlic) can be inserted into the vagina for six to eight hours. The

garlic can be threaded like a necklace with needle and cotton thread so that it can be easily removed as if it were a tampon. "Garlic tampons" or garlic capsules can be inserted intravaginally in the morning and then lactobacillus capsules can be inserted in the evening to create an environment that both inhibits growth of the offending organism and repopulates the microflora to a normal healthy state.

Garlic
Intravaginal "tampon" or capsule in the morning; intravaginal lactobacillus capsule in the evening

---

Goldenseal (*Hydrastis canadensis*) and Oregon Grape Root (*Berberis vulgaris*)

Goldenseal and Oregon grape root contain a substance called berberine that acts both as an antibacterial and immune enhancer. This immune effect is especially specific in epithelial mucus membrane tissue such as that found in the vagina, mouth, and even the stomach. Berberine has been shown to possess antimicrobial activity against a wide variety of microorganisms, some of which are found in the vagina, such as *Candida albicans, coli, Staphylococcus aureus,* and others.[23] Preparations of goldenseal and Oregon grape root have been used both orally in teas, caps, and liquid extracts, and intravaginally in douches and suppositories. Because of their ability to affect both yeast and bacteria, these two herbs would seem a logical choice in cases where multiple infectious agents are involved.

Goldenseal or Oregon grape root
Orally (capsules or liquid extracts) or intravaginally in suppositories

---

Tea Tree (*Melaleuca alternifolia*)

Tea tree oil has been studied for trichomonas, candida, and other vaginal infections. Perhaps the most impressive study used an emulsified 40 percent solution of Australian tea tree oil with 13 percent isopropyl alcohol. The study focused on 130 cases of vaginal infections: trichomonal vaginitis, 96 cases; *Candida albicans,* 4; *Trichomonas vaginalis* causing cervicitis, 30 patients. Ten patients with cervicitis were cured after four weekly treatments of washing the vaginal canal for 30 seconds and then keeping a vaginal tampon saturated with the solution in place for 24 hours. Twenty of the cervicitis patients were successfully treated with a 20 percent solution. In the 96 cases of trichomonal vaginitis, clinical cures were seen with the application of six treatments (see Treatment Plan for *Trichomonas vaginalis* for specifics).[24] Various tea tree oil preparations have demonstrated antimicrobial activity against *Staphylococcus aureus* and *Candida albicans,* thereby showing its usefulness in diverse situations.[25]

Tea tree oil

Emulsified 40 percent solution of Melaleuca alternifolia *oil with 13 percent isopropyl alcohol: wash vaginal canal for 30 seconds once a week for 4 weeks; then use vaginal tampon saturated with solution for 24 hours following each washing.*

Herbal Combinations

Many different herbs can be prepared in combinations for suppository use or even douching. Powdered herbal mixes of myrrh, echinacea, usnea, goldenseal, marshmallow, geranium, yarrow, and calendula are often used by herbalists and naturopathic physicians. Each herb has its own special feature, whether it's antimicrobial, immune-enhancing, soothing to the membranes, or antifungal. These suppositories can be made at home with powdered herbs and cocoa butter or can be purchased from a natural food store or an alternative health care practitioner.

Other Therapeutic Agents

Lactobacillus

Although we often think of only *Lactobacillus acidophilus,* several species of lactobacillus populate the vagina. The predominant species of lactobacillus isolated from the vagina of healthy women remains controversial. Several mechanisms are possible for how lactobacillus does its remarkable job. A low vaginal pH is believed to be a primary mechanism controlling the composition of the vaginal microflora. Lactic acid is produced by the metabolism of lactobacillus, and although there may be other ways in which the vagina maintains its normal acidic environment, the role of lactobacilli seems evident. Lactobacilli thrive at an acidic pH of 3.5–4.5, and these values are indeed found in the normal vagina throughout the menstrual cycle.

Lactobacilli have also been shown to interfere with how pathogenic (disease-causing) bacteria adhere to and colonize the cells of the vagina.[26] Hydrogen peroxide production is another well-recognized antagonist to problematic bacterial populations. There are strains of lactobacilli that produce hydrogen peroxide (H_2O_2). A lack of H_2O_2-producing lactobacilli predisposes a woman to bacterial vaginosis by allowing the overgrowth of *Gardnerella* and other anaerobic bacteria. Lactobacilli also act directly as antibacterials[27] and may function as an immune stimulant locally in controlling microbial levels in the vagina.

Lactobacillus orally and intravaginally is one of the most important aspects of effectively treating yeast and bacterial vaginitis. Women who have H_2O_2-producing lactobacilli in the vagina are less likely to have bacterial vaginosis or candida vaginitis.[28] These same lactobacilli are also toxic to *Gardnerella vaginalis* (the predominant organism in the vagina of women with BV).[29] Although probably not the sole factor, the vaginal pH is lowered by the predominance of these lactobacilli, and the acidity of the vagina is maintained. The bacteria that cause bacterial vaginosis thrive in a higher pH of 5.0–6.0 and cannot readily survive in the lower pH, more acid environment. In addition, the lactobacilli compete with other bacteria for the utilization of glucose, which is necessary for the production of the lactic acid.

The concept that lactobacilli might be useful when supplied in the diet or intravaginally dates back to the 1890s. While scientists have vacillated on the value of lactobacilli in prevention or treatment, patients in need have not. In fact, lactobacillus therapy is quite popular both with alternative practitioners and with women who seek simple self-treatment methods. Dr. Eileen Hilton published the results of a study in 1992 on the daily ingestion of yogurt containing *Lactobacillus acidophilus* in women with recurrent candidal vaginitis. In the women who ate eight ounces of the yogurt daily, there was a threefold decrease in infections and in candidal colonization when compared to the women who did not eat the yogurt.[30]

Another method that is popular is the application of lactobacilli directly into the vagina. Douching used to be a popular method, but since research has shown that douching may contribute to infertility and pelvic infections, a safer and more convenient method is available by introducing lactobacillus capsules or tablets into the vagina.[31] This can be done once or twice daily for a few days or even several weeks. Alone or in combination with other vaginal or oral therapies, lactobacillus is the key to establishing normal vaginal microflora, preventing recurring infections, as well as treating acute candida and bacterial infections of the vagina. However, buyer beware. There is a great deal of variability in lactobacillus products and yogurt products regarding the actual presence of lactobacillus. For yogurt, make sure the label lists lactobacillus, and choose a brand without sweeteners. Some yogurts and encapsulated products make claims that they contain *L. acidophilus* but, when tested,[32] they did not, moreover, they had contaminants. When purchasing encapsulated products, it may be worth requesting product analysis information to assure quality.

Lactobacillus

Eat 8 oz unsweetened live-culture yogurt daily; use an intravaginal tablet or gelatin capsule once or twice daily for a few days to several weeks

---

Boric Acid

Nothing impresses me more than the success rate of boric acid suppositories for the treatment of candida vulvovaginal infections. In one study, 100 women with chronic resistant yeast infections who had failed extensive and prolonged conventional

therapy were treated with 600 mg boric acid vaginal suppositories twice a day for two or four weeks. This regimen was effective in curing 98 percent of the women who had previously failed to respond to the most commonly used antifungal agents.[33] Once daily boric acid suppository use for four days per month during the menses for four consecutive months was also clearly indicated as the treatment of choice for preventing recurrence.

Clinical effectiveness doesn't really get any better than this. Boric acid works most of the time, it's inexpensive, and it's easy to use. The only downside I have observed is that if the tissue has been irritated enough by the infection, burning can occur when the boric acid passes over this tissue. Using vitamin E oil or lanolin or even Vaseline on the external genitalia to protect the tissue from the boric acid seems to avert any significant discomfort. In a study that compared boric acid with the more conventionally prescribed nystatin, cure rates for boric acid were 92 percent after 10 days and 72 percent after 30 days, whereas the nystatin cure rates were 64 percent and 50 percent, respectively.[34]

Boric acid

Acute: 600-mg vaginal suppositories twice a day for 3–7 days; chronic: 600-mg vaginal suppositories twice a day for 2–4 weeks; prevention: 600-mg vaginal suppository 4 days per month during menses for four consecutive months

---

Gentian Violet

Most herbal suppositories, including boric acid and tea tree oil, should be avoided during pregnancy. The goal is to find a remedy that is effective for the mother-to-be but is also safe for the fetus. An old treatment such as gentian violet may be just the thing. In the 1950s, this was the most commonly used and favorite treatment of gynecologists. Although it can be painted onto the cervix and the vaginal wall, the signature blue stain can be disconcerting; moreover, it requires a speculum insertion to apply.

A more desirable preparation and one appropriate for home use is a gentian violet gel made up according to the following formula:

Gentian violet	0.2 percent
Lactic acid	3.0 percent
Acetic acid	1.0 percent
Polyethylene glycol base	

The effects of this preparation were reported in a study undertaken in 1950.[35] Patients were given disposable vaginal applicators, with the recommendation to use one dose daily at bedtime. If a complete cure was not achieved in 12 days, 12 more days were added. Of 191 cases studied, 78 percent were considered cured, and 12 percent were significantly improved. The remaining 3 percent had modest improvement, and 7 percent showed no improvement at all.

Gentian violet is available only by prescription in certain states and is therefore only available through a licensed health care practitioner. You may be able to find a milder strength available without a prescription. Put a few drops of the over-the-counter concentration onto a tampon, if you want to try using it on your own.

Gentian violet

See a licensed health care practitioner for prescription. Use one vaginal applicator daily at bedtime for 12 days.

Iodine

Yeast and trichomonal vaginitis infections can often occur simultaneously. In some instances, after treatment for trichomonas, a yeast infection may flare up. Local therapy that can treat both would obviously be desirable. Iodine in the form of povidone-iodine preparations is a logical solution. There is another example of an older successful treatment that got left behind in the face of more modern, mass-market pharmaceuticals. Once again, the simple and inexpensive is worth trying first.

A regimen of treatment for vaginitis combining the use of a povidone-iodine solution for swabbing, a povidone-iodine vaginal gel for application at night, and a povidone-iodine douche for use in the morning was evaluated in 93 courses of treatment in 87

patients with yeast or trichomonal vaginitis, or a combination of both. In the yeast vaginitis cases, symptoms were cleared in one to three weeks in all 74 courses of treatment. In four of five patients with trichomonal vaginitis, symptoms were cleared within three weeks. In 14 courses for combined infections, symptoms were cleared within three weeks in 13.[36]

Method of use: Paint the cervix and vagina with a povidone-iodine solution on day one. Then apply one applicatorful of a povidone-iodine gel (approximately 5 gm) at bedtime, douche the next morning, using a dilution of 2 tablespoonfuls of the povidone-iodine in one quart of warm water. This is

---

Iodine

See licensed health care practitioner for six-day regimen using povidone-iodine preparations.

SAMPLE TREATMENT PLAN FOR BACTERIAL VAGINOSIS

Guidelines

- Provide systemic and local immune enhancement.
- Restore vaginal flora.
- Use natural antimicrobials.

Two-week minimum regimen

- Avoid refined foods and simple carbohydrates.
- Take goldenseal and/or Oregon grape root capsules: 2 caps, 1–2 times daily taken orally.
- Take garlic capsules: 1 cap, 1–2 times daily taken orally.
- Eat 8 oz plain yogurt daily or take 3 *lactobacillus* capsules daily between meals.
- Insert one *lactobacillus* capsule into vagina every morning.
- Insert one goldenseal and/or Oregon grape root powder capsule into vagina every evening.
- Paint the cervix and vagina with povidone-iodine twice each week. (A speculum exam would be the most desirable method of doing this.)
- Avoid vaginal sexual activity during course of treatment to avoid re-infection and to reduce irritation to inflamed tissues.

SAMPLE TREATMENT PLAN FOR CANDIDA VAGINITIS

Acute vaginitis

- Avoid alcohol, sugars, and refined carbohydrates.
- Eat 8 oz acidophilus yogurt daily.
- Take 3 *lactobacillus* capsules daily between meals.
- Boric acid powder capsules: Insert morning and evening for 3–7 days in mild cases and up to 14 days for resistant cases.

Chronic vaginitis

- Avoid sugars, refined carbohydrates, alcohol, fermented foods.
- Eat 8 oz acidophilus yogurt daily or take 3 *lactobacillus* capsules daily between meals.
- Garlic capsules: 1 cap, 1–2 times daily by mouth.
- Boric acid powder capsules: Insert into vagina morning and evening for 14 days. Repeat for an additional 14 days if responding, but not completely resolved after the first 2 weeks.

Prevention of recurrence

- Avoid sugars, refined carbohydrates, alcohol, and fermented foods.
- Eat 8 oz acidophilus yogurt or take 2 *lactobacillus* capsules daily between meals.
- Garlic capsules: 1 capsule daily by mouth.
- Boric acid powder capsules; insert 1 capsule once daily at bedtime during menstruation only for 4 consecutive months.

During pregnancy

- Avoid sugars, refined carbohydrates, alcohol, and fermented foods.
- Eat 8 oz acidophilus yogurt or take 2 *lactobacillus* capsules daily between meals.
- Garlic capsules: 1 capsule daily by mouth.
- Gentian violet: Insert one vaginal applicator at bedtime for 12 consecutive nights. (Alternate method: Purchase over-the-counter low dose liquid, apply several drops to end of tampon, and insert nightly for 12 consecutive nights.)
- Avoid boric acid, herbal, or iodine suppositories.

SAMPLE TREATMENT PLAN FOR TRICHOMONAS VAGINALIS INFECTION

- Avoid sugars, refined carbohydrates, and alcohol.
- Tea tree oil: 40 percent water-miscible emulsified solution with 40 percent *M. alternifolia* oil and 13 percent isopropyl alcohol.

  1. Thoroughly wash the vulva and vagina with pHisoHex followed by a thorough water rinse.
  2. Dry the area.
  3. Topical application on the vulva and washing of the vagina with a 1 percent solution of the basic medication (i.e., 0.4 percent *M. alternifolia* oil), using approximately 15 cc.
  4. Insert a tampon that has been saturated with the solution and remove in 24 hours.
  5. Daily vaginal douches of 1 percent of the basic medication (i.e., 0.4 percent *M. alternifolia* oil) in one quart of water.

Repeat step 3 once per week for up to 6 weeks and step 5 for up to 7 weeks. Consider povidone-iodine treatment as described on page 285 instead of tea tree oil. The tea tree oil treatment is unreasonably long, although it has been successfully studied in more women.

- Eat 8 oz acidophilus yogurt daily for 1 month or take 3 *lactobacillus* capsules daily between meals.
- Consider goldenseal, echinacea, garlic, licorice, and myrrh for systemic botanical immune support.

done for six nights and mornings, but, if the condition is not resolved, it can be continued for as long as three more weeks. Although I rarely recommend douching, some women may find it appropriate to clear this condition.

✧ *Conventional Medicine Approach*

The accurate diagnosis of vaginitis is critical. Incorrect self-diagnosis or guesswork on the part of the practitioner can lead to unnecessary and ineffective treatment, thus prolonging the symptoms.

TABLE 18.1 **CDC Guidelines for Intravaginal Treatment of Yeast Vaginitis**

Drug	Regimen
Butoconazole 2% cream	5 g for 3 days
Clotrimazole 1% cream (OTC)	5 g for 7–14 days
Clotrimazole vaginal tablet (OTC)	100 mg, 4 times per day for 7 days; or 100 mg, twice daily for 3 days
Clotrimazole vaginal tablet	500 mg, single dose
Miconazole 2% cream (OTC)	5 g for 7 days
Miconazole suppository	200 mg for 3 days
Miconazole suppository (OTC)	100 mg for 7 days
Terconazole 0.4% cream	5 g for 7 days
Terconazole 0.8% cream	5 g for 3 days
Terconazole suppository	80 mg for 3 days
Terconazole 6.5% ointment	5 g single-dose

Candida

Uncomplicated, acute candidal infections can be treated with one of a variety of products. The "feminine itch" is so common that no fewer than 66 prescription drugs and 45 over-the-counter preparations are currently marketed to deal with this problem. Despite the latest "third-generation" anticandidal preparations, women continue to be plagued by the occurrence and recurrence of candidal vulvovaginal infections. Approximately 25 percent of women with symptoms of vulvovaginal candidiasis do not respond to initial therapy. Up to 50 percent of these women have problems with recurring, chronic vulvovaginal candidiasis.

The Centers for Disease Control (CDC) recommends treatment guidelines including both intravaginal and oral agents (see Table 18.1). There are many to choose from—some of them are over-the-counter (OTC) items; others are prescription items.

Oral medications are recommended as alternative regimens; these include fluconazole, ketoconazole, and itraconazole, all of which may be just as effective as the topical agents. As many as 84 percent of women prefer the oral therapy over the intravaginal therapy since it is far more convenient and much less messy. Fluconazole is the only single-dose oral agent for the treatment of yeast vaginitis. Not only is the single-dose oral agent effective against yeast vaginitis and comparable to the results seen in the 7-day intravaginal regimens, in many instances it is the most cost-effective therapy. Single-dose oral fluconazole was curative in 76 percent of women versus 72 percent cured using a 7-day intravaginal clotrima-

zole 100-mg tablet.[37] Many women can treat their known yeast vaginitis with the increasingly available OTC medications. More resistant cases may require some of the prescription drugs or the single-dose agents. Treatment of male partners is usually not necessary but may be considered if the partner has symptoms, or if the woman has chronic candida vaginitis or symptoms that are resistant to treatment.

An increasing number of cases of candida vaginitis are not due to *Candida albicans* and are in fact non-*albicans* species, which may be resistant to several of the OTC antifungal agents and may require the use of prescription antifungal agents.

Bacterial Vaginosis

The immediate goal of therapy is to relieve signs and symptoms related to the bacterial overgrowth. The recommended conventional regimen is a 7-day oral metronidazole, 500 mg twice daily or 250 mg three times daily. Since many women experience some digestive symptoms from oral metronidazole, intravaginal 0.75 percent metronidazole gel (5 g inserted in the vagina twice daily) for five days is often preferred. Other treatment regimens are seven days of 2 percent clindamycin cream (5 g intravaginally), or seven days of oral clindamycin (300 mg twice daily). Oral clindamycin at this dosage appears to be effective but may be associated with a higher incidence of diarrhea. Randomized, controlled trials have demonstrated the overall cure rate of oral metronidazole to be 95 percent for the seven-day regimen, and 84 percent for the 2-gram single-dose regimen.[38] A single oral dose (2 g) of metronidazole is also an effective option, but nausea and vomiting may occur, and it may be slightly less effective.

With all metronidazole medications, patients should avoid using alcohol until 24 hours after completion. In pregnant women, medication use in the first trimester is controversial, and clindamycin cream is preferred. Clindamycin cream or metronidazole gel may be recommended for the second and third trimesters. Some intravaginal creams may weaken the latex used in condoms, cervical caps, and diaphragms, so be cautious using these items.

Treatment of the male partner remains controversial. Most studies have not demonstrated an improved cure rate or lower re-infection rate with treatment of the partner with the first episode.[39] Most practitioners would consider that if the patient has repeated episodes of bacterial vaginosis, treatment of her partner with an oral regimen may be helpful.[40]

Trichomoniasis

The recommended treatment for women with trichomoniasis is single-dose oral metronidazole (2 g). An alternate recommended regimen is 500-mg oral metronidazole twice daily for seven days. Be forewarned of possible nausea and vomiting with this single dose use, although less than 10 percent of patients experience this. These medications have demonstrated 95 percent cure rates in scientific controlled trials. Again, metronidazole is contraindicated in the first trimester of pregnancy, but the oral single-dose regimen (2 g) may be used in the later stages of pregnancy. Intravaginal preparations are not effective in eliminating trichomonas but may relieve symptoms and can then be used after delivery.

The male sexual partners of women with trichomoniasis must be treated during the same time period, and intercourse should be avoided until both partners are cured. If both partners are without symptoms and the course of therapy is complete, cure can be assumed. A follow-up test can also be utilized. Resistant trichomonal infections are rare; however, in cases where the patient has been compliant and the male partner has been treated, a resistant strain should be considered. The treatment of resistant trichomoniasis may require high dosages of metronidazole (more than 2.5 g per day). This is then combined with intravaginal metronidazole sup-

positories, 500 mg once or twice daily for a minimum of 10 days. These are prepared by a pharmacist.

Conventional management of all forms of infectious vaginitis can be complicated due to the wide variety of vaginal preparations available. This has been further complicated because some of these are over-the-counter and self-administered by the woman, whereas others are prescribed. Although these OTC preparations have provided increased options for women without the expense of an office visit, she may not be treating the right condition or the right organism. This then can delay effective and appropriate treatment or could perpetuate a health problem that is actually a result of a chronic underlying disorder. As technology continues to improve and offers women home test kits plus further education, these mistakes and delays will hopefully become rare.

❦ Seeing a Licensed Primary Health Care Practitioner*

The most appropriate way to assure an accurate diagnosis is to see a licensed health care practitioner who is familiar with the clinical picture of various forms of vaginitis, can perform a physical exam, knows what to test for, and can collect those samples during your exam. Accurate diagnosis is the most important key to efficient and appropriate treatment, whether the therapies are natural or pharmaceutical. If you know what kind of infection you currently have and choose self-treatment, it is essential to recognize when and if self-treatment isn't working and to seek professional care at that time. The most important times to seek that care is when infections recur more than three times per year, if you have a chronic infection that doesn't fully resolve, or when you are pregnant. Specific testing can be done, but, more important, a licensed practitioner can help to determine if underlying disorders are contributing to the vaginal infections; this can then be investigated. All the alternative therapies discussed in this chapter should be considered safe for home use except for pregnant women. What is not safe is completely avoiding treatment or neglecting to seek help at the appropriate time.

---

*N.D. = Naturopathic Doctor; M.D. = Medical Doctor; D.O. = Osteopathic Doctor; N.P. = Nurse Practitioner; P.A. = Physician's Assistant.

GENERAL EXERCISE PROGRAM

There is strong and rapidly accumulating evidence that muscular exertion reduces cancer risk. The following recommendations are based on a review of recent scientific literature on physical exercise and cancer risk reduction:

1. To prevent injuries, begin each exercise session with Joint Warming Exercises and end each exercise session with Basic Stretches (see following pages).
2. Exercise six days a week. Walk or do moderate hiking on your day off.
3. Alternate aerobic (cardiovascular) with strength (weight lifting) exercises.
4. Take one day off each week.
   - Forget about your work, your bills, your problems. Seek peace in the woods or at the mountains.
   - Refresh your being with pure air, pure water, simple food, and communion with nature.
   - Hike moderately, read a good book, lie down and look at the sky or the birds, or take a nap.
   - This is your day of recreation. Let nothing interfere with it.
5. Calculate your Training Heart Rate (THR) for aerobic exercise. THR is defined as the range of heart beats per 10 seconds that is safe for your heart and will strengthen it.

- Calculate your Maximum Heart Rate (MHR); MHR = 220 minus your age (in years).
- Calculate your Training Heart Rate (THR) as a percentage of MHR.
  - If you are just beginning, multiply MHR by 60 percent and 70 percent THR (beats per 60 seconds) = MHR times .60 and .70.
  - Otherwise, multiply MHR by 70 percent and 85 percent THR (beats per 60 seconds) = MHR times .70 and .85.
  - Divide result obtained above by six to calculate THR per 10 seconds.
- As an example, let us calculate THR for a 50-year-old woman, who is beginning to exercise.
  - MHR = 220 – 50 = 170 beats per 60 seconds.
  - THR per 60 seconds
    170 times .60 = 102
    170 times .70 = 119
  - THR per 10 seconds
    102 divided by 6 = 17
    119 divided by 6 = 20
  - THR range = 17–20 beats per 10 seconds
- For this woman, the recommendation would be: After three minutes of aerobic exercise, check your pulse for 10 seconds. If it is less than 17, increase pace. If more than 20, reduce pace. Repeat procedure every three minutes or so to the end of the exercise session.

Joint Warming Exercises

The following exercises are designed to protect the joints against injury from weight-bearing exercise. These exercises should be performed before any cardiovascular or strength workout.

1. NECK
   Rotate neck gently to left 5 times, then to right 5 times.

2. SHOULDERS
   Rotate shoulders forward 10 times, then backward 10 times.

3. ELBOWS, WRISTS, and FINGERS
   Begin with arms bent, elbows against the sides of body, hands forming a fist against shoulders. Then extend arms fully, directly in front of you, while opening hands and extending fingers. Return to initial position. Repeat 10 times.

   Same as above, but this time raise your hands above your head. Don't forget to open hands and extend fingers as you extend your arms above your head. Repeat 10 times.

4. TRUNK and WAIST
   Bend your trunk at the waist from right to left and from left to right. Avoid stiffening your muscles or applying force as you do this exercise. Perform the exercise as a gentle rocking movement from side to side. Alternate right to left for 20 counts.

5. HIPS
   "Hula-hoop" exercise. Perform full circles with your hips rotating clockwise 10 times. Repeat rotating counterclockwise 10 times.

6. HIPS and KNEES
   Bring right knee close to chest by using both hands around knee and gently pulling with your arms. Repeat with left knee. Count to 20.

7. KNEES
   Standing on left leg, gently bend and extend the right leg 20 times. Repeat exercise with the left leg, 20 times while standing on right leg.

8. ANKLES
   Standing on left foot, rotate right ankle inward 10 times and then outward 10 times. Repeat exercise with left ankle by standing on right foot.

Basic Stretches

General Guidelines:

- Stretch at the end of the exercise session, when muscles are warm.
- Hold stretch steadily—do not bounce.
- Accept a bit of discomfort but avoid pain—do not push.

1. CALVES, HAMSTRINGS, BACK, NECK
   Standing, feet apart about shoulder width, toes pointing forward, knees straight.

   Let head and trunk fall forward and down. Let arms hang down. Allow gravity to push down your trunk so that your fingertips will get closer and closer to your toes, without forcing.

   Relax in this position for 30 seconds (over several weeks, increase gradually to 60 seconds).

2. INNER THIGH, LOW BACK
   Standing, separate feet as much as possible, knees straight.

   Bend trunk forward at the hips, let arms and head hang down comfortably.

   Relax in this position for 20 seconds.

3. INNER THIGH, RIGHT SIDE OF THE BODY, LEFT HAMSTRINGS
   Same position as in #2.

   Rotate trunk over left leg and let your trunk and arms hang along the left leg with hands trying to reach the left foot.

   Relax in this position for 20 seconds.

4. INNER THIGH, LEFT SIDE OF BODY, RIGHT HAMSTRINGS
   Repeat same stretch as in #3, but do it with trunk and arms hanging along the right leg.

   Relax in this position for 20 seconds.

5. TIBIALIS, QUADRICEPS, ABDOMINALS, CHEST, FRONT OF NECK
   On hands and knees, thighs and arms perpendicular to the floor.

First stretch: Keeping hands and knees in place and arms extended, move trunk forward until your abdomen touches the floor. Then raise your head up and back so that you can see the ceiling.

Hold this position for about 20 seconds.

Second stretch: Keeping hands and knees in place and arms extended, move trunk backward until

Sample Conditioning Exercise Program: 8 Weeks

Sunday, Tuesday, Thursday	Monday, Wednesday, Friday	Saturday
Aerobic	Strength	Rest

Sunday, Tuesday, Thursday — Aerobic

- Joint warming exercises.
- Walk briskly for 15 minutes. Gradually increase to 30, 45, or 60 minutes, over a period of 4–6 weeks.
- Basic Stretches.
- Other possibilities:
  Jog, run, swim, cycle, row, play a sport (e.g., tennis), skate, ski, or water exercise.
- Friction entire body, from feet up (30 seconds), with dry washcloth.
- Shower.
- Joint warming exercises.
- Walk briskly for 15 minutes.
- Dumbbell exercises.

Monday, Wednesday, Friday — Strength

Week 1: begin with a weight that allows you to do 10–12 repetitions (reps) of each exercise easily.
Week 2: increase weight, 10 reps.
Week 3: 10 reps, 2 sets per exercise.
Week 4: increase weight, 10 reps, 2 sets.
Week 5: increase weight, 10 reps, 2 sets.
Week 6: increase reps to 12, 2 sets.
Week 7: increase weight, 12 reps, 2 sets.
Week 8: increase weight, 12 reps, 2 sets.
Basic Stretches.
Friction entire body, from feet up (30 seconds), with dry washcloth.
Shower.
- See #4 on page 289.

More Advanced Strength Training

(Probably best to join a health club, fitness club, gymnasium, or a similar organization)

Weeks 9–12: Divide workout into body parts and do two sets per exercise.

Day	Exercise	Reps	Week 9 Set 1	Week 9 Set 2	Week 10 Set 1	Week 10 Set 2	Week 11 Set 1	Week 11 Set 2	Week 12 Set 1	Week 12 Set 2
Day 1										
All parts	**Warm–up**	5–10 mins								
Chest	Bench press	8–10								
Biceps	Arm curl	8–10								
Abdominals	Easy crunches	8–10								
All parts	Stretch	5–10 mins								
Day 2										
All parts	**Warm–up**	5–10 mins								
Back	Pull–down to chest	8–10								
Triceps	Arm extension	8–10								
Abdominals	Easy crunches	8–10								
All parts	Stretch	5–10 mins								
Day 3										
All parts	**Warm–up**	5–10 mins								
Legs	Squat or leg press	8–10								
Calves	Heel raise	8–10								
Shoulders	Press behind neck	8–10								
All parts	Stretch	5–10 mins								

Weeks 13–16: Divide workout into body parts and do two sets per exercise.

Day	Exercise	Reps	Week 9		Week 10		Week 11		Week 12	
			Set 1	Set 2	Set 1	Set 2	Set 1	Set 2	Set 1	Set 2
Day 1										
All parts	**Warm–up**	5–10 mins								
Chest	Bench press	8–10								
Biceps	Arm curl	8–10								
Abdominals	Easy crunches	8–10								
All parts	Stretch	5–10 mins								
Day 2										
All parts	**Warm–up**	5–10 mins								
Back	Pull–down to chest	8–10								
Triceps	Arm extension	8–10								
Abdominals	Easy crunches	8–10								
All parts	Stretch	5–10 mins								
Day 3										
All parts	**Warm–up**	5–10 mins								
Legs	Squat or leg press	8–10								
Calves	Heel raise	8–10								
Shoulders	Press behind neck	8–10								
All parts	Stretch	5–10 mins								

your buttocks touch your heels. Let head down, forehead against the floor.

Relax in this position for 20 seconds.

Remember:

1. Work out on alternate days.
2. Take a mouthful of water between sets.
3. For each repetition: breathe out during the effort phase of the repetition, breathe in during the relaxation phase.
4. If, after a workout, the exercised muscles are sore for more than 48 hours, reduce the weight and/or the number of repetitions.
5. Most injuries from exercise result from doing "too much, too fast, too soon."
6. Warm up for 5–10 minutes before the workout. Joint mobility exercises are excellent for this purpose.
7. From week to week increase weight slightly so that you can continue to perform the same amount of repetitions per exercise as in the previous week.
8. After 16 weeks of this conditioning program, you may

- increase the number of sets per exercise
- modify your routine to include other exercises
- concentrate on body areas that need extra work.

Preventing Exercise Injuries

Prevention of exercise injuries revolves around several guidelines:

1. **Stretching**

   Stretching exercises should be engaged in *after* every exercise session, especially concentrating on the muscle groups that have been utilized during the exercise session. For walkers and runners, this means concentrating on posterior leg muscles and the lower back and the front of the chest. For cyclers, this means the quadriceps and posterior leg muscles and upper back. For swimmers, the shoulder joints especially should be stretched as well as the lower back and calves.

2. **Strengthening**

   Often muscle imbalances can create injury problems. For knee problems in runners, for example, often the hamstrings are too strong and the quadriceps are too weak, so progressive resistance exercises for the knee (extension) can be performed, both for prevention and treatment. If the shin area is giving problems or might potentially be a future problem, the anterior leg muscles can be strengthened through toe raising resistive exercises (with stretching of the calf muscle which is often too strong).

3. **Warming Up and Down**

Slow aerobic exercises should always precede and follow hard aerobic exertion. Five to ten (5–10) minute transition periods between rest and exercise and then rest are important to help the metabolic, circulatory, and neuromuscular systems adapt without injury or trauma.

A recommended warmup is Joint Warming Exercises (see p. 290).

4. **Proper Equipment**

Safety equipment and quality footwear are important for all sports. For the runner this may mean reflective tape and $50 to $100 shoes; for the cycler, this means a hard helmet, for the racquet ball player, goggles, etc.

5. **Gradual Progression**

The number-one cause of musculoskeletal problems is overuse—too much, too fast, too soon. A conservative beginning, with gradual progression, is the most important injury prevention practice and is readily available. Many beginner exercisers are too overzealous initially and soon acquire injuries that thwart future exercise.

6. **Moderation**

Avoid too much of any one activity. Several different activities can help prevent overspecialization and then muscle imbalances and overcompulsion.

7. **Responsibility of the Individual**

The individual's responsibility is to stay within the tolerance of her or his own musculoskeletal system. Individual judgment and common sense should be utilized to "listen" to one's body, making adjustments when necessary. This can mean avoiding that extra three miles of running or that extra set of squats, being regular in training, ob-

taining adequate rest and optimal nutrition, and seeking a balanced approach.

8. **Be Willing to Rest: An important equation in exercise is**

$$\frac{E + R = F}{\text{(exercise) (rest) (fitness)}}$$

In other words, it takes both exercise and adequate rest to build fitness. Either alone will not do it. Often beginner exercisers will sacrifice sleep time to get up and exercise. Chronic fatigue may result, and the whole purpose of exercise—to feel better—is negated. It's important to get both rest and exercise.

9. **Exercise Technique**

Various aerobic activities require special techniques to avoid injury. Flexibility exercises demand stretching below the pain threshold. Regarding aerobic activities such as running or jogging, it is important to keep the body in an upright posture, the arms at a 90° angle, swinging from the shoulder. The feet should land almost flat-footed with the weight well back toward the heel. Only sprinters should run on their toes. Breathing should be through the mouth and nose in a regular fashion. Overall, the body should be loose, natural, and poised. Each sport should be studied to ensure adequate technique.

Abbreviated General Exercise Program

Aerobic Exercise

Beginner

- Allow at least 6 weeks for conditioning of your heart: exercise very moderately.
- Exercise at a training heart rate (THR) that is 60–70 percent of your maximum heart rate (MHR).
- Walk for 15 minutes. Increase time of exercise gradually to 30 minutes over the 6-week period.

More Advanced

- For 10 weeks, increase THR to 65–75 percent of MHR.
- Walk for 30–45 minutes.

Advanced

- Increase THR to 70–85 percent of MRH.
- Walk for 45–60 minutes.
- Introduce variations in program. For example, do interval training: Walk fast for 5 minutes and then jog for 30 seconds. Repeat combination 3 times during workout.

Strength Exercise

Beginner

- Follow program of exercise planned for you by an exercise specialist.
- Allow at least 8 weeks for conditioning of your muscles and joints: exercise very moderately and increase weight gradually every week, as you get stronger.

More Advanced

- For 6 weeks, do 10 reps, 2 sets.
- Keep increasing weight every week, gradually.

Advanced

- Divide workout into upper body exercises on alternate days.
- Do 10 reps, 3 sets of each exercise.

Preventing Injury from Strength Training

- Work with an exercise specialist to show you the safe way to use weights.
- Do not compete with anyone but yourself.
- Begin with very light weight, so that you can perform 12–15 repetitions of the exercise easily. Increase weight very gradually.
- Avoid holding your breath while lifting. Breathe in during relaxing part of exercise and breathe out during effort part of exercise.
- Rest and take a mouthful of pure water between exercises.
- Warm-up for 3–5 minutes before weight lifting exercises and stretch the muscles used during the exercise session after the workout.

❧ *Speak Pregnancy Exercises**

1. **Cobbler's pose**

   This exercise helps the pelvic organs by promoting circulation of blood in this area. It also helps to assure the correct position of the pelvis. This exercise can be done as often as you like and can be used in general as a sitting position.

   When sitting in this position, you should be able to feel a stretch on the inside of your thighs, vagina, and hip joints. You may also feel stretching in your knees and ankles.

   Sit on the floor with your back straight and legs stretched out in front. You can sit against a wall to support the lower back.

   Bend your knees and let your knees relax to the side bringing the bottom of your feet together. The soles of your feet should now be touching with the outside ankle region resting on the floor. Pull your pressed-together feet as close to the opening of your vagina as possible. Open out your thighs and let your knees lower toward the floor. Breathe deeply.

2. **Kneeling with knees apart**

   This position helps to alleviate low back pain and decrease tension in the pelvis and pelvic joints. The pelvic joints open and the muscles are able to relax and lengthen in the low back and pelvis. Stretch only as far as you can without bending your back, and then hold this position, while breathing deeply. You should be able to feel the stretch in the vaginal region and in the knees and ankles.

   Kneel on the floor with knees as wide apart as possible, the top of your feet on the floor and your toes pointing in toward each other. Try to sit between your feet with your buttocks on the floor or sit on top of your heels.

   Move slowly forward from the hips, keeping your buttocks down as much as possible and then lean forward and place your palms on the floor in front of you with both arms straight. Try resting on your arms, keeping your back straight. You should feel a stretch in the vagina.

   Try a gently rocking movement shifting your weight from your arms to your legs.

   ---

   *Adapted from *Health* magazine, (December 1993): 28–30.

Breathe deeply while trying to stay in this position for a minute or longer, then come up and resume a normal sitting position.

3. **Pelvic floor exercises**

   The exercise will help your pelvic-floor muscles relax if you do it often enough. This will prove to be helpful in the second stage of labor, and it may prevent a tear when giving birth.

   This exercise should be done daily, especially in the third trimester.

   Stand with your feet about two feet apart. Squat down and end up squatting on the balls of your feet. Lean forward onto your hands, keeping your arms and back straight, and open your knees wide apart pointing them to the outside.

   Tighten your pelvic-floor muscles, pulling them in as if you are trying to stop yourself from urinating. Hold for several seconds and then slowly let go. Repeat 3 to 5 times.

   Repeat the exercise again, but this time let go in four stages a little at a time. Repeat the exercise again, and this time picture your baby's head passing through your pelvis during the second stage of labor. Each time you breathe out, imagine that your baby is continuing to pass through your vagina as you release your pelvic muscles.

4. **Pelvic tuck-in**

   One of the health problems during pregnancy can be strain on the lower back due to the extra weight. This exercise strengthens the buttocks muscles and will increase support to the lower back and prevent back pain. This exercise also helps to stabilize the pelvis which can prevent back pain. A gentle rocking movement added to the exercise can be good practice for labor and lessen pain and ease the passage of the baby through the birth canal.

   Position yourself on the floor on all fours: hands and knees. Your knees should be about one foot apart. Pull in and tighten your buttocks, pulling your pelvis so that your back arches like a cat's back when it's afraid or angry. Hold this for 10–15 seconds and then let go. Do this repeatedly at least 6 repetitions. Do the exercise a little bit faster, rocking your pelvis gently up and down along with your back motion.

5. **Legs against the wall**

   This exercise will stretch the large muscles along the inner thighs from the pubic bone to the knees.

   Caution: During pregnancy, some women may become dizzy if they lie flat on their backs. If this occurs, avoid this exercise and any others that involve lying on your back.

   You will feel a stretch in the inner thighs during this exercise. You may feel stiff in the beginning, but this will let up as you practice more and become more limber.

   A. Sit sideways next to a wall, so that one hip is touching the wall. Then turn facing the wall with your legs up in the air against the wall. You will now be lying on your back with the bottom of your buttocks against the wall and your feet perpendicular to the floor, but your legs straight and extending up the wall. Stretch your arms over your head on the floor.

   B. Now pull your feet down the wall while bending your knees as if you are sitting on the wall. Your feet should be about shoulder width apart. Extend your arms over your head onto the floor and breathe deeply into your belly. Relax your back and press the small of your back into the floor.

   C. Now bring the bottoms of your feet together and pull your feet down close to the vaginal area. Extend your knees to the side, pressing them toward the wall with your hands.

   When you are done with the exercise, roll over slowly onto your side, and then sit up on the floor.

HORMONE SUPPORTIVE AND HORMONE REPLACEMENT OPTIONS FOR MENOPAUSE

Phytoestrogens

Product name	Company	Dose	Source	Equivalence to 0.625 Premarin
Cimicifuga Extract Plus	Vitanica	40 mg/cap 2–4 caps/day	Black cohosh	Unknown

Comments: Contains a standardized extract of black cohosh, 2.5 percent triterpene glycosides (1 mg), 40 mg per cap. Also contains traditional dried whole root, 85 mg per cap.

Remifemin	Phytopharmica Enzymatic Therapies	20 mg/tablet 2 tablets/day	Black cohosh	Unknown

Comments: Contains triterpene glycosides calculated as 27 deoxyactein. 1 tablet contains 20 mg per cap.

Women's Phase II	Vitanica	2–6 caps/day	Burdock root, licorice root, wild yam root, dong quai, motherwort	Unknown
Meno–caps	Wise Woman Herbs	2–6 caps/day	Motherwort, dong quai, burdock, chaste tree, black cohosh, licorice, motherwort	Unknown
Compounded Vitex/Alfalfa	Gaia Herbs	30 drops 3 to 4 times daily	Chaste tree, alfalfa, cactus, St. John's wort, sage, wild oat, motherwort, lavender oil	Unknown
Pulsatilla, Vitex Compound	HerbPharm	30–60 drops 3 to 4 times/day	Chaste tree, pulsatilla, licorice, motherwort, black cohosh	Unknown
Phyto-est	BioTechnologies	3–6 caps/day	Soybean	Unknown

Comments: 3 capsules contains 45 mg of isoflavones.

Product name	Company	Dose	Source	Equivalence to 0.625 Premarin
Women's Transition	Pioneer Life	2–6 caps/day	Chaste tree, dong quai, licorice, black cohosh, motherwort, rice bran oil	Unknown
Meno-fem	Prevail	2–6 caps/day	Rice bran oil, dong quai, wild yam, licorice, ginseng, chaste tree, other	Unknown

Comments: There are over 300 phytoestrogen plants, some of which are medicinal and others edible. In addition to the plants mentioned below, a short list includes flax, red clover, fennel, hops, wild yam, and kudzu.

Natural Hormones

Product name	Company	Dose	Source	Equivalent doses
Phyto B	Bezwecken	8 pellets/day, (4 sublingual twice daily)	Soybean, Mexican wild yam, licorice	Unknown (see comments)

Comments: 8 pellets contain 1.6 mg estriol, 0.2 mg estrone, 0.2 mg beta-17 estradiol, 66 mg progesterone. Estriol is considered to have been between 25–40 percent of the activity of estradiol or estrone. If you calculate based on the 40 percent of the high side), then this formula is equivalent to 1.04 mg of estradiol. (Estrace = 1 mg beta estradiol). A cautionary note, however, is that equivalent doses of sublingual delivery methods have not been determined.

Osta B3	Bezwecken	8 pellets/day (4 sublingual twice daily)	Soybean, Mexican wild yam, licorice	Unknown (see comments)

Comments: 8 pellets contain 2 mg estriol, 50 mg progesterone. If you calculate based on estriol being only 40 percent of the activity of estradiol, then this is equivalent to 0.8 mg of beta-17 estradiol (as in Estrace). See cautionary note above.

Ostaderm	Bezwecken	½ tsp/day (transdermal, ¼ tsp twice daily)	Soybean, Mexican wild yam, licorice	Unknown (see comments)

Comments: ½ tsp contains 2 mg total estrogens: 1.6 mg estriol, 0.2 mg estrone, 0.2 mg beta-17 estradiol, 66 mg progesterone. Apply cream to palms, chest, inner forearms, inner thighs. Best to rotate sites. Transdermal absorption equivalent doses have not been determined.

Ostaderm V	Bezwecken	½ tsp/day (transdermal, ¼ tsp twice daily)	Soybean, Mexican wild yam, licorice	Unknown (see comments)

Comments: This product contains the same information as Ostaderm but has a decreased amount of alcohol and is meant to be applied to the external genital tissue.

Compounded tri–estrogens	Compounding pharmacies	Individualized prescription	Soybean, Mexican wild yam	Estimated (see comments)

Comments: The current common practice is for a tri-estrogen compound to be composed of 80 percent estriol, 10 percent estrone, and 10 percent beta-estradiol. This is based on a laboratory determination made by Dr. Jonathon Wright that he determined was most similar to normal body physiology. There is some question that this was based on urinary levels and not on serum levels. Further study and research are needed to determine the accuracy of these percentages. If you are seeking a dose similar to Estrace 1 mg (Premarin 0.625), calculate the estradiol and estrone first. Generally, these two are the same. Then calculate estriol on a ratio of 80 percent/10 percent/10 percent (E3/E1/E2). Figure that estriol has only

Product name	Company	Dose	Source	Equivalent doses

25–40 percent of the activity of estradiol. A total day's dose is actually divided into two capsules such that you take 1 cap twice daily. A typical formulation is E3 1 mg/E1 0.125 mg/E2 0.125 mg per cap. 1 cap twice daily. This formula is called tri-est 2.5 mg. Estrace 1 mg = Premarin 0.625 = approximately Tri-est 2.5 mg. Progesterone is added to the formula and should be a minimum of 40 mg twice daily to adequately oppose the estrogen and protect the uterus from endometrial hyperplasia. Some practitioners formulate 100 mg twice daily or more. Custom formulas can be made of any combination of one or more of the estrogens and with or without progesterone. *Examples:* estriol/progesterone; estriol/estradiol/progesterone. One of the more important advantages of using natural hormones is that they can be completely individualized to the dose and combination most appropriate for the patient. These formulations can also be made into creams, gels, or intravaginal preparations.

Product name	Company	Dose	Source	Equivalent doses
Oral micronized progesterone (OMP)	Compounding pharmacies	Individualized prescription	Mexican wild yam	200 OMP equivalent to 10 mg Provera

Comments: The Postmenopausal Estrogen/Progestin Intervention (PEPI) Trial determined that OMP 200 mg/day for 12 days per month adequately opposed 0.625 conjugated equine estrogens and prevented endometrial hyperplasia.

Intravaginal estriol	Compounding pharmacies	Individualized prescription	Soybean	Unknown

Comments: A common prescription is 0.5 mg of estriol in 1 gram of cream, but any strength can be made. A typical regimen of this prescription is to use once each night for two weeks followed by twice weekly for eight months or more. These formulations can be combined with natural progesterone in the formula.

Progon B	Bezwecken	8 pellets/day (4 sublingual twice daily)	Mexican wild yam	Unknown (see comments)

Comments: 8 pellets contain 100 mg USP progesterone. Equivalent doses for sublingual products have not been determined in relationship to either OMP or Provera (medroxyprogesterone acetate-MPA).

Pro-Gest	Transitions for Health, Inc.	¼ tsp twice daily	Mexican wild yam	¼ tsp delivers 20 mg precutaneous progesterone

Comments: 2-ounce tube contains 900 mg USP progesterone. Percutaneous dose equivalents to oral micronized progesterone (OMP) have not been determined. Apply to palms, chest, inner forearms, or inner thighs. Rotate application sites.

Pro-Gest SL (supplement drops)	Transitions Health, Inc.	6 drops twice daily	Mexican wild yam	3 drops delivers 10 mg
Maxine's Feminique	Country Life	¼ tsp twice daily	Mexican wild yam	¼ tsp delivers approximately 11 mg

Comments: Contains 457 mg USP progesterone/1-oz jar.

Progonol	Bezwecken	½ tsp/day (transdermal, ¼ tsp twice daily)	Mexican wild yam	¼ tsp delivers 33 mg transdermally (see comments)

Comments: A 2-oz tube contains 1.995 mg. Transdermal dose equivalents have not been determined. Apply to palms, chest, inner forearms, or inner thighs.

Progesterone transdermals	Compounding pharmacies	Individualized prescriptions	Mexican wild yam	Many strengths available for compounding in gels or creams

Comments: Transdermal (topical) wild yam products and progesterone products exist on the market today with great variability in contents. Be aware that there are wild yam extracts that contain little or no natural progesterone; there are wild yam extracts that contain small amounts of natural progesterone; then there are products that contain more than 400 mg of progesterone per ounce of cream. They all have a time and a place for their use. Know what you need and know what you are getting. The following is a list of available products that were evaluated by Aeron Life Cycles Labs to contain more than 400 mg USP progesterone per ounce. These are the only creams that have a significant amount of natural progesterone that is then bioavailable. Wild yam extract products with little to no progesterone have therapeutic value due to wild yam but not due to progesterone. It is currently generally accepted that the body cannot convert wild yam to progesterone. Natural progesterone is made by extracting either diosgenin from Mexican wild yam or stigmasterol from soybeans. It is then converted to USP progesterone in a manufacturing laboratory via enzymatic chemical reactions. Natural progesterone is biochemically identical to endogenous progesterone produced by the corpus luteum due to ovulation. To learn more about natural hormones, see *Natural Woman, Natural Menopause* by Marcus Laux, N.D. (Morrow Publishing).

Natural Progesterone Creams with More Than 400 mg per ounce

Product	*Company*	*Product*	*Company*
Pro-Gest	Transitions for Health, Inc.	Femarone-17	Wise Essentials
Progonol	Bezwecken	Progest-1 Complex	Kenogen
PhytoGest	Karuna	Angel Care	Angel Care
PureGest	BioVita	Renewed Balance	American Image Marketing
Pro-Alo	HealthWatchers System	Serenity	Health and Science
NatraGest	Broadmoore Labs, Inc.	Natural Balance	South Market Service
Happy PMS	HM Enterprises, Inc.	Ultimate Total Woman	New Science Nutrition
Equilibrium	Equilibrium Lab	Natural Woman	Products of Nature
Pro-G	TriMedica	Fair Lady	Village Market
ProBalance	Springboard	Marpé Wild Yam	Green Pastures
BioBalance	Elan Vitale	Progessence	Young Living
Edenn Cream	SNM	Feminique	Country Life
Kokoro Balance Cream	Kokoro, LLC		

Product name	*Company*	*Dose*	*Source*	*Equivalent doses*
Intravaginal suppositories	Compounding pharmacies	Individualized prescription	Mexican wild yam	Many strengths available
Sublingual lozenges	Compounding pharmacies	Individualized prescriptions	Mexican wild yam	Many strengths available for formulating
Crinone	Wyeth-Ayerst	8% intravaginal	Mexican wild yam	1 applicator delivers 90 mg progesterone
		4% intravaginal		1 applicator delivers 45 mg progesterone

Comments: Crinone delivers natural progesterone in a "bioadhesive gel" to the endometrium with low levels of systemic absorption. Data on file at Wyeth-Ayerst document proven endometrial effect in opposing estrogen for use in HRT: one applicator vaginally (of either 4 percent or 8 percent) every other day for 12 days each month (6 doses per month). Consult other sources for use as part of an Assisted Reproductive Technology (ART) treatment for infertile women with progesterone deficiency.

Prometrium	Solvay	100 mg	Mexican wild yam	200 mg = 10 mg Provera

Additional Natural Hormones

Natural testosterone (available from compounding pharmacies)
Natural testosterone creams/gels (available from compounding pharmacies)
DHEA (available over-the-counter and compounding pharmacies)
Pregnenalone (available over-the-counter and compounding pharmacies)

Friendlier Conventional Hormones

Product name	Company	Dose	Source	Equivalent doses
Estrace	Mead-Johnson (division of Bristol-Myers Squibb)	0.5 mg, 2.0 mg, 1.0 mg	Soybean	1 mg = 0.625 Premarin

Comments: This ERT contains beta-estradiol. When swallowed, it is metabolized to estrone. Best absorbed when taken with food.

Product name	Company	Dose	Source	Equivalent doses
Ortho-Est	Ortho	0.75 mg, 1.5 mg	Mexican wild yam, soybean	0.75 mg = 0.625 Premarin

Comments: Contains estropipate (estrone sulfate).

Product name	Company	Dose	Source	Equivalent doses
Ogen	Pharmacia Upjohn	0.75 mg, 1.5 mg	Mexican wild yam, soybean	0.75 mg = 0.625 Premarin

Comments: Contains estropipate (estrone sulfate).

Product name	Company	Dose	Source	Equivalent doses
Estraderm	Ciba-Geigy	0.05, or 0.1 mg/day	Mexican wild yam, soybean	0.5 mg = 0.625 Premarin Patch changed 2 times/weekly. Patch cannot be cut.
Vivelle	Ciba-Geigy	0.035, 0.05, 0.075, 0.1 mg	Mexican wild yam, soybean	0.05 mg = 0.625 Premarin Patch changed 2 times/weekly. Patch can be cut to modify dose.
Alora	Proctor and Gamble	0.05, 0.075, 0.1 mg/day	Mexican wild yam, soybean	0.05 mg = 0.625 Premarin Patch changed 2 times/weekly. Patch can be cut to modify dose.
Climara	Berlex Laboratories	0.05, 0.1 mg/day	Soybean	0.05 mg = 0.625 Premarin Patch changed once per week. Patch can be cut to modify doses.
FemPatch	Parke-Davis	0.025 mg/day	Plant-derived	0.025 mg = 0.3 Premarin Patch changed once per week. Patch cannot be cut.

Product name	Company	Dose	Source	Equivalent doses
Estrace cream	Mead-Johnson	2 g every night for 2 weeks; then 1 g 3 times a week	Soybean	0.1 mg estradiol per gram
Ogen	Pharmacia Upjohn	2.0–4 g/day for 3 weeks with 1 week off	Mexican wild yam, soybean	1.5 mg per gram

Less-Friendly Conventional Hormones

Product name	Company	Dose	Source	Equivalent doses
Premarin	Wyeth-Ayerst	0.3 mg, 0.9 mg	Pregnant mare's urine	0.625 mg = 0.625 mg Premarin

Comments: Made of conjugated equine estrogens (CEE). Contains 50 percent estrone along with 10–12 conjugated estrogens (equilins, equinalins, alpha estradiol, beta estradiol).

Menest	SmithKline Beecham	0.3 mg, 0.625, 1.25, 2.5 mg	Mexican wild yam, soybean	0.625 = 0.625 Premarin

Comments: Contains esterified estrogens which are 75–85 percent sodium estrone sulfate and equilin sulfates.

Estratab	Solvay	0.3 mg, 0.625, 1.25 2.5 mg	Mexican wild yam, soybean	0.625 = 0.625 Premarin

Comments: Contains esterified estrogens which are 75–85 percent sodium estrone sulfate and equilin sulfates.

Premarin Cream	Wyeth-Ayerst	0.5–2 g/day for 3 weeks with 1 week off	Pregnant mare's urine	0.625 mg per gram
Estring	Pharmacia Upjohn	2 mg delivered over 90 days	Mexican wild yam, soybean	Not applicable

Comments: Contains alpha estradiol. Placed in the vagina like a diaphragm; minimal systemic absorption.

Provera	Bristol-Myers	Continuous: 2.5 mg Cycled: 5.0 or 10 mg	Synthetic	Gold standard for comparison

Comments: Provera is the most widely used and tested progestin. Medroxyprogesterone acetate (MPA) may cause PMS-like side effects in some women (40 percent reported), including breast tenderness, water retention, depression, and irritability.

Micronor	Ortho	0.35 mg continuous	Synthetic	Unknown. Typical continuous dose
Megace	Bristol-Myers	20 mg	Synthetic	Unknown

Comments: Usually used twice a day for hot flashes and vasomotor symptoms.

Cycrin (MPA)	Wyeth-Ayerst	Continuous: 2.5 mg Cycled: 5.0 or 10 mg	Synthetic	Same as Provera
Amen	Carnrick Labs	5.0 or 10.0 mg	Synthetic	Same as 5.0 or 10.0 Provera

Additional Products in This Category

Estratest (esterified estrones with methylestosterone) available in E 1.25 mg and T 2.5 mg or half-strength (HS) with E 0.625 mg and T 1.25 mg.

Prempro (daily doses of Premarin 0.625 mg and MPA 2.5 mg).

Premphase (Premarin 0.625 mg for days 1–28 and MPA 5.0 mg for days 14–28).

Methyl testosterone (compounding pharmacies).

CombiPatch (Estradiol/Norethindrome acetate) 0.05/0.14 mg per day.

Premarin with methyl testosterone: Premarin 0.625 plus methyl-test 5.0 mg.

Note: This chart was compiled as a reference and in no way represents a recommendation of any product for any particular patient or clinical situation. An attempt was made to be accurate, but this is not guaranteed.

PROCEDURES AND PRACTICES

Breast Self-Exam

The breast self-exam should be done in three steps:

1. The first step is a visual exam in front of a mirror: Look at your breasts with your arms at your sides, then hold your arms overhead clasping your hands behind your head. Next place your hands on your hips and roll your shoulders forward and bow forward slightly as you pull your shoulders and elbows forward. Inspect both breasts for swelling, changes in skin (dimpling, puckering, discoloration, or scaling of skin), or changes in your nipples including retraction or discharge.
2. The second step is to lie down and place a small pillow or folded towel under your right shoulder and your right arm behind your head. Press firmly with the pads of your fingers and move your left hand over all parts of your right breast in an up and down motion as if you are tracking a vertical line in rows next to each other. Pay extra attention to the area between the breast and the armpit, including the armpit itself. Gently squeeze the nipple to check for discharge. Check the left breast with your right hand in the same way.
3. The third step is standing. With your left arm behind your head, use your right hand to examine your left breast. Move your fingers up and down in vertical rows pressing firmly with the pads of your fingers. Repeat this on the right breast.

(Adapted from the American Cancer Society)

Alternating Sitz Baths

Obtain two large tubs that you are able to sit in. Fill one half full with hot water (bath water temperature). Fill the other one half full with ice cold water. Sit in the hot water for three minutes and then quickly sit in the cold for 30 seconds. Repeat this three times in succession. Quickly get dressed or put on a robe or blankets so as not to become chilled. The room where you are doing the treatment should be comfortable and warm.

Castor Oils Packs

Materials needed:

1. Wool flannel cloth
2. Plastic sheet (medium thickness)
3. Bath towel
4. Two safety pins
5. Bowl
6. Castor oil
7. Saran wrap
8. Baking soda

Instructions

Fold a piece of wool or cotton flannel so that it is three layers thick and is approximately 12 inches square. This size is recommended for abdominal and pelvic applications. Pour castor oil into the bowl. Place the cloth in the bowl to saturate the flannel; wring it out so it is not dripping. Place the plastic sheet on the bed where you will be lying down. Apply the cloth to the designated bodily area. Then cover the pack with a piece of plastic wrap. Wrap a towel around the entire area and fasten it with safety pins. Lie down and avoid becoming chilled. The pack should stay in place for a minimum of one hour but may be worn longer. After removing the castor oil pack, clean the skin with soda water (two teaspoons of baking soda added to a quart of water).

The castor oil pack may be saved in a plastic bag or container for future use. It can be used repeatedly for a number of treatments.

Infusions

An infusion is a simple tea made with one or more herbs steeped in boiled water. To make an infusion, weigh out one ounce of dry herbs. Add one pint (two cups) of boiling water to the herbs. Some herbs will taste better if you use more than two cups of water. Steep the herbs for ten to twenty minutes. Herbs that are steeped longer will become stronger. Strain the tea through a metal-wire or bamboo tea strainer. Drink throughout the day.

BODY MASS INDEX ACCORDING TO HEIGHT AND WEIGHT

Body Mass Index

	19	20	21	22	23	24	25	26	27	28	29	30	31	32	33	34	35	36
Ht(in)									*Body weight (lb)*									
58	91	95	100	105	110	114	119	124	129	133	138	143	148	152	157	162	167	172
59	94	99	104	109	114	119	124	129	134	139	144	149	154	159	164	169	174	179
60	97	102	107	112	117	122	127	132	138	143	148	153	158	163	168	173	178	183
61	101	106	111	117	122	127	132	138	143	148	154	159	164	169	175	180	185	191
62	103	109	114	120	125	130	136	141	147	152	158	163	168	174	179	185	190	196
63	107	113	119	124	130	135	141	147	152	158	164	169	175	181	186	192	198	203
64	111	117	123	129	135	141	146	152	158	164	170	176	182	187	193	199	205	211
65	114	120	126	132	138	144	150	156	162	168	174	180	186	192	198	204	210	216
66	118	124	131	137	143	149	156	162	168	174	180	187	193	199	205	212	218	224
67	121	127	134	140	147	153	159	166	172	178	185	191	198	204	210	217	223	229
68	125	132	139	145	152	158	165	172	178	185	191	198	205	211	218	224	231	238
69	128	135	142	149	155	162	169	176	182	189	196	203	209	216	223	230	236	243
70	133	140	147	154	161	168	175	182	189	196	203	210	217	224	231	237	237	244
71	136	143	150	157	164	171	179	186	193	200	207	214	221	229	236	243	250	257
72	140	148	155	162	170	177	185	192	199	207	214	221	229	236	244	251	258	266
73	143	151	158	166	174	181	189	196	204	211	219	226	234	241	249	257	264	272
74	148	156	164	171	179	187	195	203	210	218	226	234	242	249	257	265	273	281
75	151	159	167	175	183	191	199	207	215	223	231	239	247	255	263	271	279	287
76	156	164	172	181	189	197	205	214	222	230	238	246	255	263	271	279	287	296

RESOURCES

Nutritional and Herbal Products

Formulations Developed by Dr. Tori Hudson by Vitanica

Product	Purpose
Breastblend	Breast cancer prevention
Cardioblend	Heart disease prevention
Crampbark Extra	Menstrual cramps
Cranstat Extra	Urinary tract infections
Fibroblend	Fibrocystic breasts
Herbal Symmetry	Multi-herb daily
Herpblend	Herpes simplex
Iron Extra	Iron deficient anemia
Ipriflavone	Extra osteoporosis prevention
Maternal Symmetry	Prenatal multivitamin
Opti-Recovery	Surgery support
Osteoblend	Osteoporosis prevention
Phytoestrogen Herbal	Phytoestrogen powder
Sleepblend	Insomnia
Slow Flow	Menstrual flow reduction
Uplift	Depression
Veinoblend	Varicose veins
Women's Phase I	Premenstrual syndrome
Women's Phase II	Menopause support
Women's Symmetry	Multivitamin-mineral
Yeast Arrest	Yeast vaginitis

Single Herb Standardized Extract Formulations by Vitanica

Product	Ingredients
Cimicifuga Extract Plus	Black cohosh
Ginger Extract Plus	Ginger
Gingko Extract Plus	Gingko
Horse Chestnut Extract Plus	Horse Chestnut
Soy Choice	Soy isoflavones
St. John's wort	St. John's wort
Vitex Extract Plus	Chaste tree berry

Cervical Dysplasia Products by Bezwecken

Vitamin A suppositories
Herbal C suppositories
Condyloma (Papillo) suppositories
Escharotic Kit
Vag Pack suppositories

Soy Products

Products	Company
Soy Choice	Vitanica
Soy Essentials	Health From the Sun
Nutra Soy	NutraSoy
Genisoy Powder	Genisoy
Phytoestrogen Herbal	Vitanica

Natural Hormone Creams

Product	Company
Progest	Transitions for Health
Ostaderm	Bezwecken
Ostaderm V	Bezwecken
Others	Compounding pharmacies

Standardized Herbal Extracts

Herbs	Company
Gingko, chaste tree, black cohosh, St. John's wort, ginger, horse chestnut	Vitanica
Red clover (Promensil)	Novogen

Other reputable suppliers of standardized herbal extracts are Enzymatic Therapies, Phytopharmica, and Madis Botanicals.

Herbal Tinctures Are Available from the Following Companies:

Avena Botanicals
Eclectic Institute
Gaia Herbs
Herb Pharm
Materia Medica
Wise Women Herbals

Uterine Fibroid Herbal Formulations from *Gaia Herbs*

Scudder's Alterative
Echinacea/red root compound
Fraxinus/Ceonothus compound
Gelsemium/Phytolacca compound
(Turska formula)

Other Products

Product	Company
Mixed natural carotenes (Betaplex)	Scientific Botanicals
Liquid folic acid (Folirinse)	Scientific Botanicals
Lomatium isolate	Eclectic Institute

Nutritional and Herbal Companies

Vitanica (Dr. Tori Hudson's Women's Health Product Line)
P.O. Box 1285
Sherwood, OR 97140
1-800-572-4712

Avena Botanicals
Rockland, ME 94841
(207) 594-0694

Eclectic Institute
14385 SE Lusted Road
Sandy, OR 97055
1-800-332-4372

Enzymatic Therapies
Greenbay, WI 54311
1-800-225-9245

Gaia Herbs
108 Island Ford Road
Brevard, NC 28712
1-800-831-7780

Genisoy Products Co.
Fairfield, CA 94533
1-888-436-4769

Health from the Sun
P.O. Box 840
Sunapee, NH 03782
1-800-447-2229

Herb Pharm
P.O. Box 116
Williams, OR 97544
1-800-599-2392

Madis Botanicals
375 Huyler Street
South Hackensack, NJ 07606
(201) 440-5000

Materia Medica, Inc.
112 Hermosa SE
Albuquerque, NM 87108
(505) 232-3161

Novogen
6 Landmark Square
Stamford, CT 06901
1-888-890-6721

Nutra Soy
Narula Research
107 Boulder Bluff Trail
Chapel Hill, NC 27516
(919) 967-7621

Prevail
2204-8 NW Birdsdale
Gresham, OR 97030
1-800-248-0885

Transitions for Health
621 SW Alder
Portland, OR 97205
1-800-888-6814

Tyler Encapsulations
2204 NW Birdsdale
Gresham, OR 97030
(503) 661-5401

For Licensed Practitioners Only

Bezwecken
15495 SW Millikan Way
Beaverton, OR 97006
1-800-743-2256

Metagenics
1010 Tyinn Street #26
Eugene, OR 97402
1-800-338-3948

NF Formulas
9775 SW Commerce Circle
Suite C-5
Wilsonville, OR 97070

Phytopharmica
825 Challenger Drive
Green Bay, WI 54305
1-800-553-2370

Priority One
715 West Orchard
Bellingham, WA 98225
1-800-443-2039

Pure Encapsulations
490 Boston Post Road
Sudburg, MA 01776
1-800-753-2277

Scientific Botanicals
P.O. Box 31131
Seattle, WA 98103
(206) 527-5521

Thorne Research
25820 Highway 2 West
P.O. Box 25
Dover, ID 83825
1-800-228-1966

Wise Woman
P.O. Box 279
Creswell, OR 97426
1-800-532-5219

Compounding Pharmacies

International Academy of Compounding
Pharmacists
P.O. Box 1365
Sugarland, TX 77487
(713) 933-8400
(900) 927-4227

Apothecure
13720 Midway Road
Dallas, TX 75244
1-800-969-6601

Bajamar Women's Health Care
9609 Dielman Rock Island
St. Louis, MO 63132
1-800-255-8025

Belmar Pharmacy
8015 West Alamed Avenue
Lakewood, CO 80226
1-800-525-9473

College Pharmacy
3503 Austin Bluffs Parkway, Suite 101
Colorado Springs, CO 80918
1-800-888-9358

Lloyd Center Pharmacy
1302 Lloyd Center
Portland, OR 97232
1-800-358-8974

Madison Pharmacy Associates
429 Gammon Place
P.O. Box 9641
Madison, WI 53715
1-800-558-7046

Women's International Pharmacy
5708 Monona Drive
Madison, WI 53716-3152
1-800-279-5708

Clinics, Naturopathic Colleges, and Organizations

A Woman's Time, P.C.
Dr. Tori Hudson
2067 NW Lovejoy
Portland, OR 97209
(503) 222-2322

Women's Institute of Natural Medicine
(Postgraduate training in women's health
and natural therapies)
Dr. Tori Hudson
2067 NW Lovejoy
Portland, OR 97209
(503) 222-2322

National College of Naturopathic Medicine
049 SW Porter
Portland, OR 97201
(503) 499-4343

Bastyr University
14500 Juanita Drive NE
Bothell, WA 98011
(425) 602-3100

Southwest College of Naturopathic Medicine
and Health Sciences
2140 East Broadway
Tempe, AZ 85282
(602) 990-7424

Bridgeport University
126 Park Avenue
Bridgeport, CT 06601
(203) 576-4552

Canadian College of Naturopathic Medicine
2300 Yonge Street
P.O. Box 2431
Toronto, ON M4P1E4
(416) 486-8584

American Association of Naturopathic Physicians
P.O. Box 20386
Seattle, WA 98102
(206) 323-7610

American Holistic Medical Association
6728 Old McLean Village Road
McLean, VA 22101
(703) 556-9728

American College of Obstetricians and
Gynecologists
Resource Center
401 12th Street SW
Washington, DC 20024

The American Herbalists Guild
P.O. Box 746555
Arvada, CO 80006
(303) 423-8800

American Botanical Council
P.O. Box 12006
Austin, TX 78711
(512) 331-8868

American Herb Association
P.O. Box 1673
Nevada City, CA 95959

Herb Research Foundation
1007 Pearl Street
Boulder, CO 80302
(303) 449-2265

Books and Publications

Women's Bodies, Women's Wisdom by Christiane Northrup, M.D. (Bantam)

Health Wisdom for Women, a newsletter by Christiane Northrup, M.D. (Phillips Publishing, Inc., 1-800-211-8561)

Dr. Susan Love's Hormone Book by Susan Love, M.D. (Random House)

Dr. Susan Love's Breast Book by Susan Love, M.D. (Addison-Wesley)

Natural Woman, Natural Menopause by Marcus Laux, N.D., and Christine Conrad (HarperCollins)

Books by Susan Lark, M.D. (Celestial Arts Publishing):
PMS Self-Help Book
Fibroid Tumors and Endometriosis
Anxiety and Stress
Anemia and Heavy Menstrual Flow
Menstrual Cramps
Women's Health Companion
The Estrogen Decision

The Pause by Lonnie Barbach, Ph.D. (Signet Health)

Preventing and Reversing Osteoporosis by Alan Gaby, M.D. (Prima Publishing)

Breast Cancer: What You Should Know by Steve Austin, N.D., and Cathy Hitchcock, M.S.W. (Prima Publishing)

Total Breast Health by Robin Keuneke (Kensington)

Herbal Prescriptions for Better Health by Donald Brown, N.D. (Prima Publishing)

Encyclopedia of Natural Medicine by Michael Murray, N.D., and Joe Pizzorno, N.D. (Prima Publishing)

Encyclopedia of Nutritional Supplements by Michael Murray, N.D. (Prima Publishing)

The Healing Power of Herbs by Michael Murray, N.D. (Prima Publishing)

The Hormone of Desire by Susan Rako, M.D. (Harmony Books)

Menopause Naturally by Sadja Greenwood, M.D. (Volcano Press)

The Complete German Commission E Monographs by Mark Blumenthal (American Botanical Council)

Alternative Medicine: The Definitive Guide by Burton Goldberg Group (Future Medicine Publishing)

Health Notes Online
1125 SE Madison Street
Portland, OR 97214
(503) 234-4052

Natural Pharmacy, edited by Skye Leninger, D.C. (Prima Publishing)

Quarterly Review of Natural Medicine
Natural Products Research Consultants
1125 SE Madison Street, Suite 209
Portland, OR 97214
(503) 234-4052

What Your Doctor May Not Tell You About Menopause by John Lee, M.D. (Warner Books)

Estrogen, The Natural Way by Nina Shandler (Villard)

HerbalGram
P.O. Box 12006
Austin, TX 78711

Additional Publications and Tapes by Dr. Tori Hudson

Gynecology and Naturopathic Medicine
Tori Hudson, N.D.
TK Publications
2067 NW Lovejoy
Portland, OR 97209
(503) 222-2322

Women's Health Update, The Complete Collection of Townsend Letter Columns 1992–1997
Tori Hudson, N.D.
TK Publications
2067 NW Lovejoy
Portland, OR 97209
(503) 222-2322

Herbal Educational Services (tapes)
P.O. Box 57
Swans Island, ME 04680
1-800-252-0688

Tree Farm Communications (tapes)
1-800-468-0464

REFERENCES

Chapter One: Abnormal Uterine Bleeding

1. Phipps W, Martini M, Lampe J, Slavin J, Kurzer M. "Effect of flaxseed ingestion on the menstrual cycle." *J Clin Endocrin Metab* 1993; 77(5):1215–19.
2. Cassidy A, Bingham S, Setchell K. "Biological effects of a diet of soy protein rich in isoflavones on the menstrual cycle of premenopausal women." *Am J Clin Nutr* 1994; 60:333–40.
3. Olsson H, Landin-Olsson M, Gullberg B. "Retrospective assessment of menstrual cycle length in patients with breast cancer, in patients with benign breast disease, and in women without breast disease." *J Natl Canc Inst* 1983; 70:17–20.
4. Juneja H, Murthy S, Ganguly J. "The effect of vitamin A deficiency on the biosynthesis of steroid hormones in rats." *J Biochem* 1966; 99(1):138–45.
5. Lithgow D, Politzer W. "Vitamin A in the treatment of menorrhagia." *S A M J* 1977; 51:191–93.
6. Biskind M. "Nutritional deficiency in the etiology of menorrhagia, metrorrhagia, cystic mastitis and premenstrual tension: Treatment with vitamin B complex." *J Clin Endocrin Metab* 1943; 3:227–34.
7. Cohen J, Rubin H. "Functional menorrhagia: treatment with bioflavonoids and vitamin C." *Curr Therap Res* 1960; 2(11):539.
8. Weiss R. "Herbal Medicine." *Ab Arcanum*, Sweden, 1988.
9. Amann W. "Removing an obstipation using Agnolyt." *Ther Gegenew* 1965; 104(9):1263–65.
10. Sliutz G, Speiser P et al. "Agnus castus extracts inhibit prolactin secretion of rat pituitary cells." *Horm Metab Res* 1993; 25:253–55.
11. Probst V, Roth O. "On a plant extract with a hormone-like effect." *Dtsch Me Wschr* 1954; 79(35):1271–74.
12. Bleier W. "Phytotherapy in irregular menstrual cycles or bleeding periods and other gynecological disorders of endocrine origin." *Zentralblatt Gynakol* 1959; 81(18): 701–9.
13. Milewica A, Gejdel E et al. "*Vitex agnus castus* extract in the treatment of luteal phase defects due to hyperprolactinemia: results of a randomized placebo-controlled double-blind study." *Arzneim-Forsch Drug Res* 1993; 43:752–56.
14. Macalo N, Jain R, Jain S et al. "Ethnopharmacologic investigations of ginger (*Zingiber officinale*)." *J Ethnopharm* 1989; 27:129–40.
15. Kelly R, Lumsden M et al. "The relationship between menstrual blood loss and prostaglandin production in the human: evidence for increased availability of arachidonic acid in women suffering from menorrhagia." *Prostaglandins and Leukotrienes in Medicine* 1984; 16: 69–77.
16. Mowrey D. *The Scientific Validation of Herbal Medicine.* Cormorant Books, 1986;188.
17. Kuroda K, Takagi K. "Physiologically active substances in Capsella bursa-pastoris." *Nature* 1968; 220(5168): 7078–708.

Chapter Two: Amenorrhea

1. Wabisch M, Hauner H et al. "Body fat distribution and steroid hormone concentrations in obese adolescent girls before and after weight reduction." *J Clin Endocrin Metab* 1995; 80(12):3469–75.
2. Jeghers H. "Skin changes of nutritional origin." *N Engl J Med* 1943; 228:678–86.
3. Almond S, Logan R. "Carotenemia." *N Engl J Med* 1942; 2:239–41.
4. Robboy M, Sato A, Schwabe A. "The hypercarotenemia in anorexia nervosa: a comparison of vitamin A and carotene levels in various forms of menstrual dysfunction and cachexia." *Amer J Clin Nutr* 1974; 27:362–67.

5. Pops M, Schwabe A. "Hypercarotenemia in anorexia nervosa." *JAMA* 1968; 205:533–34.

6. Frumar A, Medrum D, Judd H. "Hypercarotenemia in hypothalamic amenorrhea." *Fertil Steril* 1979; 32: 261–64.

7. Page S. "Golden ovaries." *Aust NZ J Obstet Gynecol* 1971; 11:32–36.

8. Richards S, Chang F et al. "Serum carotene levels in female long-distance runners." *Fertil Steril* 1985; 43(1): 79–81.

9. Heaney R. "Nutritional factors and estrogen in age-related bone loss." *Clin Invest Med* 1982; 5:147–55.

10. Weiss R. *Herbal Medicine.* 1988. Ab Arcanum, Sweden.

11. Amann W. "Removing an obstipation using Agnolyt." *Ther Gegenew* 1965; 104(9):1263–65.

12. Probst V, Roth O. "On a plant extract with hormonelike effect." *Dtsch Me Wschr* 1954; 79(35):1271–74.

13. Losh E, Kayser E. "Diagnosis and treatment of dyshormonal menstrual periods in the general practice." *Gynakol Praxis* 1990; 14(3):489–95.

14. Sliutz G, Speiser P et al. "Agnus castus extracts inhibit prolactin secretion of rat pituitary cells." *Horm Metab Res* 1993; 25(5):253–55.

15. Jarry H, Leonhardt S, Wuttke W. "*Agnus castus* as dopaminergous effective principle in mastodynon N." *Zeitschrift Phytother* 1991; 12:77–82.

16. Milewica A, Gejdel E et al. "*Vitex agnus castus* extract in the treatment of luteal phase defects due to hyperprolactinemia. Results of a randomized placebo-controlled double-blind study." *Arzneim-Forsch Drug Res* 1993; 43:752–56.

17. Liske E, Duker E. "Cimicifuga racemosa in clinical practice and research." *Ars Medici* 1993; 7:1–8.

18. Duker E, Kopanski L, Jarry H, Wuttke W. "Effects of extracts from Cimicifuga racemosa on gonadotropin release in menopausal women and ovariectomized rats." *Planta Medica* 1991; 57:420–24.

19. Gifford R. "Historical note on the treatment of amenorrhea with water pepper." *J Reprod Med* 1972; 9(3):143–45.

20. Ogier T. "Amenorrhea treated successfully with the water pepper." *Charleston Med J* 1846; 1:298–300.

21. Cann C, Martin M, Jaffe R. "Duration of amenorrhea affects rate of bone loss in women runners: implications of therapy." *Med Sci Sports Ex* 1985; 17:214.

22. Boyden T et al. "Sex steroids and endurance running in women." *Fertil Steril* 1983; 39:629.

23. Bullen B et al. "Induction of menstrual disorders by strenuous exercise in untrained women." *N Engl J Med* 1985; 312:1349.

24. DeSouza M et al. "Adrenal activation and the prolactin response to exercise in eumenorrheic and amenorrheic runners." *J Appl Physiol* 1991; 70:2378.

25. Prior J, Vigna Y. "Ovulation disturbances and exercise training." *Clin Obstet Gynecol* 1991; 34:180.

26. Bonen A. "Recreational exercise does not impair menstrual cycles: a prospective study." *Int J Sports Med* 1992; 13:110.

27. Hetland M et al. "Running induces menstrual disturbances but bone mass is unaffected, except in amenorrheic women." *Am J Med* 1993; 95:53.

28. Walberg J, Johnston C. "Menstrual function and eating behavior in female recreational weight lifters and competitive body builders." *Med Sci Sports Exerc* 1991; 23:30.

29. Walberg-Rankin J, Edmonds C, Dwazdauskas F. "Diet and weight changes of female bodybuilders before and after competition." *Int J Sport Nutr* 1993; 3:87.

30. Bonen A. "Exercise-induced menstrual cycle change." *Sports Med* 1994; 17:392.

31. Rogol A et al. "Durability of the reproductive axis in eumenorrheic women during one year endurance training." *J Appl Physiol* 1992; 72:1571.

32. Sandoval W, Weyward V, Lyons T. "Comparison of body composition, exercise and nutritional profiles of female and male body builders at competition." *J Sports Med Phys Fitness* 1989; 29:63.

33. Kleiner S, Bazzarre T, Litchford M. "Metabolic profiles, diet, and health practices of championship male and female bodybuilders." *J Am Diet Assoc* 1990; 90:962.

34. Lamar-Hildebrand N, Saldanha L, Endres J. "Dietary and exercise practices of college-aged female bodybuilders." *J Am Diet Assoc* 1989; 89:1308.

35. Greene J. "Exercise-induced menstrual irregularities." *Comp Ther* 1993; 19:116.

36. Ramos R, Warren M. "The interrelationships of body fat, exercise, and hormonal status and their impact on reproduction and bone health." *Sem Perinatol* 1995; 19:163.

37. Williams N et al. "Strenuous exercise with caloric restriction: effect on luteinizing hormone secretion." *Med Sci Sports Exerc* 1995; 27:1390.

38. Wolman R et al. "Menstrual state and exercise as determinants of spinal trabecular density in female athletes." *Br Med J* 1990; 301:516.

39. Ronkainen H et al. "Physical exercise-induced changes and season-associated differences in the pituitary-ovarian function of runners and joggers." *J Clin Endocrin Metab* 1985; 60:416.

40. Kleiner S, Bazzarre T, Ainsworth B. "Nutritional status of nationally ranked elite bodybuilders." *Int J Sport Nutr* 1994; 4:54.

41. Baird D. "Amenorrhea, anovulation and dysfunctional uterine bleeding." In De Groot L, ed. *Endocrinology,* 3 ed. New York: WB Saunders, 1995:2059–79.

42. Ferrari C, Crosignani P. "Medical treatment of hyperprolactinaemic disorders." *Hum Reprod* 1986; 41:74–79.

Chapter Three: Cancer Prevention

1. Ames B, Gold L, Willet W. "The causes and prevention of cancer: an epidemiologic exercise." *JAMA* 1995; special issue on cancer: 1–9.

2. Colditz G. "Relationship between estrogen levels, use of hormone replacement therapy, and breast cancer." *J Natl Cancer Inst* 1998; 90:814–23.

3. Perera F. "Uncovering new clues to cancer risk." *Scien Am* May 1996; 54–62.

4. Brunet J, Ghadirian P, Rebbeck T et al. "Effect of smoking on breast cancer in carriers of mutant BRCA1 or BRCA2 genes." *J Natl Canc Inst* 1998. May 20 90(10):761–66.

5. Welp E, Weiderpass E, Boffetta P et al. "Environmental risk factors of breast cancer." *Scand J Work Environ Health* 1998. Feb; 24(1):3–7.

6. Ishibe N, Hankinson S, Colditz G et al. "Cigarette smoking, cytochrome P450 1A1 polymorphisms, and breast cancer risk in the Nurses' Health Study." *Canc Res* 1998. Feb 15; 58(4):667–71.

7. Morabia A, Bernstein M, Ruiz J et al. "Relation of smoking to breast cancer by estrogen receptor." *Int J Canc* 1998. Jan 30; 75(3):339–42.

8. Barbone F, Austin H, Partridge E. "Diet and endometrial cancer: a case-control study." *Am J Epid* 1993; 137:393–403.

9. Le M, Moulton L, Hill C et al. "Consumption of dairy produce and alcohol in a case-control study of breast cancer." *JNDI* 1986; 77(3):633–36.

10. Knekt P, Jarvinen R, Seppanen R et al. "Intake of dairy products and risk of breast cancer." *Br J Canc* 1996; 73(5):687–91.

11. Kato I, Miura S, Kasumi F et al. "A case-control study of breast cancer among Japanese women: with special reference to family history and reproductive and dietary factors." *Breast Canc Res Treat* 1992; 24(1):51–59.

12. Cramer D et al. "Galactose consumption and metabolism in relation to the risk of ovarian cancer." *Lancet* 1989; 2:66–71.

13. Bleiker E, van der Ploeg H, Hendriks J, Ader H. "Personality factors and breast cancer development: a prospective longitudinal study." *J Natl Canc Inst* 1996; 88:1478–82.

14. Chen C, David A, Hunnerley H et al. "Adverse life events and breast cancer: case-control study." *BMJ* 1995; 311:1527–30.

15. Cooper C, Faragher E. "Psychosocial stress and breast cancer: the inter-relationship between stress events, coping strategies and personality." *Psych Med* 1993; 23:653–62.

16. Fox C, Harper A, Hyner G, Lyle R. "Loneliness, emotional repression, marital quality, and major life events in women who develop breast cancer." *J Comm Health* 1994; 19(4):467–82.

17. *NCI Surveillance, Epidemiology, and End Results Program*, 1998. Available at http://www.cancer.org/statistics/cff98/graphicaldata.html.

18. Baird D, Umbach D, Lansdell L et al. "Dietary intervention study to assess estrogenicity of dietary soy among postmenopausal women." *J Clin Endocrin Metab* 1995; 80:1685–90.

19. Stoll B. "Eating to beat breast cancer: potential role for soy supplements." *Ann Onc* 1997; 8(3):223–25.

20. Adlercreutz H, Mazur W. "Phyto-estrogens and Western diseases." *Ann Med* 1997; 29:95–120.

21. Willett W, Hunter D, Stampfer M et al. "Dietary fat and fiber in relation to risk of breast cancer." *JAMA* 1992; 21:2037–44.

22. Yuan J, Wang Q, Ross R et al. "Diet and breast cancer in Shanghai and Tianjin, China." *Br J Cancer* 1995; 71:1197–1200.

23. Lubin F, Wax Y, Modan B. "Role of fat, animal protein, and dietary fiber in breast cancer etiology: a case-control study." *J Nat Canc Inst* 1986; 77:605–12.

24. van Veer P, Kolb C, Verhoef P et al. "Dietary fiber, beta-carotene and breast cancer: results from a case-control study." *Int J Canc* 1990; 45:825–28.

25. Baghurst P, Rohan T. "High-fiber diets and reduced risk of breast cancer." *Int J Canc* 1994; 56:173–76.

26. Adlercreutz H, Hamalainen E, Gorbach S et al. "Diet and plasma androgens in postmenopausal vegetarian and omnivorous women and postmenopausal women with breast cancer." *Am J Clin Nutr* 1989; 49:433–42.

27. Adlercreutz H, Fotsis T, Hockerstedt K et al. "Diet and urinary estrogen profile in premenopausal omnivorous and vegetarian women and in premenopausal women with breast cancer." *J Steroid Biochem* 1989; 34:527–30.

28. Chatenoud L, Tavani A, La Vecchia C et al. "Whole grain food intake and cancer risk." *Int J Canc* 1998; 77(1):24–28.

29. Lund E, Bonaa K. "Reduced breast cancer mortality among fishermen's wives in Norway." *Canc Caus Control* 1993; 4:283–87.

30. Rylander L, Hagmar L. "Mortality and cancer incidence among women with a high consumption of fatty fish contaminated with persistent organochlorine compounds." *Scand J Work Environ Health* 1995; 21(6):419–26.

31. Amagase H, Milner J. "Impact of various sources of garlic and their constituents on 7,12-dimethylbenz[a]antracene binding to mammary cell DNA." *Carcinogenesis* 1993. Aug; 14(8):1627–31.

32. Sundaram S, Milner J. "Impact of organosulfur compounds in garlic on canine mammary tumor cells in culture." *Canc Lett* 1993. Oct 15; 74(1–2):85–90.

33. Liu J, Lin R, Milner J. "Inhibition of 7,12-dimethylbenz[a]anthracene-induced mammary tumors and DNA adducts by garlic powder." *Carcinogenesis* 1992. Oct 13(10):1847–51.

34. Ip C, Lisk D, Stoewsand G. "Mammary cancer prevention by regular garlic and selenium-enriched garlic." *Nutr Canc* 1992; 17(3):279–86.

35. Hussain S, Jannu L, Rao A. "Chemopreventive action of garlic on methylcholanthrene-induced carcinogenesis in the uterine cervix of mice." *Canc Lett* 1990. Feb; 49(2):175–180.

36. Dorant E, van den Brandt P, Goldbohm R. "Allium vegetable consumption, garlic supplement intake, and female breast carcinoma incidence." *Breast Canc Res Treat* 1995; 33(2):163–70.

37. Schardt D, Schmidt S. "Garlic: clove at first sight?" *Nutrition Action Healthletter* 1995. July/August:3–5.

38. Hunter D. "Diet and breast cancer." *Proc Anu Meet Am Assoc Canc Res* 1996; 37:643.

39. Franceschi S, Favero A, Decarli A et al. "Intake of macro-nutrients and risk of breast cancer." *Lancet* 1996; 347:1351–56.

40. Hilakivi-Clarke L. "Mechanisms by which high maternal fat intake during pregnancy increases breast cancer risk in female rodent offspring." *Breast Canc Res Treat* 1997. Nov; 46(2–3):199–214.

41. Henson D, Block G, Levine M. "Ascorbic acid: biologic functions and relation to cancer." *J Nat Canc Inst* 1991; 83(8):547–50.

42. *National Cancer Institute.* Vitamin C. http://cancer-net.nci.nih.gov/clinpdq/therapy/Vitamin_C.html.

43. Luo S, Sourla A, Labrie C et al. "Combined effects of dehydroepiandrosterone and EM-800 on bone mass, serum lipids, and the development of dimethylbenz(A) anthracene-induced mammary carcinoma in the rat." *Endocr* 1997; 138:4435–44.

44. Katiyar S, Mukhtar H. "Tea antioxidants in cancer chemoprevention." *J Cell Biochem Suppl* 1997; 27:59–67.

45. Nagata C, Kabuto M, Shimizu H. "Association of coffee, green tea, and caffeine intakes with serum concentrations of estradiol and sex hormone-binding globulin in premenopausal Japanese women." *Nutr Canc* 1998; 30(1):21–24.

46. *National Cancer Institute.* "Breast cancer prevention trial shows major benefit, some risk." http://207.121.187.155/NCI CANCER TRIALS/zones/PressInfo/1b.html, 1998.

47. Thune I et al. "Physical activity and the risk of breast cancer." *N Engl J Med* 1997; 336:1269.

48. Rennie J, Rusting R. "Making headway against cancer." *Scien Am* 1996 Sept:59.

49. Cramer D, Harlow B, Titus-Ernstoff L et al. "Over-the-counter analgesics and risk of ovarian cancer." *Lancet* 1998; 351(9096):104–7.

Chapter Four: Cervical Dysplasia

1. American Cancer Society. "Cancer facts and figures." Atlanta: American Cancer Society, 1995; 6.

2. Holly E. "Cervical intraepithelial neoplasia, cervical cancer, and HPV." *Ann Rev Pub Health* 1996; 17:69.

3. Syrjanen K. "Spontaneous evolution of intraepithelial lesions according to the grade and type of the implicated human papillomavirus (HPV)." *Eur J Obstet Gyn Reprod Biol* 1996; 65:45.

4. Herrero R, Potischman N, Brinton L et al. "A case-control study of nutrient status and invasive cervical cancer." *Am J Epid* 1991; 134(11):1335–46.

5. Slattery M, Abbott T, Overall J Jr. et al. "Dietary vitamins A, C, and E and selenium as risk factors for cervical cancer." *Epid* 1990; 1:8–15.

6. Basu J, Palan P, Vermund S et al. "Plasma ascorbic acid and beta-carotene levels in women evaluated for HPV infection, smoking, and cervix dysplasia." *Canc Detect Prev* 1991; 15:165–70.

7. Brock K, Berry G et al. "Nutrients in diet and plasma and risk of in situ cervical cancer." *J Natl Canc Inst* 1988; 80(8):580–85.

8. Schneider A, Shah K. "The role of vitamins in the etiology of cervical neoplasia: an epidemiological review." *Arch Gynecol Obstet* 1989; 246:1–13.

9. Guo W, Hsing A et al. "Correlation of cervical cancer mortality with reproductive and dietary factors, and serum markers in China." *Intl J Epid* 1994; 23(6): 1127–31.

10. Ziegler R, Brinton L, Hamman R et al. "Diet and the risk of invasive cervical cancer among white women in the United States." *Am J Epid* 1990; 132(3):32–45.

11. Palan P, Mikhail M, Basu J, Romeny S. "Beta-carotene levels in exfoliated cervicovaginal epithelial cells in cervical intraepithelial neoplasia and cervical cancer." *Am J Obstet Gynecol* 1992. Dec; 167(6):1899–1903.

12. Van Enwik J, Davis F, Bowen P. "Dietary and serum carotenoids and cervical intraepithelial neoplasia." *Int J Canc* 1991; 48:34–38.

13. Palan P, Romney S, Mikhail M, Basu J. "Decreased plasma beta-carotene levels in women with uterine cervical dysplasias and cancer." *J Nat Canc Inst* 1988; 80(6):454–55.

14. Hudson T. "Consecutive case study research of carcinoma in situ of cervix employing local escharotic treatment combined with nutritional therapy." *J Nat Med* 1991; 2:6–10, 19.

15. Hudson T. "Escharotic treatment for cervical dysplasia and carcinoma in situ." *J Nat Med* 1993; 4(1):23.

16. Wylie-Rosett J, Seymour L, Romney N et al. "Influence of vitamin A on cervical dysplasia and carcinoma in situ." *Nutr and Canc* 1984; 6(1):49–57.

17. Meyskens F, Surwit E et al. "Enhancement of regression of cervical intraepithelial neoplasia II (moderate dysplasia) with topically applied all-trans-retinoic acid: a randomized trial." *J Natl Canc Inst* 1994; 86(7):539–43.

18. Graham W, Surwite E, Weiner S, Meyskens F. "Phase II trial of beta-all-trans-retinoic acid for cervical intraepithelial neoplasia delivered via a collagen sponge and cervical cap." *West J Med* 1986; 145: 192–95.

19. Wassertheil-Smoller S, Romney S, Wylie-Rosett J et al. "Dietary vitamin C and uterine cervical dysplasia." *Am J Epid* 1981; 114(5):714–24.

20. Romney S, Duttagupta C, Basu J et al. "Plasma vitamin C and uterine cervical dysplasia." *Am J Obstet Gynecol* 1985. April 1; 151(7):976–80.

21. Butterworth C, Hatch K, Gore H et al. "Improvement in cervical dysplasia associated with folic acid therapy in users of oral contraceptives." *Am J Clin Nutr* 1982; 35:73–82.

22. Whitehead N, Reyner F, Lindenbaum J. "Megaloblastic changes in the cervical epithelium: association with oral contraceptive therapy and reversal with folic acid." *JAMA* 1973; 226:1421–24.

23. Streiff R. "Folate deficiency and oral contraceptives." *JAMA* 1970; 214:105–8.

24. Lyon J, Gardner J, West D et al. "Smoking and carcinoma in situ of the uterine cervix." *Am J Pub Health* 1983; 73:558–62.

25. Basu J et al. "Smoking and the antioxidant ascorbic acid: plasma, leukocyte, and cervicovaginal cell concentrations in normal healthy women." *Am J Obstet Gynecol* 1990. Dec; 163(6Pt1):1948–52.

26. Vessey M, Villard-Mackintosh L, McPherson K et al. "Mortality among oral contraceptive users: 20-year follow up of women in a chort study." *Br Med J* 1989; 299:1487.

27. Parazzini F, La Vecchia C, Negri E et al. "Oral contraceptive use and invasive cervical cancer." *Int J Epid* 1990; 19(2): 259.

28. Brinton L. "Oral contraceptives and cervical neoplasia." *Contr* 1991; 43:581.

29. Kjaer S, Engholm G, Dahl C et al. "Case-control study of risk factors for cervical squamous-cell neoplasia in Denmark. III. Role of oral contraceptive use." *Canc Causes Cont* 1993; 4(6):513.

30. Coker A, McCann M, Hulka B et al. "Oral contraceptive use and cervical intraepithelial neoplasia." *J Clin Epid* 1992; 45(10)1111.

31. Schiffman M, Bauer H, Hooever R et al. "Epidemiologic evidence showing that human papillomavirus infection causes most cervical intraepithelial neoplasia." *J Natl Canc Inst* 1993; 85:958.

32. Ursin G, Peters R, Henderson B et al. "Oral contraceptive use and adenocarcinoma of the cervix." *Lancet* 1994; 344:1390.

33. Goodkin K, Antoni M, Blaney P. "Stress and hopelessness in the promotion of cervical intraepithelial neoplasia to invasive squamous cell carcinoma of the cervix." *J Psychosom Res* 1986; 30:67–76.

34. Antoni M, Goodkin K, Helder L. "Psychosocial stressors, coping, and cervical neoplasia in 3 samples studies from 1981–1990." In *12th Annual Scientific Sessions of the Society of Behavioral Medicine*. Rockville, Md.: Society of Behavioral Medicine, 1991:128.

35. Paavonen J et al. "Cervical neoplasia and other STD-related genital and anal neoplasias." In Holmes K et al, eds. *Sexually Transmitted Diseases*, 2d ed. New York: McGraw-Hill, 1990:561.

Chapter Five: Contraception

1. Lader L. *The Margaret Sanger Story and the Fight for Birth Control*. 1st ed. Garden City, N.Y.: Country Life Press, 1955.

2. Brown S, Eisenberg L, eds. "The Best Intentions; Unintended Pregnancy and the Well-Being of Children and Families." Committee on Unintended Pregnancy; Division of Health Promotion and Disease Prevention. Institute of Medicine. Washington, D.C.: National Academy Press, 1995.

3. Sperhoff L, Glass R, Kase N. *Clinical Gynecologic Endocrinology and Infertility*. 5th ed. Baltimore: Williams and Wilkins, 1994.

4. Hatcher R et al. *Contraceptive Technology*. 16th ed. New York: Irvinton Publishers, Inc. Contraceptive Technology Communications, Inc., 1994.

5. Collaborative Group on Hormonal Factors in Breast Cancer. "Breast cancer and hormonal contraceptives: collaborative reanalysis of individual data on 53,297 women with breast cancer and 100,239 women without breast cancer from 54 epidemiologic studies." *Lancet* 1996; 347:1713H.

6. Speroff L, Carolyn L, Westhoff C. "Breast disease and hormonal contraception: resolution of a lasting controversy." *Dialog in Contracep* 1997; 5(3): 1–4.

7. Shojania A, Hornady G. "The effect of oral contraceptives on folate metabolism." *Am J Obstet Gynecol* 1971; 111(6):782–91.

8. Webb J. "Nutritional effects of oral contraceptive use: a review." *J Reprod Med* 1980 Oct; 25(4):150–56.

9. Morre K, ed. "Public Health Policy Implications of Abortion." A Government Relations Handbook for Health Professionals. Washington, D.C.: *ACOG*, 1990.

Chapter Six: Endometriosis

1. Mishell D, Stenchever M et al. *Comprehensive Gynecology*. St. Louis, Mo.: Mosby; 1997.

2. Koninckx P, Ide P, Vandenbroucke W, Brosens I. "New aspects of the pathophysiology of endometriosis and associated infertility." *J Repro Med* 1980; (6): 257–60.

3. Simpson J, Elias S, Malinak L, Buttram V. "Heritable aspects of endometriosis." *Am J Obstet Gynecol* 1980. June; 137:327–31.

4. Cramer D, Wilson E et al. "The relation of endometriosis to menstrual characteristics, smoking, and exercise." *JAMA* April; 255(14):1904–8.

5. Woodworth S, Singh M et al. "A prospective study on the association between red hair color and endometriosis in infertile patients." *Fertil Steril* 1995 Sept; 64(3):651–2.

6. D'Hooghe T, Bambra C et al. "The prevalence of spontaneous endometriosis in the baboon (Papio anubis, Papio cynocephalus) increases with the duration of captivity." *Acta Obstet Gynecol Scand* 1996. Feb; 75(2):98–101.

7. Harrop-Griffiths J, Katon W et al. "The association between chronic pelvic pain, psychiatric diagnoses, and childhood sexual abuse." *Obstet Gynecol* 1988 Apr; 71:589–94.

8. Koninckx P, Oosterlynck D et al. "Deeply infiltrating endometriosis is a disease whereas mild endometriosis could be considered a non-disease." *Ann NY Acad Sci* 1994. Sept; 333–41.

9. Lanzone A, Marana R. "Serum CA-125 levels in the diagnosis and management of endometriosis." *J Repro Med* 1991. Aug; 36:603–7.

10. Gould S, Shannon J, Cunha G. "Nuclear estrogen binding sites in human endometriosis." *Fertil Steril* 1983:520–24.

11. Sampson J. "Peritoneal endometriosis due to the menstrual dissemination of endometrial tissue into

the peritoneal cavity." *Am J Obstet Gynecol* 1927. Oct; 14:422–69.

12. Dmowski W, Steele R et al. "Deficient cellular immunity in endometriosis." *Am J Obstet Gynecol* 1981. Oct; 141: 377–83.

13. Noble L, Simpson E et al. "Aromatase expression in endometriosis." *J Clin Endo Metab* 1996; 81:174–79.

14. Dmowski W, Steele R et al. "Deficient cellular immunity in endometriosis." *Am J Obstet Gynecol* 1981. Oct; 141: 377–83.

15. Peterson N, Hasselbring B. "Endometriosis reconsidered." *Med Self Care* 1987. May–June; 52–55.

16. Rier S, Martin D et al. "Immunoresponsiveness in endometriosis: implications of estrogenic toxicants." *Envir Health Perspect* 1995; 103(Suppl 7):151–56.

17. Koninckx P, Meuleman C et al. "Suggestive evidence that pelvic endometriosis is a progressive disease, whereas deeply infiltrating endometriosis is associated with pelvic pain." *Fertil Steril* 1991. April; 55(4): 759–65.

18. Koninckx P, Martin D. "Treatment of deeply infiltrating endometriosis." *Curr Opin Obstet & Gynec* 1994. June; 6(3):231–41.

19. D'Hooghe T, Bambra C et al. "The effects of immunosuppression on development and progression of endometriosis in baboons (Papio anubis)." *Fertil Steril* 1995. Jul; 64(1):172–78.

20. Nomiyama M, Hachisuga T et al. "Local immune response in infertile patients with minimal endometriosis." *Gynecol and Obstet Invest* 1997; 44:32–37.

21. Halme J, Becker S. "Increased activation of pelvic macrophages in infertile women with mild endometriosis." *Am J Obstet Gynecol* 1983. Feb; 145:333–37.

22. Muscato J, Haney A et al. "Sperm phagocytosis by human peritoneal macrophages: a possible cause of infertility in endometriosis." *Am J Obstet Gynecol* 1982; 144:503–10.

23. Wilson T, Hertzog P et al. "Decreased natural killer cell activity in endometriosis patients: relationship to disease pathogenesis." *Fertil Steril* 1994. Nov; 62(5): 1086–8.

24. Oosterlynick D, Meuleman C et al. "Immunosuppressive activity of peritoneal fluid in women with endometriosis." *Obstet Gynecol* 1993. Aug; 82(2):206–11.

25. Garzetti G, Ciavattini A et al. "Natural killer cell activity in endometriosis: correlation between serum estradiol levels and cytotoxicity." *Obstet Gynecol* 1993. May; 81(5): 665–68.

26. Gleicher, N, El-Roeiy A et al. "Is endometriosis an autoimmune disease?" *Obstet Gynecol* 1987. July:70:115–22.

27. Gleicher N, Pratt D. "Abnormal (auto)immunity and endometriosis." *Int J Gynecol Obstet* 1993; 40(Suppl): S21–27.

28. Mathur S, Peress M et al. "Autoimmunity to endometrium and ovary in endometriosis." *Clin Exp Immunol* 1982; 50:259–66.

29. Galle P. "Clinical presentation and diagnosis of endometriosis." *Obstet Gynecol Clin North Am* 1989. Mar; 16(1):29–42.

30. Baron J. "Beneficial effects of nicotine and cigarette smoking: the real, the possible and the spurious." *Br Med Bull* 1996. Jan; 52(1):58–73.

31. McCann S, Freudenheim J et al. "Endometriosis and body fat distribution." *Obstet Gynecol* 1993. Oct; 82:545–49.

32. Malinak R. ACOG Technical Bulletin. *Endomet* 1993. Sept:1–6.

33. Holloway M. "An epidemic ignored." *Scient Amer* 1994. Apr:24–26.

34. Rier S, Martin D et al. "Immunoresponsiveness in endometriosis: implications of estrogenic toxicants." *Envir Health Perspect* 1995; 103(Suppl 7):151–56.

35. Mayani A, Barel S et al. "Dioxin concentrations in women with endometriosis." *Human Reprod* 1997. Feb; 12(2):373–75.

36. Davis D, Bradlow H. "Can environmental estrogen cause breast cancer?" *Scient Amer* 1995 Oct:166–72.

37. Pauci A, Braunwald E et al. *Harrison's Principles of Internal Medicine.* New York: McGraw-Hill; 1998.

38. Hill M, Goddard P et al. "Gut bacteria and etiology of cancer of the breast." *Lancet* 1971. Aug; 472–73.

39. Portz D, Elkins T. "Oxygen free radicals and pelvic adhesion formation: I. blocking oxygen free radical toxicity to prevent adhesion formation in an endometriosis model." *Int J Fertil* 1991; 36(1):39–42.

40. Goldin B, Adlercreutz H et al. "Effect of diet on excretion of estrogens in pre- and postmenopausal women." *Canc Res* 1981. Sept; 41:3771–73.

41. Murray M, Pizzorno J. "Digestion and elimination." *Encyclopedia of Natural Medicine.* California: Prima Publishing; 1998.

42. Kappas A, Anderson K et al. "Nutrition-endocrine interactions: Induction of reciprocal changes in the delta-5alpha-reduction of testosterone and the cytochrome P-450-dependent oxidation of estradiol by dietary macronutrients in man." *Proc Natl Acad Sci* 1983. Dec; 80:7646–49.

43. Michnovicz J, Bradlow H. "Altered estrogen metabolism and excretion in humans following consumption of indol-3-carbinol." *Nutr & Cancer* 1991; 16:59–66.

44. Leibovitz B, Mueller J. "Bioflavonoids and polyphenols: medical applications." *Ins for the Study of Opt Nutr* 1993; 2(1):17–35.

45. Leung A. *Encyclopedia of Common Natural Ingredients Used in Food, Drugs and Cosmetics.* New York: Wiley & Sons, 1980:17.

46. Yudkin J, Elisa O. "Dietary sucrose and oestradiol concentration in young men." *Ann Nutr Metab* 1988; 32:53–55.

47. Grodstein F, Goldman M. "Relation of female infertility to consumption of caffeinated beverages." *Am J Epid* 1993; 137:1353–60.

48. Tremblay L. "Reproductive Toxins Conference—Pollution Prevention Network." *Endomet Assoc Newsletter* 1996; 17(5–6):13–15.

49. Anderson R. "The immunostimulatory, anti-inflammatory and anti-allergic properties of ascorbate." *Adv Nut Res* 1984; 6:19–45.

50. Leibovitz B, Siegel B. "Ascorbic acid and the immune response." *Adv Exp Med Biol* 1981; 135:1–25.

51. Alexander M et al. "Oral beta-carotene can increase the number of okT4 cells in human blood." *Immunol Lett* 1985; 9:221–24.

52. Gerster H. "Anticarcinogenic effect of common carotenoids." *Internat J Vit Nutr Res* 1993; 63:93–121.

53. Ongsakul M et al. "Impaired blood clearance of bacteria and phagocytic activity in vitamin A deficient rats." *Proc Soc Exp Biol Med* 1985; 178(2):204–8.

54. Watson R. "Effect of ß-carotene on lymphycyte subpopulations in elderly humans; evidence for a dose-response relationship." *Am J Clin Nutr* 1991; 53:90–94.

55. London R, Sundaram G et al. "Endocrine parameters and alpha-tocopherol therapy of patients with mammary dysplasia." *Canc Res* 1981 Sept; 41:3811–13.

56. Butler E, McKnight E. "Vitamin E in the treatment of primary dysmenorrhea." *Lancet* 1955; 1:844–47.

57. Moncada S et al. "Leucocytes and tissue injury; the use of eicosapentaenoic acid in the control of white cell activation." *Wien Klin Wochenschr* 1986; 98(4):104–6.

58. Biskind M, Biskind G. "Effect of vitamin B complex deficiency on inactivation of estrone in the liver." *Endocr* 1942; 31:109–14.

59. Kiremidjian-Schumacher, Stotsky G. "Selenium and immune responses." *Environ Res* 1987; 42:277–303.

60. Spallholtz et al. "Immune response of mice fed diets supplemented with selenium." *Proc Soc Exper Biology & Med* 143:685–869.

61. Murray M, Pizzorno J. "Immune Support." *Encyclopedia of Natural Medicine*. Calif.: Prima Publishing, 1998.

62. Decapite L. "Histology, anatomy and antibiotic properties of vitex agnus castus." *Ann Fac Agr Univ Studi Perugi* 1967; 22:109–26.

63. Baba K, Abe S et al. "Antitumor activity of hot water extract of dandelion, Taraxacum officinale—correlation between antitumor activity and timing of administration." *Yakugaku Zasshi* 1981. June; 101(6):538–643.

64. Chevallier A. "Leonurus cardiaca." *Encyclopedia of Medicinal Plants*. New York: Dorling Kindersley Limited, 1996.

65. Tamaya T, Motoyama T et al. "Steroid receptor levels and histology of endometriosis and adenomyosis." *Fertil Steril* 1979; 31:396–400.

66. El-Roeiy A, Dmowski W et al. "Danazol but not gonadotropin-releasing hormone agonists suppresses autoantibodies in endometriosis." *Fertil Steril* 1987; 70:115–19.

67. Malinak R. "Endometriosis. *ACOG Tech Bull* 1993; 184:1–5.

68. Kettel L, Murphy A et al. "Treatment of endometriosis with the antiprogesterone mifepristone (RU486)." *Fertil Steril* 1996. Jan; 65(1):23–28.

69. Fedele L, Bianchi S et al. "The recurrence of endometriosis." *Ann NY Acad Sci* 1994. Sept:358–63.

70. Redwine D. "Conservative laparoscopic excision of endometriosis by sharp dissection: life table analysis of reoperation and persistent or recurrent disease." *Fertil Steril* 1991; 56:628–34.

71. Lu P, Ory S. "Endometriosis: current management." *Mayo Clin Proc* 1995. May; 70:453–63.

Chapter Seven: Fibrocystic Breasts

1. Love S et al. "Fibrocystic 'disease' of the breast: a non-disease." *N Engl J Med* 1982; 307:1010.

2. Page D, Dupont W. "Indicators of increased breast cancer risk in humans." *J Cell Biochem Suppl* 1992; 16G:175.

3. Devitt J et al. "Risk of breast cancer in women with breast cysts." *Can Med Assoc J* 1992; 147:45.

4. Sterns E. "The natural history of macroscopic cysts in the breast." *Surg Gyn Obstet* 1992; 174:36.

5. Hentes D. "Does diet influence human fecal microflora composition?" *Nutr Rev* 1980; 38:329–36.

6. Minton J, Foeking M, Webster D, Matthews R. "Caffeine, cyclic nucleotides, and breast disease." *Surg* 1979; 86:105.

7. Ernster V, Mason L, Goodson W et al. "Effects of caffeine-free diet on benign breast disease: a randomized trial." *Surg* 1982; 912:263–67.

8. Lubin F et al. "A case-control study of caffeine and methylxanthine in benign breast disease." *JAMA* 1985; 253(16):2388–92.

9. Shawer C, Brinton L, Hoover R. "Methylxanthine and benign breast disease." *Am J Epid* 1986; 124(4):603–11.

10. Marshall J, Graham S, Swanson M. "Caffeine consumption and benign breast disease: a case-control comparison." *Amer J Pub Health* 1982; 72(6):610–12.

11. La Vecchia C et al. "Benign breast disease and consumption of beverages containing methylxanthines." *JNCI* 1985; 74(5):995–1000.

12. Boyle C et al. "Caffeine consumption and fibrocystic breast disease: a case-control epidemiologic study." *JNCI* 1984; 72(5):1015–19.

13. Boyd N, McGuire V, Shannon P et al. "Effect of a low-fat high-carbohydrate diet on symptoms of cyclical mastopathy." *Lancet* 1988. July 16; 2(8603):128–32.

14. Rose D et al. "Effect of a low-fat diet on hormone levels in women with cystic breast disease. I. Serum steroids and gonadotropins." *J JCK* 1987; 78(4):623–26.

15. Abrams A. "Use of vitamin E in chronic cystic mastitis." *N Engl J Med* 1965; 272:1080.

16. Solomon D, Strummer D, Nair P. "Relationship between vitamin E and urinary excretion of ketosteroid fractions in cystic mastitis." *Ann NY Acad Sci* 1972; 203:103.

17. London R et al. "Clinical response and urinary excretion of 11-desoxy-17 ketosteroids and pregnanediol following alpha-tocopherol therapy." *Breast* 1978; 4:19.

18. London R et al. "Mammary dysplasia: Endocrine parameters and tocopherol therapy." *Nutr Res* 1982; 7:243.

19. Meyer E et al. "Vitamin E and benign breast disease." *Surg* 1990; 107(5):549–51.

20. London R et al. "The effect of vitamin E on mammary dysplasia: A double-blind study." *Obstet Gynecol* 1985; 65(1):104–6.

21. London R et al. "Endocrine parameters and alpha-tocopherol therapy of patients with mammary dysplasia." *Canc Res* 1981; 41:3811–13.

22. Pye J et al. "Clinical experience of drug treatment for mastalgia." *Lancet* 1985; 2:373–77.

23. Pashby N et al. "A clinical trial of evening primrose oil in mastalgia." *Br J Surg* 1981; 68:801–24.

24. Band P et al. "Treatment of benign breast disease with vitamin A." *Prev Med* 1984; 13:549.

25. Estes N. "Mastodynia due to fibrocystic disease of the breast controlled with thyroid hormone." *Amer J Surg* 1981; 142:102.

26. Eskin B, Bartushka D, Dunn M et al. "Mammary gland dysplasia in iodine deficiency." *JAMA* 1967; 200:691–95.

27. Ghent W et al. "Iodine replacement in fibrocystic disease of the breast." *Can J Surg* 1993. Oct; 35(5):453–60.

28. Lee, J. *What Your Doctor May Not Tell You about Menopause.* New York: Warner Books, 1996.

29. Fisher B et al. "Breast cancer prevention trial shows major benefit, some risk." Press release, *Nat Canc Inst Canc Trials,* 4/1998.

Chapter Eight: Genital Herpes

1. Guyatt G, Feeny D, Patrick D. "Measuring health-related quality of life." *Ann Int Med* 1993; 118: 622–29.

2. Wild D, Patrick D, Johnson E, Berzon R, Wald A. "Measuring health-related quality of life in persons with genital herpes." *Qual Life Res* 1995; 4:532–39.

3. Griffith R, DeLong D, Nelson J. "Relation of arginine-lysine antagonism to herpes simplex growth in tissue culture." *Chemo* 1981; 27:209–13.

4. Griffith R et al. "Success of L-lysine therapy in frequently recurrent herpes simplex infection." *Derma* 1987; 175:183–90.

5. McCune M, Perry H, Muller S, O'Fallan M. "Treatment of recurrent herpes simplex infections with L-lysine monohydrochloride." *Cutis* 1984; 34:366–73.

6. Terezhalmy G, Bottomley W, Pelleu G. "The use of water-soluble bioflavonoid-ascorbic acid complex in the treatment of recurrent herpes labialis." *Oral Surg* 1978; 45(1):56–62.

7. Starasoler S, Haber G. "Use of vitamin E oil in primary herpes gingivostomatitis in an adult." *NYS Dent J* 1978; 11:384–85.

8. Fitzherbert J. "Genital herpes and zinc." *Med J Austr.* 1979; 1:399.

9. Wolbling R, Leonhardt K. "Local therapy of herpes simplex with dried extract from Melissa officinalis." *Phytomed* 1994; 1:25–31.

10. Muldner V, Zoller M. "Antidepressive wirkung eines auf den wirkstoffkomplex hypericin standardisierten hypericum-extrakes." *Arzneim Forsch* 1984; 34:918.

11. Beutner K. "Valacivlovir; a review of its antiviral activity, pharmacokinetic properties, and clinical efficacy." *Antiviral Res* 1995; 28:281–90.

12. Beauchamp L, Krenitsky T. "Acyclovir prodrugs: the road to valaciclovir." *Drugs Future* 1993; 18:619–28.

Chapter Nine: Heart Disease

1. U.S. Dept Health and Human Services, National Center for Health Statistics. "U.S. mortality data tapes, 1968 to 1983." Washington, D.C.: U.S. Dept. of Health and Human Serv, 1984.

2. Wenger N, Speroff L, Packard B. "Cardiovascular health and disease in women." *N Engl J Med* 1993; 329:247.

3. Havlik R, Feinleib M, eds. "Proceedings of the conference on decline in coronary heart disease mortality." NIH publication no. 79-1610. Bethesda, Md.: Nat Inst of Health, 1979.

4. Matthews K, Meilahn E, Kuller L et al. "Menopause and risk factors for coronary heart disease." *N Engl J Med* 1989; 321:641.

5. Rich-Edwards J, Manson J, Hennekens C, Buring J. "The primary prevention of coronary heart disease in women." *N Engl J Med* 1995; 332:1758–65.

6. Manson J, Colditz G, Stampfer M et al. "A prospective study of obesity and risk of coronary heart disease in women." *N Engl J Med* 1990; 322:882–89.

7. Wilson P, Garrison R, Castelli W et al. "Prevalence of coronary heart disease in the Framingham offspring study: role of lipoprotein cholesterols." *Am J Cardiol* 1980; 46:649.

8. Wuerst J Jr., Dry T, Edwards J. "The degree of coronary atherosclerosis in bilaterally oophorectomized women." *Circ* 1953; 7:801.

9. Higgins M, Thom T. "Cardiovascular disease in women as a public health problem." In Wenger N, Speroff L, Packard B, eds. *Cardiovas Health and Dis in Women.* Greenwich, Ct.: Lelacq Communications, 1993.

10. Freeman R. "Hormones and heart disease." *Meno Mgmt* 1996; 5(2):10–15.

11. Grodstein F, Stampfer M. "The epidemiology of coronary heart disease and estrogen replacement in postmenopausal women." *Prog Cardiovasc Dis* 1995; 18:199.

12. Derby C, Hume A, McPhillips J et al. "Prior and current health characteristics of postmenopausal estrogen replacement therapy users compared to non-users." *Am J Obstet Gynecol* 1995; 173:544.

13. Speroff L et al. "Postmenopausal hormone therapy and the cardiovascular system." A Supplement to *Contemp Obstet Gynecol* 1997, June.

14. Hulley S, Grady D et al. "Randomized trial of estrogen plus progestin for secondary prevention of coronary heart disease in postmenopausal women." *JAMA* 1998; 280(7):605–13.

15. Sullivan J. "Estrogen therapy: mechanisms of cardioprotection." *Prog Cardiovasc Dis* 1996; 38:211.

16. Kannel W, Wilson P. "Risk factors that attenuate the female coronary disease advantage." *Arch Intern Med* 1995; 155:57–61.

17. Gordon T, Castelli W, Hjortland M et al. "High density lipoprotein as a protective factor against coronary heart disease: the Framingham Study." *Am J Med* 1977; 602:707–14.

18. Summary of the second report of the National Cholesterol Education Program (NCEP) Expert Panel on Detection, Evaluation, and Treatment of High Blood Cholesterol in Adults.

19. Love S. *Dr. Susan Love's Hormone Book.* New York: Random House, 1997.

20. Bass K, Newschaffer C, Klag M et al. "Plasma lipoprotein levels as predictors of cardiovascular death in women." *Arch Intern Med* 1993; 153:2209–16.

21. Manson J. "A prospective study of maturity-onset diabetes mellitus and risk of coronary heart disease and stroke in women." *Arch Intern Med* 1991; 151(6): 1141.

22. Barrett-Connor E, Bush T. "Estrogen and coronary heart disease in women." *JAMA* 1991; 265:1861.

23. Kemp H Jr., Elliott W, Gorlin R. "The anginal syndrome with normal coronary arteriography." *Trans Assoc Am Phys* 1967; 80:59.

24. Walton C, Goldsland I, Proudler A et al. "The effects of the menopause on insulin sensitivity, secretion, and elimination in non-obese, healthy women." *Eur J Clin Invest* 1993; 23:466.

25. Reaven G. "Pathophysiology of insulin resistance in human disease." *Physiol Rev* 1995; 75(3): 473–85.

26. Zavaroni I, Mazza E, Dall'aglio P et al. "Prevalence of hyperinsulinaemia in patients with high blood pressure." *J Int Med* 1992; 231:235–40.

27. Bogardu C, Lillioja S, et al. "Relationship between degree of obesity and in vivo insulin action in man." *Am J Phys* 1985; 248(S): E286–E91.

28. Ornish D, Brown S, Scherwitz L et al. "Lifestyle changes and heart disease." *Lancet* 1990; 336:129–33.

29. Kaplan N. "Non-drug treatment of hypertension." *Ann Int Med* 1985; 102:359–73.

30. Yehuda S, Carasso R. "Modulation of learning, pain thresholds, and thermoregulation in the rat by preparations of free purified alpha-linolenic and linoleic acids: determination of the optimal omega 3-to-omega 6 ratio." *Proc Natl Acad Sci* 1993 Nov 1; 90(21):10345–49.

31. Murray M, Beutler J. *Understanding Fats and Oils.* Encinitas, Calif.: Progressive Health Publishing, 1996.

32. Mata P et al. "Effect of dietary monounsaturated fatty acids on plasma lipoproteins and apolipoproteins in women." *Am J Clin Nutr* 1992; 56:77–83.

33. Linder M. *Nutritional Biochemistry and Metabolism with Clinical Applications.* 2d ed. Norwalk, Conn.: Appleton and Lange, 1991.

34. Adler A, Holub B. "Effect of garlic and fish-oil supplementation on serum lipid and lipoprotein concentrations in hypercholesterolemic men." *Am J Clin Nutr* 1997; 65:445–50.

35. Albert C et al. "Fish consumption and risk of sudden cardiac death." *JAMA* 1998; 279:23–38.

36. Vahouny G, Kritchevsky D. *Dietary Fiber in Health and Disease.* New York: Plenum Press, 1982.

37. Kris-Etherton P, Krummel D. "Role of nutrition in the prevention and treatment of coronary heart disease in women." *J Am Diet Assoc* 1993; 93:987–93.

38. Ripsin C, Keenan J, Jacobs D et al. "Oat products and lipid lowering: a meta-analysis." *JAMA* 1992; 267(24): 3317–25.

39. Resnicow K, Barone J, Engle A. "Diet and serum lipids in vegan vegetarians: a model for risk reduction." *J Am Diet Assoc* 1991; 91:447–53.

40. Robertson J, Brydon W, Tadesse K. "The effect of raw carrot on serum lipids and colon function." *Am J Clin Nutr* 1979; 32:1889–92.

41. Block G. "Fruit, vegetables, and cancer prevention: a review of the epidemiological evidence." *Nutr Cancer* 1992; 18:1–29.

42. Kohlmeier L, Hastings S. "Epidemiologic evidence of a role of carotenoids in cardiovascular disease prevention." *Am J Clin Nutr* 1995; 62(Suppl):1370S–76S.

43. Stringer M et al. "Lipid peroxides and atherosclerosis." *Br Med J* 1989; 298:281–84.

44. Anderson J, Johnstone B, Cook-Newell M. "Meta-analysis of the effects of soy protein intake on serum lipids." *N Engl J Med* 1995. Aug 3; 333(5):276–82.

45. Trowell H, Burkitt D, Heaton K. *Dietary Fibre, Fibre Depleted Foods and Disease.* New York: Academic Press, 1985.

46. Skrabal F, Aubock J, Hortnagl H. "Low sodium/high potassium diet for prevention of hypertension: probable mechanisms of action." *Lancet* 1981. Oct 24; 2(8252):895–900.

47. Langford H. "Dietary potassium and hypertension: epidemiological data." *Ann Int Med* 1990; 98:770–72.

48. Puccio E, McPhillips J, Barrett-Connor E, Ganiats T. "Clustering of atherogenic behaviors in coffee drinkers." *Am J Pub Health* 1990; 80(11):1310–13.

49. Werbach M. *Nutritional Influences on Illness,* 2 ed." Tarzana, Calif.: Third Line Press, 1996.

50. Kark J, Friedlander Y, Kaufmann N, Stein Y. "Coffee, tea and plasma cholesterol: the Jerusalem lipid research clinic prevalence study." *Br Med J* 1985; 291(6497): 699–704.

51. Williams P, Wood P, Vranizan K et al. "Coffee intake and elevated cholesterol and apolipoprotein B levels in men." *JAMA* 1985; 253(10):1407–11.

52. Forde O et al. "The Tromso heart study: coffee consumption and serum lipid concentrations in men with hypercholesterolaemia: a randomized intervention study." *Br Med J* 1985; 290:893–95.

53. Garland M, Barrett-Connor E, Wingard D. "Coffee, plasma cholesterol, and lipoproteins. A population study in an adult community." *Am J Epid* 1985; 121(6): 896–905.

54. Lindahl B et al. "Coffee drinking and blood cholesterol—effects of brewing method, food intake and lifestyle." *J Int Med* 1991; 230(4):299–305.

55. Klag M et al. "Coffee intake and coronary heart disease." *Am J Epid* 1994; 4:425–33.

56. Tverdal A et al. "Coffee consumption and death from coronary heart disease in middle aged Norwegian men and women." *Br Med J* 1990; 300:566–69.

57. Raloff J. "New heart risk from too much coffee?" *Science News* 1997. Jan 11; 151:22.

58. Ginsburg E et al. "Effects of alcohol ingestion on estrogens in postmenopausal women." *JAMA* 1996; 4(276):1747–51.

59. Longnecker M, Berlin J, Orza M, Chalmers T. "A meta-analysis of alcohol consumption in relation to risk of breast cancer." *JAMA* 1988; 260:652–56.

60. Willett W, Stampfer M, Colditz G et al. "Moderate alcohol consumption and the risk of breast cancer." *N Engl J Med* 1987; 316:1174–80.

61. Longnecker M, Newcomb P, Mittendorf R et al. "Risk of breast cancer in relation to lifetime alcohol consumption." *J Natl Canc Inst* 1995; 87:923–29.

62. Spencer H et al. "Alcohol—osteoporosis." *Am J Clin Nutr* 1985; 41:847.

63. Hyman S, Casseman N. "Alcoholism." In Rubenstein E, Federman D, eds. *Scientific American Textbook of Medicine.* New York: Scientific American Inc., 1997: 13(III):1–14.

64. Murphy G, Lawrence W, Lenhard R. *American Cancer Society Textbook of Clinical Oncology*, 2d ed. Atlanta: American Cancer Society, 1995.

65. Princen H, van Poppel G, Vogelezang C et al. "Supplementation with vitamin E but not beta-carotene in vivo protects low density lipoprotein from lipid peroxidation in vitro. Effect of cigarette smoking." *Arterioscler Thromb* 1992. May; 12(5):554–62.

66. Simons L, Von Konigsmark M, Balasubramaniam S. "What dose of vitamin E is required to reduce susceptibility of LDL to oxidation?" *Aust N Z J Med* 1996; 26(4): 496–503.

67. American Heart Association Scientific Session 1992, Nov. 17.

68. Stampfer M, Hennekins C, Manson J et al. "Vitamin E consumption and the risk of coronary disease in women." *N Engl J Med* 1993; 328:1444–49.

69. Stephens N, Parsons A, Schoefield P et al. "Randomised controlled trial of vitamin E in patients with coronary disease: Cambridge Heart Antioxidant Study (CHAOS)." *Lancet* 1996; 347:781–86.

70. Belizzi M et al. "Vitamin E and CHD: the European paradox." *Eur J Clin Nutr* 1994; 48:822–31.

71. Frei B. "Ascorbic acid protects lipids in human plasma and low-density lipoprotein against oxidative damage." *Am J Clin Nutr* 1991; 54:1113S–18S.

72. Hallfrisch J et al. "Ascorbic acid and plasma lipids." *Epid* 1994; 5:19–26.

73. Simon A. "Vitamin C and cardiovascular disease: a review." *J Am Coll Nutr* 1992; 11:107–25.

74. Brown W. "Niacin for lipid disorders." *Postgrad Med* 1995; 98:185–93.

75. Illingworth D et al. "Comparative effects of lovastatin and niacin in primary hypercholesterolemia." *Arch Intern Med* 1994; 154:1586–95.

76. Arsenio L, Bodria P, Magnati G et al. "Effectiveness of long-term treatment with pantethine in patients with dyslipidemias." *Clin Ther* 1986; 8:537–45.

77. Maggi G, Donati C, Criscuoli G. "Pantethine: a physiological lipomodulating agent, in the treatment of hyperlipidemias." *Curr Ther Res* 1982; 32:380–86.

78. Alleva R et al. "The roles of coenzyme Q10 and vitamin E on the peroxidation of human low density lipoprotein subfractions." *Proc Nat Acad Sci USA* 1995; 92: 9388–91.

79. Altura B. "New perspectives on the role of magnesium in the pathophysiology of the cardiovascular system." *Magn* 1985; 4:226–44.

80. Davis W, Leary W, Reyes A, Olhaberry J. "Monotherapy with magnesium increases abnormally low high density lipoprotein cholesterol: a clinical assay." *Curr Ther Res* 1984; 36:341–45.

81. Gawaz M. "Antithrombocytic effectiveness of magnesium." *Fortschr Med* 1996. Sept 20; 114(26):329–32.

82. Ravn H, Vissinger H, Kristensen S, Husted S. "Magnesium inhibits platelet activity—an in vitro study." *Thromb Haemost* 1996. July; 76(1):88–93.

83. Ravn H, Vissinger H, Kristensen S et al. "Magnesium inhibits platelet activity—an infusion study in healthy volunteers." *Thromb Haemost* 1996. June; 75(6):939–44.

84. Altura B, Altura B. "Magnesium in cardiovascular biology." *Scientific American, Science and Medicine* 1995. May/June:28–37.

85. Patki P et al. "Efficacy of potassium and magnesium in essential hypertension: a double-blind, placebo-controlled, crossover study." *Br J Med* 1990; 301:521–23.

86. Hopkins P, Wu L, Wu J et al. "Higher plasma homocysteine and increased susceptibility to adverse effects of low folate in early familial coronary artery disease." *Arterioscler Thromb Vasc Biol* 1995; 15:1314–20.

87. Boushey C, Beresford S, Omenn G, Motulsky A. "A quantitative assessment of plasma homocysteine as a risk factor for vascular disease. Probable benefits of increasing folic acid intakes." *JAMA* 1995; 274:1049–57.

88. Landgren F, Israelsson B, Lindgren A et al. "Plasma homocysteine in acute myocardial infarction: homocysteine-lowering effect of folic acid." *J Int Med* 1995; 237:381–88.

89. Selhub J, Jacques P, Bostom A et al. "Association between plasma homocysteine concentrations and extracranial carotid-artery stenosis." *N Engl J Med* 1995; 332:286–91.

90. Franken D, Boers G, Blom H et al. "Treatment of mild hyperhomocysteinaemia in vascular disease patients." *Arterioscler Thromb Vasc Biol* 1994; 14:465–70.

91. Silcken D, Dudman N, Tyrrell P. "Homocysteinuria due to cystathionine beta-synthase deficiency—the effects of betaine treatment in pyridoxine-responsive patients." *Metab* 1985; 12:1115–21.

92. Van den Berg M, Boers G, Franken D et al. "Hyperhomocysteinaemia and endothelial dysfunction in young patients with peripheral arterial occlusive disease." *Dur J Clin Invest* 1995; 25:176–81.

93. Franken D, Boers G, Blom H et al. "Treatment of mild hyperhomocysteinaemia in vascular disease patients." *Arterioscler Thromb Vasc Biol* 1994; 4:465–70.

94. Ubbink J, Vermaak W, van der Merwe et al. "Vitamin requirements for the treatment of hyperhomocysteinemia in humans." *J Nutr* 1994; 124:1927–33.

95. Rimm E et al. "Folate and vitamin B$_6$ from diet and supplements in relation to risk of coronary heart disease among women." *JAMA* 1998; 279(5):359–64.

96. Appel L et al. "Does supplementation of diet with 'fish oil' reduce blood pressure?" *Arch Int Med* 1993; 153:1429–38.

97. Nordoy A. "Is there a rational use for n-3 fatty acids (fish oils) in clinical medicine?" *Drugs* 1991; 42(3):331–42.

98. Allman M, Pena M, Pang. "Supplementation with flaxseed oil versus sunflowerseed oil in healthy young men consuming a low fat diet: effects on platelet composition and function." *Eur J Clin Nutr* 1995; 49: 169–78.

99. Toshitsugu I et al. "Effects of gammalinolenic acid on plasma lipoproteins and apolipoproteins." *Athero* 1989; 75:95–104.

100. Bordia A, Josh H, Sanadhya Y. "Effect of garlic oil on fibrinolytic activity in patient with CHD." *Athero,* 1977; 28: 155–59.

101. Lawson L. "Bioactive organosulfur compounds of garlic and garlic products." In Kinghorn A, Balandrin M, eds. *Human Medicinal Agents from Plants.* Washington, D.C.: American Chemical Society, 1993: 306–30.

102. Silagy C, Neil A. "Garlic as a lipid lowering agent, a meta-analysis." *J Roy Coll Phys London* 1994; 28:39–45.

103. Warshafsky S, Kramer R, Sivak S. "Effect of garlic on total serum cholesterol." *Ann Int Med* 1993; 119: 599–605.

104. Silagy C, Neil A. "A meta-analysis of the effect of garlic on blood pressure." *J Hyper* 1994; 12:463–68.

105. Norwell D, Tarr R. "Garlic, vampires, and CHD." *Osteopath Ann* 1984; 12:276–80.

106. Srivastava K. "Effects of aqueous extracts of onion, garlic and ginger on platelet aggregation and metabolism of arachidonic acid in the blood vascular system: in vitro study." *Prostagl Med* 1984; 13:227–35.

107. Gujaral S, Bhumra H, Swaroop M. "Effect of ginger oleoresin on serum and hepatic cholesterol levels in cholesterol fed rats." *Nutr Rep Int* 1978; 17:183–89.

108. Satyavati G. "Gugulipid: a promising hypolipidaemic agent from gum guggul (Commiphora wightii)." *Econ Med Plant Res* 1991; 5:47–82.

109. Nityanand S, Srivastava J, Asthana O. "Clinical trials with gugulipid, a new hypolipidaemic agent." *J Assoc Phys India* 1989; 37:321–28.

110. Petkov V. "Plants with hypotensive, antiatheromatous and coronary dilating action." *Am J Chin Med* 1979; 7:197–236.

111. Wegrowski J, Robert A, Moczar M. "The effect of procyanidolic oligomers on the composition of normal and hypercholesterolemic rabbit aortas." *Biochem Pharm* 1984; 33:3491–97.

112. Van Acker S, Berg D, Tromp M et al. "Structural aspects of antioxidant activity of flavonoids." *Free Rad Biol Med* 1996; 20:331–42.

113. Hertog M, Hollman P. "Potential health effects of the dietary flavonol quercetin." *Eur J Clin Nutr* 1996; 50:63–71.

114. Hertog M et al. "Dietary antioxidant flavonoids and risk of coronary heart disease. The Zutphen elderly study." *Lancet* 1993; 342:1007–11.

115. Hertog M, Kromhout D, Aravanis C et al. "Flavonoid intake and long-term risk of coronary heart disease and cancer in the Seven Countries Study." *Arch Intern Med* 1995; 155:381–86.

116. Facino R et al. "Free radicals scavenging action and anti-enzyme activities of procyanidines from Vitis vinifera: a mechanism for their capillary protective action." *Arzneim Forsch* 1994; 44:592–601.

117. Hertog M et al. "Dietary antioxidant flavonoids and risk of coronary heart disease. The Zutphen elderly study." *Lancet* 1993; 342:1007–11.

118. Sacco R et al. "Leisure-time physical activity and ischemic stroke risk: the Northern Manhattan Stroke Study." *Stroke* 1998; 29:380.

119. Jennings G. "Mechanisms for reduction of cardiovascular risk factors by regular exercise." *Clin Exper Pharma Physiol* 1995; 22:209.

120. Fraser G, Phillips R, Harris R. "Physical fitness and blood pressure in school children." *Circ* 1983; 67: 405.

121. Roman O et al. "Physical training program in arterial hypertension: a long-term prospective follow-up." *Cardiol* 1981; 67:230.

122. Fielding R. "The role of progressive resistance training and nutrition in the preservation of lean body mass in the elderly." *J Am Coll Nutr* 1995; 14:587.

123. Gordon J et al. "The Singapore youth coronary risk and physical activity study." *Med Sci Sports Exerc* 1998; 30:105.

124. Abe T et al. "Relationship between training frequency and subcutaneous and visceral fat in women." *Med Sci Sports Exerc* 1997; 29:1549.

125. Snyder K et al. "The effects of long-term, moderate intensity, intermittent exercise on aerobic capacity, body composition, blood lipids, insulin and glucose in overweight females." *Int J Obes Relat Metab Disord* 1997; 21:1180.

126. Ward D et al. "Physical activity and physical fitness in African-American girls with and without obesity." *Obes Res* 1997; 5:572.

127. Tanaka H, DeSouza C, Seals D. "Absence of age-related increase in central arterial stiffness in physically active women." *Arterioscler Thromb Vasc Biol* 1998; 18:127.

128. Williams P. "High-density lipoprotein cholesterol and other risk factors for coronary artery disease in female runners." *N Engl J Med* 1996; 334:1298.

129. Thune I, Njolstad I, Lochen M, Forde O. "Physical activity improves the metabolic risk profiles in men and women: the Tromso Study." *Arch Intern Med* 1998; 158:1633–40.

130. Niaura R et al. "Exercise, smoking cessation, and short-term changes in serum lipids in women: a preliminary investigation." *Med Sci Sports Exerc* 1998; 30: 1414–18.

131. Gibbons L, Mitchell T. "HDL cholesterol and exercise." *Your Patient and Fitness* 1995; 9:68e.

132. Shephard R. "What is the optimal type of physical activity to enhance health?" *Br J Sports Med* 1997; 31:277.

133. Ferrauti A, Weber K, Struder H. "Effects of tennis training on lipid metabolism in recreational players." *Br J Sports Med* 1997; 31:322.

134. Code R et al. "Effects of aerobic exercise training on patients with systemic arterial hypertension." *Am J Med* 1984; 77:785.

135. *UT Lifetime Health Letter,* April 1993.

136. Hagberg J et al. "Effect of weight training on blood pressure and hemodynamics in hypertensive adolescents." *J Pediatr* 1984; 104:147.

137. Leddy J et al. "Effect of a high or low fat diet on cardiovascular risk factors in male and female runners." *Med Sci Sports Exerc* 1997; 29:17.

138. Coats A et al. "Effects of physical training in chronic heart failure." *Lancet* 1990; 335:63.

139. Coats A. "Exercise rehabilitation in chronic heart failure." *J Am Coll Cardiol* 1993; 22:172A.

140. Madsen B et al. "Prognostic value of plasma catecholamines, plasma renin activity, and plasma atrial natriuretic peptide at rest and during exercise in congestive heart failure: comparison with clinical evaluation, ejection fraction, and exercise capacity." *J Card Fail* 1995; 1:207.

141. Nishiyama Y et al. "Oxidative stress is related to exercise intolerance in patients with heart failure." *Am Heart J* 1998; 135:115.

142. Blair S et al. "Physical fitness and all-cause mortality: a prospective study of healthy men and women." *JAMA* 1989; 262:2395.

143. Lavie C, Milani R. "Effects of cardiac rehabilitation and exercise training in obese patients with coronary artery disease." *Chest* 1996; 109:52.

144. Ades P et al. "Skeletal muscle and cardiovascular adaptations to exercise conditioning in older patients." *Circ* 1996; 94:323.

145. Thompson P. "The cardiovascular complications of vigorous physical activity." *Arch Int Med* 1996; 156:2297.

146. *Health and Nutrition Newsletter.* "Is exercise worth the risk of a heart attack?" Columbia University, School of Pub Health & Inst of Human Nutr, 1(1):2.

147. Cox, M. "Exercise for mild coronary artery disease." *Phys Sports Med* 1997; 25:35.

148. Arnold E. "The stress connection. Women and coronary artery disease." *Crit Care Nurs Clin North Amer* 1997; 9:565.

149. Blumenthal J et al. "Stress management and exercise training in cardiac patients with myocardial ischemia." *Arch Intern Med* 1997; 157:2213.

150. Kaplan N. "Non-drug treatment of hypertension." *Ann Int Med* 1985; 102:359–73.

151. The Writing Group for the PEPI Trial. "Effects of estrogen or estrogen/progestin regimens on heart disease risk factors in postmenopausal women." *JAMA* 1995; 273(3):199–208.

152. Shangold M, Tomai T, Cook J et al. "Factors associated with withdrawal bleeding after administration of oral micronized progesterone in women with secondary amenorrhea." *Fertil Steril* 1991; 56:1040–47.

153. Chen F, Lee N, Soong Y. "Changes in the lipoprotein profile in postmenopausal women receiving hormone replacement therapy." *J Reprod Med* 1998; 43:568–74.

154. Rylance P, Brincat M, Lafferty K et al. "Natural progesterone and antihypertensive action." *Br Med J* 1985; 290:13–14.

155. Miyagaw K, Rosch J, Stanczyk F, Hermsmeyer K. "Medroxyprogesterone interferes with ovarian steroid protection against coronary vasospasm." *Nat Med* 1997; 3:324–27.

156. Miyagaw K, Vidgoff J, Hermsmeyer K. "Ca release mechanism of primary drug-induced vasospasm." *Am J Physiol* 1997; 272:H2645–54.

157. Laux M, Conrad C. *Natural Woman, Natural Menopause.* New York: HarperCollins, 1997.

158. Hargrove J, Maxson W, Wentz A, Burnett L. "Menopausal hormone replacement therapy with continuous daily oral micronized estradiol and progesterone." *Ob/Gyn* 1989; 73(4):606–12.

159. Staland B. "Continuous treatment with natural oestrogens and progestogens. A method to avoid endometrial stimulation." *Maturitas* 1981; 3:145–56.

160. Nishibe A, Morimoto S, Hirota K et al. "Effect of estriol and bone mineral density of lumbar vertebrae in elderly and postmenopausal women." *Nippon Ronen Igakkai Zasshi* 1996; 33:353–59.

161. Walter E, Raz S, Raz R. "A controlled trial of intravaginal estriol in postmenopausal women with recurrent urinary tract infections." *N Engl J Med* 1993; 329(11): 753–56.

162. Luotola H. "Blood pressure and hemodynamics in postmenopausal women during estradiol 17-beta substitution." *Ann Clin Res* 1983; 15:9.

163. Colditz G. "Relationship between estrogen levels, use of hormone replacement therapy, and breast cancer." *J Nat Canc Inst* 1998; 90(11):814–23.

164. Walsh J, Grady D. "The treatment of hyperlipidemia in women." *JAMA* 1995; 274:1152–58.

165. Williams P. "High-density lipoprotein cholesterol and other risk factors for coronary heart disease in female runners." *N Engl J Med* 1996; 334:1298–1303.

166. Aspirin Myocardial Infarction Study Research Group. "A randomized controlled trial of aspirin in persons recovered from myocardial infarction." *JAMA* 1980; 243:661–69.

167. Loop F, Golding L, Macmillan J et al. "Coronary artery surgery in women compared with men: analyses of risks and long-term results." *J Am Coll Cardiol* 1983; 1:383–90.

168. Waters D, Higgins L, Gladstone P et al. "Effects of monotherapy with HMG-CoA reductase inhibitor on the progression of coronary atherosclerosis as assessed by serial arteriography: the Canadian Coronary Atherosclerosis Intervention Trial (CCAIT)." *Circ* 1994; 89:959–68.

169. Kane J, Malloy M, Ports T et al. "Regression at coronary atherosclerosis during treatment of familial hypercholesterolemia with combined drug regimens." *JAMA* 1990; 264:3007–12.

170. Kaplan N. *Clinical Hypertension,* 3d ed. Baltimore: Williams and Wilkins, 1982:3.

171. "HDFP Cooperative Group: five-year findings of the Hypertension Detection and Follow-up Program: II. Mortality by race, sex, and age." *JAMA* 1979; 242:2572–77.

172. MRC Working Party. "MRC trial of treatment of mild hypertension: principal results." *Br Med J* 1985; 29:97–104.

173. SHEP Cooperative Research Group. "Prevention of stroke by antihypertensive drug treatment in older persons with isolated systolic hypertension: final results of the Systolic Hypertension in the Elderly Program (SHEP)." *JAMA* 1991; 265:3255–64.

174. Dannenberg A, Drizd T, Horan M et al. "Progress in the battle against hypertension." Changes in blood pressure levels in the United States from 1960 to 1980." *Hyper* 1987; 10:226.

175. Black D. "Atorvastatin: a step ahead for HMG-CoA reductase inhibitors." *Athero* 1995; 1066:307–10.

176. Burt V et al. "Prevalence of hypertension in the U.S. adult population: results from the third National Health and Nutrition Examination Survey, 1988–1991." *Hyper* 1995; 25:305–13.

177. Smith S Jr et al. "Secondary prevention panel. Preventing heart attack and death in patients with coronary disease." *J Am Coll Cardiol* 1995; 26:292–94.

Chapter Ten: Menopause

1. McKinlay S, Bigano N, McKinlay J. "Smoking and age at menopause." *Ann Int Med* 1985; 103:350.

2. McKinlay S, McKinlay J. "The impact of menopause and social factors on health." In Hammond C, Haseltine F, Schiff I, eds. *Menopause: Evaluation, Treatment, and Health Concerns.* New York: Alan R Liss, 1989:137–61.

3. Coulam C, Adamson S, Annegers J. "Incidence of premature ovarian failure." *Obstet Gynecol* 1986; 67(4): 604–6.

4. Katz E, McClamrock H, Adashi E. "Ovarian failure including menopause, premature menopause, and resistant ovarian syndrome, and hormonal replacement." *Cur Opin Obstet Gynecol* 1990; 2(3):392–97.

5. Wilcox L, Koonin L, Pokras R et al. "Hysterectomy in the United States 1988–1990." *Obstet Gynecol* 1994; 83(4):549.

6. Williamson M. "Sexual adjustment after hysterectomy." *JOGNN* 1991; 21 (1):42.

7. Nathorst-Boos J, von Schoultz B. "Psychological reactions and sexual life after hysterectomy with and without oophorectomy." *Gynecol Obstet Invest* 1992; 34:97.

8. Cohen S, Hollingsworth A, Rubin M. "Another look at psychologic complications of hysterectomy." *IMAGE: J Nurs Schol* 1989; 21(1):51.

9. McKinlay S, Brambilla D, Posner J. "The normal menopause transition." *Maturitas* 1992; 14:103–15.

10. Kronenberg, F. "Hot flashes: epidemiology and physiology." *Ann NY Acad Sc* 1990; 592:52–86.

11. Lock M. "Ambiguities of aging: Japanese experience and perceptions of menopause." *Cult Med Psychiatry* 1986; 10:23–46.

12. Beyene Y. "Cultural significance and physiological manifestations of menopause: a biocultural analysis." *Cult Med Psychiatry* 1986; 10:47–71.

13. Kronenberg F, Downey J. "Thermoregulatory physiology of menopausal hot flashes: a review." *Canad J Physiol Pharmacol* 1987; 65:1312–24.

14. Chakravarti S, Collins W, Thom M, Studd J. "Relation between plasma hormone profiles, symptoms, and responses to oestrogen treatment in women approaching the menopause." *Br Med J* 1979; 1:983–85.

15. Shoupe D, Lobo R. "Endogenous opioids in the menopause." In Speroff L, Lobo R, eds. *Role of Opioid Peptides in Reproductive Endocrinology. Seminars in Reproductive Endocrinology.* New York: Thieme Medical Publishers, Inc., 1987:5(2):199–206.

16. McKinlay J, McKinlay S, Brambilla D. "The relative contributions of endocrine changes and social circumstances to depression in mid-aged women." *J Health Soc Behav* 1987; 28:345–63.

17. Avis N, Brambilla D, McKinlay S, Vass K. "A longitudinal analysis of the association between menopause and depression: results from the Massachusetts Women's Health Study." *Ann Epid* 1994; 4:214–20.

18. Cagnacci A, Volpe A et al. "Depression and anxiety in climacteric women: role of hormone replacement therapy." *J North Amer Meno Soc* 1997; 4(4):206–11.

19. Sherwin B. "The impact of different doses of estrogen and progestin on mood and sexual behavior in postmenopausal women." *J Clin Endocrinol Metab* 1991; 72: 336–43.

20. Henderson V, Watt L, Buckwalter J. "Cognitive skills associated with estrogen replacement in women with Alzheimer's disease." *Psychoneuroendocrin* 1996; 21(4): 421–30.

21. Jorm A, Korten A, Henderson A. "The prevalence of dementia: a quantitative integration of the literature." *Acta Psychiatr Scand* 1987; 76:465–79.

22. Henderson V, Buckwalter J. "Cognitive deficits of men and women with Alzheimer's disease." *Neur* 1994; 44: 90–96.

23. Samsioe G, Jansson I, Mellstrom D, Svanborg A. "The occurrence, nature and treatment of urinary incontinence in a 70-year-old population." *Maturitas* 1985; 7:335–42.

24. Vermeulen A. "The hormonal activity of the postmenopausal ovary." *J Clin Endocrin Metab* 1976; 42: 247–53.

25. Vermeulen A. "Sex hormone status of the postmenopausal woman." *Maturitas* 1980; 2:81–89.

26. Bachmann G, Leiblum S, Kemmann E et al. "Sexual expression and its determinants in the post-menopausal women." *Maturitas* 1984; 6:19–29.

27. Bancroft J. "Hormones and human sexual behavior." *J Sex Marital Ther* 1984; 10:3–21.

28. Sand R, Studd J. "Exogenous androgens in postmenopausal women." *Am J Med* 1995; 98(1A):76S–79S.

29. Hoberman J, Yesalis C. "The history of synthetic testosterone." *Sci Am* 1995. Feb:76–81.

30. Sherwin B, Gelfand M. "The role of androgen in the maintenance of sexual functioning in oophorectomised women." *Psychosom Med* 1987; 49:397–409.

31. Sherwin B, Gelfand M, Brender W. "Androgen enhances sexual motivation in females: a prospective crossover study of sex hormone administration in the surgical menopause." *Psychosom Med* 1985; 47:339–51.

32. Schreiner-Engel P, Schiavi R, Smith H, White D. "Sexual arousability and the menstrual cycle." *Psychosom Med* 1981; 43:199–214.

33. Davis S et al. "Testosterone enhances estradiol's effect on postmenopausal bone density and sexuality." *Maturitas* 1995; 21(3):227–36.

34. Gamble C. "Osteoporosis: making the diagnosis in patients at risk for fracture." *Geria* 1995; 50:24–33.

35. "Consensus Development Conference: prophylaxis and treatment of osteoporosis." *Osteo Int* 1991; 114–17.

36. National Osteoporosis Foundation. *The Older Person's Guide to Osteoporosis.* Washington, D.C.: National Osteoporosis Foundation; 1991.

37. Lloyd T et al. "Collegiate women athletes with irregular menses during adolescence have decreased bone density." *Obstet Gynecol* 1988; 72:639–42.

38. U.S. Dept Health and Human Services, National Center for Health Statistics. "U.S. mortality data tapes, 1968–1983." Washington, D.C.: U.S. Department of Health and Human Services, 1984.

39. Wenger N, Speroff L, Packard B. "Cardiovascular health and disease in women." *N Engl J Med* 1993; 329:247.

40. Matthews K, Meilahn E, Kuler L et al. "Menopause and risk factors for coronary heart disease." *N Engl J Med* 1989; 321:641.

41. Speroff L et al. "Postmenopausal hormone therapy and the cardiovascular system." *A Supplement to Contemporary Ob/Gyn,* June 1997.

42. Grodstein F, Stampfer M. "The epidemiology of coronary heart disease and estrogen replacement in postmenopausal women." *Prog Cardiovasc Dis* 1995; 18:199.

43. Anderson R, Wolf W. "Compositional changes in trypsin inhibitors, phytic acid, saponins and isoflavones related to soybean processing." *J Nutr* 1995; 125 (supp): 581S–88S.

44. Brzezinski A, Adlercretuz H et al. "Short-term effects of phytoestrogen-rich diet on postmenopausal women." *Menopause: J North Amer Meno Soc* 1997; 4(2):89–94.

45. Albertazzi P, Pansini F. "The effect of dietary soy supplementation on hot flashes." *Obstet Gynecol* 1998; 91(1):6–11.

46. Eden J, Knight D, Mackey R, House F. "Hormonal effects of isoflavones (abstr)." *See* Ref 51.

47. Woods M, Senie R, Kronenberg F. "Effect of a dietary soy bar on menopausal symptoms (abstr)." *J Nutr* 1995; 125(Suppl 3S):41.

48. Baird D, Umbach D, Lansdell L et al. "Dietary intervention study to assess estrogenicity of dietary soy among postmenopausal women." *J Clin Endocrin Metab* 1995. May; 80(5):1685–90.

49. Lock M. "Contested meanings of the menopause." *Lancet* 1991; 337:1270–72.

50. Adlercreutz H, Honjo H, Higashi A et al. "Urinary excretion of lignans and isoflavonoid phytoestrogens in Japanese men and women consuming traditional Japanese diet." *Am J Clin Nutr* 1991; 54:1093–1100.

51. "First International Symposium on the Role of Soy in Preventing and Treating Chronic Disease: Proceedings from a symposium held in Mesa, Arizona, on February 20–23, 1994." Published in *J Nutr* 125(Suppl 3S): 567S–909S, 1995.

52. "Second International Symposium on the Role of Soy in Preventing and Treating Chronic Disease, Brussels, Belgium September 15–18, 1996." Program and Abstract Book; proceedings published in *J Am Coll Nutr* 1996–1997.

53. Bahram H et al. "Dietary soybean protein prevents bone loss in an ovariectomized rat model of osteoporosis." *J Nutr* 1996; 126:161–67.

54. Blari H, Jordan S, Peterson T, Barnes S. "Variable effects of tyrosine kinase inhibitors on avian osteoclastic activity and reduction of bone loss in ovariectomized rats." *J Cell Biochem* 1996; 61:629–37.

55. Anderson J, Johnstone B, Cook-Nesell M. "Meta-analysis of the effects of soy protein intake on serum lipids." *N Engl J Med* 1995; 333(5):276–82.

56. Sherwin B. "Estrogenic effects on memory in women." *Ann NY Acad Sci* 1994; 743:213–31.

57. Sherwin B. "Hormones, mood, and cognitive functioning in postmenopausal women." *Obstet Gynecol* 1996; 87:20S–26S.

58. Messina M, Persky V, Setchell K, Barnes S. "Soy intake and cancer risk: a review of the in vitro and in vivo data." *Nutr Cancer* 1994; 21:113–31.

59. Adlercreutz H et al. "Dietary phytoestrogens and cancer: in vitro and in vivo studies." *J Steroid Biochem Molec Biol* 1992; 41(3–8):331–37.

60. Barnes S, Peterson G, Grubbs C, Setchell K. "Potential role of dietary isoflavones in the prevention of cancer." In Jacobs MM, ed. *Diet and Cancer: Markers, Prevention, and Treatment.* New York: Plenum Press, 1994:135–47.

61. Braden A, Hart N, Lamberton J. "The oestrogenic activity and metabolism of certain isoflavones in sheep." *Aust J of Agr Res* 1967; 18:335–48.

62. Cassidy A. "Physiological effects of phyto-oestrogens in relation to cancer and other human health risks." *Proc of the Nutr Soc* 1996; 55:399–417.

63. Nomura A, Henderson B, Lee J. "Breast cancer and diet among the Japanese in Hawaii." *Am J Clin Nutr* 1978; 31:2020–25.

64. Hirayama T. "A large-scale cohort study on cancer risks by diet—with special reference to the risk of reducing effects of green-yellow vegetable consumption." In Hayashi Y et al. *Diet, Nutrition and Cancer.* Tokyo: Japanese Scientific Society Press, 1986:41–53.

65. Lee H et al. "Dietary effects on breast cancer risk in Singapore." *Lancet* 1991; 337:1197–1200.

66. Parkin D et al. "Cancer Incidence in Five Continents." Lyon: International Agency for Research on Cancer Scientific Publications No. 120. 1992; 6:301–431, 486–509.

67. Foth D, Cline J. "Effects of mammalian and plant estrogens on mammary glands and uteri of macaques." *Am J Clin Nutr* Suppl. In press.

68. Goodman M et al. "Association of soy and fiber consumption with the risk of endometrial cancer." *Am J Epid* 1997; 146(4):294–306.

69. Thompson L, Robb P, Serraino M, Cheung F. "Mammalian lignan production from various foods." *Nutr and Canc* 1991; 16(1):43–52.

70. Adlercreutz H. "Does fiber-rich food containing animal lignan precursors protect against both colon and breast cancer? An extension of the fiber hypothesis." *Gastroent* 1984; 86:761–66.

71. Setchell K, Adlercreutz H. "Mammalian lignans and phytoestrogens: recent studies on their formation, metabolism and biological role in health and disease." In Rowland I, ed. *Role of the Gut Flora in Toxicity and Cancer.* London: Academic, 1988:315–45.

72. Rao C. *The Chemistry of Lignans.* Waltair, India: Andhra Univ. Press, 1978.

73. Hartwell J. "Types of anticancer agents isolated from plants." *Canc Treat Rep* 1976; 60:1031–67.

74. Macrae W, Towers G. "Biological activities of lignans." *Phytochem* 1984; 23:1207–20.

75. Adlercreutz H. "Lignans and phytoestrogens: possible preventive role in cancer." *Fron Gastrointest Res* 1988; 14:165–76.

76. Adlercreutz H et al. "Diet and urinary excretion of lignans in female subjects." *Med Biol* 1981; 59:259–61.

77. Adlercreutz H et al. "Determination of urinary lignan and phytoestrogen metabolite, potential antiestrogens and anticarcinogens in urine of women on various habitual diets." *J Steroid Biochem* 1986; 25:791–97.

78. Licata A, Bou E, Bartter F, Weset F. "Acute effects of dietary protein on calcium metabolism in patients with osteoporosis." *J Geron* 1981; 36:14–19.

79. Mazariegos-Ramos E et al. "Consumption of soft drinks with phosphoric acid as a risk factor for the development of hypocalcemia in children: a case-control study." *J Pediatr* 1995; 126:940–42.

80. Murray M, Beutler J. *Understanding Fats and Oils.* Encinitas, Calif.: Progressive Health Publishing, 1996.

81. Linder M. *Nutritional Biochemistry and Metabolism with Clinical Applications*, 2 ed. Norwalk, Conn.: Appleton and Lange, 1991.

82. Kris-Etherton P, Krummel D. "Role of nutrition in the prevention and treatment of coronary heart disease in women." *J Am Diet Assoc* 1993; 93:987–93.

83. Robertson J, Brydon W, Tadesse K. "The effect of raw carrot on serum lipids and colon function." *Am J Clin Nutr* 1979; 32:1889–92.

84. Block G. "Fruit, vegetables, and cancer prevention: a review of the epidemiological evidence." *Nutr Canc* 1992; 18:1–29.

85. Smith C. "Non-hormonal control of vaso-motor flushing in menopausal patients." *Chic Med* 1964; 67:193–95.

86. Russ C, Hendricks T et al. "Vitamin B$_6$ status of depressed and obsessive-compulsive patients." *Nutr Rep Intl* 1983; 27:867–73.

87. Wynn V et al. "Tryptophan, depression and steroidal contraception." *J Steroid Biochem* 1975; 6:965–70.

88. Nobbs B. "Pyridoxal phosphate status in clinical depression." *Lancet* 1974; I:405.

89. Chenoy R et al. "Effect of oral gamma linolenic acid from evening primrose oil on menopausal flushing." *Br Med J* 1994; 308:503–6.

90. Pye J et al. "Clinical experience of drug treatments for mastalgia." *Lancet* 1985; II:373–77.

91. Gately C et al. "Drug treatments for mastalgia: 17 years experience in the Cardiff mastalgia clinic." *J Roy Soc Med* 1992; 85:12–15.

92. Mansel et al. "Effects of essential fatty acids on cyclical mastalgia and noncyclical breast disorders." In Horrobin D, ed. *Omega-6 Essential Fatty Acids: Pathophysiology and Roles in Clinical Medicine.* New York: Wiley-Liss, 1990:557–66.

93. Murase Y, Iishima H. "Clinical studies of oral administration of gamma-oryzanol on climacteric complaints and its syndrome." *Obstet Gynecol Prac* 1963; 12:147–49.

94. Ishihara M. "Effect of gamma-oryzanol on serum lipid peroxide levels and climacteric disturbances." *Asia Oceania J Obstet Gynecol* 1984; 10:317.

95. Shute E. [Title not available.] *Can Med Assoc J* 1937; 37:350.

96. Christy C. "Vitamin E in menopause; preliminary report of experimental and clinical study." *Am J Obstet Gynec* 1945; 50:84–87.

97. Finkler R. "The effect of vitamin E in the menopause." *J Clin Endocrin Metab* 1949; 9:89–94.

98. McLaren H. "Vitamin E in the menopause." *Br Med J* 1949. Dec 17:1378–82.

99. Barton D et al. "Prospective evaluation of vitamin E therapy for hot flashes in breast cancer survivors." *J Clin Oncol* 1998; 16:495–500.

100. Katzenellenbogen B, Katzenellenbogen J, Mordecai D. "Zearalenones: characterization of the oestrogenic potencies and receptor interactions of a series of fungal B-resorcylic acid lactones." *Endocrinology* 1979; 105:33–40.

101. Kumagai S, Shimizu T. "Neonatal exposure to zearalenone causes persistent anovulatory estrus in the rat." *Arch Toxicol* 1982; 50:279–86.

102. Hagler W, Tyczkowska K, Hamilton P. "Simultaneous occurrence of deoxynivalenol, zearalenone, and aflatoxin in 1982 scabby wheat from the Midwestern United States." *Appl Environ Microbiol* 1984; 47:151–54.

103. Dean D, Exley D, Goodwin T. "Steroid oesterogens in plants: re-estimation of oestrone in pomegranate seeds." *Phytochem* 1971; 10:2215–16.

104. Verdeal R, Ryan D. "Naturally-occurring oestrogens in plant foodstuffs—a review." *J Food Protect* 1979; 42:577–83.

105. Kelly G, Nelson C, Waring M et al. "Metabolites of dietary (soya) isoflavones in human urine." *Clinica Chimica Acta* 1993; 223:9–22.

106. Kuhnau J. "The flavonoids, a class of semi-essential food components: their role in human nutrition." *World Rev Nutr Diet* 1976; 24:117–91.

107. Hertog M, Hollman P, Katan M, Kromhout D. "Intake of potentially anti-carinogenic flavonoids and their determinants in adults in the Netherlands." *Nutr Canc* 1993; 20:21–29.

108. Wilcox B, Fuchigami K, Wilcox D et al. "Isoflavones intake in Japanese and Japanese-Canadians." *Am J Clin Nutr* 1995; 61:901.

109. Brucker A. "Essay on the phytotherapy of hormonal disorders in women." *Med Welt* 1960; 44:2331–33.

110. Stolze H. "An alternative to treat menopausal complaints." *Gyne* 1982; 3:14–16.

111. Warneck G. "Influencing menopausal symptoms with a phytotherapeutic agent." *Med Welt* 1985; 36:871–74.

112. Stoll W. "Phytopharmacon influences atrophic vaginal epithelium. Double-blind study—Cimicifuga vs estrogenic substances." *Therapeuticum* 1987; 1:23–31.

113. Lehmann-Willenbrock E et al. "Clinical and endocrinologic examinations of climacteric symptoms following hysterectomy with remaining ovaries." *Zent Gynakol* 1988; 110:611–18.

114. Duker E et al. "Effects of extracts from Cimicifuga racemosa on gonadotropin release in menopausal women and ovariectomized rats." *Planta Medica* 1991; 57:420–24.

115. Newall C, Anderson L, Phillipson J, eds. "Cohosh, Black." In *Herbal Medicines: A Guide for Health-care Professionals*. London: Pharmaceutical Press, 1996:80–81.

116. Harnischfeger G, Stolze H. "Black cohosh." *Notabene Medici* 1980; 10:446–50.

117. Tegtmeier O. "Cimicifuga: Effective therapy in climacteric complaints." *Apotheker J* 1996; 18(7):32–36.

118. Nesselhut T, Schellhase C, Dietrich R, Kuhn W. "Examination of the proliferative potential of phytopharmaceuticals with estrogen-mimicking acting in breast carcinoma." *Arch Gynecol Obstet* 1993; 254:817–18.

119. Nesselhut T, Borth S, Kuhn W. "Influence of Cimicifuga racemosa extracts on the in vitro proliferation of mammalian carcinoma cells." Submitted for publication.

120. Zava D, Dollbaum C, Blen M. "Estrogen and progestin bioactivity of foods, herbs, and spices." *Proc Soc Experi Biol Med* 1998; 217:369–78.

121. Einer-Hensen N, Zhao J, Andersen K, Kristoffersen K. "Cimicifuga and Melbrosia lack oestrogenic effects in mice and rats." *Maturitas* 1996; 25:149–53.

122. Haller J. "Testing the progesterones." *Therpaiewoche* 1959; 9:481–84.

123. Haller J. "The influence of plant extracts in the hormonal exchange between hypophysis and ovary. An experimental endocrinological animal study." *A Geburtsh Gynakol* 1961; 156:274–302.

124. Loch E. "Diagnosis and therapy of hormonal bleeding disturbances." *TW Gynakol* 1989; 2:379–85.

125. Probst V, Roth O. "On a plant extract with a hormonelike effect." *Dtsch Me Wschr* 1954; 79(35): 1271–74.

126. Bieier W. "Phytotherapy I irregular menstrual cycles or bleeding periods and other gynecological disorders of endocrine origin." *Zentralblatt Gynakol* 1959; 81(18):701–9.

127. Harada M, Suzuki M, Ozaki Y. "Effect of Japanese angelica root and peony root on uterine contraction in the rabbit in situ." *J Pharm Dyn* 1984; 7:304–11.

128. Yoshiro K. "The physiological actions of Tang-Kuei and Cnidium." *Bull Oriental Healing Arts Inst USA* 1985; 10:269–78.

129. Hirata J et al. "Does dong quai have estrogenic effects in postmenopausal women? A double-blind, placebo-controlled trial." *Fertil Steril* 1997; 68 (6):981–86.

130. Braquet P, ed. *Ginkgolides: Chemistry, Biology, Pharmacology and Clinical Perspectives*. I, II. Barcelona: JR Prous Science Publishers, 1992.

131. Kleijnen J, Knipschild P. "Drug profiles: Ginkgo biloba." *Lancet* 1993; 340:1136–39.

132. Rudofsky V. "The effect of ginkgo biloba extract in cases of arterial occlusive disease: a randomized placebo-controlled double-blind crossover study." *Fortschr Med* 1987; 105:397–400.

133. Voberg G. "Ginkgo biloba extract (GBE): a long-term study of chronic cerebral insufficiency in geriatric patients." *Clin Trials J* 1985; 22:149–57.

134. Mancini M, Agozzino B, Bompani R. "Clinical and therapeutic effects of Ginkgo biloba extract (GBE) versus placebo in the treatment of psycho-organic senile dementia of arteriosclerotic origin." *Gax Med Ital* 1993; 152:69–80.

135. Kleijnen J, Knipschild P. "Ginkgo biloba for cerebral insufficiency." *Br J Clin Pharmacol* 1992; 34:352–58.

136. Hofferberth B. "The efficacy of Egb761 in patients with senile dementia of the Alzheimer type—a double-blind, placebo-controlled study on different levels of investigation." *Human Psychopharm* 1994; 9:215–22.

137. Kanowski S, Herrmann W, Stephan K et al. "Proof of efficacy of the Ginkgo biloba special extract EGb 761 in outpatients suffering from mild to moderate primary degenerative dementia of the Alzheimer type or multi-infarct dementia." *Pharmacopsychiatry* 1996; 29:47–56.

138. Cohen A. As reported in *OB/GYN News* 1997. July 15:19.

139. Hikino H. "Traditional remedies and modern assessment: The case of ginseng." In Wijeskera R, ed. *The Medicinal Plant Industry*. Boca Raton, Fla.: CRC Press, 1991:149–66.

140. Shibata S et al. "Chemistry and pharmacology of Panax." *Econ Med Plant Res* 1985; 1:217–84.

141. Hallstrom C, Fulder S, Carruthers M. "Effect of ginseng on the performance of nurses on night duty." *Comp Med East West* 1982; 6:277–82.

142. D'Angelo L et al. "A double-blind, placebo-controlled clinical study on the effect of a standardized ginseng extract on psychomotor performance in healthy volunteers." *J Ethnopharmacol* 1986; 16:15–22.

143. Bombardelli E, Cirstoni A, Lietti A. "The effect of acute and chronic (Panax) ginseng saponins treatment on adrenal function; biochemical and pharmacological." Proceedings 3rd International Ginseng Symposium 1980; Korean Ginseng Research Institute: 9–16.

144. Punnonen R, Lukola A. "Oestrogenlike effect of ginseng." *Br Med J* 1980; 281:1110.

145. Zayed S, Hassan A, Elghamry M. "Estrogenic substances from Egyptian glycyrrhiza glabra. II Beta-sitosterol as an estrogenic principle." *Zenralbi Veterinarmed* 1964; 11(5):476–82.

146. Davis E, Morris D. "Medicinal uses of licorice through the millennia: the good and plenty of it." *Molec and Cell Endocr* 1991; 78(1–2):1–6.

147. Miksicek R. "Estrogenic flavonoids: structural requirements for biological activity." *Proc Soc Experi Biol Med* 1995; 208:44–50.

148. Bennetts H, Underwood E, Shier F. "A breeding problem of sheep in the southwest division of Western Australia." *J Dept Agric West Aust* 1946; 23:1–12.

149. Adams N. "A changed responsiveness to oestrogen in ewes with clover disease." *J Reprod Fertil* 1981; Suppl 30:223–30.

150. Nwannenna A et al. "Clinical changes in ovariectomized ewes exposed to phytoestrogens and 17-beta estradiol implants." *Proc Soc Experi Biol Med* 1995; 208:92–97.

151. Morazzoni P, Bombardelli E. "Hypericum perforatum." *Fitoteropia* 1995; 66:43–68.

152. Harrer G, Schulz V. "Clinical investigation of the antidepressant effectiveness of Hypericum." *J Geriatr Psychiatry Neurol* 1994 (Suppl); 7:S6–S8.

153. De Smet P, Nolen W. "St. Johns wort as an antidepressant." *BMJ* 1996; 313:241–42.

154. Hudson T, Standish L. "Clinical and endocrinological effects of a menopausal botanical formula." *J Naturo Med* 1997; 7(1):73–77.

155. Hirvonen E. "Progestins." *Maturitas* 1996; 23:S13.

156. Adams M, Register T, Golden D et al. "Medroxyprogesterone acetate antagonizes inhibitory effects of conjugated equine estrogens on coronary artery atherosclerosis." *Art Thrombo Vascu Biol* 1997; 17:217.

157. Lee J. *What Your Doctor May Not Tell You about Menopause*. New York: Warner Books, 1996.

158. Simon J. "Micronized progesterone: vaginal and oral uses." *Clin Obstet Gynecol* 1995; 38(4):902–14.

159. The Writing Group for the PEPI Trial. "Effects of hormone replacement therapy on endometrial histology in postmenopausal women. The Postmenopausal Estrogen/Progestin Interventions (PEPI) Trial." *JAMA* 1996; 275(5):370–75.

160. Moyer D, de Lignieres B, Driguez P, Pez J. "Prevention of endometrial hyperplasia by progesterone during long-term estradiol replacement: influence of bleeding pattern and secretory changes." *Fertil Steril* 1993; 59(5):992–97.

161. Kim S, Korhonen M, Wilborn W et al. "Antiproliferative effects of low-dose micronized progesterone." *Fertil Steril* 1996; 65(2):323–31.

162. Lane G, Siddle N, Ryder T et al. "Dose dependent effects of oral progesterone on the oestrogenised postmenopausal endometrium." *Br Med J* 1983; 287:1241–45.

163. Gillet J, Andre G, Faguer B et al. "Induction of amenorrhea during hormone replacement therapy: optimal micronized progesterone dose. A multicenter study." *Maturitas* 1994; 19:103–15.

164. The Writing Group for the PEPI Trial. "Effects of hormone therapy on bone mineral density. Results from the Postmenopausal Estrogen/Progestin Interventions (PEPI) Trial." *JAMA* 1996; 276(17):1389–96.

165. Riis B, Thomsen K, Strom V, Christiansen C. "The effect of percutaneous estradiol and natural progesterone on postmenopausal bone loss." *Am J Obstet Gynecol* 1987; 156:61–65.

166. Frishman G, Klock S, Luciano A, Nulsen J. "Efficacy of oral micronized progesterone in the treatment of luteal phase defects." *J Reprod Med* 1995; 40:521–24.

167. Colwell K, Tummon I. "Elevation of serum progesterone with oral micronized progesterone after in vitro fertilization." *J Reprod Med* 1991; 35(3):170–72.

168. Pouly J, Bassil S, Frydman R et al. "Luteal support after in-vitro fertilization: Crinone 8%, a sustained release vaginal progesterone gel, versus Utrogestan, an oral micronized progesterone." *Human Reproduction* 1996; 11(10):2085–89.

169. The Writing Group for the PEPI Trial. "Effects of estrogen or estrogen/progestin regimens on heart disease risk factors in postmenopausal women. The Postmenopausal Estrogen/Progestin Interventions (PEPI) Trial." *JAMA* 1995; 273(3):199–208.

170. Moorjani S, Dupont A, Labrie F et al. "Changes in plasma lipoprotein and apolipoprotein composition in relation to oral versus percutaneous administration of estrogen alone or in cyclic association with Utrogestan in menopausal women." *J Clin Endocrin Metab* 1991; 73(2):373–79.

171. Ottoson U, Johansson B, von Schoultz B. "Subfractions of high-density lipoprotein during estrogen replacement therapy: a comparison between progestogens and natural progesterone." *J Obstet Gynecol* 1985; 151:746–50.

172. Prometrium (progesterone, USP) Capsules. Package Insert. Solvay Pharmaceuticals, 1998.

173. FDA package insert for Crinone 8% (progesterone gel), Wyeth-Ayers Laboratories, Inc., 1997.

174. Fanchin R, DeZiegler D, Bergeron C et al. "Transvaginal administration of progesterone: dose-response data support a first uterine pass effect." *Obstet Gynecol.* In press.

175. Toner J. "Progesterone in reproduction: Basic biology and options for exogenous delivery." In *Progesterone Use in Reproductive and Gynecologic Endocrinology: Current and Future Perspectives*. A Suppl to *Contemporary Ob/Gyn* 1997; 42(10):12–18.

176. Cicinelli E, Petruzzi D, Scorcia P et al. "Effects of progesterone administered by nasal spray on the human postmenopausal endometrium." *Maturitas* 1993; 18: 65.

177. Colditz G, Hankinson S, Hunter D et al. "The use of estrogens and progestins and the risk of breast cancer in postmenopausal women." *N Engl J Med* 1995; 332:1589–1993.

178. Stanford J, Weiss N, Voight L et al. "Combined estrogen and progestin hormone replacement therapy in relation to risk of breast cancer." *JAMA* 1995; 274:137–42.

179. Chang K, Fournier S et al. "Influences of percutaneous administration of estradiol and progesterone on human breast epithelial cell cycle in vivo." *Fertil Steril* 1995; 63(4):785–91.

180. Mashchak C, Lobo R, Dozono-Takano R et al. "Comparison of pharmacodynamic properties of various estrogen formulations." *Am J Obstet Gynecol* 1982; 144:511–18.

181. Gorrill M, Marshall J. "Pharmacology of estrogens and estrogen-induced effects on nonreproductive organs and systems." *J Reprod Med* (Suppl) 1986; 31:842–47.

182. Hargrove J, Maxson W, Wentz A, Burnett L. "Menopausal hormone replacement therapy with continuous daily oral micronized estradiol and progesterone." *Obstet Gynecol* 1989; 73(4):606–12.

183. Staland B. "Continuous treatment with natural oestrogens and progestogens." A method to avoid endometrial stimulation." *Maturitas* 1981; 3:145–56.

184. Souza M, Prestwood K et al. "A comparison of the effect of synthetic and micronized hormone replacement therapy on bone mineral density and biochemical markers of bone metabolism." *Menopause: The J North Amer Meno Soc* 1996; 3(3):140–48.

185. Ettinger B, Genent H, Steiger P, Madvig P. "Low-dosage micronized 17-beta estradiol prevents bone loss in postmenopausal women." *Am J Obstet Gynecol* 1992; 166:479–88.

186. Longcope C. "Estriol production and metabolism in normal women." *J Steroid Biochem* 1984; 20:959–62.

187. Melamed M, Castano E, Notides A, Sasson S. "Molecular and kinetic basis for the mixed agonist/antagonist activity of estriol." *Mol Endocrinol* 1997; 11:1868–78.

188. Bergink E. "Oestriol receptor interactions: their biological importance and therapeutic implications." *Acta Endocrinol* 1980; 233:S9–S16.

189. Tzingounis V, Aksu M, Greenblatt R. "Estriol in the management of the menopause." *JAMA* 1978; 239:1638–41.

190. Yang T, Tsan S, Chang S, Ng H. "Efficacy and safety of estriol replacement therapy for climacteric women." *Chin Med J* 1995; 55:386–91.

191. Perovic D, Kopajtic B, Stankovic T. "Treatment of climacteric complaints with oestriol." *Arzneimittelforschung* 1997; 25:962–64.

192. Wren B. "Oestriol in the control of postmenopausal symptoms." *Med J Aust* 1982; 1:176–77.

193. Montoneri C, Zarbo G, Garofalo A, Giardinella S. "Effects of estriol administration on human postmenopausal endometrium." *Clin Exp Obst Gyn* 1987; 14:178–81.

194. Van Haaften M, Donker G, Sie-Go D et al. "Biochemical and histological effects of vaginal estriol and estradiol applications on the endometrium, myometrium and vagina of postmenopausal women." *Gynecol Endocrinol* 1997; 11:175–85.

195. Vooijs G, Geurts T. "Review of the endometrial safety during intravaginal treatment with estriol." *Eur J Obstet Gynecol Reprod Biol* 1995; 62:101–6.

196. Hustin J, Van der Eynde J. "Cytological evaluation of the effect of various estrogens given in postmenopause." *Acta Cytologica* 1977; 21:225–28.

197. Van der Linden M, Gerretsen G, Brandhorst M et al. "The effect of estriol on the cytology of urethra and vagina in postmenopausal women with genito-urinary symptoms." *Eur J Obstet Gynecol Reprod Biol* 1993; 51:29–33.

198. Kanne B, Jenny J. "Local administration of low-dose estriol and vital Lactobacillus acidophilus in postmenopause." *Gynakol Rundsch* 1991; 31:7–13.

199. Schar G, Kochli O, Fritz M, Haller U. "Effect of vaginal estrogen therapy on urinary incontinence in postmenopause." *Zentralbl Gynakol* 1995; 117:77–80 (article in German).

200. Raz R, Stamm W. "A controlled trial of intravaginal estriol in postmenopausal women with recurrent urinary tract infections." *N Engl J Med* 1993; 329(11):753–56.

201. Nishibe A, Morimoto S, Hirota K et al. "Effect of estriol on bone mineral density of lumbar vertebrae in elderly and postmenopausal women." *Nippon Ronen Igakkai Zasshi* 1996; 33:353–59.

202. Guo-jun C, Jian-li L, Quaz Z et al. "Nylestriol replacement therapy in postmenopausal women." *Chin Med J* 1993; 106:911–16.

203. Walter S, Jensen H. "The effect of treatment with oestradiol and oestriol on fasting serum cholesterol and triglyceride levels in postmenopausal women." *Br J Obstet Gyn* 1977; 84(11):869–72.

204. Minaguchi H, Usmura T, Shirasu K et al. "Effect of estriol on bone loss in postmenopausal Japanese women: a multicenter prospective open study." *J Obstet Gyn Res* 1996; 22:259–65.

205. Nozaki M, Hashimoto K, Inoue Y et al. "Usefulness of estriol for the treatment of bone loss in postmenopausal women." *Nippon Sanka Fujinka Gakkai Zasshi* 1996; 48:83–88.

206. Nishibe A, Norimoto S, Hirota K et al. "Effect of estriol and bone mineral density of lumbar vertebrae in elderly and postmenopausal women." *Nippon Ronen Igakkai Zasshi* 1996; 33:353–59.

207. Lindsay R, Hart D, Maclean A et al. "Bone loss during oestriol therapy in postmenopausal women." *Maturitas* 1979; 1:279–85.

208. Lemon H. "Antimammary carcinogenic activity of 17-alpha-ethinyl estriol." *Cancer* 1987; 60:2873–81.

209. Lemon H. "Pathophysiologic considerations in the treatment of menopausal patients with oestrogens; the role of oestriol in the prevention of mammary carcinoma." *Acta Endocrinol* 1980; 233:17–27.

210. Lemon H. "Pathophysiologic consideration in the treatment of menopausal patients with oestrogens; the role of oestriol in the prevention of mammary carcinoma." *Acta Endocrinol* 1980; 233:217–27.

211. Pratt J, Longcope C. "Estriol production rates and breast cancer." *J Clin Endocrinol Metab* 1978; 46:44–47.

212. Follingstad A. "Estriol, the forgotten estrogen?" *JAMA* 1978; 239:29–30.

213. Lippman M, Monaco M, Bolan G. "Effects of estrone, estradiol, and estriol on hormone-responsive human breast cancer in long-term tissue culture." *Canc Res* 1977; 37:1901–7.

214. Fahraeus L. "Metabolic consequences of postmenopausal estrogen and progestogen treatment." *Acta Obstet Gynecol Scand* (Suppl) 1985; 132:19.

215. Fahraeus L, Larsson-Cohn U, Wallentin L. "L-norgestrel and progesterone have different influences on plasma lipoproteins." *Eur J Clin Invest* 1983; 13:447.

216. Ottosson U. "Oral progesterone and estrogen/progestogen therapy: Effects of natural and synthetic

hormones on subfractions of HDL cholesterol and liver proteins." *Acta Obstet Gynecol Scand* (Suppl) 1984; 127:1.

217. Hargrove J, Osteen K. "An alternative method of hormone replacement therapy using the natural sex steroids." *Infertil and Repro Med Clin of North Amer* 1995; 6(4):653–74.

218. Simon J, Klaiber E, Wiita B et al. "Double-blind comparison of two doses of estrogen and estrogen-androgen therapy in naturally postmenopausal women: neuroendocrine, psychological and psychosomatic effects." *Fertil Steril* 1996; 66:S71.

219. Sarrel P, Dobay B, Wiita B. "Sexual behavior and neuroendocrine responses to estrogen and estrogen-androgen in postmenopausal women dissatisfied with estrogen-only therapy." *J Reprod Med.* In press.

220. Dobay B, Balos R, Willard N. "Improved menopausal symptom relief with estrogen-androgen therapy." Presented at the Annual Conference of the North American Menopause Society, Sept 1996, Chicago, Ill.

221. Watts N, Notelovitz M, Timmons M et al. "Comparison of oral estrogens and estrogens plus androgen on bone mineral density, menopausal symptoms, and lipid-lipoprotein profiles in surgical menopause." *Obstet Gynecol* 1995; 85:529–37.

222. Gambrell R Jr. "Androgen therapy." In *Managing the Menopause: An update.* New York: McGraw-Hill Inc., 1989:11–16.

223. Rako S. *The Hormone of Desire.* New York: Harmony Books, 1996.

224. Morales A, Nolan J, Nelson J, Yen S. "Effect of replacement dose of dehydroepiandrosterone in men and women of advancing age." *J Clin Endocrinol Metab* 1994; 78:1360–67.

225. Mortola J, Yen S. "The effects of dehydroepiandrosterone on endocrine-metabolic parameters in postmenopausal women." *J Clin Endocrinol Metab* 1990; 71:696–704.

226. Nawata H, Tanaka S, Takajanogas R et al. "Aromatase in bone cell: association with osteoporosis in postmenopausal women." *J Steroid Biochem* 1995; 53:165–74.

227. Yen S, Morales A, Khorram O. "Replacement of DHEA in aging men and women. Potential remedial effects." *Ann NY Acad Sci* 1995; 774:128–42.

228. Casson P, Faquin L, Steutz F et al. "Replacement of dehydroepiandrosterone enhances T-lymphocyte insulin binding in postmenopausal women." *Fertil Steril* 1995; 63:1027–31.

229. Gannon L. "The potential role of exercise in the alleviation of menstrual disorders and menopausal symptoms: A theoretical synthesis of recent research." *Women & Health* 1988; 14:105.

230. Van Pelt R et al. "Regular exercise and the age-related decline in resting metabolic rate in women." *J Clin Endocrinol Metab* 1997; 82:3208.

231. Stefanick M et al. "Distribution and correlates of plasma fibrinogen in middle-aged women. Initial findings of the Postmenopausal Estrogen/Progestin Intervention (PEPI) Study." *Arterio, Throm & Vasc Biol* 1995; 15:2085.

232. Greendale G et al. "Leisure, home and occupational physical activity and cardiovascular risk factors in postmenopausal women. The Postmenopausal Estrogens/Progestins Intervention (PEPI) Study." *Arch Int Med* 1996; 156:418.

233. Ryan A et al. "Resistive training increases insulin action in postmenopausal women." *J of Geron Series A, Biol Sci and Med Sci* 1966; 51:M199.

234. Davy K et al. "Elevated heart rate variability in physically active postmenopausal women: A cardioprotective effect?" *Am J Physiol* 1996; 271:H455.

235. Davy K, Willis W, Seals D. "Influence of exercise training on heart rate variability in post-menopausal women with elevated arterial blood pressure." *Clin Physiol* 1997; 17:31.

236. Ready A et al. "Walking program reduces elevated cholesterol in women postmenopause." *Can J Cardiol* 1995; 11:905.

237. Simkin-Silverman L et al. "Prevention of cardiovascular risk factor elevations in healthy premenopausal women." *Prevent Med* 1995; 24:509.

238. Meilahn E, Becker R, Carrao J. "Primary prevention of coronary heart disease in women." *Cardiol* 1995; 86:286.

239. Poehlman E, Toth M, Gardner A. "Changes in energy balance and body composition at menopause: A controlled longitudinal study." *Ann Int Med* 1995; 123:673.

240. Ravnikar V. "Diet, exercise, and lifestyle in preparation for menopause." *Obstet Gynecol Clin NA* 1993; 20:365.

241. Hammar M, Berg G, Lindgren R. "Does physical exercise influence the frequency of postmenopausal hot flushes?" *Acta Obstet Gynecol Scand* 1990; 69:409.

242. Lucerno M, McCloskey W. "Alternatives to estrogen for the treatment of hot flashes." *Ann Pharmacother* 1997; 31:915.

243. Stevenson E et al. "Physically active women demonstrate less adverse age-related changes in plasma lipids and lipoproteins." *Am J Cardiol* 1997; 80:1360.

244. Binder E, Birge S, Kohrt W. "Effects of endurance exercise and hormone replacement therapy on serum lipids in older women." *J Am Ger Soc* 1996; 44:331.

245. Hunter G et al. "Intra-abdominal adipose tissue, physical activity and cardiovascular risk in pre- and postmenopausal women." *Int J Obes Rel Metabol Disord* 1996; 20:860.

246. Singh N, Clements K, Fiatarone M. "A randomized controlled trial of progressive resistance training in depressed elders." *J Gerontol A Biol Sci Med Sci* 1997; 52:M27.

247. Singh N, Clements K, Fiatarone M. "A randomized controlled trial of the effect of exercise on sleep." *Sleep* 1997; 20:95.

248. King A et al. "Moderate-intensity exercise and self-rated quality of sleep in older adults: A randomized controlled trial." *JAMA* 1997; 277:32.

249. Youngstedt S. "Does exercise truly enhance sleep?" *Phys Sportsmed* 1997; 25:72.

250. Driver H, Taylor S. "Sleep disturbances and exercise." *Sports Med* 1996; 21:1.

251. Naimark B et al. "Serum ferritin and heart disease: The effect of moderate exercise on stored iron levels in postmenopausal women." *Can J Cardiol* 1996; 12:1253.

252. Ryan A et al. "Resistive training increases fat-free mass and maintains RMR despite weight loss in postmenopausal women." *J Appl Physiol* 1995; 79:818.

253. Lemaitre R et al. "Leisure-time physical activity and the risk of nonfatal myocardial infarction in postmenopausal women." *Arch Intern Med* 1995; 155:2302.

254. Tanaka H, DeSouza C, Seals D. "Absence of age-related increases in central arterial stiffness in physically active women." *Arterioscler Thromb Vasc Biol* 1998; 18:127.

255. Heislein D, Harris B, Jette A. "A strength training program for postmenopausal women: A pilot study." *Arch Phys Med Rehab* 1994; 75:198.

256. Hoshino H et al. "Effect of physical activity as a caddie on ultrasound measurements of the Os calcis: A cross-sectional comparison." *J Bone Min Res* 1996; 11:412.

257. Morganti C et al. "Strength improvements with 1 year of progressive resistance training in older women." *Med Sc Sports Exerc* 1995; 27:906.

258. Jaglal S, Kreiger N, Darlington G. "Lifetime occupational physical activity and risk of hip fracture in women." *Ann Epidem* 1995; 5:321.

259. Evans W. "Effects of exercise on body composition and functional capacity of the elderly." *J Geront A Bio Sci Med Sci* 1995; 50 Spec No:147.

260. Svendsen O et al. "Effects on muscle of dieting with or without exercise in overweight postmenopausal women." *J App Physiol* 1996; 80:1365.

261. Fox A et al. "Effects of diet and exercise on common cardiovascular disease risk factors in moderately obese older women." *Am J Clin Nutr* 1996; 63:225.

262. Ready A et al. "Influence of walking volume on health benefits in women post-menopause." *Med Sc Sport Exerc* 1996; 28:1097.

263. Nelson M. Quoted in Potera C. "Choosing the best exercise for seniors." *Phys Sportsmed* 1997; 25:21.

264. Fiatarone M, O'Brien K, Rich B. "Exercise Rx for a healthier old age." *Pat Care* 1996; Oct 15:145.

265. Love S, Lindsey K. *Dr. Susan Love's Hormone Book.* New York: Random House, 1997.

266. Hulley S, Grady D et al. "Randomized Trial of Estrogen Plus Progestin for Secondary Prevention of Coronary Heart Disease in Postmenopausal Women." *JAMA* 1998; 280:605–13.

267. Gambrell R Jr. "Update on hormone replacement therapy." *Am Fam Phys* 1992; 46:87S–96S.

268. Kiel D, Felson D, et al. "Hip fracture and the use of estrogens in postmenopausal women: The Framingham Study." *N Engl J Med* 1987; 317:1169–74.

269. Sherwin B, Gelfand M. "Differential symptom response to parenteral estrogen and/or androgen administration in the surgical menopause." Transactions of the Fortieth Annual Meeting of the Society of Obstetricians and Gynecologists of Canada. *Am J Obstet Gynecol* 1985; 151:153–60.

270. Steinberg K, Thaker S et al. "A meta-analysis of the effect of estrogen replacement therapy on the risk of breast cancer." *JAMA* 1991; 266:1362.

271. Steinberg K, Smith S, Thacker S, Stroup D. "Breast cancer risk and duration of estrogen use: the role of study design in meta-analysis." *Epid* 1994; 5:415–21.

272. Collaborative Group on Hormonal Factors in Breast Cancer. "Breast cancer and hormone replacement therapy. Combined reanalysis of data from 51 epidemiological studies involving 52,705 women with breast cancer and 108,411 women without breast cancer." *Lancet* 1997; 350:1047–59.

273. Colditz G. "Relationship between estrogen levels, use of hormone replacement therapy, and breast cancer." *J Na Canc Ins* 1998; 90(11):814–23.

274. Grady D et al. "Hormone replacement therapy and endometrial cancer risk: a meta-analysis." *Obs Gynec* 1995; 85(2):304–13.

275. Rodriguez C et al. "Estrogen replacement therapy and fatal ovarian cancer." *Am J Epid* 1995; 141(9): 828–35.

Chapter Eleven: Menstrual Cramps

1. Galeao R. "La dysmenorrhea, syndrome multiforme." *Gynecologie* 1974; 25:125.

2. Harlow S, Park M. "A longitudinal study of risk factors for the occurrence, duration and severity of menstrual cramps in a cohort of college women." *Br J Obstet/Gyn* 1996; 103:1134–42.

3. Chesney M, Tasto D. "The effectiveness of behavior modification with spasmodic and congestive dysmenorrhea." *Behav Res Ther* 1975; 13:245–53.

4. Balick L, Elfner L, May J, Moore D. "Biofeedback treatment of dysmenorrhea." *Biofeedback and Self-Regulation* 1982; 7(4):499–520.

5. Harel L et al. "Supplementation with omega-3 polyunsaturated fatty acids in the management of dysmenorrhea in adolescents." *Am J Obstet Gynecol* 1996; 174(4): 1335–38.

6. Hudgins A. "Niacin for dysmenorrhea." *Am Pract Digest Treat* 1952; 3:892–93.

7. Hudgins A. "Vitamins P, C and niacin for dysmenorrhea therapy." *West J Surg Gynecol* 1954; 62:610–11.

8. Butler E, McKnight E. "Vitamin E in the treatment of primary dysmenorrhea." *Lancet*, 1955; 1:844–47.

9. Penland J, Johnson P. "Dietary calcium and manganese effects on menstrual cycle symptoms." *Am J Obstet Gynecol* 1993; 168:1417–23.

10. Sardyle R. "Dysmenorrhea and the pineal gland; letter to the editor." *Intern J Neurosc* 1992; 65:177–81.

11. Wetterberg L, Arendt J, Paunier L et al. "Human serum melatonin changes during the menstrual cycle." *J Clin Endocrin Metab* 1976; 42:185–88.

12. Hertz-Eshel M, Rahamimoff R. "Effect of melatonin on uterine contractility." *Life Sc* 1965; 4:1367–72.

13. Kavaliers M, Hirst M, Teskey G. "Aging, opioid analgesia and the pineal gland." *Life Sc* 1983; 32:2279–87.

14. MacPhee A, Cole F, Rice F. "The effect of melatonin on steroidogenesis by the human ovary in vitro." *J Clin Endocrin Metab* 1975; 40:688–96.

15. Gimeno M, Landa A, Speziale N et al. "Melatonin blocks in vitro generation of prostaglandin by the uterus and hypothalamus." *Eur J Pharm* 1980; 62:309–17.

16. Mennini T et al. "In vitro study on the interaction of extracts and pure compounds from Valeriana officinalis roots with GABA, benzodiazepine and barbiturate receptors in rat brain." *Fitoterapia* 1993; 54:291–300.

17. Hazelhoff B, Malingre M, Meijer D. "Antispasmodic effects of Valeriana compounds: an in-vivo and in-vitro study on the guinea-pig ileum." *Arch Int Pharmacodyn* 1982; 257:274–87.

18. Felter H. *The Eclectic Materia Medica, Pharmacology and Therapeutics.* Portland, Oreg.: Eclectic Medical Publications, 1985:694.

19. Jarboe C, Schmidt C, Nicholson J, Zirvi K. "Uterine relaxant properties of Vibernum." *Nat* 1966. Nov 19: 837.

20. Evans W, Harne W, Krantz J. "A uterine principle from Viburnum prunifolium." (Journal unknown). Dept. of Pharmacology, School of Medicine, U. Maryland. 1942; 174–77.

21. Haman J. "Exercises in dysmenorrhea." *Am J Obstet Gynecol* 1945; 49:755.

22. Golub L et al. "Therapeutic exercise for teen-age dysmenorrhea." *Am J Obstet Gynecol* 1958; 76:670.

23. Golub L, Menduke H, Lang W. "Exercise and dysmenorrhea in young teenagers: a 3-year study." *Obstet Gynecol* 1968; 32:508.

24. Golub L. "A new exercise for dysmenorrhea." *Am J Obstet Gynecol* 1959; 78:152.

25. Israel R, Sutton M, O'Brien. "Effects of aerobic training on primary dysmenorrhea symptomatology in college females." *J Am Coll Health* 1985; 33:241.

26. Metheny W, Smith R. "The relationship among exercise, stress, and primary dysmenorrhea." *J Behav Med* 1989; 12:569.

27. Choi P, Salmon P. "Symptom changes across the menstrual cycle in competitive sportswomen, exercisers and sedentary women." *Br J Clin Psychol* 1995; 34:447.

28. Chan W, Dawood M. "Prostaglandin levels in menstrual fluid of nondysmenorrheic and dysmenorrheic subjects with and without oral contraceptive or ibuprofen therapy." *Adv Prostaglandin Thromboxane Leukot Res* 1980; 8:1445.

29. Chan W, Dawood M, Fuchs F. "Prostaglandins in primary dysmenorrhea: Comparison of prophylactic treatment with ibuprofen and the use of oral contraceptives." *Am J Med* 1981; 70:535.

30. Dawood M. "Overall approach to the management of dysmenorrhea." In Dawood M, ed. *Dysmenorrhea.* Baltimore: William and Wilkins, 1981:261–79.

31. Dawood M. "Dysmenorrhea." *J Reprod Med* 1985; 30(3): 154–67.

32. Trobough G, Guderian A, Erickson R et al. "The effect of exogenous intrauterine progesterone on the amount and prostaglandin F_2 alpha content of menstrual blood in dysmenorrheic women." *J Reprod Med* 1978; 21:153.

Chapter Twelve: Osteoporosis

1. Gamble C. "Osteoporosis: making the diagnosis in patients at risk for fracture." *Geriatrics* 1995; 50:24–33.

2. "Consensus Development Conference: prophylaxis and treatment of osteoporosis." *Osteoporos Int* 1991: 114–17.

3. Kanis J, et al. "The diagnosis of osteoporosis." *J Bone Miner Res* 1994; 9:1137–41.

4. Cummings S, Black D, Nevitt M et al. "Bone density at various sites is predictive of hip fractures." *Lancet* 1993; 341:72–75.

5. National Osteoporosis Foundation. "The older person's guide to osteoporosis." Washington, D.C.: National Osteoporosis Foundation, 1991.

6. Melton L III. "Epidemiology of fractures." In Riggs B, Melton L III, eds. *Osteoporosis: Etiology, Diagnosis, and Management.* New York: Raven Press, 1988:133–54.

7. Matkovic V et al. "Osteoporosis and epidemiology fractures in Croatia." "An international comparison." *Henry Ford Hosp Med J* 1980; 28:116–26.

8. Matkovic V, Kilsovic D, Ilich J. "Epidemiology of fractures." In *Physical Medicine and Rehabilitation Clinics of North America.* Philadelphia: Saunders Publishing Co., 1995; 6:415–39.

9. Frost H. "Dynamics of bone remodeling." In Frost H, ed. *Bone Biodynamics.* Boston: Little, Brown and Co., 1964.

10. Seeman E, Hopper J, Bach L et al. "Reduced bone mass in daughters of women with osteoporosis." *N Engl J Med* 1989; 320:554–58.

11. Evans R et al. "Bone mass is low in relatives of osteoporotic patients." *Ann Int Med* 1988; 109:870–73.

12. Rigoti N, Nussbaum S, Herzog D, Neer R. "Osteoporosis in women with anorexia nervosa." *N Engl J Med* 1984; 311:1601–6.

13. Slemenda S et al. "Predictors of bone mass in perimenopausal women: a prospective study of clinical data using photon absorptiometry." *Ann Int Med* 1990; 112:96–101.

14. Cummings S, Nevitt M, Browner W et al. "Risk factors for hip fracture in white women." *N Engl J Med* 1995; 332:767–73.

15. Looker A et al. "Prevalence of low femoral bone density in older U.S. women from NHANES III." *J Bone Miner Res* 1995; 10:796–802.

16. Jacobsen S et al. "Hip fracture incidence among the old and very old: a population-based study of 745,435 cases." *Am J Pub Health* 1990; 80:871–73.

17. Bell N et al. "Demonstration that bone mass is greater in black than in white children." *J Bone Miner Res* 1991; 6:719.

18. Gilsanz V et al. "Changes in vertebral bone density in black girls and white girls during childhood and puberty." *N Engl J Med* 1991; 325:1597–1600.

19. Russell-Aulet M et al. "Bone mineral density and mass in a cross-sectional study of white and Asian women." *J Bone Miner Res* 1993; 8:575–82.

20. Quigley M et al. "Estrogen therapy arrests bone loss in elderly women." *Am J Obstet Gynecol* 1987; 156:1516–23.

21. Riggs B et al. "Differential changes in bone mineral density of the appendicular and axial skeleton with aging: relationship to spinal osteoporosis." *J Clin Invest* 1981; 67:328–35.

22. Edwards J, Perry H III. "Age-related osteoporosis." *Clin Ger Med* 1994; 10:575–88.

23. Melton L III, Cummings S. "Heterogeneity of age-related fractures: implications for epidemiology." *J Bone Miner Res* 1987; 2:321–31.

24. Nevitt M. "Epidemiology of osteoporosis." *Rheum Dis Clin North Am* 1994; 20:535–39.

25. Nagat de Deuxchaisnes C. "The pathogenesis and treatment of involutional osteoporosis." In Dixon A St J, Russell R, Stamp T, eds. *Osteoporosis, A Multi-disciplinary Problem.* London: Academic Press Inc. and the Royal Society of Medicine; 1983:291–333. International Congress and Symposium Series no. 55.

26. Geusens P et al. "Age-, sex-, and menopause-related changes of vertebral and peripheral bone: population study using dual and single photon absorptiometry and radiogrammetry." *J Nuc Med* 1986; 27:1540–49.

27. Vaananen H. "Pathogenesis of osteoporosis." *Calcif Tis Int* 1991; 49:(Suppl):S11–S14.

28. Lloyd T et al. "Collegiate women athletes with irregular menses during adolescence have decreased bone density." *Obstet Gynecol* 1988; 72:639–42.

29. Pfeifer M, Pollaehne W, Minne H. "Ultrasound analyses of the calcaneus predict relative risk of the presence of at least one vertebral fracture and reflect different physical qualities of bone indifferent regions of the skeleton." *Horm Metab Res* 1997; 29:76–79.

30. Licata A, Bou E, Bartter F, West F. "Acute effects of dietary protein on calcium metabolism in patients with osteoporosis." *J Geron* 1981; 36:14–19.

31. Ellis F, Holesh S, Ellis J. "Incidence of osteoporosis in vegetarians and omnivores." *Am J Clin Nutr* 1972; 25:55–58.

32. Marsh A et al. "Cortical bone density of adult lacto-ovo-vegetarian and omnivorous women." *J Am Diet Assoc* 76: 148–51.

33. Marsh A et al. "Bone mineral mass in adult lacto-ovo-vegetarian and omnivorous males." *Am J Clin Nutr* 37: 453–56.

34. Mazariegos-Ramos E et al. "Consumption of soft drinks with phosphoric acid as a risk factor for the development of hypocalcemia in children: a case-control study." *J Pediatr* 1995; 126:940–42.

35. Thom J et al. "The influence of refined carbohydrate on urinary calcium excretion." *Br J Urol* 1978; 50:459–64.

36. Silver J et al. "Sodium-dependent idiopathic hypercalciuria in renal-stone formers." *Lancet* 1983; 2:484–86.

37. Bahram H et al. "Dietary soybean protein prevents bone loss in an ovariectomized rat model of osteoporosis." *J Nutr* 1996; 126:161–67.

38. Rudman D et al. "Effects of human growth hormone in men over 60 years old." *N Eng J Med* 1990; 323:1–6.

39. Arjmandi B, Hollis B, Kalu D. "In vivo effect of 17 B-estradiol on intestinal calcium absorption in rats." *Bone Miner* 1994a; 26:181–89.

40. Felson D, Kiel D, Anderson J et al. "Alcohol consumption and hip fractures: the Framingham study." *Am J Epid* 1988; 128:1102–10.

41. Slemenda C, Hui S, Longcope C et al. "Cigarette smoking, obesity, and bone mass." *J Bone Miner Res* 1989; 4:737–41.

42. Baron J, Le Vecchia C, Levi F. "The antiestrogenic effect of cigarette smoking in women." *Am J Obstet Gynecol* 1990; 162:502–14.

43. Chapuy M, Arlot M, Duboeuf F et al. "Vitamin D_3 and calcium to prevent hip fractures in elderly women." *N Engl J Med* 1992; 327:1637–42.

44. Cumming R. "Calcium intake and bone mass: a quantitative review of the evidence." *Calcif Tissue Int* 1990; 47:194–201.

45. Chapuy M, Arlot M, Delmas P, Meunier P. "Effect of calcium and cholecalciferol treatment for three years on hip fractures in elderly women." *Br Med J* 1994; 308:1081–82.

46. Lips P et al. "Vitamin D supplementation and fracture incidence in elderly persons: a randomized, placebo-controlled clinical trial." *Ann Int Med* 1996; 124:400–6.

47. Dawson-Hughes B, Harris S, Krall E, Dallal G. "Effect of calcium and vitamin D supplementation on bone density in men and women 65 years of age or older." *N Engl J Med* 1997; 337:670–76.

48. Reid I, Ames R, Evans M, Gamble G, Sharpe S. "Long-term effects of calcium supplementation on bone loss and fractures in postmenopausal women: a randomized controlled trial." *Am J Med* 1995; 98:331–35.

49. Recker R, Hinders S, Davies K et al. "Correcting calcium nutritional deficiency prevents spine fractures in elderly women." *J Bone Miner Res* 1996; 11:1961–66.

50. Dawson-Hughes B et al. "Rates of bone loss in postmenopausal women randomly assigned to one of two dosages of the vitamin D." *Am J Clin Nutr* 1995; 61:1140–45.

51. Ooms M et al. "Prevention of bone loss by vitamin D supplementation in elderly women: a randomized double-blind study." *J Clin Endocrinol Metabol* 1995; 80: 1052–58.

52. Bourgoin B, Evans D, Cornett J et al. "Lead content in 70 brands of dietary calcium supplements." *Am J Public Health* 1993; 83:1155–60.

53. Harbey J, Zobitz M, Pak C. "Dose dependence of calcium absorption: a comparison of calcium carbonate and calcium citrate." *J Bone Min Res* 1988; 3(3):253–58.

54. Dawson-Hughes B, Dallal G, Krall E et al. "A controlled trial of the effect of calcium supplementation on bone density in postmenopausal women." *N Engl J Med* 1990; 323:878–83.

55. Smith K, Heaney R, Flora L, Hinders S. "Calcium absorption from a new calcium delivery system (CCM)." *Calcif Tis Int* 1987; 41:351–52.

56. Miller J, Smith D, Flora L et al. "Calcium absorption from calcium carbonate and a new form of calcium (CCM) in healthy male and female adolescents." *Am J Clin Nutr* 1988; 48:1291–94.

57. Cumming R, Cummings S et al. "Calcium intake and fracture risk: results from the study of osteoporotic fractures." *Am J Epid* 1997; 145(10):926–34.

58. Wood R, Zheng J. "High dietary calcium intakes reduce zinc absorption and balance in humans." *Am J Clin Nutr* 1997; 65:1803–9.

59. Wood R, Zheng J. "The acute effect of calcium supplementation on zinc absorption." *Amer J Clin Nutr* 1997; 65(6):1803.

60. Atik O. "Zinc and senile osteoporosis." *J Am Geriatr Soc* 1983; 31:790–91.

61. Frithiof L et al. "The relationship between marginal bone loss and serum zinc levels." *Acta Med Scand* 1980; 207:67–70.

62. Grossman M, Kirsner J, Gillespie K. "Basal and histalog-stimulated gastric secretion in control subjects and in patients with peptic ulcer or gastric cancer." *Gastroent* 1963; 45:15–26.

63. Recker R. "Calcium absorption and achlorhydria." *N Eng J Med* 1985; 313:70–73.

64. Blumenthal N, Betts F, Posner A. "Stabilization of amorphous calcium phosphate by Mg and ATP." *Calcif Tis Res* 1977; 23:245–50.

65. Cohen L, Kitzes R. "Infrared spectroscopy and magnesium content of bone mineral in osteoporotic women." *Isr J Med Sci* 1981; 17:1123–25.

66. Stendig-Lindberg G, Tepper R, Leichter I. "Trabecular bone density in a two-year controlled trial of peroral magnesium in osteoporosis." *Magnes Res* 1993; 6:155–63.

67. Abraham G, Grewal H. "A total dietary program emphasizing magnesium instead of calcium. Effect on the mineral density of calcaneous bone in postmenopausal women on hormone therapy." *J Reprod Med* 1990; 35:503–7.

68. Leach R Jr, Meunster A, Wien E. "I. Studies on the role of manganese in bone formation. II. Effect upon chondroitin sulfate synthesis in chick epiphyseal cartilage." *Arch Biochem Biophy* 1969; 133:22–28.

69. Nielsen F. "Boron—an overlooked element of potential nutritional importance." *Nutr Today* 1988. Jan/Feb:4–7.

70. Calhoun N, Smith J Jr, Becker K. "The effects of zinc on ectopic bone formation." *Oral Surg* 1975; 39:698–706.

71. Yamaguchi M, Sakashita T. "Enhancement of vitamin D₃ effect on bone metabolism in weaning rats orally administered zinc sulphate." *Acta Endocrinol* 1986; III:285–88.

72. Follis R Jr et al. "Studies on copper metabolism XVIII. Skeletal changes associated with copper deficiency in swine." *Bull Johns Hopkins Hosp* 1955; 97:405–9.

73. Brattstrom L, Hultbnerg B, Mardebo J. "Folic acid responsive postmenopausal homocysteinemia." *Metab* 1985; 34:1073–77.

74. Barber G, Spaeth G. "Pyridoxine therapy in homocystinuria." *Lancet* 1967; 1:337.

75. Dodds R et al. "Abnormalities in fracture healing induced by vitamin B₆-deficiency in rats." *Bone* 1986; 7:489–95.

76. Silberberg R, Levy B. "Skeletal growth in pyridoxine deficient mice." *Proc Soc Exp Biol Med* 1948; 67:259–63.

77. Benke P, Fleshood H, Pitot H. "Osteoporotic bone disease in the pyridoxine-deficient rat." *Biochem Med* 1972; 6:526–35.

78. Hyams D, Ross E. "Scurvy, megaloblastic anaemia and osteoporosis." *Br J Clin Pract* 1963; 17:334–40.

79. Erdman J, Stillman R, Lee K, Potter S. "Short-term effects of soybean isoflavones on bone in postmenopausal women." Program and Abstract Book, *Second International Symposium on the Role of Soy in Preventing and Treating Chronic Disease.* Brussels, Belgium, 1996.

80. Gennari C et al. "Effect of chronic treatment with ipriflavone in postmenopausal women with low bone mass." *Calcif Tissue Int* 1997; 61: 519–22.

81. Firooznia H, Golimbi C, Rafii M, Schwartz M. "Rate of spinal trabecular bone loss in normal perimenopausal women: ct measurement." *Radiol* 1986; 161:735–38.

82. Riggs B, Wahner H, Melton L et al. "Rates of bone loss in the appendicular and axial skeleton of women: evidence of substantial vertebral bone loss before menopause." *J Clin Invest* 1986; 77:1487–91.

83. Krohner B, Nielson S. "Bone mineral content of the lumbar spine in normal and osteoporotic women: cross-sectional and longitudinal studies." *Clin Sci* 1982; 62:329–36.

84. Marcus R, Kosek J, Plefferbaum A, Homing S. "Age-related loss of trabecular bone in premenopausal women: a biopsy study." *Calc Tiss Int* 1983; 35:406–9.

85. Baran D, Sorensen A, Grimes J et al. "Dietary modification with dairy products for preventing vertebra bone loss in premenopausal women: a three-year prospective study." *J Clin Endocr Metab* 1990; 70:264–70.

86. Prior J, Vigna Y, Schechter M, Burgess A. "Spinal bone loss and ovulatory disturbances." *N Engl J Med* 1990; 323:1221–27.

87. Prior J. "Progesterone as a bone-trophic hormone." *Endocr Rev* 1990; 11(2):386–98.

88. Adachi J, Anderson C, Murray T, Prior J. "Effect of progestins on bone." *J Soc Obstet Gynecol of Can* 1991; 13:7.

89. Prior J. "Trabecular bone loss is associated with abnormal luteal phase length: endogenous progesterone deficiency may be a risk factor for osteoporosis." *Int Proc J* 1989; 1:70–73.

90. Prior J, Vigna Y, Lentle B et al. "Cyclic progestin and calcium increase spinal bone density in women athletes with menstrual cycle disturbances." *Endocrinol Soc Abst* 1991; 73:450.

91. Prior J, Yvette V, Alojado N. "Progesterone and the prevention of osteoporosis." *Can J Ob/Gyn Women's Health Care* 1991; 3(4):178–84.

92. Lee J. "Osteoporosis reversal: the role of progesterone." *Int Clin Nutr Rev* 1990; 10(3):384–91.

93. Scientific Advisory Board, Osteoporosis Society of Canada. "Clinical practice guidelines for the diagnosis and management of osteoporosis." *Can Med Assoc J* 1996; 155(8):1113–33.

94. Writing group for the PEPI Trial. "Effects of hormone therapy on bone mineral density. Results from the PEPI Trial." *JAMA* 1996; 276(17):1389–96.

95. Souza M, Prestwood K et al. "A comparison of the effect of synthetic and micronized hormone replacement therapy on bone mineral density and biochemical markers of bone metabolism." *Menopause: The J North Amer Meno Soc* 1996; 3(3):140–48.

96. Ettinger B, Genent H, Steiger P, Madvig P. "Low-dosage micronized 17-beta estradiol prevents bone loss in postmenopausal women." *Am J Obstet Gynecol* 1992; 166:479–88.

97. Minaguchi H, Usmura T, Shirasu K et al. "Effect of estriol on bone loss in postmenopausal Japanese women: a multicenter prospective open study." *J Obstet Gyn Res* 1996; 22:259–65.

98. Nozaki M, Hashimoto K, Inoue Y et al. "Usefulness of estriol for the treatment of bone loss in postmenopausal women." *Nippon Sanka Fujinka Gakkai Zasshi* 1996; 48:83–88.

99. Nishibe A, Morimoto S, Hirota K et al. "Effect of estriol and bone mineral density of lumbar vertebrae in elderly and postmenopausal women." *Nippon Ronen Igakkai Zasshi* 1996; 33:353–59.

100. Lindsay R, Hart D, Maclean A et al. "Bone loss during oestriol therapy in postmenopausal women." *Maturitas* 1979; 1:279–85.

101. Heaney R. "Bone mass, nutrition, and other lifestyle factors." *Nutr Rev* 1996; 54:53.

102. Bassey E. "Exercise in primary prevention of osteoporosis in women." *Ann Rheum Dis* 1995; 54:861.

103. "American College of Sports Medicine: ACSM position stand on osteoporosis and exercise." *Med Sci Sports Exerc* 1995; 27:i–vii.

104. Suominen H. "Bone mineral density and long-term exercise: an overview of cross-sectional athlete studies." *Sports Med* 1993; 16:316.

105. Chow R, Harrison J, Notarius C. "Effect of two randomised exercise programmes on bone mass in healthy postmenopausal women." *Br Med J* 1987; 295:1441.

106. Pruitt L, Taaffe D, Marcus D. "Effects of a one-year high-intensity versus low-intensity resistance training program on bone mineral density in older women." *J Bone Miner Res* 1995; 10:1788.

107. Dook J et al. "Exercise and bone mineral density in mature female athletes." *Med Sci Sports Exerc* 1997; 29:291.

108. Cassel C, Benedict M, Specker B. "Bone mineral density in elite 7 to 9 yr-old female gymnasts and swimmers." *Med Sci Sports Exerc* 1996; 28:1243.

109. Dyson K et al. "Gymnastic training and bone density in pre-adolescent females." *Med Sci Sports Exerc* 1997; 29:443.

110. McCartney N et al. "Long-term resistance training in the elderly: effects on dynamic strength, exercise capacity, muscle, and bone." *J Gerontol* 1995; 50A:B97.

111. Rockwell J et al. "Weight training decreases vertebral bone density in premenopausal women: a prospective study." *J Clin Endocrinol Metab* 1990; 71:988.

112. Gunnes M, Lehmann E. "Physical activity and dietary constituents as predictors of forearm cortical and trabecular bone pain in healthy children and adolescents: a prospective study." *Acta Paediata* 1996; 85:19.

113. Hirota T et al. "Effect of diet and lifestyle on bone mass in Asian young women." *Am J Clin Nutr* 1992; 55:1168.

114. Recker R et al. "Bone gain in young adult women." *JAMA* 1992; 268:2403.

115. Prince R et al. "The effects of calcium supplementation (milk powder or tablets) and exercise on bone density in postmenopausal women." *J Bone Miner Res* 1995; 10:1068.

116. Grove K, Londeree B. "Bone density in postmenopausal women: high impact vs low impact exercise." *Med Sci Sports Exerc* 1992; 24:1190.

117. Bloomfield S et al. "Non-weightbearing exercise may increase lumbar spine bone mineral density in healthy postmenopausal women." *Am J Phys Med Rehab* 1993; 72:204.

118. Suleiman S et al. "Effect of calcium intake and physical activity on bone mass and turnover in healthy, white, postmenopausal women." *Am J Clin Nutr* 1997; 66:937.

119. Campbell A et al. "Randomised controlled trial of a general practice programme on home based exercise to prevent falls in elderly women." *Br Med J* 1997; 315:1065.

120. Bouxsein M, Marcus R. "Overview of exercise and bone mass." *Rheum Dis Clinics North Am: Osteoporosis* 1994. Aug; 20(3):787–802.

121. Erickson S, Sevier T, Christie D. "Osteoporosis in active women." *Phys Sports Med* 1997; 25:61.

122. Johnson T. "Age-related differences in isometric and dynamic strength and endurance." *Phys Ther* 1982; 62:985.

123. Rutherford O, Jones D. "The relationship of muscle and bone loss and activity levels with age in women." *Age and Aging* 1992; 21:286.

124. Lane N et al. "Long-distance running, bone density, and osteoarthritis." *JAMA* 1986; 255:1147.

125. Cooper C et al. "Childhood growth, physical activity, and peak bone mass in women." *J Bone Miner Res* 1995; 10:940.

126. Jaglal S, Kreiger N, Carlington G. "Post and recent physical activity and risk of hip fractures." *Am J Epid* 1993; 138:107.

127. Vuori I. "Peak bone mass and physical activity: a short review." *Nutr Rev* 1996; 54:S11.

128. Larkin M. "Bone up!" *Health* 1986; 33–36.

129. Schneider D, Barrett-Connor E, Morton D. "Timing of postmenopausal estrogen for optimal bone mineral density." *JAMA,* 1997; 277(7):543–47.

130. Witt D, Lousberg T. "Controversies surrounding estrogen use in postmenopausal women." *Ann Pharmacother* 1997; 31:745–55.

131. Grady D, Rubin S, Petitti D et al. "Hormone therapy to prevent disease and prolong life in postmenopausal women." *Ann Int Med* 1992; 117:1016–37.

132. Colditz G. "Relationship between estrogen levels, use of hormone replacement therapy, and breast cancer." *J Natl Canc Inst* 1998; 90:814–23.

133. Liberman U, Weiss S, Broll J et al. "Effect of oral alendronate on bone mineral density and the incidence of fractures in postmenopausal osteoporosis." *N Engl J Med* 1995; 333:1437–43.

134. Black D, Cummings S, Karpf D et al. "Randomised trial of effect of alendronate on risk of fracture in women with existing vertebral fractures: Fracture Intervention Trial Research Group." *Lancet* 1996; 348:1535–41.

135. Licata A. "Bisphosphonate therapy." *Am J Med Sci* 1997; 313(1):17–22.

136. Kasperk C, Fitzsimmons R, Strong D et al. "Studies of the mechanism by which androgens enhance mitogenesis and differentiation in bone cells." *J Clin Endocrinol Metab* 1990; 71:1322–29.

137. Geusens P, Dequeker J, Verstraten A et al. "Bone mineral content, cortical thickness and fracture rate in osteoporotic women after withdrawal of treatment with nandrolone deconoate, 1-alpha hydroxyvitamin D_3, or intermittent calcium infusions." *Maturitas* 1986; 8: 281–89.

138. Haffner S, Valdez R. "Endogenous sex hormones; impact on lipids, lipoprotein and steroid levels in postmenopausal women." *Acta Endrocinol* 1986; 11:419–23.

139. Savvas M et al. "Increase in bone mass after one year of precutaneous oestradiol and testosterone implants in postmenopausal women who have previously received long-term oral oestrogens." *Br J Obstet Gynaecol* 1992. Sept; 99(9):757–60.

140. Reginster J. "Calcitonin for prevention and treatment of osteoporosis." *Am J Med* 1993; 95 (Suppl 5A): 5A-44S–5A-47S.

141. Rico H, Revilla M, Hernandez E et al. "Total and regional bone mineral content and fracture rate in postmenopausal osteoporosis treated with salmon calcitonin: a prospective study." *Calcif Tis Int* 1995; 56: 181–85.

142. Overgaard K, Hansen M, Jensen S, Christiansen C. "Effect of calcitonin given intranasally on bone mass and fracture rates in established osteoporosis: a dose-response study." *Br Med J* 1992; 305:556–61.

143. Mitlak B, Cohen F. "In search of optimal long-term female hormone replacement: the potential of selective estrogen receptor modulators." *Horm Res* 1997; 48:155–63.

144. Draper M, Flowers D et al. "A controlled trial of raloxifene (LY139481) HCl: impact on bone turnover and serum lipid profile in healthy postmenopausal women." *J Bone Miner Res* 1996; 11:835–42.

145. Delmas P, Bjarnason N, Mitlak B et al. "Effects of raloxifene on bone mineral density, serum cholesterol concentrations, and uterine endometrium in postmenopausal women." *N Engl J Med* 1997; 337:1641–47.

146. Gregg E, Kriska A, Salamone L et al. "The epidemiology of quantitative ultrasound: a review of the relationships with bone mass, osteoporosis and fracture risk." *Osteoporosis Int* 1997; 7:89–99.

147. Hans D, Fuerst T, Duboeuf F. "Quantitative ultrasound bone measurement." *Eur Radiol* 1997; 7(Suppl 2): S43–S50.

Chapter 13: Pelvic Inflammatory Disease

1. Bauer R, Wagner H. "Echinacea species as potential immunostimulatory drugs." *Econ Med Plant Res* 1991; 5:253–321.

2. Centers for Disease Control. "Sexually transmitted diseases treatment guidelines." *MMWR* 1993; 42(RR-14): 75–81.

3. McGregor J et al. "Randomized comparison of ampicillin-sulbactam to cefoxitin and doxycycline or clindamycin and gentamicin in the treatment of pelvic inflammatory disease or endometritis." *Obstet Gynecol* 1994; 83:998–1004.

Resources:

Howes D, Marazzo J, Scott C. "Recognizing and treating PID." *A Medical Education Supplement to Patient Care.* 1994, March.

McGregor J, Hillier S, Brooker D. *New Paradigms in Women's Health: STD, PID, HIV.* U of Colorado School of Medicine, 1996.

Chapter 14: Pregnancy

1. Tulchinsky D. "Plasma human chorionic gonadotropin, estrone, estradiol, estriol, progesterone and 17-hydroxy progesterone in human pregnancies." *Am J Obstet Gynecol* 1973; 117:884.

2. Balaskas J. *Preparing for Birth with Yoga.* Mass.: Element, Inc.; 1994:37.

3. Barnes B, Bradley S. *Planning for a Healthy Baby.* London: Ebury Press; 1990.

4. Price, W. *Nutrition and Physical Degeneration.* 50th Anniv. ed. New Canaan, Conn.: Keats Publishing, Inc., 1989.

5. Strohecker J. (exec. ed.). *Alternative Medicine: The Definitive Guide.* Wash.: Future Medicine Publishing, Inc., 1994:795.

6. Dostálová L. "Correlation of the vitamin status between mother and newborn during delivery." *Dev Pharmacol Ther* 1982; 4(Suppl):45–57.

7. Mulinare J et al. "Periconceptional use of multivitamins and the occurrence of neural tube defects." *JAMA* 1988; 260(21):3141–45.

8. Truswell A. "ABC of nutrition. Nutrition for pregnancy." *Br Med J* 1985; 291:263–66.

9. Shojania A. "Folic acid and vitamin B_{12} deficiency in pregnancy and in the neonatal period." *Clin Perinatol* 1984:11:433–59.

10. Miller A, Kelly G. "Methionine and homocysteine metabolism and the nutritional prevention of certain birth defects and complications of pregnancy." *Alt Med Rev* 1996:1(4):220–35.

11. Ferris T. "Pregnancy, preeclampsia, and the endothelial cell. Edit. *N Engl J Med* 1991. 325(20):1439–40.

12. Villar J et al. "Epidemiologic observations on the relationship between calcium intake and eclampsia." *Int J Gynaecol Obstet* 1983; 21(4):271–78.

13. Taufield P et al. "Hypocalciuria in preeclampsia." *N Engl J Med* 1987; 316(12):715–18.

14. Villar J, Repke J. "Calcium supplementation during pregnancy may reduce preterm delivery in high-risk populations." *Am J Obstet Gynecol* 1990; 163:1124–31.

15. Ward N et al. "Elemental factors in human fetal development." *J Nutr Med* 1990; 1:19–26.

16. Spatling L, Spatling G. "Magnesium supplementation in pregnancy. A double blind study." *Br J Obstet Gynaecol* 1988; 95:120–25.

17. U.S. Department of Health and Human Services. "The health benefits of smoking cessation: a report of the Surgeon General." U.S. Department of Health and Human Services publication no.(CDC)90-8416. 1990: 371–423.

18. Haworth J, Ellestad-Sayed J, King J, Dilling L. "Fetal growth retardation in cigarette-smoking mothers is not due to decreased maternal food intake." *Am J Obstet Gynecol* 1980; 137:719–23.

19. Naeye R. "Abruptio placentae and placenta previa: frequency, perinatal mortality, and cigarette smoking." *Obstet Gynecol* 1980; 10:345–58.

20. Kramer M. "Intrauterine growth and gestational duration determinants." *Pediat* 1987; 80:502–11.

21. Kleinman J. "Maternal weight gain during pregnancy: determinants and consequences." NCHS Working Paper Series No 33. Hyattsville, Md.: National Center for Health Statistics, Public Health Service, U.S. Department of Health and Human Services, 1990.

22. Brown J. "Weight gain during pregnancy: what is optimal?" *Clin Nutr* 1988; 7:181–90.

23. National Center for Health Statistics. "Maternal weight gain and the outcome of pregnancy, U.S., 1980. An analysis of maternal weight gain during pregnancy by demographic characteristics of mothers and its association with birth weight and the risk of fetal death." DHHS publication no. (PHS)86-1922. Hyattsville, Md.:U.S. Department of Health and Human Services, 1986.

24. Eisenberg A, Murkoff H, Hathaway S. *What to Eat When You're Expecting*. New York: Workman Pub., 1986.

25. MRC Vitamin Study Research Group. "Prevention of neural tube defects: Results of the Medical Research Council Vitamin Study." *Lancet* 1991; 338:131–37.

26. Tamura T, Goldenberg R, Freeberg L et al. "Maternal serum folate and zinc concentrations and their relationships to pregnancy outcome." *Am J Clin Nutr* 1992:56:365–70.

27. Steegers-Theunissen R et al. "Neural-tube defects and derangement of homocysteine metabolism." Letter. *N Engl J Med* 1991; 324(3):199–200.

28. Bower D, Stanley F. "Dietary folate as a risk factor for neural-tube defects: Evidence from a case-control study in Western Australia." *Med J Aust* 1989; 150:613–19.

29. Mulinsky A et al. "Multivitamin/folic acid supplementation in early pregnancy reduces the prevalence of neural tube defects." *JAMA* 1989; 262(20): 2847–52.

30. Laurence K et al. "Double-blind randomized controlled trial of folate treatment before conception to prevent recurrence of neural-tube defects." *Br Med J* 1981; 282:1509.

31. Lucock M, Wild J, Schorah C et al. "The methylfolate axis in neural tube defects: in vitro characterisation and clinical investigation." *Biochem Med Metabol Biol* 1994; 52:101–14.

32. Jackson M, Teague T. *The Handbook of Alternatives to Chemical Medicine*. Oakland, Calif.: Lawton-Teague Pub.; 1975.

33. Weed S. *Wise Woman Herbal for the Childbearing Years*. Woodstock, N.Y.: Ashtree Publishing, 1986.

34. Simmer K, James C, Thompson R. "Are iron-folate supplements harmful?" *Am J Clin Nutr* 1987. Jan; 45(1): 122–25.

35. Editorial staff. "Excessive folic acid." *Amer Fam Phys* 1985. Oct; 32(4):290–91.

36. Doyle W et al. "The association between maternal diet and birth dimensions." *J Nutr Med* 1990; 1:9–17.

37. Heller S et al. "Riboflavin status during pregnancy." *Am J Clin Nutr* 1974; 27:1225–30.

38. Heller S et al. "Vitamin B_1 status in pregnancy." *Am J Clin Nutr* 1974; 27:1221–24.

39. Heller S et al. "Vitamin B_6 status in pregnancy." *Am J Clin Nutr* 1973; 26(12):1339–48.

40. Sahakian V et al. "Vitamin B_6 is effective therapy for nausea and vomiting of pregnancy. A randomized double-blind placebo-controlled study." *Obstet Gynecol* 1991; 78:33–36.

41. Anonymous. "Vitamin B_6 curbs severe nausea, emesis in gravida." *Fam Pract News* 1991; 21(11):10.

42. Baum G et al. "Meclozine and pyridoxine in pregnancy." *Practitioner* 1963; 190:251.

43. Marcus R. "Suppression of lactation with high doses of pyridoxine." *S Afr Med J* 1976. Dec 6:2155–56.

44. Foukas M. "An antilactogenic effect of pyridoxine." *J Obstet Gynaecol Br Commonw* 1973. Aug:718–20.

45. Temesvari P et al. "Effects of an antenatal load of pyridoxine (vitamin B_6) on the blood oxygen affinity and prolactin levels in newborn infants and their mothers." *Acta Paediatrica Scand* 1983; 72(4):525–29.

46. Klieger J et al. "Abnormal pyridoxine metabolism in toxemia of pregnancy." *Ann NY Acad Sci* 1969; 166:288–96.

47. Kirby P, Molloy A, Daly L et al. "Maternal plasma folate and vitamin B_{12} are independent risk factors for neural tube defects." *Q J Med* 1993; 86:703–8.

48. Dong A, Scott S. "Serum vitamin B_{12} and blood cell valves in vegetarians." *Ann Nutr Metab* 1982; 26:209.

49. Teratology Society. "Recommendations for vitamin A use during pregnancy." *Teratology* 1987; 35:269–75.

50. "Use of supplements containing high-dose vitamin A—New York State, 1983–1984." *MMWR Morb Mortal Wkly Rep* 1987; 36:80–82.

51. "Vitamin A policy." *Council for Responsible Nutrition News.* March 1987:1–2.
52. Martinez-Frias M, Salvador J. "Megadose vitamin A and teratogenicity." Letter. *Lancet* 1988; 1:236.
53. Rothman K, Moore L, Singer M et al. "Teratogenicity of high vitamin A intake." *N Engl J Med* 1995; 333:1369–73.
54. Kubler W. "Nutritional deficiencies in pregnancy." *Bibl Nutr Dieta* 1981; 30:17–29.
55. Hustead V et al. "Relationship of vitamin A (retinol) status to lung disease in the preterm infant." *J Pediat* 1984; 105(4):610–15.
56. Jendryczko A, Drozdz M. "Plasma retinol, beta-carotene and vitamin E levels in relation to the future risk of preeclampsia." *Zent bl Gynakol* 1989; 111:1121–23.
57. Czeizel A, Dudas I. "Prevention of the first occurrence of neural-tube defects by periconceptional vitamin supplementation." *N Engl J Med* 1992; 327:1832–35.
58. Kizer K, Fan A, Bankowska J et al. "Vitamin A—a pregnancy hazard alert." *West J Med* 1990; 152:78–81.
59. Lark S. *Women's Health Companion.* Berkeley, Calif.: Celestial Arts, 1995.
60. Rhead W, Schrauzer G. "Risks of long-term ascorbic acid overdosage." *Nutr Rev* 1971; 29(11):262–63.
61. Hammar M et al. "Calcium and magnesium status in pregnant women: a comparison between treatment with calcium and vitamin C in pregnant women with leg cramps." *Int J Vit Nutr Res* 1987; 57(2):179–83.
62. Mino M, Nagamatu M. "An evaluation of nutritional status of vitamin E in pregnant women with respect to red blood cell tocopherol level." *Int J Vit Nutr Res* 1986; 56:149–53.
63. Shah R et al. "Vitamin E status of the newborn in relation to gestational age, birth weight, and maternal vitamin E status." *Br J Nutr* 1987; 58:191–98.
64. Marks J. "Critical appraisal of the therapeutic value of alpha-tocopherol." *Vit Horm* 1962; 20:573–98.
65. Golding J et al. "Childhood cancer, intramuscular vitamin K, and pethidine given during labour." *Br Med J* 1992. Aug; 305(6849):341–46.
66. Morales W et al. "The use of antenatal vitamin K in the prevention of early neonatal intraventricular hemorrhage." *Am J Obstet Gynecol* 1988; 159:774–79.
67. National Research Council. "Recommended dietary allowances." 10th ed. Washington, D.C.: National Academy Press, 1989.
68. Ritchie L, Fung E, Halloran B et al. "A longitudinal study of calcium homeostasis during human pregnancy and lactation and after the resumption of menses." *Am J Clin Nutr* 1998; 67:693–701.
69. Laskey M, Prentice A, Hanratty L et al. "Bone changes after 3 months of lactation: influence of calcium intake, breast-milk output, and vitamin D-receptor genotype." *Am J Clin Nutr* 1998; 67:685–92.
70. Institute of Medicine. "Dietary reference intakes. Calcium, phosphorus, magnesium, vitamin D, and fluoride." Washington, D.C.: National Academy Press, 1998.
71. Chan G, McMurry M et al. "Effects of increased dietary calcium intake upon the calcium and bone mineral status of lactating adolescent women." *Am J Clin Nutr* 1987; 46:319–23.
72. Butcher H, Guyana G, Cook R et al. "Effect of calcium supplementation on pregnancy-induced hypertension and preeclampsia: a meta-analysis of randomized controlled trials." *JAMA* 1996; 275:1113–17.
73. Ward N et al. "Elemental factors in human fetal development." *J Nutr Med* 1990; 1:19–26.
74. Hemminkl E, Rimpelä U. "A randomized comparison of routine versus selective iron supplementation during pregnancy." *J Am Coll Nutr* 1991; 10(1):3–10.
75. Gabbe S, Niebyl J, Simpson J, eds. *Obstetrics—Normal and Problem Pregnancies*, 3d ed. New York: Churchill Livingston, 1996.
76. Franz K. "Correlation of urinary magnesium excretion with blood pressure of pregnancy." *Magnes Bull* 1982; 4:73–78.
77. Weaver K. *Magnesium in Health and Disease.* Jamaica, N.Y.: Spectrum Publications; 1980:833.
78. Kurzel R. "Serum magnesium levels in pregnancy and preterm labor." *Am J Perinatol* 1991; 8:119–27.
79. Conradt A. "Pathophysiology and clinical aspects of pre-eclampsia." *Z Geburtshilfe Perinatol* 1985; 189(4):149–61.
80. Argemi J et al. "Serum zinc binding capacity in pregnant women." *Ann Nutr Metab* 1988; 32:121–26.
81. Apgar J, Evertt G. "Low zinc intake affects maintenance of pregnancy in guinea pigs." *J Nutr* 1991; 121:192–200.
82. Lazebnik N et al. "Zinc status, pregnancy complications and labor abnormalities." *Am J Obstet Gynecol* 1988; 158(1):161–66.
83. Mukherjee M et al. "Maternal zinc, iron, folic acid, and protein nutriture and outcome of human pregnancy." *Am J Clin Nutr* 1984; 40(3):496–507.
84. Buamah P et al. "Maternal zinc status: A determinant of central nervous system malformation." *Br J Obstet Gynaecol* 1984; 91:788–90.
85. Bergmann K et al. "Abnormalities of hair zinc concentration in mothers of newborn infants with spina bifida." *Am J Clin Nutr* 1980; 33:2145.
86. Malhotra A et al. "Placental zinc in normal and intrauterine growth-retarded pregnancies." *Br J Nutr* 1990; 63:613–21.
87. Higashi A et al. "A prospective survey of serial serum zinc levels and pregnancy outcome." *J Ped Gastroenterol* 1988; 7:430–33.
88. Singh P et al. "Maternal hypozincemia and low-birth-weight infants." *Clin Chem* 1987; 33:1950.
89. Cherry F et al. "Plasma zinc in hypertension/toxemia and other reproductive variables in adolescent pregnancy." *Am J Clin Nutr* 1981. Nov; 34(11):2367–75.
90. Cherry F et al. "Adolescent pregnancy: Associations among body weight, zinc nutriture, and pregnancy outcome." *Am J Clin Nutr* 1989; 50:945–54.
91. Kynast G, Saling E. "Effect of oral zinc application during pregnancy." *Gynecol Obstet Invest* 1986; 21(3):117–22.
92. Hunt I et al. "Zinc supplementation during pregnancy: effects on selected blood constituents and on progress and outcome of pregnancy in low-income women of Mexican descent." *Am J Clin Nutr* 1984; 40(3):508–21.

93. Redman J. Letter. *Med Trib,* April 16, 1980.

94. O'Brien P et al. "The effect of dietary supplementation with linoleic acid and linolenic acid on the pressor response to angiotension II: a possible role in pregnancy-induced hypertension?" *Br J Clin Pharmacol* 1985; 19(3):335–42.

95. Noia G, Lippa S, Di Maio A et al. "Blood levels of coenzyme Q10 in early phase of normal or complicated pregnancies." In Folkers K, Yamamura Y. *Biomedical and Clinical Aspects of Coenzyme Q.* Amsterdam: Elsevier, 1991:209–13.

96. Essien F, Wannberg S. "Methionine but not folinic acid or vitamin B_{12} alters the frequency of neural tube defects in Axd mutant mice." *J Nutr* 1993; 123: 973–74.

97. Potier de Courey G, Bujoli J. "Effects of diets with or without folic acid, with or without methionine, on fetus development, folate stores, and folic acid-dependent enzyme activities in the rat." *Biol Neonate* 1981; 39:132–40.

98. Zeisel S. "Choline and human nutrition." *Ann Rev Nutr* 1994; 14:269–96.

99. Zeisel S, Epstein M, Wurtman R. "Elevated choline concentration in neonatal plasma." *Life Sci* 1980; 26:1827–31.

100. Garner S, Mar M, Zeisel S. "Choline distribution and metabolism in pregnant rats and fetuses are influenced by the choline content of the maternal diet." *J Nutr* 1995; 125:2851–58.

101. Sturman J. "Nutritional taurine and central nervous system development." *Ann NY Acad Sci* 1986; 477:196–213.

102. Gladstar R. *Herbal Healing for Women.* New York: Simon and Schuster, 1993:176.

103. Fischer-Rasmussen W et al. "Ginger treatment of hyperemesis gravidarum." *Eur J Obstet Gynecol Reprod Biol* 1990; 38:19–24.

104. Sternfeld B. "Physical activity and pregnancy outcome: review and recommendations." *Sports Med* 1997; 23:33.

105. Clapp J, Dickstein S. "Endurance exercise and pregnancy outcome." *Med Sci Sports Exerc* 1984; 16:556.

106. *American College of Obstetricians and Gynecologists.* "Exercise during pregnancy and the postnatal period." Washington, D.C.:ACOG, 1985.

107. Zeanah M, Schlosser S. "Adherence to ACOG guidelines on exercise during pregnancy: effect on pregnancy outcome." *JOGNN* 1993; 22:329.

108. Hatch M et al. "Maternal exercise during pregnancy, physical fitness, and fetal growth." *Am J Epid* 1993; 137:1105.

109. Rosato F. *Fitness and Wellness: The Physical Connection,* 2d ed. West Publishing Co., 1990:157.

110. "ACOG issues recommendations on exercise during pregnancy and the postpartum period." *Amer Fam Phys* 1994; 49:1258.

111. Lindblom L. "Exercise during pregnancy." *Your Patient & Fitness* 1995; 9:28e.

112. Clapp J. "Pregnancy outcome: physical activities inside versus outside the workplace." *Sem Perinat* 1996; 20:70.

113. Dye T, Oldenettel D. "Physical activity and the risk of preterm labor: an epidemiological review and synthesis of recent literature." *Sem Perinat* 1996; 20:334.

114. Bung P, Artal R. "Gestational diabetes and exercise: a survey." *Sem Perinat* 1996; 20:328.

115. Katz V. "Water exercise in pregnancy." *Sem Perinat* 1996; 20:285.

116. Carlberg K, Alvin B, Gwosdow A. "Exercise during pregnancy and maternal and fetal plasma corticosterone and androstenedione in rats." *Am J Physiol* 1996; 271:E896.

117. Bell A et al. "Fetal and maternal endocrine responses to exercise in the pregnant ewe." *J Dev Physiol* 1983; 5:129.

118. Garris D et al. "Effects of exercise on fetal-placental growth and uteroplacental blood flow in the rat." *Biol Neon* 1985; 47:223.

119. McDonald A et al. "Fetal death and work in pregnancy." *Br J Ind Med* 1988; 45:148.

120. Ahlborg G. "Physical work load and pregnancy outcome." *J Occ Environ Med* 1995; 37:941.

121. Spinollo A et al. "The effect of work activity in pregnancy on the risk of severe preeclampsia." *Aust NZ J Obstet Gynaecol* 1995; 35:380.

122. Magann E, Evans S, Newnham J. "Employment, exertion, and pregnancy outcome: assessment by kilocalories expended each day." *Am J Obstet Gynecol* 1996; 175:182.

123. Schramm W, Stockbauer J, Hoffman J. "Exercise, employment, other daily activities, and adverse pregnancy outcomes." *Am J Epid* 1996; 143:211.

124. Cohen L, Keewhan C, Wang C-X. "Influence of dietary fat, caloric restriction and voluntary exercise on N-Nitrosomethylurea (NMU)-induced mammary tumorigenesis in rats." *Canc Res* 1988; 48:4276.

125. Cohen L et al. "Inhibition of rat mammary tumorigenesis by voluntary exercise." *In Vivo* 1993; 7:151.

126. Thompson H et al. "Effects of exercise on the induction of mammary carcinogenesis." *Canc Res* 1988; 48:2720.

127. Hall D, Kaufmann D. "Effects of aerobic and strength conditioning on pregnancy outcomes." *Am J Obstet Gynecol* 1987; 157:1199.

128. Clapp J. "The course of labor after endurance exercise during pregnancy." *Am J Obstet Gynecol* 1990; 163:1799.

129. Bell R, Palma S, Lumley J. "The effect of vigorous exercise during pregnancy on birthweight." *Aust NZ J Obstet Gynaecol* 1995; 35:46.

130. Webb K, Wolfe L, McGrath M. "Effects of acute and chronic maternal exercise on fetal heart rate." *J Appl Physiol* 1994; 77:2207.

131. Pivarnik J et al. "Effects of chronic exercise on blood volume expansion and hematologic indices during pregnancy." *Obstet Gynecol* 1994; 83:265.

132. Clapp J. "Morphometric and neurodevelopmental outcome at age five years of the offspring of women who continued to exercise regularly throughout pregnancy." *J Pediatr* 1996; 129:856.

133. Spinnewijn W et al. "Fetal heart rate and uterine contractility during maternal exercise at term." *Am J Obstet Gynecol* 1996; 174:43.

134. Sternfeld B et al. "Exercise during pregnancy and pregnancy outcome." *Med Sci Sports Exerc* 1995; 27:634.

135. Horns P et al. "Pregnancy outcomes among active and sedentary primiparous women." *J Obstet Gynecol Neonatal Nurs* 1996; 25:49.

136. Ohtake P, Wolfe L. "Physical conditioning attenuates respiratory responses to steady-state exercise in late gestation." *Med Sci Sports Exerc* 1998; 30:17.

137. Clapp J, Little K. "Effect of recreational exercise on pregnancy weight gain and subcutaneous fat deposition." *Med Sci Sports Exerc* 1995; 27:170.

138. McMurray R et al. "Metabolic and hormonal responses to low-impact aerobic dance during pregnancy." *Med Sci Sports Exerc* 1996; 28:41.

139. Avery M, Leon A, Kopher R. "Effects of a partially home-based exercise program for women with gestational diabetes." *Obstet Gynecol* 1997; 89:10.

140. "A healthy body means a healthy pregnancy." *Speak* 1993, Dec:28.

141. Araujo D. "Expecting questions about exercise and pregnancy?" *Physic Sportsmed* 1997; 25:85.

142. Gold S, Sherry L. "Hyperactivity, learning disabilities, and alcohol." *J Learn Disabil* 1984; 17(1):3–6.

143. Plant M. "Drinking in pregnancy and foetal harm: results from a Scottish prospective study." *Midwifery* 1986; 2(2):81–85.

144. Earnhart C et al. "Alcohol teratogenicity in the human: a detailed assessment of specificity, critical period, and threshold." *Am J Obstet Gynecol* 1987. Jan; 156(1):33–39.

145. Peacock J et al. "Cigarette smoking and birthweight: type of cigarette smoked and a possible threshold effect." *Int J Epidemiol* 1991; 20(2):405–12.

146. Northrup C. *Women's Bodies, Women's Wisdom.* New York: Bantam, 1994:613.

147. Haglund B et al. "Cigarette smoking as a risk factor for sudden infant death syndrome." *Am J Pub Health* 1990; 80:29–32.

148. Fenster L et al. "Caffeine consumption during pregnancy and fetal growth." *Am J Publ Health* 1991; 81: 458–61.

149. Berger A. "Effects of caffeine consumption on pregnancy outcome. A review." *J Reprod Med* 1988; 33(12): 945–56.

150. Colburn T. *Our Stolen Future.* New York: Penguin Books USA, Inc., 1996.

151. O'Leary L, Hicks A, Peters J, London S. "Parental occupational exposures and risk of childhood cancer: a review." *Am J Indust Med* 1991; 20(1):17–35.

152. Kardaun J et al. "Testicular cancer in young men and parental occupational exposure." *Am J Indust Med* 1991; 20(2):219–27.

153. "Miscarriages prompt study of lead levels at USA Today." *Am Med News* 1989. April 14:61.

154. Dawson E, Kelly R. "Calcium, magnesium, and lead relationships in preeclampsia." Abstract. *Am J Clin Nutr* 1990; 51:512.

155. Editorial staff. "Aspirin-pregnancy link: lowered IQs." *Pregnancy and Childbirth: Brain/Mind Bull Coll* 1991: 13(9K).

156. Editorial staff. "Valium inhibits cell fusion in lab tests." *Pregnancy and Childbirth: Brain/Mind Bull Coll.* 1991: 12(13D).

157. Wegner C, Nau H. "Alteration of embryonic folate metabolism by valproic acid during organogenesis: implications for mechanism of teratogenesis." *Neurol* 1992; 42:S17–S24.

158. Biale Y, Lewenthal H. "Effect of folic acid supplementation on congenital malformations due to anticonvulsive drugs." *Eur J Obstet Gynecol Reprod Biol* 1984; 18:211–16.

159. Balch J, Balch P. *Prescription for Nutritional Healing.* Garden City, N.Y.: Avery Publishing Group, 1997: 442.

160. Strohecker J. *op cit,* 791, noting: Barnes B, Bradley S. *Planning for a Healthy Baby.* London: Ebury Press, 1990.

161. Bracken M et al. "Association of cocaine use with sperm concentration, motility, and morphology." *Fertil Steril* 1990 Feb; 53(2):315–22.

162. Schulick P. *Ginger: Common Spice and Wonder Drug.* Brattleboro, Vt.: Herbal Free Press, Ltd., 1994:43, citing: Fischer-Rasmussen W, Kjaer SK, Dahl C, Asping U. "Ginger treatment of hyperemesis gravidarum." *Eur J Obstet Gyn Reprod Biol* 1991. Jan 4; 38(1):19–24.

163. Carlson K, Eisenstat S, Ziporyn T. *The Harvard Guide to Women's Health.* Cambridge, Mass.: Harvard University Press, 1996.

164. Sibai B. "Hypertension in pregnancy." *Obstet Gynecol Clin North Amer* 1992; 19:615.

Chapter 15: Premenstrual Syndrome

1. Gurevich M. "Rethinking the label: who benefits from the PMS construct?" *Women and Health* 1995; 23(2): 67–98.

2. American College of Obstetrics and Gynecology (ACOG), Committee opinion. *Int J Gyn and Obstet* 1995; 50:80.

3. Mortola J. "Issues in the diagnosis and research of premenstrual syndrome." *Clin Obstet Gynecol* 1992; 35(3): 587–98.

4. DeJong R et al. "Premenstrual mood disorder and psychiatric illness." *Amer J Psych* 1985; 142:1359.

5. Nicolson P. "The menstrual cycle, science and femininity: Assumptions underlying menstrual cycle research." *Soc Sci Med* 1995; 41:77.

6. Chan A et al. "Persistence of premenstrual syndrome during low-dose administration of the progesterone antagonist RU 486." *Obstet Gynecol* 1994; 84(6):1001–5.

7. Rapkin A. "The role of serotonin in premenstrual syndrome." *Clin Obstet Gyn* 1992; 35(3):629–36.

8. Abraham G. "Nutritional factors in the etiology of the premenstrual tension syndromes." *J Reprod Med* 1983; 28:446–64.

9. Goei G, Ralston J, Abraham G. "Dietary patterns of patients with premenstrual tension." *J Appl Nutr* 1982; 34:4.

10. Abraham G. "Magnesium deficiency in premenstrual tension." *Magnes Bull* 1982; 4:68.

11. Jakubowica D. "The significance of prostaglandins in the premenstrual syndrome." In Taylor R, ed. *Premenstrual Syndrome.* London: Medical New-Tribune, 1983:16.

12. Danis R, Newton N, Keith L. "Pregnancy and alcohol." *Curr Prob Obstet Gynecol* 1981; 4:5.

13. Belfer M, Shader R, Carroll M et al. "Alcoholism in women." *Arch Gen Psych* 1971; 25:540.

14. Chuong J, Dawson E. "Critical evaluation of nutritional factors in the pathophysiology and treatment of premenstrual syndrome." *Clin Obstet Gynecol* 1992; 35:3.

15. Chakmakjian Z, Higgins C, Abraham G. "The effect of a nutritional supplement, Optivite for women, on premenstrual tension syndrome: effect of symptomatology, using a double blind crossover design." *J Appl Nutr* 1985; 37:12.

16. Adams P et al. "The effect of pyridoxine hydrochloride (vitamin B_6) upon depression associated with oral contraception." *Lancet* 1973; 1:897–904.

17. Kleijnen J, ter Jtiet G, Knipschild P. "Vitamin B_6 in the treatment of the premenstrual syndrome—a review." *Br J Obstet Gynaec* 1990; 97:847–52.

18. Ebadi M, Govitrapong P. "Pyrodoxal phosphate and neurotransmitters in the brain." In Tryfiates G, ed. *Vitamin B_6 Metabolism and Role in Growth.* Westport, Conn.: Food and Nutrition Press, 1980:223.

19. Taylor D, Mathew R, Bent T et al. "Serotonin levels and platelet uptake during premenstrual tension." *Neuropsychobio* 1984; 12:16.

20. Cohen M, Bendich A. "Safety of pyridoxine: a review of human and animal studies." *Toxicol Letters* 1986; 34:129–39.

21. London R et al. "The effect of alpha-tocopherol on premenstrual symptomatology: a double-blind study. II. Endocrine correlates." *J Am Coll Nutr* 1984; 3:351–56.

22. Puolakka J et al. "Biochemical and clinical effects of treating the premenstrual syndrome with prostaglandin synthesis precursors." *J Rep Med* 1985; 30(3):149–53.

23. Ockerman P et al. "Evening primrose oil as a treatment of the premenstrual syndrome." *Rec Adv Clin Nutr* 1986; 2:404–5.

24. Massil H et al. "A double blind trial of Efamol evening primrose oil in premenstrual syndrome." 2d Internat Symp on PMS, Kiawah Island, Sept. 1987.

25. Casper R. "A double blind trial of evening primrose oil in premenstrual syndrome." 2d Internat Symp on PMS, Kiawah Island, Sept. 1987.

26. Thys-Jacobs et al. "Calcium carbonate and the premenstrual syndrome: effects on premenstrual and menstrual symptoms." *Am J Obstet Gynecol* 1998, Aug: 444–52.

27. Haller J. "Testing the progesterones." *Therapiewoche* 1959; 9:481–84.

28. Haller J. "The influence of plant extracts in the hormonal exchange between hypophysis and ovary. An experimental endocrinological animal study." *Z Geburtsh Gynakol* 1961; 156:274–302.

29. Loch E. "Diagnosis and therapy of hormonal bleeding disturbances." *TW Gynakol* 1989; 2:379–85.

30. Wuttke W. "Cell biological investigations with Agnolyt preparations." HN 246, NH 247 Report 1992; 8:7.

31. Dittmar F. "Das pramenstruelle Spannungssyndrom." *Jiatros Gynakologie* 1989; 5(6):4–7.

32. Tamborini A, Taurelle R. "Value of standardized Ginkgo biloba extract in the management of congestive symptoms of premenstrual syndrome." *Rev Fr Gynecol Obstet* 1993; 88:447–57.

33. Steege J, Blumenthal J. "The effects of aerobic exercise on premenstrual symptoms in middle-aged women: a preliminary study." *J Psychosom Res* 1993; 37:127.

34. Johnson W, Carr-Nangle R, Bergeron K. "Macronutrient intake, eating habits, and exercise as moderators of menstrual distress in healthy women." *Psychosom Med* 1995; 57:324.

35. Prior J et al. "Conditioning exercise decreases premenstrual symptoms: a prospective, controlled 6-month trial." *Fertil Steril* 1987; 47:402.

36. Aganoff J, Boyle G. "Aerobic exercise, mood states and menstrual cycle symptoms." *J Psychosom Res* 1994; 38:183.

37. Choi P, Salmon P. "Stress responsivity in exercisers and non-exercisers during different phases of the menstrual cycle." *Soc Sci Med* 1995; 41:769.

38. Gannon L. "The potential role of exercise in the alleviation of menstrual disorders and menopausal symptoms: a theoretical synthesis of recent research." *Women & Health* 1988; 14:105.

39. Keye W Jr. "Medical treatment of premenstrual syndrome." *Can J Psychiatry* 1985; 30:483–87.

40. Sampson G. "Premenstrual syndrome: a double-blind controlled trial of progesterone and placebo." *Br J Psychiatry* 1979; 135:209.

41. Freeman E, Rickels K, Sonheimer S, Polansky M. "Ineffectiveness of progesterone suppository treatment for premenstrual syndrome." *JAMA* 1990; 264:349–53.

42. Dennerstein L et al. "Progesterone and the premenstrual syndrome: a double blind crossover trial." *Br Med J* 1985; 290:1617–21.

43. Martorano J, Ahlgrimm M, Myers D. "Differentiating between natural progesterone and synthetic progestogens: clinical implications for premenstrual syndrome management." *Compr Ther* 1993; 19(3):96–98.

44. Lee J. *Natural Progesterone: The Multiple Roles of a Remarkable Hormone.* Sebastopol, Calif.: Bll Publishing, 1995:50–52.

45. Havens C. "Premenstrual syndrome." *Post Med* 1995; 77:32.

46. Keye W. "Premenstrual symptoms: evaluation and treatment." *Comp Ther* 1988; 14:19.

47. Muse K. "Hormonal manipulation in the treatment of premenstrual syndrome." *Clin Obstet Gyn* 1992; 35(3):658–66.

48. Cullberg J. "Mood changes and menstrual symptoms with different estrogen combinations." *Acta Psychiatr Scand* (Suppl) 1972; 236:1.

49. Pearlstein T. "Hormones and depression: what are the facts about premenstrual syndrome, menopause, and hormone replacement therapy?" *Am J Obstet Gyn* 1995. Aug; 173(2):646–53.

Chapter Sixteen: Sexually Transmitted Diseases

1. Majeroni B. "Chlamydial cervicitis: complications and new treatment options." *Am Fam Phys* 1994; 49: 1825–29.
2. Rein M. "Vulvovaginitis and cervicitis." In Mandell G, Bennett J, Dolin R, eds. *Mandell, Douglas, and Bennett's Principles and Practice of Infectious Diseases*, 4th ed. New York: Churchill Livingstone, 1995; 1074–90.
3. Washington A et al. "Oral contraceptives, Chlamydia trachomatis infection, and pelvic inflammatory disease: a word of caution." *JAMA* 1985; 253:2246.
4. Bauer R, Wagner H. "Echinacea species as potential immunostimulatory drugs." *Econ Med Plant Res* 1991; 5:253–321.
5. Loginov A, Nilova T et al. "Pharmacokinetics of lipoic acid preparations and their effects on ATP synthesis, processes of microsomal and cytosole oxidation in human hepatocytes during liver damage." *Farmacol Toksikol* 1989; 52:78–82.
6. Berkson B. "Alpha-lipoic acid (thioctic acid): my experience with this outstanding therapeutic agent." *J Orthomolec Med* 1998; 13(1):1–5.
7. Murata A. "Viricidal activity of vitamin C: vitamin C for prevention and treatment of viral diseases." *Proc First Intersectional Cong Int Assoc Microbiol Soc* 1975; 3:432–42.
8. Thyagarajan S, Subramian S, Thirunalasundari T et al. "Effects of Phyllanthus amarus on chronic carriers of hepatitis B virus." *Lancet* 1988; 2(8614):764–66.
9. Meixa W, Cheng H, Li Y et al. "Herbs of the genus Phyllanthus in the treatment of chronic hepatitis B: observations with three preparations from different geographical sites." *J Lab Clin Med* 1995; 126:350–52.
10. Shiki Y et al. "Effect of glycyrrhizin on lysis of hepatocyte membranes induced by anti-liver cell membrane antibody." *J Gastroent Hepat* 1992; 1:12–16.
11. Hikino H, Kiso Y. "Natural products for liver diseases." In Wagner H, Hikino H, Farnsworth N, eds. *Economic and Medicinal Plant Research*. Vol 2. New York: Academic Press, 1988:44.
12. Mittal A, Kapur S, Garg S et al. "Clinical trial with Praneem polyherbal cream in patients with abnormal vaginal discharge due to microbial infections." *Austr NZ J Obstet Gyn* 1995; 35:190–1.
13. Misoguchi Y, Kawada N, Ichikawa Y, Tsutsui H. "Effect of Gomisin-A in the prevention of acute hepatic failure induction." *Planta Medica* 1991; 57:320–24.
14. Fujisawa K et al. "Therapeutic effects of liver hydrolysate preparation on chronic hepatitis: a double blind, controlled study." *Asian Med J* 1984; 26:497–526.
15. Centers for Disease Control and Prevention. "1993 Sexually Transmitted Diseases Treatment Guidelines." *MMWR* 1993; 42 (No. RR-14):1–102.
16. Martin D, Mroczkowski T, Dalu Z et al. "A controlled trial of a single dose of azithromycin for the treatment of chlamydial urethritis and cervicitis." *N Engl J Med* 1992; 327:921–25.
17. Centers for Disease Control and Prevention. "1997 Sexually Transmitted Diseases Treatment Guidelines."

Chapter Seventeen: Uterine Fibroids

1. Moore J. "Benign disease of the uterus." In Hacker N, Moore J, eds. *Essentials of Obstetrics and Gynecology*, 1st ed. Philadelphia: Saunders, 1986:272–76.
2. Lacey C. "Benign disorders of the uterine corpus." In Pernoll M, ed. *Current Obstetric and Gynecologic Diagnosis and Treatment*, 7th ed. Norwalk, Conn.: Appleton and Lange, 1991:732–38.
3. Wallach E. "Myomectomy." In Thompson J, Rock J, eds. *Te Linde's Operative Gynecology*, 7th ed. Philadelphia: Lippincott, 1992:647–53.
4. Cramer S, Robertson A, Ziats N et al. "Growth potential of human uterine leiomyomata: some in vitro observations and their implications." *Obstet Gynecol* 1985; 66:36.
5. Wilson E, Yang F, Rees E. "Estradiol and progesterone binding in uterine leiomyomata and in normal uterine tissues." *Obstet Gynecol* 1980; 5:20.
6. Puuka M, Kontula K, Kauppila A, Janne O, Vihdo R. "Estrogen receptor in human myoma tissue." *Mol Cell Endocrinol* 1976; 6:35.
7. Pollow K, Geilfuss J, Boquoi E, Pollow B. "Estrogen and progesterone binding proteins in normal human myometrium and leiomyoma tissue." *J Clin Chem Clin Biochem* 1978; 16:503.
8. Buttram V Jr, Reiter R. "Uterine leiomyomata: etiology, symptomatology and management." *Fertil Steril* 1981; 36:433–45.
9. Golden B et al. "Estrogen excretion patterns and plasma levels in vegetarian and omnivorous women." *N Engl J Med* 1982; 307:1542–47.
10. Goodman M, Wilkens L et al. "Association of soy and fiber consumption with the risk of endometrial cancer." *Am J Epid* 1997; 146(4):294–306.
11. Dean D, Exley D, Goodwin T. "Steroid oestrogens in plants: re-estimation of oestrone in pomegranate seeds." *Phytochem* 1971; 10:2215–16.
12. Verdeal R, Ryan D. "Naturally-occurring oestrogens in plant foodstuffs—a review." *J Food Protec* 1979; 42: 577–83.
13. Price K, Fenwick G. "Naturally occurring oestrogens in foods—a review." *Food Addit Contam* 1985; 2:73–106.
14. Miksicek R. "Estrogenic flavonoids: structural requirements for biological activity." *Proceed Soc Exper Biol Med* 1995; 208:44–50.
15. Bennetts H, Underwood E, Shier F. "A breeding problem of sheep in the southwest division of Western Australia." *J Dept Agric West Aust* 1946; 23:1–12.
16. Saloniemi H, Wahala K, Nykanen-Kurki P, Saastamoinen I. "Phytoestrogen content and effect of legume fodder." *PSEBM* 1995; 208:13–17.
17. Kallela K, Heinonen K, Saloniemi H. "Plant oestrogens: the cause of decreased fertility in cows. A case report." *Nord Vet Med* 1984; 36:124–28.

18. Adams N. "Cervical mucus and reproductive efficiency in ewes after exposure to oestrogenic pastures." *Aust J Agric Res* 1977; 28:481–89.

19. Folman Y, Pope G. "Effect of norethisterone acetate, dimethylstilbestrol, genistein, and coumestrol on uptake of oestradiol by uterus, vagina, and skeletal muscle of immature mice." *J Endocrin* 1969; 44:213–18.

20. Shutt D, Cox R. "Steroid and phyto-oestrogen binding to sheep uterine receptors in vitro." *J Endocrin* 1972; 52: 299–310.

21. Medlock K, Branham W, Sheehan D. "Effects of coumestrol and equol on the developing reproductive tract of the rat." *PSEBM* 1995; 208:67–71.

22. Messina M, Persky V, Setchell K, Barnes S. "Soy intake and cancer risk: a review of the in vitro and in vivo data." *Nutr and Canc* 1994; 21(2):113–31.

23. Parkin D et al., "Cancer Incidence in Five Continents." Lyon: International Agency for Research on Cancer Scientific Publications No. 120. 1992; 6:301–431, 486–509.

24. Lipschutz A. "Experimental fibroids and the antifibromatogenic action of steroid hormones." *JAMA* 1942; 120:71.

25. Goodman A. "Progesterone therapy in uterine fibromyoma." *J Clin Endocrinol Metab* 1946; 6:402.

26. Lee J. *What Your Doctor May Not Tell You about Menopause.* New York: Warner Books, 1996.

27. Rein M, Barbieri R, Friedman A. "Progesterone: a critical role in the pathogenesis of uterine myomas." *Am J Obstet Gynecol* 1995; 172(1):14–18.

28. Friedman A, Hoffman D, Comite F et al. "Treatment of leiomyomata uteri with leuprolide acetate depot: a double-blind, placebo-controlled, multicenter study." *Obstet Gynecol* 1991; 77(5):720–25.

29. Nakamura Y, Yoshimura Y, Yamada H et al. "Treatment of uterine leiomyomata with a luteinizing hormone-releasing hormone agonist: the possibility of nonsurgical management in selected perimenopausal women." *Fertil Steril* 1991; 55(5):900–5.

30. Stovall T, Ling F, Henry L et al. "A randomized trial evaluating leuprolide acetate before hysterectomy as treatment for leiomyomas." *Am J Obstet Gynecol* 1991; 164 (6 Pt 1):1420–25.

31. Hufnagel V. *No More Hysterectomies.* New York: NAL Books, 1988.

32. Rouret R et al. "Recourse to particular arterial embolization in the treatment of some uterine leiomyoma." *Bull Acad Natl Med* 1997; 181(2):233–43.

33. Berkeley A, DeCherney A, Polan M. "Abdominal myomectomy and subsequent fertility." *Surg Gynecol Obstet* 1983; 156:319.

34. Woner-Muram H, Muram D, Gillieson M. "Uterine myomas in pregnancy." *J Can Assoc Radiol* 1984; 35:168.

Chapter Eighteen: Vaginitis

1. Biswas M. "Bacterial vaginosis." *Clin Ob Gyn* 1993; 36(1):166–76.

2. Gravett M, Nelson H, DeRouen T et al. "Independent associations of bacterial vaginosis and Chlamydia trachomatis infection with adverse pregnancy outcome." *JAMA* 1986; 256(14):1899–1903.

3. Watts D, Eschenbach D, Kenn G. "Early postpartum endometritis: the role of bacteria, genital mycoplasmas, and chlamydia trachomatis." *Obstet Gynecol* 1989; 73:52.

4. Horowitz B, Giaguinta D, Ito S. "Evolving pathogens in vulvovaginal candidiasis: complications for patient care." *J Clin Pharmacol* 1992; 32(3):248–55.

5. Horowitz B. "The role of non-albicans candida in vulvovaginal candidiasis." *J Clin Pract Sexual* 1991; 7 (special issue):16–20.

6. Hillier S. "Yeast vaginitis self-diagnosis incorrect in 2 out of 3 women." *Ob Gyn News* 1994. July 1.

7. Odds F. "Candidosis of the genitalia." In Odds F, ed. *Candida and Candidosis*, 2d ed. London: Balliere Tindall, 1988:124.

8. Faro S. "Systemic vs. topical therapy for the treatment of vulvovaginal candidiasis." *Infect Dis Obstet Gynecol* 1994; 1:202–8.

9. Horowitz B. "The role on non-albicans Candida in vulvovaginal candidiasis." *J Clin Pract Sexuality* 1991; 7 (special issue):16–20.

10. O'Connor M, Sobel J. "Epidemiology of recurrent vulvovaginal candidiasis: identification and strain differentiation of Candida albicans." *J Infect Dis* 1986; 54:358–63.

11. Horowitz B, Edelson S, Lippman L. "Sexual transmission of Candida." *Obstet Gynecol* 1987; 69(6):883–86.

12. Horowitz B, Giaquinta D, Ito S. "Evolving pathogens in vulvovaginal candidiasis: implications for patient care." *J Clin Pharmacol* 1992; 32(3):248–55.

13. Thomason J, Gelbart S. "Trichomonas vaginalis." *Obstet Gynecol* 1989; 74:536–41.

14. Lossick J. "Epidemiology of urogenital trichomoniasis." In Honinberg B, ed. *Trichomonads Parasitic in Humans.* New York: Springer Verlag, 1989:311–23.

15. Wolner-Hanssen P et al. "Clinical manifestations of vaginal trichomonas." *JAMA* 1989; 264:571–76.

16. Elegbe I, Botu M. "A preliminary study of dressing patterns and incidence of candidiasis." *Am J Public Health* 1982; 72:176–77.

17. Heidrich F, Berg A, Bergman J. "Clothing factors and vaginitis." *J Fam Prac* 1984; 19(4):491–94.

18. Doderlein A. "Die Scheidensekretuntersuchugen." *Zentralbl Gynakol* 1894; 18:10–14.

19. Ant M. "Diabetic vulvovaginitis treated with vitamin E suppositories." *Am J Obstet/Gynecol* 1954; 67(2):407–9.

20. Adetumbi M, Javor G, Lau B. "Allium sativum (garlic) inhibits lipid synthesis by Candida albicans." *Antimicrob Agents and Chemother* 1986; 30(3):499–501.

21. Moore G, Atkins R. "The fungicidal and fungistatic effects of an aqueous garlic extract on medically important yeastlike fungi." *Mycologia* 1977; 15:466–68.

22. Cavallito C, Bailey J. "Allicin, the antibacterial principle of Allium sativum. Isolation, physical properties and antibacterial action." *J Am Chem Soc* 1944; 66:1950–51.

23. Amin A, Subbaiah T, Abbasi K. "Berberine sulfate: antimicrobial activity, bioassay, and mode of action." *Can J Microbiol* 1969; 15:1067–76.

24. Pena E. "Melaleuca alternifolia oil: its use for trichomonal vaginitis and other vaginal infections." *Obstet Gynecol* 1962; 19(6):793–95.

25. Williams L, Home V. "A comparative study of some essential oils for potential use in topical applications for the treatment of the yeast Candida albicans." *Aust J Med Herbal* 1995; 7(3):57–62.

26. Chan R, Bruce A, Reid G. "Adherence of cervical, vaginal and distal urethral normal microbial flora to human uroepithelial cells and the inhibition of adherence of gram-negative uropathogens by competitive exclusion." *J Urol* 1984; 131:596–601.

27. Andersson R, Daeschel M, Hassan H. "Antibacterial activity of plantaricin SIK-83, a bacteriocin produced by Lactobacillus plantarum." *Biochimie* 1988; 70:381–90.

28. Hillier S, Krohn M, Klebanoff S, Eschenbach D. "The relationship of hydrogen peroxide-producing lactobacilli to bacterial vaginosis and genital microflora in pregnant women." *Obstet Gynecol* 1992; 79(3):369–72.

29. Klebanoff S, Hillier S, Eschenbach D, Waltersdorph A. "Control of the microbial flora of the vagina by H_2O_2-generating lactobacilli." *J Infec Dis* 1991; 164:94–100.

30. Hilton E, Isenberg H, Alperstein P, France K, Borenstein M. "Ingestion of yogurt containing lactobacillus acidophilus as prophylaxis for candidal vaginitis." *Ann Int Med* 1992; 116:353–57.

31. Hilton E, Rindos P, Isenberg H. "Lactobacillus GG vaginal suppositories and vaginitis." *J Clin Microbiol* 1995; 33(5):1433.

32. Hughes V, Hillier S. "Microbiologic characteristics of lactobacillus products used for colonization of the vagina." *Obstet Gynecol* 1990; 75(2):244–48.

33. Jovanovic R, Congema E, Nguyen H. "Antifungal agents vs. boric acid for treating chronic mycotic vulvovaginitis." *J Rep Med* 1991; 36(8):593–97.

34. Van Slyke K, Michel V, Rein M. "Treatment of vulvovaginal candidiasis with boric acid powder." *Am J Obstet Gynecol* 1981; 141(2):145–48.

35. Waters E, Wager H. "Vaginal mycosis in pregnancy: an improved gentian violet treatment." *Am J Obstet Gynecol* 1950; 60(4):885–87.

36. Ratzan J. "Monilial and trichomonal vaginitis: topical treatment with povidone-iodine preparations." *Calif Med* 1969; 110:24–27.

37. Sobel J, Brooker D, Stein G et al. "Single oral dose fluconazole compared with conventional clotrimazole topical therapy of Candida vaginitis." *Am J Obstet Gynecol* 1995; 172:1263–68.

38. Centers for Disease Control and Prevention. "Sexually Transmitted Diseases Treatment Guidelines." *MMWR* 1993; 42(No. RR-14):1–102.

39. Homes K. "Lower genital tract infections in women: cystitis/urethritis, vulvovaginitis, and cervicitis." In Holmes K, Mardyh P, Sparling P, Wiesner P, eds. *Sexually Transmitted Diseases.* 2d ed. New York: McGraw Hill; 1990:527–45.

40. Pheifer T, Forsyth P, Durfee M et al. "Nonspecific vaginitis: role of Haemophilus vaginalis and treatment with metronidazole." *N Engl J Med* 1978; 298:1429–34.

INDEX

('b' indicates boxed material; 'i' indicates an illustration; 't' indicates a table)